Up Wi' The Bonnets!

The History of

Dundee Football Club

1893 - 2007

BY

NORRIE PRICE

PUBLISHED BY NORRIE PRICE

AUTHOR'S NOTE

Fourteen years have elapsed since *Up Wi' The Bonnets* was first published and as well as the updated history, this new edition features many fresh images and memorabilia with colour throughout. Hopefully, you will judge it worthy of our famous old club. My first experience of a professional football match came in September 1962 when my grandfather and uncle took me to see Dundee play Aberdeen at Dens Park on my twelfth birthday. That was just three days after the famous 8-1 victory over Cologne but it was another European Cup tie - against Anderlecht in the quarter-final some six months later - that remains my most memorable experience.

The Dark Blues' European Cup exploits had made them the talk of the town - and Scotland for that matter - and the match was a total sell-out. There were 40,000 fans at Dens that night and I can clearly recall the roars of the huge crowd as we scurried to the ground from our parking place about a mile away. Dundee fought their way to a 2-1 win and great was the excitement as the huge crowd spilled out onto the streets at the end. Entry into the European Cup semi-final in 1963 proved the pinnacle of Dundee Football Club's now 114-year-old history but despite the uncertainty of recent years, it is hoped that the incredible loyalty shown by the fans will soon see the club return to the higher echelons of Scottish football.

ACKNOWLEDGEMENTS

I would like to express my gratitude to the many people who assisted in this publication. Martins the Printers have consistently turned out a quality product. Eddie Flann, David Young and Craig Thomson were a great help, Jim Hendry was a key man in the first edition, for which I got great encouragement from my late father, Ron Hill and Peter Shepherd, and thanks, too, to my wife Lorraine for her diligent proof-reading. I am grateful to DC Thomson's Calum Laird and Bill McLaughlin for the use of so many fine photos with a special mention for Anne Swadel in Photofiles for her unstinting support. Dave Martin (Fotopress) provided many top quality shots as did Mirrorpix, SNS Group, Alan Richardson (Pix-AR), Ian Hendry (Postcard Club of Dundee), David Young and George Ashton. Others who provided information, advice or memorabilia were ex-Dundee directors Ian Gellatly, Bob Hynd, Steve Martin, while former Dark Blues who assisted were Jim Paton, Harry Smith, Archie Coats, Tommy Gallacher, George Hill, Doug Cowie, Bert Henderson, Sammy Kean (coach), Bobby Cox, Alex Hamilton, Alan Gilzean, Doug Houston, Ian Phillip, Dave Johnston, Eric Sinclair, Bobby Glennie, Cammy Fraser and Keith Wright.

Other contributors were Charlie & Alan Beat, Alex Benvie, Stephen Borland, John Brown, Bob Douglas & David Walker (all DC Thomson), Dave Forbes, Joanna Fraser (Aberdeen Journals), Mark Gallacher, Scott Glenday, Alastair & Ken Gibb, Andy & Gordon Gurvan, David Halliday, Jim Hill, John Hunter, Simon Inglis, Gareth Jennings (DCT), Jimmy & Mabel Lorimer, Doug Lowe and Grace Gough (The Herald), Paul Lunney, Gordon McBrearty (Hampden Museum), Kevin McCarra (Scotland on Sunday), Jack Murray, Mark Robertson, Kenny Ross, Dave Roy, Peter Rundo, Cyril Rice (Daily Record), Bob Slessor, Kerry Black & Charlie Taylor (The Scotsman), Derek Souter & Craig McGregor (DJS Services), Dave Thomson, Jim Thomson, Sandy Watson, Jim Wilkie, Ken Winter (Tayport Printers), David Kett & Local History staff at Dundee Central Library, and staff at The Scottish Football League, The Scottish Football Association and The English Football League.

This edition published October 2007. (First published 1993).   ISBN 978 0 9521426 4 5   Printed by Martins the Printers, Seaview Works, Spittal, Berwick Upon Tweed (01289-306006).

          Cover design by Craig McGregor DJS Services. Layout, publication, distribution by Norrie Price.

Glory night - Dundee demolished Cologne 8-1 in the European Cup at Dens in September 1962. From left - Bobby Cox, Bert Slater, Bobby Seith, Bobby Wishart, Andy Penman, Gordon Smith, Alan Cousin, Alan Gilzean, Hugh Robertson, Ian Ure and Alex Hamilton.

Dark Blue Legend - Dundee supporters get ready to give it their all before the Scottish Cup Final at Hampden in 2003. Those on the top tier display their magnificent flag immortalising Billy Steel, the legendary Dundee and Scotland star of the 1950s.

Fotopress

Heavenly view - Dens Park, the home of Dundee Football Club showing the top of the Provost Road terracing with the old stand to the left. It is 1960 and the new south enclosure and floodlighting system have transformed the ground.

DC Thomson

CONTENTS

TOP - Dundee Harbour Trustees' boardroom. ABOVE - The Albion Hotel in Tally Street at the corner of the Overgate where it was proposed that *Our Boys* and *East End* should merge to become Dundee Football Club.

Dundee Central Library

Dundee F.C.'s opening game against Rangers at West Craigie Park on August 12th, 1893. Dundee are in the blue and white stripes of East End. (BACK, left to right) Adam Marshall (trainer), Mr Sandy Spalding, Willie Thomson, Mr David McEwan, Mr Tom Shaw, James Brown, Bill Ferrier, Mr James McIntosh, Bill McKie, Mr J. Black (referee), Dave Craig, Sandy Keillor, Mr James Petrie (president). MIDDLE - Bill Longair, Bob Petrie. FRONT - John Craik, Jimmy Dundas and Sandy Gilligan.

Alistair Gibb

CHAPTER ONE

Hectic, Happy, Days

As the Nineteenth Century moved into its final decade, the game of Association Football had continued to grow in popularity. Although there was evidence of the game in various earlier forms, organised football in Scotland began with the formation of the Scottish Football Association in 1873 and a new competition, the Scottish Cup, was initiated.

Initially football was played on an amateur basis and Queen's Park were the early pace-setters with nine Scottish Cup wins between 1873 and 1893. The Scottish Cup apart, games consisted of local competitions in addition to friendlies against other Scottish and English sides.

In 1883 the Forfarshire Football Association was formed with twelve of its 18 clubs based in Dundee. Although an unknown Dundee side lost 5-1 to Glasgow's Alexandra Athletic on January 1st, 1875, the city's earliest known senior club was St Clement's who were formed in 1876. The following year heralded the formation of East End, Our Boys and Strathmore, and in 1879 - the year of the Tay Bridge disaster - they were joined by Dundee Harp.

There was intense local rivalry and a rapid growth in public awareness and interest. On September 19th, 1885, a huge crowd saw Our Boys lose 3-1 to Harp at East Dock

John Cameron (Our Boys) - a signatory to Dundee Football Club's application to join the Scottish League. David Thomson

Street in the second round of the Forfarshire Cup. The result served to exacerbate previous disharmony amongst the players and officials of Our Boys and, soon afterwards, several players walked out, later forming a new club called "Wanderers".

The Forfarshire Cup was then a keenly contested affair and, between 1883 and 1893 the trophy was won no less than four times by Arbroath, three times by Harp and once each by Montrose and Our Boys. Even in these early days, the best players were very much in demand and with professionalism introduced to the English League in 1885, many Scots stars were lured south.

In 1890, an 11-club Scottish League was formed and it quickly proved a big success. None of the Dundee clubs were included, and, with lucrative friendlies against leading Scottish or English sides now restricted to New Year or Easter, their income was significantly diminished.

Season 1891-92 saw the formation of an eight-team Northern League and the first championship was shared by Our Boys and East End, both of whom had originated in the Morgan Street area of Dundee. East End, who had started at Clepington Park (now Tannadice), vacated their ground at Pitkerro Park and moved to Carolina Port, which was situated in the dock area on the site now occupied by J. T. Inglis and the potato merchants, Pattullo Barr.

The newly-opened ground, which was leased from Dundee Harbour Trustees, also had running and cycle tracks. And, with a 12,500 capacity including a 1,500-seater stand, it compared favourably with most other Scottish football grounds at that time.

Our Boys played at West Craigie Park to the north of the Arbroath Road, on a site now occupied by part of Baxter Park Terrace and Park Avenue. In late 1892, however, "The Blues" suffered a severe setback when their grandstand - described by the *Dundee Advertiser* as a "primitive contraption" - was extensively damaged by fire and, with the dressing-rooms destroyed, changing facilities consisted of a wooden hut in the north-west corner of the ground.

On January 7th, 1893, Our Boys and East End fought out

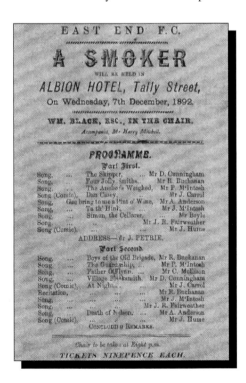

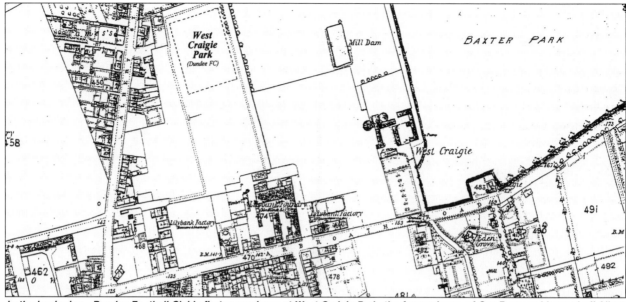

In the beginning - Dundee Football Club's first ground was at West Craigie Park, the former home of Our Boys and located off Albert Street to the north of the Arbroath Road. BELOW - Mathers Hotel in Whitehall Place at the corner of Dock Street. Dundee Central Library

a 4-4 draw on a snow-covered West Craigie Park. Ten minutes from time, the crowd broke through the ropes and, when an East End official remonstrated with them, he was pelted with snowballs.

He was forced to beat a hasty retreat and the focus of attention switched to the centre-circle. "There", in the words of *The Advertiser*, "a couple of young bloods exchanged blows" and, with the committee man safely in the dressing rooms, it was thought prudent to bring the game to an early conclusion.

Both clubs were ambitious and, wearying of the monotonous round of local fixtures, they yearned for the grander stage of national competition. Early in 1893, an amalgamation was proposed but this was strenuously opposed by members of both clubs.

Nevertheless, the formation of the Scottish League and the continuing drain of the best Scots players to England had already taken its toll and, when professionalism was legalised in Scotland on May 2nd, the writing was on the wall for Dundee's senior clubs.

On May 13th, Mr Andrew Buttar, an official of Our Boys, who was also president of the Dundee Charity Football Association, made his views clear while presenting the Charity Shield Cup at the Albion Hotel in Tally Street. He highlighted the splintered football support within the city and strongly advocated that Our Boys and East End should amalgamate and apply for admission to the Scottish League.

Early Dundee heroes - (TOP, left to right), Johnny Darroch, Sandy Keillor, Adam Marshall (trainer), Bill Longair and Jimmy Dundas. David Thomson

This had the desired effect and it was finally agreed that East End and Our Boys would merge to form Dundee Football Club. On May 20th, the two clubs met at Mathers Hotel in Whitehall Place and a formal application for membership was prepared for submission to the Scottish League AGM that was to take place on June 12th.

Hibernian, St Bernards and Cowlairs had also applied for election with Dundee while the bottom three clubs, Renton, Abercorn and Clyde were applying for re-election. Dundee, Renton and St Bernards were successful and 10 days later the former officials of East End and Our Boys reconvened to appoint office-bearers for the newly-formed club.

James Petrie (East End) became the first president with Andrew Buttar (Our Boys) vice-president, William Black (East End) business secretary, Andrew Williamson (Our Boys) match secretary and W. McLean and J. M. Forbes as the joint-treasurers. Other committee members were J. MacIntosh, E. Fleming, T. McKee, D. McVicar, A. Spalding, W. K. Murray and W. Saunders.

Although many had previously doubted the practicalities of an amalgamation between the pair, it was accepted as a logical step and now local fans could anticipate regular clashes with Scotland's elite.

It was expected that Dundee would play at Carolina Port. But, when the lease was surprisingly given to Strathmore, the new club resolved to play at West Craigie Park, the former home of Our Boys. This required a considerable amount of renovation and the new Dundee F.C. committee was also kept busy with fund-raising and the assembly of a team worthy of Scottish League status.

And, although Scottish international outside-left Sandy Keillor and the goalkeeper Bill McKie were signed from Montrose, most of the players were drawn from the two amalgamated clubs. Ferrier, Longair, Petrie, Craik, Dundas and Gilligan came from East End while Brown, Craig, Thomson, McInroy and Salmond were from Our Boys.

On Saturday, August 12th, 1893 - it was truly the Glorious Twelfth for the city's growing army of football fans - the new side opened their Scottish League campaign. And they were right in at the deep end with a home game against Rangers from Glasgow.

As you would expect, there was great excitement amongst the fans who made their way to the ground. Only the better-off could afford the luxury of a hansom cab and, although many took the juggernaut steam trams - which often became stuck on the incline approaching Victoria Road - most made their way on foot.

In those days, a working man could spend an enjoyable Saturday for very little money. A glass of beer cost a penny and a half and with admission costing 6d (3d for boys), there was a crowd of around 5,000 for the visit of the Light Blues.

The Dundee side for this historic game was: McKie; Brown, Ferrier; Craig, Longair, Petrie; Thomson, Craik, Dundas, Gilligan, Keillor. No fancy formations or defensive football then - plain and simple, it was two full-backs, three half-backs and five forwards, and into attack.

After falling two goals behind, inside-left Sandy Gilligan scored Dundee's first-ever goal. This sparked a revival in which Sandy Keillor and Jimmy Dundas found the net and, at full-time, the fledgling homesters could be well pleased with their point from an exciting 3-3 draw.

The following week, Celtic departed with a 4-1 win and, although the next two games brought away successes over Renton (3-2), and Leith (5-3), Dundee managed to record only four wins from 13 games by mid-December.

To bolster the side, Dundee signed Harp goalkeeper Francis Barrett and the experienced Aston Villa defender, George Campbell. Just as significantly, Carolina Port was acquired when Dundee took over the financially struggling Athletic Grounds Company, holders of the lease with the Dundee Harbour Trustees.

Scottish League 1893-94						
	P	W	D	L	F A	Pts
Celtic	18	14	1	3	53-32	29
Hearts	18	11	4	3	46-32	26
St Bernards	18	11	1	6	53-39	23
Rangers	18	8	4	6	44-30	20
Dumbarton	18	7	5	6	32-35	19
St Mirren	18	7	3	8	49-47	17
Third Lanark	18	7	3	8	38-44	17
Dundee	18	6	3	9	47-59	15
Leith Athletic	18	4	2	12	36-46	10
Renton	18	1	2	15	23-57	4

Soon afterwards, Dundee moved to Carolina Port while the "dispossessed" Strathmore amalgamated with Johnstone Wanderers and became known as Dundee Wanderers playing at Clepington Park. It proved an expensive move for

Through the mists of time - one of the earliest action pictures involving Dundee F.C. against unknown opponents at Carolina Port in the 1890s. Dundee are wearing the blue and white vertical stripes of East End and are attacking the visitors' goal. Note the pavilion and wooden stand on the right - the latter was dismantled and re-erected on the south side of Dens Park in 1899.   Dundee Central Library

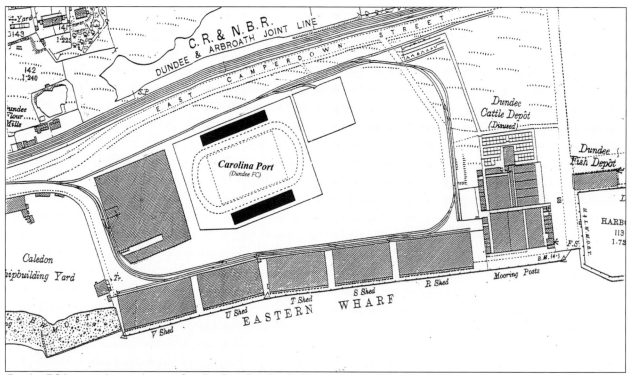

Dundee F.C.'s second ground was at Carolina Port. But despite its excellent facilities "The Port" was not served with public transport and remained relatively inaccessible to most fans.

Dundee Central Library

The club was founded in 1893 when two teams, Our Boys and East End, joined forces. For six seasons they played at Carolina Port, where a rubbish dump made a free "grandstand".

Dundee for, after the considerable expense of refurbishing West Craigie Park, they now inherited debts of around £600 from the Athletic Grounds Company.

Nevertheless, a covered stand was erected at Carolina Port and the roofless West Craigie structure - which became known as "the three-penny stand" - was brought to the opposite end of the ground. But, at a cost of £2,000 - a substantial amount in those days - these renovations were later to prove a significant financial burden for the club.

Dundee, who alternated between the dark blue of Our Boys and the blue and white stripes of East End, could boast some fine players and despite being labelled "the ten-bobbers" - initially they had paid a modest 10/- per week with a bonus of 2/6d per point - they had attracted many top local stars.

In March 1894, goalkeeper Francis Barrett, centre-half Bill "Plum" Longair and left-winger Sandy Keillor - all Dundonians - became the first Dundee players to represent Scotland in a 2-1 triumph over Ireland in Belfast.

Longair was also selected against Wales and England, but injuries prevented him turning out which meant that the Irish game would be his only international appearance. The following year, Barrett earned his second cap against Wales while the moustached Keillor, said to be "the best-known

player north of the Forth" by one critic, gained another three caps to take his total to six. Two of these were previously gained with Dundee's Angus neighbours Montrose, the club he would later rejoin in 1902.

In their first two seasons, Dundee finished eighth in the 10-team Division One but, on both occasions, they gained re-election. In 1894-95, centre-forward Jimmy Dundas played for the Scottish League against the Irish League and the Dark Blues had a highly successful run in the Scottish Cup.

Wins over the Aberdeen club Orion (a) 5-1, St Mirren (h) 2-0, and Celtic (h) 1-0, took them to the semi-finals with the visit of Celtic, league champions and cup finalists for the past two seasons, attracting a 12,000 crowd - a record attendance for Dundee at Carolina Port. It proved a great occasion as the home team fielded: Barrett; Darroch, Campbell; Dundas, Longair, Keillor; Thomson, McInroy, Maxwell, Sawyers and Gilligan.

Willie Sawyers went on to score the game's only goal and,

Grand Football Match.

Semi-Final Scottish Cup-Tie.

RENTON

VERSUS

DUNDEE.

DUNDEE ATHLETIC GROUNDS.

KICK-OFF AT 3.15 P.M.

SEE OFF-SIDE RULE.

MURDOCH & PATERSON, PRINTERS, DUNDEE.

Ticket from Dundee v Renton Scottish Cup-tie at Carolina Port.   Alex Benvie

within weeks, the former Clyde inside-left would gain his one and only Scottish cap against Wales along with his team-mates Francis Barrett and Sandy Keillor.

Those were hectic but happy days at Carolina Port and, within seven days of beating the mighty Celtic, Dundee completed an Old Firm double with a highly credible 2-1 home win over Rangers.

Dundee's semi-final clash with Renton attracted 8,000 fans to the "Port" but, with the scores tied at 1-1 (remarkably both were own-goals!), a late penalty miss by Sawyers meant a trip westwards for the replay.

After trailing 2-0, Dundee managed to scramble a 3-3 draw before a crowd of 20,000 at Hampden but Renton made no mistake in the second replay at Parkhead. This time nearly 30,000 fans saw the Dunbartonshire side win 3-0 and, sadly, Dundee's hopes of cup glory were over.

The semi-final alone had been watched by over 55,000 fans and Dundee's share of the gate receipts was most welcome for, in addition to the expenditure on West Craigie and Carolina Port, considerable amounts had previously been spent on players like Barrett, Campbell, Maxwell, Sawyers, Fleming and Darroch. And, despite the windfall that the cup adventure had brought to the coffers, it was necessary to sell Willie Maxwell, a future Scotland international, to the English club, Stoke City.

Nevertheless, over the next two seasons Dundee managed to finish in fifth place despite some severe setbacks. In their opening season, they had crashed 10-3 to St Mirren at Paisley but, on October 20th, 1895, a visit to Celtic Park resulted in an 11-0 rout. That defeat remains the heaviest in the club's history although Dundee had been severely handicapped by the loss of Longair late in the first half, with left-back Ferrier also unable to resume after half-time.

Some weeks later, Dundee players wore black armbands in the home game against Clyde. This was in no way due to the

In 1898 Barney Battles played 90 minutes of a Scottish Cup tie with a poisoned left arm in a sling.

Parkhead debacle, but was a mark of respect for reserve player Harry Jackson, who had recently drowned in the wreck of the ill-fated SS Principis. It soon became evident that the Parkhead result was a one-off but, although the Dark Blues quickly recovered, underlying financial difficulties came to a head early in 1896.

The ground rent was payable six months in advance and, although the home club retained two-thirds of the drawings, Dundee were only attracting an average of 5,000 to Carolina Port. Generally their away games involved expenses of £35 and often they received only the minimum guarantee of £15.

No home games remained, and when Dundee made an early cup exit to Third Lanark, losing 4-1 in Glasgow on January 15th, the only source of revenue lay in the traditional Easter holiday fixtures against touring English sides.

Club officials came in for fierce criticism and, at the April AGM only two members of the old committee survived with Messrs Petrie, Williamson and Black amongst those who departed from office.

On March 21st, 1896, Keillor became the first Dundee player to score for his country in a 4-0 win over Wales at Carolina Port. It was the first international to be held in the Juteopolis and, with Dundee right-winger Bill Thomson also included, the game attracted a crowd of 11,700.

In a bid to balance the books, Dundee's new committee arranged a close-season tour of England. They met famous names like Woolwich Arsenal, Corinthians, Nottingham Forest, Millwall, Southampton and Sheffield United but, despite providing some desperately needed income, even sterner measures would have to be implemented.

Sawyers was released, while Gilligan and Thomson were transferred to Bolton Wanderers. In addition, Longair joined Sunderland with Barrett moving to Newton Heath (later Manchester United). To replace Barrett, Dundee secured Burnley keeper Jack Hillman, while Everton's Scottish international right-back Bob Kelso, Hearts right-half Barney Battles and R. Blyth from Preston North End proved to be equally astute signings.

The new-look team took time to settle but successive wins over Rangers (h) 3-2, St Mirren (h) 3-2, Abercorn (a) 7-1, and Celtic (a) 1-0 at the end of 1896-97 had allowed Dundee to again finish a respectable fifth. Several Scottish clubs had raised much-needed capital by becoming limited liability companies. But, when Dundee did likewise in March 1897, only 500 of the 2,000 £1 shares were taken up.

Next season, "Plum" Longair returned and, despite slipping to seventh in the league, home wins over Partick Thistle (2-1), St Mirren (2-0) - Barney Battles played with a poisoned arm in a sling - and Hearts (3-0), again took Dundee to the Scottish Cup semi-final. Barring their way to the final were Kilmarnock, leaders of Division Two, and an 11,000 Rugby Park crowd saw Dundee field: Hillman;

Bill Longair - a legendary figure in the history of Dundee Football Club. Here he sports the pale blue and white stripes of East End with the Forfarshire Cup prominent. W. Longair

FOOTBALL IN DUNDEE.

ENTHUSIASTIC PUBLIC MEETING.

FORMATION OF A NEW COMMITTEE.

A public meeting was held in the Gilfillan Hall last night for the purpose of considering the position of football in the city, and the proposed formation of a new committee to carry on the Dundee Football Club, at present in liquidation. The hall was packed, and, in fact, the services of two policemen were retained at the door to keep back the crowd from the doors. Bailie Robertson presided, and there were also on the platform—Bailie Urquhart, Councillor Macaulay, Messrs E. Quirk, A. Gow, Gregor M'Gregor (Perth), J. Cameron, J. Petrie, A. Williamson, W. Anderson, T. Shaw, D. Mackintosh, and others.

Bailie Robertson addresses the meeting

Crisis meeting - at the Royal British Hotel on the High Street at the top end of Castle Street. Dundee Central Library

Kelso, Burgess; Battles, Longair, Gilligan; McVean, Clark, McArthur, Willocks, Malloch.

McVean put Dundee ahead in five minutes and they got a second when an attempted clearance by the Killie keeper struck Malloch and rebounded into the net. The Ayrshire side were undeterred and, after pulling one back before half-time, they went on to win 3-2 although they lost 2-0 to Rangers in the final.

However, with Dundee's financial situation continuing to deteriorate, it was often a struggle to pay the players and, at the end of the season, it was little surprise when most of the top men walked out following an acrimonious dispute.

Amongst them were Longair, who joined Broughton United, and Kelso, who had only recently captained Scotland against Ireland. Only Hillman and Keillor of any repute remained and, in October 1898, the Scottish international became the first Dundee player to receive a benefit match. The visit of Celtic attracted a 5,000 crowd from which Keillor received £143 for his loyalty.

By then, the popular Hillman had also departed. Club officials accused the English keeper of "not trying" in a 6-3 pre-season humiliation by Dundee Wanderers. Local pride had been at stake and, after a two-month suspension, during which the keeper unsuccessfully appealed to the Scottish League, Hillman was transferred back to Burnley for £175.

The departure of so many experienced players had left the Carolina Port side fatally weakened. By early December,

Dundee had lost their previous nine games and, with only three from a possible 26 points, they lay anchored to the bottom of the league.

Average home gates had slumped to 3,500 and, with the club fast heading for bankruptcy, the players were called to a crisis meeting on Thursday, December 8th. The directors offered to pay all expenses for the away match against Celtic out of their own pockets if the team would take the chance of getting sufficient gate money for their wages. The players refused and match secretary Dan McIntosh had no option but to cancel the game.

Dundee Football Club now appeared doomed but the Scottish League's determination to save their most Northerly club led to the sending of this telegram: "League wish to support you. Send deputation through to Horse Shoe Bar, Drury Street, 6.30 Wednesday, December 14th. Don't part with players meantime."

At the emergency meeting in Glasgow, the League offered to guarantee Dundee's wages and travelling expenses for the four remaining league games. They would make good any deficit not covered by gate receipts up to a limit of £25 but the Dundee board, who blamed the crisis on their inherited debts, saw it as only a temporary respite.

Secretary, Mr W. G. Andrew confessed himself "Sick of the affair" and, after rejecting the offer, intimated that the club would go into liquidation. However, with the co-operation of the current officials, Messrs Cameron and Anderson had attended on behalf of the earlier Dundee F.C. manage-

Football enthusiasm. Scene at the door of the hall.

ment. They accepted the League's offer and pledged that the club would continue.

John Cameron was as good as his word and, although some players had already departed, Dundee fulfilled their Ibrox fixture against Rangers on Saturday, December 17th. The Carolina Port side went down 7-0 but their efforts would prove worthwhile.

> **FOOTBALL.**
> **DUNDEE CLUB TO BE WOUND UP.**
> Dundee Football Club, which, during the season, has had little public support and great trouble with its players, is to be wound up. Last night the players were asked to give their services on Saturday without wages, but refusing, the directors were obliged to wire the match with the Celtic off. During the year its liability has been considerably reduced. The overdrawn bank account was brought down from £400 to £200. The debt to clubs that were creditors last season was reduced £60, and £100 of arrears on wages was paid. The present debts amount to £350, owing to other clubs.

The same day, a shareholders' meeting was held in the Royal British Hotel in Dundee. The Dundee Football and Athletic Club Ltd. had debts of £400 and, apart from the stands, assets were virtually nil. It was decided to put the club into voluntary liquidation but not before a deal had been struck between the new owners and the receiver.

Crucially, it was agreed that the stands and players would remain with the club and the Scottish League were happy to waive their rights to the players' registrations. And although it could be said that this was a new Dundee - just plain Dundee Football Club - the Scottish League, who were delighted that the north-east club would continue, considered the Carolina Port side as the same team.

Equally, the people of Dundee had no intention of allowing the club to die and, three days later, a public meeting was held at a packed Gilfillan Hall. Lively discussion ensued and a new Dundee F.C. committee was formed. Amongst them was the influential Bailie John Robertson (president) and he was ably assisted by old Dundee faithfuls John Cameron, Andrew Williamson, Sandy Spalding, George Walker, David McEwan, Tom Shaw, William Anderson, Sandy Gow, Dan McIntosh and William Wallace.

According to Robertson, the club required an annual income of £2,600 and, with extensive liabilities, including £200 due to other clubs, various fund-raising activities were proposed. Dundee went on to finish bottom of the league but they were re-elected to Division One and later a highly successful bazaar raised a most welcome £600.

Carolina Port had a superb playing surface, but it was too remote and with no public transport in that direction, large crowds only turned out for "big games". Even then, hundreds preferred the free view from the legendary "Burning Mountain", a smoking slag heap at the adjacent Gas works on the Broughty Ferry Road side of the ground.

The new management were to prove the saving of Dundee. They were men of integrity and foresight and when the Harbour Trustees intimated that an expansion of the docks could mean the closure of Carolina Port, new quarters were sought in the north of the town.

Gussie Park was considered but finally it was decided to lease some agricultural land bordered by Provost Road and Dens Road. After lengthy negotiations, a 10-year lease was obtained but only after Bailie John Robertson and two others gave personal guarantees for £120. Many, however, were sad to leave their old stamping ground and 60 years later Sandy Ogilvie, a Dundee exile in the United States, spoke nostalgically of "The good old days at Carolina Port!"

The new ground, just 300 yards along the road from Clepington Park, would be called Dens Park. And, after a

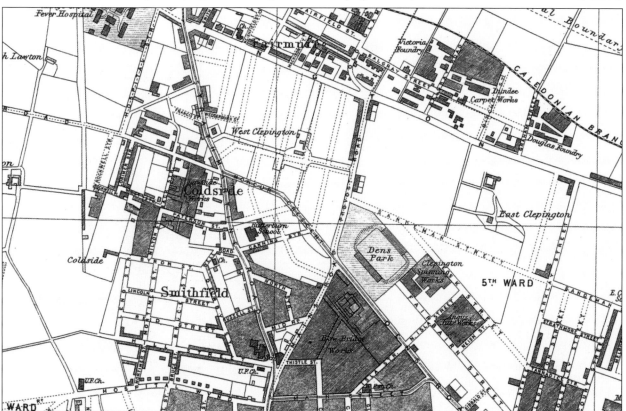

In 1899, Dens Park became home for Dundee Football Club. This location map dated 1905 shows Dens Park - Clepington Park on Esk Street is not marked - on the northern outskirts of the city well before Caird Park and the Kingsway were built. Dundee Central Library

13

Life saver - the battered cover of a programme for Dundee F.C.'s bazaar in 1899, an event which helped save the club from extinction. David Thomson

busy close season, during which the Carolina Port stand was dismantled and re-assembled on the south side and another built on the north side of the new ground, Dens Park was officially opened by Lord Provost McGrady on August 19th, 1899.

Delightful weather prevailed as a crowd of around 10,000 assembled to show their appreciation of the committee's efforts and £217-3-6d was taken at the gate. A number of ladies and gentlemen occupied a special platform in front of the South Stand as the Provost praised Bailie Robertson for successfully converting what had previously been steeply sloping arable land.

On behalf of the committee, Bailie Robertson said the new ground had been achieved by "Putting stout hearts to a stiff brae" and he welcomed the timely cash assistance which had been forthcoming from the Lord Provost down to the poorest working man.

The prodigal Longair had returned and nine local players were included in Dundee's side against St Bernard's at the official inauguration of Dens Park: T. Stewart; Watson, White; Baird, Longair, Keillor; T. Low, Steven, Robertson, McDiarmid, H. Stewart.

Bailie Robertson kicked off for the visitors but Dundee had to content themselves with a 1-1 draw with Dundonian Fred McDiarmid later awarded a medal for netting Dundee's first goal at their new ground. And, with the 20th Century just three months away, a bright new era was about to dawn for Dundee Football Club.

Players and officials of Dundee F.C. and St Bernards with local dignatories at the opening of Dens Park on August 19th, 1899. DC Thomson

14

CHAPTER TWO

Brave New World

Throughout 1899, Dundee's financial situation had stabilised and, the following year, the club became a Limited Liability Company once again. Appropriately, Bailie Robertson was appointed chairman with Messrs Cameron, Williamson, Walker and Spalding making up the board of directors.

The move to Dens Park was to prove the turning point in Dundee's fortunes. With the astute Willie Wallace in charge of team affairs, sixth place was attained and, despite finishing seventh the following season, only five from 19 home games had been lost since the advent of the new regime. This ensured a healthy home support which served to further strengthen the club's financial footing.

In addition to his part-time managerial post, Wallace was also club secretary and, since the turn of the Century, he had been ably assisted by "Plum" Longair. The stalwart defender, who continued playing until 1902, was now trainer but another local man, Peter Allan, would play an equally important role.

Renowned as a top local scout, Allan had sent many talented Scots to leading English sides and in a shrewd move, he was coaxed to Dens and soon there was a steady influx of stars, many from south of the Border.

In 1901-02, Dundee slipped to ninth place, but after successfully gaining re-election, they mounted their strongest title challenge to date. The 1902 AGM had shown a considerable loss of £785-16-5d but six successive wins at the start of the season saw home gates climb steadily from below 10,000 to a regular 15,000.

Remarkably, only 12 goals were conceded throughout the 22-game campaign of 1902-03. The attack, however, could only find the net 31 times, and Dundee - dark blue and white were now their official colours - had to settle for second place, six points behind Hibs. Crucially, the Dens Parkers had lost both meetings with the Easter Road side - by the only goal in Edinburgh and 3-0 at Dens - but the Scottish Cup would bring a measure of revenge.

Home wins over Barholm Rovers (walkover) and Nithsdale Wanderers (7-0) set up a third-round clash with the league leaders on February 7th, 1903. Now in their ninth year of existence, the Dark Blues had one of their best-ever teams and five special trains took over 4,000 Dundonians to Edinburgh for the game.

A stirring contest finished 0-0 before a 15,000 crowd. A total of £330-17s was taken at the gate with the stand yielding a further £91-18s. The tie was replayed in Dundee the following Saturday and, with local enthusiasm at fever

THE "SCOTTISH TEAMS" SERIES

DUNDEE

GROUND DENS PARK DUNDEE.

Good old Dundee!

pitch, there were unprecedented scenes at Dens Park.

Before kick-off, the gates were closed with thousands of desperate fans still clamouring for entry. Inside, there was congestion behind both goals with youngsters hoisted over the heads of their elders and deposited on the track for safety.

Outside the enclosure, desperate fans finally wrenched open a gate and hundreds more rushed in. And, despite a baton charge by several constables, the mob continued to pour through the breach. Many fans were knocked over by the falling gate and trampled by the oncoming crowd. There were fears of a disaster similar to that at Ibrox in 1902 but, although many were seen to limp away, there were no serious injuries.

The game itself was another no-scoring thriller and, although the official attendance of 24,000 (receipts were £665-16-3d) was a new Dens record, it was believed that at least 2,000 more had gained admission by illegal means. The previous record had been the 17,000 present for a third-round Scottish Cup tie against Celtic in February, 1901.

Dundee had fielded: Muir; Darroch, Sharp; Halkett, P. Robertson, Boyle; Bell, White, Dickson, MacFarlane, T. Robertson. Billy Muir was a brilliant goalkeeper while the full-back partnership of Johnny Darroch, now in his second spell at Dens, and Jimmy Sharp was second to none. At centre-half, inspirational captain Peter Robertson was a dominant figure with the hard-running Sandy MacFarlane the mainspring in Dundee's attack.

Ibrox Park was the venue for the second replay and, with Fred McDiarmid still on the injury list, Jim Jeffray was brought in

William Wallace - Dundee's first manager in 1899.

for Dicky Boyle at left-half. Once again, there was little between the sides but, 25 minutes from time, the deadlock was finally broken.

A wind-assisted effort by the brilliant Alan Bell sailed high past Hibs Scottish international keeper, Harry Rennie, and that was enough to put Dundee into the last four! The tie had aroused enormous interest and the 35,000-plus attendance brought takings of £1,009, the first time either club had exceeded a four-figure sum.

In the semi-final, Dundee were paired with Hearts at Dens but, despite providing extra accommodation, the attendance was a couple of thousand down on the Hibs tie. Disappointingly, a dour struggle ended 0-0 and, in the replay at Tynecastle, a late goal by Porteous ended Dundee's dream of Scottish Cup glory.

Nevertheless, Dundee had earned rich pickings. £960 was taken from the three meetings with Hibs and the semi-final ties also proved lucrative - the bumper 32,000 (£650) Tynecastle gate being a record outwith Glasgow at the time.

In 1904, Third Lanark managed their solitary title success but it was the green and white of Celtic that would dominate Scottish football for the next six years. The next few seasons saw a gradual expansion of the league and, by 1907, Division One consisted of 18 clubs. In this period, Dundee were unable to attain their earlier heights as they finished in mid-table and failed to progress beyond the third round of the Scottish Cup.

A significant factor in the Dark Blues' decline was the loss of skipper Peter Robertson in December, 1903. Just nine months after appearing for Scotland against Ireland the centre-half suffered serious knee damage in a 7-1 win over Motherwell at Dens. Sadly, his career was over and the Dark Blues could manage only four wins from their remaining 14 league games.

The hard-tackling Sharp was a product of the local East Craigie Juniors and, in 1904, a crowd of 13,000 saw him captain Scotland in a 1-1 draw against Wales in the first-ever international to be held at Dens. Soon afterwards, Sharp joined Fulham but team-mate Sandy MacFarlane, who had also played against Wales, was destined for a long and distinguished career at Dens. Signed from Newcastle United in 1901, the inside-left gained a further three caps with the Dark Blues and would later become manager of the Dens Park club.

Summer 1905 saw the arrival of centre-half Herbert Dainty from Notts County and outside-left Jack Fraser from Southampton. Each would play their part in a Dens revival but, although Fraser went on to gain a Scottish cap, it was the hard-tackling Englishman who would prove the foundation of Dundee's success.

That August, left-half Fred McDiarmid was rewarded for his six years service when his benefit game against Rangers

Wm. Longair (Trainer)　　Wm. White　Jas. Turnbull　Wm. Muir　　Jas. Sharp　Peter Robertson (Captain)

Wm. Wallace (Manager)　　Allan Bell　John Darroch　　R. Boyle　G. Henderson　Alex. M'Farlane　Fred. M'Diarmid

AGNEW & SON. PHOTO

RELIABLE SERIES

DUNDEE FOOTBALL CLUB, 1902-1903.

So near - Dundee F.C. Season 1902-03 - Scottish League Division One runners-up and Scottish Cup semi-finalists.　Ian Hendry - Postcard Club of Dundee

A view of Dens Park in the early 1900s looking northward towards Clepington Road. This postcard was sent by right-back Johnny Darroch who has marked his presence with an X. The stand was later extended beyond the corner flag.
Jack Murray

attracted a 4,000 crowd to Dens. In his early days, McDiarmid had been a left-winger and, at the turn of the Century, he formed a deadly combination with his brilliant inside partner, Tommy McDermott.

McDermott, who one fan later compared favourably with the great Billy Steel, had been transferred to Celtic in 1902 and later went on to play for Everton and Chelsea. However, in the summer of 1906, this brilliant dribbler returned to Dens and, with the team further strengthened by the arrival of Southampton left-half Bert Lee, Dundee made a strong challenge for the championship. An 18-game unbeaten run raised hopes of title success, but the Dark Blues could only manage one win in their last seven games to finish second, seven points behind Celtic.

Since 1902, Dundee had built a formidable home record with only 13 defeats in 101 league games at Dens. Muir was a key man in a consistently solid defence and, in March 1907, he kept goal for Scotland against Ireland at Parkhead. Soon afterwards, he joined Bradford City, but Lochee lad Bob Crumley, signed earlier from Newcastle, was to prove a worthy successor.

Billy Cox had finished top scorer with 21 goals - by far the highest total for a Dundee player at that time. But, along with right-half Geordie Henderson, he was surprisingly allowed to join Hearts in time for their Scottish Cup Final clash with Celtic.

Dundee, however, had lined up Portsmouth's John Hunter, a centre-forward with a deadly scoring reputation and a man whose exploits would soon figure large as the club gunned for their first domestic triumph. Known as the "Sailor" due to his distinctive rolling gait, the experienced Hunter netted 18 goals as the Dark Blues again made a strong challenge in the 1907-08 season.

But, despite a 16-game unbeaten run, another spring slump saw them finish a disappointing fourth, seven points behind League Champions Celtic. According to the local press, McDermott had become "quite rotund" and he was replaced

Boardroom memoir - George Chaplin's Scotland strip which he wore against Wales at Dens Park in 1908.
Jimmy Lorimer

by Geordie Langlands, a recent signing from Forfar. And, when the dashing outside-right Jimmy Bellamy was secured from the London club Woolwich Arsenal, Dundee's prospects for the new campaign appeared all the brighter.

Earlier that year, left-back George Chaplin had been capped in Scotland's 2-1 win over Wales at Dens with the Scots kitted out in the colours of Lord Roseberry. But, in October, he was transferred to Bradford City for what was described as "a goodly sum" after losing his place in the Dundee team to his elder brother John.

In recent seasons, Dundee had been regarded as one of Scotland's top footballing sides. They employed a close-passing style and with quality forwards like Bellamy, Langlands, Hunter, MacFarlane and Fraser, many a mazy pattern was weaved past opposing defences.

Hunter was in deadly form and his 29-goal tally, five more than the Scottish League record, took the Dark Blues within an ace of championship success. In January 1909, the "Sailor" netted three in a 4-0 home win over Rangers and, the following month, a Dens record crowd of 29,000 anticipated a repeat in the second round of the Scottish Cup.

Disappointingly, the tie ended in a no-scoring draw and the Dark Blues went down 1-0 in the replay but, by April 24th they remained top of the league, a position they had held since the turn of the year.

Division One 1908-09						
	P	W	D	L	F A	Pts
Dundee	30	22	6	6	70-32	50
Clyde	33	20	6	7	60-37	46
Celtic	30	20	5	5	60-19	45

Dundee's lead might have been greater for, in March, with the prolific Hunter on Scotland duty in Wales, they had lost 2-1 to Morton at Dens. That failure proved fatal as Celtic took six points from their last four games in a five-day spell to pip Dundee for the title by a single point, albeit with a jittery 2-1 win at Hamilton in their final game.

Surprisingly, Dundee's league performances in 1909-10 were dogged by inconsistency but glory was just around the corner. The first round of the Scottish Cup paired them with non-league Beith and, with the Ayrshire side agreeing to "sell" home advantage, the tie was played at Dens Park. On a frosty surface, Bellamy missed an early penalty but, despite going ahead through Comrie, Beith fought back for a 1-1 draw. The game had attracted 9,000 fans but 3,000 fewer saw the replay in which Langlands gave Dundee the narrowest of wins.

At the next stage, the Dark Blues entertained Falkirk, who were challenging strongly at the top of the league, and around 20,000 turned out in the expectation of a close game. Dens was a mudbath but, after a Hall shot was controversially adjudged to have crossed the line, further goals by Bellamy and Hunter clinched a 3-0 win.

In the third round, Dundee travelled to Motherwell. On the train going through, MacFarlane took ill and so Hunter went to inside-left and former Newcastle centre Sandy Hall came in to score all the goals in a 3-1 win.

Next came Hibs for what proved a marathon semi-final. In a repeat of 1903, there were no-scoring stalemates at Dens and Easter Road before the second replay again went to Glasgow. This time Parkhead was the venue for another gruelling struggle but a typical headed counter by Hunter took Dundee into their first-ever Scottish Cup Final.

In the other semi-final, Clyde, who had earlier beaten Leith, Rangers and Queen's Park, had stunned Scottish football by eliminating the mighty Celtic, who were by then

heading for their sixth successive championship.

The Parkhead side had held the cup for two years and might have made it three in a row had the trophy not been withheld after the serious rioting when the replayed final between Celtic and Rangers ended in a 1-1 draw. Other than interruptions for two World Wars, this remains the only year without an outright Scottish Cup winner. Nevertheless, Dundee were confident of success and a mood of optimism was abroad in the Jute City.

Until December, Dundee's league performances had shown little of last term's consistency but, by 1910, the team was again firing on all cylinders. By the time of the Cup Final, only one game from fifteen had been lost and, despite Clyde's Old Firm successes, Dundee were favourites to win the trophy at the 75,000 capacity Ibrox Park.

However, it was Clyde who began confidently and, by half-time, goals by Chalmers and Booth put them 2-0 ahead. Both were the result of poor defending by Dundee but, with both sides producing some grand football, there was no let-up in the action.

As the minutes ticked away, Dundee showed little sign of making the breakthrough and thousands of their fans faced the prospect of a bleak journey home. Many of the 60,000 crowd had made their way to the exits and Clyde officials were so certain of victory that their chairman had already prepared his cup-winning speech.

With three and a half minutes remaining, a long ball was sent down the middle. Hunter refused to give up the chase and, as Watson attempted to clear, the ball flew off the inrushing Dens centre and into the net. Some maintained it was an "own-goal" although the referee later confirmed Hunter as the scorer. But, no matter which route the ball had taken, Dundee were back in the hunt.

Caution was thrown to the wind and, with 30 seconds remaining, the Dark Blues' efforts were rewarded by a corner. Bellamy sent over a perfect cross and Langlands crashed the ball high into the net.

Dundee supporters were ecstatic although many downcast souls were already on their way to the railway station! The players too were in buoyant mood and Dens skipper Bert Lee was heard to declare: "I'll eat the Tay Bridge if we don't win the replay!" However, many Dens fans were unable to afford an Ibrox return the following Saturday and, with the onset of stormy weather, only 20,000 passed through the gates.

The Dark Blues made one change, Bert Neal being preferred to Jimmy Lawson at right-back. Torrential rain turned the pitch into a quagmire but, despite half-an-hour of extra-time, neither side could score. The blustery conditions proved too much for young Jackson of Clyde. He collapsed in the mud and was carried from the field some minutes from the end.

The physically stronger Dens Parkers had held the edge and were now clear favourites in the second replay at Ibrox on Wednesday, April 20th. McEwan replaced the injured Chaplin at left-back as Dundee lined up: Crumley; Neal, McEwan; Lee, Dainty, Comrie; Bellamy, Langlands, Hunter, MacFarlane, Fraser. Clyde had been unchanged in the first two games but now Wylie and Wyse were brought in for Stirling and Jackson, their team lines reading: McTurk; Watson, Blair; Walker, McAteer, Robertson; Wyllie, McCartney, Chalmers, Wyse, Booth.

Days of Yore - a 1910 rooftop view of Dundee's High Street and the Overgate which would soon be awash with celebrating fans.

Dundee were shocked when Chalmers put Clyde ahead in three minutes. The Shawfielders sat back and, as Dundee pushed forward, Bellamy headed the equaliser from a 15th minute corner. Once again, it was a keenly fought contest in stamina-sapping conditions. Ten minutes after half-time, MacFarlane hirpled on the wing but Dundee would not be denied. "Sailor" Hunter broke through and, after beating former Dens Park centre-half McAteer, he sent the ball past McTurk from a narrow angle.

Desperately Clyde laid siege to the Dundee goal. But, with Crumley and Dainty outstanding in defence, there was no further scoring. And, when referee Dugary blew for full-time, caps and sticks were thrown in the air by jubilant Dens fans in the 24,000 crowd.

"Sailor" Hunter

It was an emotional ex-Baillie Robertson who accepted the trophy for, according to the Dens Park chairman, "It had been the height of the club's ambition to win the Scottish Cup." The names of Dundee's Cup-winning side would long be remembered especially that of John "Sailor" Hunter, whose winning goal ensured that the cup would come east to Dens Park.

The official Dundee party was cheered off from Glasgow's Buchanan Street Station and although it was 11 o'clock before the train steamed into Dundee, a huge crowd awaited their arrival. Anxious to avoid any demonstration, the party decided to alight at Magdalen Green but when confronted by large crowds, they carried on!

The explosion of detonators told the 20,000 crowd at the West Station that their heroes had arrived. Then, as ex-Bailie Robertson emerged holding the trophy, thunderous roars rent the night air! Dock Street was jammed with happy, shouting people but, despite the chaos, players and officials

Great was the joy - huge crowds gathered in the city streets to cheer Dundee's Cup triumph. This caricature depicts the scenes on Victoria Road.

managed to clamber aboard the horse-drawn coach that awaited them there.

The police struggled to keep control. Halfway up Union Street, the horses were unyoked and scores of enthusiastic fans took over. Slowly, the coach progressed along High Street, Meadowside and into Victoria Road on its way to Dens Park. There the horses were put back to ascend the brae but many fans had also climbed onto the brake and, eventually, the back axle collapsed under the excess weight!

Guarded by police, the triumphant Dundee party continued on foot, waving the Cup as they went. When they reached Dens, there were great celebrations as the waiting crowd roared themselves hoarse. It was the early hours before things quietened down and players and officials went on to dine at the Royal British Hotel.

It was a night to remember for all concerned. Dundee had taken a marathon ten games to secure the silverware but, watched by a total of 214,000 fans, it had proved a money-spinner for the Dens Park club. The final alone had attracted 104,000 and, after expenses, £3,336 was shared between the two clubs. And, with the aid of local subscriptions, the Dens players received a healthy bonus of £40 per man.

A dream come true! - Dundee F.C.'s Scottish Cup-winning squad of 1909-10 (BACK, left to right) Bert Neal, George Langlands, Jimmy Bellamy, William Wallace (secretary-manager), Herbert Dainty, Sandy Hall. MIDDLE - Mr David McEwan (director), Bob McEwan, George Comrie, Bill Longair (trainer), Jack Fraser, John Chaplin, Mr George Walker (director), Bob Crumley. SITTING - Mr John Cameron (director), John Hunter, ex-Bailie Robertson (chairman), Bert Lee (captain), Mr Andrew Williamson (director), Sandy MacFarlane, Mr Sandy Spalding (director). FRONT - Jimmy Lawson and Daniel McCann.
DC Thomson

At the start of the following season, the Scottish Cup was displayed before Dundee's game against Hibs at Dens. A life-long supporter of the Dark Blues, Charlie Beat was 87 years old at the start of 1993. Nostalgically, he recalled: "I can remember the players coming round the pitch with the Cup but I've no recollection of the game itself. I was only five at the time and, with my mother and father working in their own shop, my aunt always took me to Dens to get me out of the way!"

"We always went to the small enclosure between the South Stand and the pavilion and would arrive at 12 o'clock because the ground filled up quickly when the works came out at mid-day. Dens Park was still on the outskirts of the town in those days and there was a small track behind the East terracing. This was bordered by various small-holdings and behind part of the North Stand there were rows of cabbages!"

However, although they made a strong challenge until Christmas, Dundee again had to settle for sixth place in the league championship. Cup hero Sailor Hunter was soon on the move to Clyde but, with former Rangers and Hearts Scottish international R. C. Hamilton signed as his replacement, the Dark Blues remained a top side. Hamilton no longer had the speed of old but his clever play brought him 20 goals and, in a surprise international recall, he scored another in Scotland's 2-2 draw at Cardiff.

Wins over Hibs (h) 2-1, Partick (a) 3-0 and Rangers (h) 2-1 - the match against the Ibrox side attracted a new crowd record of 30,000 to Dens - brought hopes of a second successive Scottish Cup Final appearance. However, despite taking a two-goal lead early in the second half of the Douglas Park semi-final against Hamilton, Dundee became complacent and the relegation-threatened Accies went on to win 3-2.

Soon afterwards, a 2-0 defeat to Rangers ended Dundee's incredible 39-game unbeaten run at Dens. Remarkably, it was only their second home defeat in 58 games since February 1908 but, coupled with the shattering cup upset, it marked the end of a golden era for the Dark Blues.

Of the Cup-winning squad, Hunter, Chaplin (to Manchester City), and McCann (Celtic), had all already gone. Crumley gave way to Manchester City's Scottish international keeper Jack Lyall -

"UP WI' THE BONNETS O' BONNIE DUNDEE"

The Scottish Cup Comes to Tayside.

THE BEST FINAL SEEN FOR YEARS.

Unparalleled Scenes of Enthusiasm in the City.

DUNDEE DEFEAT CLYDE BY 2 GOALS TO 1.

Dundee F.C. before the opening game of 1909-10 including eight of the side that went on to lift the Scottish Cup. (BACK, left to right) William Wallace (manager), John Chaplin, Jack Fraser, Bert Lee, Bert Neal, Bob Crumley, Jimmy Dundas (linesman). FRONT - Jimmy Bellamy, George Langlands, Sandy McFarlane, Herbert Dainty, Alex Menzies, Jimmy Lawson, Bill Longair (trainer). Ian Hendry Postcard Club of Dundee

Glory goal - R.C. Hamilton has just scored for holders Dundee in the Scottish Cup quarter-final at Dens on February 25th, 1911. The Dark Blues went on to win 2-1 before a new record attendance of 30,000. The old North Stand, later demolished after the present one was completed in 1921, has been extended almost to the corner. Inset - Bob Crumley (left), Jack Fraser (right)

Courtesy of Dundee F.C.

GALLAHER'S CIGARETTES.

H. DAINTY,
DUNDEE, 1909-10.

another Dundonian - and, in the close-season, Herbert Dainty, Bert Lee and Bob McEwan also moved on.

In April of 1910, Herbert Dainty's Dens testimonial against Rangers had attracted a crowd of 8,000. The popular centre-half, who had scored an astonishing 24 goals - only seven of them penalties - in six seasons at Dens, had been a key man for Dundee and his departure to Bradford City came as a severe blow. Dainty soon returned to Scotland but there was now a rift between him and the Dens board and, despite having business interests in Dundee, he joined Ayr United before later returning to the Jute City to turn out for the recently formed Dundee Hibs.

Dundee signed 14-times capped Scottish international right-half Andy Aitken from Leicester but, as they entered a period of decline, they could finish no higher than seventh in the three seasons before the outbreak of war in August 1914.

August 1913 had seen the return of Geordie Langlands at the age of 26 to Forfar. He was the last survivor of Dundee's 1910 Cup-winning side, with Sandy MacFarlane, who had made a then record 333 appearances in his 12 years at Dens, joining Chelsea earlier that summer.

Right-back Tom Kelso followed in the footsteps of his uncle, Bob Kelso, when he appeared for Scotland against Wales the following March but, shortly afterwards, he moved on to Rangers. George Philip (24), was another who had emerged as a top performer. After two seasons at centre-half he was switched to centre-forward and, after scoring fourteen goals in 12 appearances, he was transferred to Sunderland for a Dens Park record fee of £1,500 just before the end of the 1913-14 season.

Meanwhile, international tensions had escalated and, in August, Britain joined France and Russia and went to war against Germany and the Central Powers. The Great War had begun and, although Scottish League football continued, it became largely irrelevant compared to the horrors of the Western Front. British Generals had predicted that the war would be over by Christmas but, with the opposing armies reaching a stalemate in the Flanders mud, the fighting was to

continue for another four horrendous years.

At the outbreak of war it was agreed that admission be reduced from 9d to 3d. In addition, players' wages would decrease by around 25 per cent with a maximum of £1 weekly but this was ignored by many of the top clubs.

The Dark Blues were no longer amongst the elite. Their fortunes had continued to deteriorate and, in 1916-17, they finished sixteenth in what had become an Old Firm-dominated top Division of twenty clubs after the scrapping of Division Two in 1915.

A number of Dundee players were enlisted and although some, such as young Alec Troup and Dave Hutcheson served on the Western Front, others remained locally and continued to turn out for the Dark Blues. Very little newspaper space was now devoted to the reporting of football and even the match reports included the players' military ranks such as "Private" MacDonald, "Sergeant" Brown and "Sapper" Ferguson.

NT BAYONET ARGES.
Y ROUTS GERMANS ALTKIRCH.
OWNS TAKEN.

KITCHENER'S CLARION CALL TO SCOTLAND

100,000 MEN WANTED IMMEDIATELY.

GREAT RESPONSE TO "PEOPLE'S JOURNAL" APPEAL.

Lord Kitchener, Secretary of State for War, to Editor, "People's Journal":—

"I appeal to the men of Scotland. Their King and Country need them. We require 100,000 men at once for service. Go to your nearest Post Office or Recruiting Station and answer your country's call."

God Save the King.

WHY LORD KITCHENER WANTS SCOTSMEN.

THE NEVER-DYING FAME OF THE HIGHLAND REGIMENTS.

DOUGHTY DEEDS.

THE "PEOPLE'S JOURNAL" FIERY CROSS.

One of the more amusing wartime footballing stories concerned the demise of the Dens Park mascot. A Mr Gow was the Dundee F.C. groundsman and, in addition to his normal duties, he kept some animals including a giant parrot, a monkey and a goat.

For some years, the goat had been club mascot but, with the onset of war and a drop in gates, cuts had to be made. And, in *The Dundee Post* of November 14th, 1914 came the sad news - the Dens Park goat was no more!

In 1917, Dundee, along with Aberdeen and Raith Rovers, were asked to withdraw from the Scottish League to minimise the travelling of their predominantly West of Scotland opponents. A North-East League was formed and one notable "guest" for the Dark Blues was Aberdeen goalkeeper George Anderson, who would later become such an influential figure at Dens. By then, the Great War had almost run its course and, on November 11th, 1918, hostilities finally ceased with the signing of the Armistice in Versailles.

F.&J SMITH'S CIGARETTES

DUNDEE.
A TROUP.

CHAPTER THREE

Post–War Boom

After a two-year absence from league football, little was expected from Dundee in the 1919-20 season. The Dens board now comprised John Cameron (chairman), Andrew Williamson (vice-chairman), William McIntosh (treasurer), William Lindsay, N. D. Dickson, P. T. Jackson and Robert Paterson and one of their first moves was to appoint former Dens favourite Sandy MacFarlane as the club's new manager.

Earlier that year, William Wallace had intimated his resignation after 20 years service. Unlike his predecessor, MacFarlane would be full-time but he faced a daunting task in re-establishing the Dark Blues amongst Scotland's elite.

Throughout the war years, Dundee had fielded a young side but, although recognising that left-back David "Napper" Thomson, right-half Bert McIntosh, centre-forward Davie Brown and left-winger Alec Troup were talented performers, the new manager realised that new blood was required and several new signings were made.

On August 23rd, 1919, 20,000 fans attended Dundee's opening home game against Third Lanark. The Dark Blues fielded: Capper; Raitt, Thomson; McIntosh, Nicoll, Hutchison; D. McDonald, Buchan, D. Brown, W. Brown, Troup - and goals by Buchan, Davie McDonald, and Thomson with a penalty, brought a 3-1 victory.

Only seven points were taken from the first nine games and it was soon clear that some of the newcomers were not up to scratch. This could not be attributed to bad management since the interruption by the war made the form of individual players, many of whom had fought at the front, a matter of inspired guesswork. Right-back Davie Raitt (Lochgelly Juniors), and centre-half Dyken Nicoll (Forfar), were the pick of the bunch and, to the credit of the Dens Park board, they continued to improve the playing staff.

In the opening 13 games, centre-forward Davie Brown, who had scored 77 goals for Dundee since 1914, found the net another eleven times. Surprisingly, he was transferred to Stoke City that October but former Hearts centre Johnny Bell - a Lochee lad - took his place and went on to finish the season with 28 goals!

The Dark Blues were further strengthened by the arrival of right-winger Archie Rawlings (Rochdale), Motherwell left-half John Jackson, who had played against Dundee in the 1910 Cup Final, and inside-men Donald Slade (Fulham), and Jim McLaughlin (Clydebank). It was the experienced Rawlings who provided the vital spark and, by mid-December, a successful run saw Dundee slip into third place behind Rangers and Celtic.

Sandy MacFarlane - the first full-time boss.

And, although Scottish Cup hopes ended with a 3-1 home defeat by Celtic before a 34,000 record home crowd, the Dens Parkers went on to finish fourth, their highest league placing for eleven years.

However, there had been a controversial end to the season. Two days after crashing 6-1 to league leaders Rangers at Ibrox, Dundee faced second-placed Celtic at Parkhead. Four minutes from the end, the score remained 1-1 but, when Celtic's Adam McLean reacted angrily to a tackle by Bert McIntosh, several ruffians ran from the terracings and onto the pitch.

McIntosh, who was Dundee captain, was attacked and the referee chased from the field. Many of the Celtic support believed that Dundee had "lain down" to Rangers and were now determined to thwart the Parkhead title challenge. The game was abandoned and the result later deemed to stand but only a hasty intervention by players of both sides had defused a potentially explosive situation.

That March, Dundee purchased Dens Park for £5,000 and, soon afterwards, it was announced that a new 5,000-seater grandstand would replace the existing North Stand. Nine-and-a-half years of the lease had remained but when it was heard that a neighbouring works was negotiating to buy the north side of the ground, the board had moved decisively to secure the club's future.

To raise capital, there was a new share issue but, contrary to the hopes of many fans, Dundee F.C. remained a private company and only around 30 selected persons were invited to take up the available shares.

Nevertheless, Dundee's prime aim was to have a successful team on the field and more top men were brought to Dens. Sam Irving, the Northern Ireland international half-back was signed from Blyth Spartans while former Dens Parker George Philip returned from Sunderland for £500.

A five-game unbeaten run saw Dundee make a promising start to their 1920-21 campaign. Irving, who was a splendid ball-player, brought composure to the side and, with Bell repeating his scoring exploits of the previous season, the Dark Blues again finished fourth.

As in the early 1900s, much of the success was down to Dundee's solid defence and it was claimed that centre-half Nicoll could head the ball as far as many could kick it! But although right-back Davie Raitt was a traditional hard-

Dundee F.C. Season 1920-21 (BACK, left to right) John Jackson, Dyken Nicoll, Davie Raitt, Tom Gibbon, David "Napper" Thomson, George Philip, Sam Irving. FRONT - Davie McDonald, Johnny Bell, Donald Slade, Alec Troup.

DC Thomson

tackling defender, his full-back partner David Thomson, while equally solid, had a different approach.

Nicknamed "Napper" due to his cool play, Thomson scorned the big punt upfield and invariably would find his man with an accurate pass. Here was a full-back before his time, yet, surprisingly, the stylish defender made only one international appearance for Scotland when he played in the first post-war game against Wales in February 1920.

"Napper was no soft touch," recalled Charlie Beat. "Shoulder charges were part and parcel of the game in those days. One of Thomson's specialities was to run alongside an opponent until he got him on one leg, then wham! I can still remember the headline in *The Saturday Post* after a game against Albion Rovers. It read: 'Ribchester (Rovers' right-winger) got a Ribtester from Napper at Dens!' Napper was a great back, better than Dodds and McStay of Celtic, but like Troup, he found it was a lot easier to get a game for Scotland if you were playing for a team from Glasgow."

Although Johnny Bell had scored 53 league goals over the past two seasons, much of his success was down to left-winger Alec Troup. Signed from Forfar in 1915, Troup was a great favourite with the fans and although only 5'5" tall, his dazzling wing play and pinpoint crosses made him a constant menace to opposing defences.

Nevertheless, Sandy MacFarlane was concerned at the lack of height in attack and to rectify matters, he signed David Halliday (St Mirren), and Walter Bird (Blackburn Rovers), with Airdrie's Willie Fotheringham arriving as a replacement goalkeeper for Tom Gibbon.

On September 17th, 1921, the new stand, designed by the renowned football stadium architect Archibald Leitch, was officially opened before the league game against Ayr United at Dens. A Willie McLean goal gave Dundee a 1-0 win

before a 20,000 crowd as they fielded: Fotheringham; Raitt, D. Thomson; Irving, W. Thompson, Nicoll; Ross, W. McLean, Bell, Bird, Troup.

The imposing new structure was in stark contrast to the antiquated South Stand but, just three months later, the former Carolina Port stand was razed to the ground. The fire began soon after Dundee's 2-0 home win over Hamilton on December 24th and appeared to be caused by a lit match or cigarette end that had been dropped during the game.

It had been raining but, fanned by a strong breeze, the dry wooden structure was soon ablaze from end to end. The Fire Brigade were unable to prevent its destruction although valuables and documents were carried to safety and the adjoining pavilion was preserved intact.

Curiously, the burnt-out stand, which had been insured, was to have been dismantled and sold at the end of that season. However, this did not prevent rumours of an insurance fraud with Jimmy Guthrie, a Dundee player of the 1930s, later telling of three previous outbreaks of fire in the same stand. According to him, a dutiful groundsman had doused the flames on each occasion before eventually getting the sack!

Johnny Bell was back on the score-sheet against the Accies but his form had shaded and,

> **OLD STAND AT DENS PARK DESTROYED BY FIRE.**
>
> The south or old stand at Dens Park was totally destroyed on Saturday by an outbreak of fire which engulfed the structure not long after the spectators had left the Dundee-Hamilton game.
>
> The cause of the blaze, which, it is estimated, created damage amounting to about £1200, is presumed to be the dropping of a lighted match or cigarette-end by some of the occupants of the stand during the progress of the match.
>
> Fanned by a strong north-westerly breeze, the flames, despite the fact that rain was falling at the time, soon held the dry wooden erection in their grip, and the Fire Brigade, under Firemaster Weir, directed their efforts to save the reserve stand, which adjoins it, and the latter, though slightly damaged, was preserved.
>
> At a time when the conflagration threatened to envelope the stand from end to end the officials, along with willing assistants, conveyed all valuable movables and documents to a place of safety.
>
> It is a singular coincidence that the stand, which is now a skeleton of fantastically.

soon afterwards he was replaced by the powerful Davie Halliday who had impressed as a left-winger with Queen of the South and St Mirren. And, by the end of the season, Halliday's 25-goal tally did much to ensure Dundee finishing fourth in the league for the third successive season.

Dundee's post-war gates had averaged 15,000 but the new £55,000 stand proved a massive burden on the club's finances. The board had been strengthened by the addition of Mr A. P. McBain but, in January, 1922, the club lost one of their greatest servants with the death, at the age of 60, of vice-chairman Andrew Williamson, who had owned a tobacconist's shop in West Port. Williamson was one of the founder members of Dundee F.C. and had also been on the committee which had resurrected the club in 1898.

The approach of the 1922-23 campaign heralded the departure of Davie Raitt to Everton. A "substantial" fee was received and the fans were somewhat placated by the arrival of two experienced forwards. Outside-left Jock McDonald was signed for £1,000 from Blackburn Rovers while Davie McLean, the ex-Forfar and Celtic favourite was secured from Bradford Park Avenue.

McLean settled quickly and taking advantage of the fine service provided by Alec Troup, he soon found the net on a regular basis. "Wee Troupie" was an original touchline terror and would certainly have made more than the four Scottish international and two Scottish League appearances he managed while at Dens, had it not been for Alan Morton of Rangers, who was regarded as the finest winger in Britain at the time.

For long enough, Troup had played with the handicap of a loose collarbone and often, without apparent cause, the shoulder came out and the winger would pull up. On came the trainer and with one thump, the shoulder would be back in place and Troup would carry on as if nothing at all had happened!

By early January, Dundee lay two points behind league

Davie Halliday - hit a Dens record 38 league goals in 1923-24.

leaders Rangers with 32 points but, astonishingly, the brilliant Troup was allowed to join Everton for £4,000 just two weeks later.

The wee winger had been a key man and without him the Dark Blues could manage only nine points from their remaining eleven games. That left them seventh and, despite improving two places the following term, the downward trend had been confirmed.

Many speculated that payments for the new stand had necessitated the transfers of Raitt and Troup. But, although Jock McDonald was a ready-made replacement for Troup, no fewer than eight players were tried in an effort to find a suitable successor to Raitt.

The 1923-24 season saw McLean and Halliday develop a potent partnership. The advent of the awkward but hard-running Halliday meant McLean switching to inside-right. There he became the "general" of the team, cleverly controlling play and thrilling the fans with his thundering long-range shots.

McLean's experience brought out the best in Halliday and, that term, the big centre rattled in 39 goals, one more than his total for the previous two seasons at Dundee. Remarkably, thirty-eight of those had been scored in league games, a tally that remains a Dens Park record to this day.

The summer of 1923 had seen the Dark Blues undertake their first-ever overseas tour. A lengthy journey by boat and train took them to Spain where they won four of their seven games including a 2-0 triumph over the famous Real Madrid. The tour was a great success and, the following year, Dundee returned.

Again there was a bright start with 2-0 and 2-1 victories against Barcelona - who had won both meetings in 1923 - before Dundee met Real Madrid. But, with the visitors lead-

Dens Park in October 1921 - in the foreground lies the South Stand and pavilion, the former brought from Carolina Port in 1899. On the far side is the newly erected North Stand, which is still going strong to this day.

DC Thomson

Up Wi' The Bonnets - a glorious view of Dens Park in its then rural surroundings in August 1925 when Morton were defeated 3-0. Sam Irving is on the ball with Jock Ross, Willie Rankine, Napper Thomson, Finlay Brown and Jock Britton the other Dundee men.   Sandy Watson

ing 1-0, the game exploded when the Spanish referee, who had officiated from the shade of the stand with a lemon in his hand, awarded Real a soft penalty.

The Dundee players were incensed by this and, when the referee placed the ball on the spot, an exasperated Willie Rankine kicked it into the net!

At this, the official tried to strike Rankine but he was quickly pushed away by the Dens centre-half. Rankine was then ordered off but, when he refused to go, six armed policemen were asked to intervene. Willie was having none of it and, after shaking them off, the entire Dundee team walked from the field.

There was uproar amongst the 6,000 crowd and only the intervention of manager Sandy MacFarlane and treasurer William McIntosh ensured the completion of the game. The score ended 1-1 but, when the sides played again the following day, twice as many fans saw the Dark Blues record a most satisfying 2-1 win.

Two years earlier, the strapping Rankine had taken Dyken Nicoll's place at centre-half. But although there were plenty of characters onfield, there were also others off it such as the war veteran so movingly described in *The Sporting Post*: "Along the track, Blind Jock padded as usual, grinding out

music from his melodeon and doing rather well financially."

Surprisingly, the 1924-25 campaign began badly and, by Christmas, Dundee lay twelfth with only 18 points from 20 games. Sandy MacFarlane had been the architect of Dundee's post-war success but he now felt compelled to resign and responsibility for team affairs was temporarily assumed by club treasurer William McIntosh.

The slump continued with only two wins from the next six league matches before inside-left John Rankine was signed from Doncaster Rovers. The hard-working newcomer soon brought a better balance to the team and home wins over lower league sides Johnstone (5-0), and Lochgelly United (2-1), took Dundee to the third round of the Scottish Cup. Since the war, the Dark Blues had twice reached the quarter-finals but few expected them to overcome their next hurdle against cup-holders Airdrie, who currently lay second in Division One.

However, when the sides met on February 21st, Willie Rankine was successful in blotting out Airdrie's live-wire Scotland centre-forward, Hughie Gallacher. And with the Broomfield attack effectively shackled, goals by McLean, Duncan and Halliday gave Dundee a 3-1 win in the Dens Park mud.

The game had been watched by a crowd of 22,373 (receipts £901) though almost 7,000 fewer would see Dundee struggle against lowly Broxburn in the quarter-final. But with 15 minutes remaining, the stalemate was broken. Irving sent over a corner and Halliday bundled keeper and ball into the net to put Dundee into the last four. Shoulder to shoulder contact with the keeper was part and parcel of the game in these days!

In the semi-final, the luck of the draw brought them a fifth successive home tie against Hamilton Accies and 29,814 (£1,184) passed through the Dens Park turnstiles. Dundee had most of the play but, despite Duncan equalising an early goal by the Douglas Park men, the homesters were unable to land the killer punch.

Easter Road was the venue for the replay and this time Dundee made no mistake. In 15 minutes, Davie McLean cracked in the opener from a tight angle and, near the end, John Rankine clinched a place in the Final for the Dens men with a second goal.

Now, Dundee could anticipate a Hampden clash with Celtic although only the casting vote of SFA chairman Mr White of the Parkhead club had ensured that the Queen's Park ground got the nod over Ibrox!

Since the war, Celtic had regularly finished in the top three, winning the championship and Scottish Cup once each. Both sides had lost just one of their last 11 games but, with a 5-0 semi-final triumph over Rangers and a recent 4-0 home win over Dundee, the Parkhead side were strong favourites to go on and win the trophy.

All Dundee's players were fit but there was disappointment for right-half Colin McNab who had appeared in both semi-final ties. The youngster had played over 20 first-team games that term but Dens skipper Jock Ross, a regular since 1921, had recovered from injury and would lead the side out for the Scottish Cup Final.

A fascinating contest was in prospect as Dundee lined up: Britton; Brown, Thomson; Ross (captain), W. Rankine, Irving; Duncan, McLean, Halliday, J. Rankine and Gilmour. Celtic: Shevlin; W. McStay, Hilley; Wilson, J. McStay, MacFarlane; Connolly, Gallacher, McGrory, Thomson and McLean.

Former Albion Rovers keeper Jock Britton had taken over from Fotheringham, who had moved to Morton the previous summer. At full-back, "Napper" Thomson was partnered by Finlay Brown, who had emerged as a capable successor to Davie Raitt. Like Celtic, the Dark Blues had an experienced midline but, although there was little between the sides defensively and the respective inside men looked well-matched, Celtic appeared to hold an edge on the wings.

On the right, Dundee fielded Charlie Duncan, normally an elusive inside-forward, with young reserve left-back Jock Gilmour continuing to deputise for the injured veteran Jock McDonald out on the left wing.

A number of special trains travelled from Dundee and 6,000 supporters gave the Dark Blues a great cheer as they took to the field. The 75,137 crowd was the second largest for a Scottish Cup Final thus far and, curiously, Tom Dougray, who had refereed Dundee's Cup Final win in 1910, was again in charge.

Davie McLean - put Dundee ahead in Final.

Against the odds, it was Dundee who dominated the opening stages and in 30 minutes they went ahead. Taking a pass from Halliday, McLean slipped the ball to Duncan. The winger crossed and under pressure from the inrushing Halliday, Shevlin could only palm the ball out to Gilmour. The youngster headed goalwards but hit the bar and, as the ball dropped between two of the Celtic defenders, McLean rushed in to score.

Half-time arrived with Dundee deservedly ahead but, after the interval, Celtic produced their customary cup-tie spirit. For long spells only Halliday, Duncan and Gilmour were upfield as Celtic pounded the Dens defence and just 19 minutes remained when Celtic were awarded a free-kick 40 yards from the Dundee goal.

Taking a short pass from Wilson, Patsy Gallacher - father of Tommy Gallacher, who was to be a major Dens star of the 1940s and 50s - set off on a run. Incredibly, he managed to wriggle his way past several lunging tackles before running the ball into the net.

Although now at the veteran stage, 31-year old Gallacher had caused havoc in the Dens defence and with three minutes remaining Thomson brought him down at the edge of the box. MacFarlane lofted over the free-kick and when the prolific Jimmy McGrory headed home - from an offside position according to some - it was all over for Dundee.

The Dark Blues were criticised for their negative approach after the interval and many believed that Willie Knox, an experienced winger, should have played on the right. However, despite their disappointment, it was hoped that Dundee would reproduce their best form next season.

In June, former Celtic full-back Alex McNair (42), was appointed Dundee manager. The likeable McNair had made 15 appearances for Scotland and was held in great esteem

Dundee from the Law Hill, looking towards Dens Park.

THE SUNDAY POST, APRIL 12, 1925.

HOW DUNDEE LOST THE LEAD AND THE BIG CUP BATTLE.

ALL ABOUT THE PLAYERS—FRANK AND FEARLESS CRITICISM.

BY CAPTAIN BOB.

CELTIC I have always described as up-hill fighters.

I was confident—before the game— that the Parkhead boys would do the trick, would carry on the tradition of the club, would win despite any frowns that capricious Fortune might cast their way.

That was before the game. After forty-five minutes' play I was not so confident. Dundee had scored. Dundee had revealed ability in attack, resolution in defence, and an all-round crispness which augured well for their success.

If Dundee had realised—as I realised—the advantage of a leading goal they would have won. But they didn't. Their inside men played a defensive game merely, instead of supporting their wingers and their centre as they had done in the first half.

Usually he overdoes the Gallagher part, and so upsets his colleagues.

But in that last forty-five minutes! He was IT, a helper, a raider, and an inspiration to the young fellows in whom the Celtic officials had put their trust.

His goal, a chancy thing, was of incalculable value. It was the sort of goal that does not impress of itself, but means a world of encouragement to the scoring side.

Encouragement! We saw what that goal meant to Celtic in the closing stages. They completely outplayed Dundee. Cool and crafty as "Napper" Thomson was, dashing as Brown was, intelligent and intuitive as Britton was, the tide could not be stemmed.

Celtic's second goal — from M'Grory's header off a free kick lobbed in by M'Farlane—put Dundee out of the Cup. A good goal, a clever goal, and that Jimmy Quinn described as " masterly."

Rather remarkable are these Celtic youngsters. Hilley, for example. I am sure he has never played so well since he joined the Parkhead club. Some say that Willie

players, some old in the game, some newcomers.

Outstanding was Thomson, a shrewd, full-back, a man with heart and head. Many times he busted in opportunely. I heard someone shout, " Play the game, Napper!" when he walked coolly over the midway line and neatly placed M'Grory offside.

What was wrong? Was " Napper " to be blamed for using his wits to outwit a less astute opponent? I hope not.

Brown did well. He kept a close grip of M'Lean, and so close that Adam never attained his usual standard. And I say that, knowing that the Celtic left winger was one of the most dangerous men in the Parkhead team.

Sam Irving played a fairly steady game. So did Jock Ross. But the " big noise " was undoubtedly W. Rankine, a relentless spoiler, a player who never faltered.

I am sure Ross and Irving will acknowledge Rankine's power, will agree with me that to him they are indebted for assistance in troublous times. The centre half was

throughout the game. However, his task would be all the harder following the departure of the transfer-seeking Davie Halliday to Sunderland for £4,000.

In 1924, the 23-year-old centre had been capped for the Scottish League against their English counterparts. He was just the latest in a widespread exodus of top Scots to go to England but, with a scoring record of 103 goals in 147 games for Dundee, such a prolific scorer would be hard to replace. Halliday was to be a big success down south and, over the next four seasons, he scored a phenomenal 162 goals in 175 games for Sunderland and only the consistency of Hughie Gallacher kept him out of the Scotland side.

Although Dundee were the city's major club, the recent promotion of Dundee United brought added interest to the local game. A £300 deal saw Jock McDonald join the Tannadice side but, in an astute move, Forfar's Willie Cook was signed to take his place on the left-wing.

Apart from Dundee Wanderers' brief flirtation in 1894-95, Dundee had been the city's only Scottish League club until the emergence of Dundee Hibs in 1909. The Hibs had been formed to represent the Roman Catholic community in Dundee but, like their forerunners, Dundee Harp, who had gone defunct in 1897, their existence had been a continual struggle.

After their relegation from Division Two in 1922, Dundee Hibs returned the following year despite protestations by William

Alex McNair - was the Dark Blues third manager.

McIntosh that the city could not support two clubs. Dundee again objected when they proposed changing their name to Dundee City to gain wider appeal, but later they accepted the name of Dundee United.

Predictably, Dundee finished seven points above their struggling neighbours but, without the deadly Halliday and with McLean's influence on the wane, the Dens Parkers could only finish a disappointing tenth in the table.

Dundee took three points out of four from United but found it hard going against their less-fancied opponents. On November 21st, 1925, a crowd of 18,000 turned out for the first-ever league derby at Dens. The usually reliable "Napper" Thomson missed a penalty as the rivals drew 0-0 but a goal by Davie McLean ensured a 1-0 win at Tannadice just seven weeks later. There was keen rivalry between the sides and, during the Tannadice clash, Willie Cook and United's Dave Walker were ordered off.

In the close season, goalkeeper Jock Britton was transferred to Spurs while Sam Irving, who had made 10 appearances for Northern Ireland, moved on to Cardiff City. Big English keeper Bill Marsh took over in goal with Jock Thomson coming in at left-half. Both were promoted from the reserves although manager McNair also made a number of signings including Joe Cassidy, the ex-Celtic forward who made four appearances for Scotland in the early 1920s.

That term, Dundee were a much-improved side. And, although a new Dens record crowd of 37,471 saw them fall 4-2 to Celtic in the third round of the Scottish Cup, they finished a respectable fifth in the league.

Encouragingly, right-half Colin McNab had emerged as a

real driving force and, with Andy Campbell netting 30 league goals, including four in a 5-0 derby win over Dundee United at Dens, the future looked bright.

However, it would prove a transitional period as familiar names continued to depart. After a re-signing dispute, left-back Napper Thomson was placed on the transfer list, while the redoubtable Willie Rankine, who had earlier gained a Scottish League cap against the Irish League, was sold to Bradford City for £4,000.

The loss of Rankine came as a severe setback, and after four defeats in the opening five games of the 1927-28 season - including a 2-0 reverse at lowly Bo'ness - Alec McNair resigned in October. Dundee did not have their problems to seek and, on October 27th, the players' pavilion was destroyed by fire.

Two months later, Sandy MacFarlane, who had spent almost three years at Charlton Athletic, returned for his second spell in charge at Dens. But although he made a number of signings in an attempt to restore the club to its former glories, the erratic results continued.

One of his first captures was Kilmarnock defender Jim Paton, who became a regular at full-back the following season. In March 1993, Mr Paton (90), who was believed to be the club's oldest surviving former player, was a guest of honour at the Centenary Dinner in the Angus Hotel. He was full of praise for Sandy MacFarlane: "Sandy was a gentleman and a real player's man. He was a good manager and, unusually for a manager in those days, he would train with the players."

In the Scottish Cup, a 4-2 win over Stranraer at Stair Park

DUNDEE MANAGER APPOINTED

LOCAL FOOTBALLER TO TAKE CHARGE AT DENS PARK

Jimmy Bisset was the next man in charge at Dens.

set up a second-round clash with Dundee United. Honours were even in a six-goal Tannadice thriller and a solitary counter by Willie O'Hare was sufficient to take Dundee through in a replay at Dens Park.

At this time, the Dark Blues had their strongest-ever English contingent and no fewer than six Southerners - Marsh, Townrow, Godfrey, Craddock, Whitlow and Lawley - were included for Dundee's third-round tie against Dunfermline at Dens. However, this did not prevent the Fifers from winning 2-1, with George Lawley netting a consolation counter for the Dark Blues.

Recent years had seen an alarming drop in Dundee's previously high standards - 5-1 away defeats by Rangers, St Johnstone and Falkirk and a 7-2 Dens drubbing by Hearts had left them in fourteenth place after the loss of 80 league goals and, inevitably, changes would have to be made

Sandy MacFarlane's renewed "love affair" with Dundee was to prove short-lived and, in May 1928, he resigned before rejoining Charlton Athletic. Dundee United boss Jimmy Brownlie was strongly tipped to take over but it was the lesser known Lincoln City manager Jimmy Bissett (31), who had played for the Dundee reserves in season 1919-20 prior to playing for Everton, Middlesbrough, Rochdale and Lincoln, who was the directors' choice.

Dundee F.C. Season 1925-26 - (BACK, left to right) Trainer John Vickers, Henry Nicholson, Jock Ross, Jock Britton, David "Napper" Thomson, Davie McLean. FRONT - Alec Ross, Sam Irving, Finlay Brown, Willie Rankine, Jimmy Hunter, Willie Cook. Behind is the pavilion which burned down in 1927.

DC Thomson

A Dens Park vision - famous football stadium architect Archibald Leitch, who was later knighted, designed Dundee's North Stand and it features as the centre-piece of his plan for a redeveloped Dens Park.

Bob Hynd/Simon Inglis

The new manager had arrived at a difficult time. After walking out due to his wages dispute, "Napper" Thomson had not kicked a ball all season. Now, with little sign of a settlement, the long-serving defender who had joined Dundee from Fairfield Juniors in 1913, finally decided to hang up his boots. The popular Thomson had made 384 appearances for Dundee and his acrimonious departure marked a sad end to a great career.

In the immediate post-war era, an entertainment-starved population provided a captive audience for football. As football boomed, there were huge gates all over the country but, as a world-wide recession took effect, many fans could no longer afford the 1s admission fee introduced in 1919. By 1927-28, there was a widespread drop in attendances and Dundee's home gates which had averaged 15,000 in 1919-20 slumped to around 7,200.

A considerable amount remained outstanding on Dundee's new stand and, coupled with the decrease in gate receipts, some harsh decisions were made. The reserve team was scrapped and the Dens Park board indicated their willingness to consider offers for any of their top players.

The Bissett era made an inauspicious start and, with the centre of defence again looking suspect, Dundee continued to struggle. Colin McNab was sent off during a fiercely contested clash with Rangers at Dens Park, in which, although Dundee had lost 3-2, Willie Cook had been in dazzling form.

The elusive winger was a marvellous ball player, straight from the Alec Troup mould, but, in December 1928, the prevailing financial climate saw Dundee's latest star turn sold to Bolton for what was another substantial

Hugh Ferguson

transfer fee of £3,000. Cook's departure further drained the fans' ever-diminishing morale and worse was to come.

Wins over King's Park and Brechin brought a Scottish Cup derby clash with Dundee United for the second successive season. Fully 23,000 saw the sides draw 1-1 at Dens but this time the Dark Blues were stunned when the Division Two club went on to triumph 1-0 in the replay.

The misery continued and a paltry eight points from their remaining eleven games saw Dundee complete their programme in eighteenth place, just three points clear of relegated Third Lanark. Only the ineptitude of their fellow strugglers had saved the Dark Blues from the drop and the achievements of earlier years remained but a distant dream.

In an effort to stop the rot, Bissett paid £500 for Cardiff City's ex-Motherwell centre-forward, Hugh Ferguson. The prolific Ferguson, then aged 34, had netted 283 goals for the Fir Parkers between 1916 and 1925, and he went on to hit another 77 goals for Cardiff City, who of course also included ex-Dark Blue Sam Irving.

Ferguson had scored the only goal in Cardiff's FA Cup Final win over Arsenal in 1927, although season '28/9 saw the Welsh club relegated from the First Division. However, his move to Tayside was to end in tragedy. Somehow, he did not hit it off and, after only two goals in 17 games, the centre found himself out of the team by December.

On the evening of January 8th, 1930, Ferguson left his digs, telling his landlady he was going to the pictures, but tragically he was found dead in the gas-filled Dens pavilion - by then in the main stand - next morning. As the player had lost form, his self-confidence had drained and unknown to anyone he had suffered a severe nervous breakdown.

CHAPTER FOUR

Depressing Times

The death of Ferguson cast a dark cloud but on a more positive note, the defence had been stiffened by the introduction of Lochee United centre-half Tom McCarthy. Another local lad, inside-right Jimmy Robertson, showed his flair in attack while Andy Campbell, out for 18 months through illness, again displayed his scoring touch by netting 20 goals that term.

There was a derby double over newly-promoted Dundee United (both 1-0), then wins over Morton (h) 2-0, St Johnstone (h) 4-1 and Airdrie, 2-1 in a second replay at Ibrox, took Dundee to their first Scottish Cup quarter-final since 1925.

Their opponents were Hearts but, although the Dens gate was boosted to 31,000 (£1,250) by the return of Alec Troup from Everton, Dundee could only manage a 2-2 draw before going down 4-0 in the replay at Tynecastle.

That result heralded the departure of left-half Jock Thomson to Everton but, with local talent like half-backs Willie Blyth (Lochgelly), and Scott Symon (Dundee Violet), continuing to break through, a promising start was made to the 1930-31 campaign.

By the middle of October, fourth-placed Dundee had taken 17 points, half their previous season's total. And, despite eventually slipping to eighth, there was renewed optimism in the Dens Park camp. After a 10-1 Dens romp against Fraserburgh in the first round of the Scottish Cup, Dundee were paired with the all-conquering Rangers at Ibrox.

The Light Blues were heading for their eighth title win in nine years but, in the day's biggest shock, goals by Andy Campbell and Jimmy Robertson gave Dundee a 2-1 win. They fielded: Marsh; Brown, Gilmour; McNab, McCarthy, Blyth; Gavigan, Ritchie, Campbell, Robertson, Troup.

In the next round, the Dark Blues faced Aberdeen and for the second time in three years the Dens Park record attendance was smashed. This time 38,099 (receipts £1,526.14s) witnessed a 1-1 draw but it was the Dons who progressed to the quarter-finals with a 2-0 win in the Pittodrie replay.

Since the mid-1920s, Marsh, Brown, Gilmour, McNab and Campbell had been stalwarts for Dundee and, in October 1930, Jock Gilmour and Colin McNab were capped for Scotland against Wales. The following year, the battling

Dens forwards at Ibrox in 1930 - Peter Gavigan, Andy Campbell, Jim Craigie, Jimmy Robertson and Alec Troup. DC Thomson

McNab played against England at Hampden and, along with Jimmy Robertson, he was included in Scotland's European tour party. Both Dens Park players appeared against Austria and Italy with Colin McNab also capped against Switzerland. And, in 1932, the red-headed right-half made his sixth and final international appearance against England at Wembley.

COLIN McNAB
DUNDEE

Just like big Jimmy Robertson, inside-left Harry Smith was a local lad who had also been signed from Dundee's Logie Juniors. Smith, who was a guest at the club's Centenary Dinner of 1993, was at Dens between 1930 and 1933 and as he explained: "Dundee were not particularly successful then but the team was crammed with personalities. English goalie Bill Marsh was a giant of a man and, at 6'2" and well over 14 stone, he dominated his goal area. He had enormous hands and was well known for clutching the ball - rain-sodden or not - one-handed!"

Marsh had a grocer's shop in Ann Street and one of the many stories about the great custodian concerns the Dundee supporter who showed but grudging admiration for the goal-keeper. "I'll admit that Marsh is a braw goalie," he said, "but, meh goad, he canna cut a slice o'ham!"

Smith went on: "Finlay Brown and Jock Gilmour were backs of the highest calibre and both were tough as teak. Colin McNab was as fine an attacking half-back as ever pulled on a Dundee jersey while Eckie Troup remained a tricky customer on the wing."

"Jimmy Robertson and the prolific Andy Campbell were marvellous characters. Campbell of the slicked-back hair

was a big, bustling centre, who was very good in the air, while the long-legged Robertson was a marvellous entertainer and a firm favourite with the fans. Curiously, three of that team - Jock Gilmour, Tom McCarthy and myself - later became tram drivers in Dundee."

In 1931-32, Lew Morgan replaced Finlay Brown at right-back although the veteran defender would remain as assistant-trainer until the outbreak of World War Two. By 1931, Dundee had completed payments on their new stand but, instead of a further onfield improvement, things went from bad to worse. The Dark Blues finished the '31/2 campaign in eleventh place and, the following season, the loss of 77 goals with six goals conceded to Rangers, Motherwell and Ayr United, saw them slip to a lowly fifteenth.

Throughout the years, some massive turnouts for cup-ties at Dens indicated the tremendous crowd potential in the city of Dundee. But, while large crowds would attend the big games, they were not prepared to follow the fortunes of a club so apparently content with mediocrity. The board had lost touch with the aspirations of the footballing public and the hunger for success, so evident in the early 1920s, had all but disappeared.

In 1932, greyhound racing had been introduced to Dens Park but, despite receiving £2,000 from the racing syndicate involved, Dundee reported a loss of £1,096 for the 1932-33 season. Gates had tumbled to an average of 5,300 and for months there had been rumblings of internal strife at Dens.

Matters came to a head when it was announced that the players would no longer get summer wages. Throughout the season, their pay would be £4 per week with an extra £1 for league or Scottish Cup games. This was little more than the minimum and when Gilmour, McCarthy, Robertson and Morgan applied for the dole, all four were put up for sale.

Dundee F.C. 1933-34 - (BACK) Johnny Brown (trainer), Tom McCarthy, Lew Morgan, Bill Marsh, Scott Symon, Tom Smith, Jimmy Guthrie.
FRONT - Willie Blyth, Johnny Murdoch, Jimmy Robertson, Morgan Mackay, Jock Gilmour, Pat Lee, Danny Paterson, Harry Smith. DC Thomson

In May 1933, Jimmy Bissett "resigned" after five years in charge. And although former Dens stalwart Sam Irving applied for the vacancy, it was another Irishman, ex-Rangers full-back Billy McCandless, at that time player-coach with Ballymena United, who was appointed as the new manager.

Ten days later, Dundee treasurer William Mcintosh resigned from the board after a series of disagreements with his fellow directors. McIntosh had been a grand servant to the Dark Blues. He had been a director for over 20 years and had also been an influential figure at the SFA, where, until recently, he had been treasurer and his departure marked the end of a long period of continuity at Dens.

New boss - ex- Ranger Billy McCandless

At the AGM, held in the Mathers Hotel the following month, Mr Alex McBain (chairman) and Mr P. T. Jackson did not apply for re-election and D. P. How, Frank Graham and John Ford joined Walter Simpson, Robert Paterson, William Hood and James Meechan on the board. Simpson, who along with How and Graham was a wealthy jute merchant, became chairman with Paterson combining duties of vice-chairman and secretary.

Meanwhile, Billy McCandless had been busy. There was no longer a peg for Alec Troup, and the 37-year-old veteran rejoined Forfar. Andy Campbell, who had scored 106 goals in 201 games for Dundee since 1926, was another to be released and, like Jock Ross four years earlier, he also joined Division Two neighbours, Dundee United.

Following a renegotiation of terms, all the "rebels" had re-signed while the attack was strengthened by the arrival of former Scottish international right-winger Johnny Murdoch from Motherwell and the left-wing pairing of Pat Lee and Danny Paterson from Ballymena.

And, minor investments though they were, the Dark Blues made their most encouraging start for many years. Eleven points were taken from the opening eight games but, though Queen of the South were on the wrong end of an 8-0 thrashing at Dens, the revival proved short-lived with fourteen of the next 20 games ending in defeat.

The arrival of left-winger Harry Kirby from Belfast Distillery brought an improvement but, in December, Jimmy Robertson, last season's top scorer with 22 goals, the same as Jimmy Balfour - his Christian name was David - in '31/2, was transferred to Birmingham City for £1,250. St Mirren's Bobby Rankin was obtained as a replacement but, with the defence continuing to creak ominously, the Dark Blues had to settle for twelfth place in the league.

And, although the new board had made an honest effort to put the club back on the football map, only Murdoch and Kirby of the five newcomers, had looked the part. At the end of the season, Murdoch moved on with the long-serving Colin McNab - a great servant to the club - also departing to join Arbroath.

Dundee were fortunate to get Ayr United's Tommy Robertson as a replacement for the departed Johnny Murdoch but Billy McCandless did an even better bit of business when he again raided his homeland to land centre-forward Archie Coats from Northern Irish club, Bangor.

After a disappointing spell with Portsmouth, the chunky 23-year-old centre-forward had been a prolific scorer in the Irish League. Like Kirby, Coats had cost £500 but he settled quickly and his 30 league goals in the 1934-35 season were a major factor as Dundee finished eighth in the league.

And, although veterans like Marsh and Gilmour had played their part in the team's improvement, Lew Morgan, Scott Symon and Jimmy Guthrie were other key men for the Dark Blues. Symon had successfuly been switched to centre-half while Morgan had taken over at right-back from Finlay Brown in 1932 and it came as a bitter blow when both men requested a move.

Symon claimed he would not re-sign under any condition and, although Dundee were adamant that they were not for sale, both were transferred to English First Division side Portsmouth shortly after the start of the 1935-36 season.

Much of manager McCandless's signing activity had been concentrated on Northern Ireland and Wales. Coats and Kirby had proved their worth but, although left-back Len Richards (Dundalk), and inside-left Billy Phillips (Aberdare), were useful additions, several others were not up to the mark and the Dark Blues had to be content with twelfth place in the championship.

Amongst those given free transfers was long-serving defender Jock Gilmour, who had made 369 league and cup appearances for the Dark Blues since his arrival from Bathgate in 1924. Another to depart was trainer Johnny Brown who had been at Dens since 1926. He resigned after a dispute with the players and his place was taken by Jimmy Stewart.

Initially, the Dens greyhound racing venture had proved successful but its popularity had waned and, in 1936, the dogs had run their final race. Now, only the much criticised floodlighting standards remained as evidence of the dogs but, with the Dens Road banking considerably raised and wide terracing completed all around the pitch, the ground capacity was extended to 45,000.

Legendary figure - giant goalkeeper Bill Marsh played a total of 417 games for the Dark Blues.　Stephen Borland

All at sea - it's New Year's Day 1936 as Tommy Robertson prepares to take a corner for Dundee against Aberdeen at the flooded T.C. Keay end at Dens. A small group of fans can be seen on the snow-covered terracing. RIGHT - Jimmy Guthrie who was Dundee skipper from 1934 to 1937.   Stephen Borland/Bob Hynd

Recently, Johnny Darroch, a defensive stalwart from the club's early days, had retired at the age of 66 from his job as attendant at Dundee's Public Baths. And, in December 1936, memories of those heady days were further recalled when international football returned to Dens Park after an absence of twenty-eight years.

A crowd of 23,858 saw Scotland left-back Bobby Ancell of Newcastle United taken off with a broken leg as Scotland went down 2-1 to Wales. But local fans were destined to see more of this stylish defender, who would return as a Dundee player and later as manager.

Little had been done to strengthen the team for the 1936-37 campaign although right-back Bobby "Tiger" Rennie and inside-left Arthur Baxter, a local lad, both established themselves in the side. Archie Coats netted 27 goals to take his total to 83 in three seasons as Dundee finished ninth. Since 1930, Dundee had failed to progress beyond the third round of the Scottish Cup and the pattern continued when they lost 1-0 to Clyde in a third-round replay at Dens.

Although stocky, Archie Coats was only 5'7" tall and, at 10 stone, many reckoned he would come off second best in his tussles against the strapping six-footers employed by most Scottish clubs. Coats, however, had been a revelation and had shown himself well able to take a goal with either foot. Coats praised manager McCandless for giving him some sound advice: "Billy was a canny man. When I first arrived, he advised me to get close in to the opposing centre-half and I wouldn't get hurt. It worked a treat for I did well and, although I once got seven stitches in a head wound, I never missed a game in my six seasons at Dens."

Financially, Dundee were on a sound footing and, despite a £5,673 outlay on wages and bonuses and another £837 on salaries for the manager and trainer, the 1937 AGM had showed a surplus of £1,939.

Neither Billy McCandless nor Jimmy Stewart would remain at Dens very much longer. Stewart became trainer at Portsmouth, while long-standing rumours of McCandless's departure proved correct. The Irishman had been unsuccessful in his efforts to revitalise the club and it was now 15 years since Dundee had finished in the top four of the league.

An abortive approach was made for former St Johnstone manager Tommy Muirhead. Tom Craig (Falkirk), and Tom Jennings (Third Lanark), then turned down the job before ex-Rangers and Scotland half-back and former Newcastle United boss Andy Cunningham was appointed manager.

Almost immediately, inside-right Jimmy Guthrie was transferred to Portsmouth, where, with old team-mate Lew Morgan, he played - as captain - in their F.A. Cup winning team against Wolves in 1939, to emulate other notable ex-Dens men who boasted F.A. Cup winner's medals like Johnny Darroch (Bury, 1900), Willie Cowan (Newcastle, 1924), Sam Irving (Cardiff, 1927, and Willie Cook (Bolton, 1929).

Cunningham's first signings were Anglos, Bobby Regan (Manchester City) and Harry McMenemy (Newcastle). Now Dundee's forward-line read: Regan, Baxter, Coats, McMenemy and Kirby and initially this proved a potent blend. Six straight wins over Arbroath (a) 3-0, Clyde (h) 4-1, Arbroath (h) 1-0, Morton (a) 2-0, Queen of the South (h) 4-1, and Aberdeen (a) 3-2 were followed by a 3-2 reverse at Clyde, before a 2-0 home win over Queen's Park put the Dark Blues back on the winning trail.

In September, Dundee had two players in the Scottish

League team to play the Irish League. Tom Smith was at left-half and, although Arthur Baxter had cracked in nine goals in the opening nine games, Archie Coats was the other Dens Park representative.

Two months later, Bill Marsh, who had made a then record 417 league and cup appearances since arriving from Chelsea in 1924, was transferred to Kilmarnock. The Dark Blues had a keeper of tremendous promise in the form of 19-year-old Johnny Lynch and, perhaps sensing his Dens days were numbered, Marsh, who had recently received £500 from a benefit game against Portsmouth, had sold his grocer's shop in Ann Street some months earlier.

Dundee's revival had brought the fans flocking back but, despite holding a three-point lead over Rangers and Motherwell in October, their early form was not maintained. By November 6th, they had slipped to fifth. At the start of December they lay seventh and, as the slump continued throughout January 1938, they plummeted to fifteenth, with only one win in their previous 11 games.

The signs were ominous, particularly after a 4-2 defeat by Albion Rovers in the first round of the Scottish Cup. Already manager Cunningham had tried to strengthen his side and previous regulars like Rennie, Evans and Smith had been dropped. Regan had not lived up to his reputation and, in October, right-winger Jimmy Boyd was signed from Bury with left-half Harry Sneddon arriving from Blairhall three months later.

Outside-left Sam Roberts was signed from Rangers and, on February 5th, he made his debut against his former club at Dens. It was a vital game for both sides. Any further slips would put Dundee in serious danger of relegation while Rangers, who had beaten the Dark Blues 6-0 at Ibrox in October, were keen to maintain the pressure on the front-runners Celtic and Hearts.

A crowd of 15,000 saw Dundee line up: Lynch; Cowie, Richards; Laurie, Morgan, Sneddon; Boyd, Baxter, Coats, McMenemy, Roberts. Against the run of play, Venters put Rangers ahead in 18 minutes but, playing down the slope with a strong wind behind them, Dundee hit back strongly. Goals by Baxter (22 pen., 40) and Coats (27, 38) put them in the driving seat. Not surprisingly, the Dark Blues were given a standing ovation as they went off at the interval.

And, although Rangers made big effort after the break, Dundee were to finish the stronger. In 83 minutes, Baxter grabbed his hat-trick after a Coats header rebounded from a post and, two minutes from time, Boyd sent the Dens fans home in raptures when he made it 6-1.

Dundee had been worthy victors and, despite a 1-0 reverse to Partick Thistle at Firhill, yet another 6-1 scoreline was recorded, against St Johnstone at Dens. And, after taking only two points from their next four games, the Dark Blues again hit the goal trail with a 5-1 win over Ayr United at Dens.

Nevertheless, Dundee faced a tricky run-in and, by the last day of the season, two defeats by league leaders Celtic and another by third-placed Falkirk, left them in the thick of the relegation battle. Morton had long been doomed but any one of seven others could now accompany them to Division Two.

A win at Ayr would guarantee Dundee's survival but, with virtually the same line-up that had recently beaten the Somerset Park men convincingly, they could only manage a no-scoring draw. "We were quite happy with the result when we came off the park for we thought that would be enough to keep us up," said Coats. "However, when the other results were brought in to the dressing room, it was a real shock to us all!"

Incredibly, all the other games had gone badly for Dundee. Queen of the South had beaten Rangers 3-2 at Ibrox, Clyde had won 3-1 at Morton and Hamilton and St Mirren had both managed home draws with Queen's Park and Falkirk. It was an unexpected combination of results and, despite accumulating 32 points, the unfortunate Dens men had finished nineteenth with Kilmarnock, Queen of the South, Ayr United, St Mirren and Hamilton just one point above.

Apart from 1898, when the club had faced extinction, it was the lowest point of Dundee's 45-year history. They had netted 70 league goals, their highest tally for 11 years, but the defensive problems which had plagued the club for over a decade, had remained. No fewer than 74 goals had been conceded throughout the league campaign and the continuing failure to rectify the problem now meant a spell in Division Two.

Andy Cunningham would remain in charge and the directors pledged the continuation of full-time football. Boyd, Richards, Regan and McMenemy were sold and, with the reserve team again scrapped to cut costs, Dundee began the 1938-39 season with only 13 players which included reserve goalkeeper Galloway. Indeed, the Dark Blues were so short that an appeal was made for players to ensure that the club's public trial would go ahead!

Dundee F.C. Season 1937-38 (BACK, left to right) Bobby Adamson, Andy Cowie, Bill Marsh, Bobby Rennie, Tom Smith, John Evans. FRONT - Bobby Regan, Arthur Baxter, Archie Coats, Harry McMenemy and Norman Kirby. DC Thomson

Prolific scorer - Archie Coats netted 132 goals for Dundee. S Borland

Encouragingly, around 7,000 saw a 5-0 win over Brechin at Dens on the opening day of '38/9 but, although this suggested a prompt return to Division One, the policy of the Dens Park management was severely criticised when only one of the next five games resulted in a win.

On September 10th, Dundee were left with acute defensive problems when centre-half Jimmy Morgan broke his leg against Edinburgh City. The following week there was a 3-0 defeat by rivals Dundee United at Tannadice and, despite trouncing Forfar 10-2 at Dens, an astonishing 6-5 home reverse at the hands of lowly East Stirling indicated where the problems lay.

Earlier, John Evans, who had lost his place to Morgan, had been placed on the transfer list. But, despite a renewed effort to re-sign him, the Welshman opted for Division One side Motherwell with Dundee getting inside-left Charlie McGillivray in exchange.

In October, Willie Cook, now 35 years of age, returned from Bolton while right-half George Stewart from Clyde and inside-right Bobby Wilson from Arnot were secured in minor deals. The previous season, Baxter had finished top scorer with 24 goals but, after struggling to find the net, he lost his place to Wilson and was subsequently sold to Barnsley in December.

Although slower, Cook had lost none of his touchline trickery and with McGillivray, who scored a hat-trick on his debut against East Stirling, proving an excellent foil to the ever-dangerous Coats, Dundee had no problem in finding the net. However, in early December, the experienced Andy Cowie was transferred to Aberdeen for £1,000 and, by the end of 1938, the once proud Dark Blues lay in the lower reaches of the table with only six wins from 21 games.

Former Dundee United centre-half Bill Masson, the father of 1992 Dens chief executive and director Alan Masson, was signed from Montrose and his arrival helped stabilise the defence. Disappointingly, however, Dundee lost 1-0 to Clyde in a Scottish Cup first-round replay at Dens - the third time in four years that they had narrowly lost out to the battling Shawfield Stadium outfit.

Bill Masson described manager Andy Cunningham as: "A big amiable man who could lay down the law when necessary. He got on well with the players and in his team talk he was very thorough in analysing the player's strengths and weaknesses."

However, the former defender was much more critical of the board. In Masson's first game for the Dens Parkers, Dundee had gone down 2-1 at Forfar and on the journey back to the Jute City all one particular director had talked about was "money, money, money!"

Nevertheless, they were a much improved side and, on March 18th, the Dark Blues met city rivals United at Dens. They fielded: Lynch; Rennie, Kirby; Stewart, Masson, Sneddon; Melville, Wilson, Coats, McGillivray, Cook. This time Dundee made no mistake and goals by McGillivray and Wilson brought a comfortable 2-0 win before a very healthy 12,500 crowd.

It was a disastrous campaign, for, although losing just one of their last 15 games, Dundee were unable to make up lost ground and finished a disappointing sixth behind Cowdenbeath, Alloa, East Fife, Airdrie and Dunfermline.

The Dark Blues scored 99 league goals but 63 had been conceded to their Division Two opponents and gates which had averaged 7,000 at the start had dwindled to only a couple of thousand diehards by the end of the season.

Meanwhile, the menace of Hitler's Nazi Germany continued to darken the Continent of Europe. In turn, the Sudetenland, Austria and Czechoslovakia had crumbled but, despite the imminent threat of war, the Scottish football season began as usual in August 1939.

Dundee started well with wins over Raith Rovers (h) 5-1, Airdrie (a) 4-2, and Dumbarton (h), 3-1 and, on September 2nd, a 1-1 draw at Morton maintained their position at the top of Division Two. Germany, meanwhile had invaded Poland and, when Britain and France declared war the following day, all further competition was suspended.

It was soon realised that football would maintain the morale of the population and, in October, new leagues were formed. Due to travel restrictions and petrol rationing, these were played on an East-West regional basis. Players' wages were fixed at £2 per week plus expenses and crowds of no more than 8,000 were allowed at games for fear of German air attacks. Dundee went on to finish sixth in the Eastern Division, later losing 4-2 on aggregate to Third Lanark in the first round of the Scottish War Cup.

Andy Cunningham - Dundee manager from 1937 until 1940 when the club closed due to the Second World War. DC Thomson

The crowd rolls up for another big match at Dens but War clouds were on the horizon and soon Scottish League football would be reorganised on a regional basis.   DC Thomson

R. RENNIE

Increasingly, local players volunteered or were called up for military service and, with a £1,400 loss the previous season and average home gates of only 3,000, Dundee decided to close down for the duration of the war. On May 18th, 1940, they played their final game against Falkirk at Dens and goals by Adam, Coats (2), and McGillivray brought a 4-2 win before some 3,000 fans. The Dark Blues had fielded: Mathieson; Peattie, Rennie; Ross, Morgan, Masson; Kirby, Adam, Coats, McGillivray and Cook.

For the next four years, Dens Park was utilised as a store for the Decontamination (Food) Service but, by early 1944, the tide of the war had turned and, with Britain and her allies on the offensive, moves were made to restart football at Dens Park.

In 1939, Dundee's board of directors had consisted of James A. Galloway (chairman), David P. How (vice-chairman), Frank Graham, Robert Paterson, James Meechan, William Hood and James W. Simpson. Since then, How had died, Hood and Meechan had retired while Paterson did likewise in 1944 after a lengthy illness.

How and Simpson's 3,000 shares had been purchased by a consortium of local businessmen and at a board meeting on April 1st, Messrs. Galloway and Graham were joined by John Thomson, Murray Wilkie, James Gellatly and Jack Swadel. At the AGM, which was held the following month, John Thomson was elected chairman with Murray Wilkie as vice-chairman but, more significantly, George Anderson, another member of the consortium was co-opted onto the board and would look after team affairs.

Anderson had been a director at Aberdeen Football Club and had previously played in goal for the Pittodrie club although he had also made a number of guest appearances

for the Dark Blues towards the end of the Great War.

In 1939, Aberdeen manager David Halliday - Dundee's prolific scorer of the 1920s - went off to the War and, along with fellow-director Charles Forbes, Anderson assumed the responsibilities of caretaker-manager. It was a job which he relished but, with the Pittodrie post reserved for the return of Halliday, George Anderson saw the potential at Dens Park and made his move.

A Northumbrian, he owned a thriving ice cream and confectionery business in the Granite City and, as a well-known figure in footballing circles, his numerous contacts soon brought several astute signings. These included goal-keeper Reuben Bennett (Hull City), left-back Bobby Ancell (Newcastle) and forwards Willie Anderson (Hibs) and Ronnie Turnbull (Jeanfield Swifts).

On August 5th, 1944, two months after the D-Day landings, Dundee returned to action against the British Army at Dens. They lost 7-0 but, with their opponents fielding a near international eleven and including many household names like Frank Swift, Joe Mercer and Matt Busby, this was certainly no disgrace.

Dundee's side, complete with guests, contained only two players - Bobby Rennie and Sam Roberts - who had been on their books four years earlier: Bennett; Rennie, Ancell; Fenton (West Ham), Gray (Morton), Cox (Third Lanark); Miller (Partick Thistle), Turnbull, Anderson, Auld, Roberts.

Anderson moved sharply to secure Tommy Gray and for good measure he also signed another Morton player, Gibby McKenzie. That season, Dundee competed in the 10-team North-Eastern Division. This was split into two series of 18 games but, after winning the first, they could only finish fourth in the second.

At the AGM in May, there was another boardroom shuffle. Former chairman James Galloway stood down and was replaced by local builder Andrew Clark. With the war in Europe almost over, Scottish League football restarted in

Football is back! Dens Park re-opens in August 1944 as skipper Bobby Ancell presents the Dundee team to officials before the game against the British Army.
DC Thomson

1945. Dundee went on to win the 1945-46 'B' Division Championship by ten clear points but, with clubs given a year's grace to "put their house in order", there would be no promotion or relegation until the following season.

In the newly-initiated League Cup, Dundee fell 3-1 to Rangers in the Hampden quarter-final and the other cup competitions also brought disappointment. There was a 3-2 aggregate defeat by Hibs in the Scottish Victory Cup and, in the semi-final replay of the Supplementary Cup, the Dark Blues lost 2-1 to Airdrie at Broomfield.

Throughout the war, Scottish based "guest" players were permitted and between 1944 and 1946, Dundee fielded ex-England international outside-left Reggie Smith of Millwall and half-backs, Tommy Gallacher of Queen's Park and Third Lanark's Sammy Cox.

The balding Smith, who was serving with the RAF at Leuchars, was a great favourite at Dens. In March 1946, his move became permanent with Willie Anderson going to Millwall in exchange. The Dark Blues had also wanted to sign Cox. But, as an amateur he was free to move on and, at the end of the season he joined Rangers where he went on to make twenty-five appearances for Scotland.

Throughout that season, players had returned to Dens after "demob" and the retained list read: Allan, Laurie, Lynch, Rennie, Sneddon and Wattie, who had all been at the club before the war, plus Follon and Hill who had both been provisionally signed in 1939-40. All the rest were George Anderson signings - Ancell, Andrews, Beaton, Bennett, Clark, Cowie, Dickson, Ewen, Gray, Jones,

JULIUSSEN

Red-Letter Day At Dens Park

STRONG ARMY ATTRACTION FOR REOPENING GAME

By Unomi

TO-DAY is a red-letter day in Dundee football. It sees the reopening of Dens Park for regular play after a closure of over four years.

Joyner, Juliussen, Lawrie, Marshall, McKenzie, McIntosh, Ouchterlonie, Rattray, Robertson, A. Smith, R. Smith, G.T. Stewart, G. Stewart, Stirling, Thomson and Turnbull. Eight players were released - Adam, Kirby, Masson, Roberts and Wilson - all from pre-war days - plus Auld, Ruse and Warnock.

Bobby Wilson had been held for four years in a German Prisoner of War camp, but one who would not come back was 1930s favourite Tom Smith - killed while serving with the Fleet Air Arm in the early days of the war. Another with Dark Blue connections to perish was Arthur Baxter - he returned from Barnsley and played for Dundee United in the 1940 Scottish War Cup Final - who fell in the Normandy campaign of 1944.

Prolific pre-war scorer, Archie Coats, made two appearances after being demobbed in the autumn of 1945. Time, however, had taken its toll and with scorers of the calibre of Turnbull and Juliussen now on the books, Coats was allowed to go. The centre-forward had managed 132 league and cup goals in 202 games for the Dark Blues, a Dens total unsurpassed until the early 1960s. And, had it not been for the War, he may well have gone on to become Dundee's all-time top goalscorer.

In the close season, Dundee toured Germany and Austria and returned unbeaten after four games against British Army sides. That July, Willie Arbuckle, who had been Dundee's trainer-masseur since 1936, died after an illness and his post was taken by former Dundee United trainer Willie Cameron.

CHAPTER FIVE

Post-War Revival

Although Dundee began as strong title favourites, George Anderson continued to strengthen the side. Veteran inside-man Johnny Pattillo, who had been Aberdeen's top scorer two seasons earlier, arrived for a bargain £1,000, while top Juniors Ally Gunn and Jimmy Toner were signed from Elmwood and Fauldhouse United respectively.

In the opening game, a Joyner hat-trick helped Dundee crush East Fife 6-2 at Methil and, despite a 1-1 draw with Airdrie at Dens, wins over Dundee United and Arbroath left them top of the table by September 1946.

The Tannadice derby was a dour struggle for the 21,000 fans and Dundee's luck held good when a United shot came off the underside of the bar and struck Bennett before being cleared. A second-half penalty put United ahead but opportunist goals by Juliussen and Turnbull in the last 25 minutes gave Dundee a 2-1 win.

However, all was not plain sailing, and after crashing 4-2 away to East Fife in the Supplementary Cup quarter-final, the Dark Blues fell 2-1 in the league at Dumbarton. These setbacks proved temporary and a 6-2 win over Alloa at Dens was the springboard for a 14-game winning run. By late December, Dundee remained top of the league

while sectional wins over Raith Rovers and Stenhousemuir earned their place in the League Cup quarter-finals.

Spearheaded by the bustling Bert Juliussen, Dundee's attack could do no wrong and, by December 7th, high scoring wins over Raith Rovers (a) 4-2, Stenhousemuir (h) 4-2, Cowdenbeath (a) 8-2, Dunfermline (a) 5-2, Albion Rovers (h) 6-2, and St Johnstone (a) 5-1 took their goal tally up to 53 goals from twelve league games.

The powerful Juliussen was typical of centre-forwards of that era. Exciting to watch and possessing a tremendous left-foot shot, the Englishman's shoot-on-sight policy had already brought him 13 goals to add to the 36 league and cup goals netted the previous season. "Big Julie" had served with the Black Watch and, although he had been a war-time guest across the road at Tannadice, George Anderson had stepped in to pay £2,000 for his transfer from Huddersfield Town in July 1945.

There was often fierce debate whether Juliussen or another big Englishman, Ronnie Turnbull, should play at centre. Juliussen could turn a game with a couple of flashing shots but the more mobile Turnbull was the better play-maker. Nevertheless, when Juliussen was injured in November, Turnbull soon demonstrated his scoring ability by netting four goals against Albion Rovers.

Halcyon days - director-manager George Anderson (top) was the architect of Dundee's post-war revival. The fans returned in their thousands and here large crowds queue outside the Dens Road turnstiles before the Scottish Cup tie with Celtic in 1947. DC Thomson

Near thing - Bert Juliussen looks on as Ronnie Turnbull's shot goes over to the relief of the Celtic defence. DC Thomson

Dundee could also boast the tightest defence in the league. Reuben Bennett was first-choice keeper with long-serving Johnny Lynch, who had earlier rejected a move to Cardiff City, in reserve. Gerry Follon had turned in some brilliant performances since replacing Alec McIntosh at right-back and later that season he was honoured by the Scottish League against the Irish League. He was partnered by the experienced Bobby Ancell, twice capped for Scotland in his pre-war Newcastle days, with another old hand, Tommy Gray, at centre-half.

Much of Dundee's inspiration came from half-backs Gibby McKenzie and Reggie Smith with Johnny Pattillo and Ernie Ewen a deadly scoring combination at inside-forward. George "Pud" Hill and Frank Joyner had begun the season as first-choice wingers but Ally Gunn's sparkling form soon earned him the right-wing slot with Hill switching to the left.

Second-placed Airdrie lay four points behind, and three days after Christmas, a 15,000 crowd saw a thrilling encounter at Broomfield. With the scores locked at 1-1, Bennett bravely returned after receiving six stitches to a head wound, but, 13 minutes from time, he was helpless when Airdrie netted the winner. Ironically, the sturdy custodian had recently shown concern that his own misplaced punches were causing injury to his defensive colleagues in crowded goalmouths!

In the Ne'erday derby with Dundee United at Dens, Dundee wore numbered jerseys for the first time and goals by Ronnie Turnbull and Ernie Ewen ensured a 2-0 win. And with £3,130 taken from the 24,000 crowd - Dundee's top league gate that term - it certainly underlined the importance of the derby to both city clubs.

Turnbull had scored 11 goals in eight games and, when Juliussen resumed, he was retained at centre with Juliussen

at outside-left. There, "Julie" proved less effective but that did not discourage interest from Everton, Portsmouth and 'A' Division Motherwell. Dundee, however, valued promotion more highly than cash in the bank and they rejected £9,000 bids from Everton and Motherwell.

Dundee's league position was consolidated by a further seven points that month but it was the Scottish Cup clash with Celtic which caught the imagination of the footballing public. All 36,000 tickets (priced at 5/- and 3/6d for the stand, 2/6d for the enclosure and 1/6d for the ground) were quickly snapped up with thousands more disappointed.

The Dark Blues showed little respect for their 'A' Division opponents and a raging 25-yarder from Ewen put them ahead after quarter of an hour. In 62 minutes, Turnbull added a second and, although McAloon pulled one back for Celtic in the dying minutes, Dundee held on to win. McKenzie and Smith were the architects of a famous victory and this augured well for Dundee's top league return - for few disputed that they would go up.

George Anderson was a man of vision and, in preparation for 'A' Division football, St Johnstone left-half Alfie Boyd was signed for £4,000 in the face of fierce competition. A former Dens ball-boy, Boyd had threatened to emigrate to South Africa unless he got a move, and reluctantly, Saints had parted with their skipper.

Anderson's forward planning was soon vindicated for, on February 1st, a late Pattillo goal earned a 2-2 draw away to Albion Rovers and promotion was assured. Now the Dark Blues could concentrate on cup competitions and, in the second round of the Scottish Cup they coasted to a 3-0 win over Albion Rovers at snow-cleared Dens. In the League Cup quarter-final, Dundee were paired with North-East rivals Aberdeen - again managed by Davie Halliday - and, despite losing 4-2 on aggregate, both ties were closely fought affairs.

Stung by this reverse, Dundee's response was immediate. On Saturday, March 8th, they ran up a 10-0 win over Alloa at muddy Recreation Park. Ronnie Turnbull was rested, and

Albert Juliussen

Albert Juliussen celebrated his return to centre with six cracking goals.

This was a Dens Park club record but, incredibly, the 10-0 scoreline was repeated in the next game which was against Dunfermline at home. Once again, Juliussen was in sensational form, and this time he went one better, hitting a remarkable seven goals!

Jubilant Julie In Dundee Goal Rush

ALLOA, 0: DUNDEE, 10

DUNDEE, 10: DUNFERMLINE, 0

Dundee F.C. Season 1946-47 'B' Division Champions - (BACK, left to right) George Anderson, Gerry Follon, Gibby McKenzie, Reuben Benett, Tommy Gray, Johnny Lynch, Bobby Ancell, Reggie Smith, Jack Swadel (director). FRONT - Bert Juliussen, Ally Gunn, Johnny Pattillo, Ronnie Turnbull, Ernie Ewen, George Hill, Frank Joyner, Willie Cameron (physiotherapist).

DC Thomson

Significantly, Boyd had come in at left-half with Smith at outside-left and this further enhanced an already potent mix. Clearly, Dundee were a class above most of their 'B' Division opponents and, with an average home gate of nearly 14,000, their attendances were also of 'A' Division standard.

The Scottish Cup quarter-final provided Dundee with an early chance of revenge over Aberdeen and it proved an epic encounter for the 38,000 Dens crowd. At half-time, Dundee led through Ewen but, despite going all out for another, Aberdeen's South African centre-forward Stan Williams equalised on the hour.

Dundee Football Club Ltd.
Scottish Cup - 4th Round
Dundee v. Aberdeen or Morton
DENS PARK, DUNDEE
SATURDAY, 15th MAR.
1947 Kick-off-3 p.m.
This portion to be retained. Tickets sold subject to conditions on back. Robt. Crichton, C.A., Sec.
GROUND 1/6
Including Tax
Enter by Turnstile No. **5**
SEE PLAN ON BACK
No. 299

The score remained 1-1 at full-time and, although the Pittodrie men dominated, the game was still deadlocked after another 30 minutes of extra time. A fixture pile-up meant the game would have to be played to a finish, hence a further 10 minute "sudden death" period and, with 129 minutes on the clock, Williams scored the winner for the Dons. Dundee had been unlucky but the deadly Juliussen had taken considerable punishment and Aberdeen's close marking tactics had paid off.

Nevertheless, the 'B' Division Championship was clinched by decisive home wins over Dumbarton (4-0), Raith (5-2) and Ayr (6-2) with Airdrie finishing runners-up, three points behind. The Dundee goal tally had amounted to an impressive 134 in 35 league and cup games with Ewen and Juliussen each netting 33, although the big Englishman had played twelve games less through injury.

After nearly 10 years out of the top flight, the Dark Blues were back and now the bowler-hatted Anderson was the toast of the city! The promotion side had been based on experience but, looking to the future, Anderson had shrewdly blooded talented youngsters like wing-half Doug Cowie and inside-left Peter Rattray.

According to outside-left George Hill, the Dens boss was adept at teambuilding: "George Anderson had a good eye for talent and, in a very short time, he put together a successful side. He liked to win by playing attractive football but, although he abhorred rough play, he would occasionally remind players that Dens Park was not a Sunday School."

"The boss was a master of man-management. He treated players and staff like men and he was well respected. In those days, there were no complex instructions before a game. Mr Anderson would simply tell us to go out and enjoy ourselves and the senior professionals would organise things on the park."

Promotion success was rewarded by a close-season tour of Denmark and Sweden, while at Dens the old wooden perimeter fence was replaced by a white-painted retaining wall with regular bands of blue.

By this time, Stirling and Ouchterlonie had moved on to Reading and Ayr United and Joyner, McIntosh, Rennie and Sneddon had been freed. And in preparation for the new campaign, the Dens squad was strengthened by the addition of centre-forward Alec Stott from Portsmouth and former wartime centre-half Bob Bowman from Alloa.

The 1947-48 season kicked off with the League Cup and Dundee's section included 'A' Division sides Rangers, Celtic and Third Lanark. On August 9th a great start was made with a 5-0 win over Thirds at Dens. With Bennett and Juliussen injured, Dundee fielded: Lynch; Follon, Ancell; McKenzie, Gray, Boyd; Gunn, Ewen, Turnbull, Smith, Hill. Many in the bumper 24,000 crowd wondered whether

A classic pose - goalkeeper Johnny Lynch was a Dens stalwart from 1935 to 1951.   DC Thomson

understanding that he might return to the North of England if a suitable offer was received and, reluctantly, George Anderson agreed to the transfer.

Nevertheless, the momentum was maintained with four points from the next three games before 1947 ended with defeats by Morton (h) 0-4, Rangers (h) 1-3, and Queen of the South (a) 2-5. Dundee United outside-left "Piper" Mackay then arrived in exchange for reserve centre-half Jimmy Dickson plus cash with Dundee also signing Hibs keeper Jock Brown for a "substantial" fee.

Curiously, Dundee now had four goalkeepers. Bennett was troubled by a knee injury and, in October, Partick Thistle's Jimmy Steadward was signed as a back-up for Lynch. Steadward had looked shaky in the Christmas Day defeat by Rangers, prompting the signing of Jock Brown, whose debut had been marked by a 7-0 win over Clyde at Dens.

Pud Hill was one of Dundee's outstanding performers that day. Tommy Gallacher was full of praise for the wee winger, "Although small in stature he lacked nothing in tenacity and that allied to his speed and ability to beat a man made him a big favourite with the Dens Park fans."

Dundee's veterans might struggle in the sweltering heat, but they were soon reassured by a dazzling display with Ernie Ewen netting a well-deserved hat-trick.

The euphoria was short-lived for, after dropping three points in away games against the Old Firm, Dundee crashed 5-1 to Third Lanark at Cathkin. The following week they bounced back with a 4-1 win over Celtic at Dens but there were violent scenes on the terracing with widespread bottle-throwing by disgruntled Celtic fans.

Veteran Gibby McKenzie, such an influential performer in the previous season's promotion run, had struggled in the opening games and, in late August, former wartime guest Tommy Gallacher was signed from Queen's Park. He was the son of famous Celt Patsy Gallacher and, having enjoyed his earlier spell at Dens, he was more than delighted to sign professional forms for Dundee. Doug Cowie was also challenging strongly for a regular first-team place and, in October, McKenzie moved on to Airdrie.

Dundee settled quickly into the 16-team 'A' Division and, by November 15th, they lay fifth, five points behind league leaders Hibs, having taken twelve points from their opening 10 games. Now they faced a tough test in Edinburgh against the talented Easter Road side who had narrowly finished runners-up to Rangers last season. Ronnie Turnbull equalised Eddie Turnbull's early goal for Hibs but Dens hopes of a well-merited point were dashed when Gordon Smith scored the winner two minutes from the end.

Turnbull was now Dundee's regular centre and, the following week, he took his season's tally to twelve, netting both goals in Dundee's 2-0 win at Motherwell. An earlier exchange deal for Newcastle winger Tommy Pearson had fallen through but, only days later, Turnbull was on his way to Sunderland for £8,000. He had re-signed on the

Jack Johnson and Jorgen Neilsen, befriended in the close-season tour of Denmark, had been Dundee's guests since early December. Their reserve appearances had attracted good crowds to Dens and when the stylish Johnson appeared for the first-team against Hearts at Tynecastle on January 17th, he capped an impressive display by scoring the only goal of the game!

The following week, the Edinburgh side gained their revenge with a 4-2 Scottish Cup success at Dens, and eight weeks later there was further disappointment for the Dundee fans. Soon after scoring his 20th goal of the season, transfer-seeking Bert Juliussen was sold to Portsmouth for £10,000. "Julie" had scored many spectacular goals and was a big favourite at Dens but, although his departure sparked off a barrage of criticism, George Anderson was adamant that there was no room for unhappy players at Dens.

The Dens boss had remained in Aberdeen, where he was a town councillor as well as owner of a thriving confectionery business. He would travel the 66 miles to Dundee twice a week although the day-to-day training was organised by Willie Cameron and Andy McCall, with assistance from senior players like Reggie Smith and Bobby Ancell.

Young reserve centre George Stewart came in for the remaining five games and, despite failing to score, three wins, including a 3-2 victory over new champions Hibs at Dens, saw Dundee finish a credible fourth after their first season "upstairs".

The loss of the high scoring Turnbull and Juliussen was a blow but the framework of a fine side remained. Jock Brown was by this time first-choice keeper with Follon and Ancell at full-back. Boyd had replaced the injured Gray at centre-half for much of the season and, with Gallacher and Cowie now established at wing-half, this trio would prove the cornerstone of Dundee's success over the next five seasons.

Despite Mackay's arrival, Gunn, Ewen, Pattillo and Hill remained the regulars up front but another clue to Dundee's success was the excellent cover provided by quality fringemen such as Johnny Lynch, Bob Bowman, Jack Bruce, Andy Irvine, Peter Rattray and George Stewart.

Murray Wilkie had succeeded Bailie John Thomson as chairman in August 1946, but, at the AGM in July 1948, he retired and was replaced by vice-chairman James Gellatly. George Anderson became the new vice-chairman with Messrs Thomson, Clark, Swadel, Graham and Bob Crichton (secretary) making up the board.

Anderson believed in fostering local talent and he again found his home territory fruitful when he captured two talented forwards, George Christie and Syd Gerrie from the Aberdeen juniors. The astute Dens boss had actually spotted Christie's potential two years earlier and, after farming him out to Banks O'Dee Juniors, had given him a job at his Granite City sweetie factory!

The league campaign began brightly with six points from the opening four games but, when East Fife shocked the Dark Blues with a 5-2 win at Dens on Wednesday September 1st, home fans in the 29,500 crowd turned angrily on their team.

It was a temporary setback. By mid-November, Dundee lay just two points behind joint leaders East Fife and Hibs and had reached the semi-finals of the League Cup. Qualifying comfortably from sectional ties against Albion Rovers, Falkirk and Motherwell, the Dark Blues beat Alloa 3-1 in the quarter-final replay after a 1-1 draw at Dens.

With only two defeats in 16 games, Dundee prepared confidently for the Hampden semi-final with Rangers on November 20th. They fielded: Brown; Follon, Ancell; Cowie, Gray, Boyd; Gunn, Gallacher, Pattillo, Smith and Mackay. At the end of the previous season, Reggie Smith had made only fleeting appearances before joining non-league Corby Town as player-manager. But in October, he returned to Dens and made a fine comeback in a 1-0 win over Celtic at Parkhead.

Gale-force wind and rain had slashed the Hampden attendance to 50,996 and, on winning the toss, Rangers skipper Jock Shaw chose to play with the elements.

Dens favourites - Gerry Follon and Tommy Gallacher.   DC Thomson

Tragically, Dundee were 3-0 down after only seven minutes with stalwart centre-half Tommy Gray taken off injured at the opening goal in just two minutes. Although he returned to limp on the wing, a fourth Rangers goal after 25 minutes finished the Dens men, who had only a late Smith penalty as any consolation in a 4-1 defeat.

Later, Dens Park skipper Bobby Ancell confirmed that Rangers had chosen ends as well as kicking off, and for his oversight referee Livingstone later received a severe reprimand! Nevertheless, the Hampden disappointment was quickly forgotten and, by the end of 1948, Dundee lay third, two points behind pace-setters Hibs.

The Dark Blues lacked a finisher of the quality of Juliussen or Turnbull and although Stewart, Gerrie and Stott were all tried at centre, none seemed the answer. In October, Dundee United's Welsh inside-forward Jack Court was signed for £1,000 with Wolves centre Jack Malloch arriving for a similar fee soon afterwards. Neither were to make much impact and, in one of football's great ironies, Stott returned to score four in Dundee's 6-0 win over Albion Rovers, shortly after Malloch's arrival.

On New Year's Day, a 3-1 win at Aberdeen set Dundee up for the Dens clash on January 2nd with new leaders Rangers, who lay one point behind. As kick-off approached, the turnstiles were closed one by one and, with thousands still milling outside, scores of fans clambered over the walls with hundreds more climbing onto the roofs of T.C. Keay's, Densfield and Bowbridge Works.

At the foot of Provost Road the pressure of the crowds burst open the big iron gates and around 2,000 fans swept past police into the ground. Some fans wanted out due to the crush but gatemen were reluctant to open the gates due to the large crowds outside desperate for entry. And although the official attendance was given as 39,975, an estimated 45,000 were in the ground with another 5,000 outside.

Marshall put Rangers ahead in 10 minutes but, within 60 seconds, Ewen thundered a long-range equaliser past Brown and there was no stopping Dundee. Urged on by the huge home crowd, Dundee twice hit woodwork before Stott scored in 23 minutes and, with only eight minutes remaining, Dens Park erupted when the same player headed a third!

That left Dundee top at the halfway stage and, over the next two months, they continued to set the pace. There were wins over Hearts (a) 1-0, Morton (h) 3-1, Albion Rovers (h) 5-0, Queen of the South (a) 1-0, a 4-4 draw with Partick Thistle at Firhill, with the only reverse being a

On your marks - George Anderson prepares Ernie Ewen, Alfie Boyd, Tommy Gallacher, Syd Gerrie and Alec Stott for some sprint training.   Mark Gallacher

Boom time at Dens Park. The Dundee v Rangers match in January 1949 recorded an official attendance of 39,975 but it was estimated that another 5,000 fans gained entry by illegal means.

DC Thomson

3-0 away defeat by strong-going East Fife.

Meanwhile, Dundee had progressed to the Scottish Cup quarter-final by beating St Johnstone (h) 6-1 and St Mirren (a) 2-1 after a 0-0 draw at Dens, before getting a third-round bye. The bustling Alec Stott, who was from nearby Newbigging, would never lay claim to being the most skilful of forwards. However, since his recall to the first-team on Christmas Day, the big centre had found the net on a regular basis and his four-goal haul against the men from Muirton took his season's tally to an impressive 24 goals.

On March 5th, 37,000 noisy fans saw Dundee and Hearts produce a classic quarter-final tie in the Tynecastle mud. Soon after the break, Gerrie put Dundee 3-2 ahead but the game hung in the balance until near the end when Hearts were awarded a penalty. Reuben Bennett, deputising for Lynch, made a splendid save and, soon afterwards, Pattillo clinched matters for Dundee.

George Anderson firmly believed that a strong half-back line was essential for success and like the influential McKenzie-Gray-Smith midline in the 1946-47 promotion side, much of Dundee's inspiration now came from Tommy Gallacher, Doug Cowie and Alfie Boyd.

All three were capable of pushing forward. As one might expect from an ex-inside-forward, the silky Gallacher was an accomplished ball-player. Cowie was outstanding in the air and just as comfortable on the ground, while the elegant Boyd - also noted for his aerial prowess - was another polished performer.

That season, Dens skipper Alfie Boyd had represented Scotland against the British Army. He had also been a reserve against Wales in Cardiff and, along with Tommy Gallacher, had played in Scotland's League international against England.

With seven weeks of the season now remaining, Dens hopes of a league and cup double were dented by an incredible result at Paisley. Dundee had dominated but a Pattillo penalty miss proved fatal as St Mirren went on to win 6-1 in only Dundee's second defeat in 16 games.

Seven days later, a 4-3 Dens win over Hibs allowed the Dark Blues to regain the leadership and with seven games left they held a one-point advantage over the Edinburgh side and Rangers. Shortly after half-time, Dundee had trailed 3-1 but, inspired by tremendous support from the terracing they recovered to score a stunning three goals within the space of seven minutes.

The Scottish Cup draw paired Dundee with Clyde and, as was their custom for all big games under Anderson, the players were taken to the Pitlochry Hydro for their pre-match preparation. Dundee were favourites to win the Easter Road tie but only late goals by Gunn then Stott with

44

a penalty, took the game to extra-time where there were no further scoring.

Dundee had been fortunate to survive but things looked good when an early Milligan own-goal put them ahead in the Hampden replay.

However, instead of pressing home their advantage, Dundee handed the initiative to Clyde and goals by Bootland in 36 and 62 minutes gave the more enterprising Shawfield side a deserved passage into the final where they would meet Rangers.

Top gun - Alec Stott equalled Davie Halliday's 39 goals in a season record from 25 years earlier.

Nevertheless, 3-2 wins over Third Lanark (a) and Celtic (h), a 2-2 draw away to Morton and a 3-1 win over Falkirk at home maintained the Dens Park challenge. By now Hibs were out of contention but Rangers showed no sign of slipping. Dundee remained one point behind but, on April 23rd, with the Ibrox men involved in the Scottish Cup

Final, a 4-2 win over Partick Thistle at Dens restored the Dark Blues to the top of the league.

Three days later there were 25,000 at Dens for the visit of Motherwell in the second-last game. Following a long throw by Hill, Pattillo cracked home the opener in 28 minutes but the Fir Park side levelled before half-time. Then midway through the second period, Stott brushed aside Paton to head a controversial winner with Motherwell claiming in vain that he had used an elbow.

Now the Dark Blues were poised for their first championship win in their 56-year history. Rangers 1-0 win at Morton left them one point behind and a Dundee success in their final game at Falkirk would clinch the title no matter what the Light Blues did against lowly Albion Rovers at Coatbridge. The high-scoring Bairns - whose assistant-manager Bob Shankly was later destined for great things with the Dark Blues - would be no pushover, as Dundee had recently had to fight all the way for a 3-1 win at Dens.

On Saturday April 30th, there were 17,000 at a sun-drenched Brockville with thousands from Dundee hoping to see their heroes take the title. The Dark Blues lined up: Lynch; Follon, Irvine; Gallacher, Cowie, Boyd; Gunn, Pattillo, Stott, Gerrie, Hill.

PENALTY MISS IN WAR OF NERVE

By WILLIE ALLISON

FALKIRK 4   DUNDEE 1   (H.T.

Scorers: Falkirk—Inglis (64 mins.), Aikman (72), Alison ... Dundee—Stott (80).

... than a football match. If we ... "tragedy" in the game, then ... bitterness.

... at Brockville but whose thoughts ... George Anderson as he went on to the ...

THE SPORTING POST,

DUNDEE FLOP AT

Penalty Save Inspires Falkirk

The total eclipse of Dundee's forward line cost them the championship in a fast, but never very scientific, game.

Stott's penalty miss at the crucial stage was the real start of downfall. It seemed to increase the nervous tension which was in their play from the start. The classy touches which have bu...

IT WAS BLACK BROCKVILLE

THERE were many strange features about the championship decided at Brockville. Falkirk, with no worries, were calm...

So near and yet so far - Alec Stott's penalty in the final league game at Brockville is saved by Bairns keeper George Nicol with the score at 0-0. Falkirk went on to win 4-1 and shatter Dundee's title dream.

DC Thomson

DUNDEE F.C.

The "Dark Blues" Down the Years

Dundee F.C. Season 1948-49 - 'A' Division runners-up and semi-finalists in League Cup and Scottish Cup. (BACK, left to right) George Anderson (director-manager, Tommy Gallacher, Gerry Follon, Johnny Lynch, Andy Irvine, Doug Cowie, Alfie Boyd, Reggie Smith (trainer). FRONT - Ally Gunn, Johnny Pattillo, Alec Stott, Syd Gerrie and George Hill.

DC Thomson

The pitch was very firm but although the Dark Blues made heavy weather of things in the opening stages they looked to have got the vital breakthrough three minutes before half-time. Hill beat three men before being brought down in the box and Stott, currently Scotland's top scorer with 38 goals, stepped forward to take the kick. Right-footed he directed a shot towards the bottom right-hand corner but, unfortunately, he had not made a clean connection and George Nicol was able to turn the ball round the post.

Hill took the corner but with Gerrie's header looking net-bound, the Falkirk keeper made another magnificent save. The interval did little to settle Dundee's nerves and Falkirk's pressure finally paid off with two goals in an eight-minute spell. With 12 minutes remaining, Stott pulled one back but any hopes of a revival were quickly dashed by another two goals by Falkirk shortly afterwards.

All with Dundee connections were devastated. Rangers had won 4-1 at Coatbridge and it was a downcast Dens party that departed from Brockville. The penalty miss had come at a crucial stage but the Dark Blues had played nothing like their best. The light ball had been a problem for both sides but, right from the kick-off Dundee had looked a nervy lot. There was none of the usual flair and the forwards could make little of a stuffy Falkirk defence.

Many of the Dundee players were later critical of the pre-match build-up. When the Dens party arrived at Brockville they were met by the usual pre-match banter from the Falkirk players as they went inside.

"That day, George Anderson was a bag of nerves - even more so than normal," recalled Tommy Gallacher. "He said it was better to keep away from all that stuff since it could be upsetting and he told us all to get into the dressing room. At that he locked the door and for the next hour all callers were ignored. Tension built up with every minute and by kick-off nerves had taken over."

Nevertheless, George Hill felt that Dundee - widely regarded by the critics as the best footballing side in Scotland that season - had been desperately unlucky not to take the title: "In December, Third Lanark's Polish winger Staroscik palmed the ball into the net for a late equaliser at Dens while, the following month, East Fife's Henry Morris charged Lynch and the ball into the net only a minute into the game and both "goals" were allowed to stand!"

Scottish League 'A' Division 1948-49						
	P	W	D	L	F A	Pts
Rangers	30	20	6	4	63-32	46
Dundee	30	20	5	5	71-48	45
Hibs	30	17	5	8	75-52	39
East Fife	30	16	3	11	64-46	35
Falkirk	30	12	8	10	70-54	32
Celtic	30	12	7	11	48-40	31
Third Lanark	30	13	5	12	56-52	31
Hearts	30	12	6	12	64-54	30
St Mirren	30	13	4	13	51-47	30
QOS	30	11	8	11	47-53	30
Partick Thist.	30	9	9	12	50-63	27
Motherwell	30	10	5	15	44-49	25
Aberdeen	30	7	11	12	39-48	25
Clyde	30	9	6	15	50-67	24
Morton	30	7	8	15	39-51	22
Albion Rovs.	30	3	2	25	30-105	8

CHAPTER SIX

Star Quality

At the end of the season, Dundee undertook a three-game tour of Belgium and Northern France. Prior to that, Bennett, Brown, Bruce and Mackay were released with Tommy Gray moving on to Arbroath. In addition to George Anderson, Dundee's backroom team consisted of Willie Cameron (trainer-masseur), Jackie Kay (assistant-trainer) and wartime inside-left Andy McCall (reserve-team trainer).

Now they were joined by the recently retired Reggie Smith (trainer-coach) and with Ancell, Lynch, Pattillo and Ewen also at the veteran stage, Anderson signed Everton winger Johnny McIlhatton (£5,000) and full-backs Alan Massie - an Aberdeen "free" - and Jack Cowan from Canada's Vancouver University.

In the League Cup, Dundee were grouped with Clyde, Motherwell and Partick Thistle. Their opening match against Clyde at Dens was watched by a 28,500 crowd but only a late goal by Ewen ensured a 1-1 draw. The Dark Blues continued to disappoint and, with confidence at rock-bottom, only three points were taken from the six sectional ties.

There was a distinct lack of punch up front. Alec Stott had lost his lethal touch and he was replaced by Jimmy Fraser, a recent signing from Aberdeen minor football. After some changes, Dundee began to field a more settled side and, by early November, a gradual recovery saw them up alongside the Old Firm, just one point behind league leaders St Mirren.

The pacy Fraser had formed a useful partnership with inside-right Peter Rattray and later that month the out-of-favour Alec Stott was allowed to join Partick Thistle for £6,000. Jack Cowan was now established at left-back in preference to Irvine and Massie. He had been recommended by ex-Dunfermline manager and former referee Bobby Calder, who was a friend of George Anderson's. Calder had an excellent eye for footballing talent and this was later to be more fully exploited by Aberdeen.

In early December, Dundee were unfortunate to lose 2-1 to Hibs at Dens but, by the end of 1949, they had slipped to fourth, six points behind the Easter Road outfit. For the first time in recent seasons, injuries and illness had taken their toll. Behind the scenes, Willie Cameron had suffered a stroke while George Anderson himself was not in the best of health.

Cowie, Rattray, Follon, Gallacher and Ewen were all out for lengthy spells but Johnny Pattillo again demonstrated his versatility by switching to centre-half with Boyd reverting to a more creative role at left-half. With Fraser and Stewart

Jack Cowan - the Canadian left-back was a tower of strength for Dundee.

struggling to find the net, Gerrie moved to the centre and scored four in the New Year encounters against Aberdeen (h) 1-1, Motherwell (a) 2-0, and Hearts (h) 3-1. Third-placed Hearts had won their last 12 games but in the event, two-goal Gerrie far outshone his much-vaunted counterpart, Willie Bauld.

Any lingering title ended with defeats at Clyde and Celtic before Dundee travelled to meet Hearts in the first round of the Scottish Cup. Gerrie put Dundee ahead on the hour and it took a late counter by Bauld to keep the Tynecastle side in the Cup.

In the Monday afternoon replay, a shot by inside-right Jimmy Toner hit the bar before bouncing into the net off the unlucky Tynecastle keeper. Wardhaugh equalised before half-time but, despite the loss of left-winger Jimmy Andrews through injury, the score remained 1-1. In extra-time, the Dark Blues looked like holding out until Gerrie went off with a pulled muscle but, now reduced to nine men, they finally succumbed when Bauld got the winner near the end.

With little to play for, Dundee's season finished with six successive defeats, culminating in a 6-2 humiliation by Hearts at Tynecastle, to leave the Dens Parkers a disappointing sixth in the league.

Although it was now a transitional period, plenty of talented players remained with the cultured Doug Cowie again on the fringes of full international honours. He was chosen as Scotland's reserve against Switzerland at Hampden and both he and the £20,000-rated Syd Gerrie were the subject of considerable English interest.

The previous August, 17-year-old Bill Brown had been signed from Carnoustie Panmure after a successful trial against Hibs at the opening of Dundee Violet's Glenesk Park. The young keeper had replaced the injured Lynch for the last eight games and, despite his tender years, looked a player of immense potential.

In April, Jimmy Steadward and Jack Court were released. Earlier, Jack Malloch had joined St Johnstone and between them the trio, who had cost a considerable amount, had managed only 10 first-team games.

To add some much-needed punch, Arbroath centre-forward Ernie Copland was signed for £4,000 after an impressive Forfarshire Cup performance against Dundee, while centre-half Willie Roy from Aberdeen and keeper Gordon Rennie from St Mirren were both obtained on free transfers.

Once again, Dundee struggled in the League Cup with only two wins from ties against Falkirk, St Mirren and Hibs. The Dens game with Hibs was abandoned after 68 minutes due to flooding. The visitors had led 2-0 but with the Easter Road men taking sufficient points to reach the next stage, there was no need for a replay.

The players had been heavily barracked at Dens and although this was nothing new, it had never been as widespread. Peter Rattray was a particular target and, upset by this treatment, he asked for a transfer. Reluctantly, Anderson sold him to Plymouth in exchange for £7,000-rated former Aberdeen centre-forward Stan Williams, plus £3,000.

Many fans were shocked by the move and more particularly at the high valuation placed on the player but in the next home game against Hearts, the 25,000 crowd got right behind the team. Just back after a lengthy re-signing dispute, Lynch pulled a muscle and the goalkeeper had to hirple on the wing, but the team were lifted by the tremendous support and went on to win 1-0.

Willie Cameron had retired. Former Dens keeper Reuben Bennett became Reggie Smith's new assistant and soon their newly-devised training schedules had the Dundee players amongst the fittest in the land.

The genial Anderson was a highly persuasive character. But although he had already signed stars like Juliussen, Smith, Boyd, Gallacher, Cowie and Brown, none could compare with his latest signing coup. On September 21st, 1950, Dundee F.C. called a press conference and a beaming Anderson declared: 'Gentlemen, I want to introduce you to Billy Steel, ex-Derby County and now of Dundee!'

The club had paid a Scottish record fee of £23,500 for one of the best-known players in British football. Twenty-seven-

Billy Steel - the all-action Dundee forward remains a legendary figure in Dens Park folklore. *DC Thomson*

year-old Steel was an established Scottish international having joined Derby from Morton for a world record fee of £15,000 in 1947. The inside-left had a somewhat volatile personality and, after refusing to re-sign for Derby, had returned to Scotland that summer proclaiming that, if necessary, he would give up the game.

In August, Anderson had offered £18,000 for his transfer but negotiations broke down when Derby demanded a fee of £25,000. Steel had been given training facilities at Ibrox but, when Rangers declared they would not be making a signing offer, the Dens boss moved quickly to clinch a deal. In contrast to the previous talks which had taken place in the full glare of publicity, Anderson had slipped onto a southbound train at Glasgow with a coat over his head. And, after agreeing a fee with Derby, he returned to make his triumphal announcement!

When asked what it felt like to be a £23,500 player, the self-assured Steel replied: "Nothing to it. I'm used to this sort of thing. When I left Morton I needed a suitcase to carry my share of the fee!"

Two days later, 34,000 fans, around 8,000 more than normal, turned out for Steel's debut against Aberdeen at Dens. Dundee fielded: Brown; Follon, Cowan; Gallacher, Cowie, Boyd; Gunn, Toner, Williams, Steel, Andrews. The Dons, who had also wanted Steel, provided stiff opposition and Scotland international keeper Fred Martin looked in unbeatable form.

Clearly, the flaxen-haired Steel lacked match practice but his clever positioning and masterly touches were an inspiration and with only 19 minutes remaining, Dens Park erupted as Dundee's new hero scored with a low shot! Near the end, Toner made it

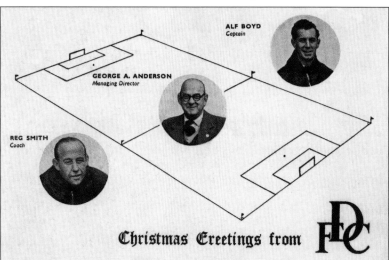

ALF BOYD
Captain

GEORGE A. ANDERSON
Managing Director

REG SMITH
Coach

Christmas Greetings from

Season's greetings - a Dundee F.C. Christmas card from 1950. *Stephen Borland*

2-0 and, when Steel emerged from the dressing room after the game, there were hundreds of schoolboys clamouring for the new star's autograph.

Steel had been an automatic choice for Scotland since 1947 and further caps against Wales and Northern Ireland that autumn made him Dundee's first full international since Colin McNab's Wembley appearance against England in April 1932.

The stocky inside-forward had brought power and imagination to the front-line and, by mid-November, Dundee led 'A' Division with only one defeat in 10 games. With Lynch back between the sticks, only six goals had been conceded yet, despite Steel's fine approach work, only 13 goals had been scored. Once again, centre-forward was proving a problem position but although Fraser, who had broken his leg in August, Stewart, Gerrie, Copland and Williams were all tried, none had looked particularly effective.

In May, the balance sheet had shown a profit of £951-3-7d but, only the previous year's profit had overturned a trading loss of £2,921-8-9d. Steel's transfer fee had come from the directors' own pockets and, in November, three players were sold to balance the books. Gerrie, who had been replaced by Steel, joined Hull City for £12,000, McIlhatton was sold to Raith Rovers for £3,000 and Stewart went to St Mirren for £2,500. Veteran defender Bobby Ancell was now thirty-eight and a month earlier he had decided to hang up his boots to become manager of 'C' Division Berwick Rangers.

In late December, a 37,400 crowd saw Billy Steel inspire Dundee to a 2-0 win over Rangers at Dens. Dundee's newly acquired Continental rubber boots - George Hill believed they were the first team in Scotland to use them - had allowed them to keep their feet on the frosty, but heavily sanded pitch and goals by Gunn and Ewen did little to reflect their true superiority. Dundee's title challenge continued and, by early March, they lay two points behind league leaders Hibs who had played two games less.

Steel had quickly become the pin-up boy at Dens and Tommy Gallacher recalled his somewhat unorthodox approach to training: "In those days our fitness schedule consisted of lapping the track, running up and down the terracing and the occasional road run. After a while Billy would drift away from the other players. He would then

Dens stars - Alfie Boyd and Tommy Gallacher feature in this festive card of 1951 - a year that brought success Jimmy Lorimer

perform an incredible selection of handsprings and acrobatics before practicing with a football. He was a law unto himself but it was great to have him on your side on a Saturday."

Centre-forward Ken Ziesing (24), and full-back Gordon Frew (23), had arrived from South Africa the previous August. On January 2nd, 1951, nearly 36,000 saw the strapping Ziesing score his first goal in Dundee's 2-1 win over Morton at Dens although Frew made a less auspicious start, putting through his own goal in the 3-1 home win against Celtic!

Steel was partnered by either Andrews or Christie on the left-wing and, with Hill switching to the right, Ally Gunn was transferred to Huddersfield for £9,000. This brought Dundee's transfer income to nearly £30,000 for the season and effectively Steel's transfer fee had now been paid.

On January 27th, Dens Park housed a 38,000 all-ticket crowd for the Scottish Cup first-round tie with Dundee United. Leading 2-0 at half-time, the Dark Blues unaccountably relaxed and had to settle for a 2-2 draw. In the Tannadice replay - played on the Wednesday afternoon four days later - Gerry Follon, a right-winger in his Junior days with Lochee Harp, was fielded at outside-right and this time a more determined Dundee went on to win 1-0.

Dens hero Billy Steel scored with a swerving 30-yard shot which completely deceived United keeper Wylie and later the internationalist cheekily claimed that he had intentionally put "screw" on the ball!

Two weeks later, a record 29,972 fans packed Muirton Park for Dundee's second-round tie with 'B' Division St Johnstone. Former Dens Parker Jack Malloch gave Saints an early lead but a Boyd penalty and counters from Christie and Ewen gave Dundee a 3-1 win.

The arrival of a big-time player like Steel and the Dark Blues's subsequent revival had ensured a gates bonanza at Dens. After getting a third-round bye, their official ground record was

Muddy day at Dens - Tommy Gallacher appeals for offside as Johnny Urquhart of Hearts shoots for goal in this cup-tie in 1948. Goalkeeper Jock Brown and Gerry Follon guard the goal. DC Thomson

No holding back - Doug Cowie goes into a crunching tackle with Aberdeen's Tommy Pearson at Dens.
                                                    Doug Cowie Jnr

smashed when a massive 40,920 packed Dens for the Scottish Cup quarter-final with Raith Rovers on March 10th. Penman put Raith ahead in three minutes but, although Christie equalised on the half-hour, another Penman goal in 61 minutes ended Dundee's hopes. The Dark Blues had dominated but, once again, lack of punch had cost them dear.

Disappointingly, successive defeats by East Fife (h) 2-4, and Airdrie (a) 0-2 ended Dundee's title hopes. And although a 2-0 home win over Raith brought a measure of revenge, it brought little consolation as the Dark Blues finished third, 10 points behind champions Hibs.

Only four sides had scored less than Dundee's 47 league goals and, despite using eight different centres, Steel was their top league scorer with only seven goals. In contrast, Alec Stott had proved a bargain buy for Partick Thistle, and in a year and a half at Firhill, he had already netted 39 goals.

All was not well amongst Dundee's players. During a game, Steel would constantly call for the ball and he would make a lot of noise if he didn't get it. Players like Gallacher, Cowie and Boyd were also capable of controlling the play and Steel's non-stop criticism did not go down well with his team-mates. A meeting was called to clear the air but the players were shocked when George Anderson perhaps not unnaturally sided with his biggest star. According to him, the others were jealous of Steel and they were to lay off!

Not all Anderson's signings had borne fruit. Jock Brown, Court, Mackay, Steadward, Malloch, McIlhatton, Rennie and Roy had all been released within two years of signing, while Copland had also done little of note. Nevertheless, encouraged by Steel's success, Anderson swooped to sign 29-year-old former Airdrie and Hearts goalscorer Bobby Flavell for £6,000. Flavell had walked out on Hearts and had only recently returned to Scotland after a season with Colombian side Millionairos of Bogota.

There were repercussions. On April 3rd, a board meeting was held at Dens following rumblings of discontent. John Thomson claimed that he and other directors had only learned of the Flavell signing through the press. Chairman James Gellatly expressed his confidence in Mr Anderson and, consequently, Mr Thomson offered his resignation.

This was accepted by the chairman and seconded by Frank Graham and, although local butcher Jack Swadel proposed non-acceptance, there was no seconder and with the acrimonious departure of Mr Thomson, the board now consisted of Messrs Gellatly, Anderson, Graham, Swadel, Clark and Crichton.

There was little close season break for the Dark Blues. In June, they toured Israel and Turkey and, the following month, returned to play in the St Mungo's Cup. The competition, which was for 'A' Division sides, was held by Glasgow Corporation to celebrate the Festival of Great Britain. The trophy was won by Celtic but, for Dundee, interest ended with a 4-3 first round defeat by Motherwell at Dens Park.

One familiar face was missing. Last season, Johnny Lynch had settled his dispute with the club and some brilliant performances had even brought mention of international honours. But, following his father's death in February, he had missed the Muirton cup-tie and, unable to regain his place, he was freed after 16 years at Dens. As back-up to Bill Brown, the experienced Bobby Henderson was signed on a free transfer from Partick Thistle.

That summer, Billy Steel played on Scotland's European tour but it did not prove a happy trip for the mercurial inside-left. As Scotland crashed to a 4-0 defeat against Austria in Vienna, Steel retaliated under severe provocation and consequently became the first Scotland international to get his marching orders.

Finishing touch - Bobby Flavell's eye for goal added a cutting edge to the Dundee attack.
                                                    DC Thomson

CHAPTER SEVEN

Hampden Heroes

Nevertheless, Steel was in his usual place at the start of the 1951-52 season and a promising start was made in the League Cup with a 2-2 draw at St Mirren and wins over Hearts (2-1) and Raith Rovers (5-0) at Dens. Falkirk centre-half Bobby Henderson was signed for £3,000 but made a shaky debut in a 1-0 home defeat by St Mirren. George Anderson, however, denied that his arrival would signal the departure of Doug Cowie in exchange for Bolton's Scotland international forward Billy Moir, who had been a guest of the Dens Parkers in 1945.

After going ahead in the first minute against Hearts at Tynecastle, Dundee were severely handicapped by injuries to Steel and Flavell and went down 5-2. Now St Mirren led the section on six points with Dundee and Hearts one point behind and all would rest on the final sectional ties.

Brown, Ewen, Irvine and Williams replaced Bobby Henderson, Gallacher, Flavell and Steel for the vital game against Raith Rovers at Stark's Park. Brown quickly justified his inclusion with a penalty save from Colville and goals by Williams and Christie (2) gave Dundee a 3-1 win. Meanwhile, Hearts had defeated St Mirren 3-1 and although level on points, Dundee pipped the Edinburgh side for a place in the last eight on goal-average.

In the quarter-final, a tremendous rearguard action ensured a 0-0 draw at Falkirk. The battling Bairns took an early lead in the Dens return but, by half-time, Dundee's constant pressure was rewarded by decisive goals from Steel and Ziesing. Their league form was less convincing and, on October 13th, the Dens men faced the holders Motherwell in the semi-final at Ibrox with only one win from four league games. Cowan had recovered from injury and replaced Frew at left-back and, with Hill injured, Toner switched to outside-right with Pattillo restored to the number eight jersey.

Dundee led 2-1 after a thrilling first half but the second period saw them come under intense pressure. However with 19 minutes remaining, Pattillo grabbed a third and, for good measure, Flavell added another two near the end to give a rather flattering scoreline.

Now the Dark Blues could look forward to their first post-war final. The Steel-Flavell combination had paid off handsomely with Steel making four of the goals and Flavell, restored to centre after spells on the wing, proving himself a deadly finisher with a well-earned hat-trick.

In the final, Dundee would meet Rangers who boasted no fewer than eight Scottish internationals. Four weeks earlier, Dundee had beaten the Ibrox side 1-0 at Dens and a 2-1 home win over Celtic left them in fine fettle for the Hampden final on October 27th. The Dark Blues were unchanged from the semi-final: Brown; Follon, Cowan; Gallacher, Cowie, Boyd; Toner, Pattillo, Flavell, Steel, Christie. Rangers: Brown; Young, Little; McColl, Woodburn, Cox; Waddell, Findlay, Thornton, Johnson, and Rutherford.

Cup glory - the 1951 League Cup Final at Hampden Park as Dundee keeper Bill Brown gathers from Willie Thornton of Rangers. The other Dark Blues are Tommy Gallacher, Doug Cowie and Johnny Pattillo.

DC Thomson

HOW DUNDEE TOOK THE LEAGUE CUP

THE SKIPPER'S V-GOAL STRUCK HAMPDEN DUMB

DUNDEE 3, RANGERS 2. (Half-time—0-1.)

Scorers:—Dundee—Flavell (47 min.), Pattillo (69 min.), Boyd (89 min.); Rangers—Findlay (20 min.), Thornton (88 min.).

IMAGINE 30,000 people cheering wildly away inside Hampden ten minutes after the final whistle? Sounds fantastic.

And, like the tremendous grandstand finish we had to this Cup final, it was fantastic.

Hampden has certainly seen nothing like it before.

By JACK HARKNESS

The after-match cheering. The thrill-drenched last two minutes which saw Dundee hold the cup, let it slip from their grasp, and miraculously, ever so miraculously, snatch it back again. Here was drama—ay, drama with knobs on.

Two dramatic moments at Hampden. Above—Dundee skipper ALF BOYD waves his arms in joyous abandonment just after he'd headed the winning goal. BOBBY FLAVELL is rush-

A famous day for the Dark Blues as they hit back to defeat Rangers in a dramatic finale to the 1951 League Cup Final.

George Young won the toss and to the relief of Dens skipper Alfie Boyd he chose to attack the "Rangers" end - relief because in Dundee's two unsuccessful semi-finals in the 1948-49 season, the Dark Blues themselves had kicked that way in the first half!

In the opening quarter of an hour, Dundee were in almost complete control with Steel spraying passes all over the field. But just when it seemed Dundee must score, Findlay put Rangers ahead in 21 minutes and by half-time the Glasgow giants looked well in command.

Boyd had played almost as a second centre-half with Steel lying deep but with Dundee's long-ball tactics making little impression on Rangers' "Iron Curtain", the emphasis would now be on short-passing along the ground to draw out the Ibrox defence.

Just two minutes after the interval, the ever-alert Flavell fired Christie's cross into the net despite the efforts of Bobby Brown. Now Dundee turned on the style and they were rewarded when Pattillo ran on to a Flavell pass and shot high past Brown. With only two minutes left, victory looked certain. But when Young floated a long free-kick into the Dundee goalmouth, Bill Brown was challenged by Willie Thornton and the ball floated into the net.

From the restart, Steel was fouled deep in the Rangers half. Only 30 seconds remained as he shouted the famous words: "I'll place it on your head Alfie!" and when his free-kick swirled over, Boyd lept to head home from eight yards out. The left-half was swamped by his joyous team-mates amidst a tremendous roar from the 30,000 Dundee fans in the 92,325 crowd many of whom were gathered on the terracing below the now-demolished North Stand.

It was one of the most dramatic finishes ever seen at Hampden. At the end, an ecstatic George Anderson congratulated each of the victorious Dark Blues and, chaired by Tommy Gallacher and Billy Steel, Dens skipper Alfie Boyd held aloft the glittering League Cup. "That was a wonderful moment," recalled Doug Cowie. "It was a great game but I always felt we had the edge that day and deserved to win."

It is always hard to take on either member of the Old Firm in Glasgow but Dundee had produced a grand team performance with Billy Steel an inspirational figure. Indeed, many believed that the bigger the occasion the better the mercurial inside-man played - and so it had proved!

The Dundee party got a tremendous send-off from Glasgow's Buchanan Street Station but this was nothing

And in 1951-52, when the team won the League Cup, Boyd headed in the winning goal in the closing seconds of the game.

compared to the reception given by the huge crowds at Dundee's West Station. Cowie remembers the scene: "The noise was incredible. The players mounted a special open-top bus in Yeaman Shore before going on a triumphal tour of the city centre, and there thousands of jubilant fans brought traffic to a halt in a never to be forgotten night of celebration."

Incredibly, by mid-December, the Dark Blues lay second-bottom of the league with only one win from seven outings since their Hampden victory. A recurring ankle injury had forced the influential Steel to miss a number of games but the previously reliable defence had lost four goals in successive games against Hibs, East Fife and Airdrie.

Meanwhile, left-winger Jimmy Andrews had been unable to get a regular game and, in November, the little Dens Parker joined West Ham for £10,000 with St Mirren winger Gerry Burrell making the move to Dundee a month later.

Centre-half George Merchant and inside-forward Albert Henderson were introduced from the reserves and, with Steel returning, five festive season wins, including a 2-1 success against Rangers at Ibrox, lifted Dundee to sixth. However, only two points were taken from the next three games and with all league hopes gone, Dundee looked to the Scottish Cup.

Andy Irvine, normally a left-back, was the surprise choice at centre for the first-round tie with 'B' Division Ayr United but his two goals were to pave the way for a 4-0 win at snow-covered Dens. In February, the Dark Blues cruised to a 7-1 second-round win over non-league Wigtown with a record 4,500 crammed into tiny Crammondford Park. Prior to the match, their president had jokingly offered Billy Steel half-a-dozen pies to slow him down but the Dens dynamo responded with two goals and his usual all-action display.

In the third round at Dens, 'C' Division Berwick Rangers, whose manager Bobby Ancell and centre-forward Albert Juliussen were former Dark Blues, proved stuffier opponents. But despite the loss of Pud Hill with a broken arm, an early Pattillo goal put Dundee through.

Although Dundee's indifferent league form continued, the Dens quarter-final clash with Aberdeen was a 41,000 sell-out. Ziesing got Dundee's opener with a tremendous shot, then Steel dribbled through for a second soon after the break. Further goals by Boyd, with a penalty, and Steel again emphasised the Dark Blues' superiority as they strolled into the last four of the Scottish Cup.

Steel's ankle injury was again giving concern and his influence was badly missed as a couple of defeats left Anderson's men uncomfortably near the relegation zone. But despite opting out of the Scotland v England international, the Dens star returned with his ankle

Dundee F.C.'s Scottish League Cup winning team of 1951 - (BACK, left to right) Tommy Gallacher, Gerry Follon, Bill Brown, Doug Cowie, Jack Cowan. MIDDLE - Johnny Pattillo, Frank Graham (director), Bob Crichton (secretary), Andrew Clark (director), Jack Swadel (director), Reggie Smith (trainer). FRONT - Jimmy Toner, Bobby Flavell, James Gellatly (chairman), Alfie Boyd, George Anderson (director-manager), Billy Steel and George Christie.

DC Thomson

heavily strapped up for the Easter Road semi-final against strong-going Third Lanark.

There was little between the sides but in the 27th minute a brilliant Steel dummy allowed Burrell through for the opener and, shortly before half-time, the wee maestro added a second. Thirds continued to fight but, despite the continual prompting of their Scottish international inside-man Jimmy Mason, there was no further score.

On Saturday, April 19th, 1952 Dundee faced last season's runners-up Motherwell in the Scottish Cup Final. In earlier rounds they had beaten Forfar, St Mirren, Dunfermline, Rangers, then Hearts - after a second semi-final replay - but the sides appeared evenly matched with Motherwell winning both league clashes and Dundee victors in the semi-final of the League Cup. Recently, however, Dundee had struggled against Morton (h) 2-2, Hibs (a) 1-3, and Partick Thistle (h) 0-2 and, although relegation had been avoided, the once solid defence looked strangely vulnerable.

With Bill Brown on National Service, Bobby Henderson had been in goal since January and Hill for Burrell was Dundee's only change from the semi-final: Henderson; Follon, Cowan; Gallacher, Cowie, Boyd; Hill, Pattillo, Flavell, Steel, Christie. Motherwell: Johnstone; Kilmarnock, Shaw; Cox, Paton, Redpath; Sloan, Humphries, Kelly, Watson, Aitkenhead.

A remarkable crowd of 136,274 was inside Hampden before the gates closed shortly after kick-off with another 4,000 - including 1,000 from Dundee whose special train had arrived late - locked out! This remains a record for two provincial sides and only the 1937 final between Aberdeen and Celtic (147,365) attracted a bigger attendance for a Cup Final in Scotland.

At half-time the scoreline remained blank but, after dominating the opening half-hour, wind-assisted Dundee were desperately unlucky not to be ahead. Three times

Kilmarnock cleared off the line with Dundee convinced that the third, just before the interval, was over, but Jack Mowat, who had also refereed the League Cup Final in October, waved play on. Steel had looked in match-winning form but, shadowed by Cox and often two others as well, he took some very heavy tackles and gradually faded from the game.

Motherwell slowly gained in confidence and, when Christie missed a great chance after the break, the writing was on the wall for the Dark Blues. Shortly afterwards, they were stunned by two goals within a minute by Watson and Redpath and another lightning double by Humphries and Kelly near the end made it 4-0 for the Fir Parkers. "There was never four goals between the sides," claimed Geoge Hill. "Motherwell defended well and, on the day, they got the breaks. It would have been a different story if we had scored in that first half-hour."

Motherwell's plan to mark Steel out of the game had paid off. They had also shown more speed and flair and Dundee's offside ploy had been unable to cope. Henderson and Gallacher had performed well but the gamble of playing Flavell, recently plagued with thigh and groin injuries, rather than Ziesing, had failed with only Steel showing anything up front.

In an end of season clear-out, no fewer than eleven players, including men of first-team experience like Pattillo, Ewen, Williams, Fraser and Beaton were released. The popular Johnny Pattillo, now 37-years-old, had proved a great servant in his seven years at Dens and now he returned to Aberdeen in the role of trainer-coach. In addition, South

Hampden again - Motherwell's Archie Kelly appeals for a penalty as Johnny Aitkenhead goes down after a challenge from Doug Cowie with Jack Cowan, Bobby Henderson and Gerry Follon watching anxiously.

Hampden Smash-And-Grab By Flavell

season. Only a week earlier they had pulverised the much-fancied Motherwell 7-3 at Fir Park and their brilliant forward-line of Gordon Smith, Bobby Johnstone, Lawrie Reilly, Eddie Turnbull and Willie Ormond fully merited their "Famous-Five" nickname.

On October 4th, the Tynecastle "semi" proved an enthralling encounter for the 44,200 crowd but it was Dundee not Hibs who were masters on the day. After dominating the early stages, Dundee were shocked when Reilly put Hibs ahead on the half-hour. Seven minutes after half-time, clever interpassing between Flavell and Steel ended with Steel equalising from close in.

The tide had turned and, led by the darting Steel and the dashing runs of Christie, Dundee went for the kill! And with only 10 minutes left on the clock, Flavell ended a goalmouth melee by crashing the ball past Younger for the winner.

Dundee's copybook football had Hibs chasing in vain and the Flavell-Steel double act had again paid off with Billy Steel in breathtaking form. His arrival two years earlier had sparked a Dens revival and now, remarkably, Dundee would make their third Hampden appearance in twelve months.

And with an impressive record of only one defeat in 14 games, the Dark Blues were firm favourites to retain the League Cup against 'B' Division Kilmarnock in the final in Glasgow on Saturday, October 25th.

Nine special trains took 5,000 Dundee fans to Hampden, another 5,000 travelled by bus with others making their way by private car. Sadly, George Anderson would miss the game. He was recuperating from pleurisy in an Aberdeen nursing home but, just like he had done in the semi-final, the Dens supremo would follow play via the radio commentary.

Assisted by Reuben Bennett, Reggie Smith was in charge and the only change from the semi-final was Frew for the injured Cowan with Albert Henderson again preferred to the off-form Gallacher at inside-right. Dundee: B. Henderson; Follon, Frew; Ziesing, Boyd, Cowie; Toner, A. Henderson, Flavell, Steel, Christie. Kilmarnock: Niven; Collins, Hood; Russell, Thyne, Middlemass; Henaughan, Harvey, Mays, Jack, Murray.

It was soon evident that the Ayrshire part-timers, who had beaten Rangers 1-0 in the semi-final, were not merely to provide the supporting cast. Backed by the swirling Hampden breeze and roared on by their fans in the 51,000 crowd, Killie began to take control and Dundee's defence took a first-half pounding.

Dark Blue heroes - skipper Alfie Boyd and his happy team-mates celebrate their second League Cup triumph against Kilmarnock. DC Thomson

African left-winger Basil Wilson returned to his homeland. He had arrived at Dens last September but had never made the first-team breakthrough.

Now free from injuries, Dundee made another bright start in the 1952-53 League Cup and wins over Raith Rovers (h) 2-1, Airdrie (a) 3-1, and a 2-2 draw with Clyde left them one point above the Kirkcaldy side at the halfway stage.

Perhaps with the future in mind, Boyd and Cowie had switched positions while Follon and Gallacher were replaced by Frew and Ziesing. These changes did not go down well with the fans and with Frew's form adversely affected by barracking, Follon and Gallacher - at inside-right - were recalled for the vital clash with Raith Rovers at Stark's Park. In a bruising encounter, Dundee won 2-1 with Steel settling the issue just six minutes from time.

A 3-2 win over Airdrie confirmed their quarter-final place before Dundee were held 3-3 by "bogey" team Clyde in the final game at Shawfield. There, Dundee had sported a a new outfit of dark blue and white quartered jerseys with the well-known Courier cartoonist John R Mason likening the players to the components of a prefabricated chess-board!

In the quarter-final, Dundee surprisingly fell 3-1 to 'B' Division Stirling Albion at Annfield. But within three minutes of the return, an on-form Bobby Flavell pulled one back and a comfortable 5-0 win took the Dens Parkers into the semi-final 6-3 on aggregate.

Barring their way to another Hampden appearance were league champions Hibs, who along with Dundee were currently the best footballing side in Scotland. And although Dundee had lost only once in 11 games, the Easter Road side were clear favourites having already scored 40 goals that

"Wee Hilly" - George Hill was a great Dens favourite. DC Thomson

Thanks largely to some inspired goalkeeping by Bobby Henderson the score remained 0-0 at the interval but the pattern was to continue at the start of the second period. Then at last wing-halves Ziesing and Cowie came into the game but, after Christie's long-range shot was fisted onto the bar by Niven, only a last-ditch Frew tackle saved the day. With 10 minutes left, Toner switched places with the struggling Bert Henderson and within two minutes, the move paid off.

Feinting to the wing, Toner sent through a perfect pass to Flavell and the wee centre shot low past Niven. Six minutes later, Dundee made certain. Bobby Henderson's long punt reached the Killie penalty area and, as centre-half Thyne hesitated, Flavell raced in to thump the bouncing ball into the corner of the net.

Dundee had become the first side to retain the League Cup and, although there were again joyous scenes amongst players and fans, the celebrations were curtailed due to a sudden downpour of rain. "I'll admit we were a wee bit lucky," said Doug Cowie. "We took a long time to get into our stride but at the end of the day it's goals that count and it was us that got them!"

The Dens defence had held up well but it was Flavell's opportunism that had won the day. Young Bert Henderson had been badly affected by nerves but, surprisingly, the experienced Steel, closely marked by Russell, had been a shadow of his normal self. The "root" of the problem, however, became clear a month later when the Scotland international had no fewer than eleven teeth extracted!

Fireworks, bugles and whistles greeted the Dundee team who returned back in the city with the League Cup for the second year running. When their train arrived at 8.35pm at Dundee's West Station, the Dens party was hustled through the cheering crowds onto a waiting open-topped bus. Alfie Boyd held the trophy aloft as he sat in front of his teammates on the top deck as the bus wound its way through the

Hibs v Dundee clashes were eagerly awaited by the football connoiseur.

densely packed throngs via Whitehall Crescent and Whitehall Street where cars and trams were soon brought to a standstill.

There was a large crowd in City Square but they were to be disappointed when the bus, unlike last year, continued up Reform Street and on down to West Ferry via Victoria Road.

It was, though, yet another great night to remember for the Dens Park club, and the party stopped for a small celebration at the home of chairman James Gellatly at Albany Road, before later returning to the Royal British Hotel in Dundee for a meal at 10pm.

However, a week after retaining the League Cup, a 3-2 defeat by East Fife at Methil signalled an astonishing four-month slump and by March 1953, Dundee lay near the foot of the 'A' Division league table having won just two of their previous 17 games!

Injuries had again proved unsettling. Follon, Ziesing, Flavell, Hill and, significantly, Steel had all missed games and worryingly goals were in short supply. In January's 3-2 home defeat by Raith Rovers, top scorer Bobby Flavell had been replaced by Jack Johnson. However, the Dane, who was in Scotland for the rest of the season, did not look match-fit and to make matters worse, two of Raith's goals were scored by former Dark Blue Ernie Copland who had joined the Kirkcaldy team in October 1951.

Going for goal - Dundee's Tommy Gallacher gets in front of two defenders to send a powerful header towards goal in this match against Airdrie at Dens with Bobby Flavell and George Christie ready to pounce.

Mark Gallacher

Bursting at the seams - a tightly-packed south terracing for the Dundee v Rangers match at Dens Park in February 1953. The crowd of 42,024 is the club's record home attendance and one unlikely to be surpassed.

DC Thomson

Little was going right and, after a first-round bye, the Dark Blues drew Rangers in the second round of the Scottish Cup. The Ibrox side were unbeaten in 14 games and such was the interest that 43,024 fans packed into Dens Park to smash Dundee's official ground record for the second time in two years.

Dundee played some tidy football but they had little penetration up front and rarely looked like winning. Blunders by Bill Brown - home on leave - and Gerry Follon, in a 60-second spell just after half-time, allowed Hubbard and Grierson to put Rangers ahead and there was no way back for Dundee. The £3,270 gate money brought a measure of consolation but, with two months of the 1952-53 campaign still remaining, Dundee's season was effectively over.

The Dens men had to be content with seventh place but, with Billy Steel back to his best and Doug Cowie finally gaining full international recognition, they could at least boast two players in the Scotland team which managed a 2-2 share of the spoils with England at Wembley, and again in the 2-1 defeat to Sweden at Hampden.

Centre-half Bob Henderson was freed but, included in Dundee's 17-player party to tour South Africa was old Dens Park favourite, centre-forward Ronnie Turnbull, who had recently been signed from Swansea after spells with Sunderland and Manchester City, as well as youngsters Davie Easson, Jackie Stewart and Bert Walker.

Globe-trotters - the Dens Parkers prepare to board a BOAC Comet in London before flying to South Africa.

George Hill

Dens skipper Alfie Boyd had made his last domestic appearance for the club. He had accepted a coaching post in South Africa and would remain there on completion of the tour. The two month trip was a marvellous experience for the Dundee players and officials who had flown direct from London to Johannesburg on a BOAC Comet. There were Caledonian Society functions by the score and the team made a tremendous impression with only one defeat in a gruelling 17-game schedule.

The flamboyant George Anderson was well aware of the benefits of good publicity and, as the side changed to go out against a Johannesburg Select, he came into the dressing room with a parcel. "These will take a trick out there," he said, presenting each player with a Dundee strip in the Anderson tartan. When the team took the field they were given a great reception by the local fans and the following day the newspaper headlines read: "Tartan troops from Tayside!"

George Hill with the famous tartan strip worn by Dundee in South Africa.

Back in Britain, meanwhile, Celtic had won the Coronation Cup, which was held to celebrate the Coronation of Queen Elizabeth II. Arsenal, Manchester United, Newcastle United and Tottenham Hotspur, Celtic, Rangers, Hibs and Aberdeen had participated. Certainly, Rangers had won the League Championship and the Scottish Cup but Hibs and Aberdeen had also been invited despite only finishing as runners-up.

Surprisingly, Dundee had been ignored for the domestic celebrations despite their two successive League Cup wins, while they had also finished above Celtic and Aberdeen in the league. Certainly, this prestigious tournament clashed with Dundee F.C.'s South African tour but the invitations had been made prior to final confirmation of the trip the previous October.

Tour of South Africa 1953	
Southern Transvaal (Johannesburg)	1-1
Natal (Pietermarizburg)	4-1
Natal (Durban)	5-0
Border X1 (East London)	5-0
Eastern Provine (Port Elizabeth)	5-0
Western Province (Capetown)	4-0
Griqualand (Kimberly)	2-0
Eastern Transvaal (Benoni)	4-2
Lorenco Marques X1 (Port. East Africa)	3-1
Orange Free State (Bloemfontein)	9-2
Northern Transvaal (Pretoria)	2-0
Southern Transvaal (Jo'burg)	4-0
South Africa 1st Test (Durban)	0-1
Southern Rhodesia (Salisbury)	4-1
Southern Rhodesia (Bulawayo)	8-0
South Africa 2nd Test (Jo'burg)	5-0
South Africa 3rd Test (Cape Town)	5-3

Played 17, won 15, drew 1, lost 1,
Goals scored 70, conceded 12

SOUTHERN TRANSVAAL FOOTBALL ASSOCIATION

TEST MATCH
DUNDEE FOOTBALL CLUB
vs.
SOUTH AFRICA
At RAND STADIUM, JOHANNESBURG
On SATURDAY, 11th JULY, 1953
PRICE £1 : 11 : 6

COMPLIMENTARY

GATE	BLOCK	ROW	SEAT
5	D	I	No. 13
WEST			

This portion to be retained by holder and shown on request.
NOT VALID for admission at the Outer Gates without attached voucher.
No Refund if match is not played through causes outside Association's control.

Sunny South Africa - (BACK, left to right) Jackie Stewart, Andy Irvine, Bobby Henderson, Gordon Frew. MIDDLE- Bert Henderson, Jack Cowan, Ken Ziesing, Alfie Boyd, Doug Cowie, Ronnie Turnbull, Bert Walker. FRONT - George Hill, unknown (South Africa FA), Dave Easson, Bob Crichton, Bobby Flavell, George Anderson, Billy Steel, Reggie Smith, George Christie. (absent Tommy Gallacher).

CHAPTER EIGHT

Into Decline

Returning bronzed and fit, Dundee began their second League Cup defence in devastating fashion. A razor-sharp Flavell netted four in a 6-1 thrashing of Stirling Albion at Dens. Then a 4-2 win over Clyde at Shawfield, a 1-1 draw with Partick Thistle at Dens and wins over Stirling Albion (a) 2-0 and Clyde (h) 4-2, took their haul to nine points.

A quarter-final place looked certain with Partick Thistle, two points behind, requiring to beat Dundee by three clear goals in the final game at Firhill to qualify on goal-average. With Follon and Flavell unfit, the Dark Blues fielded: Brown; Frew, Cowan; Gallacher, Cowie, Ziesing; Hill, Turnbull, Henderson, Steel, Christie.

Dundee began confidently but they were stunned when Thistle scored three in an incredible nine-minute spell before half-time. There was no way back and the loss of a fourth goal near the end made it a dismal day for the Dark Blues. The Firhill side went on to reach the final where they lost 3-2 to East Fife and Dundee could only reflect on what might have been.

Billy Steel, who trained at Shawfield during the week, had not played well. That season, he had been appointed captain but the move was not a success and the influence of Alfie Boyd was sorely missed. A 4-0 defeat in the opening league game at Falkirk resulted in Doug Cowie reverting to left-half and within a month the big Aberdonian assumed the captaincy from Steel.

Reserve centre-half Danny Malloy was brought in and quickly established himself. Other youngsters like right-half Jackie Stewart and right-winger George Carmichael were blooded more gradually. The changes were successful and, by the end of October 1953, Dundee lay second, four points behind surprise leaders Queen of the South. Home form was

Unsung hero - George Christie spent 10 years at Dens. DC Thomson

impressive and an unbeaten eight-game run at Dens included wins over Queen of the South (4-1), and current champions Rangers (1-0).

Billy Steel had always been a domineering character but, increasingly, his intolerant attitude was resented by his colleagues. On November 21st, the star was sensationally "rested" for the game with Stirling Albion and he watched Dundee's 4-1 win from the Dens Park stand. Until then, George Anderson had sided with the maestro but the latest move, he felt, was in the best interests of the team.

"Steel was one of football's greatest characters and he could beat a man any number of ways," said Tommy Gallacher. "However, he always wanted to do things his own way and, wherever he went, the fur was sure to fly. Unfortunately for us, the more his tongue wagged, the better he seemed to play!"

Meanwhile, with Carmichael, Hill and Christie competing for the wingers' jerseys, Gerry Burrell was transferred to Huddersfield in late December. Only one point had been dropped in Steel's four-game absence but players and fans alike were delighted to welcome his return for the Boxing Day game with Raith Rovers.

A 4-2 Ne'erday win over Aberdeen at Dens followed a 2-1 victory at Stark's Park to leave the Dark Blues one point behind leaders Queen of the South with a game in hand.

Bird's eye view - from the rear of the Provost Road terracing at a packed Dens Park for a cup-tie in the early 1950s. DC Thomson

Dundee's performance against Aberdeen had been their best of the season but, in a remarkable turnaround, five of the next six games ended in defeat and, by late February, their title hopes lay in ruins.

Changes were made. Henderson replaced Brown in goal, Follon was recalled with Frew replacing Cowan at left-back, Gallacher was dropped in favour of Stewart or Ziesing while the forwards were constantly shuffled - but it was all to no avail. In addition, George Anderson's health was again giving concern and, in January 1954, he was confined to bed for a number of weeks.

In the Scottish Cup, Dundee were given a first-round bye before struggling to a 1-1 draw with Albion Rovers at Coatbridge. Bill Brown saved the day with a penalty stop but Dundee made no mistake as they coasted to a 4-0 win in the replay at Dens.

On Saturday, February 27th, Dundee travelled to play 'C' Division Berwick Rangers at the next stage. Berwick were managed by Jerry Kerr, later to become such a success with Dundee United but, despite their recent unconvincing form, Dundee remained firm favourites to win.

George Anderson had recovered from illness but there were shocks when the team was announced after lunch: Brown; Frew, Cowan; Gallacher, Malloy, Cowie; Follon, Irvine, Merchant, Ziesing, Steel. The forward-line selection caused many a raised eyebrow particularly as regulars Toner and Hill were travelling reserves.

It appeared that the front men had been chosen for their strength rather than finesse as conditions at Shielfield Park were very heavy. Only Steel was a recognized attacker although big George Merchant, recently switched from centre-half to centre-forward, had scored all four goals in the replay with Albion Rovers. Ziesing was now regarded as a half-back and, although Follon and Irvine had occasionally been played up front for tactical reasons, they had never all played together.

Sadly, the move was doomed to failure. After falling a goal behind on the half-hour, Dundee faced an uphill struggle and, when Berwick scored a second in 65 minutes, there was

Safe hands - Bill Brown comes out to save watched by Dundee centre-half Danny Malloy.
DC Thomson

no way back. The Dark Blues had struggled throughout and a third Berwick goal near the end completed the humiliation. The attack had contributed little and a series of defensive blunders had ultimately proved catastrophic.

George Hill was amongst many who believed that Anderson had underestimated the opposition: "Recently the Dundee reserves had thrashed the full Berwick team in a 'C' Division game and I think the boss thought we would win no matter what side he put out. In the event, the team played so badly that, the longer the game went, the more Dundee were going to lose by."

Shortly afterwards came another blow. Cowan, Frew and Ziesing all announced their intention to return to their respective countries at the end of the season with Flavell also keen to try his luck in South Africa.

Anderson tried hard to dissuade them but, when it became obvious that their minds were made up, he declared that the "rebel four" would not play in the remaining games. This cleared the air and Dundee took nine points from their last seven games to finish fourth-equal on points, but seventh when goal-average was taken into account.

For a number of months there had been serious concern that Steel's ankle injury might finish his career. The Dens star had continued to play with his ankle doped up after repeatedly refusing to have an operation. But in the last game of the season, he displayed much of his old verve in Dundee's 6-0 home win over Partick Thistle.

Anderson had been the architect of Dundee's post-war success but, dogged by ill-health in recent years, he retired as manager although retaining his seat on the board. In 1949, Reggie Smith had been offered the post on a joint basis with Bobby Ancell but had turned it down. With his extensive experience and coaching certificates from both sides of the border, Smith appeared the logical successor to Anderson but it was veteran Rangers and Scotland centre-forward Willie Thornton who became the new Dundee boss.

It had been discovered that Billy Steel was not training regularly in Glasgow. In April, Anderson had given him an ultimatum that he must give up his job in Glasgow and train full-time at Dens and when the internationalist refused he was put up for sale. No offers were received and three months later after repeatedly refusing terms, Steel shocked Scottish football by announcing his departure for the USA.

He was to become manager of Los Angeles Danes and, with a job, a car and a house thrown in, he would earn around $600 a month - roughly four times his Dens salary! On August 12th, 1954, Dens Park idol Billy Steel (31), set sail for his new life in California and his departure together with the retiral of George Anderson marked the end of Dundee's golden post-war era.

Since their three Hampden appearances in 1951 and 1952, the Dark Blues had been in decline. Apart from the newly departed Steel, Cowan, Frew and Ziesing had also gone. Jimmy Toner was given a free transfer while Ronnie Turnbull, who was now past his best, was put up for sale.

In addition, Flavell, who had decided to remain, Follon, Irvine, Gallacher and Hill were all in the twilight of their careers and Willie Thornton's first move was to sign two experienced players. Former Rangers full-back Davie Gray - brother of former Dens stalwart Tommy - arrived on a free

Heading for goal - Tommy Gallacher dives full length to connect with a cross in the Scottish Cup replay against Albion Rovers at Dens as Billy Steel looks on. At inside-right for the day, the Dundee man beat the goalkeper but headed wide. DC Thomson

transfer from Blackburn, while ex-Falkirk inside-forward Joe Roy was signed from Clydebank Juniors.

Despite the upheaval, the Dark Blues made a bright start and only narrowly failed to qualify from a tough League Cup section. Recovering from a 3-1 reverse to Hearts at Tynecastle, they recorded successive home wins over Falkirk (3-1), Celtic (3-1), and Hearts (4-1). The games against Celtic and Hearts attracted crowds of almost 30,000 and after going to the top of the section with a 1-0 win over Celtic at Parkhead, a win in the final game at Falkirk would ensure their place in the quarter-final.

Brockville had long been a bogey ground for Dundee and the jinx continued as they crashed 4-0. Hearts, meanwhile, had qualified with a 3-2 home win over Celtic and later went on to lift the trophy with a 4-2 victory over Motherwell in the final. The slump continued and, despite some decent home results, Dundee lay in mid-table by the end of 1954. It had been a difficult spell and, in September, a disillusioned Reggie Smith - "He would have done a good job for Dundee," said Bert Henderson - severed his nine-year Dens connection to become manager of Dundee United.

Meanwhile, Willie Thornton looked to the future and, increasingly, youngsters like George Carmichael and Bert Walker and inside-men Dave Easson and Dave Dunsmuir were given their chance. Bobby Flavell, then 34, had scored many important goals for Dundee but, in late December, he was released and joined Kilmarnock soon afterwards. His successor was last year's top scorer George Merchant, who, after returning from injury had scored seven goals in five games by the end of the year.

However, three successive defeats in early 1955 soon brought urgent cries for new blood. Already that season, Dundee had been badly hit by call-ups for National Service. Stables, Stewart, Sneddon and Carmichael had all gone and with Easson's departure also imminent, Stirling Albion winger Jim Chalmers was signed for £4,000.

On January 29th, a George Merchant double brought a morale-boosting 2-1 win over Rangers at Dens. Seven days later, 58,000 saw the sides draw 0-0 in the Scottish Cup at a muddy Ibrox and Dundee were unchanged from the two previous encounters for the replay at Dens: Brown; Gray, Craig; Gallacher, Malloy, Cowie; Chalmers, Henderson, Merchant, Roy, Christie. There was little between the sides but 10 minutes from time, Gallacher headed into his own net while attempting to clear to give Rangers a 1-0 victory.

An unbeaten run from mid-February until the end of March saw Dundee take nine from a possible 12 points but this form was not maintained as they finished eighth, their lowest position since the war.

George Merchant - his move up front paid off with goals.

George Merchant - "The Merchant of Menace" - might have lacked some of the finer touches but, by the end of the season, he had netted 16 goals in 23 games. Centre-half Danny Malloy had made rapid progress and, after being named as reserve for Scotland against Hungary and the Scottish League against the League of Ireland, he played for the Scottish League against the English League and also for the Scotland 'B' team against Scotland.

In mid-March, George Hill, who had been at Dens since 1940, was released. The bed-ridden George Anderson was unstinting in his praise for the winger, declaring: "He was one of the pillars on which the post-war Dundee F.C. was built." Mr Anderson still remained on the board but, sadly, illness had wrecked his plans of easing Willie Thornton into management.

It was clearly a transitional period although, encouragingly, both Bill Brown and Doug Cowie had been on Scotland's close-season tour of Austria, Hungary and Yugoslavia. Cowie played in all three games but Tommy

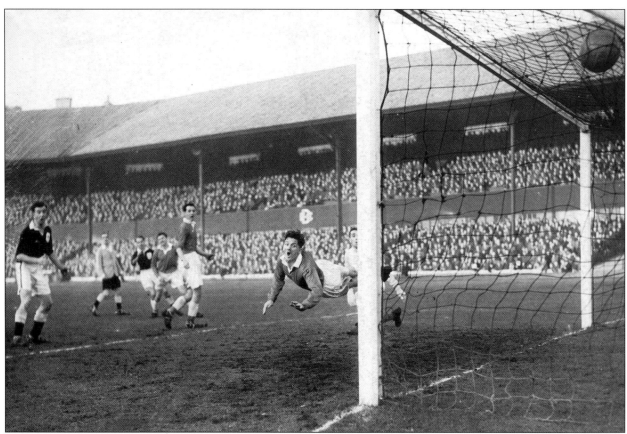

A screamer - George Christie (third left) thunders the ball into the "postage stamp" corner in this league clash with Aberdeen at Dens in January 1956. George Merchant looks on with Allister, Macfarlane, Young and Martin the Dons defenders.   Aberdeen Journals

Younger of Hibs was an automatic choice in goal and the unfortunate Brown was the only player in the 16-man party not to play.

The 1954 AGM had shown a small loss of £3-6-0d and, with average home gates dropping from 19,100 in season 1953-54 to 15,900 last term, Dundee had little to spend, and, unless there was an improvement in their playing fortunes, this trend looked sure to continue.

Earlier, reserve defender Alan Massie had joined Reggie Smith at struggling Dundee United and, in May, fringe players Archie Simpson and Jimmy Mason were amongst six players freed. Billy Steel had been badly missed at inside-forward and although Bert Henderson had proved himself a tireless worker, Dunsmuir and Roy lacked the strength and stamina to back up their undoubted skill.

An unsuccessful bid was tabled for Motherwell's Jim Forrest before Dundee turned their attention to the free transfer market. They signed inside-forwards Ivor Smith and Johnny Anderson from Aberdeen and Partick Thistle, respectively, but neither made much impact in early League Cup defeats by Airdrie (a) 0-4, and Kilmarnock (h) 1-2.

Willie Thornton then signed Falkirk right-half Gordon Black but, although unbeaten in their remaining four ties, Dundee finished one point behind section winners St Mirren. Nevertheless, they could take encouragement from a 3-0 win in their final tie at Paisley, where recently signed centre-forward Billy Ritchie from Osborne scored twice and brought some much-needed dig to attack.

Once again Dundee made a bad start to the championship. They lost 4-0 to Hearts at Tynecastle, and showing little consistency over the next few months, the glory days of the early Fifties remained a distant memory. Anderson and Smith fell from favour but, in October, Smith returned to hit four goals in a 6-3 win over Raith Rovers at Dens. Home gates continued to fall with the average down to the 12,000 mark but, despite reported interest in £10,000-rated Ian McMillan of Airdrie and Alan Brown of East Fife, no business was done.

Since Gordon Black's arrival, Tommy Gallacher had struggled for a game and, in November, he asked for a transfer. At this time, Dundee were nearly £8,000 in the red and when no move was made for Gallacher, a £15,000 deal was agreed for the transfer of Doug Cowie to Cardiff City. However, this was not to Cowie's liking and the international half-back turned down the move.

Archie McCauley, the former Arsenal and Scotland half-back who had been coach of non-league Guildford, was appointed to a similar position at Dens. However in early December, just when Dundee had moved within four points of league leaders Celtic, Danny Malloy was transferred to Cardiff City for £17,500.

The centre-half had developed into a key man for Dundee and he was regarded as a likely successor to George Young for Scotland. His departure was heavily criticised by the fans and, despite the balance sheet deficit, it was a move sadly lacking in ambition.

The following day Gordon Black played centre-half against Hibs at Easter Road but, without the commanding Malloy, Dundee crashed to a 6-3 defeat. Over the ensuing months, Black, Merchant and young Jimmy Stevenson all got their chance but none would prove the equal of Malloy.

The early weeks of 1956 brought little improvement and

Doug Cowie (on the right), pictured with Scotland International team-mate Lawrie Reilly of Hibs. DC Thomson

four successive defeats prompted Thornton into signing action. Centre-forward Jim Watt arrived from Berwick Rangers for £3,000, full-back Ed Skinner came from Arbroath for £1,450, while Chelsea keeper Dave McLaren was obtained on a free transfer.

In January, Gerry Follon was released after 283 league and cup appearances in his 16 years at Dens. Since August, the veteran defender had been in dispute with the club over non-payment of a benefit. Hugh Reid was now first-choice at right-back and, with Davie Gray also in contention, Follon suffered a further setback when he underwent a cartilage operation in November. A keen Dundee fan, Follon was another great servant to the club and, although he joined St Johnstone soon afterwards, he later expressed regret over his acrimonious departure from Dens.

The Scottish Cup campaign began with a fifth-round tie against neighbours Dundee United at snow-covered Tannadice. Milne opened the scoring for United and although Stables scored shortly after half-time, a late equaliser by outside-left Milne earned the battling Division Two outfit another chance.

For the Wednesday afternoon replay, Gray replaced Reid at right-back as Dundee fielded: Henderson; Gray, Irvine; Gallacher, Black, Cowie; Stables, Henderson, Merchant, Roy, Christie. This time the Dark Blues made no mistake and goals by Merchant, Stables and Henderson gave them a comfortable 3-0 win before a crowd of 17,000. "It was a game we expected to win for United were no big deal in those days," recalled Dens powerhouse Bert Henderson. "Conditions were a great leveller in the first tie."

In the next round, Dundee were paired with Rangers - their third Scottish Cup clash in four years. The Dark Blues had dominated the league clashes at Dens, but there was little doubt that the Ibrox side were the cup specialists. The pattern was to continue for, although Rangers were outplayed for long spells, a first-half goal by South African centre Don Kitchenbrand was enough to see them through.

By mid-March, Dundee hovered perilously near the relegation zone having taken only two points from nine games since New Year. None of the recent signings had impressed and Tommy Gallacher made a scoring return with two goals in the 3-0 home win over Partick Thistle. Still the Dark Blues were not safe and three successive defeats, including an incredible 5-4 reverse to bogey-team East Fife at Methil, again placed them in danger of relegation.

On Monday, April 9th, there was a morale-boosting 5-1 win over Manchester United in a friendly at Dens.

The brilliant play of the new English champions - including three players later to perish in the Munich air disaster of 1958 - had earned them the title of the "Busby Babes". That night, however, it was Dundee who sparkled. Encouraged, they went on to win three of the seven remaining games but, despite avoiding relegation, the Dark Blues finished a lowly thirteenth in the new 18-team league.

In recent years, George Anderson's health had deteriorated and in May he died at the age of 69. A born showman, his flair for the unexpected had made him a colourful character. His boundless enthusiasm and knowledge of the game had been a key factor in Dundee's post-war revival and his influence would be sadly missed.

Willie Thornton had rejected a lucrative offer to become manager of Preston North End, preferring to concentrate on the further development of the Dens Park youth policy. Towards the end of last term, young Alan Cousin (Alloa YM), and George O'Hara (Shettleston), had impressed and it was hoped that other recent arrivals like Bobby Cox (Osborne), George McGeachie (Falkirk High), and Doug Alexander (Westrigg Bluebell), would do likewise.

Previously, Anderson, Roy, Craig, Walker and Bobby Henderson had been released, with Tommy Gallacher and Davie Gray both available for £1,500 each. Gray was later freed while, at the age of 34, Gallacher decided to hang up his boots before opting for journalism with the *Dundee Courier and Advertiser*.

Towards the end of the previous season, Jimmy Stevenson had established himself as first-choice centre-half. Shortly, however, he was due to commence his National Service, and, as a replacement, Dundee signed Falkirk veteran Ralph McKenzie on a free transfer.

His experience was to prove invaluable and in a remarkable transformation, the Dark Blues qualified for the quarter-final of the 1956-57 League Cup. Only one point was dropped from the six sectional ties against Airdrie, Motherwell and Raith Rovers with the best performance reserved for Broomfield where Airdrie were crushed 7-1 in the final game.

There was a new fighting spirit about the side. Bert Henderson had moved back to right-half with Chalmers and Black forming a productive right-wing partnership in the absence of the injured Ian Stables and Dave Easson. Last season, George Merchant had scored 14 goals to finish Dundee's top marksman for the fourth successive year. Now he had netted another ten in nine games and, with little

prospect of a first-team berth, Billy Ritchie moved on to Stirling Albion of Division Two.

Things had not gone well for Billy Steel in America. After only six games he had been dropped by the Los Angeles Danes then, following

Tommy Gallacher hung up his boots and soon made his mark in journalism. adverse publicity due to a driving offence, he moved to San Francisco where he did not play for eighteen months before joining Hollywood F.C. in January 1956.

However, out of the blue, Willie Thornton received a letter from Steel. At the age of 33, the former Dens star believed he had two or three seasons left. But although the Dundee manager agreed to his request for a trial, nothing more was heard from the mercurial Steel.

On Wednesday, September 12th, Dundee met Dundee United in the first leg of the League Cup quarter-final at rain-swept Dens. Former Dundee keeper Bobby Henderson was an absentee for United after a recent leg-break and his experience was badly missed as Dundee went on to win 7-3. Pacy right-winger Jimmy Chalmers gave United a torrid evening and his efforts were rewarded with a well-deserved hat-trick.

Three days later, Reggie Smith fielded the recently-signed Davie Gray in the Tannadice return. The experienced defender brought composure to the United defence and they went on to win 2-1 in Dundee's first reverse that term.

For the Ibrox semi-final against Partick Thistle, Dundee were on familiar lines: Brown; Reid, Irvine; Henderson, McKenzie, Cowie; Chalmers, Black, Merchant, O'Hara, Christie. Disappointingly for the 24,000 fans there was no scoring with only the dashing Chalmers showing anything up front for the Dark Blues.

However, in the midweek replay their only change was Skinner for the injured Irvine at left-back. Black missed an early chance but, thereafter Thistle took control and goals by Hogan and Wright put them 2-0 ahead after half-an-hour. Inspired by Cowie, Dundee fought back and Christie and O'Hara made it 2-2 at the interval.

For the next 15 minutes, Dundee besieged the Thistle goal only to be hit with a sucker punch when Bill Brown was deceived by a Davidson free-kick in 69 minutes. There was no further scoring and Thistle went on to play Celtic in the final which they lost 3-0. Dundee's forwards had again disappointed. But although Merchant had limped from early on, the potentially lethal Chalmers had only been switched to centre 15 minutes from the end.

After the loss of so many top stars in 1954, it had been a difficult two years for Willie Thornton. Players like Brown Irvine, Cowie, Henderson and Christie had experienced the glory days but they understood the problems facing the manager. "Under George Anderson's management, Dundee had played an all-out attacking game," said Doug Cowie.

"However, Willie Thornton did not have as many quality players at his disposal as his predecessor. The boss had played for an Ibrox side famed for its defensive qualities and it was little surprise that Dundee moved towards a more defensive formation - a trend reinforced by the arrival of Archie McCauley as coach."

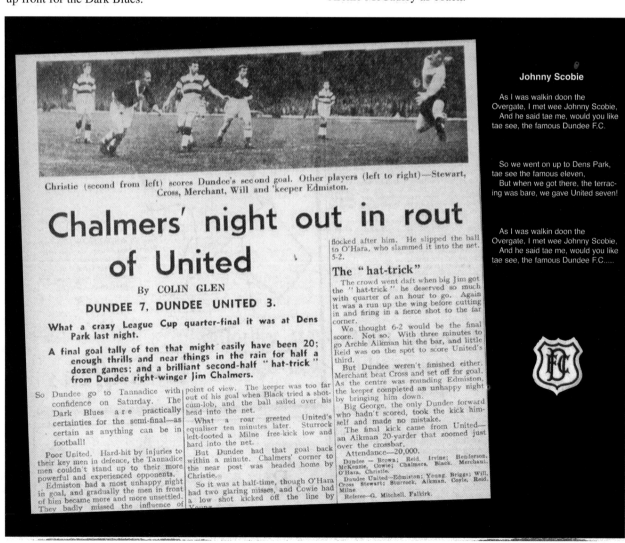

Christie (second from left) scores Dundee's second goal. Other players (left to right)—Stewart, Cross, Merchant, Will and 'keeper Edmiston.

Chalmers' night out in rout of United

By COLIN GLEN

DUNDEE 7, DUNDEE UNITED 3.

What a crazy League Cup quarter-final it was at Dens Park last night.

A final goal tally of ten that might easily have been 20; enough thrills and near things in the rain for half a dozen games; and a brilliant second-half "hat-trick" from Dundee right-winger Jim Chalmers.

So Dundee go to Tannadice with confidence on Saturday. The Dark Blues are practically certainties for the semi-final—as certain as anything can be in football!

Poor United. Hard-hit by injuries to their key men in defence, the Tannadice men couldn't stand up to their more powerful and experienced opponents.

Edmiston had a most unhappy night in goal, and gradually the men in front of him became more and more unsettled. They badly missed the influence of Young.

point of view. The keeper was too far out of his goal when Black tried a shot-cum-lob, and the ball sailed over his head into the net.

What a roar greeted United's equaliser ten minutes later. Sturrock left-footed a Milne free-kick low and hard into the net.

But Dundee had that goal back within a minute. Chalmers' corner to the near post was headed home by Christie.

So it was at half-time, though O'Hara had two glaring misses, and Cowie had a low shot kicked off the line by Young.

flocked after him. He slipped the ball to O'Hara, who slammed it into the net. 5-2.

The "hat-trick"

The crowd went daft when big Jim got the "hat-trick" he deserved so much with quarter of an hour to go. Again it was a run up the wing before cutting in and firing in a fierce shot to the far corner.

We thought 6-2 would be the final score. Not so. With three minutes to go Archie Aikman hit the bar, and little Reid was on the spot to score United's third.

But Dundee weren't finished either. Merchant beat Cross and set off for goal. As the centre was rounding Edmiston, the keeper completed an unhappy night by bringing him down.

Big George, the only Dundee forward who hadn't scored, took the kick himself and made no mistake.

The final kick came from United—an Aikman 20-yarder that zoomed just over the crossbar.

Attendance—20,000.

Dundee — Brown; Reid, Irvine; Henderson, McKenzie, Cowie; Chalmers, Black, Merchant, O'Hara, Christie.

Dundee United—Edmiston; Young, Briggs; Will, Cross, Stewart; Sturrock, Aikman, Corle, Reid, Milne.

Referee—G. Mitchell, Falkirk.

Dundee F.C. Season 1956-57 - League Cup semi-finalists (BACK, left to right) Hugh Reid, Andy Irvine, Bill Brown, Ralph McKenzie, Bert Henderson, Doug Cowie. FRONT - Jimmy Chalmers, Gordon Black, George Merchant, George O'Hara, George Christie. DC Thomson

14 games, they finished a disappointing tenth in the table.

In January, George Merchant and the long-serving "Handy-Andy" Irvine joined Falkirk in a £10,000 deal. Two months later, Falkirk won 2-1 at Dens with Merchant - a committed Dundee fan - scoring twice, but despite this, the popular pair got a tremendous reception from the home support! By then, Reggie Smith was manager at Brockville and, aided by this strong Dundee influence, the Bairns went on to win the Scottish Cup, beating Kilmarnock 2-1 in the replay.

There had been a flurry of other moves. Right-back Jim Ferguson was brought from Stirling Albion, Ed Skinner joined East Fife for £750 and, in April, Archie McCauley left to become the manager of Norwich City.

That same month, there was a humiliating 5-2 defeat by lowly Brechin City in the Forfarshire Cup. It was a result which saw the fans desert in their droves and three days later, a mere 3,000, Dundee's lowest home crowd since the war, turned out for what ended up as a 1-0 defeat by East Fife.

League form proved to be solid rather than spectacular but, by New Year, a good run left Dundee fifth, seven points behind leaders Hearts with three games in hand. The defence had looked secure with left-back Bobby Cox making an impressive debut in the 3-1 home win over Queen's Park in October. His crisp tackling and passing ability soon made him a first-team regular and he was widely tipped for Scotland Under-23 international honours.

For a number of years, Doug Cowie had been Dundee's outstanding player and the big Aberdonian was widely regarded as the most accomplished left-half in Scotland. At the start of the season he had been the subject of an abortive enquiry by Rangers but an ankle injury sustained in the recent international against Northern Ireland would rule him out for the next seven games.

The long-striding Alan Cousin was back in form at inside-right but, although the industrious Jim Watt had scored seven goals in eight games while deputising for George Merchant, he later gave way to the bustling Billy Birse.

Sadly, Dundee's improved form was not reflected at the gate with only 8,500 at home games against Queen's Park and Ayr United. Many blamed their falling crowds on the outward redistribution of the city centre population, but with attendances declining throughout Scotland, many fans wondered how Dundee could afford to retain their best players.

Five successive defeats made it a dismal start to 1957 before Dundee entertained Clyde in the first round of the Scottish Cup at Dens. A crowd of 22,000 saw Dundee dominate but they couldn't breach the Bully Wee defence. There were 10,500 at Shawfield for the replay and, after trailing 2-0, Cowie pulled one back in 71 minutes. But despite a storming finish in which the Dark Blues twice hit the woodwork, Clyde, unbeaten in 23 games, held on to win.

All Dundee's early season promise had vanished. There was little consistency up front, where Birse had not lived up to expectations and with only four wins from their final

In the close season, Willie Thornton resisted overtures to become Kilmarnock manager and Sammy Kean of Hibs was appointed trainer-coach at Dens, despite interest from ex-skipper Alfie Boyd. Former Dundee United assistant-manager Ally Gallacher was appointed chief scout but there were already signs that Thornton's youth policy had begun to pay off.

Cousin, Cox and O'Hara were now first-team regulars while others like Easson, Sneddon, Stewart, Alexander and the two Jim Fergusons - one a goalkeeper, the other a right-back - had all tasted first-team action. And over the past nine months, the influx of young talent had continued with the arrival of Jimmy Gabriel (Dundee North End), Alan Gilzean (Coupar Angus Juniors), Alex Hamilton (Westrigg Bluebell), and Hugh Robertson (Auchinleck Talbot).

Carmichael, Stables, Smith and Young were amongst nine players given free transfers, while Watt joined Queen of the South for £1,250 and Birse moved on to East Fife. Towards the end of the previous season, there had been speculation that Airdrie's Ian McMillan and Partick's George Smith were transfer targets.

Dundee, however, chose to offer £1,750 for Dundee United's talented inside-forward John Coyle and when this was rejected - United later got £8,000 from Clyde - Dunfermline's Under-23 international inside-left Felix Reilly was signed for £3,000.

Other newcomers were forwards Clive Wallace (Kirrie Thistle), and Don Watt (Dundee United), and half-backs Alec Glen (Queen's Park) and Danny McLennan (East Fife).

A study in concentration - Dundee goalkeeper Bill Brown and Hugh Reid on their toes against Queen of the South. DC Thomson

None had cost any money, Wallace arriving from the juniors with Watt, Glen and McLennan obtained on free transfers.

In the 1957-58 League Cup, the Dark Blues failed to qualify from their section which included Hearts, Kilmarnock and Queen's Park. Alan Cousin gave them a splendid start with three goals in the 5-2 win over Queen's Park at Hampden but they could only manage three more points and Kilmarnock qualified with ease.

On August 18th, Dundee's game with Hearts was abandoned at half-time with the score 0-0. Throughout the first half torrential rain had flooded the T.C. Keay end, and at the interval, the groundsman was given 10 minutes to disperse the water. However, despite a big improvement, the referee decided to abandon the match and, ironically, the water had drained completely five minutes later.

Since the abandonment had happened after the break, the disgruntled fans were not entitled to a refund and many bemoaned Dundee's failure to emulate Dundee United, who had recently erected a covered enclosure. Three days later, 16,300 saw the replayed game end 2-2 and, although this was almost 3,000 less than the first game, Dundee and Hearts were clear winners in a financial sense.

In fact, Dundee had planned to build an enclosure over the T.C. Keay and Provost Road terracings. This would have provided cover for another 20,000 fans, but problems with piling would have entailed costs of around £20,000 - a figure which was prohibitive at the time.

In their final League Cup tie, Dundee had lost 4-2 to Hearts at Tynecastle. Seven days later, they crashed 6-0 at the same ground and when further defeats left them with just one win in 10 games, it was clear that many long-standing problems remained unresolved. All the recent signings had struggled and Watt was released soon afterwards with McLennan joining Berwick Rangers a few months later.

That September, Wally Warren and Ken Whitlock - both recommended by Alfie Boyd - arrived on trial. But, like Basil Wilson five years earlier, neither of the South Africans made the first-team before returning home in November.

By then, Dundee had a settled, steady defence comprising: Brown; Reid, Cox; Black, McKenzie, Cowie though injuries meant constant changes up front. With George McGeachie sidelined by cartilage trouble, Jimmy Chalmers regained the number seven jersey but the pacy Hugh Robertson was in brilliant form on the left-wing, and soon George "Cocker" Christie was switched to the right.

Cousin and Sneddon were the established inside-forwards but the centre-forward position continued to pose problems. Cousin, Chalmers, O'Hara, Henderson and Easson were all tried before Frank McCrory was signed from Arbroath and, on his Boxing Day debut, the newcomer found the net in a 2-0 home win over Kilmarnock.

Two days later, an injury-hit Dundee included four reserves for the game at Airdrie. Right-back Alex Hamilton, centre-half Gordon Tosh, left-half Alec Glen and left-winger Arthur McIvor all made their debuts, but with Bill Brown hampered by an early shoulder injury and the novices unable to offer much protection, the Dark Blues were on the end of a 7-1 mauling. Reserve keeper Jim Ferguson deputised in defeats by Aberdeen (h) 1-2, and Raith (a) 0-4 and although Brown returned for the Dens clash with league leaders Hearts on January 4th, 1958, Dundee went down 5-0.

The Tynecastle team were on their way to a runaway title success and with players of the calibre of Dave Mackay, Alex Young and Jimmy Wardhaugh, they would finish 13 points above second-placed Rangers, losing only once and scoring a remarkable 132 goals in the process.

In the Scottish Cup, Dundee got a first-round bye before a third-minute goal by Cousin brought a narrow win against Raith Rovers at Stark's Park. They went on to control much of the third-round tie with Aberdeen at Dens but it was the visitors who went two goals ahead. And, although Robertson narrowed the deficit, Aberdeen's Bobby Wishart settled the issue with a third near the end.

The early cup exit came as a bitter blow and soon Felix Reilly and Jim Chalmers were on their way out in exchange for East Fife's Jimmy Bonthrone and Kilmarnock's Dave Curlett. Both newcomers were seasoned campaigners. They brought a better balance in attack and successive wins over Queen's Park (a) 7-2, Celtic (h) 3-3, and Falkirk (a) 2-0, in March soon dispelled any fears of relegation.

Driving rain and sleet ensured that only 5,000 hardy souls turned out for the Dens clash with Celtic - around a quarter of the normal attendance for the visit of the Parkhead side. The pitch quickly turned into a mudbath and, with both sides

George McGeachie - a real bundle of tricks.

badly affected by the freezing conditions, all were agreed that the match should never have begun.

Nevertheless, the tide had turned and, despite finishing 10th, Dundee ended the season with a 1-0 win over runners-up Rangers at Ibrox. Alan Cousin, recently capped for Scotland's Under-23's against Holland was a constant menace and, just before the interval, he headed the only goal of the game.

CHAPTER NINE

The Young Ones

That summer, Bill Brown and Doug Cowie had represented Scotland in the World Cup Finals in Sweden. It was a fitting finale to Cowie's 20-game international career but, for Brown it was only the beginning. He made his debut against France and would continue as Scotland's No. 1 keeper for another seven years.

In an end-of-season clear-out, Glen, Tosh, McIvor, Wallace and both Fergusons were released with George O'Hara joining Southend for £1,500. Dundee's growing band of full-timers was swelled by Ally Hill (Clyde), Tommy Robertson (Rangers), Frank Crossan (Sheffield Wednesday), and Ronnie Crichton (Arbroath YM). All were forwards and all had been obtained on free transfers.

There had been encouraging signs towards the end of last term and there was now an abundance of young talent at Dens. Alex Hamilton was now the regular right-back and his partnership with Bobby Cox was regarded as one of the best in Scotland. Up front, the wily Davie Sneddon and the hard-running "Shug" Robertson made a formidable left-wing alongside Alan Cousin. And, with the experienced Curlett and Bonthrone as well as McGeachie, the omens were good.

But despite opening their League Cup campaign at Dens for the first time since 1953, the Dark Blues lost 3-2 to Partick Thistle. A 2-1 win at Motherwell put them back in contention but narrow reverses to Queen of the South (a) 0-1, Motherwell (h) 2-3, and Partick Thistle (a) 2-3, ended their quarter-final hopes. Nevertheless, there was much to savour about Dundee's early-season play, particularly the emergence of 17-year-old Jimmy Gabriel, signed from Dundee North End, at centre-half.

Managed by ex-Dens Parker Bobby Ancell, Motherwell also put the accent on pure football and the League Cup ties between the pair were cracking affairs. Both clubs had benefited from operating a youth policy and in McCann, Martis, Quinn, St John, Hunter and Weir, the Fir Park men had some of Scotland's brightest youngsters.

In their opening league game, the classy Dark Blues confirmed their potential with a 5-2 win at Falkirk. Three goals were scored by Alan Cousin but the pace of new centre Ally Hill had been another key factor. The 31-year-old proved an ideal foil for the other young forwards and, by mid-October, he had netted six goals in 10 games before being sidelined by injury.

The team were now performing consistently well and by late autumn they lay in sixth place, just three points behind league leaders Hearts. Eleven points had been taken from their opening nine games and in September Gabriel and Cousin were outstanding as Dundee departed from Ibrox with a 2-1 win over Rangers.

Invariably, the athletic Cousin had played well against the Light Blues and it was little surprise when they offered £16,500 for his transfer shortly afterwards. However, the Dundee forward was a classics student at nearby St Andrews University and was happy to remain at Dens. Thus, like an earlier bid by Newcastle, the Rangers bid for the player was doomed to failure.

Inside-left Davie Sneddon had emerged as a key player for the Dark Blues in his new deep-lying schemer role and Scotland's international selectors were amongst his many admirers. He was capped for the Under-23s against Wales, later appearing, along with Gabriel, for the Scottish League against the full Scotland side - an annual fixture that always had an edge because of the Home Scots v Anglos element.

The lanky Bill Brown was now firmly established as Scotland's international keeper but, in mid-November, he was stretchered off unconscious after making a brave save

Just in time - Jimmy Gabriel beats Johnny Hubbard to the ball at Ibrox as Doug Cowie watches. Inset - Davie Sneddon. DC Thomson

Cup calamity - Bobby Cox, Bill Brown, Alex Hamilton and Jimmy Gabriel on the defensive at Fraserburgh in the Scottish Cup. The Highland League outfit caused a major upset with their 1-0 first-round win.

Aberdeen Journals

against Queen of the South at Palmerston. He received three stitches in a head wound (he later wore a protective scrum cap) and, although still groggy, returned to help Dundee towards a 3-1 win, their first at Dumfries since 1949.

The majestic Doug Cowie remained a dominant force in the middle of the park. He was well respected throughout the game and Bobby Cox was full of admiration for his former skipper: "He was superb in the air and had great vision and passing ability. In short, he was the complete player and, what's more, he played for Dundee!"

However, the rapid development of the "Thornton babes" meant less opportunities for the older players. In September, 30-year-old George Christie went to Third Lanark for £750 and Ralph McKenzie left for Inverness Caley on a free transfer. Gordon Black, earlier on offer at £1,000, was released with Jackie Stewart, who was also given a free transfer, moving on Airdrie a few months later.

At the start of 1959, Dundee took three points from Aberdeen (a) 1-1, and Raith Rovers (h) 2-0, leaving them in fourth place, three points behind league leaders Rangers. However, the tricky underfoot conditions brought about by the severe frosts of a typical Scottish winter did nothing for Dundee's silky football and successive defeats by Killie (a) 0-1, and Motherwell (a) 0-2, then Rangers (h) 1-3, brought their title hopes to an end.

In October, Alex Hamilton had lost his place to Hugh Reid after breaking his toe against Raith Rovers. However, "Hammy" returned against Rangers and Dundee were

unchanged for the Scottish Cup first-round tie up at Fraserburgh on January 31st: Brown; Hamilton, Cox; Henderson, Gabriel, Cowie; Curlett, Bonthrone, Cousin, Sneddon and Robertson.

As expected, Dundee took control but, after wasting countless chances, they were stunned when Strachan put Fraserburgh ahead a minute from the interval. After the break, Dundee continued to dominate but, with the stuffy Highland Leaguers, including veteran forward Bobby Auld - a Dens Parker in season 1944-45 - refusing to crack, there was no further score.

For the second time in five years, the Dark Blues were the victims of a "giant-killing" and for Bill Brown and Doug Cowie, who had both played at Berwick in 1954, it was a

All American - a crew-cut Doug Cowie with Albert Henderson and Andy Penman on tour in the USA.

On their way - some of the Dens Park players and officials with their families at Dundee's West Railway station prior to the squad setting off for their tour of the USA. The Dundee men are Albert Henderson, Doug Cowie, Hugh Reid, Alex Hamilton, Jimmy Gabriel, Bobby Cox, Reg Morrison, Jimmy Bonthrone, Ally Hill and manager Willie Thornton with coach Sammy Kean at front. DC Thomson

particularly bitter experience. Bert Henderson summed it up: "We did everything but score and we can only blame ourselves for that. The person I felt sorriest for was the manager Willie Thornton."

Alan Cousin's form had been affected by the earlier transfer speculation and, along with Curlett and Robertson, he was dropped for the away game against Hearts on February 7th. And to replace them, in came Ally Hill and teenage wingers Andy Penman (15), and Fred Jardine (17).

Penman had arrived at Dens a month earlier after being released by Everton due to homesickness. Just two weeks short of his 16th birthday, the Fifer remains the youngest player ever to wear the Dark Blue of Dundee and, despite a 1-0 defeat at Tynecastle the youngster did well enough to retain his place for the visit of St Mirren the following week.

However the strong-going Love Street outfit had discovered a potent blend and, with the dashing Gerry Baker netting four in a 6-4 triumph, the Buddies were shortly destined for Scottish Cup glory. It was Dundee's sixth successive defeat but, encouragingly, their scoring touch had returned. And with confidence restored, a nine-game unbeaten run saw them finish fourth behind Motherwell, Hearts and league champions Rangers.

The previous December, the death of Frank Clark at the age of 71 had reduced the board to James Gellatly, Jack Swadel, Frank Graham and Bob Crichton. In addition,

Dundee's average home attendance of 11,500 was nearly half that of 1951-52 and, without any income from a Scottish Cup run, the influential Davie Sneddon was sold to Preston for £12,000 in April.

That summer, Dundee undertook a 10-game tour of the USA and Canada. The month-long trip involved visits to New York, St Louis, Chicago, Detroit, Philadelphia, Vancouver and San Francisco. There were keenly contested clashes with English First Division side West Bromwich Albion which ended 2-2, 1-7 and 2-4, and another highlight was the emotional reunion with Billy Steel in California.

It was a fabulous experience for the Dens Parkers, but a further shock was in store. Bill Brown was unsettled and, soon after their return to Scotland, the lanky international keeper was transferred to Tottenham Hotspur for a fee of £16,500. "Dundee's loss was Tottenham's gain," according to Alex Hamilton. "Brown was a great keeper who dominated his goal area with magnificent handling. He was the best in Scotland and he went on to prove himself the best in Britain."

Although that season would mainly be remembered for the infamous defeat at Fraserburgh, the Dark Blues' league placing of fourth was their highest for eight years. And, despite the loss of two of his top players, manager Willie Thornton chose to remain at Dens after rejecting a lucrative offer of £3,000 per annum from Leeds United.

Dundee F.C. Season 1959-60 - (BACK, left to right) Alex Hamilton, Bobby Cox, John Horsburgh, Dave Curlett, Jimmy Gabriel, Doug Cowie. FRONT - George McGeachie, Jimmy Bonthrone, Alan Cousin, Bert Henderson, Hugh Robertson. DC Thomson

To make way for the younger school, Crossan, Drennan, Stevenson and Watson were released with Frank McCrory moving on to Forfar Athletic. There was now a steady stream of young talent at Dens. Hamilton, Cousin, McGeachie, Robertson and Gabriel were first-team regulars while others like Andy Penman, goalkeeper Pat Liney and left-half Ian Ure had shown promise in their brief appearances. Time and again, Dundee had beaten bigger clubs to the cream of the young talent and once at Dens, the youngsters were carefully groomed by Sammy Kean.

An abortive approach was made for ex-Scottish international winger Gordon Smith, who had been released by Hibs. He elected to join Hearts and Dundee's only newcomer was centre-half Billy Smith, who was signed on a free transfer from Rangers.

In the League Cup, Dundee's youthful side struggled to produce last season's form and they could manage only four

Parting words - Dundee's Scotland international goalkeeper Bill Brown speaks to Pat Liney prior to joining 'Spurs. DC Thomson

points from Rangers, Motherwell and Hibs. The Fir Parkers qualified for the quarter-final but, for Dundee, the misery continued when a 3-1 league reverse to Hearts at Dens left them with five defeats from their opening seven games.

John Horsburgh (22), recently signed from Penicuik Juniors, had been the surprise choice in goal, preferred to the more experienced Pat Liney and Reg Morrison (ex-Aberdeen), both of whom had been on the North American tour. However, Horsburgh's confidence was badly shaken by the loss of 16 goals in five games and Liney, signed from Dalry Thistle in 1957, stepped into the breach. Soon afterwards, Morrison joined Stirling Albion for a small fee without ever playing a first-team game for Dundee.

Like Brown, Sneddon had been a key man for Dundee and although ex-Ranger Tommy Robertson was given his chance, he was unable to exert a similar influence.

Nevertheless, the fans were given a glimpse of another three youngsters in centre-half Billy McMillan (Dalry), centre-forward Bobby Waddell (St Andrew's Swifts) and inside-left Alan Gilzean (Coupar Angus Juniors). And although Gilzean returned to Aldershot to complete his National Service soon afterwards, both McMillan and Waddell played their part in a 3-0 win at Aberdeen on September 5th.

That was to be Willie Thornton's final game in charge. Just days later, he resigned due to his wife's ill-health and returned to Glasgow to become manager of Partick Thistle. During his five years at Dens, Dundee had done little of note but it had not been an easy task for the likeable Glaswegian in his first managerial appointment.

Thornton, who, like George Anderson, watched games

from the directors' box, had nothing like the power wielded by his predecessor. Instead, he very much followed the line dictated by the board. However, he had rebuilt the side and now Dundee could boast many of Scotland's top prospects. In August 1954, there were barely enough full-timers for a game of five-a-side, but now there were 24, one of the largest full-time staffs in Scotland.

Bob Shankly (48), the Third Lanark and former Falkirk manager, was appointed as Thornton's successor. Shankly had revitalised Thirds in his two years in charge and, already that season, they had progressed to the League Cup Final which they subsequently lost 2-1 to Hearts. In addition to the new manager, the backroom staff now comprised Sammy Kean (trainer-coach), and Jackie Kay (assistant-trainer), and soon afterwards, they were joined by physiotherapist Lawrie Smith.

There was no glory start to the Shankly era. On Saturday, October 10th, a 3-1 home defeat by league leaders Rangers left Dundee near the foot of the table. They had managed only three wins from 13 games that season and, clearly, a lot of hard work lay ahead.

The Dark Blues had fielded: Liney; Hamilton, Cox; Gabriel, Smith, Curlett; McGeachie, Cousin, Hill, Henderson, H. Robertson. Smith had made his debut in place of McMillan and in the following weeks, further changes were made to the line-up.

Cowie returned after his injury, while Bonthrone replaced Henderson and Curlett moved to centre in place of Hill, who joined Bristol City for £1,500 shortly afterwards. The moves paid off and, by mid November, five successive wins took Dundee to third. And despite some disappointments, notably a 4-0 drubbing by Kilmarnock at Dens, the Dark Blues remained in fourth position by the end of January 1960.

An unchanged defence had played solidly since Cowie's return in October and Bobby Cox gained a measure of

Modest maestro - Bob Shankly would lead the Dark Blues into a glorious new era. DC Thomson

recognition when he was named as reserve for the Scottish League against the Irish League and also for the Scottish League against Scotland.

Up front, McGeachie, Cousin and Robertson were automatic choices with Bonthrone, Curlett and Henderson contesting the two other places. In December, young Andy Penman reclaimed the number seven jersey with some great displays of pace and shooting power, and Jimmy Bonthrone, now 32, who had been a great example to the youngsters, was allowed to join Stirling Albion for a small fee.

Meanwhile, Alan Gilzean, who was the last Dundee player to do his National Service, had been demobbed and, in February, a well-placed header brought him his opening goal in Dundee's 3-1 win over St Mirren at Dens.

By then, the championship was a lost cause and, after a first-round bye in the Scottish Cup, Dundee were paired with Hibs at Easter Road. After seven postponements due to bad weather, the game finally went ahead on Monday, February 29th. The pitch quickly turned into a quagmire and two goals by Johnny McLeod and a third by Bobby Johnstone extinguished Dundee's hopes of cup glory.

Less than a year earlier, Dundee had received £28,500 from the sale of Brown and Sneddon but, despite assurances that there would be no further departures, another Dens star was to take the road south. The fair-haired Jimmy Gabriel (19), had been outstanding since moving to right-half and, after appearing for the Scotland Under-23s against Wales in November, he joined Cousin in the Scottish League team against Scotland.

Everton were keen and, after an initial bid was rejected, the Dens board were unable to resist their subsequent £30,000 offer. Gabriel - a "natural" according to Doug Cowie - was given the final decision and, although happy at Dens, he elected to join the big-money Goodison outfit. Bob Shankly was bitterly disappointed at his transfer and, once again, there was a storm of protest by disgruntled Dens Park fans.

Dundee were not the only Scots club to lose their top stars to England. In recent times, Dave Mackay, (Hearts to Spurs, £30,000) and Graham Leggat (Aberdeen to Fulham for £16,000) had also moved and what was then a trickle was soon to become a torrent.

That season, a 10,000 capacity covered enclosure had been erected opposite the main stand. A new floodlighting system had also been installed and, in March, Dundee hanselled their lights with a 1-0 win over English Second Division Liverpool. The Anfield club were managed by Bill Shankly, brother of the Dundee boss, with former Dens keeper Reuben Bennett - formerly Bob Shankly's assistant at Third Lanark - as coach. The coincidences went even further for, on the very day Bob Shankly was appointed Dundee manager, the Dens directors had received a late application

Elegance and style - these were the qualities Jimmy Gabriel brought to the Dens Park ranks. DC Thomson

New-look Dens - early 1960 brought the installation of a floodlighting system as well as a covered enclosure on the south side of Dens Park.   DC Thomson

Ure; Penman, McGeachie, Gilzean, Cousin, Robertson.

Despite the absence of virus-hit skipper Doug Cowie, Dundee cantered to a 5-0 win and victories at Ayr (2-1), Aberdeen (4-1), and Raith Rovers (3-0) ensured a place in the quarter-final draw. Throughout the sectional ties, only one change was made - Waddell replacing the injured Cousin - and convincing home wins over Ayr United (3-0), and Aberdeen (6-0) confirmed Dundee's ability to make a strong challenge for honours that season.

In recent years, Dundee had been one of Scotland's top footballing sides but they had lacked the vital killer touch so necessary to achieve tangible success. Now they had a scoring sensation in Alan Gilzean, who had netted a remarkable 24 goals in his 18 senior games, including 16 in eight matches that term.

Strong in the air and with a deadly shot in either foot, Gilzean had already grabbed four hat-tricks. However, it was far from a one-man show for Dundee had uncovered a potent attacking blend.

At Everton, Andy Penman had been described as one of English football's brightest prospects. Now he was playing brilliantly and with the clever McGeachie and the industrious Cousin and Robertson also on song, the goals had flowed freely.

Earlier that year, Dundee United returned to Division One after a 29-year absence. The Black and Whites had been revitalised by the pipe-smoking Jerry Kerr and, with Dundee firing on all cylinders, the Tannadice derby on September 17th was eagerly awaited by both sets of fans. The packed 20,000 crowd saw Briggs put United ahead with a 25th-minute penalty and although Penman equalised soon afterwards, the Tannadice battlers were not to be denied. Within a minute, Tommy Campbell restored their lead and three minutes from time the big centre settled things with a decisive third goal.

Cox and Cousin had missed the game through injury, but, more significantly, Gilzean had been closely policed by giant centre-half Ron Yeats. A few days earlier, Cowie had

from none other than Bill Shankly, who was then the manager of Huddersfield Town.

Initially, Gabriel was replaced by the versatile Bert Henderson but soon the rangy figure of Ian Ure had established his claim for regular first-team football with a series of impressive displays. Of more concern was the lack of a scoring centre-forward but in late March, Bob Shankly returned from a scouting mission to find that the Dark Blues had trounced Hibs 6-3 at Dens Park. Andy Penman had scored three but Alan Gilzean had been a revelation in his new role at centre-forward.

In 90 seconds, he thundered home Dundee's opener and generally impressed with his clever distribution and powerful shooting. The big Coupar Angus boy added another six goals in the remaining four games and an unbeaten seven-game run saw the Dark Blues finish fourth behind Rangers, Kilmarnock and title-winners Hearts.

Alan Cousin had finished Dundee's top scorer for the third successive season. He had netted 17 goals in league and cup - one more than Hugh Robertson - and his sparkling form earned him Under-23 caps against England and Belgium and an appearance for the Scottish League against Wales. And as further proof of the growing Dens Park pedigree, Andy Penman had also played against the Belgians.

Only Tommy Robertson and Dougie Alexander, who had never fully recovered from a back injury, were released. Shankly, however, had made a careful assessment of his playing staff during his seven months in charge and, in early August, he paid £6,000 for Burnley right-half Bobby Seith. The previous season, the 29-year-old Monifieth-born wing-half had captained the Turf Moor side to the English First Division Championship but now he was delighted to return to his native Tayside.

Dundee began their 1960 League Cup campaign in devastating form, notching six straight wins and scoring an impressive 23 goals. For the opening tie against Raith Rovers they fielded: Liney; Hamilton, Cox; Seith, Smith,

Young talent - Alan Gilzean, Andy Penman and Hugh Robertson travel for a Scotland Under-23 international in Wales.   DC Thomson

made his comeback in the first leg of the League Cup quarter-final against Rangers at Ibrox but, despite his appearance in a deep-lying role at inside-left, the Dark Blues went down 1-0.

For the Dens return the following week, Cousin replaced the injured McGeachie but with Cox and his deputy, reserve skipper Alex Stuart, also injured, Hugh Reid came in at left-back. An early injury left Billy Smith hirpling on the wing and, by half-time, goals by Davie Wilson and Ure with an own-goal, left Dundee three down on aggregate. On the half-hour, Shankly's men appeared to have a lifeline when they were awarded a penalty but Gilzean's effort was saved by Billy Ritchie.

After the break, the Dark Blues stormed into attack and two goals by Cousin put them back in the hunt. Fifteen minutes from the end, they were awarded another penalty and this time Penman stepped up to make it 3-3 on aggregate. Now the excitement amongst the 33,000 crowd was at fever-pitch. But, with Rangers reeling, home supporters were stunned when defensive blunders allowed Ian McMillan and Ralph Brand to give the Ibrox side a 5-3 aggregate win, which was certainly not as comfortable as the scoreline seems to suggest.

Despite the loss of Smith, Dundee had been superb for much of the game and, with Division Two side Queen of the South as semi-final opponents, a great chance of reaching the Final had been lost. However, the Dens men were undismayed, and, by October 22nd, they had strung together five straight wins over Clyde (h) 4-1, St Johnstone (h) 2-1, Rangers (a) 1-0, Kilmarnock (h) 1-0, and St Mirren (a), 2-1, to go to the top of Division One.

Since his arrival one year earlier, the brusque Bob Shankly had made quite an impact. According to Alan Gilzean: "Shankly was an honest man, who called a spade a spade, and he quickly gained the players' respect with his knowledge of the game." Indeed, the manager knew exactly what

Heroic and sure - soon it would be a half-back line of Bobby Seith, Ian Ure and Bobby Wishart. DC Thomson

he wanted and, with the players honed to peak fitness by Sammy Kean, the Dark Blues were again a team to be feared in the Scottish game.

Much of their success was down to the brilliant interchanging of the forwards. In early October, Penman and Gilzean represented the Scottish League against the League of Ireland with Penman also making an appearance against the Irish League the previous month.

In addition, there was a tremendous fighting spirit which was typified by the determination of Seith, Cox and Ure. Cox had been Scotland's reserve left-back for the recent internationals against Wales in Cardiff and against Northern Ireland at Hampden and he was again named reserve for the League international against the Irish League.

In the League Cup tie against Rangers, Ure had been outstanding when switched to centre-half in place of the injured Smith. The hard-tackling Ayrshire lad was again outstanding in the 1-0 league win at Ibrox and, although Smith was to make a brief return, Ure was there to stay.

The crew-cut defender had been greatly impressed by the skills shown by Real Madrid and Eintracht in the European Cup Final at Hampden earlier that year. Each afternoon Ure returned to Dens to work on his ball control and this was soon apparent in his play. However, the centre-half was still inclined to moments of rashness and, in November, he was ordered off along with McIntyre of Ayr in a 4-2 win at Somerset Park.

The Dark Blues were unable to sustain their early-season form and, by the end of the year, they had slipped back to mid-table. Two months earlier, Penman had broken an ankle after scoring the penalty winner against Killie at Dens and, with his pace and penetration badly missed, goals were in short supply.

There was further misfortune when George McGeachie broke a leg during Dundee's 2-0 defeat at Motherwell in December and, to bolster the attack, another abortive bid was made to sign Gordon Smith from Hearts. Ronnie Crichton, Fred Jardine and Bobby Adamson were brought in from the reserves, but after five games without a win, Dundee paid £3,500 for 29-year-old Aberdeen inside-left Bobby Wishart.

The promotion of Dundee United had added much spice to the local football scene and with Wishart set to make his debut, 22,000 turned out for the Dens derby on January 7th, 1961. Despite the frosty pitch, it was an action-packed first

Driving force - Bobby Seith tangles with Dundee United inside-forward Dennis Gillespie at Tannadice DC Thomson

Rangers bogeyman - Alan Cousin scores Dundee's winner at Ibrox with centre-half Bill Paterson and keeper Billy Ritchie helpless. The Dens men were increasingly showing that they were ready to mount a real challenge to the all-conquering Light Blues. DC Thomson

half and on this occasion, there were to be no slips from the Dark Blues. In addition to scoring two goals, Wishart gave a fine display of precision passing and a third from centre-forward Adamson gave Dundee a comfortable 3-0 win.

Soon afterwards, the long-serving Bert Henderson - now 30 years of age - was transferred to St Mirren for £2,000. Always in the engine-room of the team, Bobby Cox later described him as "a hard player and a real team man - a great servant to the club." Henderson was the second experienced man to depart, Davie Curlett having joined Ayr United for a small fee a few weeks earlier.

Dundee remained in mid-table by the end of January, but a Gilzean double ensured a 4-2 Dens triumph over league leaders Rangers and this raised hopes of a Scottish Cup repeat at the same venue three days later. Penman had returned but with Seith and Cowie now sidelined through injury, Ure, Smith and Stuart made up the half-back line for the cup-tie.

A crowd of 32,000 saw Max Murray take advantage of an early Smith blunder and, with a strong wind at their backs, the Ibrox side led 4-0 at half-time. Rangers had not played particularly well but, aided by sloppy defending, their finishing had been clinical. And despite Dundee's almost total second-half domination, the Light Blues departed with a 5-1 win.

For much of the season, Dundee's plans had been disrupted by injury and, with little to play for, Bob Shankly rang the changes. Waddell, Adamson and Cousin were tried at centre and, with Gilzean reverting to inside-left after a

spell at inside-right, Wishart moved back to left-half in place of the veteran Doug Cowie.

Some erratic performances had brought the Dark Blues uncomfortably close to the relegation zone but, in March, home victories over Dunfermline (4-1), St Mirren (2-0), and Ayr United (6-1), saw them finish in a more respectable eighth position.

Encouragingly, Ure and Gilzean had played for Scotland's Under-23s against England in February. Ure, who had previously been reserve for the Scottish League against the League of Ireland, was also travelling reserve for the league international against England the following month. But although Chelsea showed interest in the fair-haired centre-half, no business was done.

Scottish football was nearing the end of an extremely competitive era. In the 15 years since the end of the war, Rangers and Celtic had enjoyed their share of Scottish Cup successes with five and two wins respectively but honours had been evenly spread with Clyde (twice), Aberdeen, Motherwell, Hearts, Falkirk, St Mirren and Dunfermline all taking the trophy. There had been an even wider spread in the League Cup with the trophy going to Rangers, Hearts and East Fife (three times each), Dundee and Celtic (twice each), and Aberdeen and Motherwell (once each).

However, although Rangers, with eight title wins, remained the team to beat for the championship, Hibs (three times), more recently Hearts (twice), Celtic and Aberdeen had played their part - and there were to be further surprises to follow!

CHAPTER TEN

Title Success

There was an inauspicious prelude to season 1961-62 when one of the club's greatest-ever players departed. In May, Adamson, Horsburgh and Jardine were released but the end of a golden era was signalled when 34-year-old Doug Cowie was placed on the transfer list. In a fine career, Cowie had won twenty full Scotland caps and in July he was appointed player-coach of Morton.

Understandably, Cowie was disappointed: "I felt I still had a year or two left and would have been happy to remain as part of the squad. However, that was for the manager to decide and I will always have fond memories of my 16 years at Dens."

Former team-mate Bert Henderson paid him this tribute: "Cowie was the best player I ever played with - even better than Steel in my opinion." His departure severed the last link with the George Anderson glory days, but as one famous veteran departed, another had arrived.

Twice previously, Gordon Smith had been a Dens transfer target but after getting a free transfer from Hearts, the illustrious right-winger had at last signed for the Dark Blues. Brought up in Montrose, Smith had played alongside Pud Hill with Dundee North End, before signing for Hibs in 1941. After a long and distinguished career at Easter Road, Smith had spent the previous two years at Tynecastle.

He had won championship medals with both Edinburgh clubs - three for Hibs and one for Hearts - and played 18 times for Scotland, but without arguing over his pedigree,

Smith was, after all, 37 years of age and many Dark Blue fans doubted the wisdom of Bob Shankly's latest signing.

In the close season, Dundee undertook a three-game tour of Iceland. There, Smith was given his chance, but his domestic debut was delayed until the third game of the new season when he had a quiet outing in the 3-2 League Cup defeat by Third Lanark at Cathkin. To accommodate Smith, Andy Penman was switched to inside-right in place of George McGeachie, where it was hoped the youngster would find more scoring opportunities.

Sammy Kean, a former team-mate of Smith's at Easter Road, had played a big part in persuading the winger to

Street battle - Gordon Smith turns to celebrate with Alan Cousin after netting Dundee's second goal. Stewart Fraser and Rolando Ugolini are the disconsolate United men. TOP - Andy Penman on the prowl but Tommy Neilson wins out this time. DC Thomson

True grit - Ian Ure chases Alex Harley of Third Lanark at Cathkin. SNS Group

finally come to Dens.

According to the coach: "McGeachie was certainly a very tricky little player but Bob Shankly was now looking for a better service for his big lads, Cousin and Gilzean. In my opinion Smith, who was far from finished, was ideal for the job.

Unfortunately for George McGeachie, he was the man to step down." And, although Dundee took only six points and failed to qualify from a section which also included Rangers and Airdrie, there were soon signs that the new-look attack was beginning to click.

In marked contrast to their poor League Cup showing, Dundee's league campaign began brightly with a 3-1 midweek win over Falkirk at Brockville before Dundee United were taken care of at Dens. Revelling in the tense derby atmosphere generated by a noisy 20,000 crowd, Dundee's deadly short-passing game tore gaping holes in the Tannadice rearguard. Goals by Penman, Smith and a Jimmy Briggs own-goal put them 3-0 ahead, and although United did pull one back after the break, Hugh Robertson settled the issue with a fourth near the end.

The joy was short-lived. A controversial penalty award for "hands" against Alex Hamilton contributed to a 3-1 defeat at Aberdeen and two changes were made for the home game with Hearts on September 23rd. Bobby Wishart returned in place of Alex Stuart at left-half, with Alan Gilzean and Alan Cousin switching places.

Now the team read: Liney; Hamilton, Cox; Seith, Ure Wishart; Smith, Penman, Cousin, Gilzean and Robertson - and that was a line-up that was destined to trip off the tongue for many decades to come.

An Alan Gilzean double brought a 2-0 win and another success, 3-1 in Glasgow against a Third Lanark side - who, spearheaded by the prolific trio of Hilley, Harley and Gray, had scored 100 league goals to finish third last term - propelled the rampant Dark Blues into top spot along with Kilmarnock and title favourites Rangers.

Dundee then produced a dazzling display of attacking football - Andy Penman weighed in with a hat-trick - to beat much fancied Killie 5-3 at Dens and another sparkling performance at Fir Park earned a 4-2 win over Motherwell. Twice Motherwell had come from behind to equalise through Willie Hunter, but late goals by Smith (71 mins), and Gilzean (76), ensured the points would go to Dens.

Observers agreed that the fare on offer that sunny afternoon was up there with the finest Scottish football had to offer. And that opinion was backed up by Shankly himself who said: "The boys played tremendous football and the Fir Park game was our finest all-round display of the season."

The vintage football continued throughout October and into November and wins over last season's Scottish Cup winners Dunfermline (a) 2-1, Partick Thistle (h) 3-2, and Celtic (h) 2-1, left Dundee three points clear of Killie and five ahead of Rangers, although the Ibrox side had two games in hand.

The clash with fourth-placed Celtic proved a real thriller, Carroll equalising after Wishart had given Dundee an early lead. But although the Parkhead side mounted a series of frenzied attacks, Dundee's more studied approach paid off when Gilzean nodded Cousin's head-flick past Frank Haffey for a 59th-minute winner.

Dundee's win did not go down well with a section of the Celtic support and *The Sunday Post* report told of "Bottles, cans, arrests and blood-stained victims". Post-match, the trouble continued in the city centre, where several bars were wrecked, particularly in the Dock Street area, and the

Close call - Alan Gilzean, who later headed the winner, beats Celtic keeper Frank Haffey only for Duncan Mackay to clear off the line with Jim Kennedy and Pat Crerand watching anxiously. TOP - Dundee goalkeeper Pat Liney was an ever-present in 1961-62. DC Thomson

Start of the rout - Alan Gilzean beats Harold Davis to head Dundee's opener past Billy Ritchie in the famous 5-1 win over Rangers at Ibrox. BELOW - the big No.10 is mobbed after completing his hat-trick.   DC Thomson

significance of Dundee's win was somewhat overshadowed by this unwelcome outbreak of violence.

Now Dundee faced their sternest test to date when they travelled to meet current champions Rangers at Ibrox on Saturday, November 11th. The Light Blues, with seven Scottish internationalists - currently Eric Caldow, Jim Baxter, Alex Scott, Ralph Brand and Davie Wilson - in their side, had already won the League Cup and were unbeaten in 21 games that season.

Nevertheless, the Dark Blues were in sparkling form and could take great encouragement from their record of three league wins and a draw over the past four seasons at Ibrox. They also now had Gordon Smith, who was proving an inspirational signing. His positioning, inch-perfect passing and crossing made him the perfect foil for the other young forwards and Cousin and Gilzean, who had both scored eleven goals, and Penman, with nine, had taken full advantage of his immaculate service.

A huge crowd had been expected but with Glasgow

enshrouded by dense fog, rumours abounded and many believed the game was off. But half-an-hour before kick-off, the worst of the fog had cleared and the game was on. Countless supporters' buses were turned back less than a mile from the ground, and only 38,000 - less than half the Ibrox capacity of that era - would witness the eagerly-awaited top-of-the-table clash.

Inspired by the brilliant Jim Baxter, Rangers took control, but at half-time the score remained at 0-0. Concerned at the amount of freedom given to Baxter, Shankly encouraged Penman to adopt a more positive role, and soon it was the Ibrox left-half doing the chasing. Just 30 seconds after the restart, Alan Gilzean finished a three-man move by heading past Ritchie and before Rangers could recover, he hit a magnificent second two minutes later.

Now well on top, Dundee switched from defence to attack with bewildering speed and it was little surprise when Gilzean got a third in 73 minutes. Brand pulled one back for Rangers with six minutes left, but, within 60 seconds, Gilzean thundered in a fourth and, two minutes from time Penman completed the 5-1 rout.

It had been a famous victory in the swirling Ibrox fog. In the first half, Dundee's defence - superbly marshalled by Ure, had been immense - and after the break, the forwards were at their brilliant best. In *The Courier*, Tommy Gallacher commented: "Over the past 16 years I've taken part in and watched my old club play some wonderful games. But I have never played in or seen a Dundee team during that period match Saturday's lot for precision finishing."

Although all in Dark Blue had played their part, few would dispute that four-goal Alan Gilzean was the hero of the hour. "Everything came off for me that day," explained the big inside-left. "However we felt we had better players than Rangers and had gone to Ibrox confident of getting a win!"

DUNDEE'S GLORY DAY -RANGERS THRASHED

RANGERS 1, DUNDEE 5.

Half-time—0-0. Scorers—Rangers—Brand (84 min.). Dundee—Gilzean (46, 48, 73, 86), Penman (88).

SO Rangers never lose a game when the chips are down? Well, just take a look at that score. At stake here was possibly Rangers' entry into next season's European Cup tournament. And that alone is big "chips" in any language.

Yet Rangers were thrashed. Not knocked off their game by a team of bustlers. Not playing it out with a man injured. Not—definitely not—on the receiving end of any bad refereeing breaks. It was a clear-cut Rangers thrashing without one single excuse to be offered by the Ibrox faithful.

But if there were no excuses, there were plenty of reasons for defeat. Eleven of them, for instance, wore Dundee jerseys.

The plain truth is that this team gave the finest exhibition of football seen at Ibrox—or any other Scottish football ground—for many a long day.

Gilzean, with four glorious goals, wasn't even a hero. He merely scored them in the normal course of events.

There were Penman and Cousin, without being greatly in evidence, ripping huge gaps in that Rangers defence.

DEVASTATING FORWARD PLAY

And, glory be, there was Gordon Smith, at 37 years of age, in this game of all games coming out well ahead of any of Rangers' five forwards.

But it wasn't only devastating forward play that set the seal on Dundee's day of glory. Because each and every one of these forwards was ever willing to go back and lend a hand to a defence that always looked as if it could very well take care of itself.

started scrawling his autograph right up and down that right touchline, much to the discomfiture of Baxter and Caldow, who just couldn't read Gordon's writing.

A goal just had to come from the right. It came all right. A low cross from a Smith corner was banged first-time into the net by Gilzean. That was that!

Only the fog coming down could now save Rangers. But the fog that did arrive wasn't nearly so dense as it was DENS—if you get what I mean.

So it continued till about six minutes from the end—a period in which Dundee treated us to all the finer arts of football.

They even showed us how carelessness can be very effectively punished. Because the ball which Brand headed home hereabouts should have been cleared long before it got this length.

Did Bob Shankly thereupon bat another eyelid? Because Gilzean not only went on to score four minutes from time his own fourth goal, but Penman added yet another with just two minutes to go.

The Ibrox debacle was complete. And what

Ibrox joy - the dramatic headline from the match report in The Sunday Post

It was a great day for the supporters as Dave Thomson, then fourteen, recalls: "I went through by train with my dad and grandfather - the legendary "Napper" Thomson - and when we got to Ibrox, the police told us the game was probably off. It wasn't and Dundee recorded one of the greatest results in their history. Buchanan Street railway station was awash with happy Dundee fans and so many others turned up at Dundee West, that you'd think we'd won the cup!"

But there was more drama to come and the Dark Blue fans who had missed the Rangers rout were rewarded with an absolute thriller at Dens a week later. Raith Rovers - fresh from a great 3-2 win over Kilmarnock - were the visitors and only an incredible fighting finish ensured victory for Dundee.

Leading 2-1 shortly after half-time, the Dark Blues found themselves 4-2 down with 27 minutes left. However, roared on by the noisy 15,000 crowd, two cracking shots by Bobby Wishart (69 mins), and Bobby Seith (86) levelled the scores, and just two minutes from time, Dens erupted when Gordon

Smith made it 5-4 with a dramatic winning goal!

"That was a real thriller but the fans got right behind us and, in the end, we deserved to win," declared right-back Alex Hamilton. It had not been one of their better displays, but the never-say-die spirit shown by the men in Dark Blue - allied to their undoubted skill - finally convinced Bob Shankly that he had potential champions in his charge.

His optimism was justified, for, by early 1962, Dundee remained top. They had gone on to extend their unbeaten run to 14 games after taking points from Hibs (a) 3-1, Stirling Albion (h) 2-2, Airdrie (h) 5-1, St Mirren (a) 1-1, and Falkirk (h) 2-1 and now they lay six points ahead of second-placed Celtic and seven above Rangers, who lay in third position.

Dundee had confounded their critics for many believed that the Dens Park challenge would evaporate abruptly as it had the previous year. Since late September, the side had been virtually unchanged with only three enforced alterations to Bob Shankly's magical mix - George McGeachie deputising for Gordon Smith against Partick and also for Alan Gilzean against Airdrie and St Mirren.

The victory at Easter Road was a hard-fought affair even though Hibs had had a lean time of it in recent years. A goal either side of half-time gave Dundee a two-goal cushion but a Stevenson counter lifted the men in green and white and things were in the balance until former Hibs favourite Gordon Smith settled matters with a third near the end.

The loss of a point to bottom-of-the-league Stirling Albion came as a shock but with Smith switched to centre-forward in the absence of Gilzean, who had injured his jaw, the Dark Blues bounced back with a convincing win over Airdrie. And although another point was dropped at Paisley, Rangers had fared even worse, slipping to defeats at the hands of Dunfermline and Aberdeen.

Frost was to wipe out Dundee's next three games but on January 6th, they made a good start to the New Year against Falkirk. Gilzean was back and, wearing sandshoes to combat the frozen pitch, the big inside-forward's ingenuity was rewarded with yet another two goals.

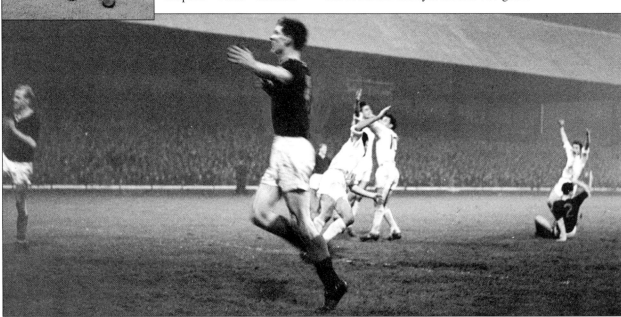

Thriller - Gordon Smith is engulfed by joyous team-mates after hitting the winner in the dramatic 5-4 win over Raith Rovers. TOP - Smith was also a great provider of goalscoring opportunities and was a master at dictating the tempo of Dundee's play. DC Thomson

Netbound - the great run continues as Alan Gilzean fires home the opener in the 2-1 win over Falkirk at Dens. Bairns keeper Jimmy Boag is grounded with John Lambie too late to prevent the ball going in.
DC Thomson

Top Positions - January 24th, 1962						
	P	W	D	L	F A	Pts
Dundee	21	18	2	1	60-29	38
Rangers	20	13	4	3	52-21	30
Celtic	21	12	5	4	56-27	29

Then came a 2-0 victory over Hearts at Tynecastle - a significant milestone since Dundee's last win in Gorgie had been away back in 1948-49! Gordon Smith had been badly shaken in a car crash prior to the game, but he insisted on playing against his former team-mates and contributed to both first-half goals scored by Cousin and Gilzean.

Hard-fought home wins over Aberdeen, Third Lanark and St Johnstone, all by 2-1, stretched their unbeaten run to eighteen - 20 games if a 4-2 Dewar Shield Final win over St Johnstone and the 8-2 rout of Swedish champions Elfsborg Boras in a friendly are included - and by January 24th, 1962, the high-flying Dark Blues held an eight-point advantage over favourites Rangers at the top of Division One!

Lifelong Dundee fan Peter Shepherd recalls these halcyon days: "A group of us were in our mid-teens and we used to turn up at Dens soon after the gates opened at 1.30 pm. There were always long queues at the Boy's Gate at the foot of Provost Road, and when we got up the steps, we would lean on a crush barrier and watch all the fans pouring into the ground."

"The winning run lifted the crowds from around 12,000 up to 16,000 or 17,000. We had followed the team for a few years but that season we knew we were watching something special. We stood halfway up the west terracing in the thick of the "Provie Road choir". There was plenty to shout about then and the tremendous atmosphere was enhanced by the high walls of the Bowbridge Jute works just across Dens Road!"

Three days after defeating St Johnstone, a bumper 22,000 crowd turned out for the Scottish Cup first-round clash with St Mirren at Dens. In recent games, Dundee had lived dangerously - scoring late, late winners against

the Perth Saints and the Dons - and there were signs that the strain was beginning to tell.

Some fans were even heard to voice concern how their favourites could possibly cope with a cup run on top of their points-gathering exertions. But there was no need for such anxiety as the Paisley side - managed by former Dens scoring ace Bobby Flavell - showed the greater commitment and a 38th-minute goal by George McLean meant yet another early cup exit for the Dark Blues. It also signalled the end of their long unbeaten run and although disappointed many hoped that without this burden the Dens men might now return to their early season form.

On February 3rd, an 89th-minute goal by Alan Cousin, when his cross-cum-shot was adjudged to have been carried over the line by goalkeeper Sandy McLaughlin, earned a creditable 1-1 draw at Kilmarnock but, seven days later, a 3-1 reverse to Motherwell at Dens signalled the start of an alarming Dundee slump.

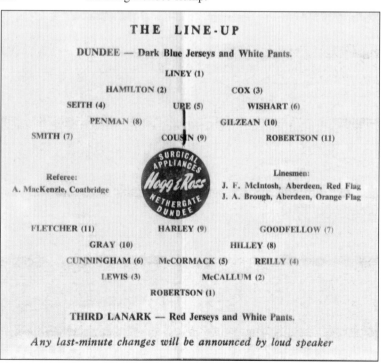

THE LINE-UP

DUNDEE — Dark Blue Jerseys and White Pants.

LINEY (1)

HAMILTON (2)   COX (3)

SEITH (4)   URE (5)   WISHART (6)

PENMAN (8)   GILZEAN (10)

SMITH (7)   COUSIN (9)   ROBERTSON (11)

Referee: Linesmen:
A. MacKenzie, Coatbridge   J. F. McIntosh, Aberdeen, Red Flag
                             J. A. Brough, Aberdeen, Orange Flag

FLETCHER (11)   HARLEY (9)   GOODFELLOW (7)

GRAY (10)   HILLEY (8)

CUNNINGHAM (6)   McCORMACK (5)   REILLY (4)

LEWIS (3)   McCALLUM (2)

ROBERTSON (1)

THIRD LANARK — Red Jerseys and White Pants.

Any last-minute changes will be announced by loud speaker

Disaster day - Partick Thistle's Billy Hainey blasts the final goal past Pat Liney in Dundee's 3-0 defeat at Firhill. DC Thomson

Top Positions - March 8th, 1962						
	P	W	D	L	F A	Pts
Rangers	26	19	4	3	70-26	42
Dundee	26	18	3	5	60-40	39
Celtic	26	15	6	5	66-32	36
Dunf'line	27	16	4	7	64-36	36

In his report in *The Courier,* ex-Dundee defender Gerry Follon observed: "Over their long run of success Dundee have established a reputation for smooth football. However, the sharp incisive game which earlier "dissected" Rangers has deteriorated into a soft, side-of-the-foot, pattern-weaving type of model."

Ominously, there were further defeats by Partick Thistle (a) 0-3, Celtic (a) 1-2, and Dunfermline (h) 1-2, with Dundee hitting rock-bottom at Firhill on February 24th. There appeared to be no stopping Rangers either and when they beat Motherwell for their ninth successive league win four days later, they went a point clear of Dundee at the top.

The Ibrox men had played a game more but it was a huge blow for Dundee, who, in just over a month, had seen their seemingly unassailable eight-point lead disappear. Too many players had started to believe in the team's invincibility and as their attitude slackened, the tide had turned in the other direction.

The loss of six goals in two games was of great concern but the return of inspirational skipper Bobby Cox, who had missed three games through injury, brought a big improvement against strong-going Celtic on March 3rd. Wishart got the opener, but, with Smith hirpling from a thigh injury, Celtic recovered to score two goals in the last 10 minutes to keep themselves on the fringes of the title race.

Without Smith, Dundee had lacked the guile to penetrate Dunfermline's well-organised sweeper system, which was masterminded by Northern Ireland international full-back Willie Cunningham - later to become Pars manager - and with Rangers now three points ahead, many doubted Dundee's ability to recover the ground they had lost.

Following their premature Scottish Cup exit, Dundee had fixed up glamour friendlies with Arsenal, who had taken an early tumble in the English FA Cup. In February, the Dens Parkers had impressed in a 2-2 draw at Highbury but there was to be no morale-boosting victory in the Dens return three weeks later, with the Gunners getting the only goal of the game

Now came the crucial clash with Rangers at Dens on Wednesday, March 14th. Home fans in the 35,000 crowd were dismayed to find that ace scorer

Alan Gilzean was out with flu with Bobby Waddell in his place. However, Gordon Smith was back while the brilliant Jim Baxter - still on National Service but generally available to Rangers - would miss out after the Army insisted he play in an Inter-Services match against the Navy.

Understandably, most fans felt that Dundee - three points behind with an inferior goal-average and without a victory in their last eight games - just had to win. On a hard, slippy pitch, the game was played at a frantic pace but with both sides badly affected by the tension, the game ended goal-less even though Rangers had been handicapped with injured centre-half Doug Baillie limping out on the wing for almost 70 minutes.

Nevertheless, Dundee had recovered their fighting spirit and, a few days later, they were back on the winning trail with a 3-2 victory over Raith Rovers in Fife, finishing March with further successes against Hibs (h) 1-0 and Stirling Albion (a) 3-2. It had been hard going at Kirkcaldy, where Shankly's men had twice come from behind before Andy Penman's 82nd-minute winner and, on March 24th, there were ironic cheers at half-time after a dire first-half display against Hibs.

However, news that Rangers were 1-0 down to Dundee United at Ibrox transformed things. Within seven minutes, Alan Cousin burst through and, after initially failing to connect, Bobby Waddell bundled the ball into the net. That proved to be the winner and when it was found that the Ibrox scoreline had remained unchanged, there was a great cheer from the home dressing room.

Ball boys danced with joy and there were beaming smiles from delighted officials, for United's shock win had brought Dundee within a point of their Glasgow rivals.

Fresh hope - Bobby Waddell's header is saved by Ronnie Simpson of Hibs with Jim Easton in pursuit. The centre later got the winner to put Dundee back in the title hunt. DC Thomson

Mayhem at Broomfield - Dundee players surround the referee and successfully appeal for a penalty after an Airdrie defender handled. BELOW - joyous scenes following Alan Gilzean's late winner against Dundee United at Tannadice.

DC Thomson

It came as a great lift for players and fans alike and Ian Ure remarked: "It made a big difference to us. The whole team put more into it. We knew this was our big chance and now we're in the hunt again." That was exactly the sentiment in the local press with *The Courier* headlines exhorting: "Now go to it, Dundee!"

There had almost been a slip-up at Annfield. The Dark Blues had played some neat, precise football but their approach was too casual. Twice Stirling Albion levelled before Gilzean - back after missing three games through illness - accepted a 50-yard pass by Smith before thumping home the winner with 12 minutes left.

Injuries, illness and loss of form had brought changes to the regular line-up. The crew-cut Craig Brown - later to become Scotland manager - had proved a capable deputy for Bobby Cox and, when the Dens skipper returned, Brown was retained at left-half until he, too, was affected by cartilage trouble. Up front, the marauding Bobby Waddell had also done well but, for the nail-biting title run-in, manager Shankly reverted to his battle-hardened old guard.

Dundee's remaining games that would decide their fate were against: Airdrie (a), Dundee United (a), St Mirren (h), St Johnstone (a); while Rangers faced: Dunfermline (h), Celtic (a), Aberdeen (a), and Kilmarnock (h).

On April 7th, two Penman goals - the second a disputed penalty when Dens players persuaded referee Willie Brittle to consult his linesman after Airdrie defender Shanks palmed the ball clear - earned Dundee a 2-1 win in a backs-to-the-wall display at Broomfield. However, Rangers had also won by beating Dunfermline 1-0 at Ibrox and the derby games on the spring holiday Monday now took on a crucial significance.

There was a tremendous cup-tie atmosphere amongst the 20,000 all-ticket crowd at Tannadice. It proved to be an action-packed thriller with the home side in no mood to lie down to their more illustrious rivals. In 15 minutes, Jim Irvine deservedly put United ahead only for Gilzean to level with a long-range effort just before the break.

The battlers in black and white looked the likelier to break the deadlock but, with just four minutes remaining, Gilzean took a pass from Wishart, flicked the ball between his legs

then thundered a 25-yard shot high into Ugolini's top left-hand corner for the winner!

After the game there were scenes of jubilation amongst the Dundee players and fans and that evening their title hopes were further boosted when Rangers could only draw 1-1 with Celtic. Now the pair were neck-and-neck and, although Rangers by then had a vastly superior goal-average, the championship was set for a dramatic finale.

"That derby win was a huge step for us," said ace scorer Alan Gilzean. "It was always going to be a tricky hurdle, but, having cleared it, we knew we had an easier finish than Rangers."

That season, Dundee's success had been reflected at international level. On April 14th, Alex Hamilton was in the Scotland side which ended a 25-year Hampden hoodoo with a memorable 2-0 win over England. As well as Hamilton (4 caps), Ian Ure (2), and Hugh Robertson (1), had also made the

Night of drama - St Mirren keeper Bobby Williamson is beaten by Andy Penman's rocket shot for the decisive second goal. Earlier, Pat Liney had made a brilliant penalty save and BELOW - the goalkeeping hero is mobbed by delighted young fans. DC Thomson

full international breakthrough and, in November, all three were in the Scotland team which lost 4-2 after extra-time in the World Cup play-off against Czechoslovakia - the eventual runners-up to Brazil - at the Heysel Stadium in Brussels.

In addition, Hamilton (2), Ure (2), and Gilzean (1), gained Scottish League caps with Gilzean (2), Robertson (2), and Penman (1), all representing the Scotland Under-23s. And, in February, no fewer than five Dundee players - Hamilton, Seith, Ure, Cousin and Gilzean - were selected for the Scotland v Scottish League trial at Hampden.

On the evening of Wednesday, April 24th, Dundee entertained St Mirren in their penultimate game. After their second-round defeat of Dundee, the Paisley outfit, winners of the trophy in 1959, had gone on to reach the Scottish Cup Final which they had lost 2-0 to Rangers at Hampden just five days earlier. Now the "Buddies" desperately required points to avoid relegation and there was a nervy start by both sides. Dundee's luck held when George McLean hit the post with an early header, but shortly before half-time, Alan Cousin put them ahead with a low shot from 18 yards.

Encouraged by news that Rangers trailed 1-0 at Pittodrie, the Dark Blues went all-out for a second goal but with 12 minutes remaining, St Mirren were awarded a penalty when Smith was adjudged to have handled. The home players protested bitterly, but although referee Willie Syme consulted his linesman, the award stood.

Paisley skipper Jim Clunie aimed the spot-kick for the top left-hand corner but Pat Liney twisted in mid-air to claw the ball to safety. Four minutes later, Andy Penman made it 2-0 and as the 20,000 crowd celebrated, the 19-year-old was engulfed by his joyous team-mates.

At the end, jubilant fans invaded the pitch and when the announcer confirmed that Aberdeen had won 1-0, a great roar swept the ground. Dundee were two points ahead and one point from their final game against relegation-threatened St Johnstone would clinch the championship!

Liney's penalty save was a pivotal moment and years later the keeper recalled: "There was uproar when it happened at the Provie Road end with Ian Ure and Gordon Smith at the forefront of the protests. It was quite a while before the kick was taken and a photographer from *The Daily Express* who I knew had time to come up from behind the other goal."

"I had a good record of saving penalties and by the time the kick was taken, there was huge pressure on Clunie. I made the save high to my right, just where my father - a St Mirren fan - had previously said he would put it. Andy Penman scored at the other end and the rest, as they say, is history!"

Thirteen years earlier, Dundee's title hopes had died on the last day at Brockville but, this time, there was a grim determination to make amends. Saturday, April 28th was a gloriously hot day and there were around 20,000 Dundee fans amongst the 26,500 shirt-sleeved Muirton crowd.

"There was no question of Dundee playing for a draw and before the game the players were brimful of confidence. They just knew they were going to win," said Sammy Kean. In his book, *Ure's Truly*, Ian Ure later told of an attempt to fix the game: "A message was passed to the players that they could collect £50 each if they made it a draw. The idea was treated with contempt and only served to double our determination."

Dundee fielded: Liney; Hamilton, Cox; Seith, Ure Wishart; Smith, Penman, Cousin, Gilzean and Robertson. St Johnstone: Taylor; McFadyen, Lachlan; Little, J. Ferguson, Donlevy; McIntyre, Townsend, McVittie, A. Ferguson and Thomson.

There were a lot of battlers in that Perth line up - none more so than inside-left Alex Ferguson, later to demonstrate just how much he enjoyed winning - and hated losing for that matter - as a manager of Aberdeen and Manchester United.

The pitch was bone-hard and, with both teams affected by the tension on the terracing, the initial exchanges were scrappy. Dundee had an early scare when Hamilton had to clear off the goal-line, but in 24 minutes they went ahead.

Smith made ground up the right and when his swirling cross came over, Gilzean sent the huge travelling support wild with delight when he headed past Bill Taylor. This settled Dundee and with the influential Seith and Smith spreading play intelligently, the Dark Blues took control.

The Perth side made crude attempts to break their rhythm but to no avail. In 59 minutes, Gilzean ran on to a brilliant long ball from Hamilton and beat centre-half Jim Ferguson, before cracking in his 27th goal of the season. Just eight minutes later, Penman crashed in a third via the crossbar from 18 yards and, from then to the finish, with the title in the bag, Dundee were able to turn on the style.

Double shuffle - the long-striding Alan Cousin leaves a St Johnstone defender trailing at Muirton. BELOW - Bobby Wishart wins a midfield tussle with Saints Jim Townsend.

Dundee's Road to the Title			
1961			
Aug 23rd	Falkirk	(a)	3-1
Sep 9th	Dundee Utd	(h)	4-1
16th	Aberdeen	(a)	1-3
23rd	Hearts	(h)	2-0
30th	Third Lanark	(a)	3-1
Oct 7th	Kilmarnock	(h)	5-3
14th	Motherwell	(a)	4-2
21st	Dunfermline	(a)	2-1
28th	Partick Thistle	(h)	3-2
Nov 4th	Celtic	(h)	2-1
11th	Rangers	(a)	5-1
18th	Raith Rovers	(h)	5-4
25th	Hibernian	(a)	3-1
Dec 2nd	Stirling Albion	(h)	2-2
16th	Airdrie	(h)	5-1
23rd	St Mirren	(a)	1-1
30th	Falkirk	(h)	2-1
1962			
Jan 13th	Hearts	(a)	2-0
17th	Aberdeen	(h)	2-1
20th	Third Lanark	(h)	2-1
24th	St Johnstone	(h)	2-1
Feb 3rd	Kilmarnock	(a)	1-1
10th	Motherwell	(h)	1-3
24th	Partick Thistle	(a)	0-3
Mar 3rd	Celtic	(a)	2-1
7th	Dunfermline	(h)	1-2
14th	Rangers	(h)	0-0
17th	Raith Rovers	(a)	3-2
24th	Hibernian	(h)	1-0
31st	Stirling Albion	(a)	3-2
April 7th	Airdrie	(a)	2-1
9th	Dundee Utd	(a)	2-1
25th	St Mirren	(h)	2-0
28th	St Johnstone	(a)	3-0

A fourth goal was chalked off but there was no further scoring and at full-time, pandemonium reigned as thousands of Dundee fans rushed on to the pitch to congratulate their heroes. As the crowd chanted their names, the players went up to the directors' box in the stand, before later relaxing in the bath with champagne.

Dark Blueprint - Bob Shankly with Sammy Kean on the left.

Rangers had drawn 1-1 with Kilmarnock at Ibrox and the Dark Blues were champions by a three-point margin. Amidst joyous scenes, Dundee fans cheered skipper Bobby Cox and his colleagues from the field, but for Saints there was only misery. All their rivals had picked up vital points and unfortunately for the Perth club, they were relegated on goal-average.

Cox later described it as his greatest moment in football: "We knew we had some great players and over the past two seasons, the youngsters had matured. Bob Shankly's judgement was sound and he moulded a great team." The gritty Dundonian himself was a key man in the title success and according to Sammy Kean: "His influence was immense. He was a real tiger, a born winner who just never gave up."

Exuberant supporters gave the Dundee team bus a noisy escort back from Perth. With thousands lining the streets, the players got a tumultuous welcome when they appeared on the balcony of the Council Chambers in Dundee's City Square. Later, the players and officials had drinks at the chairman's home before going for a meal in a city hotel and then there were parties galore.

The Sporting Post

No. 2951. SATURDAY, APRIL 28, 1962. 3d

Lighting-Up, 9.12 p.m.; Moon, 3.43 a.m.-12.40 p.m.

IT'S DUNDEE'S LEAGUE

No.1 - Alan Gilzean heads home against Saints as the huge Dundee support prepares to celebrate.

No. 2 - Alan Gilzean turns away after netting his second goal and soon afterwards Andy Penman made it 3-0.

Full-time - a grinning Bobby Seith and Andy Penman are engulfed as jubilant Dundee supporters invade the pitch.

So happy - Alan Gilzean and Alex Hamilton with fans.

Hail the 'Dee - Dens skipper Bobby Cox shows his joy.

Party time - Dundee F.C. players and officials celebrate with Lord Provost McManus at Dundee's City Chambers.

Dundee F.C. - Scottish League Champions 1961-62 - (BACK, left to right) Gordon Smith, Andy Penman, Bobby Seith, Alex Stuart, Pat Liney, Bobby Wishart, Craig Brown, Bobby Waddell, Lawrie Smith (physio), Alan Gilzean, Ian Ure. FRONT - Sammy Kean (coach), Alex Hamilton, Jack Swadel (director), Bobby Cox, James Gellatly (chairman), Alan Cousin, Bob Crichton (secretary, Hugh Robertson, Bob Shankly (manager). Inset - George McGeachie.

DC Thomson

Scottish League Division One 1961-62						
	P	W	D	L	F A	Pts
Dundee	34	25	4	5	80-46	54
Rangers	34	22	7	5	84-31	51
Celtic	34	19	8	7	81-37	46
Dunfermline	34	19	5	10	77-46	43
Kilmarnock	34	16	10	8	74-58	42
Hearts	34	16	6	12	54-49	38
Partick This.	34	16	3	15	60-55	35
Hibernian	34	14	5	15	58-72	33
Motherwell	34	13	6	15	65-62	32
Dundee Utd.	34	13	6	15	70-71	32
Third Lanark	34	13	5	16	59-60	31
Aberdeen	34	10	9	15	60-73	29
Raith Rovers	34	10	7	17	51-73	27
Falkirk	34	11	4	19	45-68	26
Airdrie	34	9	7	18	57-78	25
St Mirren	34	10	5	19	52-80	25
St Johnstone	34	9	7	18	35-61	25
Stirling Alb'n	34	6	6	22	34-76	18

It was a fitting climax to a wonderful season for, after a 19-game unbeaten run, Dundee recovered from a slump to collect 15 points from their last eight games. Their title success would long be remembered for they had played with a wonderful, flowing style much admired by top football journalist Bob Crampsey: "That Dundee team was exquisite, far and away the best footballing side Scotland produced."

It had also been a great achievement to pip Rangers, for, in the three seasons between 1961 and 1964, the Ibrox club would claim no fewer than seven of the nine domestic trophies on offer. Certainly, Willie Thornton had left some of Scotland's brightest stars at Dens, but Bob Shankly had brought in men like Seith, Wishart, and Smith and they had given the side the perfect balance of youth and experience.

For the elegant Gordon Smith it was his fourth championship medal with three different Scottish provincial clubs - a record that stands to this day. He no longer had the pace of old but his ability to hold the ball and his eye for an opening had brought out the best in the other young forwards, particularly Gilzean, with whom he appeared at times to have an almost telepathic understanding.

Liney had been a steady keeper - brilliant when needed - while the full-back combination of Hamilton and Cox was arguably the best in Scotland. Ure had been immense at pivot while the assurance and passing ability of Seith and Wishart ensured a steady supply of ammunition for Dundee's deadly forwards.

On the left, the dashing Robertson balanced the more deliberate play of Smith on the other flank while the inside trio of Penman, Cousin and Gilzean had played a key role in the free-flowing football on display that season. Gilzean finished top marksman with 24 league goals, Penman weighed in with seventeen while Cousin - master of the double shuffle - found the net fifteen times.

Front page - "Shug" Robertson reads all about Dundee's great day.

The backroom team of Bob Shankly, Sammy Kean, Lawrie Smith and Jackie Kay had played a vital part in the side's success but remarkably, Dundee had used only 15 players and they had been fortunate to have top calibre men like Brown, McGeachie, Stuart and Waddell as back-up.

CHAPTER ELEVEN

Taking Europe by Storm

Dundee made the most of their title celebrations but in May it was back to business when they took part in the prestigious New York Tourney. Normally this honour went to the runners-up, but, with Rangers emerging as title favourites in the spring, the Scottish League had nominated the Dark Blues.

And although results against Reutlingen (West Germany) 0-2, Hajduk Split (Yugoslavia) 3-3, Guadalajara (Mexico) 3-2, Palermo (Italy) 1-1, and FC America (Brazil) 2-3, were not particularly successful - the skilful Brazilians topped the section with Dundee finishing second-bottom - the Dens men had gained invaluable experience of continental football.

Over the past two years, their only taste of European action had been the Friendship Cup games against French side Valenciennes - a 1-0 defeat in France and a 4-2 victory at Dens - and an 8-2 home stroll against Swedish outfit Elfsborg in a friendly. But if manager Shankly had any major doubts about his team for the forthcoming European Cup campaign, they were not certainly not reflected in a summertime spending spree.

His only acquisitions were Queen's Park left-winger Doug Houston (19), and the experienced Liverpool and former Falkirk keeper Bert Slater (28), for £2,500. Earlier, Ronnie Crichton, Billy McMillan and Billy Smith had been released but, worryingly, no fewer than six of the championship side had refused Dundee's £25-a-week re-signing terms - a basic wage bettered only by Rangers and Celtic.

On the evening of the club's public trial - which was rained off - the deadlock was broken when Hamilton, Penman and Robertson re-signed. Next day, Seith also came to terms and star men Ure and Gilzean did likewise shortly afterwards. Said Ure: "It was simply a matter of pounds, shillings and pence. I'm happy at Dens and now I can get my dander up for Saturday's derby with United!"

As champions, Dundee had hoped to kick off the 1962-63 season at Dens but instead they opened with a League Cup tie against Dundee United at Tannadice. Two changes were made from the regular side - Bert Slater was in for Pat Liney, with Craig Brown deputising for the injured Bobby Seith.

A 25,300 crowd packed the revamped United ground, but although two goals each from Alan Gilzean and Walter Carlyle meant it was level pegging at half-time, the Dark Blues conceded a late goal to lose 3-2. A few days later, the championship flag was unfurled before a 60th-minute Smith goal earned Dundee a 1-0 win over Celtic to leave all four teams - Hearts completed the section - with two points.

The championship win was also honoured by a civic reception in Dundee's City Chambers but there were now only

Strong man - Ian Ure was a giant at the heart of the Dundee defence.

flashes of the old magic on the park. Dundee could manage only one victory - 2-1 against United at Dens, courtesy of a double by centre-forward for the day Gordon Smith - from their remaining four ties and Hearts went on to win the section and ultimately, the League Cup itself.

Following a frank exchange of views amongst players and coaching staff, Andy Penman asked for a transfer. But when the home supporters sung his praises during the League Cup victory over city rivals Dundee United, the youngster was quick to withdraw his request for a move.

In the European Cup preliminary round, Dundee were paired with Cologne with the first leg to be played at Dens. The West German champions, who were amongst the favourites for the trophy, included World Cup star Karl Snellinger as well as several other internationals. And having lost five of their opening seven games - three times to Hearts, who they had also played in the opening league game - few gave the Dark Blues much hope of success.

Brown, Stuart, Waddell, Houston and young centre Kenny Cameron had been introduced from the reserves, but it was no real surprise when most of the old guard were recalled for Dundee's first European tie on Wednesday, September 5th: Slater; Hamilton, Cox; Seith, Ure, Wishart; Smith, Penman, Cousin, Gilzean, Robertson.

In nine minutes, Hemmersbach was pressurised into heading a Penman cross into his own net, and in quick succession, Wishart and Robertson added two more. Cologne were stunned as a confident Dundee took command and further goals by Gilzean and Smith gave the Dark Blues a sensational 5-0 lead at half-time. A new force was in the process of making Europe sit up and notice.

German keeper Ewart did not appear for the second half. He had been accidentally concussed in a second-minute collision with Cousin and Regh took over in goal. The home offensive continued and goals by Penman and Gilzean, with

German champions smothered in 8-goal avalanche

By TOMMY GALLACHER

DUNDEE 8 — COLOGNE 1

Not even the most fervent Dundee supporter in his wildest imagination could ever have forecast the result of this fantastic European Cup match.

Speculation beforehand even favoured a win for Cologne. But in all the pre-match bluff and ballyhoo Dundee turned out to be the ace kidders of all!

At Dens Park last night Dundee turned on a magnificent brand of cultured precision football that far outshone any of their performances in bringing home the league title.

But they came prepared to shoot on sight and prove themselves worthy champions of Scotland. And prove it they did against a talented German team who never recovered from Dundee's opening onslaught.

An inspiration

There is no doubt about it, Dundee's three-goals-in-three-minutes spell soon after the start paved the way for this great victory.

reply, they just could not contain Dundee's brilliance long enough to settle to a game.

A great header by Gilzean put Dundee four goals ahead after only 26 minutes, and Gordon Smith made it 5-0 just before the interval to further emphasise Dundee's superiority.

Any slight chance the Germans had of staging a fight-back disappeared when they resumed without keeper Ewart and right-back Regh wearing the goalkeeper's sweater.

Ewart collided with Alan Cousin early in the game, but no one had realised the extent of his injury.

Against the 10 men Dundee continued to be devastating. Within four minutes Penman made it 6-0 with a beautifully-judged header from a Robertson cross,

Goal storm - Alan Gilzean (top) and Andy Penman add to Dundee's total at Dens.

two, made it 8-0 before the ball bounced in off Hamilton's leg for a Cologne consolation. As the goals went in, the roars of joy from the 24,500 crowd could be heard clearly as far away as the harbour, and at the end, hundreds of young fans invaded the pitch to congratulate their heroes.

It was one of Dundee's best-ever displays. In the build-up to the match, any potential threat from the Dark Blues had been dismissed by Cologne and despite the loss of their keeper, the Germans had been almost totally eclipsed. The Dark Blues had continually opened up play with long balls to the wings and with 23 shots to Cologne's six, their superiority was clear for all to see as a BBC commentary by Kenneth Wolstenholme told all of Britain about this magnificent display.

Alex Hamilton was full of praise for Gordon Smith: "He encouraged me to overlap and, along with Bobby Seith, we made a formidable right-wing trio. When I came up, Smith would play back to Seith before moving inside to create space for me on the outside. We used to play some great triangular stuff and time and again Bobby would open things up with a lob out to the wing!" Bob Shankly's verdict after the excitement had died down was typically low key: "The boys rose to the occasion as I expected them to."

Following the New York experience, the manager had intended switching from 2-3-5 to a 4-2-4 formation. Seith and Ure would play in central defence with Penman falling back to right-half. This was tried in practice but, after repeatedly losing to the reserves, the new tactics were scrapped!

One change had been made, however. The Dark Blues had started the season with a new crew-necked strip, but in a shrewd psychological move, they had reverted to their title-winning V-necked jerseys against Cologne. Needless to say, the "losers" crew-necked outfit was never worn again.

Three days later, Dundee returned to the bread and butter of league football but it took a last-gasp Gilzean header to salvage a 2-2 draw against Aberdeen at Dens. Another three points were then taken from Dundee United (a) 1-1, and newly-promoted Clyde (h) 2-0, before heading for Cologne, but many believed the second leg was a mere formality.

However, trouble was brewing. A German newspaper had published a photograph showing Cousin "punching" the unfortunate Ewart at Dens and Cologne players openly talked of revenge.

Bert Slater - heroic figure in the battle of Cologne.

Backed by around 40,000 horn-blowing fans, Cologne took heart from an early penalty goal by Habig and Dundee were forced on the defensive as the tough-tackling Germans threw everything into all-out attack.

In 27 minutes a dazed Slater was led off with a head injury after saving at the feet of Cologne centre-forward Mueller.

Although Cologne officials attempted to put him in a waiting ambulance, the groggy keeper refused to go and, with his head heavily bandaged, Slater returned on the right-wing after the interval. By then, stand-in goalkeeper Andy Penman had conceded a further two goals and Dundee's lead started to look increasingly vulnerable.

Skipper Bobby Cox

Within five minutes, the gallant Slater resumed in goal, but shortly afterwards he was impeded as Cologne reduced the leeway to 8-5 on aggregate. Now the Dark Blues were under intense pressure and, on the hour, they were unfortunate not to lose another goal when Habig hit the bar with a second penalty. That was the turning point for, although Cologne continued to attack, Slater was an inspiring figure in goal and the beleaguered Dundee defence held firm in the face of severe intimidation.

Throughout the match, Dundee players had been kicked and punched and at the end there was a near riot when they were attacked by hundreds of German fans. Only the intervention of British soldiers from the Rhine Army prevented serious injuries. Gordon Smith described the game as "the dirtiest in my 22 years in football" and, not surprisingly, the Dundee party refused to attend the official reception given by Cologne.

Back home the Dark Blues maintained their title challenge by taking six points from games against Rangers (a) 1-1, Falkirk (h) 2-1, Hibs (a) 2-2, and Kilmarnock (h) 1-0, and after a seven-game unbeaten run, they had moved to within four points of league leaders Hearts. The Dens men had rediscovered their form and now interest returned to the European campaign where they would meet Portuguese champions Sporting Club of Lisbon in the next round.

The first leg was played on Wednesday, October 23rd before 48,000 noisy fans in the Portuguese capital of Lisbon. Despite the incessant home pressure, Dundee defended solidly and were unfortunate to lose the only goal just two minutes from the end. Slater punched a Geo shot on to the bar, but when the ball bounced down, the referee adjudged it to have crossed the line and awarded a goal. Later, though,

Alan Gilzean confessed that he felt that Dundee were lucky to get off so lightly against the classy Portuguese!

The following Saturday, Dundee lost 2-0 at Dunfermline, but the narrow deficit from Lisbon ensured a near 32,000 turn-out for the Dens return a few days later. Dundee were at full-strength, with Robertson - now recovered from injury back in place of Houston, who had played in Portugal.

Roared on by the large crowd, the Dark Blues attacked from the start and, in 13 minutes Gilzean swept a low shot past Carvalho then just before half-time Cousin headed a second from a Smith corner to make it 2-1 overall.

There was no stopping Dundee and soon after the interval, Gilzean completed his second European hat-trick with two goals in a six-minute spell. Effectively, the tie was over and, although Figueredo netted a consolation goal, the Dark Blues were convincing 4-2 aggregate winners.

The green-and-white-hooped Portuguese were neat enough in possession but, like Cologne, they had been swept aside by Dundee. AC Milan, Anderlecht, Benfica, Dukla Prague, Feyenoord, Reims and Galatasaray had also reached the quarter-finals but despite that formidable queue forming to grab the ultimate prize, the Sporting Club president firmly believed that Dundee could go on to win the European Cup.

"These European nights were very special," recalled Alan Gilzean. "The Dundee public turned out in their thousands and although we had a very good side, the atmosphere generated by the huge crowds gave us a tremendous lift."

However, the European adventure was to take its toll. The Dark Blues' domestic form clearly began to slump and by the first week of 1963, they lay a massive nine points behind the league leaders Rangers. Gone was the rapier-like play which had earlier destroyed

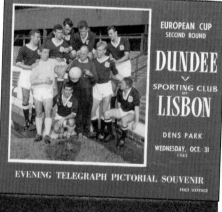

Hat-trick hero - Alan Gilzean ghosts in to head the fourth goal past keeper Carvalho to complete his second European Cup hat-trick in the 4-1 win over Sporting Lisbon at Dens.

DC Thomson

Big freeze - Ian Ure heads clear from Aberdeen's Tommy Cummings in the Ne-erday clash at a frosty Pittodrie. Lewis Thom and Charlie Cooke are the other Dons while goalkeeper Bert Slater and George Ryden are the men in Dark Blue.

Aberdeen Journals

On song - Andy Penman in action against Willie Wilson of Hibs in the Scottish Cup.

DC Thomson

Cologne and Sporting and defeats in Glasgow by Third Lanark (3-4), and Clyde (2-3), who were both struggling in the league - brought the Dark Blues sharply back to earth.

In December, Alan Gilzean equalled Bert Juliussen's 1947 record when he scored seven goals - a Scottish record six in the first-half - in Dundee's 10-2 win over Queen of the South at Dens. However, Queen's keeper George Farm had been stretchered off after a 12th-minute collision with the Dens crackshot, with the score 2-1 in Dundee's favour at the time.

The next European challenge for Dundee was to overcome Belgian champions Anderlecht. The first leg was scheduled for Brussels on February 13th but due to the Arctic weather conditions throughout Europe, it was postponed until March 6th.

Since early January, the football programme had been almost totally wiped out and by the time of the Anderlecht match, Dundee had managed only two competitive games. Both were Scottish Cup games and, although played on snow-covered surfaces, the Dark Blues had progressed to the third round at the expense of Inverness Caley (a) 5-1, and Montrose (h) 8-0.

The Montrose game had gone ahead on February 5th and just days before leaving for Brussels, the Dens men were fortunate to get some much-needed practice in a friendly with East Fife at Methil.

Anderlecht appeared formidable opponents. In the last round, they had beaten the mighty Real Madrid, who had won the European Cup five times in the previous seven years. The Belgians had nine internationalists, including the brilliant Joseph Jurion and Paul Van Himst, and Dundee were given little chance.

However, within 60 seconds of the start, the 60,000 Heysel crowd were stunned when Gilzean put Dundee ahead from a pinpoint Smith cross. The Belgians proceeded to play some fine flowing football but, in 20 minutes, Gilzean scored again with a 20-yard shot. Nine minutes from the break, Anderlecht pulled one back from the penalty spot, but just after half-time, Cousin struck to make it 3-1 for Dundee.

Anderlecht continued to press, and Ure and Cox both cleared shots off the line. Once again, Bert Slater was performing heroics in goal and, with 19 minutes remaining, Smith shattered the Belgians with a decisive fourth goal.

In an enthralling tie, the Dark Blues had shown great

Fame game - Dundee's European Cup campaign caught the imagination of football fans all over Britain and here Liney, Penman, Seith, Hamilton, Ryden, Robertson, Stuart, Wishart and Gilzean face the TV cameras prior to the quarter-final against Anderlecht <small>DC Thomson</small>

Smash-and-grab tactics had Belgians reeling

By TOMMY GALLACHER

ANDERLECHT 1, DUNDEE 4.

Dundee, Scottish League champions, and European Cup shockers extraordinaire, have done it again!

Given little chance against Anderlecht, Belgian champions and conquerors of the fabulous Real Madrid, Dundee shattered and stunned the 60,000 crowd at Heysel Stadium, Brussels, last night.

Not only did Dundee break their goal-scoring "duck" on the Continent, but they are the first team to score against Anderlecht at home in this competition.

In a simply fantastic game, sportingly played throughout, Dundee pulled off the biggest "smash-and-grab" raid surely ever witnessed on the Continent.

They scored four, and they did so with less than 20 per cent. of the play.

Played it cool

To thoroughly appreciate the win, it must be realised that Anderlecht were a very good side, but they were inclined to over-elaborate from first to last.

There is still the second leg to come at Dens next

crowd of wildly-enthusiastic Dundee supporters who invaded the pitch at the final whistle.

But this was by no means a one-man show. Typical of the way the whole team played was that skipper Bobby Cox and Ian Ure, the outstanding players in the Dundee defence, between them saved six scoring attempts on the line.

No fancy frills

Dundee will be accused of playing a defensive game. I don't believe they did.

Before the game Bob Shankly said they would suit their style of play to that of the opposition. And that is how it worked out.

Dundee under pressure fell back on top of their goal

91

Dark Blue relief - Alan Cousin takes the cheers from delighted team-mates after his 78th-minute equaliser against Anderlecht at Dens ensured Dundee's place in the European Cup semi-final.

Stand D ENTER AT TURNSTILES 34-36
ROW P PRICE . . . £1
Nº . 10
Dundee v.
Royal Sporting Club Anderlechtois
D E N S P A R K
WEDNESDAY, 13th MARCH, 1963
Kick-off, 7.30 p.m.
THIS PORTION TO BE RETAINED
In the event of this game being Postponed this Ticket will be Available on the new date
ON NO ACCOUNT WILL MONEY BE REFUNDED — PLEASE TAKE YOUR SEAT EARLY

stamina on the heavy pitch and, although forced back by the home onslaught, they had been deadly in their lightning breaks from defence.

The standing ovation from the knowledgeable football folk of Brussels told its own story and Alan Ireland, one of around 100 Dundee fans at the game recalled with pride: "To this day I can still see Bobby Cox running along the track with his arms in the air at full-time."

Said the Dens skipper: "This was Dundee at their very best, Anderlecht were a polished outfit but we took all they could throw at us and when they allowed us space to play, we were lethal."

Now Dundee had a great chance of reaching the last four. Their brilliant performances on the European stage had caught the imagination of Dundee's footballing public. Despite losing 1-0 at Airdrie three days earlier, the March 13th return against Anderlecht was a 40,000 sell-out - the biggest attendance at Dens since 1953.

It was the white-and-mauve-clad Anderlecht who dominated much of the opening period and on the half-hour, the roars of the crowd were silenced when "Dynamite" Jack Stockman put the Belgians ahead. After half-time, it was a different story - gradually Dundee grew stronger on the muddy surface and the pressure finally paid off when Alan Cousin equalised in 78 minutes.

A tremendous roar of relief rent the night air for, until then, the clever Belgians had remained in contention. Eight minutes from time Gordon Smith swept home the winner for a 6-2 aggregate victory. And as the huge crowd surged into

the surrounding streets, they could be justly proud as Dundee took their place amongst Europe's elite.

Gilzean had been quieter than usual. Six stitches were required in a foot wound in Brussels and he had missed the Airdrie game. The stitches were removed before the home tie and, although not fully fit, the inside-left proved the perfect decoy with two Belgian defenders following him everywhere.

Five days later, Gilzean headed the winner in Dundee's 1-0 win over Hibs in the third round of the Scottish Cup. In the quarter-final against Rangers at Dens, 37,000 rain-soaked fans saw a thrilling encounter finish 1-1. Both goals came from the penalty spot with the Dark Blues a shade fortunate to get a second chance.

On April 3rd, nearly 82,000 were inside Ibrox when the gates were locked, leaving countless thousands on the streets. Early in the game, Hamilton headed an own-goal but a Gilzean double had put Dundee ahead shortly after half-time. In 74 minutes, Ralph Brand scored from a dubious penalty and two minutes from time the Rangers sharp-shooter got the winner in a game which Dundee had scarcely deserved to lose.

Dundee now appeared to be reserving their best performances for the big games and since beating Anderlecht their league form had been disappointing. Nineteen-year-old Kenny Cameron scored the winner in a 2-1 win over Partick Thistle at Dens, but successive defeats by Celtic (a) 1-4, Queen of the South (a) 0-1, and Hibs (h) 1-3, did little for Dundee's morale. The players vehemently denied that they were saving themselves for the European Cup and in Gordon Smith's view: "Dundee were the team everyone wanted to beat with few breaks going our way."

In *The Sporting Post*, "Rambler" felt that Dundee had begun to develop a "Gilzean complex", and now that he was so tightly marked, they required to vary their tactics. More significantly, perhaps, Bob Shankly showed little inclination to alter his strongest team, but four games in eight days had

Dundee F.C. Season 1962-63 - European Cup semi-finalists. (BACK, left to right) Alex Hamilton, Bobby Seith, Ian Ure, Bert Slater, Bobby Wishart, Bobby Cox. FRONT - Sammy Kean (coach), Gordon Smith, Andy Penman, Alan Cousin, Alan Gilzean, Hugh Robertson, Bob Shankly (manager). BELOW - Barison outjumps Bert Slater for Milan's fourth in the San Siro with Alex Hamilton helpless. DC Thomson

clearly taken its toll on veterans Smith - now 38 - and Seith and Wishart, who were both 32 years old.

Nevertheless, Dundee lay just two games away from the European Cup Final. They faced a formidable task in disposing of Italian giants AC Milan, coached by the highly-rated Nereo Rocco, who had earlier beaten Union Sportif of Luxembourg (aggregate score 14-0), English champions Ipswich Town (4-2), and Galatasary of Turkey (8-1), while the Dark Blues had the added complication of playing twice a week to clear the domestic backlog.

As excitement mounted over the first leg in Milan, there was extensive press coverage and Dundee's European Cup run even reached the dizzy heights of a slot on BBC television's midweek *Sportsview* - Peter Dimmock et al. However, Dens fans complained bitterly about semi-final ticket prices - nearly double those of previous rounds and almost triple those for league games. The stand was priced £2 and £1-10s, the enclosure 12/6d, and the ground 7/6d, whereas the normal admission price for a league game was 3/- and many accused the board of blatant profiteering.

Meanwhile, Dundee's indifferent league form continued. A 5-1 home win over St Mirren was followed by defeats by Dundee United (h) 1-2, and Motherwell (a) 1-2, but, more seriously, Bobby Cox had damaged a cartilage at Fir Park just two days before the flight to Milan. Nevertheless, the Dens party were in fine spirits when they arrived in Italy, and they unfurled their Lion Rampant for the waiting pressmen before travelling to their headquarters at Bergamo.

Dundee's stunning progress had not gone unnoticed on the Continent where Ure - regarded by many as the best centre-half in Britain - Gilzean and Smith were particularly highly rated. Milan, though, had nine full internationalists - including Jose Altafini, who had played in two World Cups (in 1958 for Brazil, then in 1962 for Italy), centre-half Cesare

Maldini, Giovanni Trapattoni and Italian football's Golden Boy Gianni Rivera - and they were firm favourites to win.

Bobby Cox and his deputy Craig Brown, were both out through injury and Alex Stuart made his European debut before a boisterous 78,000 crowd at the impressive San Siro Stadium. Dundee lined up: Slater; Hamilton, Stuart; Seith, Ure, Wishart; Smith, Penman, Cousin; Gilzean, Houston.

This time it was Dundee's turn to lose an early goal when Dino Sani put Milan ahead in three minutes but, midway through the first half, Cousin headed the equaliser after a fine run by Penman. This settled Dundee and by half-time the Italians were having some anxious moments.

There had been problems for the Dark Blues. Bert Slater

93

had been pestered by a battery of camera men firing flash bulbs around his goal while the Spanish referee and linesmen had shown a clear bias towards the Latins, making it almost impossible for the Dundee players to tackle without being penalised.

At the interval, there was great optimism in the Dundee dressing room but this would soon turn to dismay. Houston shot past the post after he was clean through then, in quick succession, Barison and Mora found the net with flashing headers, both of which were controversial.

Benitez had appeared to be over the byeline before crossing for Barison's goal while Altafini - standing on the Dundee goal-line - had clearly been offside at the third goal. At first Senor Caballero had given offside but, when one of the linesmen ran on to the pitch furiously waving his flag, that decision was changed.

Now Dundee were in disarray and 13 minutes from time they were stunned by another lightning 1-2 from Milan wingers Barison and Mora. After a promising first half, Dundee had disappointed with the inspirational qualities of skipper Bobby Cox badly missed. All five goals had come from high crosses and the normally reliable defence was surprisingly vulnerable with even Ure struggling to cope.

Milan were certainly a top side but, according to the Dundee players, not as good as Cologne or Anderlecht. Indeed, there was every indication that the Dark Blues had been cheated, for the Spanish referee was found to have accepted extravagent gifts from the Italian club prior to the game and subsequently he was banned on various other charges of bribery.

Fielding an

"Hammy" - Alex Hamilton was a Scotland regular

unchanged side from the San Siro, Dundee faced an uphill struggle in the Dens return on Wednesday May 1st. And encouraged by the roars from a vociferous 38,000 crowd, they attacked from the start although it was soon clear that the Italians would defend in depth.

Play was never allowed to flow due to the constant interruption for fouls and there were few opportunities at goal for the much-improved Dundee. But, with half-time approaching, Gilzean finally broke the deadlock when he rose to head Smith's cross past Milan goalkeeper Ghezzi.

Soon after the interval, Penman had the ball in the net again but the goal was disallowed for offside against Gilzean. And although Milan were unfortunate not to concede a penalty when Smith was blatantly punched in the box, there was no further scoring. Throughout, Smith - Milan probably regarded him as the key playmaker - and the deadly Gilzean had taken some terrible punishment and, with six minutes remaining, the frustrated inside-man lashed out at his Peruvian marker Benitez, and was ordered off.

The hard pitch and strong wind had not helped in a tension-ridden game but Dundee had done Scotland proud. Indeed, many felt they might have become the first British side to reach the European Cup Final had they been drawn against either of the other semi-finalists, holders Benfica (Portugal), who went on to lose 2-1 to Milan, or Feyenoord (Holland). And with the final at Wembley, Dundee would have backed themselves against anyone, according to Ian Ure!

Due to the fixture backlog caused by the severe winter weather, the Scottish season was extended to the end of May. But, despite taking eight points from their remaining six games, Dundee could only finish ninth and, sadly, there would be no European football next term.

Evening Telegraph Pictorial Souvenir

EUROPEAN CUP
SEMI-FINAL

DUNDEE v MILAN

DENS PARK, DUNDEE
WEDNESDAY, 1st MAY, 1963

Mayhem - another flashpoint in the AC Milan game at Dens. With Dundee needing to pull goals back, the Italians were happy to see play halted at every turn and they made sure the Dark Blues never had the chance to get into their stride.

DC Thomson

CHAPTER TWELVE

Goals Galore

In **May**, Hamilton and Ure, both regulars in the Scotland team, had asked away and with Gilzean also unsigned, the break-up of an outstanding Dundee side looked on the cards. However, in the close-season, Gilzean and Hamilton finally put pen to paper. Hamilton had struggled in Scotland's tour games against Norway and Eire and was dropped for the final match with Spain. And, holding out for a transfer, he felt, would be detrimental to his international career.

Ure, though, had not come to terms and vowed, "never to kick another ball for Dundee". He had not received any wages since June and, after making an abortive attempt to claim £3-7-6d per week unemployment benefit, he was offered a sales job by millionaire washing-machine magnate and Arsenal supporter John Bloom. Shortly after the start of the season, Dundee finally agreed to consider offers for their fair-haired star and, on August 22nd, Ure joined Arsenal for a Scottish record fee of £62,500.

The loss of Ure was a severe blow for as well as being an international class centre-half, he was a great favourite of the fans. Later, Bob Shankly told of an English club who had offered him the keys to a £5,000 Bentley - if Ure could be steered "in the right direction". The Dundee manager, however, had done all in his power to hold on to Ure but had finally had to admit defeat.

Meanwhile, almost secondary to all the transfer drama, Dundee had begun the season with a bang. In the League Cup, there were four straight wins against Third Lanark (a)

2-1, Airdrieonians (h) 2-1, Dunfermline (h) 4-1, and Third Lanark (h) 3-2.

With Dundee back on song, the fans were again turning up to Dens in big numbers and they were certainly rewarded with some exciting performances. Andy Penman was in devastating form as the much-fancied Pars were put to the sword, before a well-taken Alan Gilzean hat-trick subdued the men from Cathkin in the scorching summer sun.

Wing ace - Hugh Robertson brought balance on the left.

Against the Pars and Thirds, Bob Shankly had fielded: Slater; Hamilton, Cox; Seith, Ryden, Stuart; Penman, Houston, Cousin, Gilzean, Robertson. But without the injured Stuart, Dundee went down 4-1 at Airdrie and now they needed a point from their last game at Dunfermline to reach the quarter-final. Defeat would put the Fifers through on goal-average but Dundee rose to the occasion. Trailing 2-1 at the interval, two goals each by Gilzean and Cameron finally earned them a 4-3 win in an East End Park thriller with Pars boss Jock Stein taking time to comment on Dundee's new-found hardness.

Craig Brown had made a rare appearance - at left-half - but almost immediately he was sidelined with a knee injury, a recurring problem that was to blight his career at Dens. A bright start though was made in the league with 1-1 draws against Rangers and Dundee United at Dens and a 4-2 win over Aberdeen at Pittodrie. The encounter with Rangers was a torrid affair. Brand put the champions ahead with an early penalty but Bobby Seith levelled with a raging 30-yard drive.

The home games with Rangers and Dundee United had pulled in bumper attendances of 34,000 and 22,000 respectively and, on Wednesday, September 11th, 25,000 fans turned out for the quarter-final tie against strong-going Hibs at Dens.

Alan Gilzean, Andy Penman and Bobby Waddell were all on target but, with the defence less than convincing, the Dark Blues had

Thriller - games between Dundee and Dunfermline in the early 1960s were exciting affairs. Here Alan Gilzean eludes Jim Thomson to head past Jim Herriot at East End Park.

All smiles - Alan Gilzean and Alex Hamilton chat with fellow Scotland international Campbell Forsyth after Dundee's league win over Kilmarnock at Dens.

DC Thomson

impressed in Scotland wins over Norway (6-1) and Wales (2-1) at Hampden.

On December 7th, a 1-1 draw at Kilmarnock kept Dundee just one point behind the Rugby Park outfit and three behind league leaders Rangers. But, by early 1964. their title hopes lay in tatters after defeats to Partick Thistle (a) 0-2, Rangers (a) 1-2, Aberdeen (h) 1-2, and Dundee United (a) 1-2.

The Dark Blues had struggled badly in the Ne'erday clash with Aberdeen but there was a big improvement in the following day's derby with Dundee United at Tannadice. At half-time, Dundee led 1-0 through Gilzean and, although effectively reduced to nine men after injuries to Houston (cracked collar-bone) and Cameron (twisted ankle), it took a late goal by Ian Mitchell to give the men in black and white full points with a 2-1 win.

The Dark Blues, however, took heart from a plucky display and, by early March, wins over Forres Mechanics (a) 6-3, Brechin City (a) 9-2, and Forfar Athletic (h) 6-1, had taken them to the quarter-finals of the Scottish Cup. In the league, only one point had been dropped in games against Third Lanark (h) 6-0, East Stirling (a) 5-1, Queen of the South (h) 6-2, Motherwell (a) 2-2, Hibs (h) 3-0, Dunfermline (a) 2-1, and St Mirren (h) 9-2. Once again, Dundee lay on the fringes of the title race.

These indeed were the halcyon days. In just over eight weeks, the Dens men had netted an amazing 54 goals with a virtually unchanged team: Slater; Hamilton, Cox; Seith,

to settle for a 3-3 draw in a game they should have won.

In the Easter Road return, Dundee paid the price for their slackness. Few breaks went their way and goals by Neil Martin and Gerry Baker gave Hibs a 2-0 win and a semi-final tie with Division Two pace-setters Morton.

However, the setback was temporary and Dundee soon returned to their winning ways. Once again, Rangers and Kilmarnock were the pace-setters at the top of the league but, without the distractions of European football, Dundee were able to mount a strong challenge. By late November, they had taken 21 points from their opening 14 league games and, despite the loss of Ure, their squad looked very strong.

Bobby Waddell - got his share of the goals for Dundee.

The crew-cut George Ryden had made an encouraging start as Ure's successor while Alex Stuart - a revelation in his new, more attacking role - had played impressively since replacing Bobby Wishart at left-half. Bobby Waddell had established himself up front, while Doug Houston had shown his versatility in a number of positions, but Alan Gilzean remained the number one danger for Dundee.

On October 19th, the inside-left scored all the goals in Dundee's 4-0 win at Easter Road. Gilzean had always been capable of finding the net, but he was also a fine leader of the line. He often displayed some brilliant touches and this was evidenced by his third goal at Easter Road.

A long through ball pierced the Hibs defence but despite arriving a split second before keeper Ronnie Simpson, "Gillie" did not shoot. Instead, he hooked the ball back over his head with his right foot before calmly turning to loft it over Simpson's outstretched arms with his left.

It was a classically executed finish and it was no surprise when he made his full international debut in November. With Denis Law the regular choice at inside-left, Gilzean was handed Ian St John's number nine jersey and he

Dundee Football Club Limited

DUNDEE

v.

.... HEART OF MIDLOTHIAN ....

AT DENS PARK, DUNDEE

...... on Saturday, 21st March, 1964.......................

Gate Receipts	Adults	£1375 : 16 : -
	Boys	£ 181 : 11 : 6
Less Referee and Linesmen's Expenses		: :
		£1557 : 7 : 6
League Levy	%	: :
Net Total	- - -	£ : :
Half Share	- - -	£778 : 13 : 9

Secretary.

9172 Adults @ 3/.
2421 Boys @ 1/6

Ryden, Stuart; Penman, Cousin, Waddell, Gilzean and Cameron. Alex Hamilton was a constant danger courtesy of his fast attacking forays up the right, while the introduction of Alex Stuart with his powerful long-range shooting, brought added drive to the half-back line.

Up front, the goal-hungry forwards were full of menace and, although Alan Cousin had dropped into a deeper role, bustling Bobby Waddell and the eager Kenny Cameron were enjoying blossoming reputations as goal-grabbers supreme.

On the right-wing, the pacy Andy Penman was back to his best. Already, he had scored 23 goals and, in December, he was again capped for Scotland's Under-23s against Wales. However, even Penman was outshone by the scoring exploits of Alan Gilzean - "Gil-zean, Gil-zean" roared the fans - and almost every weekend, newspaper headlines screamed about his deadly touch and clinical finishing.

The popular Gilzean had a tremendous rapport with the Dens Park faithful and his second goal against Forfar on February 15th was his 40th of the season, one more than Alec Stott's Dens Park record of 39 in season 1948-49. The "Gillie" goals came thick and fast and, incredibly, his hat-trick in the 9-2 rout of St Mirren was his fifth of the season.

In January 1965, a bribes case which also involved a number of top British players such as England internationals Peter Swan and Tony Kay, resulted in St Mirren goalkeeper Dick Beattie being jailed for taking payment to "throw" games. And although it was Dundee's 5-1 home win over Saints in 1963 which featured in the prosecution evidence, Beattie again made some spectacular blunders in the 9-2 game, though there was no denying the deadliness of Gilzean.

Lifelong supporter Bill Dryden recalled: "It was a wonderful time to be a Dundee fan for there were goals galore and no shortage of heroes. We were probably spoiled by the

Hammy and the Hamsters - Kenny Cameron, Alex Stuart, Alex Hamilton. FRONT - Craig Brown and Hugh Robertson. DC Thomson

quality of player we had back then but we were young and just lapped it up. After the games, we would wait behind the main stand to collect the players' autographs."

The emergence of the younger school meant there was no longer a place for veterans Gordon Smith and Bobby Wishart. Their spell at Dens had coincided with some of the greatest moments in the club's history and, in February, Smith, now approaching 40 years of age, was released at his own request.

George McGeachie had also moved on. Last season, he had started work as an industrial chemist on Teeside after a dispute at Dens. He was placed on the transfer list at £5,000 and, in January 1964, he joined Fourth Division Darlington for £2,000. Another to go was Championship team goalkeeper Pat Liney. He had lost his place to Bert Slater and after a year and a half in the reserves, he was transferred to home town team St Mirren for £4,000.

Dundee's spectacular scoring had put them amongst the favourites for the Scottish Cup and there was a bumper 30,443 crowd (receipts £4,653) for their quarter-final tie with Motherwell - conquerors of Hearts in the previous round - at Dens. However, with just one win from their last eight clashes against the 'Well, the Dark Blues clearly found the men in

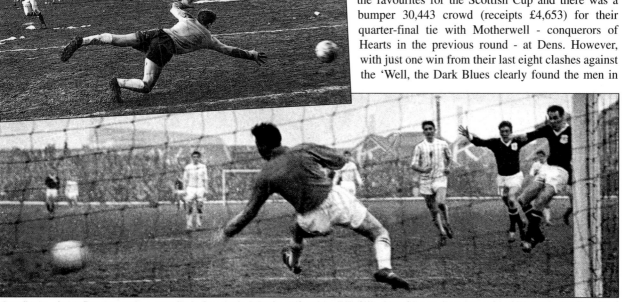

Cup fiesta - Andy Penman nets a penalty in Dundee's 9-2 win at Brechin. BELOW - Alan Gilzean fires home his 40th goal - his final total was 52 goals - in the 6-1 win over Forfar to set a new Dens Park record for League and Cup goals scored in a season. DC Thomson

Eleven Dens Dynamos

DUNDEE 9, ST MIRREN 2.

Half-time—4-0. Scorers—Dundee—Gilzean (18, 48, 68 min.), Waddell (36, 43), Cousin (41), Cameron (51, 58), Penman (76). St Mirren—Ross (50), Beck (79).

A ND the Saints went lurching in! What a thrashing the bewildered Buddies took from the dazzling Dens Parkers.

FORRES MECHANICS 3, DUNDEE 6.

-5. Scorers—Forres—Shaw (44 min.), A. McIvor (49), Anderson ll (6), Gilzean (9), Penman (12), Stuart (20), Cousin (22), Cameron (65).

cess of giving North fans a football treat, and booki in the next rour Cun. Dundee were remind e's not won unti rk side decided to wi ey proceeded to do so minutes. idn't reckon on was a game from slipping g 68 minutes. had obviously said d before Forres settle ld, Dundee might hav the first five minut the Forres saviour as art belted the ball go ll scored a cute one w eith pass close in to

earth Dundee

Six Goals— And Dundee Were Unlucky!

DUNDEE 6, QUEEN OF THE SOUTH 2.

Half-Time — 2-1. Scorers — Dundee—Cameron (13, 26 min.), Gilzean (46, 48, 61), Penman O.S. — Rodger (42), 0).

scored six, but it have been more. Why ause of good form by er new management Not because of the Jim Rodger and Maurice because of the loss of den in 16 minutes. f these reasons was en of South were not Division standard. The were not outstanding. ee simply didn't miss ll. reasons were three-le bit of bad luck. An f good goalkeeping by a teeny-weeny touch of

Back To The Good Old Days At Dundee

DUNDEE 6, THIRD LANARK 0.

(Half-time—2-0.)

Scorers:—Gilzean (25, 88 min.), Penm (43), Waddell (45½), Cousin (49), Camer (77).

S TORMING back to form with a supe display of goal-snatching in the seco half Dundee showed their three festi

EAST STIRLING 1, DUNDEE 5.

ime 0-1. Scorers—East Stirling—Coburn Cousin (45, 58), Waddell (62, 68), Gilzea EE finished looking like honours

Free Wheel Downhill For Dundee

BRECHIN CITY 2, DUNDEE 9.

Half-time—2-2. Scorers — Brechin City —Pollock (24½ min.), Wyles (44). Dundee Penman (1½, 74 pen.), Waddell (24), Cousin (47, 52), Gilzean (67, 69, 83), Cameron (87).

S LAUGHTER in the sunshine. Glebe Park at the final whistle looked like the

Goals galore - the early months of 1964 brought an absolute deluge of goals for the men who wore the Dark Blue!

Cup fever - George Ryden clears from Motherwell's Joe McBride.

claret and amber something of a bogey team. Kenny Cameron got the opener for Dundee soon after half-time but, with only seconds remaining, Ryden rashly conceded a free-kick and Joe McBride - that well-travelled centre-forward with the deadly finish - stepped up to fire in a last-gasp equaliser for Motherwell.

Four days later, a crowd of 26,280 (receipts £3,692) turned up for the Fir Park replay and they would be rewarded with a cup-tie classic. The teams were level with a goal apiece at half-time but, in 62 minutes, Gilzean gave Dundee the lead.

Shortly afterwards, McBride levelled but Dundee were not to be denied and, roared on by a huge travelling support, goals by Cameron (70 mins), and Waddell (78), clinched their place in the semi-finals.

Also through to the last four were Rangers, Kilmarnock and Dunfermline, who, along with Dundee, were currently rated the best clubs in Scotland. The draw paired Dundee with Kilmarnock at Ibrox while Rangers and Dunfermline would meet at Hampden.

In the event, however, the Dark Blues' semi-final preparations were far from ideal with successive defeats by Airdrie (a) 1-3, and Hearts (h) 2-4, ending their long unbeaten run and with it any lingering hopes of a second title success.

On the night of the Airdrie game, Alan Gilzean and Alex Hamilton, who had earlier missed Dundee's 3-1 home defeat by Motherwell while on Scotland duty, had turned out for the Scottish League against the English League. Young Steve Murray, at the tender age of 19, deputised for Gilzean but his debut was witnessed by a meagre Broomfield crowd of only 802.

Three times in the last four years, Killie had finished runners-up in the league. Their manager Willie Waddell was a renowned tactician and, along with Dunfermline's Jock Stein, he had taken the revolutionary step of visiting the famed Inter Milan coach Hellenio Herrerra at the San Siro to observe his coaching methods at first-hand.

With Bobby Waddell ruled out of the semi-final with a stomach injury, Kenny Cameron was moved to centre with Hugh Robertson, whose form had dipped towards the end of the year, recalled on the left-wing.

There was little between the sides as first-half play raged from end to end. Slater made a miraculous save from a point-blank Brian McIlroy header before Gilzean broke the deadlock with a goal from close range on the half-hour. After the break, Killie continued to battle but Dundee responded with some brilliant man-to-man football and, although Scotland keeper Campbell Forsyth was in top form, further goals had to come.

Penman scored a second 17 minutes after the break and an own-goal by Jim McFadzean in 77 minutes and another by Gilzean two minutes later gave Dundee a convincing win. Now, the Dark Blues could look forward to their first Scottish Cup Final since 1952 and Rangers, who had beaten Dunfermline 1-0 just across the city, would be their opponents.

The irrepressible Alex Hamilton was in brilliant form and off the field, too, he was making the headlines. He was now the proud owner of a gleaming white Jaguar car and, along with four of his team-mates - Craig Brown, Kenny Cameron, Hugh Robertson and Alex Stuart - the Dens star had formed a pop group, Hammy and the Hamsters, who, the day before the Cup Final, released a single: "My Dream Came True!"

Along with the likes of Bill Brown, Jim Baxter and Denis Law, Hammy was a regular for Scotland and, prior to the Scotland v England clash at Hampden, he modestly declared himself "The greatest full-back in Europe." His promise that the renowned Manchester United and England left-winger Bobby Charlton would get "scarcely a kick of the ball!" was just spot on and, with Alan Gilzean heading the game's only goal, it proved a famous day for Dundee.

Their build-up to the Cup Final went reasonably well. At Parkhead, they conceded two late goals in a 2-1 defeat but wins over Killie (h) 2-1, St Johnstone (h) 2-1 - the first attempt to play this game was abandoned at half-time due to flooding with Saints leading 1-0 - and Partick Thistle (h) 5-2, left their fans convinced that Dundee's name was on the Scottish Cup!

Goals against Celtic and Kilmarnock had taken Gilzean within reach of his half-century and 12,000 Dens fans roared their approval when their idol reached his target with a

double against Partick Thistle. The Dens men were in fine fetttle and by Scottish Cup Final day on April 25th, 1964, they had lost only three from 19 games since early January.

Rangers had enjoyed great success under the management of Scott Symon, former Dens stalwart of the 1930s, and had

Semi-Final thrills - Bert Slater pulls off a miraculous save from Killie's Brian McIlroy. BELOW - Andy Penman tucks away the decisive second goal to put Dundee on the road to the Final.

Hampden bound - all set for the 1964 Scottish Cup Final (BACK, left to right), Sammy Kean (coach), Alex Hamilton, Alan Cousin, Bert Slater, George Ryden, Alex Stuart, Bobby Seith, Bob Shankly (manager). FRONT - Andy Penman, Bobby Waddell, Bobby Cox, Kenny Cameron, Alan Gilzean, Hugh Robertson.

DC Thomson

suffered just one defeat in 18 starts over the same period. But although the mighty Ibrox side had already won the League Cup and the League Championship, the Dark Blues were a side for whom they had the greatest respect. In recent years, the sides had been well matched and, despite the rain, there were 25,000 Dundee fans amongst the 120,982 crowd at Hampden.

Bookings were less commonplace in Scottish football these days - indeed a caution would often be treated as a major happening by the nation's sports pages. Bobby Cox had received his third caution of the season in the Ibrox semi-final but his two-week suspension expired three days before the final.

And so, with Bobby Seith recovered from a thigh strain which had caused him to miss the previous two games, and with esteemed Old Boy Ian Ure in the stand to see his former team-mates, the Dark Blues were unchanged from the semi-final and lined up: Slater; Hamilton, Cox; Seith, Ryden, Stuart; Penman, Cousin, Cameron, Gilzean, Robertson.

Rangers: Ritchie; Shearer, Provan; Greig, McKinnon, Baxter; Henderson, McLean, Millar, Brand, Wilson.

The Scottish Cup rule of that time was that, in the event of a colour clash, both teams would have to change and that explained why Dundee lined up in an all-white strip while Rangers wore blue and white stripes with white shorts and red socks. The referee was Mr Hugh Phillips of Wishaw - widely recognized as Scotland's best of that era.

Early on, Dundee impressed with Penman making some penetrating runs and there was bad luck when Cameron's shot was blocked. The ball spun to Robertson and only a goal-line clearance by Bobby Shearer saved the day for Rangers. Penman continued to look dangerous but with the other forwards unable to make much headway against the tough-tackling Ibrox defence, he got little support.

Rangers harassing tactics ensured that the game was played at a frantic pace and Dundee found little time to settle. Wing halves Seith and Stuart were forced to do a lot of chasing and Dundee's passing began to go astray. Rangers gradually took command and by half-time, only some brilliant saves and uncanny anticipation by Slater kept the scores level. After the break, Dundee again took the initiative but soon Slater was back in action, repeatedly thwarting Rangers with his courageous saves.

In 71 minutes, Jimmy Millar outjumped Ryden to a Willie Henderson cross and headed for goal. Ralph Brand dummied brilliantly and, with Slater wrong-footed, the ball bounced gently into the net. Straight from the restart, Stuart found Cameron in the inside-left position and from 12 yards he hooked a fierce shot past Billy Ritchie! Now Hampden was in uproar and, although Rangers continued to dominate a breath-taking struggle, a replay looked increasingly likely.

Pick it out - Dundee have just gone a goal behind at Hampden and Kenny Cameron gives the best possible reply as he volleys the ball beyond the reach of keeper Billy Ritchie with Rangers defenders Ron McKinnon and Bobby Shearer helpless.   DC Thomson

The No. 1 Man - Bert Slater, Dundee's hero in the Final, grabs the ball on the deck watched by Dark Blues (from left), Cox, Ryden, Seith, Cousin and Hamilton and Rangers men McLean, Brand and Baxter.

DC Thomson

As time ran out, there was an almost unbelievable tension. Wee Willie Henderson had been in international form down the right but, with only 90 seconds remaining, he made ground down the opposite flank before crossing for the ever-dangerous Millar to head past Slater. Dundee tried desperately for an equaliser but, with the final whistle about to blow, Brand made it 3-1 after another great run by Willie Henderson.

The brave Slater had been Dundee's best - to such an extent that to Dens fans the game became known as Slater's Final. Other Dens stand-outs were Hamilton, Seith, Stuart, Penman and Cousin. Gilzean, however, had been strictly policed by John Greig and, disappointingly, had made little impression, moreso since he injured an ankle before the break.

Bobby Cox had been thrilled to lead Dundee out before such a huge crowd, but the Dens skipper was bitterly disappointed at the result. With two minutes left we had started to think about the replay. Rangers played very well but we lost our concentration in the dying minutes and that was fatal," said Cox.

Dundee had not been at their best and, although Rangers had been deserved winners on the day, there was at least the consolation of a healthy cheque and a place in the following season's European Cup Winners' Cup.

Still, the season was not over and in May, Dundee took part in the new Summer Cup competition. This consisted of four sections grouped on a regional basis with Dundee placed alongside Aberdeen, Dundee United and St Johnstone. The Dark Blues looked jaded after their Hampden appearance and, despite losing only one of their six games, they failed to qualify for the last four. Aberdeen, who had finished 13 points behind sixth-placed Dundee in the league, won the section and went on to the final where they lost to Hibs.

There was no doubting the hero status that had been bestowed by Dens fans on Alan Gilzean, who, that term, had

Ace scorer - Alan Gilzean headed the only goal in Scotland's 1-0 victory over England at Hampden in 1964. "Gillie - The King" netted 169 goals in 190 competitive games for Dundee.

scored an amazing 55 goals for club and country. Now, however, the popular scoring ace refused to re-sign and, like Ure before him, he demanded a transfer. Previously, stars like Gabriel and Ure had been allowed to go, but Bob Shankly was adamant that Gilzean would stay for he was a key man at Dens.

Since 1962, Dundee had made around £120,000 from the Ure transfer and from runs in various cup competitions, yet little had been spent on players. Gilzean's terms would be expensive to meet but many supporters felt it would be money well spent.

The impasse continued and with Gilzean on the sidelines, Dundee lost four of their opening five games of the new season, failing to qualify from their League Cup section comprising Dundee United, Motherwell and Falkirk. Two of the defeats had come from section winner's United - 3-2 at Dens and 2-1 at Tannadice - and, disturbingly, that meant that Dundee had beaten their city rivals only once in their eight meetings since April 1962.

Shankly was well aware of the team's failings. In the absence of Gilzean, another proven goalscorer was required but bids for Motherwell's Joe McBride and Sammy Wilson of Falkirk had proved unsuccessful. There were also question marks over the form of centre-half George Ryden but, despite reported interest in Dickie Rooks of Sunderland and St Mirren's Jim Clunie, no business was done.

With morale at a low ebb, sweeping changes were made for the League Cup tie with Motherwell at Dens. Out went Slater, Cox, Seith, Cameron and Houston and in came Ally Donaldson, Alex Totten, John Phillips, Jocky Scott and Hugh Robertson. Apart from Robertson, all were youngsters making their first league appearance but the gamble paid off with an astonishing 6-0 win!

A Waddell treble, two from Penman and one from Cousin were the names on the scoresheet but the name on everyone's lips was that of 16-year-old inside-left Jocky Scott, who had been a revelation with his strong direct running. That summer, the Aberdonian had been released by Chelsea but had quickly signed for Dundee after impressing in their pre-season public trial.

Three days later, Scott played his part in Dundee's 3-1 win at Falkirk but, late on, the starlet was to claim the headlines

Local hero - Bobby Cox on the ball for Dundee. DC Thomson

again, this time for the wrong reason when he got his marching orders after a clash with Bairns centre-forward Sammy Wilson.

Dundee were back on song and a 3-1 home win over Aberdeen set them up for the Tannadice clash with Dundee United. Lewis Thom put Jerry Kerr's men ahead in 28 minutes but seven minutes later, Cousin equalised with a well-judged lob. Soon after half-time, the in-form Bobby Waddell made it 2-1 and a late double by Scott completed an eagerly awaited derby success.

On September 19th, Dundee avenged their Cup Final defeat with a crushing 4-1 win over Rangers at Dens. Forrest netted an early goal for the Ibrox men but Dundee replied in devastating style courtesy of goals from Stuart, Cousin and Robertson with two - the second of which, a blistering finish after a mazy 40-yard run, prompted *The People's Journal* to describe it as the "Goal of the Season". Recently appointed skipper Alex Hamilton had revelled in Dundee's superiority and, near the end, he cheerfully conducted the victory chants of the joyful home support.

After five successive wins, Gilzean's absence had almost been forgotten but the growing euphoria soon subsided after defeats by Motherwell (a) 1-2, Falkirk (a) 2-4, Kilmarnock (h) 1-3, and Hearts (h) 1-2. At Falkirk, Slater and Seith were

Perfect view - Dark Blue attackers Hugh Robertson and Bobby Waddell get a close-up as Alan Cousin's lob sails into the net past the despairing dive of United keeper Sandy Davie for the opener in Dundee's 4-1 win. DC Thomson

recalled with reserve centre-half Norrie Beattie replacing the erratic George Ryden. Nine minutes from time, Dundee had led 2-1 but a series of appalling defensive blunders contributed to a 4-2 defeat.

New blood was required and, in late October, 24-year-old Hibs centre-half Jim Easton was signed for £7,000 with Birmingham centre-forward Alex Harley arriving for £12,000 shortly afterwards.

In December 1963, Easton had captained the Scotland Under 23s against Wales but, soon afterwards, he suffered a broken leg for the second time in his career. Before joining the St Andrews outfit, Harley

Keeper's ball - Norrie Beattie, Alan Cousin and Alex Hamilton watch anxiously as Ally Donaldson comes for a cross against Real Zaragoza in the European Cup-Winners Cup tie at Dens. DC Thomson

had been a prolific scorer, first for Third Lanark (42 goals in '60/1) - for a spell under Bob Shankly - then for Manchester City, who had paid £18,000 for his transfer in August 1962.

Their arrival plus the return of Gilzean, who had signed a two-month contract in October, coincided with wins over St Mirren (a) 2-0, Dunfermline (h) 3-1 and Celtic (a) 2-0. None of the trio, however, were eligible to play in the second round of the European Cup Winners Cup since all had signed after the August 15th deadline and, although Dundee appealed that Gilzean was a retained player, it was to no avail.

The Dark Blues had been given a first-round bye but, on Wednesday, November 18th, European football returned to Dens with the visit of Zaragoza from Spain. Encouraged by the roars of the 21,000 crowd, Steve Murray headed Dundee into an early lead only for Zaragoza to reply with a lightning double midway through the first half.

From then until the interval, the Spaniards turned on the style but, after the break it was all Dundee. Two minutes from time, Houston grabbed the equaliser but the Dark Blues were to regret their misses with Gilzean's opportunism sorely missed.

In the return leg, Robertson gave Dundee an early lead but, just before half-time, Zaragoza's brilliance was rewarded with two goals from their international winger Lapetra. Dundee had struggled to contain the lively Spaniards and, with Cox hirpling on the wing after pulling a muscle, they were unable to recover the 4-3 deficit.

Meanwhile, the race for Gilzean had hotted up. On November 25th, Torino, Spurs, Sunderland and Wolves were amongst a host of clubs present as he netted his fourth goal in five internationals in Scotland's 3-2 win over Northern Ireland at Hampden. Ten days later, Gilzean headed a brilliant hat-trick in Dundee's 4-4 draw with St Johnstone at Dens. Sadly, it was his last appearance for the club. His contract expired soon afterwards and he refused to sign another.

This time, Dundee agreed to listen to offers and, on December 16th, the scoring ace joined Tottenham Hotspur

for a new Scottish record fee of £72,500. "We all knew there was big money to be made in England," said Gilzean. "Once I began to mix with the big earners in the Scotland team, it was only a matter of time before I left Dundee."

"In those days all the players were paid the same and I had to move to better myself. I could have stayed and there might have been further glories but football is a fickle game. For example, Doug Cowie was one of Dundee's all-time greats and yet when he left, the club wouldn't even let him train at Dens Park. However, those were great times at the club and I was glad to be part of them!"

Since making his Dundee debut in 1959, Gilzean had scored an astonishing 169 goals in 190 competitive appearances and his would be a hard act to follow. "Gillie" would prove just as big a hero at White Hart Lane. By the end of his career in 1974, he had added another 133 goals giving him a remarkable total of 302 goals in 629 games for Dundee and 'Spurs, with another twelve from his 22 appearances in the Dark Blue of Scotland.

Handy Andy - a caricature of Dundee's Andy Penman.

The Dundee board knew there would be unrest at Gilzean's transfer and they made a swift move to appease the fans when within 48 hours, they paid £40,000 for Aberdeen inside-forward Charlie Cooke, a record fee between Scottish clubs. The talented 22-year-old had already been capped for the Scottish League and the Under-23s and Dons fans were devastated at his departure to their North-East rivals. The newcomer settled quickly, but some indifferent results left Dundee in mid-table by the end of January 1965.

It had been a season of transition for the Dark Blues. In August, Bobby Wishart (34), had joined Airdrie while the experienced Bert Slater and Bobby Seith had dropped out of the side. In addition to Cooke, Easton and Harley were newcomers and, with Ally Donaldson and Steve Murray having only recently made their first-team breakthrough, it was becoming apparent that it would take time to perfect the blend.

On February 6th, Dundee met St Johnstone in the first round of the Scottish Cup at Muirton. There was a large contingent of Dens fans in the 17,000 crowd but any hopes of another successful cup run were dashed by a 19th minute goal from Saints former Thistle inside-man Neil Duffy.

The cup defeat came as the last straw for Bob Shankly and, less than two weeks later, he resigned. Earlier, Shankly had turned down the post of Kilmarnock manager and, according to former Dundee chairman Ian Gellatly, he had also been approached by Rangers director Matt Taylor about a possible move to Ibrox. However, in March he was appointed manager of Hibernian in place of Jock Stein who had just taken over at Celtic.

It was known that Shankly had been unhappy for some time over the transfer of top players like Gabriel, Ure and now Gilzean. In particular, he was bitterly disillusioned at the transfer of Gilzean and he did not mince his words. A year earlier, the Dens boss had been offered a new contract by Dundee. However, it had never been signed and although club officials made desperate efforts to persuade him to stay, Shankly's mind was made up.

His successor was former Dundee full-back Bobby Ancell, who had produced a fine footballing side at Motherwell after spells at Berwick Rangers and Dunfermline. Along with Reggie Smith, Ancell had been offered the Dens post in 1949 while both were on the playing staff, but it was an arrangement they found unacceptable with the powerful figure of George Anderson still dominant in the background.

Ancell would remain at Motherwell until April 1st and Sammy Kean took over as caretaker-manager. However, on February 27th, Cameron and Penman scored three goals each as Dundee hammered the league leaders Hearts 7-1 at Tynecastle. Two weeks earlier, the Dens men, who had fielded: Donaldson; Hamilton, Cox; Cousin, Easton, Stuart; Murray, Penman, Cameron, Cooke, Robertson, had torn title-chasing Kilmarnock apart in a 4-1 win at Rugby Park and a repeat performance from that same eleven had also humbled Hearts.

Bobby Ancell - a familiar face back at Dens

The lanky Donaldson had already been capped for the Scotland Under-23s against Wales and had also appeared with Penman and Cooke against England at that level. Penman and Cooke, along with half-backs Cousin and Stuart, were key men in the Dens "engine room" and with the goals flowing freely, Dundee lost only one of their remaining nine games to finish sixth. Andy Penman finished top scorer with 29 goals, while Kenny Cameron - always a danger in and around the opposition penalty box - weighed in with 14 goals after regaining his place from the disappointing Alex Harley.

Although Dundee's recovery had come too late to mount a title challenge, they had strongly influenced the eventual destination of the championship. By late March, the title

Kenny Cameron

Dundee Massacre Leaders

HEARTS 1, DUNDEE 7. (Half-time—0-3.)

Scorers:—Hearts—Cousin (o.g. 85 min.); Dundee —Penman (pen. 15, 25, 50), Cameron (26, 62, 76), Cousin (55).

NO, this wasn't Murrayfield—though the way Dundee kept ramming home the scores with rugger-style regularity, it must have felt like it to the demoralised Hearts.

This was Dundee in their "Kilmarnock" form. Just as they tore the flag-challenging Rugby Parkers apart a fortnight ago, they reduced the league leaders to selling their progressive probing of the honesters' defensive anatomy.

Cousin's and Stuart's astute positioning and deadly accurate passing

chase had developed into a four-horse race between Kilmarnock, Dunfermline, Hearts and Hibernian and all were to suffer at the hands of Dundee for, after beating Killie and Hearts, the Dens Parkers had also gone on to thwart Dunfermline (a) 3-3, and Hibs (h) 2-1, at a critical stage in the chase for the championship flag.

Hearts, however, could feel the most aggrieved. They had lost 2-0 to Killie in their final game at Tynecastle and that result gave the Ayrshire team their first-ever championship success on goal-average. The margin had been by 0.04 of a goal and their 7-1 trouncing at the hands of Dundee had undoubtedly caused much of the damage!

Meanwhile, another two of Dundee's championship-winning squad had moved on. Bobby Waddell had faded after a bright start to the season and, in March, he was transferred to Blackpool for £10,000. A month earlier, Craig Brown - later to become manager of Clyde and Scotland - had joined Falkirk for £6,000.

The Dark Blues had finished the season in top form and with 102 goals to their credit they were expected to do well in the Summer Cup. Disappointingly, they were unable to reproduce their recent sparkle and four of the six ties ended in defeat. Even worse, Dundee United, who had taken the imaginative step of signing quality Scandinavians like Lennart Wing, Finn Dossing, Orjan Perrson and Mogens Berg - had triumphed in both derbies, 4-1 at Dens and 3-2 at Tannadice, and went on to lose the final to Motherwell.

Coming on top of other recent reverses to their neighbours, 4-2 in the league at Dens and 1-0 in the Forfarshire Cup Final, these setbacks were further blows to Dundee's ever-diminishing esteem and increasingly the fans clamoured for signings to be made.

CHAPTER THIRTEEN

Changing Faces

August 1965 marked the beginning of a new era at Dens. In May, Sammy Kean had been appointed manager of Falkirk and Bobby Seith (34), who, that summer, had hung up his boots, took over as first-team coach. Physiotherapist Lawrie Smith had also departed - Gerry Stevenson was his replacement, and now the highly successful Shankly-Kean-Smith backroom team was no more.

On the playing side, some familiar faces had also gone. The previous season, Hugh Robertson had missed only a handful of games, but, in a shock move, he joined Dunfermline for £13,000 in May. In addition, 1964 Cup Final star Bert Slater had been released along with Alex Harley, Alex Totten - later to become a successful manager - John Phillips and Phil Tinney.

"The signing of Harley had been one of Shankly's few errors of judgement," claimed Sammy Kean. "He was a pale shadow of the player that had left Third Lanark a few years earlier and he struggled badly at training." After only four goals in 10 appearances, Harley had lost his place to Kenny Cameron. It was evident that his lifestyle was no longer compatible with that of a professional footballer and, after a short spell with Irish club Portadown, he died two years later at just 30 years of age.

Gilzean's goal urge had been badly missed and Morton's 21-times capped Danish international centre, Carl Bertelsen (26) - scorer of 20 goals for the Cappielow men in 1964-65 - was signed for £10,000. A £20,000 bid was also made for another of Morton's Danish internationals, right-back Kai Johansen, but he chose to join Rangers instead.

Last term, Dundee had scored over one hundred goals, but, alarmingly, 73 had been conceded. Now Bobby Ancell's clear priority was to tighten his shaky defence and with that in mind he decided Dundee would play in a 4-2-4 formation. With the pre-season public trial a thing of the past, the Dark Blues undertook a short tour of North-West England and proceeded to defeat Manchester City 2-1 and Tranmere Rovers by two goals to nil.

OFFICIAL MAGAZINE OF DUNDEE F.C. SUPPORTERS' CLUB

Big shot - Alex Stuart was famed for his powerful shooting. SNS Group

Dundee's League Cup campaign began with a 1-0 defeat at Motherwell then an enthralling no-scoring draw with Dundee United before 25,000 at Dens Park. A Kenny Cameron double then earned a 2-0 win over Celtic in Glasgow but, with victory in sight against Motherwell at home, a late own-goal by Jim Easton followed by a Bert Howieson counter, allowed the visitors to depart with both points.

Only two points separated the four teams, but, to retain any hope of qualifying, Dundee had to beat section leaders Dundee United at Tannadice on Wednesday, September 1st. Amidst a tension-ridden atmosphere, goals by Cameron (38 mins, 46) put Dundee in the driving seat before Gillespie pulled one back with a 61st-minute penalty. However, 19 minutes from time, Murray settled the issue when he sent a low shot past keeper Donald Mackay.

According to *The Daily Record*: "This was vintage Dundee, compact in defence and needle sharp in attack". Now, a win in their final game with Celtic would clinch a place in the quarter-final unless Dundee United won by five clear goals at Motherwell. The section table looked thus:

	P	F	A	Pts
Celtic	5	8 - 6		6
Dundee	5	6 - 4		5
Dundee Utd	5	7 - 8		5
Motherwell	5	6 - 9		4

Dundee fielded that season's regulars: Donaldson; Hamilton, Easton, Stuart, Houston; Cousin, Cooke; Penman, Murray, Bertelsen, Cameron. Jock Stein, however, had learned from Dundee's 2-0 win at Parkhead, and with the influential Cooke marked out of the game by John Divers, Celtic went on to win 3-1. Cooke and Cousin were the vital "linkmen" in Dundee's set-up, but, as one journalist later commented: "Where there should have been four, there were two and vice-versa. It was chaotic!"

Manager Ancell was far from happy with his side's showing and six days later, 27-year-old Clyde inside-

No chance - Ally Donaldson is helpless as John Hughes of Celtic cracks home a powerful 30-yarder. Alex Stuart, Alan Cousin, Doug Houston and Jim Easton are the other Dundee defenders.

DC Thomson

New man - Jim McLean was signed from Clyde.

forward Jim McLean was signed for £10,000. Next day, McLean, who had caused Dundee problems in the past, was played on the left-wing in the league clash with Dundee United at Dens. After a seven-game absence, Bobby Cox was also back after settling his dispute with the club over his non-payment of a £50 SFA fine imposed for his sending off at Dunfermline last season. But, with the over-elaborate Dark Blues lacking the aggression of their city rivals, the result was a humiliating 5-0 defeat.

The following week, there was a welcome 3-2 win at Aberdeen, but the Dark Blues were to be plagued by inconsistency. Although clever enough, Bertelsen had done little to justify his scoring reputation and, in October, Cameron, who had started the season on the left-wing, was switched to centre. The move paid dividends and, by the end of November, Dundee lay sixth after taking seven points from their next four games.

The long-serving Alan Cousin had lost the number four jersey to Charlie Cooke although just five months earlier, the big schoolteacher had been voted Dundee's "Player of the Year". Now surplus to requirements, he was allowed to rejoin Bob Shankly at Hibs for £15,500 and another vital component of the title-winning season had become history.

In September, Donaldson, Hamilton, Penman and Cooke played in the Scottish League's 6-2 win over the Irish League at Hampden, while Alex Hamilton gained further full caps against Northern Ireland and Poland. Sadly, the Hampden World Cup tie against Poland ended disastrously. Near the end, the Poles snatched two late goals to win 2-1 and Hamilton found himself dropped for the next match against Italy at Hampden.

John Greig did well in his place, scoring the only goal of the game, and Hammy's international career was over. Hamilton had missed only one international since making his Scotland debut in autumn 1961 and his appearance against Poland that October was his 24th cap - a Dens Park record to this day.

Ironically, as Hammy's international career was ending,

that of a Dens colleague was about to begin. Charlie Cooke had been in brilliant form and, in November, he got his first full cap against Wales at Hampden. He starred in Scotland's 4-1 win and was retained for the game against Italy in Naples. This time the Scots, minus several top stars, crashed 3-0 but the classy Dens midfielder emerged with great credit.

Dundee were unable to maintain their momentum and wintry weather at the turn of the year saw a downturn in form with four defeats in five games, including a 2-1 defeat by Dundee United in the Tannadice derby on January 3rd, 1966.

In the Scottish Cup, the first-round tie with East Fife was postponed because of a flu epidemic amongst the Dundee players. After two inches of snow had been cleared from Dens, the match went ahead on Wednesday, February 9th. Bobby Cox opened the scoring in 14 minutes and further goals by Penman (3), McLean (2), Stuart (2) and Cameron gave Dundee a convincing 9-1 win.

The second-round draw gave Dundee a home tie with the vastly improved Celtic. In November, Ally Donaldson had been included in the Scotland squad for the Hampden game with Italy. Recently, however, he had struggled and, for the Celtic match, he was replaced by John Arrol (21), who had arrived from East Stirling for £3,000 six months previously.

Watched by a 29,000 crowd (receipts £5,719), Celtic made a great start when McBride - a £22,000 bargain buy from Motherwell - scored in five minutes. Arrol brilliantly saved a Hughes penalty, but, against the run of play, Chalmers made it 2-0 just on half-time and there was no way back for the Dark Blues.

Five days later, Dundee crashed 5-0 to Celtic in the league at Parkhead and after an abortive attempt to lure Jimmy Millar from Rangers, two signings were made. In early March, Ancell paid £12,000 for Falkirk's Northern Ireland centre-forward Sammy Wilson and Carl Bertelsen, who had scored only six goals in 22 appearances, went to Kilmarnock for £10,000. Then, shortly afterwards, Cowdenbeath right-back Bobby Wilson was signed for £8,000.

Bobby Wilson replaced the out-of-favour Alex Hamilton and soon proved himself an accomplished performer. Although never the quickest, the balding Sammy Wilson led his line well and he was exceptionally dangerous in the air.

Meanwhile, Murray and Cooke had switched places. Revelling in the freedom of his attacking role, Cooke performed brilliantly in Dundee's 6-2 win over Stirling Albion at Dens and his superb form did not go unnoticed.

In early April, Chelsea manager Tommy Docherty announced his "interest" and, shortly afterwards, Cooke asked for a transfer. On April 25th, Cooke was presented with the Dundee "Player of the Year" trophy but, less than 24 hours later came the shock news that he had been transfered to Chelsea for £72,500!

The mercurial Cooke had been at Dens for only 16 months and there was a storm of criticism over his transfer. Unlike Ure and Gilzean, he had been under contract, but Dundee's directors maintained that Cooke had been sold to avoid another protracted transfer saga.

There had been only two defeats in nine games since the arrival of the Wilsons, but the Cooke move on top of earlier transfer demands by Penman and Hamilton saw morale hit rock bottom. Having endured the slow handclap during feckless home performances against Aberdeen (1-2), and Partick (1-1), successive 2-0 defeats by Dunfermline at Dens, and Motherwell at Fir Park brought the curtain down on a miserable season.

Just four years after the championship success of 1961-62, Bobby Ancell's first full season in charge had seen Dundee finish a disappointing ninth. The departure of Ure and Gilzean had prompted the break-up of the title-winning side and since then, there had been a steady decline. Certainly, signings had been made. Within the past two years, around £100,000 - more than the Old Firm combined - had been spent on eight players, but too often their quality had not matched expectations.

The loss of Cooke was yet another blow. The £40,000 spent on his transfer had proved a wise investment and the ex-Dons star had progressed to full international level. In contrast, Harley and Bertelsen - who had cost far less - had made little impact in their brief Dens careers and there was little to indicate that more recent signings like Jim McLean, Bobby Wilson and Sammy Wilson would significantly improve the club's fortunes.

There had also been much criticism of Dundee's 4-2-4 system. Although marginally less goals were conceded, far fewer had been scored. Celtic had successfully evolved an attacking 4-2-4 plan but often Dundee's version had verged on the more defensive 4-3-3 set-up. Across the road, however, the enterprising Dundee United had continued to improve and after finishing four places above Dundee, they would participate in next season's Fairs Cup.

The long-serving Hugh Reid (signed 1954), and George Ryden (signed 1958), were amongst those released and after reported interest in Willie Hunter (Motherwell), Craig Watson (Morton), and John Madsen (Hibs), three other signings were made.

Clyde's 21-year-old attacker Alex Bryce arrived for £28,000, Sunderland's Northern Ireland Under-23 international winger Billy Campbell (22), for £3,000, while Preston's Dundee-born defender, Ron Selway (21), came on a free transfer. That summer, Bryce had featured in John Prentice's Scotland squad for the Hampden internationals with Brazil and Portugal and much was expected of the former Clyde star.

It was now 1966 and although England's World Cup success was not universally acclaimed in Scotland, the competition gave everyone a lift and a crowd of 15,000 turned out for Dundee's pre-season friendly against Chelsea at Dens. The match was part of the Charlie Cooke transfer deal but a lack-lustre home display in a 2-1 defeat did not auger well for the League Cup sectional ties against Aberdeen, St Johnstone and for the fourth time in five seasons, local rivals Dundee United.

Last season, Andy Penman had again been Dundee's top scorer. In March, he netted in the Scottish League's 4-3 win over the English League and two months later he gained his first full cap in the 3-0 defeat by Holland at Hampden. Penman was given the number nine jersey for the opening League Cup tie at Tannadice but the experiment did not succeed, with two late goals giving United a 2-0 win.

On the half-hour, Alex Bryce retired with a knee injury but, with one substitute now permitted for an injured player, Kenny Cameron took his place. However, there was little evidence of improvement and the Dark Blues took only four points from their remaining League Cup ties.

Aberdeen, now under the iron rule of Eddie Turnbull, had qualified for the quarter-finals with a 100 per cent record but in the opening league game, Dundee took their revenge with a 2-1 home win. In a battling performance, much of the credit went to the wingers, 19-year-old Highlander Derek McKay and Billy Campbell, and the increased accent on attack again paid off the following week with a welcome 4-1 win over Dundee United at Tannadice.

Soft-shoe shuffle - Dundee's brilliant midfielder Charlie Cooke gets a lecture after a derby clash with Ian Mitchell.   DC Thomson

Thunderbolt - Andy Penman fires home from the edge of the box beating a Celtic defence soon to help win the European Cup in Lisbon. Kenny Cameron looks on with Hughes, McNeil, Clark, Auld and Murdoch the Celts.

DC Thomson

On September 24th, Dundee met League Champions Celtic in their next game at Dens and the 28,500 crowd were treated to an action-packed thriller. Penman put Dundee ahead with a 30-yard "floater" only for Lennox to equalise three minutes later.

Just after half-time, came a bizarre incident. A linesman took ill and Dundee's 12th man Alex Kinninmonth was asked to run the line! A replacement was soon found and Kinninmonth later substituted for the injured Bobby Wilson. With 15 minutes left, Celtic were awarded a disputed penalty when Houston was adjudged to have handled on the goal-line. Hughes took the kick, but although Donaldson twice saved, Chalmers netted from the second rebound.

Sadly, the revival did not last with only one win from the next five games. Ron Selway had proved an uncompromising defender but, after breaking his toe in the 4-1 win at Tannadice, he missed the next five games. Others, like Bryce, Campbell and both Wilsons had also been adversely affected and these injuries had an unsettling effect.

Bobby Seith had become an influential figure as coach, but despite an appeal by the players for him to stay, he departed to take up a similar post with Rangers in November. Bruce Hay of Clyde took over with former Dens players Gerry Follon and Jimmy Toner continuing to look after the reserves. Another well known ex-Dark Blue, Andy Irvine was doing a sterling scouting job and two of his notable signings in this period were John Duncan and Iain Phillip.

That season, the Provost Road terracing had been completely concreted and a new £20,000 enclosure providing cover for 5,000 fans was erected. However, the new structure had originally been planned for the T.C. Keay end and stretched only half the width of the terracing without covering the bottom 30 steps.

By New Year, Dundee had recovered to lie fourth but with just two points taken from their next five league games, they looked to the Scottish Cup. On January 28th, the Dark Blues met strong-going Aberdeen in the first round at Dens. They fielded: Arrol; Hamilton, Easton, Stuart, Houston; Murray, Kinninmonth; Scott, Cameron, McLean, Bryce. Penman had

not recovered his match fitness after receiving a three-inch leg gash at Dunfermline and was substitute.

At half-time the Dark Blues trailed 1-0 but, when Jimmy Wilson scored a second in 48 minutes, the floodgates opened and home fans amongst the 23,000 crowd were forced to endure a humiliating 5-0 defeat. No-one doubted that Dundee had plenty of skill but there was all too often a sad lack of fighting spirit. "Jinky" Jimmy Smith and the dashing 19-year-old future Scotland cap Davie Robb had been their main tormentors. Robb was a Broughty Ferry lad, who, ironically, had trained at Dens before joining Aberdeen!

Two weeks later the nightmare continued with a 5-3 reverse at Motherwell. Since the start of 1967, Dundee had lost an astounding 29 goals in eight games, with five goals conceded on four separate occasions. With changes inevitable, the experienced Alex Hamilton, who had regained his place in September, and Jim Easton were replaced by Bobby Wilson and George Stewart and soon Dundee's fortunes took an upward turn.

Nine points were taken from matches against Partick Thistle (h) 0-0, St Johnstone (a) 3-0, Ayr United (h) 3-0, Hibs (a) 1-2, Stirling Albion (h) 2-0 and St Mirren (a) 5-0 and, with four games left, a Fairs Cup place remained possible.

At the start of the 1965-66 season, Hamilton and Penman had received substantial signing-on fees after putting pen to paper on long-term contracts but, after repeated transfer requests, both were put up for sale. In particular, Dundee had no wish to lose the accomplished Penman. But, when he threatened to do a "Billy Steel" and join the new U.S. rebel league, they were faced with the loss of a substantial transfer fee and the die was cast.

Following their disastrous cup defeat by Berwick Rangers, Rangers had transfer-listed strikers Jim Forrest and George McLean. Initially a Penman-Forrest swop was agreed but Forrest instead opted to join Preston North End. Celtic and Newcastle were also interested in Penman but, in April, the £55,000-rated Dens star joined Rangers in exchange for George McLean plus £30,000.

McLean (24), had scored 80 league and cup goals in 112

games since joining Rangers from St Mirren in early 1963 but he was ineligible for Dundee's remaining games, having signed after the transfer deadline. Nevertheless, Dundee now had a settled team and the good run continued with wins over Clyde (a) 3-1, Dunfermline (h) 3-1, and Airdrie (a) 4-1 before the 1966-67 season ended with a 1-1 draw with Rangers at Dens. And with only one defeat in their previous 10 games, there were positive signs that the Dark Blues were back on the rails.

Arrol and his defence of Wilson, Stewart, Stuart and Cox looked secure while the hard-working and skilful Murray and Bryce provided the ammunition for the front-men. Up front, Sammy Wilson had formed a telling partnership with top scorer Jim McLean and with Campbell and Scott providing the pace, there was now an attractive attacking blend.

That summer, the upward trend was confirmed by an 11-game unbeaten tour of the USA. There were encouraging 4-2 wins over English champions Manchester United and English Cup winners Chelsea with a second game against the Stamford Bridge side ending in a 2-2 draw.

Kenny Cameron had faced a constant battle for a first-team place and the arrival of George McLean would make the situation no easier. And so, on the eve of the new season, the chunky striker joined Kilmarnock for £10,000.

Dundee's growing optimism was further boosted by a 3-0 pre-season friendly win over Millwall at Dens before they surprisingly found themselves in the first-round draw of the Fairs Cup! It had been expected that runners-up Rangers, third-placed Clyde and Hibs, in fifth place, would be the

Scottish representatives. But, with only one club allowed per city then and Rangers already "representing" Glasgow, unlucky Clyde found themselves replaced by the sixth-placed Dens Park club.

In the League Cup, Dundee opened with a 0-0 draw with Hibs at Dens but, by the halfway stage, 2-1 wins over Clyde (a), and Motherwell (h), left them level with Bob Shankly's side at the top of the section. The Edinburgh return with Hibs looked like being decisive and on Saturday, August 26th, the fans were treated to a classic at a sun-drenched Easter Road.

Dundee made a great start and with Campbell in dazzling form, they led 3-2 at half-time. In 52 minutes, Hibs were awarded their second penalty of the match but, although Joe Davis had earlier netted from the spot, Arrol made a crucial save from his second attempt. That proved to be the turning point and, 15 minutes from the end, George McLean settled the issue with a fourth goal for Dundee.

Although Jocky Scott had given way to the more experienced McLean, the Dens machine continued to run smoothly and wins over Clyde (h) 1-0, and Motherwell (a) 5-2, ensured a quarter-final place against East Fife from Division Two. In the first-leg, Steve Murray, who had developed into a top-class midfielder, scored the only goal of the game and a 4-0 win in the return eased the Dark Blues into the last four of the competition.

Ever the soccer purist, Bobby Ancell had put together a good blend of youth and experience and already George Stewart was being favourably compared to Ian Ure, a

Dundee F.C. Season 1967-68 (BACK, left to right) George Stewart, Jim Easton, Ally Donaldson, John Arrol, George McLean, Ron Selway. MIDDLE - Bobby Wilson, Davie Swan, Stevie Murray, Jim McLean, Alex Hamilton, Sammy Wilson, Jocky Scott. FRONT - Bruce Hay (coach), Alex Bryce, Billy Campbell, Bobby Cox, Kenny Cameron, Derek McKay, Bobby Ancell (manager). DC Thomson

defender who had never been adequately replaced. Bobby Wilson (23), had also made rapid progress and, in early September, he gained a Scottish League cap against the Irish League in Belfast.

Billy Campbell

Only St Johnstone now stood between Dundee's third League Cup Final appearance but, by the night of the Tannadice semi-final on October 11th, their early form had shaded. Only four points were taken from five league games and Dundee's 24-game unbeaten run had ended with a 4-2 defeat at Aberdeen.

Nevertheless, progress had been made in the Fairs Cup at the expense of Dutch side DWS Amsterdam. At Amsterdam's Olympic Stadium, Arrol made a great penalty save but, with the floodlighting of a dubious quality, Dundee were not unhappy to finish just 2-1 behind.

In the Dens return on October 4th, Sammy Wilson delighted the 15,000 crowd when he went in to fire the ball wide of Schrijvers for a fourth-minute equaliser. The Dutch made things hard for the Dark Blues before Jim McLean scored from a 60th minute penalty. But, near the end, McLean headed his second to give Dundee a 4-2 aggregate win.

St Johnstone had talented forwards like Kenny Aird and Alex McDonald and were certain to prove a hot handful in the League Cup semi-final. Both sides were affected by the tension amongst the 18,000 Tannadice crowd but, just before the interval, the deadlock was broken when Gordon Whitelaw headed St Johnstone into the lead.

After the break, Dundee went flat out for the equaliser and, with the speedy Campbell causing havoc on the right, Saints defender George Millar was twice pressurised into putting the ball through his own-goal. Campbell continued to torment and in 72 minutes he was downed by Benny Rooney in the box. Up stepped Jim McLean to net from the spot and Dundee's Hampden place was assured.

In the final, Dundee would meet Celtic, winners of last season's domestic treble and 7-1 conquerors of Morton in the other semi-final. Six months earlier, the Parkhead men had become the first British side to win the European Cup and, with Dundee's preparations upset by defeats from St Johnstone (h) 1-4, and Rangers (a) 0-2, the Parkhead team were strong favourites to win the Hampden showdown on Saturday, October 28th.

At Ibrox, Dundee had dominated for long spells but had missed vital chances. Two changes were made for the final. Donaldson and Cox dropped out in favour of Arrol and Bryce with Houston stepping back from midfield as Dundee lined up: Arrol; B. Wilson, Stewart, Stuart (capt), Houston; Murray, J. McLean; Campbell, G. McLean, S. Wilson, Bryce. Sub. - Cox. Celtic: Simpson; Craig, McNeill, Clark, Gemmell; Murdoch, Auld; Chalmers, Lennox, Wallace, Hughes. Sub. - O'Neill. Referee Bobby Davidson (Airdrie).

On a bright autumn day, there were 66,000 on the Hampden slopes including around 10,000 from Dundee. The Dark Blues hoped to contain the early Celtic onslaught and settle to their own short-passing game but, with just 10 minutes played, they found themselves 2-0 down.

In eight minutes, Billy McNeill beat Dundee's hesitant defence to a corner and nodded back for Steve Chalmers to head the opener. Four minutes later, John Hughes appeared to foul Houston as he bored in on goal but as Arrol awaited the referee's whistle, the big winger fired home.

Nevertheless, Dundee did settle and, in 25 minutes, Sammy Wilson set up George McLean for an opportunist goal. Dundee's studied football had Celtic rattled and they nearly equalised when George McLean again broke through only to shoot over the bar. After the break, Dundee continued to worry Celtic but with 17 minutes left Chalmers sped through a square looking Dens defence to put the Parkhead side 3-1 ahead.

Then, Jim McLean scored from close in after a corner but as Dundee swept forward, Bobby Lennox pounced on a defensive mix-up to make it 4-2. Dundee refused to submit and with five minutes left George McLean reduced the leeway when he swept past two defenders before clipping the ball past Ronnie Simpson. Almost the whole Dundee team pushed up in a desperate attempt to equalise but within 60 seconds they were cruelly punished when Willie Wallace broke away to make the final score 5-3 for Celtic.

In an enthralling game, Murray, Stewart and big George McLean were Dundee's best. However, defensive errors had cost them dear and a bitterly disappointed Bobby Ancell hinted that he might have chosen the wrong team. Alex Bryce had been a big disappointment while Doug Houston, who had only played a handful of games at left-back, had struggled to contain a rampant John Hughes in the vital opening stages.

Dundee dangerman - George McLean bursts through to score against Rangers at Dens with Erik Sorensen and Kai Johansen helpless. The big striker netted 35 goals in the 1967-68 season.

DC Thomson

Not an earthly - John Arrol is beaten all ends up by Bobby Lennox's shot for the fourth Celtic goal in the League Cup Final at Hampden with Steve Chalmers looking on. DC Thomson

SCOTTISH LEAGUE CUP FINAL

CELTIC v DUNDEE

HAMPDEN PARK GLASGOW
Saturday 28th October 1967
Kick-off 3 p.m.
Official Programme - · · · 1s

The switch of Hughes to the right-wing was a major factor in Celtic's devastating start and this was yet another masterly move by the legendary Jock Stein. Doug Houston himself agreed: "The damage was done in that opening spell. Celtic just overwhelmed us and from then on we were always up against it. And although we eventually settled to a good game, they always had the edge."

Significantly, Bobby Cox returned for the Fairs Cup clash against Royal Liege of Belgium four days later - Houston moving to midfield with Bryce relegated to the substitute's bench. A disappointingly low crowd of 12,000 was shocked by the loss of an early goal but the Dark Blues recovered and two Alex Stuart "specials" and a header by Sammy Wilson gave them a deserved 3-1 win.

The arrival of George "Dandy" McLean had seen last season's top marksman Jim "Beano" McLean drop back to midfield alongside the energetic Steve Murray. Jim McLean was a studied footballer and although he had never been universally popular with the fans, he adapted well to his new midfield-general role.

Dundee's league form was giving cause for concern. There had been only two wins from the opening 10 games but, on November 15th, they again demonstrated their flair for the big occasion with a stunning 4-1 win in Liege. And although it had essentially been a great team display, George McLean had taken star billing by netting all four of Dundee's goals! McLean was a character both on and off the field and Doug Houston told of the big striker's triumphant return to the dressing room in Liege. "You'd better take the number off

my jersey Mr Ancell, and replace it with S for Superman," quipped McLean.

Surprisingly, Dundee continued to struggle in the bread and butter games and by late January they lay twelfth. Up front, George McLean had already scored 22 goals, but he was still capable of missing the easiest of chances. However, a shaky defence shouldered much of the blame and, despite the return of Ally Donaldson and Jim Easton, there were some incredible scorelines like Partick Thistle (h) 3-4, Celtic (h) 4-5, and Kilmarnock (h) 6-5.

In the Scottish Cup, transfer-seeking Alex Kinninmonth grabbed a late winner at Cowdenbeath to set up a second-round tie against league leaders Rangers at Dens and on February 17th, Tannadice Street played host to two cup games. The Dundee v Rangers clash kicked off at 3pm before a crowd of 33,000, while the Dundee United v Hearts game which started an hour earlier drew a crowd of 9,000.

Seven days earlier, Dundee had lost 4-2 to Rangers in the league at Dens but the cup-tie was a tighter affair. On the hour, Rangers went ahead when the ball bounced in off Stewart's knee but the Dark Blues fought back to equalise through Billy Campbell. In the replay, Orjan Perrson gave Rangers an early lead only for Sammy Wilson to level soon after the break. But with Rangers reeling, George McLean, who had taken a roasting from the 54,000 Ibrox crowd, missed two good chances and, in extra-time, Rangers went on to win 4-1.

It had been a bad season for knee injuries. Ron Selway was still recovering from cartilage and knee ligament complications from last season, while Alex Hamilton and Bobby Cox had undergone surgery for similar complaints early in the current campaign. In February, Dens skipper Alex Stuart had required a cartilage operation with Alex Bryce following suit a few months later.

Billy Campbell (twice), and Sammy Wilson (once as substitute), followed in the footsteps of 1920s star Sam Irving when they were capped for Northern Ireland, although both were forced to withdraw from the international against Wales which had clashed with the Scottish Cup replay against Rangers. In February, Steve Murray was capped for Scotland's Under-23s against England and, shortly afterwards, he replaced the injured Stuart as Dundee skipper.

After getting a third-round bye, Dundee met FC Zurich in the Fairs Cup quarter-final. Earlier, the well-organised Swiss side had beaten Barcelona, Nottingham Forrest and Sporting Lisbon but on a windy night in March, a late scrambled goal by Easton gave Dundee a 1-0 win before a 13,500 crowd. Seven days later, the Dens men came under intense pressure at the Letzgrund Stadium in Zurich. Only George McLean was left up front but, 10 minutes from half-time, Sammy Wilson outjumped the home keeper to head a fine goal.

That put Dundee 2-0 ahead on aggregate and, with no further scoring, they would now meet last season's finalists Leeds United in the semi-final. In previous rounds, the "method-men" of Elland Road had defeated Hibs (2-1), and Rangers (2-0) and with household names like David Harvey, Billy Bremner, Jack Charlton, Norman Hunter, Eddie Gray, Peter Lorimer and Johnny Giles, they had already won the League Cup and were battling it out with Liverpool and the two Manchester clubs for the English Championship.

In contrast, Dundee's European progress had been overshadowed by some dismal displays on the domestic front. Home results were particularly disappointing and with an average home league gate of 8,900 it was clear that success abroad was only worthwhile if reinforced by similar success at home. The supporters were very critical of Dundee's rather unadventurous approach in home games while, in turn, the players were often unnerved when appearing before the hard-to-please Dens support.

Nevertheless, 24,500 turned out for the first-leg tie against Leeds at Dens on May 1st as Dundee lined up: Donaldson; B. Wilson, Easton, Stewart, Swan; Murray, Kinninmonth, J. McLean; Campbell, S. Wilson, G. McLean. Subs.- Arrol, Houston, Scott. Leeds United: Harvey; Reaney, Charlton, Hunter, Cooper; Bremner, Madeley, Giles; Greenhoff, Lorimer, Gray. Subs. - Edmunds, Hibbett, Belfitt

Dundee started well but were shocked when Paul Madeley headed past Donaldson in 26 minutes. Ten minutes later, Kinninmonth's header from a free-kick was cleared off the line by Cooper and Bobby Wilson had the Dens faithful cheering when he headed an opportunist equaliser. After the break, the white-shirted Leeds pulled utility-man Madeley back into defence and, with Dundee unable to make much impression, the game petered out to a 1-1 draw.

With away goals counting double, Dundee looked a more positive side in the Elland Road return before a near 29,000 crowd. Selway, recently recovered from his knee trouble, deputised for toothache victim Bobby Wilson with Houston and Scott replacing Swan and Kinninmonth, while Sprake and Jones came in for Harvey and Charlton.

In the first period, Dundee pushed forward but could make no headway against the strong Leeds defence. After half-time, the redoubtable Billy Bremner rallied his men, and, following a spell of intense pressure, it was fellow Scot, Eddie Gray, who scored the winner nine minutes from time. And though very disappointed, Dundee had done themselves proud and it was little surprise when the powerful Elland Road side went on to lift the Fairs Cup, defeating Ferencvaros of Hungary 1-0 on aggregate in the final.

Magic moment - Sammy Wilson, George McLean and Steve Murray watch as Bobby Wilson (on left) heads the equaliser against Leeds in Dundee's Fairs Cup semi-final at Dens. TOP - George Stewart is outjumped by England international Jack Charlton. DC Thomson/Scotsman

CHAPTER FOURTEEN

Master Tactician

After 11 years at Dens, Alex Hamilton, who was now 30 years of age, had been freed along with Norrie Beattie and five of the younger players. The former international defender would continue his career with South African club Addington and, although many were sorry to see Hammy's departure, Bobby Wilson had already proved a worthy successor.

The previous season had been something of a marathon for Dundee who had played 55 competitive games. They did well to reach the latter stages of the League Cup and Fairs Cup but poor league form had seen them finish a lowly ninth in the Division One league table.

Pre-season friendlies in England did not auger well for the approaching campaign. After winning 1-0 at Third Division Hull, the Dark Blues lost 2-0 at Dens to First Division Queen's Park Rangers before crashing 8-0 to Second Division Millwall at The Den. After 80 successive appearances, Jim McLean was dropped for the League Cup opener against Kilmarnock and, in one of football's ironic twists, he joined the Rugby Park side for £3,000 just five days later.

With Sammy Wilson and George McLean also out through injury and suspension, John Duncan was brought in alongside Jocky Scott for his first-team debut. It was a telling combination and a dazzling display brought an emphatic 4-0 win over the Ayrshire side. Only two points were taken from the next three ties against Hearts (a) 1-2, Airdrie (h) 1-1, and Kilmarnock (a) 2-2 but a Duncan hat-trick in a 4-0 midweek win over Hearts at Dens revived Dundee's quarter-final hopes.

On Saturday, August 31st, the Dark Blues met section leaders Airdrie, who lay one point ahead, in the final game at Broomfield. Dundee appeared to revel in this "cup-tie" confrontation and, urged on by a vociferous travelling support, goals by McLean (40 mins, 86) and Duncan, earned a convincing 3-0 win. Division Two Stranraer posed few problems in the quarter-final and, after a 4-0 win at Stair Park, Scott and McLean scored three each in a 6-0 goal romp at Dens.

Once again, league form was poor and defensive lapses proved costly in early games with Aberdeen (h) 4-4, Dundee United (a) 1-3, and St Johnstone (h) 2-3. Nevertheless, the youthful striking partnership of John Duncan and Roddy Georgeson - both 19 years of age - looked impressive. The fair-haired Georgeson, who last season had been sent off against Raith Rovers, was a polished performer, while Dark Blues fan Duncan, from Morgan Academy, had already shown his scoring flair with nine goals in ten appearances.

Debut day - new Dens Park boss John Prentice with trainer Bruce Hay before his first game against Clyde. DC Thomson

Like his boyhood hero, Alan Gilzean, Duncan was also strong in the air and he soon gained the nickname "Gillie" but, more unusually, he preferred to wear rugby boots, which, he claimed, gave him a more powerful shot.

At the end of September, manager Bobby Ancell (56), announced his resignation although he would remain as youth coach. It had taken the quietly spoken Ancell - described by some of his former players as "one of football's gentlemen" - two years to rebuild the side. However, despite the subsequent improvement, the Dens boss had become disillusioned after the 8-0 mauling at Millwall and, in the belief that the club required a younger man at the helm, he recommended 42-year-old Falkirk boss John Prentice as his successor.

Formerly a player with Rangers and Falkirk, Prentice had been boss of Arbroath and Clyde before becoming Scotland's first full-time manager in March 1966. Prentice was well-respected for his knowledge of the game but seven months later, he was sacked by the SFA for allegedly seeking employment in Canada.

His career in charge of playing matters at Dens began with a 3-2 home defeat by Clyde, a result which left him unimpressed by the lack of fight and organisation shown by his new charges. However, four days later, Dundee had the opportunity of reaching their second successive League Cup Final when they met Bob Shankly's Hibs in the midweek semi-final at Tynecastle. Duncan and Selway were replaced by Sammy Wilson and Stewart as Dundee lined up: Donaldson, B. Wilson, Easton, Stewart, Houston; Murray, Bryce; Campbell, McLean, S. Wilson, Scott. Sub. - Selway.

McLean put Dundee ahead after a sixth-minute corner but, within 30 seconds, Stein had equalised. The sides were evenly matched and the 19,752 crowd were treated to an absolute thriller as play raged from end to end.

Increasingly, Dundee looked like winning, particularly when Allan McGraw was stretchered off in 74 minutes with the Hibs substitute already on. The Dark Blues continued to press but, two minutes from time, the heavily bandaged McGraw, who had returned after lengthy treatment, forced home the winner in a goalmouth scramble.

Dundee had missed some great chances but it was Hibs who would proceed to meet Celtic in the final. Although 31-year-old Sammy Wilson had won four Northern Ireland caps in his time at Dens, he was never the most mobile and, now past his best, it came as little surprise when he was sold to Coleraine for £2,000 soon after the semi-final.

All action - Dens Park skipper Steve Murray. DC Thomson

However, Prentice felt that Duncan and Georgeson were not ready for regular first-team football and the experienced former Clyde striker Joe Gilroy (25), was signed from Fulham for £15,000. It looked like money well-spent when Gilroy scored in his first two games against Arbroath (a) 2-1, and Hearts (h) 3-1 but, by the end of 1968, he had

managed only two more.

Like Bob Shankly, John Prentice appeared rather dour but he shared his predecessor's burning desire for success. Naturally, the new boss wanted the game played his way and, accordingly, changes were made.

But, although the "goals-against" column was significantly improved by mid-January, a lack of scoring power meant Dundee continued to languish in the lower regions of the league.

Last season, Dundee had been unfortunate not to win both local derbies - 2-2 at Dens and 0-0 at Tannadice. Now United had once again gained the ascendancy when they ran out 3-1 winners in September and, on January 2nd, 1969, their 2-1 success at Dens put them alongside Celtic at the top of the table.

Now Dundee's hopes rested on a good Scottish Cup run and, on January 25th, they entertained the previous season's runners-up Hearts in the first round. In seven minutes, Scott beat Cruickshank for the opener but, almost immediately, George Fleming equalised. Nevertheless, Dundee had looked the stronger and, just before half-time, Bryce crossed for Campbell to head home. However, offside was given, and 18 minutes from the end of a dour struggle, Tommy Traynor scored the winner for Hearts.

Too often Dundee's build-up was laborious and, despite the presence of some skilful players, there was insufficient pace and power for a successful side. Rangers apart, Celtic's supremacy had gone virtually unchallenged since 1965 and an abysmal 14,000 cup crowd was clear evidence that thousands of disillusioned Dens fans had simply drifted away. In 1963-64, Dundee's average home league gate was close to 15,000 but, with a considerable deterioration in standards since then, attendances had almost halved.

PRICE: SIXPENCE

OFFICIAL PROGRAMME

DUNDEE FOOTBALL CLUB
LIMITED

LEAGUE CHAMPIONSHIP
DUNDEE v. DUNDEE UNITED N° 296
Thursday, 2nd January, 1969

Cairdsport at MELDRUMS
for all football gear and sports equipment.
The "know-how" of two of Dundee's leading
sports stores is now at your service.
Suppliers to Dundee Football Club.
Enquiries are invited from Club Secretaries.
REFORM STREET, DUNDEE Telephone 26855

Derby thrills - Joe Gilroy, Ally Donaldson and Davie Swan watch as United's Ian Mitchell appeals in vain that the ball has crossed the line after Bobby Wilson executes a last-gasp clearance at Dens.
DC Thomson

Under Prentice, the tactics varied from 4-3-3 to 4-4-2 with the strikers, usually Gilroy, McLean and Scott, holding up the ball until support from midfield arrived. Northern Ireland winger Billy Campbell now lay deeper and, although not as effective as before, he gained further caps against Turkey and the USSR.

Last season, the mercurial McLean had scored 23 league goals and had been capped for Scotland against Holland. But he had not thrived on the new style of play and had scored only two league goals by the

Lethal touch - Jocky Scott was an excellent finisher.

time Dundee's finances, severely hit by falling gates, saw him transferred to Dunfermline for £22,000 in March.

The nucleus of the side was now built round Donaldson, Wilson, the versatile Houston - at sweeper, left-back or midfield - Murray, Easton, Stewart, Campbell, Scott, Gilroy and Bryce. The hard-working Alex Kinninmonth, who had been at Dens since 1960, was now a midfield regular, while transfer-seeking Davie Swan looked like making the left-back slot his own. Arrol, Stuart, Cox, McKay, Duncan and Georgeson had slipped from the picture but another two youngsters, left-back Davie Johnston and midfielder Jim Steele, had given some promising displays.

The pattern of inconsistency continued until the end of the season as Dundee finished tenth. Their tally of 46 league goals was their lowest for 16 years although, encouragingly, three points had been taken from the last three games against Rangers (h) 3-2, (a) 1-1, and Celtic (h) 1-2.

That April, the long-serving Bobby Cox (35), and Alex Stuart (28), were amongst those released. Over the previous year, Cox had been plagued by injury and, in February, he had undergone the sixth knee operation of his career. He had been a stalwart throughout his 13 years at Dens and only Doug Cowie and Bill Marsh had bettered his 411 league and cup appearances for the club.

Stuart, famed for his thundering left-footed free-kicks, had joined Dundee from Aberdeen East End in 1958. Like Cox, he was a firm favourite with the fans, but had never fully recovered from his cartilage operation a year earlier. Derek McKay was the only other player of first-team experience to leave. He was snapped up by Aberdeen and, a year later, made a fairy-tale appearance in the Scottish Cup Final, when he scored twice in the Dons' 3-1 triumph over Celtic.

With the end of the decade in sight, it looked like being another hard season for Dundee. There was little money to spend and the only significant signing was 31-year-old centre-half Jim Fraser on a free transfer from Clyde. In the League Cup, the Dark Blues recovered from a 3-1 opening day reversal to St Johnstone at Perth. Five points were taken from Partick Thistle (h) 4-0, (a) 1-0, and Kilmarnock (h) 0-0, and now their quarter-final hopes hinged on the clash with the vastly-improved St Johnstone at Dens.

A 13,400 crowd saw Dundee play well but a badly mis-judged header by Stewart gave the visitors a 2-1 win. Saints'

manager Willie Ormond had blended a fine attacking side and, with stars like Kenny Aird, Henry Hall and the brilliant John Connolly, they deservedly progressed to the final, only to lose narrowly to Celtic.

Dundee's league campaign began badly with only one win from their opening six games. It had been hoped that the experienced Fraser would stiffen the defence but after eight appearances he was dropped and did not appear again in the first-team that season.

Once again, John Prentice's biggest problem was a shortage of goals. A proven scorer was urgently required and, in mid-September, Dundee paid £14,000 for Raith Rovers striker Gordon Wallace. A local lad, he had been provisionally signed for the Dark Blues in 1960 but was never called up.

Wallace went on to play for Montrose and Raith Rovers and in 1968 was voted Scotland's Player of the Year after scoring 30 goals for Raith and finishing top marksman in Division One. The newcomer made his debut in the derby clash with Dundee United at Dens, but despite scoring Dundee's equaliser, a controversial late penalty by Gillespie gave United a 2-1 win.

On November 1st, a double by former Dens star Andy Penman helped Rangers to a 3-1 win over a lethargic Dundee at Ibrox. In his match report, John McKenzie, billed as the Voice of Football by *The Daily Express* was scathing in his criticism of Dundee. "They were," he claimed, "a ghost squad in Dark Blue, run by people who appear to settle for doing just enough to keep out of trouble. The team has a soft centre and lack the will to succeed." Performances had indeed been indifferent throughout John Prentice's 13-month reign, but the Ibrox debacle was to prove a watershed for the Dens Park club.

By the end of the year, Wallace had scored nine goals. In addition, his subtle play made him the ideal foil for the pace and power of Jocky Scott and, with midfielder Alex Bryce at last looking the part, a vastly-improved Dundee lay sixth in the league. Since October, home form - comprising six wins and a draw - had been particularly encouraging and there were 12,000 crowds for the wins over high-flying Hibs (1-0), and Aberdeen (2-0) at the turn of the year.

Following an abortive enquiry for Kilmarnock pivot Jackie McGrory, transfer-listed Jim Easton had successfully

Ace scorer - Gordon Wallace was to transform Dundee's fortunes.

returned to defence at the expense of George Stewart. The rangy Jim Steele had brought some much-needed dig to midfield alongside accomplished players like Steve Murray, Alex Bryce and Alex Kinninmonth.

And with Gordon Wallace and Jocky Scott now forming a telling partnership up front, and a traditional winger no longer in vogue, Billy Campbell began to struggle for a place. Meanwhile, there had been a couple of notable departures. In October, Bobby

Dundee F.C. Season 1969-70 (BACK, left to right) Ron Selway, Steve Murray, Jim Easton, Ally Donaldson, George Stewart, Doug Houston, Alex Bryce. FRONT - Billy Campbell, Alex Kinninmonth, Gordon Wallace, Jocky Scott, Jim Steele. DC Thomson

Ancell - Prentice couldn't get him out the door quickly enough according to former chairman Ian Gellatly - was released for economic reasons and two months later, John Arrol, who had been reserve to Ally Donaldson for the past two years, joined Dunfermline for £3,000.

On January 2nd, 1970, the Dark Blues were brought back to earth with a bump. On a Tannadice pitch resembling the Arctic tundra, Dundee insisted on playing their usual neat man-to-man style of play and United's more direct approach paid off with a 4-1 win.

Ex-Dark Blue Kenny Cameron was Dundee's chief tor-men-tor with two goals, but the writing had been on the wall when a careless Easton pass-back gave United a 2-0 lead after half-an-hour. Incredibly, Easton four times, and Stewart three, had together managed to score no fewer than seven own-goals since 1965.

Nevertheless, early Scottish Cup successes over Albion Rovers (a) 2-1, and Airdrie (h) 3-0, came as a confidence booster and set the Dark Blues up for a tricky-looking quarter-final tie against Division Two East Fife at Bayview.

The Methil side included former Dens centre Bobby Waddell and ex-Motherwell and Hibs star Pat Quinn, but it was Dundee midfielder Alex Bryce who fired in the only goal after 13 minutes. Dundee had the edge in midfield and although East Fife fought hard, they had rarely looked like equalising before a healthy 14,995 crowd.

In recent years, Scottish football had seen an upsurge in terracing violence and a half-time battle between rival fans beneath the covered enclosure caused hundreds to spill on to the pitch to escape. The trouble was quickly contained but this alarming trend would further contribute to already declining attendances.

For the first time in six years, Dundee were through to the last four of the Scottish Cup. The other semi-finalists were Aberdeen, Celtic and Kilmarnock but Dundee had the misfortune to land Celtic - the current league leaders and League Cup holders - who in recent years had swept all before them.

In January, Bobby Wilson had joined Joe Gilroy on the sidelines with a long-term knee injury, but the versatile Ron Selway had done well in his place. However, there was a shock when Dundee took the field for the Hampden clash with Celtic on Saturday, March 14th.

Skipper Stevie Murray had failed a late fitness test and would not play. There were 64,000 in the ground as Dundee lined up: Donaldson; Selway, Easton, Stewart, Houston; Campbell, Bryce, Steele, Kinninmonth; Wallace, Scott. Sub. - Georgeson. Celtic: Williams; Hay, McNeill, Brogan, Gemmell; Johnstone, Murdoch, Callaghan; Macari, Wallace, Lennox. Sub. - Auld.

In the first half, Dundee played it tight hoping to frustrate Celtic's swift-flowing moves and although under intense pressure, a combination of stout defending and good fortune kept the scoreline blank.

In 57 minutes, Lou Macari put Celtic ahead, but it was Dundee's turn to celebrate with an equaliser six minutes later. Campbell began the move with a great run and Wallace sent the ball low last Evan Williams for an opportunist goal. From then on the Dark Blues grew in confidence but with a replay looking increasingly likely as the game moved towards its final stages, fate was to intervene.

That season, Ally Donaldson had conceded just 38 goals in 35 games and his fine form was rewarded with another Scottish League cap against the Irish League in November. At Hampden, he had performed heroically in the face of a Parkhead onslaught but, with only eight minutes remaining, he was unable to hold Tommy Gemmell's sweeping cross and the ever-alert Lennox was on the spot to score.

Dundee's chance of glory had gone but they could take great encouragement from their performance with the tenacious Jim Steele a real stand-out in midfield. There had been a good Dundee support but, following the terrifying scenes of bottle-throwing and violence perpetrated by Celtic fans at the 1967 League Cup Final, it was only when segregation was introduced many years later that most Dens fans felt safe enough to openly support their team in Glasgow.

The cup run had brought some much-needed revenue but, within hours of the final whistle at Hampden, the inspirational Steve Murray, who had signed a two-year contract at the start of the season, was on his way to Aberdeen for a fee of £47,500. Average home gates were less than 8,000 and, according to John Prentice, the transfer had been a financial necessity.

The Dark Blues were unbeaten at Dens since September and home wins over second-placed Rangers (2-1), Morton (2-1), and Partick Thistle (4-1), kept alive their hopes of a Fairs Cup place. Disappointingly, however, home defeats by St Johnstone (0-2), and Celtic (1-2), saw Dundee finish sixth when another four points would have taken them to fourth spot and a place in Europe.

That close season, there were some significant changes to the Dens Park staff. Jim McLean returned as first-team coach in place of Bruce Hay, who had gone to South Africa, with transfer-seeking Davie Swan going to Kilmarnock in exchange. At the end of the previous term, eight players had been released although only one, Roddy Georgeson, had made any first-team appearances.

Another to go was the unsettled Billy Campbell. He joined Motherwell in exchange for former Newcastle, Aberdeen and Morton winger Jimmy Wilson (31), and other new faces were Clyde defender Dave Soutar on a free transfer and 20-year-old Queen's Park keeper Mike Hewitt.

Dundee's dismal pre-season record continued with losses at English Second Division Millwall (0-5), and Third Division Walsall (0-2), before Fourth Division Southend were beaten 5-0 at Dens. However, in the League Cup, Dundee were a side transformed. A late Kinninmonth goal brought a 1-0 home triumph over St Mirren and further wins over Ayr United (a) 2-1, Kilmarnock (h) 2-0, Ayr (h) 4-1, and St Mirren (a) 2-0, assured them of a place in the last eight.

After only a handful of appearances over the past two years, John Duncan was back in the team. Duncan was now a better all-round player and, along with Gordon Wallace and Jocky Scott, he completed a deadly striking partnership.

On Wednesday, September 9th, Dundee met Celtic at Dens in the first-leg of the League Cup quarter-final. The Parkhead side began brilliantly and when Jimmy Johnstone netted twice within two minutes midway through the first half, things looked bleak for Dundee.

Following the break, the pattern of non-stop Celtic attacks continued until Kinninmonth pulled one back on the hour. As the tide began to turn, Scott equalised and Wallace was later unlucky to see his shot come off a post.

After nine minutes of the Parkhead return, Lou Macari appeared to punch the ball from Donaldson's grasp before finding the net. Although the infuriated Dens keeper chased referee Bobby Davidson to the halfway line, the goal stood and, 3-0 behind at half-time, the Dark Blues eventually went down 5-1 and went out 7-3 on aggregate.

Bad break - Ally Donaldson and Alex Kinninmonth are helpless as Bobby Lennox pounces to net the winner for Celtic in the 1970 Scottish Cup semi-final at Hampden.

That month, Dundee had also been eliminated from the Texaco Cup by Wolves while managing just one point from their four league games. The English First Division side had stars like Jim McCalliog, Frank Munro, Bobby Gould and Derek Dougan and, like Leeds in 1968, looked physically stronger than Dundee in their 2-1 first-leg win at Dens. The Molineux return ended in a 0-0 draw but, despite their cup exit, Dundee could be proud of their battling performance.

After their bright start, Dundee were again looking suspect down the middle. Easton and Stewart had begun as first-choice pairing but, once again, the enigmatic Stewart put through his own goal past a luckless Ally Donaldson in the home game against St Mirren.

Various permutations were made from Easton, Stewart, Houston and Selway, before 19-year-old reserve defender Iain Phillip got his chance. The tall youngster, groomed by Broughty United amateurs, but signed from Junior club Broughty Athletic in 1968, quickly established himself with some classy displays and soon there was a marked improvement in defence.

Phillip's breakthrough coincided with a Dens revival and, by the end of 1970, a run of 12 games with only one defeat, left Dundee fifth, just two points behind third-placed Rangers. John Prentice now had the makings of a good side and he took great encouragement from the performances of his younger players like Phillip, Steele, Duncan, Hewitt and Johnston.

The Dens manager was highly regarded by his players according to skipper Doug Houston: "He was the most astute manager I ever played for. He brought out the best in players and Alex Kinninmonth and Alex Bryce, who had done little before his arrival, made tremendous progress under his management. Prentice was a tactician before his time and was one of the first in Scotland to use three at the back. When appropriate, Jim Steele, Iain Phillip and myself would defend with full-backs Bobby Wilson and Dave Johnston pushing forward to give a four-man midfield. It used to work a treat!"

However, at New Year, Dundee were brought back to earth when they lost 3-0 to league leaders Aberdeen up at Pittodrie

Loyal servant - Doug Houston was an influential figure at Dens.   DC Thomson

and two weeks later there was an astonishing 8-1 defeat by Celtic. Certainly it was true that the Dark Blues had not beaten the high-flying Parkhead side since August 1965, but, in league clashes at Dens, only one goal had separated the sides over the previous 11 years.

The Dundee boss accepted part of the blame. Prentice had believed that his much-improved

Driving force - Jim Steele leaps high to head home against Ayr United in a League Cup tie at Dens.   DC Thomson

team should "have a go" rather than employ their usual "hit-on-the-break" tactics against the pacy Parkhead men. Despite trailing 2-0, Dundee had played well in the first half but when Celtic got a third on the hour, the home side collapsed. Iain Phillip later recalled: "I will never forget that one, it was the Jimmy Johnstone show, he just ran amok and in that form the wee man was virtually unstoppable."

After five years at the top Celtic remained Scotland's outstanding team but Prentice stormed: "It was humiliating, no professional team should ever lose by seven goals." Dundee's struggles continued the following week although they did manage a 1-0 win over Division Two club Partick Thistle in the Scottish Cup.

With 19 minutes remaining, left-back Davie Johnston put Dundee ahead with a diving header but, with Thistle pressing hard there was an incredible let-off in the dying minutes. Donnie McKinnon's netbound header was clearly palmed over the bar by Bobby Wilson, but, quite amazingly, neither the referee nor his linesman had seen the incident and Thistle were out of the Cup, their angry protests ignored.

Even the Dens diehards sympathised with the unlucky men from Maryhill, and there was a storm of booing at full-time. Nevertheless, the Dark Blues were grateful to reach the second round and another goal by Johnston and one from his full-back partner Bobby Wilson earned a comfortable 2-0 win over Stirling Albion at Dens.

In the quarter-final, Dundee met a vastly improved Hibs at Easter Road. Former England international centre Joe Baker had been a great favourite a decade earlier and his Easter Road return had helped spearhead the recent Hibernian resurgence.

The match, which attracted an attendance of 21,710, proved to be hard and uncompromising and Phillip was moved from his usual position at sweeper to do a man-marking job on influential Hibs midfielder Pat Stanton. A running feud between Baker and the Dens defence culminated in Stewart going off injured and it was little surprise when the Hibs striker and Steele later found themselves in the referee's notebook. Just before half-time, Jimmy O'Rourke put Hibs ahead with a penalty and, with the Dens forwards

Dundee F.C. Season 1971-72 - (BACK) - Bobby Wilson, Iain Phillip, Mike Hewitt, Ally Donaldson, George Stewart, Dave Johnston, Jim McLean (coach). MIDDLE - John Prentice (manager), Bobby Robinson, Ian Scott, Jim Steele, Ron Selway, Duncan Lambie, Maurice Friel (physiotherapist). FRONT - Alex Bryce, John Duncan, Alex Kinninmonth, Doug Houston, Gordon Wallace, Jocky Scott, Jimmy Wilson.

unable to make any impression, there was no further scoring as Dundee tumbled out of the Cup.

Seven days later, the Dark Blues gained revenge with a 1-0 win over Hibs at Dens and, with only two defeats from their last nine games, they qualified for the following season's UEFA Cup (formerly the Fairs Cup) by finishing in fifth position in the league.

There was a new enthusiasm at Dens and at last there were signs that better times lay ahead. The Dark Blues had finished two points ahead of Dundee United but their rivals' recent 3-2 win at Dens now meant that Dundee had not won a league derby since September 1966.

In contrast, Dundee had enjoyed an impressive Dens record against Rangers in recent years and this ascendancy was maintained when Jocky Scott scored the only goal in their 1-0 win in April.

For years, Scott had been a player of tremendous potential and, assisted by the promptings of Wallace, he was now one of the most feared strikers in Scotland. Last season, Wallace had scored 23 goals to finish top scorer, with Scott contributing 11, but now Scott had managed 21 goals, with Duncan and Wallace chipping in with 15 and 14 goals apiece.

Scott's fine play had not gone unnoticed by Scotland boss Bobby Brown and in June the Dens attacker was called into the international squad. And, after appearing as a substitute in the 1-0 defeat by Denmark in Copenhagen, he excelled in a left-wing role against Russia in Moscow although Scotland again lost by the only goal.

However, these were to prove Bobby Brown's last games in charge. The new Scotland manager was none other than former Chelsea boss Tommy Docherty - the man who had released Scott from Stamford Bridge in 1964 - and, effectively, Jocky's international career was over.

That summer, Dundee participated in a mini-tournament in Portugal. Atletico Madrid were beaten 2-0 but defeats by Sporting Lisbon (0-1), and Norwich City (3-5), ended the Dens Park interest. For their pre-season preparations, the Dark Blues opted for a tour of Northern France and Belgium. All four games against Boulogne (3-0), Beerschot (2-1), La Louvieroise (2-1), and FC Liege (2-0) were won and John Prentice, who had used the trip to experiment with players and tactics was well pleased.

A dispute over a benefit payment had resulted in a Dens suspension for Ally Donaldson and former Hibs keeper Thomson Allan was signed after some impressive performances on the tour. Remarkably, Allan and two other signings - Falkirk midfielder Bobby Robinson and Dundee United striker Ian Scott - had been obtained on free transfers and all three would prove excellent acquisitions

Earlier, nine players, including the experienced Jim Easton, Jim Fraser, and Joe Gilroy had been released. Since John Prentice's arrival almost three years ago, no fewer than 28 players had been given free transfers, Perhaps significantly, twenty-one were youngsters who had never made the first team and there appeared to be serious doubts over the quality of the players now being produced by the Dens Park scouting system.

Spot king - Jocky Scott places a penalty behind Hamish McAlpine in the 6-4 win over United who are now wearing Tangerine. DC Thomson

A "new look" Dundee, now sporting a first-choice outfit of white jerseys, dark blue shorts and red socks, narrowly failed to qualify from their 1971-72 League Cup section containing Aberdeen, Clyde and Falkirk. Three points were taken from the section favourites Aberdeen but, despite finishing with eight points, it was the unfancied Falkirk who qualified with one point more.

After a three-year absence from Europe, Dundee met Danish side Akademisk Boldclub in the first round of the UEFA Cup. On September 15th, goals by Bryce (2), Wallace and Lambie brought a comfortable 4-2 first-leg victory at Dens before only 9,000, their lowest home attendance to date for a European tie. The Danes posed few problems in the Copenhagen return and, shortly after half-time Duncan scored the only goal with a header to give Dundee a 5-2 aggregate win.

"John Prentice and Jim McLean had developed a good partnership and there was a tremendous team spirit at this time," said Doug Houston. "McLean would do the shouting and bawling but Prentice was the unflappable type. He could see what was going on and adjust things with a few words at half-time."

At home, Dundee continued to impress and, by late October, they lay fifth having lost just twice in their opening seven games. On September 11th, two goals each by Bryce, Wallace and Jocky Scott brought an amazing 6-4 Dens triumph over Dundee United and, the following Saturday Gordon Wallace grabbed four in a 5-2 win over East Fife at

Methil to emphasise Dundee's progress.

Remarkably, the derby win was Dundee's first home success over Dundee United in the league since 1961. In the past, the close control and ball skills of Alex Bryce had often caused problems for United and the transfer-seeking midfielder, whose recent appearances had mainly been as substitute, was recalled for the derby. It was an inspired move and, with Bryce dictating play and carving through the visiting defence at will, Dundee led 2-1 at half-time.

Jocky Scott made it 3-1, cheekily delaying his scoring shot until challenged by three United defenders, and further goals by Bryce and Scott, with a penalty, made it 5-1 after 65 minutes. United pulled one back only for Wallace to make it 6-2 soon after. But, with a rout in prospect, Dundee took their foot off the pedal and the loss of two late goals took the shine off a brilliant display. "It could have been the biggest slaughter since the Little Big Horn," claimed Jocky Scott. "However, it was still a moment to savour for it ended a run of six successive derby defeats."

In October, Billy Steel made his first visit to Scotland since his departure in 1954. His return to his old stamping ground coincided with a 4-0 win over Falkirk and the old maestro declared himself "delighted" at his old team's performance.

In the second round of the UEFA Cup, Dundee were paired with old European Cup rivals Cologne. That term Mike Hewitt had been an ever-present in goal but Ally Donaldson had finally resolved his differences with the club and the more experienced keeper was recalled for the first leg in Cologne. In the first half, the Dark Blues were content to soak up the pressure although Lambie was unlucky to have a "goal" disallowed for pushing an opponent.

Just after the break, Cologne took a controversial lead when Rupp's short corner was dummied by Flohe only for

PEOPLE'S Journal

DUNDEE EDITION

No. 5939   Saturday, November 6, 1971   Price 2½p

● Dundee F.C. gave the greatest performance in their history with a fightback which flummoxed Cologne on Wednesday evening. So they deserve front page treatment.

THE WINNER!

● Duncan scores his hat-trick and the Dundee players tear back to the centre to try for another. And they got it (right).

NIGHT OF MADNESS!

" WE Shall Not Be Moved " echoed from the Dens dressing-room after that fantastic win over Cologne in the U.E.F.A. Cup on Wednesday evening.

The players were delirious; the fans were dancing and hugging one another on the terracing; " Hail, Hail, The 'Dee Are Here," echoed throughout the ground.

Dundee were back in the big-time again after the greatest game of the century at Dens Park.

DUNCAN SCORES HIS SECOND—IT'S 2 - 2 AND THE FIGHT - BACK IS ON.

Rupp himself to set up Sheermann to score! Two consecutive touches from a corner kick were not in the rule-book but the dummy had confused the referee as well as the Dundee defence and the goal stood. And despite a 75th-minute equaliser from Kinninmonth, Lohr got Cologne's winner, seven minutes from time.

Nevertheless, a disciplined display had given Dundee high hopes of overturning the 2-1 deficit and on November 3rd, an enthusiastic 15,500 Dens Park crowd saw them line up: Donaldson; B. Wilson, Johnston; Steele, Phillip, Houston; Duncan, Kinninmonth, Wallace, J. Scott, Lambie. Subs - I. Scott, J. Wilson.

Dundee stormed into attack and after a 12th-minute corner, Duncan levelled the scores with a header. The youthful home side continued to attack, but the Germans - inspired by the brilliant Overath - were a constant danger with their lightning attacks and goals by Simmet (35 mins) and Flohe (59), stunned the crowd to silence. Dundee now needed three goals to overcome Cologne's 4-2 aggregate lead.

In 69 minutes, Duncan pulled one back and, roared on by a vociferous home support, the big striker scored again with six minutes left. The scores were now level at 4-4 but, with away goals to count double in the event of a tie, the Dark Blues had to score again to stay in the competition.

U.E.F.A. CUP — THIRD ROUND, 2nd LEG
DENS PARK, WEDNESDAY, 8th DECEMBER, 1971
KICK-OFF 7.30 p.m.

DUNDEE   **A. C. MILAN**

THE LINE-UP

DUNDEE		A. C. MILAN
1	Hewitt	1 Codicini
2	R. Wilson	2 Sabadini
3	Johnston	3 Zignoli
4	Steele	4 Anguiletti
5	Phillip	5 Schnellinger
6	Houston	6 Biasolti
7	Duncan	7 Villa
8	Ford	8 Bennetti
9	Wallace	9 Bignon
10	J. Scott	10 Rivera
11	J. Wilson	11 Pragi

Shirts — WHITE   Shirts — BLACK and RED
Pants — WHITE   Pants — WHITE

Referee : Monsieur Wurtz
Linesmen : Monsieur Didier
Monsieur Petit

3

Another close thing - Doug Houston's long-range shot slips over the bar with AC Milan keeper Cudicini beaten.   DC Thomson

In a near-electric atmosphere there was now an almost continuous roar from the terracing. With three minutes left, substitute Jimmy Wilson was bundled off the ball and a penalty given. However, the Belgian referee was persuaded to consult a linesman and he changed his decision to a dropped ball.

Cologne were now under intense pressure and, 60 seconds later, Steele and Duncan both had shots cleared off the line before Bobby Wilson stepped in to crash home the winner! Amidst incredible scenes of joy, Dundee held on to win and later *The Peoples Journal* described the nerve-tingling contest as: "The greatest that century at Dens". Few who attended would have disagreed.

Dundee's next opponents were AC Milan, another of their European Cup foes from 1963, but only one player from each side remained from the previous clash. Doug Houston had played in both ties as had Milan's famous Italian international midfielder Gianni Rivera (29). In the first leg at the San Siro Stadium, Dundee employed a defensive formation - Iain Phillip playing as a sweeper behind a back four of Wilson, Stewart, Steele and Johnston and, despite the loss of an early goal, the tactic proved sound. However, shortly after half-time, a misunderstanding between Stewart and Donaldson saw the defender send the ball into an empty net and a third from Benetti gave Dundee an uphill task for the second leg.

In the Dens return on December 8th, Dundee showed two changes from the side that had beaten Cologne at home -

Stewart and Jimmy Wilson coming in for Johnston and Kinninmonth. A grimly determined Dundee besieged the visitors' goalmouth and in 38 minutes their persistence was rewarded when Wallace headed a Lambie cross past giant goalkeeper Cudicini. After the break, the relentless pressure continued but a rampant Dundee were unable to breach the well-organised Milan defence which wasted time at every opportunity.

Before the game, much talk had centred on the brilliant Rivera, but on the night the Italian star was eclipsed by the immaculate performance of Broughty Ferry boy Iain Phillip. Another to impress was the pacy Dens winger Duncan Lambie (19), who had been signed from Armadale Thistle earlier that year. The former Falkirk boot-boy emerged as a player who revelled in the big-match atmosphere and his direct running had given Milan all sorts of problems.

With 16 minutes remaining, he fired a shot from 30 yards and, although the ball rebounded from the post, John Duncan was on the spot to score. Urged on by the 15,500 crowd, the Dark Blues tried desperately for another to take the game to extra-time. In the end it was to no avail but Dundee's had been an exhilerating performance, well worthy of the crowd's standing ovation.

The game had been lost in Milan but, as the watching former Dens boss Bob Shankly later commented: "If Dundee had got the early goal they deserved they would have won hands down. The crowd gave them great support but how many will be at Dens for the next home game?"

CHAPTER FIFTEEN

Fortress Dens

Shankly's remarks were highly significant. Four days earlier, John Prentice announced that he would resign at the end of the year because of his increasing disillusionment with the game. He cited the constant battle against falling gates and the necessity of selling star players to balance the books. His future, would now, he believed, lie outwith football, and initially at any rate, in the family bagpipe-making business in Canada.

Davie White - was the new Dundee manager.

Since his arrival in October 1969, Prentice had moulded Dundee into a highly effective side. Players were introduced as part of an overall plan and, in youngsters like Steele, Phillip, Johnston, Lambie and Hewitt and shrewd signings such as Allan, Robinson, Ian Scott and, more recently, Bobby Ford, who had arrived from Falkirk in exchange for Alex Bryce, the Prentice legacy would prove a framework for future success.

Celtic's six-year dominance of the domestic game had seen gates tumble at other Scottish grounds and, two weeks later, the point Shankly had made was amply illustrated when only 4,800 passed through the gates for the visit of Kilmarnock. Previously, the Dens boss had been forced to part with George McLean and Steve Murray and now there were indications that the swashbuckling Jim Steele, recently included in Scotland's squad to play Belgium at Pittodrie, might also be allowed to go.

In his year and a half as coach, Jim McLean had become an equally influential figure. He was well respected for his knowledge of the game, and although he demanded much in terms of effort, the players had never been fitter. But, prior to the game in Milan the players had been told that McLean was to become manager of Dundee United, a decision hastened by McLean's continuing rift with directors James and Ian Gellatly.

McLean had seemed the logical choice as Prentice's successor but former Clyde and Rangers boss, Davie White was named as the new Dundee manager and, in a remarkable parallel with Reggie Smith's departure 17 years earlier, Jim McLean made the short trip to Tannadice.

McLean was bitter that his contribution to Dundee's revival had gone unrecognised and to make matters worse, he had previously clashed with White when both had played for Clyde - curiously under the management of John Prentice. However, it was Jim McLean's move to Dundee United rather than Davie White's arrival at Dens which would significantly alter the balance of power in the city for years to come.

Earlier that year, Ian Gellatly, the second son of Dundee chairman James Gellatly, had become a director following the death of secretary Bob Crichton, the board now consisting of both Gellatlys and well-known Tayside builder John Bett, who had been appointed in 1968.

Said Ian Gellatly: "We had known for a number of months that John Prentice wanted out of football. That was a blow because he and Jim McLean had done a good job and things were progressing nicely. We also knew that Dundee United were desperate to get McLean, whom we regarded as an excellent young coach."

"However, when we asked John Prentice whether he thought McLean was managerial material, his response was negative. You can only go on what the professionals advise you, but, unfortunately for us, McLean went on to prove himself the outstanding coach in Scottish football over the next 20 years."

Dons dumped - John Duncan runs through to beat Aberdeen keeper Bobby Clark with George Murray and Tommy McMillan helpless.

Air power - Ian Scott gave Dundee an added aerial threat and here he heads in a vital goal in the League Cup tie against Dumbarton.

Dundee's new management team of Davie White and his coach, former Rangers "iron-man" Harold Davis, took over on January 1st, 1972 and, after draws with Aberdeen (h) 1-1, Dundee United (a) 1-1, and East Fife (h) 0-0, high-scoring wins over Hearts (a) 5-2, and Ayr United (h) 5-1, took Dundee to fourth in the league.

The Dens euphoria was to be short-lived. It was little surprise when Ally Donaldson was sold to Falkirk for £10,000 but news that the popular Jim Steele gone to Southampton for £70,000 on January 24th came as a bitter blow. Earlier that month, Steele along with Hewitt and Phillip had appeared for Scotland's Under-23s against the West German Olympic XI but the red-headed midfielder had indicated his desire to move south should Dundee make a European exit.

Steele quickly made his mark at the Dell and played in Southampton's F.A. Cup winning team against Manchester United in 1976, to emulate other former Dens stars like Bill Brown, for 'Spurs v. Leicester City, (1961) and v. Burnley (1962), Jimmy Gabriel, for Everton v. Sheffield Wednesday (1966), Alan Gilzean, for 'Spurs v. Chelsea (1967), and Charlie Cooke - a loser in 1967 - for Chelsea v. Leeds (1970).

The Dens board looked to have been unduly hasty for gates had been showing an upward trend. In the Scottish Cup, a 3-0 win over Queen of the South at Dens set up a fourth-round clash against Celtic in Glasgow. A crowd of 47,000 saw Dundee make a bright start, but without the power and determination of Steele, they struggled after losing an early goal and, inspired by Kenny Dalglish, Celtic ran out 4-0 winners.

Nevertheless, Dundee recovered to make a strong challenge for a UEFA Cup place. On Monday, April 10th, headed goals by Ian Scott and Stewart earned a 2-0 win over Rangers at Dens to complete a league double over the Light Blues - cracking goals by Kinninmonth, Wallace and Johnston had earned them a 3-2 win in an Ibrox TV spectacular in November - but the loss of five home points from their last four games left Dundee three points adrift of fourth-placed Hibs.

Unlike the previous term, fifth place was insufficient to secure a European place and Aberdeen, Rangers and League Cup winners Partick Thistle would be Scotland's UEFA Cup representatives. Nevertheless, it had been another season of improvement with only seven games lost and a tally of 41 points - their highest since 1967. That form was continued on a close-season tour of New Zealand and Southern Australia, where the Dark Blues scored 53 goals as they recorded seven straight wins.

Earlier, Alex Kinninmonth, Ron Selway, George Falconer and Dave Soutar were named on Dundee's free transfer list and the only new signings were defenders Alec Pringle (23), and Bobby Mathieson (18), who had both been released by Hibs. Falconer, who had played alongside Wallace at Stark's Park, was signed from Raith Rovers for £5,000 in November 1970, but he made only one first-team appearance.

In the 1972-73 League Cup there was seeding for the first time, each section containing two teams each from Divisions One and Two with the top two sides qualifying for the second round. Dundee made a devastating start with John Duncan netting five in the 8-2 crushing of East Stirling at Firs Park. The pattern continued and wins over Clyde (h) 2-1, (a) 1-0, Motherwell (a) 3-1, (h) 2-1 and East Stirling (h) 3-0, saw the Dens men progress with a 100 per cent record.

With George Stewart suspended for the opening three games, Bobby Robinson had proved an excellent sweeper alongside Iain Phillip and when Stewart returned, a midfield place was found for the pacy ex-Falkirk man. In the second round, Dundee crashed to a shock 3-0 defeat at Dumbarton. But, inspired by the darting runs of Jocky Scott, there was a remarkable turnaround in the Dens return. Goals by Ian Scott (37 mins), and Wallace (50, 74) levelled the scores and, in a dramatic finale, Duncan netted the winner four minutes from time.

On September 16th, Dundee went down 2-1 in a scrappy Tannadice derby only to bounce back with a sensational 2-0 win over league leaders Celtic at Dens, their first home success against the Parkhead side since 1961. In recent years, Dundee had successfully utilised the height of Duncan, Stewart and Ian Scott at dead-ball situations and, once again, the tactic paid off. In eight minutes, Stewart flicked on a near-post corner by Jocky Scott for Ian Scott to head home and five minutes later, 19-year-old John Gray made it two.

Dundee's defence had been superbly marshalled by Iain Phillip but, astonishingly, the elegant defender was on his way to Crystal Palace for £95,000 just two days later. It was yet another devastating blow for the Dens Park fans. Last season, Phillip had appeared in the League international against England and was included in the full Scotland squad to play Peru at Hampden. Phillip and Steele had been recognised as the backbone of Dundee's much-improved side and now both were gone.

After Steele joined Southampton, Davie White had stated: "Although clubs cannot survive on gate receipts alone, there is no reason why any other top players should have to go." Clearly, the three-man board of James and Ian Gellatly and John Bett disagreed and, in their haste to sell, they were to stand accused of showing a sad lack of ambition.

Earlier that month, Dundee had beaten Norwich City 2-1 at Dens in the Texaco Cup but, without the composure of Phillip, they fell 2-0 at Carrow Road and went out 3-2 on aggregate. Phillip's departure had unsettled Jocky Scott and the influential midfielder, who was keen to have the security of a long term contract, demanded a transfer. However, there was no question of Scott being allowed to go and, with players like Allan, Robinson, Ford and Ian Scott breaking through, there remained a formidable squad at Dens.

On October 7th, Hibs, joint-leaders and holders of the Dryburgh Cup, were beaten 1-0 at Dens Park and a few days later a Gordon Wallace goal sealed a 1-0 win over Celtic in the first leg of the League Cup quarter-final. Dundee had always enjoyed a reputation for producing top-class goalkeepers and the red-shirted Thomson Allan served notice that he would maintain the tradition with a brilliant display against the eager Celtic attack.

In the Parkhead return, Dundee trailed 3-1 before Jocky Scott capped a tremendous fightback with a 25-yard scoring shot on the hour. That levelled the aggregate scores, but the drama continued into extra-time and, with no further score, it was agreed that Glasgow's Hampden Park would house the replay on Monday, November 20th.

In that game, after controlling the early play, Jocky Scott put Dundee ahead in 19 minutes. But, with Johnstone and Dalglish in tantalising mood, Celtic replied four times by half-time and there was no way back. Over the previous two years, Dundee's defensive play had shown a big improvement and, rather surprisingly, all Celtic's goals had come from high crosses.

The three ties with Celtic had attracted a total of 97,500 fans but, despite this additional income, there were no new signings. Instead, Davie White continued to blood reserves like full-back Bobby Mathieson, midfielders Alec Pringle and Ian Anderson and forwards John Gray, Ian Smith and Duncan McLeod.

Nevertheless, Dundee continued to prosper and, by early February, they lay fifth, a placing that might have been even higher but for a sticky period at the start of 1973. In the Ne'erday game at Pittodrie, the brilliant Hungarian, Zoltan Varga inspired the Dons to a 3-1 win. But, despite a comfortable 3-0 win over Dundee United at Dens - where two-goal John Duncan had outshone United's much-vaunted Andy Gray - valuable points were dropped in visits to the top two sides, Celtic (1-2), and Hibs (1-1).

In the Scottish Cup, a crowd of 10,618 saw Dundee win 3-0 at Dunfermline, who were back in Division Two for the first time since 1955. The next round involved a trip to far-off Stranraer where goals by Duncan (4), Wallace (3), Houston and Ian Scott ensured a 9-2 romp and, on March 17th, the Dens men met Montrose in the quarter-final. Before a Links Park record attendance of 8,893, Dundee crushed the battling "Gable Endies" and, now into the last four, the draw paired them with Celtic while Hearts and Rangers would contest the other tie.

Duncan, Wallace and Scott had continued their lethal scoring partnership and, by the time of the Hampden clash with

Something extra - Davie White appeals for greater effort as the League Cup-tie at Parkhead goes into extra-time. New Dens hero, keeper Thomson Allan, finds something to smile about but Celtic had the last laugh in the replay. DC Thomson

Near thing - Thomson Allan is beaten all ends up and Bobby Robinson, Bobby Wilson and Dave Johnston can only watch anxiously as this shot from Bobby Lennox zips over the bar in the Scottish Cup semi-final at Hampden. DC Thomson

Celtic, the trio had contributed 69 goals. Duncan alone had netted 39 and with recent 6-0 wins over Morton and Arbroath at Dens, the Dark Blues were confident of success.

There was only one change from the team which had lost 4-1 to Celtic at Hampden in November, Dave Johnston replacing Alec Pringle in defence as Dundee lined up: Allan; B. Wilson, Robinson, Stewart, Johnston; J. Wilson, Houston, J. Scott, I. Scott; Duncan, Wallace Substitute - Ford. Celtic: Hunter; McGrain, McNeill, Connelly, Brogan; Murdoch, Hay, Callaghan; Dalglish, Deans, Lennox. Substitute - Johnstone.

Although Dundee remained unbeaten at Dens all season, only three away wins had been recorded. They looked particularly vulnerable in the West and, sadly, this trend was to continue at Hampden. The high-scoring front men got little support from their overworked midfield and only a tremendous defensive display ensured a 0-0 draw before a crowd of 54,428. For the replay on Wednesday, April 11th, Bobby Ford replaced Jimmy Wilson while Billy Semple, recently signed on a free transfer from Rangers, won a seat on the bench.

In the first half, the pattern remained unchanged and, although Dundee looked more aggressive after the interval, the game again ended in stalemate. In extra-time, Jock Stein shrewdly switched George Connelly to midfield and, lifted by the promptings of the talented Fifer, goals by Johnstone (102 mins, 110) and Dalglish propelled the Parkhead side into the Scottish Cup Final.

The Dark Blues were sound defensively but, although recognised as one of the best footballing sides in Scotland, it was clear more dig and attacking pace were required to achieve any tangible success. Throughout the season, they had shown themselves to be past masters at pulling teams into a web of defensive covering before mounting deadly counter attacks. But, explained Dave Johnston: "It was the same old story in the important games against Celtic. We were powder-puff up front and rarely looked like scoring. Our only chance was to keep it tight at the back in the hope that we might snatch something."

Nevertheless, six points from their remaining four games enabled Dundee to finish fifth for the third successive season and, once again, they would compete in the UEFA Cup. John Duncan had finished Scotland's top scorer with 40 goals and in March, his exploits were rewarded with a Scottish League cap against the English League, the big striker responding with two goals in a 2-2 draw with strike partner Jocky Scott coming on as a substitute.

Earlier, however, Duncan, who was now playing out the option clause of his contract, had submitted a transfer request and another star seemed set to go. Dundee had taken big money from their lucrative cup runs, yet, rather than build on the current side, they were already planning to replace Duncan. A bid was made for Ally McLeod - top scorer in the Division Two - but the St Mirren striker chose instead to join Southampton.

However, it was not Duncan who was next to leave Dens Park. On the final day of the season, influential skipper Doug Houston (30), was the subject of a shock £30,000 move to Rangers. Just hours earlier, the long-serving midfielder had scored the equaliser in the 2-2 draw with Hearts at Dens but long-standing disagreements between the articulate midfielder, a qualified coach, and Davie White over coaching and tactics hastened his departure.

According to Dave Johnston: "Doug Houston and Gordon Wallace were great thinkers of the game and both were disciples of the Jim McLean way of thinking. There was no love lost between Davie White and Jim McLean and, perhaps understandably, Davie was resentful of McLean's continuing influence."

CHAPTER SIXTEEN

Hampden Glory

At the end of May 1973, the balance sheet had shown a £78,459 profit but only the sale of Phillip and Houston for £122,500 had prevented a substantial loss. That summer, abortive bids were made for Celtic's Harry Hood and Aberdeen's Steve Murray. Hood elected to remain at Parkhead and, although Dundee's £50,000 bid for Murray was accepted by the Pittodrie club, the former Dens skipper opted instead to join Celtic.

Nevertheless, there had been one significant arrival. Tommy Gemmell (28), had been signed on a free transfer from Nottingham Forest and Davie White was hoping the ex-Celtic and Scotland defender might provide the necessary leadership to win a major trophy.

From the start of that season, two substitutes would be allowed. And, in the League Cup, there would be an experiment whereby players could not be offside within the 18-yard box which would extend to both touchlines.

For the first time since its inception in 1971, Dundee had qualified for the Drybrough Cup which was contested by the four top-scoring teams in Divisions One and Two. An extra-time own-goal by former Dundee defender Ron Selway brought a 1-0 win over Raith Rovers at Dens but, in the semi-final, the Dark Blues crashed 4-0 in a disappointing performance against Celtic at Parkhead.

Undaunted, Dundee went on to qualify from their League Cup section. Bobby Wilson scored the only goal in a 1-0 opening day win over St Johnstone and victories over Partick Thistle (a) 3-0, (h) 4-0, and Hearts (h) 2-1, meant just one point from the game against nearest rivals Hearts at Tynecastle would take them through to the next stage. Alec Pringle was played as a sweeper behind the back four and, with Donald Ford and Drew Busby well policed, a 0-0 draw was achieved.

In the absence of the suspended Stewart, the injured Bobby Wilson, and Duncan who remained unsigned, the full depth and versatility of the squad had become evident. With Gemmell and Pringle solid down the middle, Robinson adopted a more constructive role in midfield. Last term, Ian Anderson (18), and John Gray (20), had made only fleeting appearances but both were now featuring more regularly.

Meanwhile, John Duncan had finally re-signed following Dundee's rejection of a £50,000 bid by Celtic. And although former Celtic and Crystal Palace forward John Hughes spent a trial period at Dens, he was not offered terms.

The second stage of the League Cup produced two thrilling ties with Dunfermline. A late strike by Gray gave Dundee a 3-2 win at East End Park and, although former stalwart Alex Kinninmonth twice equalised for the Pars in the Dens return,

Hot shot - John Duncan netted an impressive 40 goals in 1972-73 and here he heads for goal against St Johnstone at Dens. DC Thomson

Out first time - George Stewart gets in a header in the UEFA Cup tie against Dutch club Twente Enschede. BELOW - Tommy Gemmell in training with Thomson Allan, Bobby Robinson, George Stewart, Ian Scott, Mike Hewitt, Bobby Wilson and Duncan Lambie. DC Thomson

the Dark Blues went through to the quarter-finals, with a 5-4 aggregate scoreline.

Despite their League Cup progress, Dundee had taken only four points from their first seven league games. And although unbeaten in 29 home games over the previous 17 months, there had already been Dens defeats that season to Dundee United, East Fife and Celtic, all by the only goal.

Their unbeaten home record in Europe had also gone. On Wednesday, September 19th, a crowd of 11,210 saw the Dark Blues get a footballing lesson as they fell 3-1 to Dutch aces Twente Enschede in the first round of the UEFA Cup. On the half-hour, Allan raced 40 yards from goal only to be lobbed from near the halfway line. After the break, Stewart equalised with a header but, almost immediately, Twente regained their lead before adding a third near the end.

Sadly, a spectator had run onto the pitch and wrestled with a linesman, an incident which resulted in Dundee receiving a £1,370 fine. At this time Dutch football was at a peak and Twente, who included the brilliant Frans Thyssen, confirmed their superiority with a 4-2 win in Holland to qualify 7-3 on aggregate for the next round.

By mid-October, Dundee lay perilously near the foot of the league and to strengthen the team Iain Phillip was brought back from Crystal Palace for £40,500. Phillip had never settled in London but his Dens return sparked a revival with five successive wins over Arbroath (a) 4-2, Ayr (h) 2-1, Clyde (h) 1-0 (in the League Cup), St Johnstone (a) 4-1 and Dumbarton (h) 2-1.

In the first leg of the League Cup quarter-final, a Duncan goal gave Dundee a 1-0 win over Clyde following a dour struggle at Dens. There was far more action in the Shawfield return but, although Clyde twice drew level, Dundee slipped into the last four by the odd goal in five.

Celtic, Rangers and Kilmarnock were the other semi-finalists but, for once, fortune favoured the Dark Blues, who would meet Division Two side Killie with the Old Firm battling it out for the other place in the final. Ominously,

Dundee had just crashed 5-1 to Dunfermline at Dens. They had been without the injured Duncan, Wallace and Stewart but only Wallace was still missing from the Hampden semi-final clash with Killie on Wednesday, November 28th.

The miners' strike had developed into a national energy crisis that would soon bring down Edward Heath's Conservative Government but, despite some doubts over an evening kick-off, the game went ahead. The floodlights were powered by a generator producing only a third of the normal power and this heightened the eerie atmosphere amongst the sparse 4,682 crowd.

Dundee were slow to settle but, 10 minutes after the break, Gemmell broke the deadlock with a skidding shot which eluded Killie keeper Jim Stewart. The Ayrshire side continued to battle but, although Gemmell twice headed netbound shots off the line, the Dark Blues held on to win.

In the final, they would meet Celtic who had defeated Rangers 3-1. The Parkhead side had continued to dominate Scottish football and, with a cup record of nine wins, two draws and only one defeat against Dundee since 1966, they were strong favourites to take the trophy.

Once again, Stewart and Wallace were injury doubts but both were in Dundee's line-up for the League Cup Final on Saturday, December 15th: Allan; B.Wilson, Stewart,

Phillip, Gemmell (capt.); Duncan, Robinson, Ford, Lambie; Wallace, J. Scott. Subs - I. Scott, Johnston. Celtic: Hunter; McGrain, McCluskey, McNeill (capt), Brogan; Murray, Hay, Callaghan; Hood, Dalglish, Wilson. Subs - Johnstone, Connelly.

For days, there had been blizzard conditions all over Scotland and doubts over the game taking place continued right up to the unprecedented kick-off time of 1.30pm, brought forward to allow for extra-time in daylight if necessary. It had taken Dundee's coach three hours to reach Glasgow through snowbound roads and, as a result, the players pre-match meal had been a hurried affair.

Conditions were appalling with snow and sleet turning to driving rain which continued throughout the game. The pitch itself was bone hard with slush and pools of water later forming after relentless rain. It was also an uncomfortable afternoon for the fans - the terracings were a sea of mud and, outside Hampden, there were deep pools of slush and water.

Neither club wanted it played and, although referee Bobby Davidson deemed the game on, the 29,974 attendance was, not surprisingly, the lowest-ever for a League Cup Final.

Occasionally, players slipped and the ball would bounce and skid awkwardly, but, in the circumstances it was an entertaining game. There was a sharp contrast in style - Celtic wanting to run with the ball while Dundee opted for a more studied passing game. It was the Dark Blues who were more successful and, in the first half, they created four scoring chances to Celtic's one. After the interval, though, conditions

Magic moment - Gordon Wallace wheels to chest down Bobby Wilson's free-kick and tuck the ball beyond the reach of Celtic goalkeeper Ally Hunter for Dundee's winning goal in the 1973 League Cup Final at Hampden.
Glasgow Herald/Ron Hill

Another view of the Gordon Wallace winner with the Dundee players rushing to celebrate and the Celtic men barely able to believe it. The backdrop shows the sparse attendance brought about by the shocking weather and power crisis.   DC Thomson

It's Dundee's Cup - Tommy Gemmell receives the League Cup trophy as Thomson Allan celebrates.   Glasgow Herald

worsened and chances became few and far between.

Only 14 minutes remained when Bobby Wilson was fouled by Paul Wilson on the halfway line. The right-back took the kick himself and sent the ball curving towards Wallace just inside the Celtic box. The striker had his back to the goal and was surrounded by three Celtic defenders. But in one movement he took the ball on his chest before turning to sweep a low shot past the diving Ally Hunter.

Celtic tried to move up a gear, but Dundee were not to be denied although Murray went close. Near the end, Celtic appealed desperately for a penalty when Jimmy Johnstone went down in the box, but the referee was not impressed. The downpour had continued but, at the final whistle, there was no dampening the enthusiasm of the Dundee players and fans.

Thomson Allan had been immaculate in goal and, although Celtic had forced 13 corners to Dundee's five, most of the menace had come from the Dark Blues. Wallace had scored a memorable winner but when asked about his goal, he modestly declared: "Ach, I just turned and hit it!" Although Dundee's third League Cup success had been achieved by solid teamwork, the swashbuckling Tommy Gemmell had been an inspirational skipper. John Duncan had been a revelation in a deeper role on the right with Wallace and Phillip also outstanding.

Later the players, officials and their wives celebrated in Dundee's Angus Hotel, but half a dozen of the squad left the reception early to visit former Dens coach Jim McLean whom they believed had done so much to improve their game. "We felt it was a good idea at the time," said Iain Phillip. "But on reflection it was a silly thing to do. Davie White was pretty upset and later, we were all fined."

For too long, Dundee had existed in the shadow of illustrious predecessors, but since 1970 there had been a steady improvement. Now the breakthrough had been made and according to director Graham Thomson: "It was only the beginning." A local businessman, Mr Thomson and William Lyburn, a farmer, had been appointed to the board at the start of the season. Thomson talked of future plans for the club and over the next five years visualised that Dens Park would become an all-covered stadium with additional seating and much-improved snack bar and toilet facilities.

Seven days after the Hampden triumph, Dundee paraded the League Cup before the league game against Motherwell at Dens. However, it proved a disappointing afternoon as the visitors departed with a 1-0 win. A cold, swirling fog had limited the attendance to only 6,000 and, to complete their misery, Dundee skipper Tommy Gemmell was sent off after a heated exchange with a linesman.

GEMMELL-INSPIRED DUNDEE

CELTIC 0, DUNDEE 1.

Half-time 0-0. Scorer—Wallace (75 min.).

WE have copied the Continentals a lot in recent years. So maybe we should pick their brains a bit more and follow the example of those countries who have decided that all cup finals should be played in the spring or summer.

That way they get the kind of weather showpiece games deserve.

Having said that, let's now look at this Scottish League Cup Final.

It kicked off at the unearthly hour of 1.30 p.m. It was played in continuous sleet and rain. The pitch was bone-hard underneath, yet coated with a top of shallow mud. Not surprisingly in the circumstances, it attracted a crowd of less than 30,000.

All that must be kept in mind when trying to paint a

By Jack Harkness

picture of this Dundee-Celtic battle. Because it ruined any chance this game had of being a classic cup final.

That said, don't let us take any credit from Dundee. They deserved to win. Also the goal that mattered, scored by Gordon Wallace, was fit to win any game, anywhere.

MASTERPIECE

Dundee played it close. They worked in packs. So their short-passing game gave them less margin for error. In other words, on the treacherous surface, they had the ball much more often under control than Celtic.

The winning goal was a masterpiece.

Over came a free kick from Wilson. It dropped near Celtic's penalty spot. Gordon Wallace was facing his own goal when the ball came to him. But he whirled round like lightning and, on the turn, unleashed a terrific grounder which careered well out of Hunter's reach.

There were still 15 minutes to go. So Celtic brought on their subs. First Johnstone replaced the injured Harry Hood, then Connelly came on for David Hay, who had been seldom in the fray.

NO PENALTY

The Parkhead side began to look more dangerous than they had been all through. A Steve Murray header took the paint off the top of the bar. Then Johnstone tumbled in the box mid great roars for a penalty.

I thought it was a spot kick — until the Dundee men pointed out that Jimmy had been floored by one of his own players.

The general picture of the first half was of Celtic having corner after corner—yet the real near things were at Hunter's end!

STARS FOR MERIT

DUNDEE		CELTIC.	
★★★★	ALLAN	★★★	HUNTER
★★★★	WILSON	★★★★★	McGRAIN
★★★★★	GEMMELL	★★★	BROGAN
★★★★★	FORD	★★★★★	McCLUSKEY
★★★★★	STEWART	★★★★	McNEILL
★★★★	PHILLIP	★★★★★	MURRAY
★★★★★	DUNCAN	★★★★★	HOOD
★★★★	ROBINSON	★★	HAY
★★★★★	WALLACE	★★	WILSON
★★★★	SCOTT	★★★	CALLAGHAN
★★★★	LAMBIE	★★★	DALGLISH
★★★★	Referee — R. H.	Subs.—	
	DAVIDSON, Airdrie.	★★★	JOHNSTONE
		★★★	CONNELLY

In the first minute we got an example of the conditions the players were being asked to overcome.

Tommy Gemmell, off balance, kicked his own player, George Stewart, on the chin. Stewart had to go off and get a pad to stop the bleeding.

But it wasn't all crazy stuff like that.

There was the time Scott went right through the middle. When he was in danger of being crowded out, he cleverly back-heeled the ball into the tracks of Duncan. John's first-time sizzler went inches over the crossbar.

Then we had Duncan coolly beating Hunter in a race for the ball only to find Brogan popping up and scrambling it away for a corner.

Just on the interval, too, Ford lofted the ball over the bar from eight yards' range when it looked easier to score.

In all this, there wasn't much joy for Celtic. In fact, the biggest cheer which came from their fans all afternoon was when Jimmy Johnstone came on as substitute.

But even wee Jimmy needs the ball to show his wares. And, with Dundee continuing their possession football, opportunities coming the wee man's way were few and far between

MAN-OF-THE-MATCH

Also it must have been galling to the Celtic fans to see Tommy Gemmell stamp his personality so much on this final. It was the sort of occasion which suited big Tam's happy-go-lucky type of play.

His standard of performance, in addition to his leadership, made him, in my book, the player of the day.

Celtic's best were McGrain, McCluskey, McNeill, Murray and Hood. Their three inside men never really got to grips with the game.

Dundee hadn't a weakness. Playing almost above themselves were Gemmell, Stewart, Ford, Duncan and Wallace. But every man jack in the side played his part in taking the League Cup to Dundee.

But no more finals like this at Hampden, please.

Crowd—27,974.

CRIME COUNT.

CELTIC—11 fouls—11 points.
DUNDEE—11 fouls—11 points.

Printed and Published in Great Britain by D. C. Thomson & Co., Ltd., 144 Port Dundas Road, Glasgow G4 0HZ. Telephone 041-332

Dundee F.C. Season 1973-74 - League Cup winners and Scottish Cup semi-finalists - (BACK, left to right) Eric Ferguson (physio), Bobby Wilson, Dave Johnston, Iain Phillip, Thomson Allan, George Stewart, Bobby Robinson and Bobby Ford. FRONT - Davie White (manager), Jimmy Wilson, Ian Scott, Gordon Wallace, Tommy Gemmell, John Duncan, Jocky Scott, Duncan Lambie, Alec Pringle and Harold Davis (coach).

George Ashton

Razzle dazzle - Jocky Scott was at the peak of his form. SNS Group

At the turn of the year, a four-game unbeaten spell, including a 2-1 success against Dundee United at Tannadice provided an ideal build-up for the Scottish Cup. The continuing energy crisis and the resultant three-day week had brought the introduction of Sunday football. And, on Sunday, January 27th, 1974, Dundee faced a difficult tie at Aberdeen, where a turn-out of 23,574 was well up on the expected figure.

In 30 minutes, a long-range drive by Dave Johnston was deflected past a static Bobby Clark and Dundee were on their way. From then on, they were never seriously troubled, and a late goal by Robinson clinched a 2-0 win at a ground where they had not won since 1965.

With confidence high, successive Sunday wins over Partick (h) 4-1, and league leaders Celtic (a) 2-1, set the

Dens men up for their second-round clash with Rangers on February 17th. The popularity of Sunday football had brought a 50 per cent increase in gates in Scotland. There had been 40,000 fans for Dundee's visit to Parkhead, but even that was dwarfed by a near 65,000 crowd for the cup-tie at Ibrox the following Sunday.

Throughout the first half, Dundee came under pressure, but disciplined defensive work ensured the scoreline remained blank. Five minutes after the break, Jocky Scott scored from a Jimmy Wilson cut-back and the Dark Blues took control. They were brimful of confidence, and Rangers had no answer to their slick-passing movements as further goals by Duncan (70 mins, 76) put the result beyond doubt.

David Norrie, then 17 years old, was in the main stand that Sunday: "It was a fantastic experience although I only went at the last minute after my brother Scott took ill and I accompanied his pal on the bus. In the second half, Dundee took them apart. The movement off the ball and the controlled, precision passing was a joy to behold and of course Johnny Duncan and Jocky Scott were great finishers. At the start it looked like we only had a couple of hundred fans but by the end, it was clear that there were a good few thousand!"

In 1969, Davie White had been sacked from Ibrox despite two relatively successful years in charge. A sound tactician, the Dens boss would alter his side and tactics according to the opposition. He had anticipated that Rangers would make use of the high ball through the middle to Derek Parlane and his gamble on the aerial power of Stewart, recently recovered from a troublesome groin injury, had paid off handsomely. Now a strict disciplinarian, White claimed: "It is said we are slowly becoming a good team, but as far as I am concerned we already are!"

The quarter-final against Eddie Turnbull's Hibs - currently

Dundee have that double Cup look

DUNDEE EARN CUP-TIE

ABERDEEN 0, DUNDEE 2

ABERDEEN can have absolutely no complaints about elimination from the Scottish Cup. Dundee's victory—their first at Pittodrie since 1965—was thoroughly merited. On chances, the Dark Blues' winning margin could have been more pronounced.

The element of luck, which is inseparable from football, particularly of the cup-tie variety, contributed to Dundee's win in two important respects.

The visitors' opening goal came from a deflection off Dons' midfield man Jim Henry's legs and a second-half shot by Arthur Graham which was worthy of an upright and goalkeeper...

By Alastair Macdonald

RANGERS ARE WHITE-WASHED

By John Mackenzie

Rangers 0, Dundee 3. (H.T. 0—0)
SCORERS: Scott (50min.), Duncan (70, 76).

DANDY DUNDEE have done it again! Davie White's warriors not only bundled Rangers out of the Scottish Cup yesterday, they left the Ibrox men ragged and demoralised.

And yesterday's famous victory followed hard on the shock defeat of Celtic at Parkhead last week.

The Dens Parkers have declared that the football world must now sit up and take notice.

Almost 40,000 fans turned out on a glorious Sunday afternoon, and it's tragic that this pitifully poor Rangers team did nothing to maximise the impression that it would be worth while coming here.

All the skill, competence and flair came from a Dundee team that seemed to sense early in the game that they had only to keep on playing football to gain disillusioned Rangers apart.

It was going. And how magnificently it got there.

It's a grim-faced Rangers manager Jock shakes hands with Dundee manager after the match at Ibrox.

Persistence

The Sunday Post, March 10, 1974. 35

15 ELECTRIFYING MINUTES

HIBS 3, DUNDEE 3.

Scorers—Hibs—Gordon (3). Half-time 0-1. Dundee—J. Scott (24), Wilson (31), Duncan (34).

IMAGINE a football match on TV—but played at twice the normal camera speed! Then that was Easter Road, that was.

It finished up a draw. The fairest verdict, because both teams fully deserved to fight it out again.

From start to finish both sides went at it hell and... at times maybe more body...

Two minutes later Cropley was booked for a foul on Ford. Sixty seconds later Gordon put Hibs into the lead with a great header.

Hibs fans were still cheering this goal when, lo and behold, Jimmy Wilson brought them back to earth with a smashing shot from 25 yards.

But there was more — much more — to come.

In 54 minutes John Duncan shot Dundee into the lead again with a low 18-yarder.

JACK HARKNESS'S

Just four minutes later Alan Gordon notched his hat-trick amid amazing scenes of excitement. This goal was almost a side-footing home a...

"Bring On The Celtic"

A DENS PARK GALA NIGHT TO REMEMBER

AS vital statistics, 25—31—40 is not a combination calculated to win Miss World competitions—or make men leave home.

As vital minutes in time on the way to a Scottish Cup semi-final with Celtic, they will ever be remembered by Dundee fans sent home happy last night.

For it was in the 25th, 31st and 40th minutes of their replay with Hibs at Dens Park that Dundee climaxed brilliant play to demolish their visitors.

After full-back Wilson struck again in that 40th minute, rushing in on an advance of incredible speed and precision, Hibs looked a punch-drunk party.

WHILE after the interval they were allowed to raise something of a gallop—Dundee having become more security-minded—skipper Stainson and his men were patently afflicted by a hangover.

They had lost faith in themselves and showed it by careless squandering of free kicks and haphazard...

Dundee cup magic - Bobby Robinson (top) nets against Aberdeen, while Bobby Wilson makes it 3-0 against Hibs to clinch a semi-final place.

second in the league - produced an electrifying encounter for the 28,236 Easter Road crowd. Jocky Scott gave Dundee a half-time lead but, within 15 minutes of the restart the lead changed twice before Alan Gordon completed his hat-trick to make it 3-3! Hibs had played their part in a footballing fiesta, but according to Scotland boss Willie Ormond: "Dundee were currently the best side in Scotland."

Dundee's Scottish Cup run had caught the imagination of the footballing public. After an earlier postponement due to the waterlogged pitch, it was like the good old days when a bumper crowd of 30,881 rolled up to the Dens replay on Monday, March 19th. There were long queues at every gate, with many unable to gain admission until half-time.

By then, however, the game was all but over. Deadly

finishing by Jocky Scott (25 mins), Duncan (31), then Bobby Wilson (40), had put Dundee 3-0 ahead and, with no further score, they joined Celtic, Dundee United and Hearts in the last four of the tournament.

The Dark Blues had lost only twice in 15 games since their Hampden triumph in December and there was now a firm belief that they could also go on to win the Scottish Cup. However, the semi-final draw decreed that Dundee would again meet old adversaries Celtic on Wednesday, April 3rd, with outsiders Dundee United and Hearts also meeting at Hampden three days later.

Dundee had won their previous two clashes with Celtic and, following a 5-1 win at Dunfermline four days earlier, they were again confident of success. Gordon Wallace, only recently recovered from injury, was on the bench alongside Alec Pringle, and the inclusion of Jimmy Wilson was the only change from the League Cup winning side.

Deadly - Jocky Scott scores Dundee's second goal against RWD Molenbeek in the UEFA Cup but it was the slick Belgians who went through. BELOW - Dundee's Scotland international keeper Thomson Allan saves as John Greig of Rangers moves in. DC Thomson

This time Celtic - for whom, once again, the midweek semi-final was virtually a home game - were not prepared to allow Dundee the time and space for their usual short-passing game and the Dens forwards made little headway against some fierce tackling.

On countless occasions, Jimmy Johnstone had tormented the Dundee defence and just before half-time he capped another dazzling display by netting the only goal of the game. Sadly, it was Dundee's worst display in months and their bitter disappointment was compounded when city rivals United reached the final on beating Hearts 4-2 after a replay.

It had been a long season, but although 11 league games remained, there was little incentive for the Dark Blues, whose League Cup win had already ensured them a place in the UEFA Cup. A 2-1 win over Rangers at Ibrox ensured that they again finished fifth in the league but Dundee's five-year supremacy over the Light Blues finally ended with a 3-2 defeat on April 29th.

Nevertheless, it had been a successful season and another highlight was the international recognition afforded to two of the club's outstanding players. In March, Thomson Allan (28), made his Scotland debut against West Germany in Hamburg, with Bobby Robinson, who had earlier appeared for the Scotland Under-23s against Wales, coming on as substitute for Kenny Dalglish.

Allan, Robinson, Duncan and Jocky Scott were all named in Scotland's 40-strong preliminary squad for that summer's World Cup Finals in West Germany. Scott, who earlier had been favourably compared with the great Johann Cruyff by an English scout, was in great form but Allan, who gained a second cap against Norway in early June, was the only Dens player to make Scotland's final twenty-two.

As the 1974-75 season approached, there was a feeling of keen anticipation amongst the Dens fans. John Duncan and George Stewart, who were two of Dundee's key men, had recently signed four-year contracts and long-term prospects appeared bright. The League Cup success, the thrilling Scottish Cup run and the progress of Allan and Robinson to full international level had brought credibility and now Dundee were tipped for further honours.

Of the nine players released, only John Gray and Ian Smith had started a first-team game. May's balance sheet had shown a £93,436 loss, but although a bid was made for Jim O'Rourke of Hibs, the out-of-favour striker chose to join St Johnstone - and there were no major signings.

In the Dryburgh Cup, John Duncan netted all three goals in Dundee's 3-2 extra-time win over Queen of the South at Palmerston before 22-year-old Bobby Hutchinson was signed for £20,000 from Montrose after Gordon Wallace's leg break in pre-season training. The striker made a scoring debut in the Drybrough Cup semi-final against Celtic at Dens and it seemed that his 60th minute goal would be the winner. But, 30 seconds from the end, a slack Gemmell pass allowed Paul Wilson to equalise and Celtic went on to win 2-1 in extra-time.

Dundee's reign as League Cup holders was to prove short-lived. They displayed little of the previous season's flair and only four points were taken from Hibernian, Rangers and St Johnstone. In recent seasons, the Easter Road side had been one of Scotland's top clubs and, after winning the section, they went on to reach the final.

Early league form was disappointing with three defeats, including a 3-0 trouncing away to Dundee United, in the opening five games. The Tannadice derby had kicked off at 6.30pm on the Saturday evening to avoid clashing with the Leuchars Air Display and the Benson and Hedges Golf Tournament which was being held at St Andrews. In the event, the 11,000 crowd was down on figures for recent seasons and a lethargic looking Dundee were well beaten.

Throughout the 1960s and early '70s attendances in Scotland had continued to fall. There had been frequent discussions on league reconstruction but these had always been blocked by smaller clubs. However, clandestine meetings by Scotland's "big six" of Rangers, Celtic, Hearts, Hibs, Aberdeen and Dundee had brought the threat of a breakaway league and finally it was agreed that a 10-10-14 set-up would commence in season 1975-76 with all clubs now able to channel their energies into competing for places in the new leagues.

In the first round of the UEFA Cup, Dundee met the Belgian side RWD Molenbeek and a solid defensive display in the Brussels suburb left them with a far from unsurmountable 1-0 deficit for the Dens return on October 2nd.

There, Duncan levelled the scores with a 12th-minute header, but it was not long before the classy Belgians took control. Teugels and Beskamp gave them a 3-1 aggregate lead at half-time, but Jocky Scott pulled one back when Dave Johnston's free-kick slipped through the defensive wall. The 9,709 crowd provided great support but, although Dundee continued to press, two goals by Wellens in the last 21 minutes gave Racing White a 5-2 aggregate win.

As expected from a team containing nine internationals from Belgium, Holland and Denmark, Racing White were well organised and extremely dangerous on the break, but Dundee's defence had struggled badly without the injured George Stewart. Sadly, director John Bett took ill at the game and his death shortly afterwards reduced the board to four - James and Ian Gellatly, Graham Thomson and William Lyburn.

It was to prove Dundee's last European night for 29 years and, alarmingly, much of the sparkle of recent seasons had gone. Wallace had been badly missed, and with Duncan plagued by a groin injury and Hutchinson still finding his feet, the Dark Blues had struggled to find the net.

Just 14 months earlier, John Duncan had settled his differences and signed a long-term contract. Now, he again demanded a move and when he asked to be left out of the side, Dundee reluctantly agreed to his transfer. On October 17th, 10 years after the departure of Alan Gilzean, Duncan followed in his hero's footsteps and joined Tottenham Hotspur for a new Dens record fee of £140,000.

This came as a big blow to the club and there had also been a flurry of other moves. Duncan Lambie, who had never realised his earlier potential, was sold to St Johnstone for £15,000. Alec Pringle went to Clyde on a free transfer and reserve keeper Mike Hewitt moved to U.S. club Tampa Bay for £2,500. Earlier, Dundee had paid £5,000 for Brechin City keeper Eric Martin and, in mid-October, the Falkirk winger Wilson Hoggan (26), was signed for a fee of £35,000.

Season 1974-75 Price 6p
DUNDEE F.C.
Official Programme and Club News
Dens Park, Dundee

Ian Scott assumed Duncan's role as main striker before he in turn was replaced by the bustling Bobby Hutchinson. By mid-December, Dundee lay sixth and with goals in short supply, the highly experienced Hibs striker Alan Gordon (30), was signed for a fee of £12,000. The new man made his debut as a half-time substitute against league leaders Celtic at Dens. However by then the Parkhead side led 3-0, and inspired by three-goal Kenny Dalglish, they went on to win by six goals to nil.

Off the field, at any rate, the club appeared to be moving in the right direction and in December, the new Dundee F.C. Social Club, described as the finest club premises in town, was opened in Thistle Street, just a goal kick away from Dens Park.

On January 4th, 1975, Gordon Wallace made a welcome comeback against Dundee United at Dens. George Stewart ensured that United's highly rated young striker Andy Gray was given little chance to shine and Wallace's clever distribution and unselfish running was another major factor in Dundee's 2-0 success.

The return of Wallace heralded a resurgence in the team's fortunes. By mid-March, the Dark Blues had lost only one of their previous 11 games and had again reached the semi-final of the Scottish Cup. In the opening rounds, there were awkward away ties against Clyde and St Johnstone but well-taken goals by Alan Gordon and Ian Anderson brought 1-0 wins to take Dundee through to the last eight.

Cracking goal - Bobby Hutchinson fires Dundee in front against title-chasing Rangers at Dens with Ibrox keeper Stewart Kennedy and Tom Forsyth helpless . Fotopress

Cup joy - Gordon Wallace celebrates with Bobby Robinson and Ian Anderson in the tie against Hearts but once again Celtic would prove the stumbling block.   DC Thomson

On March 8th, 27,000 saw a quarter-final thriller between Dundee and Hearts at Tynecastle. Most of the accomplished football came from Dundee but only a last-gasp header by Wallace secured a 1-1 draw. In the Dens replay, a 22,197 crowd had to wait half-an-hour for the first goal when Stewart headed Dundee into the lead from a corner.

Two minutes later, Hoggan outpaced the Hearts defence for Hutchinson to add a second. Ralph Callachan then pulled one back with a penalty and, just on half-time, Drew Busby headed a sensational equaliser. After the break, play raged from end to end but in 59 minutes, Wallace sprung the offside trap and Robinson volleyed in the decisive goal.

For the third successive season, fate conspired to pair Dundee with Celtic in the semi-final. Again they would play at Hampden in midweek, with the weaker sides, Airdrie and Motherwell, meeting at the same venue three days later. By the night of the Hampden clash on April 2nd, Dundee remained sixth, but their UEFA Cup hopes had faded after taking only four points from Rangers (h) 1-2, Clyde (a) 1-0, St Johnstone (a) 1-3, and Dumbarton (h) 2-1.

Hutchinson opened the scoring against Rangers in 90 seconds. But, despite Colin Stein being sent off in the first half - an incident which caused widespread crowd trouble - the league leaders recovered to win 2-1. It was a crucial result for the Light Blues who were destined to go on to take

the title, bringing to an end Celtic's famous nine-in-a-row run of flag triumphs.

Central defender Alec Caldwell and midfielder or defender Ian Anderson, both only 19 years old, were now featuring regularly in the side and, in February, the cultured Anderson was included in the Scotland Under-23 squad to play in Wales. Veteran winger Jimmy Wilson (33), was now no longer in the first-team picture and, in March, he joined Division Two club Falkirk on a free transfer.

After a three-month absence, Iain Phillip had returned against Dumbarton but a recurrence of his foot injury ruled him out of the semi-final with Celtic. There were 40,720 at Hampden as the teams lined up - Dundee: Allan; Wilson, Anderson, Stewart, Gemmell; Robinson, Ford, J. Scott, Hoggan; Wallace, Hutchinson. Subs - Gordon, Johnston. Celtic: Latchford; McGrain, McNeill, Connelly, McCluskey; Glavin, Hood, Callaghan; Dalglish, Lennox, Wilson. Subs - Johnstone, MacDonald.

The Parkhead side were no longer the invincibles of old, and with the brilliant Dalglish effectively shadowed by Ford, Robinson and Scott spearheaded several lively attacks in a bright opening 20 minutes for Dundee. Celtic's defence had looked shaky, but with a lack of penetration up front, the Dens men began to over-elaborate in midfield and the initiative was lost.

After half-time, play became scrappy but, in 58 minutes, Ronnie Glavin broke the deadlock when he robbed Gemmell to send a low shot past Allan from 12 yards. Shortly afterwards, Gordon replaced Hutchinson, but apart from a late desperate flurry, the Dark Blues were unable to maintain their attacking momentum.

In recent years, Dundee had too often failed when the chips were down, and once again, the glamour of a Scottish Cup Final appearance had eluded them. The Dark Blues played some clever football but only Bobby Ford had stamped his authority on the game.

Revenge was gained with a 2-1 win over Celtic at Parkhead, but although a Premier League place was ensured by finishing sixth, there would be no European football the following season.

Although Thomson Allan and Bobby Robinson were omitted from Scotland's European Championship squads in the autumn, Allan was in the travelling party to Spain in February, while Robinson gained further caps against Sweden (a), Northern Ireland (h), and as a substitute against Romania (a).

Bobby Robinson - Dundee and Scotland midfielder

In the close season there were changes to the backroom staff. Harold Davis had been a strict disciplinarian but now he departed to set up a hotel business in the North of Scotland. Hugh Robertson was promoted to first-team coach with George Blues taking charge of the second string. And, after three successive Scottish Cup semi-final defeats, Davie White warned that the playing staff would also have to be reshaped.

CHAPTER SEVENTEEN

Premier Torment

Several youngsters were given their chance on the pre-season tours of Sweden and the Scottish Highlands in which all six games were won. There were encouraging performances from right-back John Martin and midfielder Gordon Strachan and the 18-year-olds were again prominent in Dundee's 2-1 win over Arsenal on the new £12,000 playing surface at Dens. For the past two seasons, the red-headed Strachan had been voted Scotland's outstanding reserve player. Now he had outshone the former England World Cup-winning midfielder Alan Ball and many likened him to a youthful Billy Bremner.

However, the Dark Blues then fell 2-1 on aggregate to Motherwell in the preliminary round of the Anglo-Scottish Cup and failed to make any impact in their League Cup section containing Hibs, Ayr United and Dunfermline. The Easter Road side, league runners-up for the past two seasons, topped the section, but a jaded Dundee could only manage four points to finish third and Dens boss Davie White admitted that too heavy a pre-season programme had been undertaken.

Ian Scott was no longer in the plans and although it was no surprise when he was released at his own request, Jocky Scott was the subject of a shock move to Aberdeen. The £40,000-rated midfielder who had been at Dens since 1964 moved to his home-town team in exchange for Dons left-winger Ian Purdie (22), plus £15,000.

Now came the start of the new 10-team Premier League. Each club would play the others four times, but with two sides to be relegated, many felt the penalty for failure to be too harsh. Dundee United boss Jim McLean was amongst those who favoured a 12-12-14 format, and he predicted that there would be an increased emphasis on defensive football.

On top of a basic wage of £60 per week, the Dundee players would get £5 appearance money, with a £30 win bonus and an additional £10 for each successive victory. And although considerably less than the £100 per week paid by the Old Firm, this compared favourably with other clubs.

On August 31st, Dundee made a promising start with a 3-2 win over Aberdeen at Dens. Bobby Ford's 90th-second goal proved to be the first in the Premier League, and although the Dons led 2-1 at half-time, late goals by Tommy Gemmell (82 mins, pen) and Wilson Hoggan (88), clinched the points for the strong-running Dark Blues.

History in the making - the first goal in the Premier League and the scorer is Dundee's Bobby Ford as he leaves Willie Miller stranded to head the ball past static Aberdeen keeper Bobby Clark.

DC Thomson

Despite a disappointing 6,067 attendance, the game had been a superb advertisement for the Premier League, but Dundee were soon to discover just how volatile the new set-up could be. By October 4th, defeats by Celtic (a) 0-4, Hearts (h) 2-3, and Ayr United (a) 1-2, and draws against Rangers (h) 0-0, and Hibs (a) 1-1, left them bottom, before wins over St Johnstone (h) 4-3, and Dundee United (a) 2-1, bounced them back up to sixth place just three points behind league leaders Celtic!

In both Tayside derbies, Dundee had come from behind to grab a late winner and each time Gordon Wallace had netted a vital counter. The following week, he again scored against high-flying Motherwell at Dens, but a series of defensive blunders saw Willie Pettigrew net four as the Fir Parkers departed with a 6-3 win.

After a quarter of the programme, Dundee remained sixth but, with the defence creaking alarmingly, 22 goals had been lost. Initially, George Stewart had been partnered by Iain Phillip or Bobby Robinson, but the return of the experienced Gemmell allowed Robinson - the subject of interest by Rangers - to revert to midfield alongside Strachan and Ford. An improvement brought excellent home wins over strong-going Celtic (1-0), and Hibernian (2-0) and, although lying seventh at the halfway stage, only another eleven goals had been conceded.

At the turn of the year, the defensive problems returned with a real vengeance when nine goals were lost in three successive matches against Motherwell (a) 2-3, Aberdeen (h) 1-3, and Celtic (a) 3-3. That was the signal for Davie White to ring the changes and, on January 10th his decision to field five players under the age of 21 - Derek Laing, Dave McIntosh, George Mackie, John Martin and Gordon Strachan - was rewarded with a 4-1 win over Hearts at Dens Park.

The promise was short-lived and, after a 3-1 defeat at Ayr, Dundee made a shock Scottish Cup exit to First Division leaders Falkirk at Dens. On the snow-cleared surface, Laing gave Dundee the best possible start with a goal in 30 seconds, but the Bairns recovered to win 2-1, with former Dark Blue Jimmy Wilson netting the decisive goal. Davie White was scathing in his post-match comments and he complained bitterly about the team's "sheer lack of character".

With reserve keeper Eric Martin set to emigrate to South Africa, Dundee paid £7,000 to bring 32-year-old Ally Donaldson back to Dens. Thomson Allan remained Dundee's number one keeper, but, along with Bobby Robinson, his international career had made little progress. In December, he was on the bench for the game against Romania at Hampden but, despite an injury to the established custodian David Harvey, it was Partick Thistle's Alan Rough who went on to establish himself as Scotland's top keeper over the next seven years.

Bobby Robinson had been named in Scotland's squad for Denmark but he was forced to withdraw through injury. And, with Bruce Rioch, Archie Gemmill, Asa Hartford, Graeme Sounesss and Kenny Burns all competing for midfield places, his international days were also over.

For months, Dundee United and Ayr had been favourites to accompany struggling St Johnstone to the First Division. At the end of January, Dundee lay seven points clear of ninth-placed Dundee United but, by early April, the Premier League had become a nightmare for the Dens Park club. Over that six-game spell, United had taken eleven points, Ayr, Hearts and Dundee had managed four and Aberdeen

DUNDEE v CELTIC

Monday 1st December 1975

Bobby Wilson's Testimonial Game

SOUVENIR PROGRAMME

Price 20p

The winner - Celtic left-back Jim Brogan and keeper Peter Latchford are flat out as Bobby Robinson rushes to celebrate his goal with Gordon Wallace in the 1-0 win at Dens Park.

DC Thomson

just two. And, with five games remaining, the Dark Blues lay in ninth place although only three points separated them from the next four clubs.

On April 3rd, a disjointed Dundee had lost 2-1 in a crucial "four-pointer" against fellow-strugglers Ayr at Dens. Many believed that Ayr would be the club to go down but, significantly, the Dark Blues had failed to win any of their six clashes with the Somerset Park men that term. The injured George Stewart had been badly missed and although he returned against Ayr, a recurrence of his groin complaint ruled him out for the rest of the season.

The slump continued with a 3-0 defeat at Ibrox but, encouragingly, reserve centre-half John McPhail had performed solidly after substituting for Caldwell in 20 minutes.

The strapping youngster retained his place but the jittery Dark Blues could only manage 1-1 draws with Hibs at Dens and with the already-doomed St Johnstone at Muirton. Ironically, Saint's equaliser came from Ian Anderson, who had joined them for £10,000 after failing to hold his place at Dens.

That season, Davie White had used no fewer than nine youngsters from his highly successful reserve team. They were defenders John Martin, Dave Mackie and John McPhail, midfielders Gordon Strachan, Dave McIntosh and Tom Hendrie, and front men Derek Laing, Mitch Bavidge (a £2,000 signing from Huntly at the start of the season) and Eric Sinclair.

Derby winner - Eric Sinclair's looping header beats Dundee United keeper Hamish McAlpine all ends up to give the Dark Blues a vital derby win at Dens. DC Thomson

Of those, Martin and Strachan had shown most progress. The attack-minded Martin was being groomed as successor to the long-serving Bobby Wilson (32), whose Testimonial against a Celtic select at Dens in December had attracted a crowd of 5,790 - but it was the elusive Strachan who quickly endeared himself to the fans with his trickery and apparently boundless energy.

Earlier that season, many established Dens stars, including Robinson, Phillip, Wilson, Wallace and Gemmell had been dropped, but the mounting pressure saw White revert to his most experienced side. In February, a late Tom McAdam goal had given Dundee United a 1-0 win over Dundee at Tannadice but the Dens derby clash on Wednesday, April 21st was now crucial to both city clubs.

Top scorer Gordon Wallace was out with an injured knee as Dundee lined up: Allan; Wilson, McPhail, Gemmell, Johnston; Hoggan, Phillip, Ford; Hutchinson, Sinclair, Purdie. Subs. - Martin, Bavidge. Dundee United: McAlpine; Rolland, Houston, Narey, Kopel; Forsyth, Fleming, Rennie; Hall, Hegarty, McAdam. Subs. - Copland, Reid.

Amidst a tension-ridden atmosphere nearly 14,000 saw a fiercely contested game. Just before half-time, Eric Sinclair was brought down in the box and Gemmell crashed home the resultant penalty. Shortly after the break, Sinclair headed a second and, although United pulled one back 15 minutes from time, the Gemmell-inspired Dundee survived a nailbiting finish.

Having trailed their city rivals by a point prior to kick-off, it had been a massive two points for the Dark Blues. Three days later they travelled to fourth-placed Motherwell but although Davie White's men went ahead through a 14th-minute goal by Bobby Hutchinson, former Hibs and Arsenal winger Peter Marinello levelled the scores.

Super Sinclair - the Dens youngster has just headed the winner against Motherwell in the last game of the season. It was a brave performance but Dundee were to lose their Premier League place on goal-difference.   DC Thomson

Normally, it would have been an excellent result but, elsewhere, wins for Aberdeen, Hearts and Ayr had taken the Dons and Hearts beyond Dundee's reach. Certainly, Dundee United had lost 1-0 at home to Rangers but four days later, they took advantage of their game in hand to leap-frog the Dark Blues with a 2-0 home win over Hibs at Tannadice.

Wizard - Gordon Strachan thrilled the Dens Park fans

On Saturday, May 1st, Dundee were unchanged for the third successive game as they wound up their campaign against Motherwell at Dens. A win was essential and backed by tremendous vocal support from the 7,661 crowd, the buoyant Dark Blues attacked from the start.

Ten minutes after half-time the pressure paid off when Sinclair headed Purdie's perfectly flighted free-kick past Stewart Rennie. There was no further scoring and, when news of Ayr's 5-3 home defeat by Celtic came through, there were wild celebrations on the terrracings.

Now, Dundee could only sweat it out in the hope that Ayr or Dundee United might slip up in their final fixture. However, it was not to be. On May 3rd, Ayr beat Motherwell 2-1 at home and, two days later, Dundee United battled their way to a shock 0-0 draw with Rangers at Ibrox, a result all the more surprising considering Rangers had won the domestic "treble".

Those results left Ayr two points ahead with Dundee, Dundee United and Aberdeen all on 32 points. But, with an inferior goal-difference, largely down to the loss of 62 goals, it was the Dark Blues who took the drop.

Ian Gellatly, who, in recent months had taken over as chairman from his ailing father James Gellatly, had been at Ibrox: "It was sheer agony that night and little did I know that game was to put Dundee into such decline. We had never been out of the top six over the past six seasons, and I thought we had as good a group of players as anyone."

A late resurgence had brought seven points from the last five games and if the same attitude had been displayed throughout the season, there would have been no question of relegation. The Premier League had proved fiercely competitive and Dundee's realisation that skill would have to be sacrificed for a tougher approach had come too late.

Certainly, the defence had been shaky for much of the season but matters had not been helped by a string of injuries to key men like Robinson, Stewart, Phillip, Hutchinson and Strachan. Davie White had used a total of 24 players throughout the season but there had only been a settled side towards the end of the campaign.

In retrospect, too many youngsters had been brought in and it could also be claimed that the departure of the experienced Jocky Scott, still just 28 and destined to play his part in Aberdeen's 1976 League Cup triumph, had been premature.

Few could argue that good fortune had deserted Dundee in the last desperate days of the relegation struggle. On April 28th, Ayr's home game against Motherwell was postponed when the Scottish League accepted the Somerset Park club's appeal that eight of their players were injured. And, when the game was played five days later, Motherwell had little incentive, having seen their UEFA Cup hopes disappear with that 1-0 defeat at Dens.

Premier League 1975-76							
(Bottom Placings)							
	P	W	D	L	F	A	Pts
Hearts	36	13	9	14	39 - 45		35
Ayr Utd	36	15	5	16	48 - 57		35
Aberdeen	36	11	10	15	49 - 50		32
Dundee Utd	36	12	8	16	46 - 48		32
Dundee	36	11	10	15	49 - 72		32
St Johnstn.	36	3	5	28	28 - 79		11

In addition, 'Well's top scorer Willie Pettigrew had not played. He, along with Tom Forsyth, Colin Jackson and Derek Johnstone of Rangers, was in the Scotland squad preparing for the Home international series, which began on May 6th against Wales at Hampden.

The Scottish League requested that the players be released in order that Dundee's relegation rivals, particularly Dundee United, would not face weakened sides. In their wisdom the SFA rejected the appeal and, although upset, Dundee could do little but accept the decision.

In May, Dundee's last hope of remaining amongst the elite disappeared at the Scottish League AGM. Morton's Hal Stewart had proposed expanding the Premier League to 12 teams but his motion was withdrawn due to lack of support.

Relegation to the First Division meant a projected loss of £100,000 and, with John McPhail showing up well, the long-serving George Stewart (28), was transferred to Hibs for £37,000. There were other departures. Alan Gordon (32), retired to further his career in Chartered Accountancy. Mitch Bavidge joined Elgin City for £1,000, while Gordon Wallace (32), Bobby Wilson (33), George Mackie and Tom Hendrie were amongst eight players released.

Wallace had finished the season as Dundee's top scorer with 14 goals and had scored an impressive 115 goals in his six-and-a-half years at Dens. But, despite earlier agreeing that he could play for Seattle Sounders in the USA, the club were unhappy at the timing of his departure before the crucial game with Motherwell on May 1st.

As a replacement, former Arbroath striker Billy Pirie (27), was signed on a free transfer from Aberdeen although a move for St Johnstone skipper Jim O'Rourke failed with the player this time opting for Premier League Motherwell.

That season, Dundee sported a new strip consisting of dark blue jerseys and shorts with a red and white stripe down each side, and red stockings. And in preparation for the more physical football anticipated on the tighter First Division pitches, the Dark Blues again undertook a tour of the Scottish Highlands and returned unbeaten after four games.

Bobby Ford - gave his all for the Dark Blues.

In the League Cup, Dundee's sectional opponents would consist of Premier League clubs Motherwell, Hearts and newly-promoted Partick Thistle. But although two of the opening three games were lost, the Dark Blues took seven points to finish runners-up to the section-winners Hearts.

Encouragingly, Dundee had beaten each of their opponents and were strong favourites to lift the First Division Championship. This optimism appeared well-founded for, by the end of September, an unbeaten Dundee were top of their league, having taken 13 points from their opening eight games.

Already, Pirie had shown his worth, spearheading the team to spectacular wins over Falkirk (a) 6-1, and Hamilton (h) 5-1, and taking his scoring tally to an impressive 15 goals in fourteen games. However, it soon became apparent that Dundee were not to have it all their own way.

Three out of the next four games were lost to St Mirren (a) 0-4, Hamilton (a) 2-4, and Clydebank (a) 1-2. Now, the Dens Parkers trailed joint leaders St Mirren and Clydebank by three points and any illusions of an easy return to the top level were well and truly shattered.

Dundee had been outclassed by Alex Ferguson's kids at Love Street before squandering a two-goal lead at Hamilton, and, at Kilbowie they were flattered by the narrow margin of defeat. For although Hoggan had come close to equalising when his shot struck the bar in a late flurry, the Davie Cooper-inspired Clydebank - only recently promoted as Second Division Champions - had wasted chances galore.

Looking shaky in defence and lacking a controlling influence in midfield, new blood was urgently required. An enquiry was made for Leeds United's Peter Lorimer (33), but their interest quickly cooled when an £80,000 fee was

Near thing - Billy Pirie heads for goal against East Fife at Dens but the ball is blocked by Alan Blair. Pirie soon proved himself a prolific marksman and over the next three seasons he netted 100 goals for the Dark Blues. DC Thomson

Great save - Ally Donaldson foils Davie Robb in the Scottish Cup at Dens as John McPhail, Dave Johnston and Aberdeen's Joe Harper watch. RIGHT - two-goal Bobby Hutchinson dumped the Dons in the replay.

mentioned for the Dundee-born midfielder.

Inverness Caley's Billy Urquhart trained at Dens but no signing move was made, and the Telford Street club's prolific scorer would later join Rangers for what was a record Highland League fee.

Meanwhile, Dundee's rivals had strengthened their teams. St Mirren signed unsettled Dundee United centre-half Jackie Copland, who had earlier been offered in exchange for Iain Phillip, while Clydebank pipped the Dark Blues for the signature of Celtic midfielder Tom Callaghan.

Five months earlier, Dundee's balance sheet had shown a loss of £5,468 despite a £45,115 transfer surplus and a £14,000 donation by the Thistle Street Social Club. And, with heavy losses expected for the current season, there was clearly little to spend. Instead, Davie White had to content himself with reshuffling the team. Out went Allan, Martin and McPhail, who were replaced by Donaldson, Ford and Caldwell. It was the first time Thomson Allan had been dropped and the former international keeper immediately demanded a transfer.

Already, Dave Johnston and Dave McIntosh with cartilage trouble, Gordon Strachan with a toe-nail problem and captain Tommy Gemmell, who had varicose veins, had all required operations and, in mid-November, a pulled hamstring sidelined Billy Pirie until the end of 1976.

Many of the players had taken badly to the more physical play of the First Division. Hutchinson was sent off against Queen of the South for retaliation while Phillip asked for a move: "I was no longer enjoying the game and even applied to join the police. I did not play particularly well in the First Division. It was very intense with speed and hardness compensating for lack of skill," said the Dens sweeper. In

December, Gemmell announced his retirement following a dispute with Davie White but the matter was quickly resolved and he returned to Dens two weeks later.

The Dark Blues maintained their promotion challenge with a 10-game unbeaten run. But their rivals showed no sign of slipping and, by February 1977, they remained four points behind St Mirren and two behind Clydebank with a game less played.

On February 8th, Dundee met St Mirren in a vital clash at Love Street. Two months earlier they had lost the chance of closing the gap when their home games against St Mirren and Clydebank were postponed due to bad weather and the preliminary round of the Scottish Cup. Neither of their rivals were in any hurry to play at Dens and now these games would not take place until the end of the season.

The strong-going Paisley side had stars like Tony Fitzpatrick, Billy Stark, Lex Richardson and Frank McGarvey and included in their 22-game unbeaten run was a recent Scottish Cup win over Dundee United. Dundee had no answer to their attacking flair and only a late goal by Strachan came as any consolation in a 3-1 defeat.

The Dark Blues recovered to beat Raith Rovers 4-0 at Dens but a shock defeat by Queen of the South (h) 0-2, and another by Clydebank (a) 0-3, left them eight points behind the second-placed Bankies - the surprise packet that term.

Aberdeen midfielder Billy Williamson was a transfer target and to finance a deal it was agreed to sell Bobby Robinson to Hearts. Recently, however, the former international had joined keeper Ally Donaldson, Bobby Ford and Eric Sinclair on the part-time staff in order to study at Dundee University and, when he rejected the move, Dundee United stepped in to sign Williamson.

Dundee, meanwhile, had reached the second round of the Scottish Cup by beating St Johnstone 4-2 in a Dens replay after a 1-1 draw at Muirton. Their next opponents were League Cup winners Aberdeen, who, after narrowly escaping relegation, had been revitalised by the effervescent Ally McLeod. It proved a rousing encounter for the 17,000 Dens crowd but despite the constant home pressure which saw them earn 18 corners to Aberdeen's four, the game ended without a goal.

In the Pittodrie replay on Wednesday, March 2nd, Hutchinson headed an early goal and Dundee settled to their best form of the season. Shortly after half-time, Aberdeen drew level through Duncan Davidson but, with Phillip pushing forward from the back and Ford, Robinson and Strachan dominating the crucial midfield area, the Dens men soon regained control.

Only 14 minutes remained when Willie Miller was short with a pass-back to Bobby Clark and the ever-alert Bobby Hutchinson nipped in to net the winner. "We were brilliant that night," said Iain Phillip. "We could always raise ourselves for that kind of game and it was so refreshing being allowed to play on a big open park."

In the quarter-final, Dundee met Arbroath before a 9,558 all-ticket crowd at Gayfield but there was a shock for the large travelling support when the "Lichties" took a first-minute lead. Following a mazy dribble, Gordon Strachan equalised in the 25th minute and although Tommy Yule hit the post for Arbroath, a late headed double by substitute Eric Sinclair ensured Dundee's place in the semi-finals.

Almost inevitably, and for the fifth time since 1970, the semi-final draw paired Dundee with Celtic, while Rangers met Motherwell in the other tie. On Wednesday, April 6th,

Dundee's Hampden line-up read: Donaldson; Gemmell, Phillip, McPhail, Johnston; Strachan, Ford, Hutchinson, Purdie; Sinclair, Pirie. Subs - Robinson, Caldwell. Celtic: Baines; McGrain, Stanton, McDonald, Lynch; Doyle, Aitken, Conn; Glavin, Dalglish, Craig. Subs. - Burns, and Edvaldsson.

A crowd of 29,900 saw an enthralling game with much of the good football coming from Dundee. But with less than 10 minutes left, two goals by Joe Craig put Celtic through to an Old Firm Final. McPhail and Phillip had been defensive stalwarts and with Strachan a dazzling midfielder, Dundee had created some good chances. Pirie, however, had been tightly marked and most opportunities had fallen to an out-of-touch Eric Sinclair.

The Scottish Cup had proved only a temporary respite from the gruelling promotion struggle. Since losing at Clydebank, Dundee had lost another precious four points to Arbroath (a) 0-1, St Johnstone (a) 0-0, and Airdrie (a) 2-2 with the defeat at Arbroath involving a catastrophic series of events. Eric Sinclair had been sent off and after Billy Pirie missed a penalty, an Iain Phillip "own-goal" gave the Gayfield club a shock 1-0 victory.

Nevertheless, in recent weeks second-placed Clydebank had faltered and the gap had narrowed to six points with Dundee holding a game in hand. The Dark Blues had five games left but the Dens clash with the Kilbowie outfit on Tuesday, April 12th looked like it would be Dundee's last chance to close the gap.

Urged on by the near 9,000 crowd, Dundee surged forward but, soon after half-time, the visitors led 3-0. Hutchinson (78 mins), and Ford (86), reduced the deficit, but no equaliser was forthcoming despite their last-ditch efforts. Dundee had played well but, with Bankies keeper Jim Gallacher in top

A star in the making - but little Gordon Strachan, seen here leading Arbroath keeper Gordon Marshall and his defence a merry dance, found the going tough in the rough-and-tumble First Division. Bobby Ford and Billy Pirie are the other Dundee men. DC Thomson

Celtic again - a familiar routine at Hampden as Ally Donaldson beats Celtic's Joe Craig to the punch with Iain Phillip, Tommy Gemmell and John McPhail watching anxiously. DC Thomson

Speed merchant - but Bobby Robinson was soon to leave the Dark Blues.

form and few breaks going their way, the promotion dream was now over.

This was confirmed by a 2-2 draw with East Fife and a 4-0 humiliation by the new First Division Champions St Mirren at home. Dundee's failure to achieve promotion meant the end of the road for Davie White and, on April 26th, 1977, he resigned after nearly five-and-a-half years in the hot-seat at Dens Park.

So what had gone wrong? Davie White had been one of the new breed of tracksuit managers but after initial success between 1972 and 1975, he had found the Prentice-McLean partnership a hard act to follow.

Billy Pirie had scored a remarkable 44 goals (38 in the league) but as Iain Phillip recalled: "Billy kept winning us crates of whisky but although we laced everybody else, we struggled in the vitally important games against St Mirren and Clydebank who, it has to be said, were both very good teams."

"In my opinion, influential players like Bobby Wilson, George Stewart, Gordon Wallace and Jocky Scott should have been kept because their experience would have been invaluable. Wallace - 119 goals for Dundee - went on to score a lot of goals for United in the Premier League while Scott and Wilson both had a couple of seasons left in them."

Jocky Scott believed that the aftermath of the 1973 League Cup celebrations may have been instrumental in the team's break-up, but Phillip had his doubts since both he and Dave Johnston remained at Dens for another five years.

The First Division had consisted of 14 teams with each club playing the others three times and Dundee had been unlucky in having to face St Mirren and Clydebank twice away from home. However, the Dark Blues had finished a poor third, seven points behind runners-up Clydebank and, with all six games against the top pair ending in defeat, it was clear that a major overhaul was required at Dens.

CHAPTER EIGHTEEN

Cavalier Approach

In June, Tommy Gemmell (34), who had earlier hung up his boots, was appointed manager. His assistant would be another "Lisbon Lion" Willie Wallace with Hugh Robertson and George Blues remaining on the coaching staff. Initially, Ayr United manager and former Dens stalwart Alex Stuart had been offered the post but when he turned it down, Gemmell, who had not applied, was invited to take charge. In addition, there was now a new chief scout at Dens. Tom Arnott had recently retired after 15 years and his successor, Bill Kerr, emphasised that Dundee would concentrate on local talent.

Last season, Dundee had scored a highly creditable total of 90 league goals with the deadly Billy Pirie netting 38 and now the priority would be to tighten a defence which had conceded 117 league goals over the past two years.

Gemmell moved quickly to strengthen the team. Hard-tackling Rangers midfielder Ian McDougall (23), was signed for £12,000 while 33-year-old ex-Celtic winger Jimmy Johnstone was obtained on a free transfer from Sheffield United. Dave McIntosh was the only player of any first-team experience to be released but Ian Purdie, a first-team regular for most of his time at Dens, was not in Gemmell's plans and he was transferred to Motherwell for £15,000.

As expected, the Dark Blues' stay in the First Division had proved costly. Average home gates in the league had fallen from 8,900 in 1975-76 to around 4,500 last term and, with the May balance sheet showing an operating loss of £56,458, there was little prospect of any major signings.

The league campaign began with a 3-0 win over Airdrie at Dens but defeats by newly-relegated Hearts (a) 1-2, and Stirling Albion (h) 0-1, came as an early setback. Although still only 26 years old, Bobby Robinson had never regained the form which had brought him international honours. And, after appearing as a substitute against Airdrie, he moved down the road to join Dundee United in exchange for Billy Williamson plus £6,000.

Unfortunately, Jimmy Johnstone was no longer the wizard of old and, in mid-September, he joined Irish League side Shelbourne after only two first-team starts for Dundee. However, Ian McDougall and Billy Williamson quickly settled and, by mid-October, Dundee lay second after taking 15 points from their next eight games.

That summer, Thomson Allan, who was now a part-timer, had turned down an offer from Hearts. St Mirren were also keen but, after almost a year in the reserves, Allan was recalled to first-team action when Ally Donaldson sustained

broken ribs in the 1-1 draw at Hamilton. The big keeper would be out for a lengthy spell and with only 17-year-old Bobby Geddes, a recent £5,000 signing from Ross County, in reserve, Dundee could not afford to let Allan go.

The League Cup was now a home-and-away knock-out competition and Dundee progressed to the third round with aggregate wins over Montrose (4-1), and Berwick Rangers (5-1). Then the draw paired them with struggling Queen of the South but, although Dundee were strong favourites to reach the quarter-finals, the Dumfries side held out for a 0-0 draw in the first leg at Dens.

So far, an improved Dens defence had conceded just 12 goals in 11 games but, when shock defeats by Arbroath (h) 2-3, and Airdrie (a) 0-3, revealed that all was not well, changes were made for the Palmerston return on October 26th. Only a month earlier, the Dark Blues had won 2-0 at the same venue but now they crashed to a humiliating 6-0 defeat, surely one of the worst in the club's long history. The injured Iain Phillip had been missed but, although Queen of the South had proved something of a bogey side last term, there was no easy answer for Dundee's night of shame.

"We could do nothing right while everything they hit went in," recalled Dave Johnston. "I was turned inside out by their right-winger Dempster, a real speed merchant, and in the end we had no complaints, we just got torn apart."

Morton and Hearts were Dundee's main promotion rivals

New boss - Tommy Gemmell with Jimmy Johnstone but the ex-Celtic and Scotland maestro was past his best. Mirrorpix

Battler supreme - midfield dynamo Jim Shirra soon showed his grit and determination in a Dundee jersey and here he celebrates the third goal in the 3-1 win against Morton. DC Thomson

but, although both had also slipped recently, Tommy Gemmell was keen to bolster his side. However, according to the Dens boss there was no cash available and with the bank pressurising Dundee to reduce their over-draft, his hand had been forced.

At the start of the season, Dens starlet Gordon Strachan had been appointed club captain and his sparkling form had earned him a place on the bench for the Scotland Under-21s against Switzerland. The skilful Strachan became the target for some rough treatment and Tommy Gemmell complained that the youngster was "being kicked out of the First Division". However, the Dens boss was also critical of Strachan's lack of work rate and maintained he would be better suited to the Premier League. The red-headed mid-fielder found himself out of the side and it was little surprise when he demanded a transfer.

On October 29th, Strachan starred in the 1-1 draw with Hearts at Dens but, within days, he was on his way up to Aberdeen. Dundee received £50,000 plus Jim Shirra but with Strachan going on to make 50 appearances for Scotland, his departure for a relatively small amount would later be the cause for bitter regret.

"In hindsight, it was a bad mistake," said Ian Gellatly. "However, a board has to be guided by the manager and a couple of years previously we got our fingers burnt. We rejected an Everton bid of £150,000 for Bobby Robinson because we wanted to build the team around him and we didn't need the money anyway. Sadly, he lost form and went part-time before joining Dundee United in the swop deal for Williamson."

However, the experienced Dave Johnston sympathised with Gemmell: "Gordon was a brilliant wee player but, at that time, he hadn't learnt when to release the ball. He would

beat two men and by trying to beat a third one he could sometimes leave some of our supporting players out of position. It took him a year to get it right and establish himself at Pittodrie and, in fairness to Big Tam and the board, Dundee didn't have time on their side."

Nevertheless, the 26-year-old Shirra was a gritty performer and his drive and determination were soon evident in victories over Stirling Albion (a) 2-0, and St Johnstone (h) 5-3. There was a dramatic finale in the Tayside derby with St Johnstone. Thomson Allan was stretchered off with a head wound in 55 minutes and, with young midfielder Alan Simpson in the Dundee goal, the visitors pulled back two goals to make it 3-3. But with the Perth side pushing for the winner, Pirie netted a disputed injury-time penalty and soon afterwards completed his hat-trick to make it 5-3 for the Dark Blues.

In quick succession, another two experienced campaigners arrived at Dens. Left-back Erich Schaedler (27), capped for Scotland against West Germany in 1974, was secured in exchange for unsettled striker Bobby Hutchinson, while £15,000 persuaded Aberdeen to part with old Dens favourite Jocky Scott, previously a transfer target for Dundee United.

Strengthened by the new signings and with Pirie and Sinclair forming a deadly striking partnership, Dundee took 16 points from their 10 games since the Palmerston debacle and by New Year they topped the First Division.

The supporters warmed to Gemmell's bold style of management and, on December 24th, a bumper 12,458 crowd saw second-placed Morton crushed 3-1 at Dens. The fans liked what they saw and, nine days later, the return visit of St Johnstone attracted an attendance of 12,785, Dundee's largest home gate of the season.

Roared on by the large crowd, Dundee surged forward only to be cruelly punished in the few Perth attacks. Goals by Williamson (73 mins, 77) made it 3-3 but, with the Dark Blues putting in a grandstand finish, Connor silenced the home support with his own third and St Johnstone's fourth, just 30 seconds from time.

Slack defending had cost Dundee dear but they recovered to draw 2-2 with Hearts before a First Division (post 1976) record crowd of 19,720 at Tynecastle. Seven days later, Billy

Pirie netted four in the 6-0 Dens romp over Alloa and, with two thirds of the programme complete, the Dark Blues shared top spot with Morton and Hearts.

Once again, Dundee were matched with Celtic in the Scottish Cup and, after a three-week break due to bad weather, their first-round tie went ahead on Monday, February 6th. Burns gave Celtic an early lead only for Schaedler to level in the ninth minute. However, after holding their own throughout the first period, the loss of goals before and after half-time saw Dundee slide to a 7-1 defeat.

Tommy Gemmell had taken a gamble in fielding Iain Phillip, who had just recovered from groin and achilles tendon injuries, but the sweeper had looked well short of match fitness. Earlier, McGeachie, Johnston, Caldwell and Ford had each partnered John McPhail in central defence but, with Johnston struggling with knee trouble and the defensive problems unresolved, Dundee paid £12,000 for Aberdeen defender Bobby Glennie. The 20-year-old Lochee lad was a Dundee fan and although appearing for Aberdeen at full-back, his uncompromising performances at sweeper soon earned him the Dens Park captaincy from Jim Shirra.

The promotion battle continued to be a three-horse race but, by late-March an unbeaten eight-game run left Dundee top, one point above Hearts and three ahead of Morton who still had two games in hand.

Pirie - a quality striker according to his team-mate Eric Sinclair - was again a prolific scorer with 33 goals while Williamson had proved a shrewd capture with another 16 goals from midfield. Indeed Gemmell had shown sound judgement in his signings. McDougall, Shirra, Schaedler and Glennie had brought a much-needed touch of iron while Scott added a more subtle approach to midfield.

The Dens boss had also successfully introduced some promising youngsters. Ian Redford (17), had been a revelation as a striker, while Dave McKinnon (20), signed from Arsenal on a free transfer in 1976, and 19-year-old George McGeachie, were sound in defence or midfield. Meanwhile, John Martin and Derek Laing, two of Davie White's brightest prospects, had faded from the scene. Martin turned part-time while Laing joined Australian side Sydney Olympic after his release in February 1968.

Only five games now remained and, on April 1st, a 12,305 crowd turned out for the vital clash with third-placed Morton at Dens. Redford put Dundee ahead in only 20 seconds but 20 minutes from the end, Morton equalised through big Andy Ritchie. After the game, a bitterly disappointed Tommy Gemmell was scathing in his criticism of Glasgow referee Ian Foote. Twice he had ignored Dundee penalty claims, including one blatant handling offence in the box. More would be heard of Mr Foote but Gemmell's comments cost him a £100 fine and four days later, the damage was exacerbated with a disastrous 2-1 defeat at Dumbarton.

Now Dundee had to rely on Morton and Hearts dropping points but, with Scott, Shirra and McDougall axed, wins over Alloa (a) 5-1, and Queen of the South (h) 3-0, kept them in the hunt. By then, Morton were assured of promotion and Dundee had to take something from the prospective champions in their final game at Greenock while hoping that Hearts, with an inferior goal-difference, might slip up at Arbroath.

Star quality - but Iain Phillip suffered more frustration when Dundee were pipped for the big step-up. DC Thomson

This is how the top of the First Division looked on the morning of Saturday, April 29th, 1978.

	P	W	D	L	F A	Pts
Morton	38	25	8	5	83-39	58
Hearts	38	23	10	5	76-41	56
Dundee	38	24	7	7	88-42	55

It was to be an afternoon of drama at sunny Cappielow as Dundee lined up: Donaldson, Caldwell, Glennie, McPhail, Schaedler; McKinnon, McGeachie, McDougall; Pirie, Sinclair, Redford. Subs - Johnston, Shirra.

It was all or nothing for the Dark Blues and, encouraged by a large travelling support, Redford put them ahead after 20 minutes. Redford then went off injured to be replaced by Johnston but a recurrence of a knee problem saw the defender replaced by Shirra at the interval. Russell scored twice for Morton but, in a fighting finish, Glennie equalised and six minutes from time Pirie netted a third from an acute angle to make it 3-2.

Dundee held on to win and at full-time the Dens fans celebrated in the belief that Hearts had drawn 0-0. Sadly, the terracing euphoria was short-lived for just two minutes later the fans heard that their rivals had scored a last-minute winner to pip Dundee at the post. "We thought we had done it," recalled Bobby Glennie. "It was a bitter disappointment to discover that Hearts had won when we got back to the dressing room."

In the close-season, the club went on a seven-game tour of Western Australia, New Zealand and New Caledonia. The trip was almost a month in duration but, unlike the tour of 1972, results were mixed. Then, the Dark Blues had returned with a 100 per cent record but this time five games were won, one was drawn and there were three defeats.

The Dundee F.C. squad for the trip to Australia (BACK, left to right), Bobby Ford, Iain Phillip, Bobby Glennie, Dave Johnston, Ally Donaldson, John McPhail, Thomson Allan, George McGeachie, Ian McDougall, Alex Caldwell, Jim Shirra. FRONT - Dave McKinnon, Ian Redford, Erich Schaedler, Billy Pirie, Billy Williamson, Eric Sinclair, Jocky Scott. DC Thomson

Directors and supporters alike felt that Gemmell had done well. The new manager had put together a more competitive side and promotion had been missed by a hair's breadth. Throughout the campaign, Dundee had been amongst the pace-setters and the team's all-out attacking style which had brought 91 league goals had seen the average home gate improve by over 2,000 to a respectable 6,723 - only 1,600 less than Dundee United's average in the Premier League.

Consequently, Gemmell was rewarded with a two-year contract extension but the failure to win promotion meant further financial worries. In December 1977 a £60,000 rights issue had increased the club's share capital from £10,000 to £70,000, yet five months later the accounts showed a trading loss of £47,682. A £56,458 deficit from the previous year meant the club were now over £100,000 in the red. But, despite fears that the club might go part-time for the first time since 1947, the board declared that full-time football would continue at Dens Park.

The previous season, Tommy Gemmell had made six new signings and virtually rebuilt his side. Now there were another four new men. Motherwell defender Willie Watson (28), and Hibs forward Alex McGhee (25), each cost £8,000; former Scotland Under-23 midfielder Alan Lamb (25), was obtained on a free transfer from Port Vale while Montrose right-back Les Barr came in exchange for Bobby Ford plus a fee of £15,000.

As well as Ford, some other well-known names had gone. The long-serving Dave Johnston was appointed player-coach at Montrose while John Martin and Alan Simpson were amongst five players released. Soon after the start of the season, utility player Dave McKinnon was transferred to Partick Thistle for £10,000 while Wilson Hoggan, who had been in dispute with Dundee since the previous March, had also gone. Hoggan had spent much of last term on loan to Alloa but, following an administrative error, he was able to rejoin Falkirk as a free agent.

Dundee's 1978-79 league campaign got off to a bright start with a 1-0 win over the much-fancied Ayr United at Somerset Park but their interest in the League Cup was to prove short-lived. Two late goals gave Celtic a 3-1 win at Parkhead and Dundee never looked like recovering the deficit in a 3-0 second-leg defeat at Dens. Nevertheless, Tommy Gemmell's men had strung together a 10-game unbeaten run, including wins over closest rivals Clyde and Clydebank, and, by the end of September, Dundee were four points clear at the top of the First Division.

Willie Watson, a former Manchester United player, soon settled alongside Bobby Glennie and, with the dependable Donaldson in goal and Barr and Schaedler at full-back, there were few problems in defence. In midfield, McDougall had been replaced by the more creative Lamb but unaccountably the next 10 games brought just three wins and, by mid-December, Clydebank were level, with Ayr, Hamilton and Kilmarnock just three points behind.

On October 7th, Queen of the South were beaten 5-0 at Dens but, with the injured Pirie out for six matches with a damaged hamstring, the Dark Blues could only manage a miserly seven goals from their next nine games.

Alarmed by the slump, Dundee paid £25,000 for Motherwell's Stewart MacLaren (26), and the midfielder made his debut in the top-of-the-table clash at Clydebank on November 25th. The Bankies had lost stars like Davie Cooper, Mike Larnach and Joe McCallan and their Premier sojourn had been brief but although Dundee had the lion's share of the play, they were unable to put the ball away in a disappointing 2-1 defeat.

After an impressive start to the season, Iain Phillip had lost his place at sweeper to Willie Watson. The former Scottish League international had been unsettled for some time and, after repeating an earlier transfer request, he was put up for

148

sale. Jim McLean had long been an admirer and, soon after MacLaren's arrival at Dens, Phillip was transferred to Dundee United for a fee of £25,000.

"When Tommy Gemmell took over as manager it was the beginning of the end for me," said Phillip. "He wanted a tougher approach and I just wasn't his type although I could see the need for battlers to get us out of the First Division. Willie Wallace wasn't my cup of tea as a coach either. Things had got slack at training and when I moved up the road, I found that I was only half-fit."

Encouragingly, the Dark Blues got back on the rails with wins over Stirling Albion (h) 2-1 and Airdrie (a) 2-0 before Christmas but, with freezing weather affecting most of the country, it would be two months before Dundee returned to footballing action.

It had been an unhappy season for Jocky Scott. On returning from his summer spell with Seattle Sounders, he failed to regain his place and asked for a transfer. The former Scotland man finally made his comeback at Airdrie only to damage a disc, an injury which required an operation on his back three months later.

After almost a year out of the side, Thomson Allan, who had walked out on Dundee back in September, joined Meadowbank on loan. In February 1979, the popular keeper looked set to sign for St Johnstone but Hearts moved in to land him for £7,000. John McPhail, who had looked to have a bright future at Dens, was also out of favour and he too moved on, joining Sheffield United for £25,000.

Other sides had taken advantage of Dundee's inactivity but, on Wednesday, February 21st, the Dark Blues restarted with a vital 2-1 win over league leaders Clydebank at Dens. Both goals were scored by Ian Redford, whose progress had been recognised with a couple of appearances for the Scotland Under-21s, against Norway and the full USA XI.

Another to impress was the tricky Jimmy Murphy (21), who had only recently been signed from Junior side Bellshill Athletic. Previously the wee winger had been on the books of Celtic and Queen of the South, but despite his failure to make an impact at these clubs, Gemmell was confident that the Junior Scotland winger might develop into a real personality at Dens.

Dundee's Scottish Cup third-round tie against Falkirk went ahead at Dens on Sunday, February 25th and nearly 10,000 saw a 70th-minute Pirie penalty earn Gemmell's men a home tie against Premier League leaders St Mirren in the next round of the competition..

Twenty-four hours before the Falkirk tie, the Paisley side had won 4-1 at Tannadice but when they came to Dens, Dundee's quick tackling and use of the long ball gave them little time to settle. The Dark Blues made full use of their first-half wind advantage and, with the bustling Sinclair scoring twice, further goals by Lamb and Pirie with a penalty earned a deserved 4-1 win before a crowd of 11,140. On the day, Dundee's midfield of MacLaren, Lamb and Shirra was outstanding and one of the best footballing sides in the country had been reduced to mediocrity.

In the quarter-final, Dundee travelled to meet Rangers, winners of the previous season's domestic treble, but any hopes of a place in the last four disappeared in a four-goal Ibrox blitz in the opening half-hour. And although a double by MacLaren reduced the deficit, Rangers ran out comfortable 6-3 winners. The Dark Blues had done well to net three goals against top drawer Premier opposition and, although defensive slackness had cost them dear, they had the consolation of sharing the proceeds of the 23,000 gate.

Gemmell expressed his pleasure at Dundee's showing in the Cup but he was now concerned that they had fallen further behind in the promotion race. An arduous 16-game programme still remained and to strengthen the squad, Motherwell defender Peter Millar arrived on a free transfer.

Fifth-placed Dundee trailed league leaders Clydebank by five points, albeit with five games in hand but, by the end of March, a run of five successive wins saw them move up to third place. Thereafter, they faced a demanding schedule of two games a week but despite upsets at Dumbarton (2-3) and Kilmarnock (1-2), wins over Raith (a) 2-1, Hamilton (h) 4-3, Clyde (h) 2-0, Airdrie (a) 4-2 and Montrose (h) 1-0 left them just two points behind league leaders Kilmarnock by the beginning of May.

Now came the crucial run-in. It was at this same stage that Dundee had faltered last time around, but, with an unbeaten home record that season, and three of their remaining four games at Dens Park, promotion and the First Division Championship looked almost certain. However, no-one had bargained for two defeats within four days by relegation-

Stopped in his tracks - Billy Pirie proved an ace scorer in the First Division but Clydebank keeper Jim Gallacher always reserved his finest form for visits to Dens Park and on this occasion he is able to keep the striker at bay. DC Thomson

threatened St Johnstone (a) 2-3, and Arbroath (h) 0-2, and many fans now began to fear the worst.

On Sunday, May 6th, a crowd of 8,385 - Dundee's largest home gate in the league that season - turned out for the visit of Arbroath. They were stunned when MacLaren conceded an early own-goal and this served to further unnerve an already jittery Dundee side. Matters were not helped when the experienced Shirra was sent off along with Wilson of Arbroath and when Albert Kidd - later to join the Dark Blues - made it 2-0 with 20 minutes remaining. there was no way back for Dundee.

"There was no doubt the tension was getting to us and having so many games to play in a short time didn't help either," said Bobby Glennie. However, Eric Sinclair offered no excuses: "We were just awful that afternoon." Three of their last four games had been lost and, with Clydebank winning their final game, victory over Raith Rovers two days later was imperative.

There had been fierce competition for midfield places with MacLaren, Lamb, McDougall, Shirra, Williamson, McGeachie, Scrimgeour and Scott all in contention. Brian Scrimgeour replaced the suspended Shirra with George McGeachie again deputising for Willie Watson, who had pulled a thigh muscle at Muirton but although Dundee were again badly affected by nerves, goals by Redford and MacLaren clinched a 2-0 win, and barring a four-goal reversal in their final game, promotion was assured.

On Thursday, May 10th, Dundee faced fourth-placed Ayr United at Dens, in the knowledge that one point would clinch the title. Despite the heavy rain, the 7,692 crowd were in fine voice and the Dark Blues attacked from the start. Just before half-time, Redford headed in a Schaedler cross, only for Brian McLaughlin and Jim McSherry to put Ayr 2-1 ahead with 22 minutes remaining. But in 77 minutes, Redford headed the equaliser from a Murphy free-kick and the title was secured.

Dundee would return to the Premier League as First

Flag night - Ian Redford outjumps Ayr's Jim Fleeting to head home the equaliser that clinched the title.   DC Thomson

Division Champions and at full-time, thousands of delighted fans invaded the pitch to congratulate their heroes.

Much to the relief of the directors, Dundee were back amongst the elite of Scottish football. It had been a three-year nightmare and the consequences of a third failure would have been grave indeed.

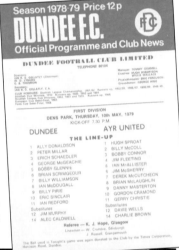

Party time - the champagne is cracked open as Dundee celebrate their return to the Premier League in May 1979.   DC Thomson

CHAPTER NINETEEN

Down Again

In his two years in charge, Tommy Gemmell had reshaped Dundee's first-team squad and now only Donaldson, Pirie, Sinclair and Caldwell remained from the start of the 1977-78 season. Last term, a more cautious style of play had tightened things at the back but, far fewer goals were scored with Pirie and Williamson well down on their previous totals.

Talented players like Robinson, Strachan and Phillip had gone as Gemmell adapted his team to the demands of First Division football. Promotion, however, had been achieved by solid rather than spectacular displays and, now, many fans doubted whether Dundee had sufficient quality to survive in the Premier League. Their concern was borne out by some unconvincing pre-season performances, the worst of which was a 5-1 defeat by Preston in a friendly at Dens.

Top scorer Billy Pirie was ruled out of the opening games with an ankle injury and, after failing to land Ayr United's ex-Celtic and Motherwell forward, Brian McLaughlin, Tommy Gemmell made the short trip to Gayfield to sign Arbroath striker John Fletcher for a fee of £20,000.

On August 11th, 1979, a crowd of nearly 18,000 watched the league opener between Dundee and Dundee United at Tannadice. Three months earlier, the city clubs had drawn 2-2 at the same ground in the Forfarshire Cup semi-final. After extra-time, Dundee had gone on to win on penalties but this time the honours belonged to United, who ran out convincing 3-0 winners.

The Tannadice side had taken the ambitious step of spending £100,000 on Motherwell sharpshooter Willie Pettigrew and, despite drawing a blank, the pacy striker had certainly caused the Dens defence all sorts of problems. However, the following week, Ian Redford confirmed his potential when he netted all four goals in Dundee's 4-1 triumph over St Mirren at Dens.

Another three points were taken from home games with Partick Thistle (2-2) and Morton (4-3), but poor away form saw the Dens Parkers in second-bottom place by the end of the first quarter of the season. Only five points had been taken and, after the loss of 26 goals in the opening nine games, there were already serious question marks over the defence, particularly over the handling of cross-balls.

In the Anglo-Scottish Cup, the Dark Blues drew 4-4 on aggregate with Kilmarnock, but qualified on the away goals rule after the second leg at Rugby Park ended 3-3. Dundee then restricted English Second Division club Sheffield United to a 2-1 win at

Eyes on the ball - Ian Redford battles it out with George Fleming in Dundee's Premier opener. DC Thomson

Bramwall Lane thanks to an ultra-defensive approach which brought howls of derision not only from Blades fans but also from those who had travelled from Tayside to witness the spectacle.

Thus, there was perhaps an element of poetic justice when former player John McPhail netted the only goal of the Dens return to see the English side safely through.

On October 20th, Dundee got their derby revenge over United in front of a 16,000 crowd at Dens with Sinclair scoring the only goal just before half-time. By then, they had reached the quarter-final of the League Cup, disposing of Cowdenbeath (7-2), and Ayr United (3-1) on aggregate.

The tournament was now sponsored by Bell's Whisky, but Dundee's chances of reaching the last four took a severe knock with a 3-1 reverse in the first leg against Hamilton at Douglas Park. In the Dens return, Dundee attacked relentlessly only to have two goals disallowed by the controversial Ian Foote. Pirie, now recovered from injury - did score near the end, but by then it was too late.

Under pressure - questions were always being asked of the Dark Blues defence and here Ally Donaldson and Bobby Glennie combine to keep Gordon Smith of Rangers at bay with Willie Watson in the background. DC Thomson

Nevertheless, the Dark Blues had adjusted to the demands of the Premier League and, in November, there were encouraging wins over Hibs (h) 2-1, Partick Thistle (a) 3-2, and Rangers (h) 3-1. At Firhill, Dundee had trailed 2-0 at half-time before mounting a stirring comeback. Peter Millar reduced the leeway with a crashing free-kick before late counters by Billy Pirie and Eric Sinclair earned a welcome away win - Dundee's first in the league that term.

Some of Gemmell's earlier signings had become surplus to requirements. Ian McDougall and Billy Williamson were out of favour, while Alan Lamb had joined St Johnstone for £6,000. Alec McGhee was also out of the plans and he was given a free transfer before going to play in the United States. Willie Watson and Stuart Turnbull had started the campaign as regulars but, with Watson struggling through injury and the 18-year-old left-back lacking experience, both had dropped out of the side.

John Fletcher, a PE teacher in a local school, remained part-time. However, he made little impact and looked short of the pace required for Premier League football. In November, Tommy Gemmell again dipped into the transfer market, this time bringing Peter Mackie (21), from Celtic for £30,000. But although the fair-haired winger, who bore an

uncanny resemblence to Kenny Dalglish, made a pleasing debut against Rangers, it was the sprightly Jim Murphy who had run the Light Blues ragged.

All season, Dundee had looked shaky down the middle. Watson, Caldwell and McGeachie did not complement club captain Bobby Glennie but, although MacLaren looked a better bet, the manager preferred to use him in midfield alongside the hard-working Jim Shirra. The Dark Blues had shown interest in former Scotland stalwart Jim Holton of Coventry and Carlisle's former St Johnstone man Iain MacDonald but just like their failed bid for experienced Celtic centre-half Roddy McDonald, no business was done.

Nevertheless, five points were taken from their next four games and by late January, Dundee lay eighth, only four points behind third-placed St Mirren. Their home record of seven wins and a draw from 10 games was impressive, but only two points had been taken from a possible 18 away from Dens.

Ian Redford, just recovered from an ankle injury, was on the mark in the 1-0 win over second-placed Morton at Dens. In his absence, Scottish Youth International striker Iain Ferguson (17), had made a scoring debut in the 3-1 home win over Kilmarnock and greatly impressed with his level of skill and powerful shooting.

Early in 1980, Willie Wallace left Dens to become manager of Australian side Apia. Hugh Robertson was appointed first-team coach while, in turn, Jocky Scott, who had never recovered full fitness after his back injury, took charge of the reserves.

Dundee's interest in the Scottish Cup was short-lived - the first-round draw pairing them with Dundee United. This was to be an infamous occasion and the clues to that had fallen into place in their most recent meeting when the Dark Blues had lost 2-0 in the league at Tannadice in a game riddled with needle. United's John Holt had been stretchered off after a tackle by Stewart MacLaren and Erich Schaedler was later red-carded for retaliation on Frank Kopel after having his jersey pulled.

In addition, Dundee United had not long since confirmed their growing superiority by lifting their first major trophy when they beat Aberdeen in the League Cup Final replay at Dens, thus depriving the Dens Park choir of their favourite song based on the fact that United hadn't managed to win anything!

And so, when the cup-tie finally came along at Tannadice on Wednesday, January 30th after an earlier postponement due to frost, Dundee had no shortage of incentives to put one over on their street rivals. Almost inevitably, there was a fiercely competitive start to the game. Pettigrew put United ahead in 30 minutes but when Shirra headed an equaliser soon afterwards, the "goal" was disallowed by referee Ian Foote, a name which had long been struck off the club's Christmas card list. By this time, Dundee were incensed, and when United added another two after half-time, the game just exploded.

In quick succession, MacLaren, booked in the first half with Millar and Murphy, then Sinclair, were sent off after off-the-ball incidents with Kirkwood and Hegarty. There were furious scenes amongst the Dundee fans and a number

were arrested after beer cans were thrown on to the pitch. Many supporters felt Sinclair had been harshly penalised when Hegarty - in their eyes by no means an innocent party - had dramatically fallen, clutching his face as the two players jostled for position at a corner-kick.

Eventually, the nine-man Dundee went down 5-1, but a bad-tempered game had been amply fuelled by inept refereeing. It was the third game that Dundee had suffered at the hands of Mr Foote, who was no stranger to controversy.

In recent seasons, Dundee's First Division gates had been  only marginally below those of Dundee United in the Premier League. However, the Tannadice side had been able to splash out a sum of £100,000 on Willie Pettigrew and after receiving a generous £400,000 from West Ham for full-back Ray Stewart, they paid a Scottish record fee to bring Eamonn Bannon from Chelsea.

These signings were growing evidence of United's ascendancy and this was brought home in the cup-tie - Pettigrew scoring four of the goals and Bannon's pace causing no end of bother for the beleaguered Dark Blue defence.

The former Hearts winger would prove an inspired signing. In contrast, Dundee had outlaid £50,000 on Fletcher and Mackie, who were players of no more than average ability. In 1964, Dundee had paid a Scottish record fee of £40,000 for Charlie Cooke but their biggest buy remained the £40,500 paid to Crystal Palace for Iain Phillip in 1973 and, ironically, he too was now at Tannadice.

Three weeks earlier, Dundee had been victims of yet another debatable refereeing decision against Partick Thistle at Dens. Just minutes from the end they had appeared to go 2-0 up when Mackie chipped the ball over Alan Rough from 25 yards. Referee Tommy Muirhead signalled a goal, but, persuaded by an angry possee of Thistle players, he

Club man - Eric Sinclair always played for the jersey and here he gets a close-up view of Jim Shirra scoring against Rangers at Dens with Ibrox left-back Ally Dawson and goalkeeper Peter McCloy helpless. DC Thomson

Last throw of the dice - Peter Mackie races in to knock home the loose ball for Dundee's fifth goal in the 5-1 rout of Celtic at Dens. That result proved a devastating blow to Celtic's title ambitions.

DC Thomson

consulted a linesman before reversing his decision. Almost immediately, the Firhill side stole away to equalise and in many ways, that typified Dundee's luck that term.

However, their disciplinary record was poor and the loss of experienced players through suspension would cost them dear. The previous autumn, MacLaren and Shirra had been sent off against Kilmarnock and Celtic respectively and with MacLaren - he now faced a further three-match ban - and Sinclair suspended, Dundee fell 3-1 to Aberdeen at Dens.

Nevertheless, the Dark Blues then managed draws with Kilmarnock (a) 1-1, Celtic (a) 2-2 and Dundee United (h) 1-1 and by the start of March they clung to eighth place, one point above the Tannadice side, who were in a surprisingly low position.

By then, the talented Ian Redford - Dundee's outstanding player - had joined Rangers for a new Scottish record fee of £210,000. With no prospects of a money-spinning cup run and with debts running to a quarter of a million pounds the board felt it was an offer they could not refuse.

At the time, however, Redford was the club's top scorer and with only eight weeks of the season remaining and the relegation battle finely poised, it was an ill-timed move. Eric Sinclair agreed: "Ian Redford was a real class act. He was clever in possession and a good finisher. His departure was a big loss to Dundee at that stage."

As a replacement, former Aberdeen striker Ian Fleming was signed from Sheffield Wednesday for £45,000 and, soon afterwards, Billy Pirie, who had made little impression in the Premier League, moved to Australia where he joined Willie Wallace at Apia.

There were narrow defeats at Paisley and Ibrox before former Everton striker Dennis Corrigan, signed on a free transfer from Svendborg of Denmark, scored in Dundee's 3-0 win over bottom-of-the-league Hibs at Dens. The Easter Road side had struggled all season and despite the presence of the mercurial George Best, were already doomed to the First Division. However, it proved but a temporary respite,

and with only one point taken from their next six games, the Dark Blues slipped to ninth with only four games remaining.

Veteran keeper Ally Donaldson had been in fine form - "He always had plenty to do," quipped Bobby Glennie - but his fellow defenders were guilty of some shocking displays. There was little craft in midfield and with Sinclair now the only danger up front - in March, the big striker scored for the Scottish League in their 2-1 defeat to the League of Ireland in Dublin - the Dark Blues were in serious trouble.

On Sunday, April 13th, Dundee had a golden opportunity to close the gap on Partick Thistle at Firhill. Previously, the Dens men had taken four points from their three meetings with the Glasgow side but paralysed by fear, they crashed 3-0 in a quite dismal display.

The Dark Blues appeared doomed but an astonishing 5-1 win over Celtic at Dens brought a glimmer of hope. In five minutes, Roy Aitken put the league leaders ahead, but, in a remarkable turnaround, goals by Ferguson (16 mins, 26 pen), Fleming (43), Sinclair (59), and Mackie (71), earned a famous victory.

"Everything went for us that day," said Bobby Glennie. "But we showed tremendous spirit and it's just a pity that that victory hadn't come a month earlier." That result paved the way for an Aberdeen title win, but Dundee's slender hopes of catching Kilmarnock or Partick Thistle were doomed to failure. Within the space of four days, both won their games in hand and, with Dundee's fate sealed, Tommy Gemmell resigned as manager.

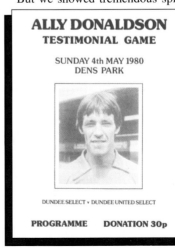

ALLY DONALDSON
TESTIMONIAL GAME

SUNDAY 4th MAY 1980
DENS PARK

DUNDEE SELECT • DUNDEE UNITED SELECT

PROGRAMME   DONATION 30p

CHAPTER TWENTY

City History Men

In May, former Dundee United goalkeeper Donald Mackay (40), was named as the new Dundee manager. Archie Knox (Forfar), Peter Lorimer (Toronto Blizzard), Bobby Wilson (Keith), and Gordon Wallace (Raith), were amongst the favourites, but the articulate Mackay, who had previously coached at Southend, Bristol City and then Danish side Norresumby Boldklub, was the surprise choice.

Donald Mackay was Dundee's new boss.

Mackay was given a two-year contract and would be responsible for all team matters. However, he would enjoy experienced back-up in what was his first managerial post. Former Dundee United boss Jerry Kerr, who had left Tannadice in 1972 after 13 years in charge, was appointed general manager and he would look after the administrative side of things at Dens. And in another move, city accountant Maurice Speedie, a former president of the Thistle Street Social Club, had joined Ian Gellatly, Graham Thomson and William Lyburn on the board of directors.

Relegation had meant the release of Alex Caldwell, Willie Watson, Peter Millar and Ian McDougall while long-serving Ally Donaldson (36), whose Testimonial against Dundee United attracted an attendance of 4,847, had decided to concentrate on his Carnoustie hotel business after refusing to come to terms.

The Mackay era began with an unbeaten four-game tour of South-West England, but more significantly, only one point was taken from the opening five league games against Dunfermline (a) 0-1, Ayr United (h) 0-0, St Johnstone (a) 0-1, Clydebank (a) 0-3 and Hibs (h) 1-2. After losing at Clydebank, it was a shattered Mackay who commented: "We wouldn't have come second in a two-horse race."

Promotion favourites Dundee now lay bottom of the First Division and, with new blood urgently needed, fruitless moves were made for strikers Alec Bruce (Preston), and Duncan Davidson (Aberdeen). Once again, Jocky Scott attempted a comeback, but, after five appearances, he finally accepted that his recurring back problem spelled the end of his days in competitive football.

In mid-September, Dundee paid a Dens record fee of £61,000 for unsettled Hearts midfielder Cammy Fraser (23). Shortly afterwards, former Aston Villa and Chelsea coach, Frank Upton, was appointed chief-coach and both newcomers would play key roles in the Dens Park revival.

Fraser settled quickly, but despite scoring in the 2-2 Dens draw with Berwick Rangers - when he also missed a penalty - and again in the 3-2 defeat at Motherwell, it was September 20th before Dundee could celebrate their first victory, a 4-0 success over Falkirk at Dens. This provided the platform for an unbeaten seven-game run and by the end of October, they lay in mid-table.

Meanwhile, the Dark Blues had reached the last eight of the Bell's League Cup with aggregate wins over Arbroath (5-0), and Premier side, Kilmarnock (5-4 on penalties after two 0-0 draws). The quarter-final draw paired them with Premier League Champions Aberdeen, but, in a scoreless first leg at Dens, Dundee were unlucky not to win.

The Dons were strong favourites for the Pittodrie return on Wednesday, October 29th, but with Murphy at his trickiest, it was Dundee who held the edge in a torrid first half. After the break, Geddes performed heroics as Dundee were pinned back, but with five minutes remaining, Fraser beat Leighton with a 15-yard drive to clinch a place in the last four.

That was Dundee's third cup success in six years at Pittodrie and, this time, the luck of the draw decreed that they would meet fellow First Division side Ayr United with Celtic meeting Dundee United in the other tie.

At Ayr, several Dens Parkers were affected by a flu virus and George McGeachie was unable to reappear after half-time. Nevertheless, only a last-gasp goal by Bobby Connor earned Ayr a 1-1 draw and there was a 9,438 crowd for the Dens return on Wednesday, November 19th.

On a rain-soaked pitch, Dundee made all the early running and Williamson scored with a low shot in 22 minutes. By half-time the picture had changed. Ayr equalised through Gerry Christie and just before the break, Dundee suffered another blow when MacLaren and Schaedler were stretchered off after a clash of heads.

Barr and Mackie substituted but, in 57 minutes, Billy McColl put Ayr ahead. There was a certain eeriness about Dens at that time as seating work had closed off the popular South Enclosure which meant that the club had temporarily lost its noisiest source of backing. Nevertheless, the Dark Blue fans - most of them having flitted to alien surroundings - excelled themselves that night. Roared on, Dundee besieged the

Erich Schaedler - taken off with a head knock.

We've done it - the celebrations after Cammy Fraser's goal in a battling performance against Ayr United clinched Dundee's place in the League Cup Final.
DC Thomson

Williamson, A. Geddes; Stephen, Sinclair. Subsitutes. - Shirra, Scrimgeour. Dundee United: McAlpine; Holt, Hegarty (capt), Narey, Kopel; Bannon, Phillip, Payne; Pettigrew, Sturrock, Dodds. Subs. - Kirkwood, Stark.

In the absence of the injured Stewart MacLaren, Bobby Glennie was given the captaincy. McGeachie came into central defence while, in midfield Shirra made way for Andy Geddes (24), a recent £20,000 signing from Leicester City.

Up front, the experienced Fleming was out with a long-term stomach injury and with Ferguson, Fletcher and Corrigan out of favour, 17-year-old Ray Stephen retained his place after netting five goals in seven appearances. Earlier that week, the mercurial Jim Murphy had been disciplined for a sub-

visitors' goal and, with the heavy pitch taking its toll on Ayr, Fraser burst through to equalise. And near the end, Sinclair crashed home the winner to send the Dens fans wild with delight.

"That was a real thriller," commented Cammy Fraser. "But we got tremendous backing from the crowd and, after beating Aberdeen in the previous round, we feared nobody." Dundee were through to their first final since 1973, but although Schaedler soon recovered from stitches to a head wound, MacLaren faced a lengthy absence after an operation for a depressed fracture of the cheekbone.

Meanwhile, Dundee United had beaten Celtic, and for the first time, the two Dundee clubs would contest a national final. A year earlier, the 27,299 crowd at the Aberdeen v Dundee United final had been lost in the vastness of Hampden. The replay was switched to Dens and the tighter ground had provided a much-improved atmosphere for the 28,984 fans. Wisely, the Scottish League had chosen the city of Jute, Jam and Journalism as the venue for the "all-Dundee final" with the toss of a coin confirming that Dens Park would again house the big game.

The Dark Blues were on a high and by League Cup Final day on Saturday, December 6th, wins over Stirling Albion (h) 5-1, and Dumbarton (a) 2-1, had elevated them to fourth place in the First Division after a 17-game unbeaten run.

Dundonian Cammy Fraser had brought drive and attacking flair to midfield and, under the direction of Mackay and Upton, the Dark Blues were emerging as a well-organised side. Nevertheless, Premier League United were League Cup holders and, with stars like Bannon, Hegarty, Narey, Phillip, Pettigrew and Sturrock, they remained firm favourites to retain the trophy. Dundee lined up: B. Geddes; Barr, Glennie (capt), McGeachie, Schaedler; Mackie, Fraser,

standard performance in a reserve game against Arbroath and to the fans' amazement, he did not even merit a place on the bench.

The 1975 Ground Safety Act which was put on the Statute Book after the Ibrox disaster in 1971, reduced the Dens Park crowd limit from 40,000 to 31,000. To further comply with new legislation, Dundee had chosen to install bench seating rather than replace the existing crush barriers and, with the South Enclosure seating recently completed, the ground capacity was reduced to 24,700 for the all-ticket final.

The tremendous demand for tickets led to thousands being disappointed and, when Dundee's allocation went on sale, long queues stretched from Sandeman Street right around the ground and back up to Tannadice Street. Dundee United fans were allocated the Provost Road terracing with Dundee fans occupying all other areas of the ground except the stand which was shared.

At kick-off, there were sporadic flurries of snow, but although United controlled the early play, it was Dundee who came closest. In 22 minutes, Sinclair headed the ball into the net after Hamish McAlpine fumbled a high cross from Schaedler only for local referee Bob Valentine to rule that the keeper had been fouled.

United were having the best of the exchanges in an untidy game, and 30 seconds from the interval, Davie Dodds found acres of room to head home a pinpoint left-wing cross from Paul Sturrock. The Tannadice side continued to dominate and when Hegarty's header came off the bar following a 60th-minute corner, Sturrock scored from close in. Soon afterwards, McAlpine sent Stephen sprawling in the box. However, no penalty was awarded and the writing was on the wall for the Dark Blues.

By then, Scrimgeour and Shirra had come on for the

ineffective Williamson and Geddes, but the pattern remained unaltered. With seven minutes left, United forced another corner and when Geddes could only parry a powerful header from Hegarty, the unmarked Sturrock made it 3-0.

Former manager Davie White felt that Sinclair had scored a good goal. Donald Mackay agreed but admitted: "We didn't play well. Slack defending cost all three goals and we just didn't compete well enough." It had been a well-behaved game with no bookings and few arrests. And although bitterly disappointed at the result, Dundee had the consolation of £19,000 in gate money, £14,000 from Bell's as runners-up plus a share of TV fees and programme sales.

Bobby Glennie and George McGeachie had fought all the way although the defensive assurance of Stewart MacLaren had been badly missed. For much of the final the midfield had played second fiddle to their Tannadice counterparts for whom Graeme Payne had been outstanding.

Ray Stephen had done well up front but Dundee had never looked like winning. The flair of Murphy might well have been a telling influence while the inclusion of Shirra from the start would have brought a better balance to midfield. Significantly, both were recalled and victories over East Stirling (a) 2-0, and Hibs (h) 1-0, took Dundee into third place, two points behind Raith Rovers and three behind leaders Hibs.

A 15th-second diving header by Sinclair proved the winner against Hibs but only a brave display by Bobby Geddes had ensured both points. An early clash with Rae resulted in severe knee ligament damage but, although heavily strapped up, Geddes bravely played on. Near the end, the courageous keeper - by this time playing the game of his life - took a bad head knock but he was once again able to play on and capped a flawless display with a miraculous save from Craig Paterson just on full-time.

In August, Dundee had signed ex-Hibs keeper Mike McDonald on a month's trial. Soon afterwards he damaged a cartilage and, with Geddes well established McDonald had been released. Now, Geddes was out for the remainder of the

Out of luck - Ray Stephen appears to have been sent sprawling by Hamish McAlpine in the League Cup Final but Bob Valentine turned down the penalty claims to the relief of Dave Narey, Paul Hegarty and John Holt.

DC Thomson

Early strike - Eric Sinclair heads Dundee into an early lead against Hibs with Billy McLaren helpless. BELOW - Jimmy Murphy gives St Johnstone's George Fleming and Duncan Lambie a torrid time at Dens.   DC Thomson

season and, initially, Dumbarton's Lawrie Williams arrived on loan. However, the Boghead keeper did little to inspire confidence. His stay coincided with seven games without a win, including a 1-0 defeat at Falkirk in the first round of the Scottish Cup, and, by mid-March, Dundee had dropped to sixth in the league, eleven points behind second-placed Raith Rovers.

Meanwhile, Jim Shirra joined Australian side Apia and, after Williams was allowed to rejoin Dumbarton, Dundee signed East Fife keeper Alan Blair on a short-term deal. The bearded custodian made a shaky start but a series of plucky displays quickly endeared him to the fans and also earned him an extended contract.

On February 28th, a waterlogged pitch caused Dundee's

home match against Dumbarton to be abandoned after just 63 minutes with the score at 0-0.

Eleven days later, the clubs met again and despite the absence of Fraser, who was suspended for three games, Dundee struggled to a 2-1 win. That was to prove the turning point and four successive wins followed against Raith Rovers (h) 3-1, Dunfermline (h) 2-0, Hamilton (a) 3-1, and Stirling Albion (a) 1-0 before a point was dropped in a no-scoring draw with Berwick at Dens.

Now Dundee lay just six points behind Raith Rovers and in early April, they faced vital home games against Raith and St Johnstone. The Stark's Park outfit were managed by former Dens striker Gordon Wallace but, despite the presence of another Dens favourite in veteran midfielder Bobby Ford, Dundee again took the points in a hard-fought 2-1 win.

Three days later a crowd of 8,586 witnessed a Tayside derby thriller against St Johnstone. With 22 minutes remaining, things looked bleak for Dundee when Schaedler went off injured with both substitutes already committed. Just four minutes earlier, Ally McCoist had equalised for St Johnstone but, in a fighting finish, goals by Scrimgeour, Mackie and Sinclair kept the Dark Blues' promotion hopes very much alive.

On April 4th, 1981 the table showed that any two from six teams could yet lay claim to the Premier League prize:

First Division (Top)			
	P	F A	Pts
Hibernian	35	59-23	50
Raith Rovers	35	48-25	48
St Johnstone	36	59-43	46
Dundee	35	59-38	45
Ayr United	36	57-39	43
Motherwell	33	57-47	41

With the finishing post in sight, Dundee faced a tricky run-in against: Dunfermline (a), Clydebank (h), Falkirk (a), and

Dundee F.C. Season 1980-81, Bell's League Cup Finalists and First Division runners-up (BACK, left to right) Donald Mackay (manager), Eric Ferguson (physio), Andy Geddes, Bobby Geddes, Ian Fleming, Les Barr, Jim Shirra, Iain Ferguson, Brian Scrimgeour, Frank Upton (coach). MIDDLE - Erich Schaedler, Ray Stephen, George McGeachie. FRONT - Billy Williamson, Peter Mackie, Jimmy Murphy, Cammy Fraser, Eric Sinclair, Bobby Glennie. (Inset - Stewart MacLaren)

Fotopress

He stooped to conquer - Eric Sinclair keeps his head down to nod home the vital goal against East Stirling at Firs Park with Ray Stephen and Brian Scrimgeour watching.   DC Thomson

Last season, the hard-working Eric Sinclair had finished top scorer with 13 league and cup goals. Now, ably assisted by pacy forwards like Ray Stephen, Jim Murphy and Peter Mackie, he was eight goals better off and his finishing would prove decisive in the final game at Firs Park. In 32 minutes Jim Murphy drifted a corner beyond the far post and, when Glennie nodded back across goal, Sinclair was on the spot to head home.

There was delight amongst the huge Dundee support in the 5,762 crowd, but it remained a tense occasion. Driven on by Cammy Fraser, Dundee held the edge but the hard, bumpy pitch made things difficult and, at time-up, only Sinclair's goal separated the teams. The fair-haired striker had always been confident of success: "I generally did well against my home town teams, particularly at Brockville, so I had no fears about our last two games."

Courageously, the Dens board had decided that Dundee would remain full-time that season. It was a policy that had cost the club around £5,000 per week, and amidst the jubilant scenes at full-time, chairman Ian Gellatly was a relieved man. Recently, Hugh Robertson, a coach at Dens since 1972, had departed in a cost-cutting exercise and the chairman rightly stated: "Tonight, our bank manager will be the happiest man in Dundee!"

East Stirling (a). A point was dropped in a 1-1 draw at East End Park before Andy Geddes got the only goal in a desperately nervy home performance against Clydebank. However, Raith's slump continued and defeats by St Johnstone, Hibs and Clydebank meant they had taken only nine points from 11 games. In addition, St Johnstone had dropped a point at East Stirling while Motherwell and Ayr had fallen out of contention.

Now promotion lay within Dundee's grasp. In a fiercely contested game at Brockville, Murphy and Stephen scored soon after half-time and, although the Bairns pulled one back, Dundee held on to win.

CHAPTER TWENTY-ONE

Tight for Cash

That close-season, the influential Frank Upton departed for a post in Kuwait and Ken Wimhurst, another with Bristol City connections, took over as chief-coach. Jocky Scott, whose Testimonial against Aberdeen at Dens had attracted around 5,000 fans on the day after the promotion-clinching game against East Stirling, would remain as reserve-coach. "Upton had formed a good partnership with Donald Mackay," according to Cammy Fraser. "Mackay was the affable type, while Upton was a no-nonsense disciplinarian."

There were also changes on the playing side. Stewart MacLaren had been unhappy at the cost of travelling to Dens from his Hamilton home. Now at the end of his contract, the Dundee skipper joined Hearts under the new freedom-of-contract arrangement and later the clubs agreed on a fee of £30,000. Billy Williamson and Stuart Turnbull were both released while Andy Geddes, who had shown some classy touches in midfield, would be sidelined from first-team action for the whole season due to cartilage trouble.

However, Donald Mackay had signed some experienced replacements. First Motherwell midfielder Albert Kidd (24), arrived for a new Dens record fee of £80,000, former St Johnstone centre-half Iain MacDonald (28), cost £45,000 from Carlisle then ex-Aberdeen full-back Chic McLelland was secured on a free transfer from Motherwell.

But despite these signings, the Dark Blues made a disastrous start to the 1981-82 season. The League Cup, no longer sponsored by Bell's, reverted to a sectional format and Dundee could only manage one point from their six ties before falling 2-0 in the league opener against Hibernian at Easter Road.

Dundee-born full-back Danny Cameron was obtained on a free transfer from Preston and, with Barr, McLelland and McKimmie already providing good cover, Erich Schaedler returned to Hibs for £12,500. Veteran keeper Ally Donaldson had only recently ended his self-imposed exile but, soon after Schaedler's departure, he also moved to Easter Road for a fee of £5,000.

There were home successes over Partick Thistle (4-2), and St Mirren (3-0), and on September 12th, a spirited performance saw Ferguson, with a penalty, and Mackie retrieve a two-goal deficit at Tannadice. However, a somewhat pedestrian rearguard of Barr, MacDonald, Glennie and Cameron was ill-equipped to handle the pace of Paul Sturrock, Eamonn Bannon and Ralph Milne and the men in Tangerine went on to record a 5-2 win.

Cash splash - Albert Kidd cost a new Dens record fee of £80,000. SNS Group

Dundee began to struggle and, by the end of October, five consecutive defeats left them at the bottom of the league. Since the inception of the Premier League, one of the two promoted sides had always gone straight back down and, already the signs were ominous for the Dark Blues.

Just four points had been taken from the first quarter of the league programme compared to eight at the same stage in 1975-76 and five in 1979-80 - and both these Premier sojourns had ended in the drop. Only Celtic had bettered their tally of 15 goals but the defence had conceded 23 league goals and this was again the main source of concern.

Last season, youngsters like Bobby Geddes, Stewart McKimmie and Ray Stephen had been introduced with great success and now the diminutive Davie Bell (18), impressed as an industrious midfielder while Iain Ferguson - a big disappointment last term - confirmed his early potential with seven goals from the opening nine league games.

Albert Kidd had not so far lived up to expectations. On September 26th, he was sent off at Cappielow along with Morton's Danny Docherty after an incident described as "a game of headers without a ball!" There had been no scoring at the time and Morton went on to win 2-0.

Donald Mackay was enraged but the lesson went unheeded. A fortnight later, Ian Fleming, who had missed most of the previous season through injury, was ordered off at Broomfield after a first-half incident with Airdrie centre-half Jim March and a weakened Dundee team ended up going down 4-2.

In late November, Jocky Scott took over as chief-coach following the resignation of Ken Wimhurst. The Englishman had been unable to settle in Dundee and, soon afterwards, there was another departure when John Fletcher, who had never been able to establish himself, joined Montrose for a fee of £5,000.

Back in the big time - Cammy Fraser, new signing Iain MacDonald and George McGeachie combine to foil Dundee United's Paul Hegarty at Dens with United's Eamonn Bannon and Dundee's Les Barr ready to step in.
DC Thomson

Although the Premier League meant glamour games against Celtic, Rangers, Aberdeen and Dundee United, it was the clashes against the sides in the lower half of the league which were crucial to Dundee's survival. In effect these games became "cup finals" but, with confidence growing, wins over Partick Thistle (a) 2-1, Morton (h) 4-1, and Airdrie (h) 3-1, lifted them above Airdrie and Partick into eighth place.

The end of the year brought frosty weather but the under-soil heating at Ibrox and Easter Road ensured the games against Rangers and Hibs went ahead. Both resulted in 2-1 defeats but, more significantly, centre-half Iain MacDonald had the misfortune to break a leg against Hibs. In his absence, however, Donald Mackay introduced 19-year-old Jim Smith and the lanky defender quickly formed a useful partnership alongside Bobby Glennie.

In the Scottish Cup, a 1-0 home win over Raith Rovers then a 3-0 Sunday success against Meadowbank earned the Dark Blues a quarter-final tie against Rangers in Glasgow. In total, both ties had attracted less than 10,000 but, although the 16,072 attendance at Ibrox brought some much needed revenue to the Dens Park coffers, it would prove the end of the cup trail for Dundee. In the 54th minute of a drab game, Mackie scorned a golden opportunity and when first Derek Johnstone then Colin McAdam scored soon afterwards, Rangers were on their way to the semi-final.

As the see-saw relegation struggle continued, Dundee slipped three points behind Airdrie and Partick Thistle but seven points from their next six games saw them back in eighth place by the end of March 1982.

Dundee's prolonged stay in the First Division had coincided with an upturn in the fortunes of Dundee United.

Historically, Dundee had carried the larger support but, more recently, the balance had swung the other way. That season, the Dark Blues had already lost 5-2 at Tannadice and 3-1 at Dens but on Wednesday, March 10th, they battled to a 1-1 draw at Tannadice with McKimmie unfortunate enough to put through his own goal.

But, although this was followed by 2-0 wins in relegation "four-pointers" at Airdrie and Firhill, Dundee's dismal disciplinary record continued. In November, Stephen had been red-carded against Morton and, when McGeachie was sent off after a clash with Partick Thistle's Alex O'Hara, he became the fourth Dens Parker to have received his marching orders that season.

Since August, clubs had retained all gate money from their own home games. Dundee's attendances, however, were

down on their previous Premier League campaigns and, with the financial situation worsening, an Extraordinary General Meeting in March determined that Dundee F.C. Limited would become a Public Limited Company. A share issue of 430,000 £1 shares would take Dundee's ordinary share capital to £500,000 and it was hoped that this cash injection would clear the club of its crippling debts.

In the light of this financial crisis, it was crucial for the club to remain in the Premier League and, for the vital midweek clash with Partick Thistle at Dens, Dundee's thirteen-man squad included Geddes, McKimmie, Smith, Ferguson, Scrimgeour, and Davidson, all of whom were under 21 years of age. Five games remained but, with Airdrie looking doomed, a home win would put Dundee a commanding six points above ninth-placed Thistle.

Donald Park put the visitors ahead against the run of play and, although Sinclair equalised on half-time, a late slip by Geddes allowed Ian Jardine's free-kick to slip tantalisingly by him for the winner.

Under pressure - Dundee's young keeper Bobby Geddes keeps Celtic's George McCluskey at bay while Brian Scrimgeour grimaces. DC Thomson

Dundee had been badly affected by nerves but, four days later, they overcame the loss of another early goal to beat Morton 2-1 at Dens. The jittery Dark Blues then crashed to Aberdeen (h) 0-5, and Rangers (a) 0-4, and although Thistle had also slipped up, they required one point from their final game against Airdrie at home on Saturday, May 15th to ensure survival. Should Thistle beat Dundee United at Firhill and Dundee lose, the Dens men would go down on goal-difference. That morning the bottom of the league table looked like this:

May 15th, 1982				
	P	F	A	Pts
Dundee	35	45-71		24
Partick This.	35	34-47		22
Airdrie	35	31-75		18

A crowd of 6,600 saw Dundee line up: Blair; McKimmie, Smith, Glennie, McLelland; Davidson, Fraser, McGeachie, Stephen; Sinclair, Ferguson. Subs. - Kidd, Mackie. Although Bobby Geddes had recovered from his career-threatening injury and had made two appearances for the Scotland Under-21s, he had recently lost confidence and Alan Blair was recalled to the team.

In only two minutes, the bearded keeper saved bravely at the feet of the inrushing Sandy Clark. His team-mates took heart and, although the sun-baked surface produced a scrappy contest, Iain Ferguson ensured Dundee's safety with the only goal of the game in 32 minutes.

Earlier that week, two legendary Dens Park figures, Billy Steel (53), and Bob Shankly (67), had died and, as thousands of rejoicing fans invaded the pitch at the end, their names were chanted along with that of the fans' latest hero - manager Donald Mackay.

Although Partick Thistle were beaten 2-1 by Dundee United in Glasgow and therefore the Dens result had not mattered, no-one grudged Mackay his moment of glory. Many felt that the club had taken a huge gamble in appointing the likeable Perth man to the post, but not only had he

guided the club to the Premier League, he had also managed to keep them there.

Les Barr, and Paul Smith, who went on to play for Dundee United, Motherwell, Dunfermline, Falkirk and Dunfermline again, were amongst those given free transfers but, with no money available for new faces, Dundee's hopes would again be pinned on youth. Eric Sinclair had little doubt that Dundee's future lay in developing their youth policy.

"Ferguson, Stephen and McKimmie had quickly proved themselves worthy of a first-team place. Fergie was a great finisher, while Ray Stephen, although not so good at finding the net, was a real power-house. Stewart McKimmie was fast and a great tackler and had all the attributes necessary to reach the top."

Dundee made a bright start to the 1982-83 League Cup, drawing 3-3 at Aberdeen before defeating Dumbarton 3-2 at Dens. And, despite losing 4-1 at rain-soaked Cappielow, a 3-2 win at Dumbarton left them level with Morton and a point behind section leaders Aberdeen. Both had still to visit Dens and Dundee had high hopes of earning a place in the quarter-finals.

At Pittodrie, Dundee had deservedly shared the spoils. Peter Mackie produced his best-ever display in a Dark Blue jersey to give the towering Doug Rougvie an uncomfortable afternoon. However, the optimism was to prove sadly misplaced and a catalogue of defensive blunders saw them crash 5-1 to Aberdeen at Dens.

Former favourite Gordon Strachan had been the main tormentor, capping a virtuoso performance with four great goals for the Dons. The brilliant midfielder had gone from strength to strength at Pittodrie and, now a regular for Scotland, it was abundantly clear that Dundee had made a gross under-valuation of his transfer value.

Changes were made and despite losing to Celtic in the league opener at Parkhead, a five-game unbeaten run against Motherwell (h) 3-1, Morton (h) 2-0, Killie (a) 0-0, Rangers (a) 1-1, and Hibs (h) 2-1, had taken the spirited Dark Blues within a point of early pacemakers Celtic.

Bobby Geddes had regained his place from Alan Blair but a nightmare performance against Aberdeen in the League

Tight-spot - Dundee's financial plight meant that the club desperately needed the game against Aberdeen to go ahead despite the atrocious underfoot conditions. Here Peter Weir comes close as Bobby Glennie and Colin Kelly watch anxiously. DC Thomson

Cup meant a prolonged spell in the reserves along with Andy Geddes and Chic McLelland. The Under-21 keeper had looked particularly vulnerable at high crosses when challenged by the likes of Doug Rougvie and Alex McLeish and Alex Ferguson's side had exploited this to the full.

Colin Kelly, who had spent much of the previous season on loan to Montrose, was given his chance. He proved a commanding keeper and, with a settled back four of Glennie, Smith, MacDonald and McKimmie, there was a big improvement in defence. In midfield, recently appointed club captain Cammy Fraser was ably assisted by Ian Fleming and Peter Mackie.

Fraser was a Dundonian and, although a Dundee United fan as a boy, had been delighted to sign for Dundee: "I had always hoped to play for one of the city clubs and it was a great honour when I was made skipper."

Alongside the swashbuckling Fraser, Fleming revelled in his new role of midfield destroyer but, in late October, he became player-manager of Brechin City with Dundee getting £5,000 in compensation.

Up front, the experienced Sinclair was partnered by Ferguson and Stephen. Both youngsters had featured in Jock Stein's Under-21 squads and Ferguson had again showed his eye for goal with nine to his credit already.

But things could alter quickly in the highly competitive Premier League, and, by mid-November, a series of single-goal defeats saw the Dark Blues alongside Motherwell at the foot of the league.

However, it was not only the slump in form that was giving concern. Since 1980, Dundee's financial situation had steadily worsened and now matters had reached crisis point. In May, a trading loss of £297,301 on top of a £264,343 loss from 1980-81 left Dundee nearly £600,000 in the red and rumours began to circulate that the club could fold by Christmas.

Only 115,000 shares had been taken up from the public share issue. This enabled Dundee to continue as a full-time club but only after directors Gellatly, Thomson, Lyburn, Speedie and the recently-appointed Fife businessman Andrew Marshall had raised their personal guarantees from £200,000 to £250,000.

Much of the expenditure had gone towards the purchase of Fraser (£61,000), Andy Geddes (£25,000), MacDonald (£45,000), and Kidd (£80,000), but freedom-of-contract meant the payment of signing-on fees when negotiating new contracts for the present staff. Now, the club faced huge interest payments on their overdraft and despite chairman Ian Gellatly's assurances that everything possible would be done to keep the club going, it was clearly a period of grave concern.

Meanwhile, there were encouraging wins over fellow-strugglers Morton (a) 2-1, and Killie (h) 5-2, although there were only 4,311 at Dens for the visit of the Ayrshire side - Dundee's lowest home attendance of the season. A crowd of 11,681 had watched Dundee's previous home game against Celtic three weeks earlier and a blank Saturday on December 4th since scheduled visitors, Rangers, were to play Celtic in the League Cup Final at Hampden had the club's bank manager twitching nervously.

The Parkhead side had been due to play Dundee United but although Dundee proposed bringing forward the Ne'erday Dens derby, the Tannadice outfit preferred an idle weekend before travelling to meet Werder Bremen in the UEFA Cup the following week. And, when a lucrative challenge match in Saudi Arabia also fell through, things looked increasingly bleak for the Dark Blues.

Dundee's next home fixture against Aberdeen was not due until December 18th and, by then, a severe frost had left Dens Park bone hard with a light covering of snow. Dundee's future was hanging by a thread but, to the board's relief, an early inspection by a local referee deemed the pitch playable, and despite Aberdeen's complaints over the state of the surface, this decision was later confirmed by match official Jim Duncan of Gorebridge.

On a bitterly cold afternoon, intermittent flurries of snow did little to improve underfoot conditions. Dundee lost 2-0 but although the first goal looked blatantly offside there were few complaints from the Dark Blues. The game had attracted only a modest 6,528 but with the Bank of Scotland threatening to call in their loan, some much-needed income had been generated.

Two weeks later, a bumper 18,109 crowd watched the Dens derby with Dundee United. This was the largest attendance in a league derby since January 1969 and Dundee's immediate financial crisis was over. The polished Tannadice side, now forging a formidable reputation in Europe, ran out 2-0 winners, but by the end of January 1983, the Dark Blues lay fifth after taking four points from their next four games.

It was hoped the club's finances would be boosted by a good run in the Scottish Cup. In the first round, Brora Rangers became Dundee's first Highland League visitors in the Cup for 52 years. Despite Dundee's non-stop attacks on the muddy Dens surface, the Brora part-timers defended gallantly but, with only 30 seconds remaining, Eric Sinclair's diving header beat Suttar to clinch a 2-1 win for the Dark Blues.

In the next round, Dundee were forced on the defensive in a dour struggle at Pittodrie. Shortly after the interval, Neil Simpson scored the only goal but there was no disgrace in losing to an outstanding Aberdeen team, who were fast heading for success in both the Scottish Cup and the European Cup-Winners' Cup.

On Wednesday, March 2nd, only 6,624 Dens fans saw Albert Kidd net in a 1-0 win over Rangers before defeats by Hibs (h) 1-0, Aberdeen (a) 1-3, St Mirren (h) 2-5, and Dundee United (a) 3-5, again plunged Dundee deep into the relegation mire. Geddes replaced Kelly for the Tannadice derby but only six minutes had elapsed before he was led off with a damaged collar-bone after a collision with team-mate Jim Smith.

Brian Scrimgeour went in goal and, despite trailing 2-0, second-half counters by Ferguson with a penalty, Kidd and Fraser put Dundee 3-2 ahead. Tragically, the stand-in keeper lost a soft goal eight minutes from time and title-chasing United went on to win by five goals to three.

Nevertheless, the Dark Blues had played with great spirit and, in a repeat performance the following Saturday, goals by Albert Kidd and Brian Scrimgeour, now restored to midfield, earned a 2-1 win over second-placed Celtic at Dens.

After an erratic start to the campaign, Albert Kidd had dropped out of the side and the club agreed to his request for a transfer. Recently, however, the popular midfielder had returned to form with four goals in four games. And when he was substituted by Ferguson near the end of the Celtic game, there were roars of indignation from home fans although the manager later explained that the change had been made for tactical reasons.

For much of the season, the Dark Blues had avoided the relegation zone and with four games remaining, no-scoring draws, at home to Kilmarnock and away to Hibs, finally ensured their place in the Premier League.

On May 4th, a 2-1 win over Rangers at Dens gave Dundee six points out of eight from the Ibrox side that term. The Light Blues' frustration was evident when their Northern Ireland international John McLelland was red-carded for kicking Iain Ferguson after full-time but, sadly for Dundee, only 4,778, a record low for the fixture, had looked on.

Three days later, Dundee's game with St Mirren at Love Street was abandoned after 23 minutes due to torrential rain. The Dark Blues had led 1-0 but in the replay, two days later, a late Frank McDougall goal gave Saints a 2-1 win.

In their final game, Dundee played host to league leaders Dundee United, who lay one point clear of Celtic and Aberdeen. A win would give United their first-ever title success but Dundee's pride was at stake and they were equally determined to put one over their local rivals.

As kick-off approached, huge crowds packed the surrounding streets and, despite the 25,000 ground capacity, the official attendance was given as 29,016. Ian Gellatly claimed there had been a misunderstanding between himself and the police over when the gates should be closed but the bearded chairman readily admitted that the £50,000 gate money was most welcome!

In a tension-packed match, United led 2-0 after 11 minutes only for Ferguson to reduce the leeway on the half-hour. As nerves began to affect the visitors, Dundee looked the likelier side but, with no further score, it was United who were left to celebrate their Premier League title win. And, as the Dens fans slipped quietly away, they could only reflect on

Under pressure - Iain MacDonald boots the ball clear against Hibs at Dens with Cammy Fraser and Jim Smith looking on.

DC Thomson

the irony of United's third trophy success in four years at Dens Park under the management of ex-Dundee player and coach Jim McLean.

That season had seen a big improvement, particularly in defence and with Dundee finishing sixth - their highest placing since 1975 - it was now hoped that the club might go on to challenge for a place in Europe. The financial position had also been improved with a much reduced trading loss of £166,364 that May.

Fanfare - a goal for Iain Ferguson with big Colin Harris and Tosh McKinlay joining the celebrations

Nevertheless, Dundee remained heavily in debt and some drastic cuts had been required. Full-time youth coach John Markie, who had been appointed a year earlier, and seven players, including Davie Bell, Danny Cameron, Chic McLelland, and Brian Scrimgeour were released with Alan Blair, Andy Geddes, Jim Murphy and Eric Sinclair placed on the transfer list.

Two signings were made. Promising 17-year-old Highland League striker Colin Hendry cost £500 from Keith while Walker McCall (31), the former Aberdeen, St Johnstone and Ayr United striker was signed from Hong Kong side, South China. It was hoped that the experienced six-foot plus McCall would complement top scorer Iain Ferguson, who had netted an impressive 30 league and cup goals over the past two seasons.

Ferguson was at the end of his contract but, after initially agreeing to a monthly deal, Dens hopes were boosted when the scoring ace put pen to paper for the rest of the season. McCall settled quickly while another to impress was 18-year-old left-back Tosh McKinlay, who had made his debut at Paisley near the end of the previous season.

However, Dundee's Premier League campaign began badly and, by the end of September, only one point had been taken from five games. The Dark Blues had been unlucky to lose to newly-promoted Hearts (h) 1-2, but heavy defeats to Aberdeen (a) 0-3, and Dundee United (h) 1-4, gave grave cause for concern.

In August, Jim Murphy had joined Ayr United for £5,000 while another Dens favourite 29-year-old Eric Sinclair, who had been out in the cold since the arrival of Walker McCall, was exchanged for St Mirren midfielder Lex Richardson (30). Richardson made his debut against Celtic at Dens but the game was to end in further disaster. After a bad foul by Davie Provan on young McKinlay, Cammy Fraser was sent off for taking retribution - a crunching tackle sent the winger flying - and the Parkhead side went on to win 6-2.

The following week, Bobby Geddes and Andy Geddes, both now recovered from injury, were recalled for the game at Motherwell. The keeper justified his inclusion by saving Andy Dornan's penalty in Dundee's 3-1 win and, with

morale boosted, five of the next eight games resulted in victory. On October 15th, a double by Ferguson and one from McCall earned a 3-2 win over Rangers at Dens and, three weeks later, a 19th-minute Peter Mackie counter at Tannadice gave Dundee their first derby win over United since October 1979.

There was fierce competition between Glennie, MacDonald and Smith for the two central-defensive positions but, in late October, it was Glennie who made the headlines when he sent a blistering 35-yard drive past Aberdeen and Scotland keeper Jim Leighton at Dens. The big defender later commented: "If the net hadn't stopped the ball, they'd never have found it!"

That season, the League Cup format had again been changed. Now, after two preliminary rounds, the 16 remaining sides were divided into four sections with the winners going on to contest the semi-finals.

Given a first-round bye, a 7-2 aggregate win over Montrose took Dundee into a section comprising Aberdeen, St Johnstone and Meadowbank. Strangely, these ties were played over a three-month period but, by Wednesday, November 30th, Dundee's eight point tally left them just one point behind section leaders Aberdeen, who they faced in the final game at Dens.

The Dark Blues had battled to a 0-0 draw at Pittodrie but their hopes of reaching the money-spinning semi-finals were dealt a savage blow just after half-time. Bobby Geddes was taken to hospital with a gashed mouth caused by a reckless Neale Cooper challenge. Ray Stephen took over in goal and, almost immediately, Aberdeen, who had opened the scoring midway through the first half, went 2-0 ahead in controversial fashion. Although a linesman flagged for offside, Dougie Bell's goal was allowed to stand and, while Fraser later pulled one back, Dundee's chance had gone.

The disappointment continued with a 2-2 draw against St Mirren at Dens before a 3-0 home defeat by Hibs brought matters to a head. And on Monday, December 12th, it was announced that Donald Mackay had resigned "by mutual consent".

Chairman Ian Gellatly agreed that Mackay had kept Dundee in the Premier League after gaining promotion and had brought through several youngsters: "Donald did well in his three-and-a-half years in charge. There is no question that he put Dundee back on an even keel but home form had been poor and the club's directors felt he could take the club no further."

In another shock move, the hard-tackling Stewart

Sold - Stewart McKimmie

McKimmie had been transferred to Aberdeen for £80,000 - a decision prompted by pressure from long-term creditors. In truth, the directors had also used some of the McKimmie transfer fee to finance Mackay's departure but with the youngster later fulfilling his promise by becoming an established Scotland player, it was another example of an Aberdeen "steal" from Dens Park.

CHAPTER TWENTY-TWO

Enter Archie Knox

The manager's chair was vacant for only four days and Dundee reversed the Aberdeen pattern when Pittodrie assistant-manager Archie Knox (40), was appointed manager with Jocky Scott confirmed as his No 2. Knox was highly respected in coaching circles and was known as a strict disciplinarian. In his youth, the new boss had supported the Dark Blues and, after three successful years alongside Alex Ferguson at Pittodrie, it was hoped he might be the man to revive Dundee's "sleeping giant".

There was to be no glory start for Knox and, although defeats by Rangers (a) 1-2, St Johnstone (h) 0-1, and Aberdeen (a) 2-5, were followed by a morale-boosting 4-1 win over Hearts at Dens, another four reverses left the Dark Blues in serious trouble.

Early in 1984, Bobby Geddes had the misfortune to break an ankle in training and a few weeks later Andy Geddes walked out and returned to his native South Africa. In late February, Dundee paid £15,000 for 22-year-old Raith Rovers striker Colin Harris but despite scoring within a minute of his debut against Rangers, the Dark Blues tumbled to a 3-1 home defeat.

Nevertheless, wins over Cowdenbeath (a) 2-0, and Airdrie (h) 2-1, took Dundee to the Scottish Cup quarter-finals and on March 10th they met strong-going Rangers at Dens. Twice the Ibrox side took the lead but goals by Ferguson and Kidd gave Dundee a well-earned draw.

With Rangers 2-1 ahead, a MacDonald header was tipped onto the bar by Nicky Walker and, after spinning high into the air, the ball came down for McCall to head home. Initially, a goal was given but, when a linesman adjudged the ball to have gone out, referee Alan Ferguson changed his mind and awarded a goal-kick! The embarrassed officials knew they had blundered and left Dens Park trying to convince anyone prepared to listen that the swirling wind had blown the ball back into play for McCall to score.

Glennie, McGeachie and McKinlay would miss the replay through suspension but Fraser and Ferguson had shrugged off injuries and would play. Smith headed Dundee into the lead and, in 63 minutes, Ferguson finished off a brilliant three-man move with a second. Things looked bleak for Rangers when Redford was ordered off after a clash with Kidd but McClelland and McPherson levelled the scores with 10 minutes remaining.

Now, the rampant Light Blues pushed for the winner but, within three minutes, Ferguson crashed a high shot past Walker to send Dundee's travelling support wild with

Big news - Dundee's appointment of Archie Knox as manager brought widespread media coverage.   Jim Hendry

delight. Rangers' 21-game unbeaten run was over and, after the full-time whistle, their Swedish international midfielder Robert Prytz was sent off for dissent.

Richardson and Mackie had excelled in their unaccustomed roles at full-back and, although Ferguson had scored two fine goals, the influential Fraser had been a key figure in midfield despite playing with a heavily bandaged thigh.

The Dens skipper, who had received a pre-match pain-killing injection after pulling a thigh muscle the previous day, had little doubt it was Dundee's best display of the season: "We outclassed Rangers that day and only a loss of concentration allowed them back in." It was hoped the Ibrox win might spark a Dens revival but, despite making it an Old Firm double with a 3-2 home win over Celtic, three successive home defeats to Hibs (1-2), Dundee United (2-5), and St Mirren (2-5), in a seven day spell soon afterwards, saw them slip to ninth alongside St Johnstone.

Meanwhile, the Scottish Cup semi-final draw had paired Dundee with Aberdeen at Tynecastle, with Celtic and St Mirren contesting the other tie at Hampden. Although the

Up for the Cup - Iain Ferguson lobs the ball past Nicky Walker in the 2-2 draw with Rangers in the Scottish Cup at Dens. Fergie went on to net twice in the 3-2 replay triumph at Ibrox. BELOW - Colin Harris beats Jim Leighton to head home a corner in the semi-final against Aberdeen but the referee ruled he had pushed the keeper.

DC Thomson

Dons were aiming for their third successive cup win, much of Dundee's hopes were pinned on the striking partnership of Ferguson and McCall.

Between them, they had already scored 39 goals that season but, with Ferguson suspended and McCall out with concussion, Dundee were dealt a further blow when Celtic refused to allow recent loan signing Jim McInally to play in the cup-tie. The former youth international full-back had been signed until the end of the season and had become a firm favourite with the fans after ending a lung-bursting 50-yard run with a great goal against Hibs.

A 17,654 Tynecastle crowd saw Dundee field: Geddes; Glennie, Smith, MacDonald, McKinlay; Fraser, McGeachie, Richardson, Mackie; Harris, Kidd. Subs. - Stephen, McGlashan. Aberdeen: Leighton; Mitchell, McLeish, Miller, Rougvie; Strachan, Simpson, Angus; Porteous, Black, Hewitt. Subs. - Bell, Cowan.

It was not to be Dundee's day for, despite looking the more aggressive in the first half, they trailed to a 28th minute Ian Porteous goal from a cleverly worked near-post corner. Ably led by Fraser, the Dons defence were put under considerable pressure but, despite having the ball in the net three times, all Dundee's efforts were disallowed by referee Brian McGinlay. In the final minute, Gordon Strachan settled matters with a second goal but Dundee were unlucky not to have earned a replay.

All efforts could now be concentrated on the relegation battle but, three days later, Dundee left it late against the already-demoted Motherwell at Dens. With only 30 seconds remaining and the score deadlocked at 0-0, the ball bounced high onto the track. Quick as a flash, Archie Knox leaped

168

from the dug-out and headed the ball to Fraser. A quick throw sent Harris away and when his cross came over, young substitute Colin McGlashan was on the spot to head the ball home.

Like the vintage Dundee side of 1963, Dundee United had reached the semi-final of the European Cup but, with Geddes in brilliant form, a tremendous rearguard action at Tannadice earned Dundee a 1-1 draw. Four minutes from time, a trip on Iain Munro led to Fraser's second red card of the season and now the influential Dens skipper would miss four of the remaining games through suspension.

After losing to Celtic (a) 0-3, and Aberdeen (h) 0-1, a late McCall goal brought a welcome 2-2 draw against Rangers at Ibrox but, alarmingly, St Johnstone's win over Motherwell had reduced Dundee's advantage to a single point. This is how the bottom of the Premier League looked:

May 5th, 1984			
	P	F - A	Pts
Hibernian	35	45-55	30
Dundee	34	47-73	24
St Johnstone	35	36-79	23
Motherwell	35	31-74	15

On Wednesday, May 9th, Dundee met Hearts at Tynecastle knowing that defeat would leave the door open for St Johnstone, who would be Dens visitors in the last game of the season. Gary Mackay put Hearts ahead in 10 minutes but the tireless McInally - now being used to great effect in midfield - equalised soon after half-time and the nervy Dark Blues held on for a 1-1 draw.

Now assured of Premier League survival due to their superior goal-difference, Dundee ended with a 2-0 win over St Johnstone at Dens. The Tynecastle game had proved a harrowing experience for Archie Knox and Jocky Scott with the assistant-manager later admitting: "It was my worst-ever night in football, worse even than the last time we were relegated."

After the narrow escape from relegation, Archie Know was determined there would be no repeat. In his view, six new faces were required to transform Dundee's fortunes but with the club still £500,000 in debt, finding the necessary finance remained the major stumbling block.

The Dens boss believed that Fraser, Ferguson and McInally could be the cornerstone of the "new Dundee" but, with all three on freedom-of-contract, there were grave doubts whether they would remain at Dens. Numerous attempts had been made to sign the on-loan McInally from Celtic but the Parkhead club faced potential embarrassment if a player they were rejecting remained in Scotland and emerged as a star.

Against that background, Dundee were surprised when Celtic declined their £40,000 offer after the Parkhead club had earlier indicated that price would secure the player's services. A solution to Celtic's difficulty was for the player to go south and in May, McInally was off to Nottingham Forest after Brian Clough was persuaded to pay £80,000 against Dundee's top bid of £47,000.

Fraser (27), and Ferguson (22), had been offered Dundee's "best-ever terms" but, following speculation that the striker might join Aberdeen in exchange for goalkeeper Brian Gunn and midfielder John McMaster, the Dens duo finally signed for Rangers.

Earlier, Dundee had rejected Rangers' £400,000 bid for the pair and, with the clubs unable to agree a fee, the Transfer Tribunal was asked to adjudicate. But, disappointingly for Dundee, Rangers were ordered to pay £200,000 for Ferguson and £150,000 for Fraser - £50,000 less than they would have received had they accepted the earlier offer.

Archie Knox was bitterly disappointed at losing his top men: "It was a big blow because you can't build anything on rubble. I was banking on signing McInally and holding on to Ferguson and Fraser. I am happy in my own mind that we did everything possible to keep our top players but just how do you replace lads like Ferguson, regardless of how much money we got for him?"

Ferguson and Fraser were not the only departures. Goalkeepers Alan Blair and Colin Kelly were amongst seven players released, while young reserve striker Colin McGlashan joined Dunfermline for £5,000 after rejecting Dundee's terms.

Meanwhile, however, the Dens boss had begun to rebuild. St Mirren centre-half John McCormack (28), arrived in exchange for Peter Mackie, John Brown (Hamilton), was obtained for £40,000, Robert Connor (Ayr United), for £50,000 and Stuart Rafferty (Motherwell), for £25,000.

And, following an unbeaten nine-game tour of West Germany and Switzerland, the squad was further strengthened by the addition of Derek McWilliams and Robert Docherty, both forwards who were previously on the books of Arsenal and St Mirren, respectively.

New signings - John McCormack, Robert Connor, John Brown, Derek McWilliams and Stuart Rafferty.

Action man - Dens attacker Ray Stephen has Craig Paterson of Rangers floundering. BELOW - John Brown cracks home the first of a double against St Mirren. DC Thomson

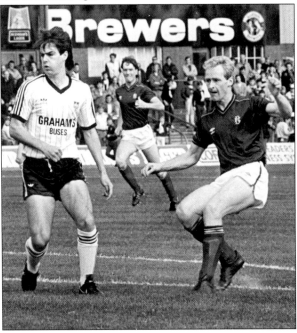

A week into the new season, experienced goalkeeper Tom Carson (25), was signed from Dumbarton on freedom-of-contract. The Boghead club valued him at £100,000, but this time Dundee were happier with the tribunal's decision. Later, the fee was fixed at £50,000, just £10,000 more than the sum Dundee had offered! That brought the spending spree to a halt although East Fife striker Gordon Durie was the next man on the wanted list if the money was to become available.

Favourable tour results and the arrival of seven new faces had rekindled the enthusiasm amongst the fans and around 500 youngsters were enrolled in the revamped Junior Dark Blues. In addition, volunteers had carried out extensive renovation at Dens with the bench seating freshly painted in dark blue, red and white paint.

Archie Knox and Andrew Marshall were to the fore in directing operations and, such was the prevailing spirit at Dens, that the pair - one the manager and the other a director - had assisted in weeding the terraces.

On the opening game of the season the Dark Blues were rather unfortunate to go down 3-2 at Aberdeen. There was another good showing in the 1-0 defeat by Hibs at Dens but, when further reverses followed at newly promoted Dumbarton (1-2) and at home to Rangers (0-2), the early enthusiasm could have been expected to waver.

But the newcomers had shown signs that they could really play and there was a belief about the place that sooner or later Dundee would click and make their mark. The turning point came in the League Cup quarter-final against Hearts at Dens on September 5th. Sponsored by Skol, the League Cup was now a knock-out tournament with all ties played to a finish in midweek. Dundee had progressed to the last eight with home wins over Hamilton (3-0), and Kilmarnock (3-0 on penalties, following a 1-1 draw after extra-time) with Tom Carson making two superb saves in the dramatic Dens penalty shoot-out.

In the quarter-final, Roddie MacDonald put Hearts ahead just before half-time. That had been against the run of play but, roared on by a noisy home support, the Dark Blues besieged the visitors' goal on the restart. Twice they hit woodwork but, with Henry Smith in tremendous form, the Tynecastle side managed to survive. Dundee had done everything but score and, at the end, they got a standing ovation from an appreciative home support.

Four days later, the promise came to fruition with a 4-3 derby triumph over Dundee United at Tannadice. Three times Dundee took the lead - through McWilliams, McKinlay and Harris - only for United to level, but, with 14 minutes remaining, John Brown powered a header past Billy Thomson for the winner.

The key to success had been in midfield where the speedy Rafferty complemented Connor's craft and the tackling and surging runs of Brown whose powerful shooting and heading ability made him a constant threat. And, as if to underline this, further goals in the 2-0 wins over St Mirren at home and Hearts at Tynecastle brought Brown's tally to three in three successive games.

"Archie Knox was a tough character, a tremendous motivator and his new signings gave the side a great boost," said Bobby Glennie. Knox's toughness was legend and the playing staff were left in no doubt about that when he strode into the dressing room for his first meeting, hung his suit jacket on the back of the door and issued the challenge: "If anyone here wants to fight, now's your chance." Knox was aware that two players had raised their hands during rows with his predecessor and his message was unmistakeable.

However, by early December, a run of eight games without a win saw Dundee slip from mid-table to the bottom alongside Morton. It was clear that Iain Ferguson had not been adequately replaced. Ray Stephen was top scorer with only four goals and, even the conversion of penalties presented a problem, with Kidd, Brown and Harris all missing in league games and Stephen drawing a blank in the penalty shoot-out with Killie.

By the end of 1984, home wins over Morton (5-1), and Hibs (h) 2-0, and a no-scoring draw at Pittodrie had elevated Dundee to seventh only for a single goal Ne'erday reverse at Dumbarton to again highlight the side's attacking deficiencies. In a game almost totally dominated by Dundee, chances galore had been squandered. One of the main culprits was big Colin Harris. He had managed only three goals in 26 games, and it was little surprise when he was exchanged for Hibs striker Graham Harvey (23), not long afterwards.

A few days later, Harvey, who had been in dispute with Easter Road boss John Blackley, made his debut against Rangers at Dens. However, it was former favourite Iain Ferguson who took the eye with two opportunist goals, although two flashing headers by Dens skipper John McCormack gave Dundee a 2-2 draw.

The influence and professionalism of Archie Knox had become increasingly evident. He firmly believed that a competitive edge was required to achieve Premier success and it was soon clear that the Dundee players had got the message. Defensive errors had largely been eliminated and, in particular, full-backs George McGeachie and Tosh McKinlay had shown a big improvement.

The previous September, Dundee had signed Arbroath right-back Stewart Forsyth (22), in exchange for Iain MacDonald plus £18,000 but, with McGeachie playing the best football of his career, the newcomer was restricted to a handful of appearances in midfield.

Towards the end of 1984, Dundee had switched to a four-man midfield. It proved a highly successful move and, by early March, a nine-game unbeaten run saw them well-placed in the league, having reached the quarter-final of the Scottish Cup. Goals by McWilliams and Connor gave Dundee a 2-1 victory over St Johnstone in a first-round Dens replay after the sides had drawn 1-1 at Muirton the night before.

The next stage took them to Ibrox where they had triumphed in such spectacular fashion in last year's competition. Rangers included seven players costing upwards of £100,000 but, although the entire Dundee team had cost only £135,000, John Brown put them ahead with an opportunist goal just nine minutes from the start.

Frantically, the homesters mounted attack after attack but they were unable to break down the well-organised Dundee defence. And, with former Dens stars like Redford, Fraser and Ferguson now in the Light Blue of Rangers, victory had been all the sweeter.

In the quarter-final, Dundee met Celtic and, with a recent 2-0 win over the Parkhead side, and only one defeat in their last 13 games, there was a near

Bomber command - John Brown beats Peter McCloy in the Scottish Cup tie at Ibrox as Graham Harvey and Craig Paterson look on. The forceful midfielder grabbed another against Celtic in the next round (top) but Dundee lost out in the Parkhead replay. DC Thomson

capacity 21,300 crowd at Dens. Dundee fielded: Geddes; McGeachie, Smith, Glennie, McKinlay; Rafferty, McCormack, Brown, Connor; Stephen, Harvey. Substitutes - McCall, Forsyth.

The crowd were treated to a cup-tie classic as play raged from end to end. In 67 minutes, pin-up boy Mo Johnston put Celtic ahead only for John Brown to head a glorious equaliser six minutes later. With Celtic on the rack, Brown blasted in a ferocious rising shot and only a desperate leap by the Glasgow club's Republic of Ireland keeper Pat Bonner prevented Dundee from taking the lead.

There were over 37,000 at Parkhead for the replay - Forsyth coming in for Harvey, leaving Stephen as Dundee's only recognised striker. Clearly, they hoped to blanket the midfield in the opening stages but a McGarvey goal in 34 minutes saw a change in tactics. At half-time, Forsyth was withdrawn in favour of McCall but, within 60 seconds of the restart, referee David Syme controversially dismissed Bobby Glennie for a heavy tackle on Murdo McLeod.

Two minutes later, Stephen levelled from close in but, despite Dundee having a 15-minute purple patch during which the large travelling support roared their approval, a second goal proved elusive. With the loss of Glennie eventually taking its toll, Celtic were able to weather the storm and take control with Johnston scoring the winner 20 minutes from the end.

Nevertheless, it had been a gallant performance and now Dundee looked towards a place in next season's UEFA Cup. However, although they recorded a 3-1 win at Ibrox - their third over Rangers in Glasgow in a year - the suspended Glennie was badly missed and three of the next four games ended in heavy defeats against Aberdeen (h) 0-4, Dundee United (a) 0-4, and St Mirren (a) 2-4.

The Dens squad was bolstered by the addition of John Waddell from Norwich. But, although the lanky utility player made only one full appearance - at right-back - home successes over Dumbarton (1-0), and Hearts (3-0), left

Dundee in fifth place with only three games remaining and on April 21st, 1985, the top Premier placings were:

April 21st, 1985			
	P	F A	Pts
Aberdeen	33	83-24	54
Celtic	32	73-27	48
Dundee United	33	63-31	43
Rangers	32	42-33	35
Dundee	33	46-50	32
St Mirren	33	41-54	32

Disappointingly, a vital point was dropped in a no-scoring draw with Jim Duffy-inspired Morton at Dens but, the following week, a thundering free-kick by Brown brought a 1-0 win over Scottish Cup finalists Celtic at Parkhead. It was the red-headed midfielder's twelfth goal of the season and, at £40,000, Archie Knox had clearly landed a bargain.

On Saturday, May 11th, Dundee played host to local rivals, Dundee United, who would meet Celtic in the Scottish Cup Final. The Dens men now trailed St Mirren by a point but they had a superior goal-difference and, should Saints drop a home point to Hearts and Dundee win, European football would return to Dens for the first time since 1974.

That term, experienced men like McCall, Richardson and Kidd had slipped out of the first-team picture but, although 19-year-olds like Derek McWilliams and Colin Hendry had been used sparingly, a sterling performance by Rab Shannon at Park-head saw the reserve skipper retained in midfield against Dundee United.

On a warm sunny day, 14,000 fans saw a hard-fought game. In 30 minutes, Rafferty set off on a 50-yard run and Connor was well-placed to ram home his hard low cross. United hit back but, with 20 minutes remaining, Bobby Geddes made his fifth penalty save of the season when he stopped Eamonn Bannon's effort. Dundee held on to win, but the euphoria was soon to subside when it was heard that St Mirren had also been victorious.

Derby joy - Robert Connor times his run to perfection and fires Stuart Rafferty's cross behind Hamish McAlpine. But although victory over Dundee United was always welcome, there was disappointment at missing out on Europe.

DC Thomson

CHAPTER TWENTY-THREE

Pipped for Europe

Only one point had separated Dundee from fourth-placed Rangers and St Mirren in fifth spot but, despite their narrow failure to qualify for Europe, the Dens Parkers' total of 37 points was easily their best Premier performance to date. Archie Knox had bought wisely and, that summer, the squad was further strengthened by the addition of 25-year-old Jim Duffy for £57,500 from Morton with former Everton striker Ross Jack obtained on a free transfer from Lincoln City.

However, with Tosh McKinlay out of contract and refusing to re-sign, the Dens boss believed his 16-strong first-team pool, which included two goalkeepers, was still four players short to compete with the resources of the current top clubs, Aberdeen, Celtic, Dundee United and Rangers over a gruelling Premier League campaign. In his opinion, successful sides required a core of 12 players committed to the club for at least four years but freedom-of-contract made this increasingly difficult to achieve.

A four-game tour of Canada and the USA in May was followed by another successful pre-season tour of West Germany and Switzerland. Then, for the first time in eight years, Dundee opened their league campaign for the 1985-86 season at Dens. But, although Connor scored twice in a 2-1 win over St Mirren, three successive defeats by newly-promoted Clydebank (a) 0-4, Dundee United (a) 0-2, and Aberdeen (h) 1-3, left them struggling near the bottom of the Premier League table.

There was not much luck in the Skol Cup either. In the first round, a last-minute header by Smith earned a 3-2 win at Stranraer but, at the next stage, the Dark Blues fell 2-1 in extra-time against First Division Hamilton. A late penalty gave Connor the chance to take the game to a penalty shoot-out but, sadly, his attempt went wide and Dundee had missed the chance of a lucrative quarter-final tie with Rangers.

Jim Duffy had arrived from Cappielow with a reputation as an outstanding defender. However, he made a shaky start to his Dens career and Dundee were dealt a further blow with news that George McGeachie would require surgery to both his ankle tendons.

However, Dundee's most pressing problems remained up front. Stephen continued to be a productive front runner but neither McCall - out of favour since turning part-time in the summer - Jack or Harvey appeared to have the necessary killer touch.

An unsuccessful attempt to bring back Ian Redford from Rangers was compounded when the former Dens star chose

Driving force - Archie Knox was a hard task-master but his players were happy to respond. DC Thomson

to join Dundee United in a £70,000 deal. Sheffield United striker Russell Black then arrived on a month's loan but, despite scoring against Aberdeen, he did little to impress and was allowed to return south.

Nevertheless, Dundee got back on the rails with wins over Motherwell (a) 3-1, Hibs (h) 1-0, and Rangers (a) 1-0 in September. Initially, Jim Duffy had been used as an orthodox central-defender but, on reverting to his more familiar role as sweeper, the former Morton star quickly justified his transfer fee. At Ibrox, Stuart Rafferty scored Dundee's winner with a spectacular long-range drive but, as the league leaders hit back, Duffy was one of the defensive rocks upon which Rangers had foundered.

That term, Smith and Shannon had occupied the full-back berths before Tosh McKinlay returned from trial periods at West Ham and Southampton. Dundee had rejected a bid from West Ham who, fearing a tribunal might place an

Dundee F.C. Season 1985-86 (BACK, left to right) Bobby Glennie, Jim Smith, John Waddell, Walker McCall, Stewart Forsyth, George McGeachie. MIDDLE - Jocky Scott (assistant-manager), Stuart Rafferty, Jim Duffy, Bobby Geddes, Archie Knox (manager), Tom Carson, John Brown, Ross Jack, Eric Ferguson (physio). FRONT - Derek McWilliams, Albert Kidd, Ray Stephen, John McCormack, Robert Connor, Graham Harvey, Rab Shannon.
DC Thomson

excessive price on the Under-21 international, had ended their interest. The Dark Blues had refused McKinlay's proposal of a monthly deal but, after turning down Southampton's offer, the young defender finally signed a one-year contract in October.

A disappointing run of defeats by Hibs (a) 1-2, Aberdeen (a) 1-4, and Dundee United (h) 0-3, left Dundee third bottom but, on Saturday, November 23rd, they recovered with a sensational 3-2 win over Rangers at Dens. It was their fourth successive win in a six-game unbeaten sequence against the Light Blues and there was little doubt that the Dark Blues held the Indian sign over the Ibrox outfit at this time.

In 17 minutes, McKinlay was red-carded for a trip on McMinn but a brilliant hat-trick by John Brown, who had been relegated to the substitute's bench against Dundee United seven days

Touch of steel - Bobby Glennie added strength and determination to defence.

earlier, turned the tide in Dundee's favour. The big midfielder had been somewhat inconsistent that season, but he always reserved his best for games against Rangers. His second goal had come from a direct free-kick and the third from a penalty. But the first, which he netted after leaving a trail of Rangers defenders in his wake, would be long remembered by the fans..

By the end of 1985, Dundee lay in mid-table just four points behind second-placed Dundee United. Jim McLean's side had continued to be a force in both Scottish and European football but, soon after beating Rangers, a 2-0 win at Tannadice saw Dundee lift the Forfarshire Cup for the first time in 14 years.

A month later, Dundee drew 0-0 at the same ground and there was a similar scoreline in the home game against Aberdeen on New Year's Day. Only ten of the 31 players on the Dark

Touch of velvet - Robert Connor brought skill and creativity to midfield. SNS Group

Blues' books when Knox took over remained and, according to the Dens boss, the club was now moving in the right direction: "Dundee are again getting their share of top youngsters and the aim is to call up two or three each season and become a successful enough side to compete for the real nuggets."

However, the side still required a major goalscorer, and with little money available, Knox indicated his willingness to sell in order to generate cash for new players. In the manager's view, prices were more realistic on the Continent and, although talks with Danish star Tommy Christensen broke down over the player's personal terms, Cologne midfielder Vince Mennie (21), the son of a British serviceman in Germany, was signed for £65,000 at the end of January.

The Dens Parkers had reached the third round of the Scottish Cup after a trip to Highland League side Nairn. Initially, the frozen surface looked as if it might present problems but, with the on-song Harvey grabbing a hat-trick, the Dark Blues eventually romped to a 7-0 win.

On his arrival, Mennie expressed his belief that he could be the man to solve Dundee's striking problems and this view was enhanced when he found the net in their 2-0 fourth-round win over Airdrie at Dens. But although that success took them into the last eight, Ross Jack - in one of his rare first-team appearances - had the misfortune to break his arm after falling awkwardly on the frosty ground.

On March 8th, Dundee entertained current champions Aberdeen in the quarter-final at Dens before a bitterly disappointing crowd of 13,188 (£26,000). This was only

4,000 more than had attended the corresponding league game at New Year and, at the same stage of the previous year's competition there had been a near full-house for the visit of Celtic.

Hewitt put the Dons in front but goals by Harvey (26 mins), and Brown (67), put Dundee in the driving seat. In midfield the silky Connor more than matched Scotland star Jim Bett, and the Dark Blues looked set for a well-merited triumph. Only 15 minutes remained when Geddes, fielding a Duffy pass-back, thought he had time to dribble the ball to the edge of the penalty box. But, unknown to him, Neil Simpson was lurking behind him and when the midfielder stole the ball from his toes, he crossed for Hewitt to head home at the far post.

Ray Stephen, now recovered from injury, replaced Colin Hendry for the Pittodrie return as Dundee lined up: Geddes; Forsyth, Smith, Duffy, McKinlay; Shannon, Brown, Mennie, Connor; Stephen, Harvey. Subs - Hendry, Glennie.

Once again, Knox's men rose to the occasion and, in 19 minutes, great work by Harvey allowed Stephen to put them ahead. As the Dark Blues turned on the style, the Aberdeen goal came under siege but, just before the interval, Eric Black headed an equaliser against the run of play.

After the break, Dundee continued to attack but referee Brian McGinlay angered the 5,000 visiting support by refusing a penalty claim when Mennie was downed in the box. However, despite their non-stop pressure, Dundee were unable to put the ball in the net and, towards the end of the 90 minutes, it was Aberdeen who had gained the upper hand.

Case for the defence - Bobby Williamson and former Dark Blue Iain Ferguson are the guilty men as Bobby Geddes hits the deck with Dundee defenders Stuart Rafferty, Jim Smith, John McCormack, Jim Duffy and Bobby Glennie appealing strongly. DC Thomson

In extra-time, this pattern continued and, with 101 minutes played, a wind-assisted cross by Peter Weir sailed above Geddes into the far corner of the net. Dundee appeared exhausted by their earlier efforts and there was to be no way back. Many in the 21,000 crowd agreed that Dundee had been unfortunate to lose and now the target was a place in the following year's UEFA Cup.

Three days later, John Brown enhanced these hopes with a penalty winner in the 2-1 triumph over Rangers at Dens. A 0-0 draw at Aberdeen then left them one point behind the Ibrox side who had played a game more with six games remaining but narrow defeats by Dundee United (h) 0-1, Celtic (a) 1-2, and Hibs (a) 0-1 again highlighted Dundee's lack of depth at a crucial stage of the season. Former Celtic and Wolves winger Danny Crainie was signed on a short-term contract but, after three appearances as a substitute, he was allowed to go.

Rangers, however, were struggling and, while Dundee were beating Motherwell 4-0 at Dens, St Mirren's win over the ailing Light Blues again put Dundee one point ahead. Victory in their last two games would give them a much-coveted European place but Dundee's cause was ill-served at Parkhead when Stephen was dismissed after an early incident with Scotland right-back Danny McGrain and Celtic went on to win 2-0.

Meanwhile, Graeme Souness was appointed Rangers manager in place of Jock Wallace and, on the penultimate day of the season, a 1-1 draw at Aberdeen allowed Rangers to overtake Dundee on goal-difference.

On May 3rd, Dundee faced league leaders Hearts, who were unbeaten in 31 games. The Tynecastle men, who had also reached the Scottish Cup Final, required one point to clinch the title from Celtic, while Dundee needed to win to maximise their European hopes.

The large visiting support swelled the Dens crowd to 19,567 but a nervy looking Hearts, some of whose players were affected by a flu-virus, appeared content to defend in depth. With seven minutes remaining, the score-line was blank and Hearts looked certainties to take the title. However, rumours that Motherwell had gone ahead at Ibrox swept through the home support and were transmitted to the players. Accordingly, Dundee, believing that Europe was now in their own hands, began to exert tremendous pressure.

Robert Connor sent in a wicked inswinging corner, and, when the ball was headed on by Brown, substitute Albert Kidd, who had only started five games all season, lashed the ball past an astounded Henry Smith. Hearts were stunned and, four minutes later, their title hopes were in tatters as Kidd played a delicate one-two with Harvey before smashing in a second,

Unfortunately, Rangers had, in fact, triumphed 2-0 and for the second successive season, European qualification had narrowly eluded Dundee. For Hearts, who had been league leaders since December, the disappointment was shattering. Almost unbelievably, Celtic had won 5-0 at Paisley to take the championship on a goal-difference of plus three and there were widespread scenes of abject misery amongst the large Tynecastle support at Dens.

Heartbreaker - Albert Kidd celebrates the first of his two late goals against Hearts at Dens. Sadly this did not gain Dundee a place in Europe but would cost the Maroons the championship on goal difference.

CHAPTER TWENTY-FOUR

Jocky's New Job

For the second successive season, Dundee had narrowly been pipped for a place in Europe. Archie Knox had built the framework of a promising side, which with some adjustment, looked capable of progressing to better things. However, on June 18th, 1986, the Knox era came to an abrupt end when it was announced that the Dens boss had resigned to become co-manager of Aberdeen alongside Alex Ferguson.

That summer, Knox had assisted Ferguson in his role of interim Scotland manager - following the death of Jock Stein - at the World Cup Finals in Mexico and, within months of his Pittodrie return, the pair would depart for lucrative management appointments with Manchester United - the sleeping giants of English football.

Knox, who had been offered a contract which he had never signed, had made a tremendous impact in his two-and-a-half years in charge. His departure came as a severe blow and the Dundee directors were particularly embittered at Aberdeen's "back-door" approach. An emergency board meeting was convened and 38-year-old assistant-manager Jocky Scott, who had spent 20 years at Dens and who had taken charge of the close-season tour of the USA while Knox was with Scotland, was appointed manager with St Mirren coach Drew Jarvie later confirmed as his assistant.

Former skipper John McCormack and John Waddell had departed on free transfers, while Ray Stephen appeared set to join either French side Mulhouse or Kaiserslautern of West Germany on freedom-of-contract. But when both deals fell through, the striker was happy to re-sign for Dundee on a one-year contract.

Since their Premier return in 1981-82, Dundee's gates had improved from an average of 7,570 to a figure of 8,952 last season. However, the financial position had deteriorated and the debts had risen from £491,848 to £665,343 over the last year. Now there were huge interest payments, and the unwelcome news that a £300,000 deal had been agreed with Hearts for the transfer of John Brown came as little surprise.

Dundee would receive £225,000 plus Hearts midfielder Andy Watson but, at the last minute, the deal collapsed when Brown failed a medical on account of a long-term knee problem. "Hearts must have been the only club in Scotland who were unaware that all Brown's cartilages had been removed," said chairman Ian Gellatly later.

In a surprise move, Jocky Scott secured former Dens striker Iain Ferguson on loan from Rangers until the end of the season. Ferguson had struggled at Ibrox but, although the

striker and Cammy Fraser had been labelled "a pair of duds" at a recent Rangers AGM, he again displayed his scoring flair with a goal in each of Dundee's home wins over St Mirren (2-1), and Hibs (3-0).

And with a crowd of 7,216 for the Hibs game - the highest against the Easter Road side since George Best had played in the corresponding game back in

In charge - Jocky Scott was now Dundee manager.

March 1982 - it seemed that Fergie might be just the personality player to bring the Dundee faithful flocking back to Dens Park.

That May, Robert Connor had appeared for Scotland against Holland in Eindhoven to become Dundee's first full internationalist since Bobby Robinson in 1975. Sadly, however, the financial situation dictated that he would have to be sold and, within days of the new season, he joined Aberdeen with Dundee getting Dons midfielder Ian Angus (24), plus £275,000.

Meanwhile, Dundee United had cast envious glances at Iain Ferguson and, in an unprecedented move, they approached Rangers for his transfer. Initially, the striker, who had no wish to go to Tannadice, rejected the move, preferring to remain at Dens in the hope of a move to England. Graeme Souness, however, was keen to sell and the player was recalled to Ibrox. And, although Dundee made a "six-figure bid", this did not match United's £140,000 offer and a £40,000 signing-on fee finally persuaded Ferguson to move to Tannadice.

Ironically, wins over Morton (a) 5-2 after extra-time, and Montrose (h) 4-0, set Dundee up for a Skol Cup quarter-final against Rangers at Ibrox just two weeks later. That game attracted an attendance of 33,000 and, had their share of the gate been available at the time, Dundee might have been able to secure Ferguson.

Already, Rangers player-manager Graeme Souness had spent over £1 million on Colin West and England internationals Chris Woods and Terry Butcher and, when Jim Smith was sent off after 25 minutes, it meant an uphill struggle for 10-man Dundee. With 15 minutes left, Fraser put Rangers ahead only for Ibrox to be shocked to silence when Forsyth volleyed home a last-gasp equaliser. However, the Light Blues continued to dominate and goals by Souness and McMinn saw them triumph 3-1 after extra-time.

Captain marvel - Jim Duffy takes time off from his defensive duties to slam home a penalty against St Mirren. DC Thomson

League re-organisation had meant the suspension of relegation for two seasons and, with Falkirk and Hamilton promoted, a 12-team Premier League now entailed a marathon 44-game league programme. By early November, Dundee lay fifth with twenty points from 17 games but, although successful against the lesser lights, all the clashes against strong-going Celtic, Dundee United and Aberdeen were lost without even a consolation goal being scored.

In September, John Brown had extended Dundee's bogey over big-spending Rangers when his swerving shot beat Woods for the only goal of the game just four minutes from time. Another top scalp was claimed with a 3-0 Tannadice win over joint leaders Dundee United, who had earlier triumphed 2-0 at Dens. Two goals by Harvey and another by Shannon made it a glory day for the Dens fans but, soon afterwards, they were stunned to hear that Ray Stephen had joined French First Division side Nancy for £150,000.

In less than five months, Dundee had lost their highly-respected manager and two top performers in Connor and Stephen. There was also the disappointment of losing Iain Ferguson to Dundee United and, when only two points were taken from their next four games and stories began to circulate that Duffy and McKinlay might also have to be sold, supporters' morale plummetted to rock-bottom.

For much of the past ten years, there had been troubled times at Dens. To rub salt into the wounds, city rivals Dundee United had flourished. Moreover, under the stewardship of former Dens player and coach Jim McLean, the Tannadice side had assembled a colony of ex-Dens stars like Redford, McInally and Ferguson with another four - Doug Houston, Kenny Cameron, Gordon Wallace and Steve Murray on their coaching staff and others like Doug Cowie, Andy Irvine and Archie Coats doing valuable scouting work. Dundee fans were bitter indeed and, led by Graham Thomson, Andrew Marshall and local property dealer Angus Cook, it was strongly rumoured that a takeover bid would be made at the AGM on December 1st, 1986.

Andrew Marshall was the club's largest shareholder with 25,000 shares, and, along with Graham Thomson in particular, he had recognised that the return of Iain Ferguson to the Dark Blue jersey had sparked fresh optimism amongst the fans. Accordingly, he felt Dundee should buy Ferguson but when this failed to materialise the progressive Marshall, who appeared to increasingly find himself at odds with decisions and an apparent lack of ambition, resigned from the Dens Park board.

Prior to the AGM, the beleaguered Mr Gellatly, whose family had been on the board since 1944, had intimated his intention to resign both as chairman and club secretary. Behind-the-scenes talks between Marshall, Thomson and Cook had paved the way for a "negotiated settlement" which would have seen Gellatly remain as a director to enable him to stay on as president of the Scottish League. But there were growing fears that he would fail to take a back seat as the incomers were insisting and the deal was off. And so the "rebels" pledged to battle it out at the AGM but the 11th-hour defection of Thomson was to prove crucial.

In the event, the shareholders opposed Gellatly's re-election and that of Maurice Speedie but these moves were defeated on a show of hands by 32-24 and 33-21 respectively. Such was the interest that around sixty shareholders, three times the normal number, were in attendance. But, after a stormy hour-long meeting, the only change was the appointment of Graham Thomson as chairman after his last-minute switch of allegiance.

The onfield crisis continued when a 2-0 defeat by Celtic at Parkhead left Dundee without a win from their last six games but their luck was about to change. Following unsuccessful moves for Manchester City's Northern Ireland international midfielder Sammy McIlroy and Falkirk striker Alan Irvine, Jocky Scott splashed out £50,000 for 23-year-

Boardroom battle - Dens directors Maurice Speedie, Ian Gellatly, Graham Thomson and Andrew Marshall pictured with commercial manager Bob McConnachie (centre). Fotopress

old Keith Wright of Raith Rovers and a further £75,000 for Dundee United's Tommy Coyne (24).

It would prove money well spent and, on December 23rd, the new striking partnership spearheaded Dundee to a 6-3 win over St Mirren with Wright netting twice on his home debut. However, despite a 2-0 home success over Hibs, three consecutive defeats left them 13 points behind fifth-placed Hearts and, with a UEFA Cup place as far away as ever, thoughts again turned to the Scottish Cup.

In their opening tie, Dundee met First Division East Fife at Dens and after an earlier postponement due to a waterlogged pitch, only a late Coyne goal earned a 2-2 draw. In the replay, there was a half-hour delay when five home players were held up by a car crash before a 4-1 win at rain-soaked Bayview took Dundee through to the fourth round.

The draw paired Dundee with Meadowbank, whose manager Terry Christie had been on the Dens Park books in the early 1960s. The well-organised First Division side

proved a tough nut to crack and although Harvey equalised an early strike by Dave Roseburgh, the slightly-built Alan Lawrence proved a constant menace to the home defence.

Tosh McKinlay, who had only recently recovered from a cartilage operation, was recalled for the replay on February 25th. But, in the eerie atmosphere of the Commonwealth Stadium, Dundee were again fortunate to escape with a 1-1 draw after extra-time.

And, as Jocky Scott and Drew Jarvie made the long walk to the dressing rooms, the pair were greeted by a storm of booing from the large Dens contingent in the 4,000 crowd. Lawrence had again run riot but, in the second replay, which was played at Dens on the

In safe hands - Bobby Geddes gathers a cross against Rangers as Jim Smith and George McGeachie stand guard. Four minutes from the end, John Brown shocked the Ibrox men with the winner. TOP - Bobby Geddes kicks the ball clear. DC Thomson

179

Power play - Dundee midfielder John Brown fires in a ferocious shot at the Clydebank goal in the 4-0 Scottish Cup quarter-final win at Kilbowie.

Stephen Borland

toss of a coin, he found Dundee's defenders in an uncompromising mood. Three days earlier, Scott's tactics of playing Glennie, Smith and Duffy at the back with full-backs Forsyth and McKinlay pushing into midfield had brought a resounding 4-1 win over Celtic at Dens. And with the elusive Lawrence effectively shackled, two second-half goals by Coyne finally earned a quarter-final tie with Clydebank on March 14th.

By then, the Dark Blues had gone 10 games without defeat and enthusiasm was further boosted by the £35,000 signing of 24-year-old Lawrence from Meadowbank. There had also been departures. Albert Kidd joined Falkirk on a free transfer while Colin Hendry, unable to consistently show the form which would later make him an international class player, rejoined his old boss Donald Mackay at Blackburn Rovers for a fee of £30,000.

In recent years, Kilbowie Park had been a bogey ground for Dundee but, cheered on by a vociferous travelling support, early goals by Wright, Coyne and Brown gave them an unassailable lead before Brown thundered home a magnificent fourth, seven minutes from time.

The semi-final draw paired Dundee with city rivals Dundee United who had also reached the UEFA Cup semi-final. The derby confrontation on Saturday, April 11th was the most important since the 1980 League Cup Final but, despite a mutual desire to play the tie in Dundee, SFA rules dictated that it should go ahead at a neutral venue. Tynecastle Park was nominated and, after a storm of protest from both sets of fans, only 13,910 turned out for an occasion confidently expected to attract a full-house back in the city of Dundee.

With two draws and a win apiece, derby honours had been shared that season but with just one defeat in 16 games, the Dark Blues were confident of success and fielded: Geddes; Forsyth, Smith, Duffy, McKinlay; Rafferty, Shannon, Brown; Jack, Coyne, Wright. Subs. - Angus, Glennie. Dundee United: Thomson; Holt, Hegarty, Narey, Malpas; McInally, Bowman, Redford; Bannon, Ferguson, Sturrock. Subs. - Gallacher, Kirkwood.

Dundee settled after a nervy start but they were stunned by

a brilliantly taken Iain Ferguson goal on the half-hour. Soon afterwards, their pressure paid off when Coyne equalised from close in and, four minutes from the break, Wright headed home a perfectly flighted cross by Coyne to give them the lead.

Shannon and the strong-running Rafferty were key men as the Dens midfield had taken control. After the restart, United began to break up Dundee's attacking pattern with a series of fouls but, although Dave Narey then Ian Redford were both booked, Rafferty's effectiveness had been curtailed by a bad thigh knock.

United gained the ascendancy and goals by Ferguson (54 mins) and Paul Hegarty 10 minutes later put them 3-2 ahead. But, although Brown had been unlucky to slip in the build-up to the second, Hegarty, who was always a threat in the air, was unchallenged when he connected with a free-kick just five yards from the Dundee goal.

However, Dundee battled grimly and, as the game again swung their way in the last quarter, Billy Thomson was twice forced into full-length diving saves from John Brown. It had been a magnificent game with not a hint of trouble amongst the two sets of fans from Tayside.

Dundee could count themselves unlucky not to get a replay but, with St Mirren reaching the final with a 1-0 win over Hearts, the Dark Blues had lost perhaps their best chance of Scottish Cup glory since winning the trophy in 1910. Said Jocky Scott: "In the second half we were second to every ball and didn't start playing again until we went 3-2 behind. Over the piece, United's experience of big-game situations saw them through."

Dundee went on to finish sixth for the third successive season having lost just three of the last 23 games. The campaign ended with a 7-3 win over Hamilton at Dens and with 18 goals in their last five matches, prospects looked bright. Harvey had finished top scorer with 17 goals with Brown contributing an impressive 13 from midfield but it was the striking partnership of Tommy Coyne and Keith

Wright that had caught the imagination of the fans.

"It was just one of those things," said Wright. "Tam and I gelled almost immediately. As well as being a lethal finisher, he was a clever player who never got the credit he deserved. I was the hard-running type and we complemented each other well." Coyne with 15 goals, and Wright with two less, had proved a deadly combination and, with Duffy, Harvey and Brown (twice) all missing penalties that season, Coyne's ability from the spot came

Breakthrough - Rab Shannon was soon a first-team regular.

as an added bonus.

News that John Brown had signed a three-year contract came as a further morale-booster in what proved an eventful close-season. In June, a fire caused an estimated £100,000 of damage to the west section of the Dens stand and two local youths were later charged with arson.

Tosh McKinlay - classy left-back with attacking flair.

Increasingly, it was accepted that football clubs could no longer survive on gate money alone. Various lotteries, including Denspools in the early 1960s had been introduced by Dundee. The club had also supplemented its income through advertising, the Dundee F.C. Shop in the city centre and ball sponsorship. However, none of those could compare with Dundee United's Taypools, which was bringing the Tannadice club some £350,000-a-year by 1975 after 18 years in existence.

In March 1985, the Dark Blues signed a jersey sponsorship with local solicitor W.G. Boyle only for the deal to collapse after intervention by the Law Society. The following season, individual players' kit was open to sponsorship and, by then, many clubs employed full-time commercial staff. In May 1986, Bob McConnachie became Dundee's first commercial manager but his stay was short-lived and he departed for another post six months later.

Early in 1987, former Dens defender Dave Johnston was appointed secretary-general manager with Allan Paul later taking over as commercial manager. On the footballing side, the backroom staff was further strengthened by the addition of ex-keeper Bert Slater as youth coach and chief scout.

It was not long before the endeavours of Johnston and Paul began to bear fruit. In August, the board announced a jersey sponsorship deal with Novafone which would earn £300,000 over the next three years while a tracksuit sponsorship by Independent Money Information Ltd. would earn a five figure sum over the same period.

Speculation that millionaire pop star Rod Sewart might become a director proved unfounded but, encouragingly, the board was increased to five by the addition of Mr Iain Bett, chairman of the Bett Group and formerly a director for a brief period after the death of his father in 1974, and Mr Jim Strachan of Galloway Mechanical Services.

However, as the 1987-88 season approached, the name of Angus Cook, who owned a Rolls Royce and was reputedly a millionaire, was featuring more and more in talk about Dundee. Following the abortive bid to oust the board, he had bought large numbers of shares - many from disgruntled fans - and had promised to pump money into the club should he take control. In June, his £150,000 bid to take charge was rejected by the board who felt it was not in the club's best interest to gain control.

Cook was by now the club's largest shareholder and, by August, he had increased his holding to 70,000 of the club's 185,000 ordinary shares, leaving him just 23,000 short of outright control. To the delight of the fans, he talked of injecting £800,000 into the club, claiming: "I cannot compromise with mediocrity for my aspirations for the club go much higher than that." Meanwhile, the board, who appeared to be moving in the right direction, were much alarmed at this turn of events and they circulated shareholders to outline the club's future strategy and appeal for support.

Away from the boardroom speculation, Dundee had reached the final of the Isle of Man International Football Festival only to lose 1-0 to English Second Division side Stoke City. Then, after a 3-0 home win over the touring Seattle Storm of the USA, their latest Premier campaign began with a 1-1 draw against Aberdeen at Dens.

Only a late equaliser by Davie Dodds prevented Dundee recording their first win over the Dons in 10 years and confirmation of the side's improvement came with excellent away wins over Falkirk (3-0) and Hibs (4-0). At Brockville, Jim Duffy was ordered off after half-an-hour but, despite his absence, the Dark Blues produced a vintage performance at Easter Road a few days later.

Their good form continued in the Skol Cup and, despite injuries to Brown (bruised ribs), and Rafferty (strained knee ligaments), 3-0 wins at Queen's Park and Meadowbank took them through to the last eight. A 2-0 home reverse to St Mirren came as a shock but with Tommy Coyne a four-goal hero in a 5-0 win over Dunfermline at Dens the following week, the Dark Blues lay third just one point behind the early pace-setters Celtic.

On Wednesday, September 2nd, Dundee met Dundee United in the Skol Cup quarter-final before a 19,817 crowd at Dens. After only six minutes, Ferguson headed Dundee in front and, for the next hour, Dundee's goal came under siege. However, brilliantly marshalled by Duffy, they survived and began to take the game back to United. In 82 minutes, Coyne broke through only for Thomson to save but three minutes later the striker made amends when he slid home a McKinlay cross.

Roared on by their exuberant fans, Dundee now put

United under severe pressure and, five minutes into extra-time, Dens erupted when Wright finished off a brilliant move by Coyne and Harvey, the latter having substituted for Mennie two minutes earlier. Jocky Scott immediately introduced a sweeper behind his back four and, despite a tense finish, there were joyous scenes amongst home fans as Dundee held on to win.

Keith Wright was overjoyed: "That was the best atmosphere I ever experienced at Dens. After a slow start, the Dundee fans got right behind us and after

Safe hands - Tom Carson with the new sponsor's logo.

Dundee F.C. Season 1987-88 - (BACK, left to right) Keith Wright, Stuart Rafferty, Stewart Forsyth, Jim Smith, John Brown, Graham Harvey, Alan Lawrence. MIDDLE - Bert Slater (coach), Steve Campbell, Ian Angus, Tom Carson, Bobby Glennie, Bobby Geddes, George McGeachie, Ross Jack, Eric Ferguson (physiotherapist). FRONT - Jocky Scott (manager), Tosh McKinlay, Rab Shannon, Jim Duffy, Vince Mennie, Tommy Coyne, Drew Jarvie (assistant-manager).

Fotopress

Hit-man - Tommy Coyne netted 37 goals in season 1987-88.

Tam equalised, they were worth an extra man."

Sadly, the euphoria proved short-lived. Just three days later, Jim Duffy (28), was carried off with an injured knee in a 2-1 defeat at Ibrox and the devastating news was that the career of Dundee's inspirational skipper was over.

His studs had caught in the turf while tackling Robert Fleck and he had suffered cartilage and severe cruciate ligament damage.

Last season, Duffy's superb form had been rewarded by an Under-21 international cap as an over-age player. Now, his organisational ability was sorely missed in defeats by Morton (a) 3-4, and Hearts (h) 1-3, and Dundee's Skol Cup hopes were further diminished when Shannon was sent off in an unruly clash with the Edinburgh side at Dens.

Nevertheless, their 11,000 allocation for the all-ticket semi-final tie with Aberdeen at Tannadice was quickly sold out and, with the suspended Shannon joining Duffy and Rafferty on the sidelines, the Dark Blues lined up: Geddes; McGeachie, Smith, Glennie, McKinlay; Mennie, Brown, Angus; Harvey, Coyne, Wright. Subs. - Jack, Forsyth. Aberdeen: Leighton; McKimmie, McLeish, W. Miller, Robertson; Bett, Irvine, Connor; J. Miller, Falconer, Hewitt. Subs. - Grant, Hackett.

With long queues still outside the ground, slack defending allowed former Dens Parker Robert Connor to put the Dons

ahead in 39 seconds. And, lacking the industrious Rafferty and Shannon and with Brown short of match fitness, Bett and Connor controlled the vital midfield area for Aberdeen. Shortly before half-time, Irvine added a second and, despite battling to the end, the Dark Blues were unable to breach the redoubtable Pittodrie defence.

Disappointingly, it was Dundee's second semi-final failure in six months and, within 48 hours, a boardroom reshuffle saw Angus Cook installed as chairman. Feeling it was time for a fresh approach, Ian Gellatly had sold 19,000 of his 23,000 shares to Cook who had also purchased the 4,000 shares owned by Iain Bett. And although Messrs Bett and Speedie resigned, Gellatly would remain on the board alongside Cook, Strachan and the deposed chairman Graham Thomson.

Soon afterwards, Hibs skipper Gordon Chisholm (27), who was on freedom-of-contract, was signed as a replacement for Jim Duffy. The clubs later agreed on a fee of £72,000, an amount partly offset by the imminent departure of Ross Jack to Dunfermline for £15,000 and Derek McWilliams to Falkirk for £5,000.

In December, Dundee met a Premier League select in a Dens Testimonial for Jim Duffy. The game drew a somewhat disappointing crowd of 6,000, whereas George McGeachie's Testimonial against Liverpool two months earlier had attracted 14,463. Unselfishly, the popular McGeachie - nicknamed "Zico" by the Dundee fans - had offered the Liverpool game to Duffy, but the Dens skipper refused. It must be said that the difference in the attendances reflected more on the attraction of Kenny Dalglish's Liverpool to Tayside than the popularity of either McGeachie or Duffy.

The introduction of Chisholm helped tighten the defence and, by the middle of that month, Dundee lay fifth after only

182

three defeats in 17 games since his arrival. Jocky Scott's men were playing with confidence and the goal-hungry partnership of Coyne and Wright netted nine goals within four days as the Dark Blues raced to spectacular away wins over Falkirk (6-0) and Morton (7-1).

A few weeks earlier, the Dark Blues had maintained their recent derby dominance with a 3-1 win over Dundee United at Tannadice. Coyne and Wright were again the key men and, although the former United man scored two opportunist goals, both were provided by the foraging Wright, who later added a third when Rafferty's long-range drive rebounded from a post.

Meanwhile, Dundee's injury woes had continued. Tosh McKinlay (ankle ligaments) had only recently returned after a 10-week absence and now came news that both Gordon Chisholm - with a damaged disc - and George McGeachie - with a recurrence of achilles tendon trouble - would miss the rest of the season. In addition, Vince Mennie would be out for a month after injuring a knee against Hearts, with Alan Lawrence later missing for six weeks with a damaged knee sustained during Dundee's successful challenge for the prestigious Tennents Sixes indoor tournament for which the club received a welcome £13,000 in prize money.

Nevertheless, Dundee remained fifth and, by mid-January, they lay seven points above sixth-placed Dundee United over whom they held a 27-goal advantage. At this stage, the buoyant Dark Blues were the Premier League's top scorers with 57 goals, 32 of which had been scored by Tommy Coyne, winner of *The Daily Record*'s "Golden Shot" award when his Ne'erday double against Dunfermline made him the first Scottish League player to score 30 goals that season.

On January 16th, Dundee met their city rivals at Dens in a clash crucial to the UEFA Cup hopes of both but, despite the homesters' early domination, the Tannadice underdogs went on to record a 2-0 win.

Just 24 hours earlier, Dundee fans had been stunned when John Brown (26), scorer of 39 goals in his three-and-a-half years at Dens, was sold to Rangers for £350,000 with Dundee also getting 21-year-old Ibrox utility-man Dave McFarlane on loan until the end of the season.

A few weeks earlier, Brown had asked away after losing his place but, on making a successful return, he rejected Jocky Scott's offer of an improved contract. In the absence of Chisholm, Brown, who was a committed Ibrox fan, had excelled in central defence. However, although Rangers had wished to beat the following day's European Cup signing deadline, and Dundee were believed to have an overdraft of £460,000, his departure was to prove ill-timed indeed.

Recently appointed Dens chairman Angus Cook insisted that there had not been any pressure from the bank and that

New man - Gordon Chisholm, seen battling with Celtic midfielder Billy Stark, was signed after injury forced Jim Duffy to retire. DC Thomson

the transfer money was available for players. But there was little sign of his much-publicised "cash-injection" and on December 18th, there had been consternation when his 51 per cent holding was put up for sale. He claimed that no local businessmen had wished to invest in the club, but, although willing to sell to anyone who could inject the necessary capital, he denied that his business might be in financial trouble.

At the 1987 AGM, held at Dens on February 22nd, 1988, a disillusioned Graham Thomson, who had been a director for 15 years, did not seek re-election. That left Cook, Gellatly and Strachan on the board, and, hopes that Andrew Marshall might return, disappeared when Cook rejected his proposal to put 200,000 unissued shares up for sale. That might have brought valuable income to the club but it may well have been a costly exercise for Cook had he wished to retain overall control.

McFarlane did little to impress and, after a handful of games, he was allowed to return to Ibrox. Ex-Brighton and Sunderland striker Gary Rowell (30), came to Dens on a month's trial but was released after only one appearance as a substitute. However, in February, Jocky Scott splashed out a Dens record fee of £100,000 for Carlisle centre-half Wes Saunders (24), with another £50,000 fee going on Dunfermline's former Dundee United and Hibs midfielder Billy Kirkwood (29).

In the Scottish Cup, Dundee progressed to the quarter-final with a 3-0 win over Brechin City in a Glebe Park replay after a 0-0 draw at Dens and a 2-0 victory over Motherwell at Dens. The second-round win over the Fir Parkers proved costly. Although far from fit, Bobby Glennie had turned out due to a shortage of central-defenders but he had limped off

Dens Park hit-men - Tommy Coyne looks on as the all-action Keith Wright outjumps Alan Main of Dundee United to head against the crossbar at Dens. Dave Narey is the other Tannadice man.

Mirrorpix

after 20 minutes with a recurrence of his groin injury and, for him, the season was over.

Once again, Dundee United stood between Dundee and a place in the last four of the Scottish Cup. But, despite the dismissal of Tannadice skipper Maurice Malpas after a 48th-minute clash with Vince Mennie, the Dark Blues were unable to break the Dens Park stalemate.

Three days later, the teams produced a thriller in the Tannadice mud. A brilliantly taken double by Bannon left Dundee two behind at half-time and with McKinlay suffering a broken ankle after yet another incident with United's Kevin Gallacher - nephew of former Dens favourite Tommy Gallacher - things looked bleak for Dundee.

However, Graham Harvey, a regular on the bench that season, came on to play a key role. He scored twice and with just seven minutes remaining, he had a third disallowed for offside. Throughout extra-time, play raged from end to end. But, with the transfer-seeking Tom Carson - deputising for the injured Geddes - making some breathtaking saves, there was no further score.

The toss of a coin took the second replay back to Dens on March 28th. By then, Carson, earlier on loan to Queen of the South, Partick Thistle, Hibs, Dunfermline and Ipswich, had lost his place after a 6-1 mauling at relegation-threatened Dunfermline and Bobby Geddes resumed in goal.

All the early pressure came from Dundee but in 24 minutes they trailed to a Joe McLeod goal and their cause was further hindered by the departure of Shannon with knee trouble. Increasingly United dominated an ill-tempered

game and, after late goals by Redford and Ferguson sealed Dundee's fate, Rafferty was sent packing for aiming a kick at Gallacher.

Although Dundee's two cup runs had earned around £150,000 in gate receipts, their Scottish Cup defeat had extended a miserable run. By mid-March, their lead over Dundee United had narrowed to two points and decimated by injuries, suspensions and loss of form, a mere seven points from 14 league games since the derby reverse in January, saw them finish seventh, six points behind fifth-placed United and two behind Hibs.

"No team could afford to lose experienced men like Jim Duffy, Gordon Chisholm and then John Brown," said Keith Wright. "Duffy and Brown in particular were a tremendous influence both on the park and in the dressing room and the loss of Brown marked the start of a real downturn in our fortunes."

The season had also turned sour for Tommy Coyne. After reaching the 30 mark at New Year he had only managed another seven goals. And, although his total of 37, of which 33 were in the league, had only been bettered by Dave Halliday's 39 (38 league) in 1923-24, Alec Stott's 39 (30 league) in 1948-49 and Alan Gilzean's 52 (33 league) in 1963-64, Coyne could only finish fifth in the race for the Adidas Golden Boot, the trophy awarded to Europe's top league marksman and ultimately won by Tanju Colak of Turkish club Galatasaray.

CHAPTER TWENTY-FIVE

Downward Spiral

The close-season heralded some notable departures. Jim Duffy turned down a coaching position at Dens to return to Glasgow. Although his contract had another year to run, Dundee agreed to his release and, after a short spell as assistant-manager at Airdrie, Duffy began the new season in charge at Falkirk.

In April, Jocky Scott's request for a two-year extension to the remaining year of his contract had been rejected and, at the end of May, the Dens boss and his assistant Drew Jarvie both resigned. At the time, Aberdeen had managerial vacancies and it came as little surprise when Scott and Jarvie, who had both played for the Dons, moved to Pittodrie soon afterwards. Scott was appointed co-manager alongside Alex Smith with Jarvie taking over as assistant-manager.

The board had made little effort to retain their services and, for the second time in two years, the Dark Blues had lost their manager to the Dons. A figure of £25,000 compensation was agreed for Scott but Jarvie was released from the remaining year of his agreement. "Their departure was a big blow for me personally," said Keith Wright. "Both had been top-class forwards and their training methods were geared to attack."

Former Old Firm bosses Jock Wallace and Davie Hay, St Johnstone's Alex Totten and Manchester United's Gordon Strachan - as player-manager - were favourites for the job. However, it was the relatively unknown Dave Smith of Plymouth Argyle who was appointed manager - Dundee's sixth since the start of the Premier League in 1975.

The Dundee-born Smith (54), had been a boyhood fan of the Dark Blues and was well acquainted with Angus Cook, who believed his management style would bring the club some much-needed publicity. Smith had played for Burnley, Brighton and Bristol City and had been a successful coach at Sheffield Wednesday, Newcastle and Arsenal before managing promotion-winning sides at Mansfield, Southend and Plymouth. Nevertheless, after 38 years in English football, many doubted that his knowledge of the Scottish game would be up to the mark, particularly as another Anglo, Ian Porterfield had recently resigned after an acrimonious stay at Aberdeen.

Dave Johnston had proved an excellent ambassador for the club in his role as general manager but, in July, it was announced that he would be departing to "return to industry". Eleven months later he took up an executive post at Pittodrie, spearheading Aberdeen's commercial activities as if to show that the "brain drain" from Dens northwards was not just confined to players, managers and coaches!

Surprise choice - Dave Smith took charge at Dens.   DC Thomson

John Campbell, who had been brought in to computerise the club's administration, took over as secretary with Angus Cook and Allan Paul sharing responsibility for commercial affairs.

Nevertheless, despite all the backroom upheaval, Dundee recorded a 2-0 home win over Newcastle United in the Dunclare Dispensers' Trophy and 12,222 fans turned out to see the Dark Blues begin their Premier programme with a 1-1 draw against Aberdeen. It was the largest league attendance for a visit by the Dons since 1972 and only the excellence of the visitors' new Dutch keeper, Theo Snelders, kept Dundee at bay.

There were also draws at Motherwell and St Mirren before home wins over Queen of the South (5-1), and Falkirk (2-1), took Dundee through to the Skol Cup quarter-finals for the second successive season. However, a 4-1 defeat by Rangers at Ibrox ended the cup run and, three days later, the Dens deficiencies were further highlighted when Dundee United went back across the road with a 3-0 win.

Dundee had been outclassed by their local rivals and, although Dave Smith had been warmly applauded after his early home successes, the Dens faithful were less than amused to see him clap their victorious neighbours from the field. "Dark days for the Dark Blues, but maybe darkest before the dawn," quoth the jovial manager. And it was this heady rhetoric rather than any soccer success that would hit the headlines in the months to come.

On September 17th, a 1-0 defeat at Hamilton left Dundee ninth but, by early November, 10 points from the next seven games, including a double over reigning champions Celtic, saw them make steady progress up the table. Tommy Coyne netted his first goal of the season in a 1-0 triumph at Dens and, in late October, the Dark Blues recovered from a 2-0 deficit to record a 3-2 win at Parkhead.

Since the arrival of Coyne and Wright, Harvey had spent prolonged spells on the bench but, with the Celtic defence struggling to handle his close control, the tricky striker had played a big part in the Parkhead triumph. After laying one on for Steve Frail, Harvey brilliantly beat two defenders to add a second and, just before half-time, his netbound

Bogey over - Tommy Coyne beats Theo Snelders for his second goal in the 2-0 triumph over Aberdeen in Dundee's first victory over the Pittodrie side at Dens since 1975. Dons defenders McKimmie and Robertson can only watch.   DC Thomson

header was rammed home by Rafferty for number three.

Four days later, Hamilton were beaten 5-2 at Dens but, with only two goals and without a single win from their next eight games, Dundee faced a crisis. On November 12th, a 1-0 home defeat by St Mirren resulted in a stormy exchange between Dave Smith and Paisley boss Tony Fitzpatrick. The Dundee manager claimed that St Mirren had not deserved to win after having only three shots at goal but the visitors had largely controlled the play and, increasingly, the Dens fans questioned Smith's unattractive long-ball tactics.

The growing disenchantment was highlighted by several indignant readers' letters in *The Courier* and soon it was also apparent that all was not well behind the scenes at Dens. By the end of the month, Harvey, Lawrence, McKinlay, Mennie and Rafferty had all submitted transfer requests and, with several others unsettled, morale hit rock-bottom when the popular Tosh McKinlay was transferred to Hearts for £300,000.

Two earlier Hearts bids had been rejected but McKinlay, represented by the agent Bill McMurdo, had intimated his intention to move when his contract expired the following June. Dens chairman Angus Cook believed his departure was inevitable and maintained that it was in Dundee's best interests to sell.

Almost immediately, there was further controversy with the announcement that Novafone had offered £300,000 for Cook's 51 per cent shareholding. They promised to invest heavily in the club but, in a typed statement to *The Courier,* Cook confirmed that although a verbal enquiry had been made by Novafone's Bob Jamieson, it had not been taken seriously and, "after I had stopped laughing," it had been rejected. This scornful public dismissal appeared to mark the end of a previously cordial relationship although, by this time, Novafone were also sponsoring Hearts.

Meanwhile, despite constant transfer speculation, no signings had been made. Fees were agreed for attacking mid-

fielders Mark Lillis of Aston Villa (£150,000), and Craig Robertson of Dunfermline (£200,000), in addition to Hearts striker Iain Ferguson (£275,000), but the players refused to join Dundee.

Hopes were raised by the arrival of Hibs winger Joe McBride (27), for £50,000 and Dunfermline defender John Holt (32), for £45,000 with the former Dundee United man, a life-long follower of the Dens Park club, delighted to get the opportunity to pull on the famous Dark Blue jersey. However, although Dundee remained five points clear of the relegation zone, single-goal defeats at lowly Hamilton and Motherwell brought a torrent of abuse towards the management.

STAR SPORT SC
DAILY STAR   Saturday, January 21, 1989

SMITH ... only five league wins

DUNDEE BOSS IN 'I QUIT' SHAKER

DAVE SMITH quit yesterday as manager of Dundee . . . after just 217 days in the job. He goes at a crucial time for the club, with a

On Hogmanay, Dundee's fortunes took a turn for the better when a Coyne double brought a well-merited 2-0 win over Aberdeen at Dens. It was their first home success against the Dons since 1975 and, even though Aberdeen were under strength, the Dark Blues - reputed to be on their highest-ever win bonus - had played with a rarely displayed passion.

However, there was little respite for the now beleaguered Dave Smith when only one point was taken from the next three games and after just seven months in charge he resigned. Smith's family had remained down south and he had found difficulty settling in Tayside. But, with only five wins from 24 league games and dressing room morale plummeting, his departure had been on the cards. And although Angus Cook claimed it was not club policy to "boot" their managers, it was later revealed that Smith had received a settlement on his £38,000 per annum, three-year contract.

Smith's eccentric style was in stark contrast to previous disciplinarians like Jocky Scott and Archie Knox and his regular absence from training had not gone down well with the players. He had not appeared to appreciate the passion for the game in Scotland and a senior player later claimed that Smith's reign had set the club back two years.

Prior to his departure, two members of the playing staff had also moved on. Vince Mennie was transferred to Falkirk for £30,000 while Bobby Glennie (31), was released after making 372 appearances in his eleven-year spell at Dens. The old warhorse had been on a monthly contract after undergoing a pelvic muscle operation at the start of the season but, soon after leaving Dundee, he was snapped up by Raith Rovers.

At that time, Glennie, whose service had been recognized with a Testimonial against Manchester City, had made the eighth-highest number of appearances for the club. Another 45 games would have put him level with goalkeeping legend Bill Marsh in second place. The defender was very disappointed to be released and, ironically, incoming manager Gordon Wallace later told him that he would have been retained.

Glennie was critical of the departed Dave Smith's style of management: "We only saw him on the Friday and Saturday. He spent the rest of the week in England and John Blackley was left to take the training." This was confirmed by Keith Wright: "The boss had some strange ideas. He said the lads should report for training at 11am to allow them a longer lie-in and it was only when John Blackley put his foot down that this was reversed."

Four months earlier, Blackley had been appointed assistant-manager to give Smith some much-needed local knowledge, with Cowdenbeath receiving compensation for their manager's breach of contract. Now, the former Hibs and Scotland sweeper took over as caretaker-manager only to see Dundee make a Scottish Cup exit to Dundee United for the third year running.

That season, Dundee had already tasted defeat in three local derbies, losing 3-0 and 1-0 at Dens and 2-0 at Tannadice, and despite holding their own in the first half-hour, Dave Bowman and Raphael Meade gave United a 2-0 lead soon after the break. By then, McBride and Kirkwood had retired through injury and although Angus reduced the leeway with a 71st-minute free-kick, Dundee were unable to equalise.

In February, Bobby Geddes became the seventh Dundee player since 1975 to be honoured with a Testimonial match. Commercial manager Allan Paul had previously been a scout with Liverpool and 9,311 fans turned out to see the Anfield side record a 3-1 win at Dens.

On February 20th, nearly a month after Dave Smith's resignation, Dundee United coach Gordon Wallace was appointed manager with John Blackley continuing as his assistant. Few fans disagreed with the choice of Wallace (44), a prolific scorer best known for his magnificent goal in Dundee's League Cup triumph back in 1973. After leaving Dundee in May 1976, he played for Dundee United and Raith Rovers and, after a spell as Raith manager, he returned to Tannadice as a coach in 1983.

The Dens board hoped that his experience of working alongside a top manager like Jim McLean would prove beneficial. Wallace had been overlooked in the much-publicised search for McLean's successor but, despite having only four months of his contract to run, he had been refused permission to talk to Dundee. Now, United protested that Wallace had been "poached" and, after being threatened with a civil action, Dundee were fined a record £5,000 by the Scottish League. Angus Cook maintained that Dundee had acted with dignity and, referring to the loss of previous managers and players, he declared that Dundee would no longer be the doormat of Scottish football.

Wallace felt there was already the basis of a reasonable side at Dens but, within two weeks, Tommy Coyne, who had

The new team - Dundee manager Gordon Wallace and his assistant John Blackley in the dug-out at Dens. DC Thomson

scored 60 goals in 109 games, was on his way to Celtic for a Dens record fee of £500,000.

Eight months earlier, Dundee had stated that neither Coyne nor Wright were for sale, "even for a million pounds", but this had not prevented approaches. In September, Cook had countered an Aberdeen approach for Wright by offering £150,000 for Davie Dodds. He also expressed an interest in Stewart McKimmie. "Both of them," claimed Cook, "were easily affordable from my personal wealth."

Aberdeen and St Mirren had both offered £400,000 for Wright and, in January, West Ham had placed a staggering £750,000 bid on the table. Dundee had resisted the temptation, but although Coyne still had 16 months of his contract remaining, he was unsettled and Gordon Wallace made it clear that he only wanted players who wished to play for the Dens Park club.

Cook had endorsed Wallace's desire to build a youth policy similar to that which had served Dundee United so well over the years, and at the AGM held soon after the new manager's arrival, he pledged that he would invest £100,000 of his own funds into such a scheme if necessary. Over 40 shareholders had been in attendance but, despite an operating profit of £224,481 - mainly from the sale of John Brown - and the reduction of the club's debts from £517,273 to £399,223, there were signs of a widening rift between the Dens chairman and many of the shareholders.

Although long-term injuries to Angus, Smith, McGeachie and Lawrence had proved disruptive, Dundee had lacked a dominant figure in midfield since the departure of Connor and Brown. Of course, Angus and Rafferty were industrious performers but, just like the experienced Holt, McGeachie and Wes Saunders, who had earlier been tried in a "midfield-destroyer" role, neither were up to the role of playmaker.

The promising Stevie Campbell (21), who had gained three Scotland Under-21 caps that season, and Steve Frail (19), had both been given extended runs but, understandably, their form had shaded. Therefore it came as little surprise when Dundee paid £70,000 for Airdrie's former Dundee United midfielder Gordon McLeod (21), with £30,000-rated Alan Lawrence going to Broomfield in part-exchange, and another midfielder, Albert Craig, was later signed on a free transfer from Newcastle United.

McLeod, who had been captain of the Scotland Under-21 side, was recovering from a cartilage operation and would not play again that season. However, home wins over Motherwell, St Mirren, Hearts and Hamilton brought nine points from the last eight games as Dundee finished eighth, 14 points clear of relegated Hamilton - the only team to go down that season.

Although Wallace felt there was room for improvement, he could take heart from the progress of some of the Dens youngsters. Already, four of the Under-18 side which reached the previous season's BP Youth Cup Final, where they lost 2-1 at Dunfermline, had appeared for the first-team. Left-back Shaun McSkimming had played once last term and, in addition to midfielders Steve Frail and Mark Craib, striker Duncan Campbell had impressed with his pace and willingness to shoot.

Having made a careful assessment of the playing staff, Gordon Wallace continued to reshape his squad and five close-season signings took his spending to the £280,000 mark. Dunfermline's Stuart Beedie (28), valued at £50,000, arrived in exchange for transfer-listed Stuart Rafferty plus £25,000. Former Eire international Alan Campbell (26), cost £60,000 from Belgian Second Division side Berchem Sport, while Gary Lennox (19), was signed from Queen's Park. All

Hat-trick hero - Dundee striker Keith Wright beats Maurice Malpas and sends a powerful header past Scott Thomson for his first goal of a hat-trick in the dramatic 4-3 victory over Dundee United at Dens. DC Thomson

three were midfielders, although the pacy Campbell had first made his name as a front runner.

Former Scotland left-back Arthur Albiston (32), was secured from West Brom for £50,000 and a further £75,000 was spent on Chelsea striker Billy Dodds (21), who last season had scored over 30 goals for Chelsea's reserves after previously impressing while on loan with Partick Thistle.

Encouragingly, star striker Keith Wright signed a three-year contract, while the promising Duncan Campbell (18), and Steve Frail were both fixed up for a further four years. The transfer-listed Ian Angus spent a trial period with Plymouth Argyle, but later returned to sign a one-year deal with Dundee.

Inevitably, there had also been departures, and in addition to Tommy Coyne, Alan Lawrence and Stuart Rafferty, reserve striker Paul Ritchie (20), had joined Angus club Brechin City, who were then managed by his father John, with the Dark Blues receiving a transfer fee of £12,000.

Loan star - Derek Ferguson showed his class while on loan from Rangers and here the midfielder battles it out with Motherwell's Northern Ireland midfielder Colin O'Neil.

There had also been changes to the backroom staff. Allan Paul departed to become commercial manager at Hearts while Billy Kirkwood, who had failed to make a full recovery from the pelvic injury he had sustained in the cup-tie against Dundee United, was appointed reserve-team coach.

As part of the 1989-90 pre-season warm-up, Dundee returned unbeaten from a four-game tour against non-League sides in North-East England before drawing 2-2 with Queens Park Rangers at Dens in the Dunclare Dispenser's Trophy match.

On the opening day of the season, Dundee travelled to newly-promoted Dunfermline, but despite taking an early lead through Beedie, they went down 2-1. Duncan Campbell's pace had caused the Fifers problems before he was helped off after a series of late tackles by Jimmy Nicholl and Doug Rougvie.

Billy Dodds took his place but, when the substitute was tripped by Nicholl soon after half-time, the former Northern Ireland international was shown the yellow card and sent off for his second bookable offence.

Seven days later, Dundee recovered to beat Dundee United 4-3 in a Dens derby thriller. The visitors led 2-0 after 24 minutes but, by half-time, Keith Wright had levelled the scores. Paatalainen made it 3-2, only for Wright to equalise on the hour and, with Dundee well on top, Joe McBride's curling free-kick beat the Tannadice wall for the winner, 17 minutes from time.

Dundee's last derby hat-trick had been scored by Jimmy Chalmers in the 7-3 League Cup triumph way back in September, 1956. Wright, however, was the first Dundee player to net three goals against Dundee United in a league game since World War Two.

The big striker had always proved a thorn in the flesh to Dundee's local rivals and he confessed: "I liked nothing better than to put one over the lads down the road." It was a habit Keith would be happy to continue in years to come.

After a first-round bye, Clyde were crushed 5-1 at Dens in the second stage of the Skol Cup. This entailed an early return to Dunfermline, but with little luck going their way, Dundee went down 1-0.

In mid-September, Angus Cook, who had earlier rejected a £1.5 million takeover bid from a group including Dave Johnston and Allan Paul, announced the formation of Discovery Group PLC. It would consist of Dundee Football Club, Discovery Developments, Discovery Investments and a new company, Discovery Leisure.

With an estimated market value of £10 million, Cook hoped for a public flotation the following May. It would be the first by a local firm for 20 years and Dundee would join Hibs as the only Scottish clubs quoted on the London Stock Exchange.

The chairman also outlined ambitious plans to develop Dens into a £15 million all-seated stadium, which would include a sports and leisure complex. The Provost Road and South Enclosure areas would be replaced by double-decker stands and underground car parking, the T.C. Keay end would be covered and seated and the main stand would also get a major refurbishment.

This concept, however, was based on a 1974 project by architectural student Peter Inglis and suspicions that Cook was "flying a kite" were heightened by a later revelation that Dundee and Dundee United had discussed the possibility of sharing a new purpose-built stadium.

Caird Park was mooted as a possible site but talks later broke down when it was found that the sale value of Dens and Tannadice would leave both clubs far short of their £5 million contributions towards the £18 million required for the new ground.

Six months earlier, both had denied holding merger talks although, perhaps significantly, Angus Cook had made an abortive attempt to alter the name of Dundee F.C. to Dundee City before the start of season 1988-89.

Cook, perhaps influenced by other owner-chairmen like David Murray (Rangers), Wallace Mercer (Hearts), and the Donald family (Aberdeen), was assuming a wider profile and, soon after taking ownership of Dundee's Queen's Hotel, came news that he proposed to build a £25 million luxury golf and country club on the outskirts of the city.

Meanwhile, the burnt-out wing stand had been restored to include a family section and, to cash in on the expanding commercial market, hospitality areas like the Billy Steel Lounge, the Premier Suite and the Executive Club Lounge, with famous names like Alex Hamilton and Bobby Cox as hosts, were created. There were also significant improvements to the boardroom, offices, dressing rooms and press-box although an application for a public house licence for the Executive Lounge was later turned down.

However, by late October, four successive defeats, including a 3-2 reverse at St Mirren after they squandered a two-goal lead, had plunged Dundee to the bottom of the league. They had taken just five points from their opening 10 games and the nightmare continued with the next 11 matches bringing just one solitary win.

On December 2nd, a late strike by substitute Albert Craig

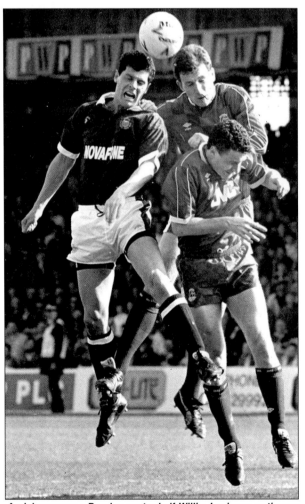

Aerial prowess - Dundee centre-half Willie Jamieson outjumps Aberdeen's Brian Irvine and Jim Bett at Pittodrie.   DC Thomson

had brought a 2-1 home victory over Motherwell but that was only their second league success of the season. By the middle of January 1990, the Dark Blues lay eight points adrift of ninth-placed St Mirren, and, having lost 52 goals in 23 games, they looked odds-on-favourites to take the drop.

That autumn, 30-year-old George McGeachie's 12-year stint at Dens ended when he joined Raith Rovers for £20,000. Of the newcomers, Gordon McLeod had looked an inventive midfielder and, with the busy Billy Dodds quickly establishing himself alongside Keith Wright, Graham Harvey moved on to Airdrie for £50,000.

Disappointingly, the more experienced signings like Albiston, who had made 18 appearances for Scotland, Campbell - capped three times for the Republic of Ireland - Beedie and Craig had struggled, although Albiston and Campbell - the former with broken ribs and a punctured lung - had been plagued by injury.

The most pressing problems lay in defence but, although regulars like Geddes and Saunders dropped out as various permutations were tried, results remained poor. In November, Partick Thistle defender Alan Dinnie (26), was signed for £95,000 but almost immediately Dundee recouped their outlay when they received a £200,000 windfall payment from Blackburn after former Dens striker Colin Hendry's £600,000 move to Manchester City.

Ironically, at a time when Dundee desperately sought a commanding pivot to play alongside Gordon Chisholm, the former Highland League player had developed into a top-class centre-half. Under an agreement made by Jocky Scott, Dundee got 35 per cent, less the £30,000 they had already received in 1987, with another £35,000 in prospect once Hendry played 50 first-team games.

At the end of November, Dundee had agreed to pay Rangers £400,000 for centre-half Scott Nisbet and midfielder Ian McCall but, like Hearts midfielder Kenny Black before them, both turned down the move. The Dens men had cast their net wide for new talent, but although several players had been on trial, no signings were made. Interest in Aberdeen stopper Brian Irvine ended when the Dons demanded £450,000, but, on January 10th, the Dark Blues signed Hamilton centre-half Willie Jamieson (27), for a Dens record fee of £125,000.

Jamieson was ineligible for the Scottish Cup first-round tie against Dundee United at Dens. This was the fourth successive season in which the clubs had met in the Scottish and, disappointingly, only 14,276 turned out for what proved a no-scoring draw. The blustery conditions were suited to Dundee's more direct approach and only three great saves by Alan Main and a goal-line clearance by Jim McInally saved the day for United. The Dark Blues would regret those misses for, in the Tannadice replay, United's John Clark crashed home the only goal 20 minutes from time in a closely contested game.

McLeod had shone against his former club, but with Beedie and Angus out injured, Dundee were short of experienced midfielders. Another abortive move was made for ex-Dens Parker Ian Redford, now with Ipswich, before Gordon Wallace did a shrewd bit of business. Scottish international midfielder Derek Ferguson (22), was signed on a

Netbound - Keith Wright grins as Billy Dodds scores against Rangers. BELOW - Jim Duffy, seen with Stuart Beedie, soon got the defence organised, but the revival came too late.

month's loan from Rangers and with his craft soon in evidence, valuable points were gained from a 2-0 home win over Hibs, a 0-0 draw with Celtic at Dens and a similar scoreline against St Mirren at Paisley.

There was now a new enthusiam amongst the Dundee support and around 1,500 fans took advantage of the directors' offer of free transport to vital relegation matches at St Mirren and Motherwell. Twenty-seven coachloads made the trip to Paisley with thirty-three travelling to Motherwell the following week. At Fir Park, Dundee dominated the early stages until two Carson blunders paved the way for a 3-1 defeat. And with ninth-placed St Mirren now nine points ahead, prospects looked increasingly bleak as the season entered its final quarter.

Meanwhile, Jim Duffy had made a shock return to Dens. Earlier that season, he had resigned as Falkirk manager after experiencing disciplinary problems with his players and, with his knee injury showing a remarkable improvement, he was given the all-clear to resume playing after intensive medical checks.

The Dark Blues had first option on the classy defender and, almost two-and-a-half years after his last competitive game, he made his return in the Forfarshire Cup Final against St Johnstone at McDiarmid Park on February 24th. Incessant rain made ground conditions treacherous, but, with the immaculate Duffy looking as if he had never been away, Dundee retained the trophy with a well-deserved 3-2 victory.

Duffy slotted in well alongside the commanding Jamieson and with skipper Chisholm pushing forward to a holding role in midfield, the Dark Blues had flourished. Derek Ferguson had brought flair to that area, but due to an ankle injury he made only four appearances in seven weeks before his return to Rangers.

However, by the end of March, six points had been taken from Rangers (h) 2-2, Dunfermline (h) 1-0, Dundee United (a) 2-1, and Aberdeen (h) 1-1 and only four points separated Dundee from fellow strugglers Dunfermline and St Mirren.

In December, Tom Carson had replaced Bobby Geddes as number one keeper, but when injury ruled him out of the game against Dunfermline, 20-year-old Alford lad Paul Mathers made the position his own with a series of top-class displays.

Despite their lowly position, the Dark Blues had done well against Dundee United and the trend was continued in a Tannadice derby punctuated by sleet storms. A headed goal by Wright, then a perfectly flighted free-kick by Shannon earned a vital win, giving Dundee six points out of eight against United that term - their highest points tally against the Tannadice outfit since the start of the Premier League in the 1975-76 season.

On Wednesday, April 4th, stout defending earned a 0-0

Great start - Alan Campbell gives Dundee an early lead in the vital game against St Mirren but a disappointing 2-1 defeat would condemn the Dark Blues to relegation.

DC Thomson

draw with second-top Hearts at Tynecastle. The game had been brought forward to allow live TV coverage by BSB for which the clubs received £50,000 each but Dundee's joy at taking a point soon evaporated when St Mirren and Dunfermline managed shock wins away to Celtic (3-0), and Motherwell (3-1), three days later.

Now Dundee trailed their rivals by five points and with four games remaining it was imperative they beat St Mirren at Dens on April 14th. There was a pre-match boost when Sammy Kean and players from the great era of the early 1960s were paraded and they got an emotional welcome from the 7,414 crowd.

The teams lined up - Dundee: Mathers; Forsyth, Jamieson, Duffy, Shannon; Craib, Chisholm (capt), McSkimming; A. Campbell, Dodds, Wright. Subs. - Craig, D. Campbell. St Mirren: Money; Wishart, Godfrey, Manley, Black; Shaw, Lambert, Martin, Kinnaird; Stickroth, Torfason. Subs. - Dawson, McDowall.

Alan Campbell gave Dundee the perfect start after just 65 seconds and they were given a great opportunity to take a two-goal lead when Wright was sent sprawling in 18 minutes. Billy Dodds, who had already netted three spot kicks that season, stepped up to take the penalty, but although his powerfully struck shot beat Money, it came crashing back off a post.

That was the turning point. Soon afterwards, a Mathers slip allowed Shaw to equalise, and as St Mirren grew in confidence, Martin put them ahead with a deflected shot in 49 minutes. There was no further score and, surprisingly, a nervy Dundee had shown little appetite for the fray.

Gordon McLeod was suspended and along with flu-victim Alan Dinnie, he had been badly missed in midfield and with Duffy clearly not recovered from the thigh injury which had caused his half-time substitution against Hearts at

Tynecastle, Torfason and Stickroth had given the Dundee defence a torrid time.

Sadly, Dundee were now doomed to relegation, and a 2-1 defeat to Motherwell at Dens on the last day of the season heralded the end of their nine-year stay in the Premier League.

Six points had separated them from safety and, despite a series of

favourable results against the top Premier sides, too many points had been lost to the other clubs in the lower reaches of the table like Dunfermline, St Mirren and Motherwell.

The Dark Blues had managed only 24 points - their lowest-ever tally in the Premier League. Defensive weaknesses in the early part of the season had set the trend and the subsequent delay in obtaining suitable replacements had cost Dundee dear. After the arrival of Jamieson, only 16 goals were conceded in 14 games compared to 49 goals lost previously and had Dinnie, Jamieson and Duffy arrived earlier, the outcome may well have been different.

Undoubtedly, Dundee had been unfortunate with injuries, particularly to experienced campaigners like Angus, Smith, Holt and Beedie, who all missed much of the season. However, the use of 29 players including youngsters like Paul Mathers, Steve Frail, Shaun McSkimming, Duncan Campbell, midfielder Grant McMartin, Kevin Bain (2 sub), John McQuillan (one sub), and midfielder Michael Kerr (one sub), gave some indication of the disarray in which the club had found itself.

CHAPTER TWENTY-SIX

Revolving Doors

Dundee, now sponsored by Kelly's Copiers, would remain full-time, but it was anticipated that relegation would cost the club in the region of £500,000 for one season in the First Division. In an effort to cut overheads, Arthur Albiston was offered a free transfer and eleven others put up for sale. They were Bobby Geddes, Jim Smith, John Holt, Ian Angus, Wes Saunders, Steve Campbell, Alan Campbell, Albert Craig, Joe McBride, Gary Lennox and John Hendry, with the transfer-seeking Rab Shannon later added to the list.

By early August, five players had moved on. Geddes, who had requested a transfer after losing his place to Carson, joined Kilmarnock for £70,000. Saunders joined former boss Dave Smith at Torquay for £60,000, Angus moved to Motherwell for £40,000, Smith went to Airdrie for £25,000, while 20-year-old Hendry, the reserve striker who had done well while on loan at Forfar, was signed by Spurs for £30,000. Their departure meant a welcome reduction in the wage bill and, with £225,000 taken in, Gordon Wallace strengthened his squad by splashing a new record fee of £150,000 on Chelsea striker Colin West (22).

Jim Duffy had been a key man in Dundee's valiant attempt to avoid relegation but, after failing to agree terms, he joined First Division rivals Partick Thistle as player-coach. The influential sweeper had received around £4,000 for signing a short-term contract with Dundee but now there was an acrimonious parting. The Dark Blues maintained they were due a transfer fee from Thistle plus £9,500, which they had repaid to an insurance company and the Players' Benevolent Fund to obtain Duffy's clearance.

Dundee wanted £50,000 although Duffy maintained it had been agreed that no fee would be required should he choose to move on. Initially, Partick offered £9,500 but, in the end, the clubs settled on a fee of £38,000 prior to the meeting of the Transfer Tribunal.

Dundee's priority was to make a swift return to the Premier League and they were soon installed as favourites for the First Division Championship - with Airdrie, Partick Thistle and Falkirk expected to be their closest challengers. Dundee fans were further boosted by the news that Keith Wright - the only First Division player selected for the Scottish League team which defeated the full Scotland XI in the Scottish League Centenary game at Hampden - was to stay with the Dens Park club.

It was hoped that a good run in the League Cup might generate some much-needed cash. In the second round, Dundee played Queen of the South at Palmerston but, with

True grit - Willie Jamieson, Gordon Chisholm and Keith Wright put Airdrie keeper John Martin under pressure. Fotopress

the sides locked at 2-2 after extra-time, the Dumfries men went through 4-1 on penalties. In the league, things did not go as planned either, and by October 13th the Dark Blues lay fourth, seven points behind pace-setters Airdrie after winning only four of their opening 10 games.

In the opening game, Dundee had been unfortunate not to beat Partick Thistle in a 1-1 draw at Dens, Jim Duffy receiving rather a stormy reception from his erstwhile admirers. On Tuesday, October 9th, a crowd of 6,360 turned out for the visit of high-flying Airdrie. The Diamonds, who had netted 27 goals in eight league games, could boast three ex-Dundee men in Jim Smith, Alan Lawrence and Graham Harvey, but the man of the moment was Owen Coyle, Scotland's top scorer with 17 league goals thus far.

Dundee produced some brilliant football but in 40 minutes, Billy Dodds was sent off for retaliation against former teammate Jim Smith, who was booked for the original foul. Throughout the second half, 10-man Dundee continued to dominate only for Alan Lawrence to slip home a shock winner near the end. The nippy Lawrence had been used as winger by Dundee but, although never a regular at Dens, he had proved a big hit in a striking role at Broomfield.

The loss of a further four points from the next four games saw Dundee slip to fifth behind strong-going Falkirk, Raith and Hamilton and much criticism was now directed at Dens Park chairman Angus Cook. His three-year reign had seen Dundee win only 35 from 125 games and they had slipped from fifth-top of the Premier League to fifth-top of the First Division. In his time at the helm, quality players like Brown, McKinlay and Coyne had departed and satisfactory replacements had not been found.

Of an estimated transfer income of £1,760,000, only £1,097,000 appeared to have been spent, yet the club desperately required a midfield playmaker. The manager was not exempt from blame, for although the accent was again on good football, some of his signings, notably the former internationalists Albiston and Campbell, had been a big disappointment. Colin West was another still to show his true form but, after a month in the reserves, he was recalled for the B&Q Centenary Cup Final against Ayr United on Sunday, November 11th.

Dundee had reached the final of the new competition by beating Alloa (a) 5-3, Raith Rovers (a) 1-0 (aet) and Kilmarnock (a) 2-0 and with Dinnie recovered from his knee injury, they fielded: Carson; Forsyth, Craib, Jamieson, Shannon; Dinnie, Chisholm, McLeod; West, Dodds, Wright. Subs. - Frail and McBride.

Ayr United: Purdie; Kennedy, McAllister, Gillespie, Smyth; McCann, Bryce, Johnston; Templeton, Graham, Weir. Subs. Evans, Walker.

Dundee carried a large support amongst the 11,506 Fir Park crowd but they were silenced when Ian McAllister put Ayr ahead in 13 minutes. Gradually, the Dens men took control and, with West causing havoc down the right, they were awarded a penalty when the flying winger was downed soon after the break. Dodds, who had missed against Meadowbank a week earlier, sent David Purdie the wrong way and 20 minutes later the wee striker put Dundee in front from an inch-perfect cross by West.

Shortly afterwards, a long-range shot by David Smyth was deflected high past Carson. This was against the run of play, and although there was no further scoring, the Dark Blues continued to dominate in extra-time. With only five minutes left and the game heading for a penalty shoot-out, Purdie made a brave save at the feet of Wright and, when the ball spun free, Dodds was on hand to complete his hat-trick from the edge of the box.

Despite widespread disquiet at the record of Angus Cook and manager Gordon Wallace - a number of banners calling for their removal had been taken down by the police - the fans had given the team tremendous support and, as the players paraded the glass trophy and ran a lap of honour, there were joyous celebrations on the terraces. It had been an enjoyable occasion and, in addition to the £10,000 prize money, the result proved a tremendous boost to morale.

There were wins over Partick Thistle (a) 3-1, and Morton (h) 1-0, before Chisholm headed a late winner at Airdrie. But although a 1-0 home win over Ayr took Dundee to the top of the table for the first time that season - Mark Craib suffered a broken leg - they were unable to maintain this form and soon slipped back to fourth place.

B&Q Centenary Cup Winners 1990 (BACK, left to right) Keith Wright, Tom Carson, Colin West, Gordon McLeod, Steve Frail, Stewart Forsyth, Willie Jamieson, Rab Shannon. FRONT - Joe McBride, Billy Dodds, Mark Craib, Gordon Chisholm, Alan Dinnie. DC Thomson

On the spot - Billy Dodds fires home a penalty against Clyde watched by team-mates Gordon McLeod and Shaun McSkimming. DCThomson

The defence had tightened up with Tom Carson, Alan Dinnie, Stewart Forsyth, Mark Craib, Willie Jamieson, Gordon Chisholm and Rab Shannon all reliable defenders. Up front, Keith Wright and Billy Dodds were the envy of most First Division teams but throughout the side there was an obvious lack of quality, particularly in midfield, where Albert Craig and Gordon McLeod had made little impact.

Too often, Dinnie and Chisholm had been used to bolster this area and, although emerging youngsters like Frail and McSkimming showed bags of promise, particularly going forward, an experienced campaigner was desperately required to pull the strings in midfield.

Home form - only four wins from 10 games - had been poor with recent gates averaging only 3,000. Angus Cook blamed the low crowds for the club's inability to buy, yet failure to gain promotion would cost another £500,000 and could mean part-time football or worse. Around 6,000 fans had travelled to the Centenary Cup Final and if home gates could be raised to this level by putting out an attractive team and the more remunerative Premier League and its financial rewards achieved, £200,000 spent on a player or two would have been a wise investment.

After a 12-game unbeaten run, Falkirk, who included the charismatic Simon Stainrod and a host of other battle-hardened players like Gordon Marshall, Brian Whittaker, Tommy McQueen, John Hughes and Alex Taylor, were clearly a threat but by the time the pair met at Brockville on January 5th, Dundee were level and there was a 10-minute delay to allow the big crowd into the ground.

It would not prove Dundee's day but although Hughes headed the only goal of a thrilling encounter, the Dens men then recorded four successive wins and by early March, they were top, one point ahead of Falkirk and five ahead of Airdrie. Since their Centenary Cup triumph, only six points had been dropped from 14 games and, with confidence mounting, Dundee's promotion hopes looked bright especially with a second team now to be promoted following the recent decision by the Scottish League to adopt a 12-12-14 format for the following season.

Home victories over Brechin (1-0), and Kilmarnock (2-0), took Dundee to the Scottish Cup quarter-finals and, on Wednesday, March 13th, they faced Dundee United at Tannadice. The game was televised live by the satellite company BSkyB - so named after a merger between BSB and Sky - but there was still a 16,228 crowd present for the first city derby for almost a year.

Despite the absence of the suspended Wright, it was an evenly contested first half. In 30 minutes, Dodds latched on to a Shannon pass before lofting the ball beyond the advancing Alan Main. However, this stung United into action and goals by Ray McKinnon, Darren Jackson and the lanky Duncan Ferguson with a header put the tie beyond the Dark Blues.

In the end, Dundee had been outclassed and all their efforts could now be concentrated on the drive for promotion. Prior to the quarter-final, however, lowly Brechin City had departed from Dens with their second league victory of the season against the hosts. Dundee had struggled against the well-organised Glebe Parkers, and once more it was the balding Ian Pryde - a constant thorn in the flesh of the home defence - who scored the winner.

That was a crushing blow to morale and although Forfar were beaten 1-0 at Dens, Dundee stumbled to away defeats against Clyde (2-4) and Partick Thistle (0-1) before ending a disastrous month with a 1-1 draw at Clydebank on March 30th. Only a late goal by Wright had saved the day at Kilbowie, and although Stuart Beedie was back for his first appearance of the season, the biggest surprise was the inclusion of former Dens skipper Cammy Fraser, who was now 33 years of age. Fraser, who had last played for Dundee in 1984, had been obtained on a free transfer from Raith Rovers just before the transfer deadline.

After two years at Ibrox, he had been forced to retire with an arthritic hip but, in 1987, he made his comeback with Raith and spent four successful seasons at Kirkcaldy. Along with Beedie, his experience would be invaluable during the nerve-wracking title run-in, particularly since key players like Wright, Shannon, Chisholm. Dodds and Dinnie had already missed recent games through suspension.

Two weeks earlier, Angus Cook had repeated that no money would be available for players to beat the transfer deadline: "In view of our home attendances, it should come as no surprise that we are not in a position to buy players. I accept the commercial reality of the situation and, while I know the business rule about speculating to accumulate, there is no way I could put the very fabric of this club at risk."

Cook's relationship with shareholders and supporters had continued to deteriorate. At the 1990 AGM held on January 30th, 1991 it had been revealed that the club had been some £600,000 in the red eight months earlier. The chairman denied that the club faced a financial crisis and the meeting, attended by around 40 shareholders, developed into a stormy two-and-a-half hour session.

His proposal to revamp Dens Park and build the golfing complex at Balumbie had failed to materialise and Discovery Leisure, including the prestigious Queen's Hotel and nine other pubs, was put into receivership with the two remaining divisions of the Discovery Group - since renamed Disgorge - later going into voluntary liquidation. Dundee Football Club, however, had been transferred from the Discovery Group to Cook's family business, Leveintac, in the summer of 1990, and was unaffected.

With seven games left, Dundee lay three points behind Falkirk and although Airdrie lay a further two points adrift, they had a game in hand. Recent form had been demoralising with the behind-the-scenes acrimony a further drain on morale and a desperately disappointing crowd of only 2,515 - the lowest at Dens all season - saw the Dark Blues scrape a 1-0 win over Morton before the crucial trip to Brockville.

There they fielded: Carson; Chisholm, Jamieson, Fraser; Dinnie, McMartin, Beedie, Shannon; D. Campbell, Dodds, Wright. Subs. Craig, Craib. Roared on by a large support in the near-10,000 crowd, the Dark Blues played as if their lives depended on the result. Only the brilliance of Bairns keeper Gordon Marshall kept them at bay although Duncan Campbell unaccountably managed to hit the post from point-blank range near the end of a 0-0 draw.

Three successive wins over Meadowbank (h) 4-0, Raith Rovers (h) 2-0, and Clyde (a) 1-0 left Dundee and Airdrie within a point of Falkirk. Now, with two games remaining, came a tough test at Kilmarnock but, once again, the Dark Blues were unable to take their chances in a no-scoring stalemate. And, although Falkirk had, as expected, clinched promotion with a 4-1 win over Ayr, upsetting news that Airdrie had defeated Partick Thistle 2-0 meant that Dundee's promotion aspirations depended on winning their final game at Hamilton in the hope that the Diamonds might slip up at Kirkcaldy.

Uproar - Dens shareholders signal a vote of no-confidence at the Extraordinary General Meeting in 1991. DC Thomson

Angus Cook - chairman from 1987 until 1991.

On May 11th, a grimly determined Dundee recovered from the loss of an early goal and in 21 minutes they were awarded a penalty. Recently, Billy Dodds had twice missed from the spot against Raith Rovers and Rab Shannon stepped forward to blast home the kick.

Midway through the second half, Dodds crashed in the winner, but although Dundee were given a well deserved ovation at the end of the Douglas Park encounter, confirmation that Airdrie had won 1-0 meant a long journey home for their dispirited legion of fans.

For everyone connected with Dundee Football Club, it was to prove an interminably long close-season. The failure to achieve promotion had deepened an already precarious financial position. In May, the accounts showed net liabilities of £1.1 million - of which £950,000 was payable within a year - and although Angus Cook insisted the club would remain full-time, it was now inevitable that players would have to be sold.

In the spring, John Holt (£10,000), and Alan Campbell (£5,000), joined Forfar while Gary Lennox moved to Brechin City on a free transfer. The experienced Arthur Albiston and Joe McBride were released. Both had been disappointing, particularly the highly-paid former Scotland international, who had earlier refused the offer of a free transfer and had made only eleven first-team appearances in his two seasons at Dens.

Over the past two seasons, reserve coach Billy Kirkwood had done an excellent job and now he was appointed to a similar post at Ibrox with Dundee receiving compensation for the remaining year of his contract. Another to go was promising 20-year-old midfielder Shaun McSkimming. In July, he was sold to Kilmarnock for £40,000 and, early the following month, the deteriorating financial situation saw Keith Wright transferred to Hibs for £500,000.

A great favourite with the fans, Wright had scored an impressive 72 goals in 185 games for the Dark Blues. Aberdeen had also been keen but with relations between the two North-East clubs at a low ebb after Jocky Scott's departure, the powerful striker had been sold to the Easter Road side.

Even this, however, had been overshadowed at the end of May when Angus Cook announced that Dundee were to mount a £4 million takeover bid for Dundee United with the amalgamated club to be called Dundee City. In his opinion, a merger was the way forward and he indicated that Tannadice shareholders could be offered up to £300 per share. However, just as Wallace Mercer had discovered during Hearts abortive takeover of Hibs 12 months earlier, he was to encounter massive resistance.

Now facing the possibility of losing their own club's identity through the proposed merger, the recently formed Dundee F.C. Shareholders' Association provided a rallying point but, with the chairman holding the power of veto with 82 per cent of the club's stock, it appeared that little could be done. However, with the support of 13 per cent of the shareholding - three per cent more than required - an Extraordinary General Meeting was held on June 8th and when repeated requests for a business plan were again ignored, the 60 shareholders present were loud in their condemnation of the board.

The controversy deepened when former club sponsor Bob Jamieson claimed that Dundee United had offered to lend him £600,000 to facilitate a takeover of Dundee. However the Tannadice Board maintained that this had been Jamieson's proposal and was one which they had immediately turned down. Another to express his interest in the club was Canadian millionaire Ron Dixon who had paid an estimated £1 million for a majority stake in the Dundee-Angus Ice Rink in 1990.

In turn, Jamieson, Dixon and Dundee F.C. Shareholders' Association chairman Steve Martin claimed that Mr Cook had offered to sell his shareholding but this was denied by the Dundee chairman. Then, in late July, Cook announced an indefinite postponement of his proposed offer to the Dundee United shareholders but there was to be further adverse publicity as a bitter war of words ensued between the Dens Park chairman and the Dundee United board.

By now, the Dens supremo faced opposition on all fronts with the great majority of fans at both clubs opposed to a merger. At the end of June, a reconstituted Dundee F.C. Supporters' Association set up the "Save the Dark Blues Survival Fund" and as a referendum on the current stewardship of the club, they called for a boycott of the Dens friendly against Wimbledon on August 3rd. The official attendance for the game, which finished 0-0, was given as 1,005 but Association chairman Alan Smith asserted that there had only been 752 fans inside the ground - a figure later confirmed by an insider at Dens.

Meanwhile, the playing squad had been strengthened by the arrival of 33-year-old striker Kevin Bremner from Peterborough United and former Lochee United and Motherwell centre-half Graeme Forbes (32), from Walsall - both on free transfers. And, despite all the close-season upheaval, Dundee began brightly with five straight wins over Clydebank (a) 2-1, Forfar (a) 4-2, Meadowbank (h) 3-1, Hamilton (h) 4-1, and Raith Rovers (a), 1-0.

Disappointingly, their Skol Cup challenge had ended prematurely when Ayr United pulled back a two-goal deficit and went on to win 4-2 after extra-time at Dens and off the field events were proceeding apace.

In September it was revealed that Bob Jamieson had offered £1 million for Dens Park with the intention of leasing it back to the club at £75,000 a year. But, just as the fans were considering the implications of the move, came the sensational news that Angus Cook had disposed of his 82 per cent shareholding and had resigned from the board.

Mr Andrew Drummond, who had been Cook's solicitor in recent years, had purchased 29.9 per cent and would assume the chair with the remaining 52.1 per cent sold to two unnamed investment companies. The new chairman denied that he was a "front-man" in a continuation of the Cook regime and within 48 hours, it was announced that Dundee would no longer

be pursuing their interest in a takeover of Dundee United.

Throughout that month, the team maintained pole position but, on October 1st, Gordon Wallace resigned to become assistant-manager at Dunfermline alongside former Dens boss Jocky Scott. His departure came just three hours before the B&Q Cup tie with Ayr United at Dens - a match they lost 2-0 - but the Dark Blues, who had intimated that the manager's contract would not be renewed at the end of the season, later received £18,000 compensation.

However, Wallace's record at Dens had not been particularly impressive. Relegation in 1989-90 had been followed by promotion failure and some of his signings, particularly the £260,000 spent on Albiston, Alan Campbell and West had proved a poor investment.

Some months earlier, former Hearts boss Alex McDonald had been lined up by Cook to replace Wallace. But now, McDonald was in charge at Airdrie and, despite interest from Donald Mackay, who had recently parted company from Blackburn, and various others, Iain Munro was named as Dundee's new manager with John Blackley remaining as his assistant.

Ironically, Munro had recently been sacked by Dunfermline. He had taken them to the Skol Cup semi-final but the Pars had struggled in the Premier League. Munro had never been accepted by the Dunfermline fans after the acrimonious departure of the popular Jim Leishman and, accordingly, his task at East End Park was always going to be a difficult one.

Meanwhile, the Dark Blues had lost the league leadership to Partick Thistle, who had departed from Dens with a 2-1 win. Thistle skipper and former Dens favourite Jim Duffy was given a sympathetic cheer when he was stretchered off with what appeared a serious knee injury, but the Dundee fans had not seen the last of the balding sweeper.

That term, Dundee had been plagued by injuries. Jamieson, West, Dinnie and Frail all missed the opening games and they were later joined by Fraser, Craig and Bremner. Before his injury, midfielder Albert Craig had netted seven goals in the opening six games while the wholehearted Bremner,

In the spotlight - new chairman and major shareholder Ron Dixon arrives at Dens.

although short of pace, had taken some of the load off the industrious Billy Dodds.

Five points had been taken from Munro's first three games in charge but performances were far from convincing and a series of poor results prompted the new Dens boss to plunge into the transfer market.

Iain Munro - got a raw deal in his short spell in charge.

Rab Shannon had not been expected to remain when his contract expired at the end of the previous season. However, the former Scotland Under-21 international had rejected an offer from Premier League Motherwell and recently a deal with Middlesbrough had collapsed with the clubs unable to agree a fee. Finally, Shannon signed a monthly contract with Dundee, but after just three appearances, he was transferred to Dunfermline in early November.

In exchange, Dundee received £125,000 with former Rangers and Bradford City midfielder Ian McCall and striker Eddie Gallagher coming to Dens. McCall, of course, had been the subject of an abortive Dens bid while at Rangers but it was the speedy Gallagher who would make the more immediate impact. League leaders Dundee faced a tricky game against third-placed Hamilton at Douglas Park but, assisted by a lightning Gallagher double in the opening minutes, they went on to win 3-1.

Seven days later, Gallagher was again on target when he netted a first-half hat-trick as Dundee romped to a 6-2 win over second-placed Partick Thistle at Firhill. And with McCall bringing some much-needed inventiveness, an eight-game unbeaten run resulted in a four-point lead over Hamilton by mid-December.

Meanwhile, the boardroom intrigue had continued. Shortly before Iain Munro's arrival, Robert Prentice - nephew of former Dens manager John Prentice - became a director, but the most significant changes were delayed until early December. After months of speculation, Ron Dixon was appointed to the board along with his Dundee-based associate Malcolm Reid - a former ice hockey star with the

Dundee Rockets in the 1960s - and Steve Martin, with James Strachan and Ian Gellatly, whose family had had a 47-year boardroom connection at Dens, stepping down as directors.

From the start of the campaign, Dundee's main promotion rivals had been Partick Thistle and Hamilton but after losing to Hamilton (h) 1-2, and Raith Rovers (a) 0-1, at the turn of the year, only goal-difference kept them ahead of the Douglas Park side. Now they faced Partick at Dens on January 4th, 1992 and, despite the absence of Dodds, who was sent off at Stark's Park, a late header by Gordon Chisholm gave Dundee a vital 1-0 win.

In January, Ron Dixon, who now owned 71 per cent of the club's stock after purchasing shares from Andrew Drummond and from the investment companies Dalelane, Bankvale and Prendrum, whose directors included Messrs Prentice, Gellatly and Drummond, became chairman with former Rangers and Falkirk chairman David Holmes joining the board as vice-chairman.

Next month, Drummond followed Prentice in resigning his directorship and both would face censure by the Takeover Panel for breaches of the City Code. And although returning as company secretary, Drummond was later struck off the Solicitors' Roll of The Law Society of Scotland for a matter unrelated to Dundee F.C. and left the club in September 1995.

Dixon outlined his plans at an Extraordinary General Meeting in February and was given a warm reception. His plans to increase the authorised share capital from 3 million to 10 million were unanimously approved and he also announced plans for an £8 million upgrading of Dens Park which included the construction of a new stand, an ice-rink-cum-conference centre plus the re-introduction of grey-hound racing.

Later, Dixon claimed that the club had been only hours away from going to the wall: "When I walked through the doors for the first time, I was met by three bankers. They said enough was enough and they were calling in the receiver. However, I talked to them and they agreed to accept a cheque for a five figure sum and wait until it cleared before doing anything."

A few days later, Dixon himself guaranteed a £25,000 fee for Falkirk's stylish striker Simon Stainrod (33). The well-travelled Englishman who was a man of many clubs includ-

Skill factor - Dundee's Ian McCall rams the ball home against Forfar at Dens as McQuillan, Chisholm and Craig look on. DC Thomson

ing Sheffield Wednesday, Sheffield United, Oldham, Stoke, Aston Villa, QPR and French sides Strasbourg and Rouen, was ineligible to play against Stirling Albion in the third round of the Scottish Cup. But although held to a 1-1 draw at Dens, an early goal by young Grant McMartin ensured their progress in the replay, which was played at McDiarmid Park due to an SFA veto on "plastic" pitches in the Cup.

That was to be Scotland Under-21 squad keeper Paul Mathers' last appearance of the season as, within 24 hours, Dundee announced the £200,000 signing of Manchester United's former Scottish international keeper Jim Leighton (33). After losing his first-team place at Old Trafford, the former Aberdeen and Scotland star had found himself in the soccer wilderness but, amidst great excitement, a near 6,000 crowd - Dundee's largest home attendance of the season, turned out to see the new signings make their debuts against Kilmarnock at Dens.

That attendance was nearly double the average home gate and, for only the second time that season, the TV cameras were at Dens. In an exciting game, both newcomers did well and, although the Dark Blues had to be content with a 1-1 draw, they still retained a four-point lead at the top.

On February 8th, Dundee travelled to meet Premier League Falkirk in the fourth round of the Scottish Cup. Stainrod was ineligible to play since Falkirk had appeared to deliberately hold up his registration to avoid having to cope with a former Bairns hero, but Leighton displayed the form that had earned him 58 Scotland caps with a series of magnificent saves. And, with Ian McCall at his tantalising best, Dundee almost caused an upset in a Brockville thriller which ended in a 0-0 draw.

Speculation had mounted over Iain Munro's future, particularly after the sacking of assistant-manager John Blackley a few days before the Brockville cup-tie. For weeks it had been rumoured that a "big-name" like Terry Butcher or Graham Roberts - both former England internationalists who had been at Ibrox at the same time as David Holmes - were to take over at Dens and on Friday, February 21st, Munro finally resigned as Dundee manager.

It was a bitterly disappointed Munro who pointed the finger at Holmes saying: "Football matters were being decided in my absence." Holmes denied this but Munro claimed he had not been consulted over the appointment of Simon Stainrod as assistant-manager. Nor had he been involved in negotiations which gave Billy Dodds a three-year contract in excess of £1,000 per week. And the final straw had been the discovery that Dundee had made a bid for Graham Roberts without his authority.

While chairman at Ibrox, Holmes had guided Rangers towards success, initially with the appointment of the high-profile Graeme Souness and thereafter by the funding of countless big-money signings. The former joiner believed that successful sides were based on strength down the middle, a philosophy which had proved successful at Ibrox after the signing of England internationals, goalkeeper Chris Woods, and central defenders Terry Butcher and Graham Roberts.

This policy was now being pursued at Dens with the arrival of Leighton and Stainrod and the targetting of Roberts and, although Holmes denied an over-involvement in footballing matters, conflict with Munro had appeared inevitable.

Star turns - Jim Leighton and player-manager Simon Stainrod. DC Thomson

Simon Stainrod was named as interim manager and after a 3-2 winning start at Montrose, the Dark Blues faced Falkirk in the cup replay at Dens. Despite live television on BSB-Sky, a crowd of 7,722 saw a finely-balanced encounter with Falkirk fortunate not to concede a 40th minute penalty when big Crawford Baptie appeared to handle in the box. On the restart, a spectacular effort by Scott Sloan put the Bairns ahead and when Mr Syme waved away another penalty claim - as he had twice done at Brockville - when Dodds was downed near the end, the writing was on the wall for Dundee.

Three days later, Dundee included Brechin City striker Paul Ritchie - brought back for £80,000 - only to go down 2-0 to second-placed Partick Thistle in Glasgow. By then, Dundee had abandoned their widely-publicised bid for Graham Roberts after being quoted a £150,000 fee. Certainly, he had at one time been high on the Holmes' shopping list to fill the manager's job - as had Falkirk boss Jim Jefferies - but Ron Dixon had put his foot down as if to prove to Holmes that he would not always be getting his own way in these matters.

The past month had been one of the most tempestuous in Dundee's history but a 5-0 home win over Stirling Albion sparked a recovery and another five points from their next three games set them up for the crucial six-game run-in. The squad was further strengthened when the promising Meadowbank midfielder Max Christie (20), was signed for £40,000 but a series of nervy performances brought draws against Meadowbank (a) 0-0, Morton (h) 2-2, and Ayr United (a) 0-0.

Billy Dodds had certainly missed the power of Keith Wright up front but the industrious striker, who was now the highest-paid player in Dundee's history, remained the main danger and his two goals against Morton took him up to the 19-goal mark. Partick, though, remained just two points behind and, with Hamilton just a point further in arrears, the Dark Blues could ill-afford any more slip-ups.

Now they faced a daunting trip to Kilmarnock, who, although out of the promotion race, had staged a revival under caretaker-manager Tommy Burns. And without the influential Stuart Beedie, who was injured, Dundee had no answer to the midfield craft of Burns. Willie Jamieson put through his own goal and when a second goal was conceded near the end, there was no way back.

Their rivals had both won and with Partick now level and Hamilton a point behind the scene was set for a grandstand finish. The club's very future remained in the balance and the remaining games, both at home, against Forfar Athletic and Montrose would decide their fate.

A Premier League return was vital to the success of Ron Dixon's future plans and the players stood to share a £100,000 bonus for winning the title and £50,000 for finishing second.

Caretaker-boss Simon Stainrod was confident of Dundee's ability to clinch the title but warned: "We must show more determination than we have of late and the senior professionals must take more responsibility in the run-in." Indeed, the presence of so many old hands had been instrumental in charting Dundee through the often stormy waters of the First Division. Gordon Chisholm and Willie Jamieson had again been the bulwark of the side and their value at set-pieces was evident with a joint contribution of nine league goals.

Young John McQuillan and Stevie Campbell were at fullback for much of the campaign, the gritty Alan Dinnie had played his part in midfield or at the back, and the defensive know-how of Stewart Forsyth, now recovered from knee ligament trouble and veteran Cammy Fraser, who had joined Montrose along with Graeme Forbes on a free transfer, had also proved invaluable.

Gordon Chisholm went into a four-man midfield as Dundee switched from their recent tactic of three at the back to a flat back-four against Forfar:- Leighton; Dinnie, Jamieson, Forsyth, S. Campbell; McQuillan, Chisholm, Beedie, McCall; Ritchie, Dodds. Subs. Gallagher, Stainrod. By half-time, there was no score but the signs were encouraging and, with the sun at their backs, the Dark Blues went ahead after 52 minutes. Interpassing between McCall and Dodds saw the ball switched to McQuillan and the youngster coolly blasted the opener into the net.

Dundee's tails were up and two minutes later, Ritchie curled in a second from 22 yards. Gary Whyte pulled one back in 77 minutes but, four minutes from time, Dens substitute Eddie Gallagher added a third to send the 5,144 crowd wild with delight. Partick and Hamilton had both lost and, after two long and expensive seasons in the First Division, Dundee were back in the Premier League.

The players had shown great character and determination in a traumatic season in which there had been three different managers, three different chairmen and boards of directors, share battles and personality clashes. It was a huge relief to all concerned, particularly those involved in the previous year's promotion failure. Left-back Stevie Campbell, a lifelong Dundee fan, said: "The recent slip-ups placed us under enormous pressure but the important thing is that we're up."

With a two point lead and a seven goal advantage over second-placed Partick Thistle, only a major reverse on the final day could prevent Dundee finishing champions. A crowd of 6,878, their largest league gate of the season, turned out for what they believed would be a promotion party against already-relegated Montrose.

It proved more of a wake for struggling Dundee and, soon after half-time, Leighton saved a penalty by Steve Craib. Seven minutes later, Campbell and Ritchie were replaced by Stainrod and Gallagher with Beedie moving to left-back but goals by Colin Maver and the dangerous Ivo Den Biemen put the Links Park men 2-0 ahead. In 75 minutes, Gallagher pulled one back but, despite a last desperate push, there was no glory finish for the Dark Blues.

Dundee fans had long since become accustomed to letdowns but defeat to lowly Montrose was totally unexpected. Nevertheless, despite the widespread disappointment, thousands of enthusiasts remained to see Dundee presented with the First Division Championship trophy.

Ron Dixon had flown in from Canada for the final game and commented: "This is the first whistlestop on a train journey down an exciting track. I have never known supporters as committed as these. We owe it to those people to get it right for next season's Premier League."

Party time - Dressing room glee after the First Division Championship had been secured despite the defeat by Montrose. (BACK, left to right) Steve Frail, Steve Campbell, Grant McMartin, Alan Dinnie, Paul Ritchie, John McQuillan, Ian McCall, Albert Craig, Billy Dodds. FRONT - Gordon Chisholm, Stewart Forsyth, Simon Stainrod, Harry Hay (sprint coach), Stuart Beedie and Eddie Gallagher. DC Thomson

CHAPTER TWENTY-SEVEN

New Look Dundee

As expected, Simon Stainrod was confirmed as Dundee's manager and, as well as a three-year contract, he would be given £1 million to spend on players. Initially, though, the aim was to re-establish the Dens Park club in the Premier League for the poor performance against Montrose had emphasised that many of the current personnel were not up to scratch. This was reflected in the free transfer list with Gordon Chisholm, Stewart Forsyth, Tom Carson, Albert Craig and Kevin Bremner all released and Mark Craib allowed to move on to Montrose for a fee of £10,000.

Club captain Gordon Chisholm (32), now looked too slow for the Premier League but, although he appeared well-placed for the vacant post of assistant-manager, David Holmes wanted John Holt, then a Forfar player and detailed contract talks had begun. However, Broughty Ferry publican John Black, soon to become a director and who was wielding considerable influence behind the scenes, now argued strongly that Jim Duffy was the man for the job.

Ron Dixon had been impressed by Duffy's leadership qualities in a game against Thistle and, when the player's Dark Blue pedigree was spelled out, the race to be Stainrod's No. 2 was effectively over. Duffy, who had told friends that he would "walk over broken glass to get back to Dens Park", was phoned by the chairman and within five minutes the deal was done.

Thistle boss John Lambie knew of Duffy's huge contribution as a player at Firhill, but he also understood his desire to break into the coaching side of the game. Accordingly, he paved the way for Duffy's return to Tayside and Thistle received £10,000 in compensation. Ironically, Gordon Chisholm, the man brought to Dens to replace Duffy when his career appeared over back in 1987, moved to Firhill where he was soon appointed to the coaching staff.

Dens interest in Celtic's £350,000-rated midfielder Peter Grant ended when the Scottish international made it clear he wanted to move south but there was no shortage of signing activity. Czechoslovakian central-defender Dusan Vrto (26), arrived from Banik Ostrava for £200,000, Dutch winger Ivo Den Bieman cost £25,000 from Montrose, Ian Gilzean (23), Gary McKeown (22), and Jamie McGowan (22), were each obtained on free transfers from Spurs, Arsenal and non-league Morecambe, respectively, while former England international Graham Rix (34), was signed from Le Havre.

The powerfully-built Gilzean, son of Dens Park scoring legend Alan Gilzean, had been a highly promising prospect at Spurs and also at Scotland Under-19 level. However, his

Sky high - Ian Gilzean heads powerfully for goal with Billy Dodds and St Johnstone's John McLelland awaiting developments.

career had been interrupted by cruciate ligament injuries requiring operations to both knees and it remained to be seen whether he would fulfil his earlier promise.

Dundee had also hoped to sign Canadian striker Alex Bunbury but, with only ten non-European Community players allowed in the Premier League, and nine permits already allocated, they lost out to Celtic, who obtained clearance for Albanian international Rudi Vata and Bunberry was allowed to go.

That season, the fans would see a new-look playing area. The stand had been refurbished with the roof and new plastic seating resplendent in blue, and to allow for the new greyhound track, sections had been removed from the front of the stand enclosure and the T.C. Keay end with the pitch moved 30 feet nearer the stand. But although the playing surface was narrower, it remained of international standard.

Former kit suppliers Matchwinner had been replaced by Asics and there had also been changes behind the scenes. In June, David Holmes resigned after his own businesses encountered severe financial difficulties but, by this stage, Ron Dixon, who had earlier stuck by Holmes when other directors pushed for his departure, had become increasingly unhappy over some aspects relating to the running of the club. He had been particularly unimpressed that Holmes had told the players that they would have to wait for their £5,600

Cool customer - Simon Stainrod looks on from the dugout as Dundee defeat Rangers 4-3 at Dens. DC Thomson

championship-winning bonus because the club was short of money and, two days later, the Canadian ensured that all the squad were paid.

Former journalist and garage proprietor Ron Hutcheson was brought in as vice-chairman, but he remained for only nine weeks. By then, Alan Masson, whose father had played for the club in the late 1930s, had been appointed managing-director and Hutcheson, whose position as vice-chairman was assumed by Malcolm Reid, stated that his had only been a "holding brief" until a suitable managing-director was found.

In March, Derek Souter had been given the post of marketing controller but now he had also gone as had lottery manager Alex Hamilton, with former chairman Andrew Drummond returning as company secretary in place of Bob Swinton. Earlier, Ian McCall had been suspended and fined after an act of gross indiscipline during a training trip to Aviemore. The skilful winger had been a key man in Dundee's promotion run but on the eve of the new season, he was allowed to join Falkirk in lieu of a £20,000 payment which was due to him.

There was an indifferent start to the new season. A 2-1 reverse to Falkirk was followed by two draws, at home with St Johnstone (1-1), and at Airdrie (0-0). Clearly, the new-comers would need time to settle but on August 15th, Dundee introduced yet another new signing, 31-year-old former Everton and Wales defender Kevin Ratcliffe, for the home clash with Rangers.

The Dark Blues fielded: Leighton; Dinnie, Duffy, McGowan, Ratcliffe; Vrto, Beedie, Rix; Den Biemen, Gilzean, Dodds. Subs. - Bain, D. Campbell. It was to prove an enthralling encounter for a crowd of nearly 13,000 and, astonishingly, Dundee included no fewer than five non-Scots, their most cosmopolitan side since the halcyon days of George Anderson in the late '40s and early '50s.

First Ivo Den Biemen, then Ian Gilzean put Dundee in

front with headed goals, only for Ally McCoist to twice bring Rangers level. After the interval, the Dark Blues continued to swarm forward and, in 63 minutes, Dodds accepted Gilzean's knock-on to sweep the ball past Ally Maxwell. In 80 minutes, the Dundee defence looked shaky when Ian Ferguson drilled home an equaliser but they were not to be denied.

Once again the ball was played forward and, when Gilzean was impeded by Richard Gough, Dundee were awarded a penalty, which Billy Dodds converted to give them a 4-3 win over an Ibrox side set to dominate the Scottish game that season. On the touchline, the dapper Stainrod had appeared in an ankle-length raincoat and fedora hat. Simon certainly knew how to grab a headline and after the match he made the most of his moment of glory, boldly saying: "We asked questions of Rangers never asked before. We went for their jugular and ripped it out. I said before the season we'd attack at all times. Now people might start believing me."

After a 3-0 Skol Cup win at Meadowbank, Dundee put up a credible performance in losing 1-0 away to Celtic in the third round, with Gilzean's dismissal just before half-time a significant factor. However, the Dark Blues were unable to reproduce the form shown against Rangers although they again played well in the 2-1 defeat by Aberdeen at Pittodrie.

The following week it all went horribly wrong when newly-promoted Partick Thistle dealt out a 6-3 hiding at Firhill and soon Dundee were isolated alongside Mother-well, Falkirk and Airdrie at the bottom of the table. It was to prove a difficult season for Simon Stainrod but although the Yorkshireman had emerged as a character in the all-too steril Premier League arena, his defence had struggled from the beginning.

Initially, Dundee had utilised an offside-trap but the ploy was abandoned when dubious refereeing decisions cost them goals and, after conceding 17 goals in the opening six league games, there was another tactical rethink. At Firhill, four of Partick's goals had arisen from defenders' inability to defend against long throw-ins. However, along with Gary McKeown, former international keeper Jim Leighton was the man to carry the can with Stainrod claiming: "At the moment, Leighton is still uncomfortable with the new pass-back rule."

Paul Mathers returned in goal, Dusan Vrto dropped back from midfield to replace McGowan at centre-half and 20-year-old Kevin Bain was brought in to shore up midfield. It was decided to adopt a tighter approach and, defensively at any rate, the improvement was soon apparent with wins over Motherwell (h) 2-1, and Dundee United (a) 1-0 and a no-scoring draw with Hibs at Easter Road.

At Tannadice, Dundee had been under pressure for much of the game but Billy Dodds netted a late winner from the penalty spot after Den Biemen was sent crashing by home keeper Alan Main. However, the hitherto sporting derby image was tarnished by the behaviour of Dundee United's Argentinian forward, Victor Ferreyra. Near the end, he spat at Jim Duffy and, at full-time, was seen to punch the Dens veteran, a misdemeanour for which he was later red-carded and subsequently allowed to return to Argentinian football.

Many had thought that Jim Duffy would concentrate on

management but with the 33-year-old quickly proving himself a commanding defender and a major asset in the first-team, former skipper John McCormack was brought in to assist with the reserves.

At the end of the first quarter of the season, Dundee lay ninth but with the Dens boss - described by Graeme Speirs in *Scotland on Sunday* as "that maverick Stainrod" - continuing to wheel and deal in the market place there were further changes to the playing staff. Out on free transfers went defensive stalwart Willie Jamieson - to Partick Thistle - and Gordon McLeod - to Meadowbank, with Kevin Ratcliffe, who had looked past his best, also departing after failing to agree terms.

In the wake of the First Division Championship triumph, the players believed the club was to pay for a holiday in Spain but instead, Ron Dixon offered them signet rings. The players declined the offer and when the story was leaked to the press, Jamieson was blamed and the chairman decreed that he would have to go.

In August, Lochore Welfare centre-half Garry Paterson had been signed for £1,000 with the junior club also receiving a set of tracksuits! The following day, the 6'4" Fifer made a dream debut when he headed home a fine goal at Aberdeen but a week later, he blotted his copybook with a headed own-goal in the Firhill debacle. Other new arrivals were former Barnsley and Sheffield Wednesday left-winger Andy Kiwomya (25), and American international left-back Steve Pittman, who had previously played for East Fife and Fort Lauderdale Strikers.

By mid-December - the halfway stage of the championship, the Dark Blues remained fourth-bottom with only 16 points from 22 games. On November 28th, a much-needed 3-1 triumph at Motherwell had ended a run of five successive defeats and although the next three games brought only two points, Simon Stainrod dived to head a last-gasp winner in a 2-1 success over Falkirk in the basement battle at Dens on December 19th.

At the start of the season, Stainrod had declared: "I'm not going to continue in the first-team, I'm not fit enough for that." However, Ian Gilzean had shaded off after a promising start and the Dens boss had made his mark with four goals in six appearances. The chunky Stainrod no longer had the speed or mobility of old but it was clear that he remained a player of skill and no little vision, especially at dead-ball situations.

Stainrod, who had earlier denied he was putting together a deal to buy out Ron Dixon - had made no secret of his search for a midfield playmaker. Previously, the board had vetoed his attempt to sign 29-year-old Dutchman Martin De Jong, since it was felt there would be little resale value. However, in early December, Ron Dixon put up £225,000 of his own money, a Dundee F.C. record fee, to sign Lyngby's Danish international midfielder Morten Wieghorst (21).

The Dane's debut coincided with a Tayside derby thriller against St Johnstone before a crowd of 5,766 at McDiarmid Park. Having lost an early goal, Dundee's problems were exacerbated when Paul Mathers was dismissed for bringing down Paul Wright just outside the box. Pittman equalised and, soon after the break, the lanky Wieghorst ghosted past three men on the edge of the box before sending a low shot past Andy Rhodes. There seemed no way back when stand-in keeper Duncan Campbell conceded three goals in 20 minutes. But in an incredible fighting finish, Billy Dodds netted twice in the final 10 minutes to salvage a point as the game finished 4-4!

Later that month, Eddie Gallagher, who had netted 12 goals in 14 First Division starts, became the eighth player of the promotion-winning squad to leave when he joined St Mirren on a free transfer. Soon afterwards, Dundee also parted company with physiotherapist Eric Ferguson (57), and Arbroath-based Jim Crosby took over two months later.

Ferguson had first arrived in 1971 and had also worked with the Scottish international team for a good number of years. "Given the opportunity, I would have continued with

Hit man - Dundee's top scorer Billy Dodds turns away after scoring against Motherwell at Dens as Stuart Beedie smiles. DC Thomson

Key man - Jim Duffy outjumps John Robertson of Hearts as Dundee battle to re-establish themselves in the Premier League. Kevin Bain and Morten Wieghorst are in the background. DC Thomson

left the Dark Blues over £800,000 in the red. Dixon went on to outline his three main targets: "A return to the glory days, a continuation of ground improvements, and to make a profit at the end of the 1993-94 financial year."

However, any great improvement in the poor financial situation would not come via the Scottish Cup. Dundee had, despite the first-half dismissal of Simon Stainrod, gone on to defeat Dumbarton 2-0 at Dens but with little threat from a strike force of Garry Paterson and Colin West - and later, Ivo Den Bieman, they had gone down 2-0 to Hearts in what turned out to be an uninspiring fourth-round tie at Tynecastle.

Dundee until I retired but the present management didn't want that," said the disappointed Ferguson, who would shortly be back on the football scene at Aberdeen.

There was much sympathy for the long-serving physio and there had been other matters of concern for the fans. In May, the police had been called to Dens to investigate allegations and counter allegations by former chairman Angus Cook and Ron Dixon respectively. And although the club appeared to be moving in the right direction on the field with a healthy influx of new blood, there were again signs of instability at boardroom level.

At the end of the year, Alan Masson left to take up "other business ventures" and with Steve Martin to follow due to personal commitments three months later, that meant no fewer than nine directors had left since September 1991. Newcomers to the board were Broughty Ferry publican John Black, local architect and former Shareholders' Association secretary Bob Hynd and Bob Paterson, administration-director of a major Dundee solicitors' firm and, firmly tongue in cheek, James Traynor of *The Glasgow Herald*, had written that: "Dundee were a club where currently there are more comings and goings than a back-street sauna."

In October, Ron Dixon had openly expressed his opinion that a merger was in the interests of the two Dundee clubs, although this was not a view shared either by Dundee United or by representatives of the DFCSA. But, when Bob Jamieson then asked the Dens chairman to "name his price", Dixon had replied: "When I arrived here I said I'd be around three to five years until we restored the fortunes of this club and I'm still on track with the original plan."

On November 19th, the charismatic Canadian, who owned 3,718,565 of the club's 5,087,063 ordinary shares told nearly 600 shareholders in the Angus Hotel that, despite the sale of Wright, Shannon and McSkimming, there had been an increased loss of almost £600,000 to May 1992, which

More significantly, Alan Dinnie, one of Dundee's most consistent performers, had been stretchered off with cruciate ligament damage - the same injury suffered by Steve Frail and Ian Durrant of Rangers - and it would be nearly a year before he would return. More recently, the Glaswegian had formed a solid partnership in central defence with either Duffy or Vrto, and Dundee were fortunate to have a ready-made replacement in Kevin Bain.

Dundee's Andy Dow

In 1989, Bain had captained the Scotland Under-16s to the Youth World Cup Final at Hampden before turning full-time with Dundee. The young Fifer had previously made a number of first-team appearances but now, at the age of 19, he looked ready to establish himself. Local boy Andy Dow (19), a left-sided attacking midfielder, was another youngster to impress and, along with Bain, he made a number of appearances for the Scotland Under-21 side that season.

Thus far, Dundee had managed to keep themselves a few points clear of the two relegation places but, by the end of January the signs looked ominous. Following a 2-0 midweek reverse to Partick Thistle at Firhill, Dundee had drawn 2-2 with bottom-markers Airdrie at Broomfield, where they retrieved a two-goal deficit despite having Den Bieman and Rix sent off by the hapless match official, Joe Timmons.

In mid-February, a 1-0 home win over St Johnstone and a 3-1 triumph over Hibs at Easter Road took them to seventh, their highest league placing of the season but a dramatic slump was to bring just three points from the next nine fixtures and, with five games remaining, Dundee lay only three points clear of second-bottom Falkirk.

By then, Dundee's defence was in disarray for Dusan Vrto (twisted knee) and Steve Pittman (broken foot bone) - had joined Alan Dinnie on the casualty list and would miss the rest of the season. The accomplished Vrto had proved extremely versatile, playing at left-back, central defence or in midfield, while the tough-tackling Pittman had also become a firm favourite.

Now, though, Stainrod bolstered the side by signing Frenchman Lionel David, a 26-year-old central-defender, formerly of La Roche and St Etienne, while the out-of-favour Ian Gilzean and Paul Ritchie returned from loan spells at Gillingham and Doncaster, respectively, and would also play their part in the battle to stay up.

On April 17th, Dundee faced a vital confrontation at Motherwell, who lay a point behind in tenth place with a game in hand. Following earlier interest by Dundee United, Dundee had placed a £1 million price-tag on the head of Billy Dodds. The fair-haired striker had managed just two goals in 18 games since mid-December, but he did well to lay on the opener for Paul Ritchie and, near the end, he netted the clincher in a 2-1 win.

Now the Dark Blues lay four points ahead of second-bottom Falkirk but they were still not clear and, on Tuesday, April 24th, a 4-0 home defeat by Dundee United coupled with wins for Motherwell and Airdrie plunged them back into the danger zone.

With Dundee down 2-0, Billy Dodds, who last summer had been made club captain in the hope that the added responsibility might calm him, had been sent off after an off-the-ball clash with Freddie Van Der Hoorn. Previously, Gilzean, McKeown, Vrto, Mathers, McGowan, Den Bieman, Rix and Stainrod had all been red-carded and that made Dodds the ninth Dundee player to be ordered off that term - a record that would cost the club a £5,000 SFA fine.

Now Dodds would miss the last three games on which could hang the club's very future. Dens boss Simon Stainrod was furious and announced that the striker had been fined a

week's wages and would be stripped of the captaincy. Dodds responded with a transfer request but was told that he would be held to the remaining two years of his contract unless a suitable offer was received.

Steve Frail and Steve Campbell had done well as stand-in full-backs and Gary McKeown's return restored some composure to midfield. Up front, the pacy Andy Kiwomya was a constant threat while Paul Ritchie looked sharp, his goal ensuring Dundee claimed a precious point in a 1-1 draw against St Johnstone at Perth.

And although Falkirk had beaten Hearts 6-0 at Brockville that day, two points from their last two fixtures would guarantee Dundee their Premier place for next season. On the morning of the crucial clash with Hibs on May 8th, the bottom of the Premier table looked like this:

	P	F A	Pts
Dundee	42	45 - 65	32
Motherwell	42	42 - 60	31
Falkirk	42	58 - 82	29
Airdrie	42	33 - 67	28

Right from the start, Dundee showed a positive attitude and, in 19 minutes, the on-form Ritchie swept home the opener. Ten minutes later, Morten Wieghorst sent a glorious half-volley past John Burridge from the edge of the box and, on the hour, Gilzean added a third as Dundee went on to win 3-1. Survival was now assured although defeats for Falkirk and Airdrie meant that they were already consigned to the First Division.

A 2-0 defeat at Parkhead saw Dundee finish tenth, five points clear of second-bottom Falkirk. But, with the Scottish League AGM deciding to re-introduce a 10-team Premier League in 1994-95, three teams would be relegated at the end of next season and, clearly, there would have to be an improvement to maintain their hard-won Premier place.

Fledgling boss Simon Stainrod had done well to keep Dundee up with some decent buys and a sprinkling of free transfer men added to the remnants of the promotion-winning side. The tireless Billy Dodds was Dundee's top scorer with 16 league goals but veteran defender Jim Duffy was another key figure, playing in forty-three of the forty-eight games and splendidly marshalling his charges throughout an arduous campaign.

The swashbuckling Stainrod was a popular figure with the supporters but reports that Dundee United were ready to appoint Jim Duffy as successor to Jim McLean prompted the Dundee-based board into two attempts - on May 11th, then after the final game of the season - to get the Englishman to step down. Clearly, the directors were willing to sacrifice Stainrod and replace him with Duffy in order to prevent the highly rated assistant-manager moving to United.

It was, of course, a similar situation to 1971 when McLean had crossed the road and transformed United and the board was anxious not to chance a repeat. Initially, Ron Dixon backed Stainrod only to later claim that Gordon Strachan was Dundee's preferred choice should he move on!

However, the Tannadice club denied any interest in Duffy and, although they subsequently appointed Ivan Golac, the Dens Park managerial uncertainty continued throughout the

Competitive streak - former Arsenal midfielder Gary McKeown shows his battling qualities in this clash with Falkirk. DC Thomson

Famous guests at the Dundee F.C. Centenary Dinner in 1993 (BACK, left to right) Alex Hamilton, Gordon Wallace, Bobby Seith, Bobby Wishart, Doug Cowie, Ian Ure, Alex Stuart. MIDDLE - Gordon Smith, Andy Penman, Alan Cousin, Tommy Gallacher, Alan Gilzean, Hugh Robertson, Sammy Kean. FRONT - Bobby Cox, Pat Liney, Craig Brown, George Hill.

turned out to be a disaster for the club. It also took me a while to sort out the real people from the imposters because of my ignorance over who should be trusted and who shouldn't. I didn't realise how deep the rot at the club ran but you don't run away at the first shot."

However, the Dens chairman still harboured ambitions for the club and commented: "We've seen that we're not going to get anywhere unless we really go for it and have decided to roll the dice and see what happens." And to back this up, in came two Polish international midfielders - the 27-year-old Piotr Czachowski, and his

whole of the close-season.

As expected, there were substantial cuts to the playing staff. Stuart Beedie, Duncan Campbell, Ian Gilzean, Graham Rix, Colin West, Andy Kiwomya, Ivo Den Biemen, Steve Campbell and Lionel David were all released, although David returned after a trial period with Sheffield United. Jim Leighton, too, had gone. He had been transfer-listed after failing to regain his place from Paul Mathers and, keen to reduce the wage bill, Dundee allowed him to join Hibernian for a nominal fee.

Andy Dow was another to depart, when he signed for Chelsea on freedom-of-contract. Dundee had valued the Under-21 international at £1 million but they were not unhappy with the £275,000 they did receive, particularly as Chelsea agreed to take just 25% (as opposed to the 50% previously agreed) of any future transfer fee should their former player Billy Dodds be sold on.

Arbroath striker Paul Tosh was signed for £100,000 but, without the experience of the suspended Duffy and Dodds and the injured Dinnie, the 1993-94 season began badly with defeats to newly-promoted Kilmarnock (a) 0-1, and Motherwell (h) 1-2, while it had taken a penalty shoot-out to get the better of lowly Meadowbank in the League Cup.

It had been a difficult 18 months for Ron Dixon and, in *The News of the World*, he admitted that mistakes had been made: "We wasted a lot of money - £200,000 for Jim Leighton, £50,000 for Graham Rix, £80,000 for Paul Ritchie and £40,000 for Max Christie. It was money flushed down the toilet and we have nothing to show for it. But that happened because the place was being run by a clique."

"I was advised that David Holmes was an experienced football man when he was appointed vice-chairman but he

countryman Dariusz Adamczuk (23), each reportedly signed for £500,000 although it was later revealed that they had cost around half that amount.

Czachowski, from Legia Warsaw, had played 45 internationals but, as a non-EEC player, he still required Home Office clearance and a Scottish League permit before he could turn out. However, the five-times capped Adamczuk, who had been signed from Eintracht Frankfurt, also held a German passport and he made his debut in the 1-1 draw with Aberdeen at Dens.

The fair-haired Pole, who had not played for two months after a dispute with his club, looked fast and skilful and played with great commitment as the Wieghorst-inspired Dark Blues deservedly took a point. Billy Dodds had withdrawn his transfer request on hearing of the new signings and the busy little striker was on the spot to ram home Dundee's goal soon after half-time.

The hard-running Tosh had ensured an uncomfortable afternoon for Dons veteran Alex McLeish but the new-found optimism quickly disappeared after a disappointing 2-1 defeat to Hibs in the third round of the League Cup at Easter Road. Bottom-of-the-league Dundee had failed to win any of their opening five games and, finally, after months of conjecture, the board installed Jim Duffy as manager in place of Simon Stainrod.

Stainrod would remain in the newly created post of Director of Football Operations, ostensibly with responsibility for the buying and selling of players as well as the development of a comprehensive youth policy and scouting system. However, by November, the flamboyant Yorkshireman had become the forgotten man at Dens and it was little surprise when he quit, before later returning to management with First Division Ayr United.

CHAPTER TWENTY-EIGHT

Dens Doldrums

There was no dream start for Jim Duffy whose first game in charge coincided with his playing return in a 2-0 league defeat by Hibs at Easter Road. Former Dundee and Dunfermline boss Jocky Scott was on the bench but speculation that he might become Duffy's assistant proved unfounded with another Dens "Old Boy", reserve coach John McCormack, later given that role.

In September, Partick Thistle's 32-year-old midfielder Ray Farningham was signed on freedom-of-contract with the fee later set at £28,500 by the Transfer Tribunal. The Dundonian made his debut in the 1-1 draw with Rangers at Dens but Garry Paterson was the stand-out, cracking home the opener then blotting out the formidable striking partnership of Mark Hately and Duncan Ferguson.

However, it was soon clear that Dundee faced a bitter battle for Premier survival as three successive defeats left them bottom, without a single win from their opening 10 games. A groin operation meant the loss of the influential Morten Wieghorst for several weeks, but on October 2nd, Dundee finally recorded their first win when a Paterson header and a spectacular 45-yard chip by Croatian trialist Dragutin Ristic earned a 2-0 success over Hearts at Dens.

Ristic, who had previously played for Benevento in the Italian Fifth Division, was signed and with Czachowski settling well in central midfield, a 2-2 draw with Partick Thistle then wins over Kilmarnock (1-0) and Hibs (3-2), all at home, took Dundee to the nine point mark by early November.

The hard-tackling Dariusz Adamczuk had regained his fitness and now looked every inch an international player, particularly in a holding role in midfield. The Pole netted the winner against Killie then impressed when switched to left-back after an injury to Steve Pittman. Near the end of another fine display against second-placed Hibs, Adamczuk was red-carded for a retaliatory tackle on Darren Jackson. That was only his eighth appearance for the Dark Blues but, a few days later, he was transferred to Serie 'A' club Udinese for a fee of around £500,000.

On November 13th, a 2-1 win over Hearts at Tynecastle brought Dundee within two points of fellow strugglers Raith Rovers and St Johnstone, with Partick Thistle three points further ahead. But when the next three games - coincidentally against their three main rivals - ended in defeat as did the Dens derby against Dundee United, it was obvious that there were major problems.

Astonishingly, it would be almost four months before their next league win and, although an attempt was made to sign Tommy Coyne from Tranmere Rovers, the former Dens scoring ace opted to join strong-going Motherwell. Nevertheless, experience did arrive in the form of 32-year-old Noel Blake, who was signed from Bradford City for £15,000. The rugged centre-half's debut coincided with a 1-1 draw with Celtic at Dens but, by early 1994, another three straight defeats left few in any doubt that Dundee were bound for the First Division.

On January 9th, came the shock news that Billy Dodds had joined relegation rivals St Johnstone along with midfielder Grant McMartin (rated at £60,000) in a total deal worth £420,000. But, although somewhat placated by the £250,000 double signing of Partick Thistle strikers George Shaw (24), and Gerry Britton (23), fans were upset that their star striker had been sold to a local club and a number of sponsors and fans were invited to meet manager Jim Duffy and the Dundee-based board.

As Duffy explained: "It was my decision and mine alone. The league position dictated that changes were necessary and, with no cash to spend, Dodds was made available. St Johnstone were the only club interested and, although Billy could have stayed, I was somewhat surprised when he chose to join another struggling club."

"I agree that Dodds is a good player but he publicly stated that he would not play for Dundee in the First Division again. In my opinion, he never really forged a telling partnership with any of the strikers - Keith Wright included - who played alongside him and he is out of contract at the end of this season."

Under the Taylor Report, Dundee had until 1997 to ensure their ground was all-seated. Unfortunately, the Football Trust had exhausted all their funds and were currently unable to pay their 50% share of the proposed £3.4 million South Stand, while local councils were unwilling to provide £1m towards the ice sports and conference centre.

Dariusz Adamczuk - Dundee's Polish international on the attack. DC Thomson

Under pressure - Garry Paterson, Steve Pittman, Jamie McGowan, Paul Tosh, Dusan Vrto, Jim Duffy and Ray Farningham watch anxiously as the ball bounces just wide of the Dundee goal in a match against Dundee United at Tannadice.   DC Thomson

Over the festive period there had been concern that Dundee had discussed sharing Tannadice with Dundee United but various rumours that the Dark Blues were about to fold were strenuously denied by Dens Park vice-chairman Malcolm Reid.

Just a solitary point had been taken from the previous nine games but the enthusiasm and running power of Britton and Shaw brought added impetus and there were four successive draws against Rangers (h) 1-1, Raith Rovers (h) 2-2, Dundee United (a), 1-1 and St Johnstone (a) 1-1. Morten Wieghorst had given Dundee a deserved lead against table-topping Rangers but, despite the heroics of Paul Mathers in a second-half pounding, Gordon Durie equalised near the end.

Gerry Britton had replaced the skilful but somewhat one-paced "Ricky" Ristic, although the clever Croatian made a dramatic substitute appearance to grab a late equaliser against Dundee United at Tannadice. Working a glorious one-two with Wieghorst he clipped the ball past the helpless Dutch goalkeeper Van de Kamp, who had earlier saved a penalty from George Shaw.

Four days later, the Dark Blues beat Clydebank 2-1 in a Scottish Cup third-round replay at Stirling Albion's Forth-bank Stadium. Dundee had struggled for long periods in the first tie at Kilbowie and only a spectacular 25-yarder by substitute Paul Tosh, six minutes from time, had maintained their interest in the cup.

Around 50 Dundee fans came on to the pitch to celebrate, and things turned ugly when some got involved in a fracas with Bankies keeper Alan Monaghan. The referee ordered both teams to the dressing rooms but order was soon restored and the match was completed despite Clydebank's demands that it should be abandoned due to the dazed state of their goalkeeper.

Dens Park officials expressed their condemnation but fears that the club might be expelled from the Cup proved groundless. The SFA executive committee were highly critical of the pitch invasion and also of Clydebank's failure to provide adequate policing. However, they decided that the fans had not intentionally stopped the match although they ordered that the Dens replay be switched to a neutral venue with both clubs later given a severe censure.

The cash-strapped Dark Blues had anticipated a 3,000 plus attendance at Dens and, although Forthbank had a 2,500 capacity, just 700 tickets were allocated to each club. Those briefs were only available from official supporters' clubs, who had to forward their fans' details to the SFA and, in the event, just 856 attended.

Goals by Gerry Britton and George Shaw gave Dundee a two-goal lead. However, the sending-off of young Neil McCann just before half-time for retaliation against Graeme Ferguson - himself sent off in the first tie - meant a second-half struggle with a late Sweeney goal putting the Dens men under severe pressure in the final minutes.

Dundee United were also at home in the fourth round and Dundee's tie against First Division St Mirren was switched to Sunday, February 20th. Barry Lavety put Saints ahead after 16 minutes but Gerry Britton levelled with a penalty and, with Wieghorst and Farningham finally stamping their authority in midfield, Shaw got a second after 56 minutes. It was an exciting game, full of flowing football, and the result remained in doubt until Britton raced through to make it 3-1, just minutes from the end.

Jim Duffy had used the Dodds cash wisely. As well as Shaw and Britton, he had fixed up promising youngsters Neil McCann, Craig Tully and Gordon Tannock on new two-and-a-half year deals. He had also raided the Highland League, spending £15,000 on 24-year-old Elgin City midfielder Mike Teasdale with another £5,000 outlaid on Keith striker Jim Hamilton (18), whose father of the same name had played for Aberdeen and East Fife in the 1970s.

French goalkeeper Michel Pageaud was signed for £70,000 from Valenciennes with Falkirk's Neil Duffy arriving in exchange for Jamie McGowan and Dragutin Ristic. In addition, Falkirk received £150,000 with Bairns keeper Ian Westwater - valued at £60,000 - also moving to Dens in a deal valued at £170,000 in total.

The Duffy move was controversial. Hearts had recently had a £210,000 bid refused but now the high-scoring midfielder appeared to be valued at just £110,000! Duffy's previous club, Dundee United, were due 25 per cent of any subsequent transfer fee less the £35,000 they had already received. Now they stood to get nothing and their suspicions were further fuelled when Westwater joined Dunfermline for

£15,000 a few weeks later, without ever making a first-team appearance for Dundee.

However, Jim Duffy was involved in a serious car crash while travelling to complete the signings, and with the manager badly shaken, it was necessary for John McCormack to finalise the deals. It was the second near miss for a Dundee player that season. In August, Lionel David had swallowed his tongue after sustaining a fractured skull during a training match and only the prompt action of physio Jim Crosby saved his life.

There was no doubting the seriousness of Dundee's league position but they were just one step away from the Scottish Cup semi-finals when they met Kilmarnock at Rugby Park on March 12th. There was little between the sides in a game played at a frantic pace. But soon after ex-Dens keeper Bobby Geddes saved a Gerry Britton penalty and his follow-up effort, Tom Brown scored with a brave diving header and that was enough to put Killie through.

Thereafter, Dundee got their fair share of league points but the other strugglers did likewise and, in late March, financial circumstances dictated the £150,000 transfer of Steve Frail to Hearts. That same month, Bob Paterson resigned as a director while Isobel Sneddon, a familiar figure in the Dens office since 1952, was another to depart.

On April 23rd, a 2-0 home defeat by Celtic finally condemned Dundee to the First Division but they would finish the season in style. A Neil Duffy goal earned a 1-1 draw with third-placed Aberdeen at Pittodrie and there was a sparkling display in a 4-0 home win over Hibs before a 0-0 draw with six-in-a-row League Champions Rangers at Ibrox ensured a dignified Premier League exit.

And although seemingly inevitable since January, a second relegation in four years came as a devastating blow and plans for ground reconstruction were put on indefinite hold. A massive eleven points had separated Dundee from safety, yet no fewer than fourteen of their 23 defeats had been by a single goal.

So why had it happened? The delayed decision on the management situation was a major factor for neither Duffy nor Stainrod had been able to implement any close-season planning. Then the team, lacking experienced men like Duffy and Dinnie, got off to a bad start and never really recovered. It then took too long to identify and rectify the deficiencies

and had Pageaud and Blake arrived earlier and Adamczuk - his transfer an excellent short-term gain (£250,000), but a strategic blunder - remained to team up with Neil Duffy, Shaw and Britton, things might well have been different.

Dundee's injury problems were part and parcel of the frantic Premier League, but continued indiscipline - Britton, Frail, Dinnie and McQuillan were all suspended - was counter-productive. Much of the damage was down to a shaky rearguard, where Paul Mathers, such an impressive performer last term, had suffered from the defensive inconsistency in front.

Frail and McQuillan were prone to lapses of concentration while Pittman was guilty of some rash challenges. The erratic Paterson was not the answer in central-defence where the veteran Jim Duffy required reliable defenders alongside him. Dinnie fitted the bill but, having been an absentee in the latter stages of season '92/3, a recurrence of his knee ligament problem restricted him to just 10 appearances last term.

However, 18-year-old Neil McCann had established himself on the left wing. He had all the skills of the traditional winger, repeatedly demonstrating his electrifying pace in beating his full-back before delivering a telling ball. Already, he had made a name for himself in the Premier League and he had also starred for the Scotland Under-21s, playing particularly well at the close-season Toulon tournament in the south of France where a number of top clubs had expressed their interest.

Craig Tully made his debut against Celtic at left-back while Jim Hamilton and right-winger Iain Anderson did well after coming off the bench against Hibs. Indeed, Anderson - just 16 years of age - had created a piece of history when he coolly placed a penalty past Scotland keeper Jim Leighton to become the youngest player ever to score in a Premier League game at that time.

Fledgling Dens boss Jim Duffy was a strong advocate of youth development: "It might not be something Dundee has been associated with in the past but the importance of a successful youth policy simply cannot be overestimated." The board agreed and Duffy's dedication and vision was rewarded by a new three-year contract. Just as significantly, Ron Dixon had repaid the £570,000 owed to the Royal Bank of Scotland and, although Dundee now owed him that amount, it was in the form of an interest-free debenture - a move that would save the club around £60,000 per annum in interest.

Dundee's Foreign Legion - Dariusz Adamczuk, Piotr Czachowski, Dusan Vrto and Dragutin Ristic grimace as a free-kick thunders past their heads. At one stage in season 1993-94 Dundee had players of seven non-British nationalities at Dens. DC Thomson

Meanwhile, the playing staff had been revamped. Twelve players - Tosh, Adamczuk, Czachowski, Farningham, Mobilio, Blake, N. Duffy, Shaw, Britton, Pageaud, Teasdale, Hamilton - had been brought in, and eleven - Adamczuk, Dodds, McMartin, Frail, Ristic, McGowan, Westwater, Armstrong, Mobilio, Christie and David - were moved on .

The sale of Steve Frail had left Dundee with a profit of £66,000 in their '93/4 accounts but Gary McKeown, Alan Dinnie and the transfer-seeking Steve Pittman failed to agree terms and began the season on monthly contracts, while Paul Ritchie and Kevin Bain, who had begun just a few games after two knee operations, were transfer-listed.

Garry Paterson joined Ayr United for £25,000, with his old junior club Lochore Welfare getting £1,875. The out-of-favour Piotr Czachowski returned to Poland and although Charlie Nicholas was offered the post of player-coach, he chose to remain with Celtic for another year despite a better offer from Dundee.

The target for 1994-95 was an immediate return to the Premier League but as Jim Duffy explained: "The First Division will be highly competitive and I see Raith Rovers and St Johnstone - who had signed Dunfermline's Northern Ireland striker George O'Boyle after selling Billy Dodds to Aberdeen for £80,000, Dunfermline and Airdrie fighting it out with ourselves for the automatic promotion place."

"Last term, we used 35 players but I have a nucleus of eight or ten men who can compete with the best in the league and I am hopeful youngsters like Jim Hamilton and Iain Anderson will push themselves into contention. We have better players than some clubs but that in itself is no guarantee of success because the best players don't always win."

Dundee's promotion challenge began well with victories over St Mirren (h) 2-0, Stranraer (h) 3-1, and St Johnstone (a) 1-0, and a draw against Airdrie (h) putting them top, two points clear of Dunfermline. And in the League Cup, Paul Tosh netted twice in a 3-0 home win over the newly formed Caledonian Thistle to ensure a plum second-round tie against Celtic at Dens on August 31st.

John Collins gave Celts an early lead but almost immediately Ray Farningham headed the equaliser. In 67 minutes, Dundee skipper Dusan Vrto - recently capped for Slovakia after the partition of the former Czechoslovakia - was ordered off for a professional foul on Paul McStay. The Celtic captain was also given his marching orders for retaliation but it was the visitors who emerged victorious with Andy Walker netting the winner.

Just days into the new season, Alan Dinnie and Steve Pittman were suspended for a serious breach of club discipline. Soon afterwards, Dinnie was transferred to Partick Thistle for £30,000 with Pittman joining him on freedom-of-contract, with his fee later fixed at £27,500 by the Transfer Tribunal.

Meadowbank left-back Mark Hutchison (19), was signed for £9,000 with ex-Dundee United midfielder Andy Cargill arriving on a free transfer but there were serious doubts over the wisdom of selling the two experienced defenders after defeats at Clydebank (2-5) and Ayr (2-3) left Dundee four points behind new league leaders Dunfermline.Then came an amazing roller-coaster of a game against the free-flowing Pars, who deservedly led until a Shaw double put Dundee 2-1 ahead after 57 minutes. Within a minute, Smith

equalised then Tosh volleyed home Dundee's third and Britton made it 4-2 with five minutes remaining. But with victory in sight, a fatal lapse of concentration allowed French to net from the spot and, within 60 seconds, Norrie McCathie headed a dramatic equaliser.

Meanwhile, the Dark Blues had made good progress in the B&Q Cup by defeating Arbroath (h) 5-0, Caley Thistle (a) 1-1 (after extra-time and penalties) and Morton (h) 2-1. Injuries, suspensions and loss of form had allowed Kevin Bain to re-establish himself and the Fifer, along with Jim Duffy, was outstanding in a floodlit semi-final thriller at Dunfermline where a 2-1 win put Dundee through to meet Airdrie in the final at McDiarmid Park.

The Dens defence had tightened up after their earlier shaky spell, and 10 points from their next four games brought them level with second-placed Airdrie, just two points behind Dunfermline. Jim Duffy's decision to rebuild his side had been vindicated with the striking partnership of George Shaw and Gerry Britton looking particularly productive - that term Shaw had found the net six times, while Britton had already scored 13 goals, four of them in a B&Q Cup match against Arbroath at Dens.

So, by the day of the B&Q Cup Final on Sunday, November 6th, the fans'enthusiasm had been rekindled with some 7,000 of the 8,844 crowd backing the Dark Blues. Dundee: Pageaud; McQuillan, J. Duffy, Bain, Vrto (capt); Tosh, Farningham, Wieghorst, McCann; Shaw, Britton. Subs. Blake, Hamilton, Thomson (gk). Airdrie: Martin; Stewart, Sandison (capt), Hay; Boyle, Harvey, Davies, Black, Jack; Cooper, Lawrence. Subs. A. Smith, T. Smith, McCulloch (gk).

Dundee began well but soon got bogged down in a tough midfield struggle. In 28 minutes, slack defending at a throw-in resulted in Harvey putting the Diamonds in front but Dundee levelled just before the interval when Hay conceded an own-goal under pressure by Gerry Britton.

In 62 minutes, a rash tackle by Tosh allowed Boyle to put Airdrie ahead from the spot but, with 14 minutes left, Gerry Britton rammed home a George Shaw cutback to make it 2-2. Neil McCann had made an indifferent start to the season after intense speculation that Celtic were keen but now he was back to his brilliant best and it was Dundee who looked the likelier winners in extra-time.

Kevin Bain - the Scotland Under-21 international was in top form.

With nine minutes remaining, a penalty shoot-out began to look increasingly likely until Michel Pageaud spilled a harmless-looking Graham Harvey shot and Diamonds' substitute big Andy Smith crashed home the winner. On a day of great disappointment, Farningham, McCann, and Wieghorst had been best for Dundee although the Danish international had been given little scope for manouevre by the uncompromising Airdrie midfielder Kenny Black.

However, the Dark Blues bounced back and, by early 1995, an eight-game unbeaten run saw them establish a six-point lead over nearest rivals Airdrie, with Dunfermline and Raith Rovers two points further behind. On December 3rd, Paul Ritchie, who had earlier turned down a £20,000 move to Montrose, netted the only goal of the game at Dunfermline to set up an intriguing home clash with Raith Rovers, the sensational conquerors of Celtic in the League Cup Final after extra-time and penalties.

In 62 minutes, Bain was red-carded for fisting a netbound shot over the bar and Dalziel put Raith ahead with the penalty. Dundee battled back and Jim Hamilton levelled from the penalty spot. Urged on by the home support, the Dark Blues went all out for the winner and it duly came when Morten Wieghorst weaved his way forward before cracking home a fierce low shot for a victory that gave them an 11-point cushion over the Kirkcaldy men.

In January, a late Jim Hamilton header earned Dundee a 2-1 Scottish Cup third-round victory over Premier League Partick Thistle. And thus far, the wiry Hamilton had looked very strong in the air with excellent ball control and passing ability.

Heat of battle - Gerry Britton is tackled by Airdrie defender Graham Hay in the B&Q Cup Final. DC Thomson

After a good spell in October, the teenager returned to the bench but later replaced the suspended Britton and retained his place when the Glaswegian returned. Now, named as Bell's Whisky's "Young Player of the Month" and with his tally of six goals in eight games alerting some top clubs, he was given a two-year extension to his contract.

Recently, Dundee had threatened to take a commanding lead but two back-to-back reverses in February - a 3-2 home reverse to second-placed Dunfermline (after Pageaud was sent off) and a dismal 1-0 defeat at Ayr - had a devastating effect on their promotion hopes. Raith Rovers were joint-top after eight successive wins and now the Dark Blues faced a double-header against Jimmy Nicholl's men, first in the Scottish Cup at Dens then at Kirkcaldy in the league.

Raith boasted an impressive array of talent - Nicholl himself, Dave Narey, Ian Redford, Gordon Dalziel and future Scotland stars Colin Cameron and Stevie Crawford. Nevertheless, Dundee deservedly led 1-0 at the interval before an injury to Blake meant Farningham - who had successfully shackled the elusive Cameron - dropping back into defence. Now Raith had the initiative and two goals in the last 19 minutes shattered Dundee's hopes of a prolonged run in the Scottish Cup.

However, the Dark Blues recovered and 10 points from their next four games - including an impressive 3-0 away win over Airdrie - their first in five attempts against the Scottish Cup semi-finalists - left them two points clear of

Dunfermline and five ahead of Raith with only seven games remaining.

On April 1st, Dundee were happy enough with a 1-1 draw from their top-of-the-table clash at Dunfermline but a similar scoreline at home against relegation-threatened Ayr United seven days later came as a massive blow. Simon Stainrod's side had been reduced to ten men before half-time but Dundee were unable to capitalise and, to exacerbate matters, George Shaw, who had earlier failed against Dundee United and Caley Thistle, missed a penalty deep in injury-time.

Now Raith were two points clear of Dundee and Dunfermline but although the suspended Gerry Britton, whose late dismissal against Ayr (his second of the campaign), and the injured Kevin Bain (ribs), and Dusan Vrto (foot), were all out for the remaining games, the under-pressure Dens men hit back. Brought in alongside Shaw, and with Tosh and McCann out wide, Jim Hamilton netted a first-half hat-trick in a 4-1 triumph against Hamilton Accies at Firhill and with the other results going their way, Dundee were again top of the First Division.

The title race was at boiling point and on April 22nd the Dark Blues faced their toughest test against strong-going Raith Rovers with nearly 8,000 in attendance at Dens. After a nervy start, Dundee dominated but it was Raith who drew first blood with a lightning counter-attack in 68 minutes. Cameron failed to connect with Wilson's speculative low cross, but Pageaud had anticipated his touch and dived too late to prevent the ball bouncing in at the far corner.

Nine minutes later, Tosh replaced Blake but this was to

Dens disaster - Michel Pageaud is unable to stop Barry Wilson's opener for Raith Rovers in the vital promotion clash at Dens. Noel Blake and Jim Duffy and Raith's Colin Cameron and Gordon Dalziel look on. BELOW - Neil McCann beats a defender but the trip to Stranraer would end in disappointment.
DC Thomson

fatally upset the defensive balance and, soon afterwards, the ever-dangerous Barry Wilson, whose father Bobby Wilson had been a big favourite at Dens, sent in a left-wing cross for Crawford to make it 2-0.

That left Dundee two points behind the leaders and without Neil McCann, who had contracted a virus while with the Scotland Under-21s in San Marino, they could only manage a 1-1 draw against struggling St Mirren at Paisley. Raith had won and although Dunfermline had also drawn, Dundee now had to win their last two games and hope that the others might slip-up.

In their penultimate game, Dundee could make little impression against St Johnstone at Dens. However, the introduction of Iain Anderson in 55 minutes turned the game and a penalty by Jim Hamilton and a late goal by George Shaw kept their promotion hopes alive. For, with Dunfermline and Raith drawing 0-0, Dundee lay three points behind the Kirkcaldy side but level with the Pars - who had a better goal-difference.

Now the Dens men had to win at Stranraer and hope for a Raith defeat at Hamilton to win the title and automatic promotion on goal-difference. Alternately, a Dunfermline slip-up at home to Clydebank would allow Dundee to pip them for the play-off position although a Pars win meant Dundee had to win by at least seven goals at Stranraer.

On a bright, sunny day, the Dark Blues had around 1,200 vociferous fans at far off Stair Park. In just nine minutes, Anderson was obstructed in the box and Hamilton converted the penalty. However, Dundee were unable to press home their advantage and it was not until the 62nd minute that Wieghorst got a second after a tremendous run from the halfway line.

Great gaps then appeared in the home defence and, after the Dane made it 3-0 in 80 minutes, only the heroics of keeper Barney Duffy prevented Dundee from running riot. Shaw and Tosh added to the tally, and at the end of an emotionally charged afternoon, Dens fans staged a pitch

invasion to cheer their heroes from the field.

By then, it was known that Raith had drawn 0-0 and Dunfermline had won 2-1, results which condemned the Dark Blues to another term in the First Division. Sadly, one more point would have guaranteed the title and Premier League football, while another two goals would have ensured a play-off with Aberdeen, who had finished second-bottom of the Premier League.

A second goal in the first half at Stair Park might well have opened the floodgates and it could be argued that the pace and power of Tosh from the start might have worn down Stranraer, with the tricky Anderson held back for later.

However, the damage had been done earlier, for, although Dundee had won more games and scored more goals than any other First Division side, they had won only three of the 12 games against their three main promotion rivals. And, even more damningly, they had managed just two points out of a possible twelve from the relegated Ayr United.

CHAPTER TWENTY-NINE

Day Out at Hampden

Jim Duffy remained committed to bringing the good times back to Dens but he was blunt about their prospects: "Since Dundee's last trophy win in 1973, the fans have had nothing but empty promises, false dawns and crushed expectations. I think there are three ways I can give them back a successful club. One is money, two is time and three is luck. I have never had any of the first and it remains to be seen whether I will get, or have any of the other two."

Meanwhile, John McQuillan had joined St Johnstone on freedom-of-contract - with Dundee receiving £87,500 compensation - while Paul Ritchie and the high-earning Noel Blake had been released. Earlier, £150,000 had been received from Polish club LKS Ptak for Piotr Czachowski and this allowed Dundee to sign former Aberdeen and Falkirk left-back Tommy McQueen (32), ex-Falkirk, St Mirren and Instant Dict (Hong Kong) centre-half Roddy Manley (30), on free transfers, with a small fee paid for Forres Mechanics midfielder Andy Matheson (21).

Jim Duffy had built a good attacking side but now they faced a tough challenge from newly relegated Dundee United as well as Dunfermline, who had been crushed by Aberdeen in the promotion-relegation play-off. St Johnstone were also expected to be in contention and Dundee's '95/96 campaign began with a hazardous trip to Perth. However, the Dark Blues made a good start, winning 2-0, before four successive draws left them third, eight points behind Dunfermline and three behind United by mid-September.

There was progress in the Challenge Cup - previously sponsored by B&Q - with a 4-2 away win over East Fife then a 3-0 victory against Cowdenbeath 3-0 at Dens. But, prior to the derby against Dundee United, only four first-team regulars were fielded in the Dens quarter-final against Stenhousemuir on September 25th. A broken leg sustained by Mark Hutchison exacerbated matters but, astutely managed by the duffle-coated ex-Dark Blue, Terry Christie, the Second Division side deservedly won 3-1 then went on to shock Dundee United in the final for their first ever trophy success.

Meanwhile, Dundee had progressed to the League Cup semi-final after a couple of dramatic encounters against Premier League opposition. On August 19th, Neil McCann hit the headlines with four goals in a 6-0 Brockville romp over lowly East Stirling to set up a third-round tie against Kilmarnock at Dens. Trailing 1-0 at half-time, the Dark Blues hit back and, in an amazing turnaround, goals by Shaw, Wieghorst and Hamilton brought them a 3-1 win.

On Wednesday, September 21st, Dundee entertained Hearts in a quarter-final tie that would prove one of the most

Double trouble - a George Shaw one-two helped overcome Hearts.

enthralling games ever seen at Dens. By the 90 minute mark the score-line was 3-3 and, after 30 minutes of extra-time, the sides were deadlocked at 4-4 before a penalty shoot-out saw Morten Wieghorst fire home the decisive kick.

The Dane had only played after passing a late fitness test but it would be his finest-ever performance in a Dark Blue jersey. A George Shaw double shortly before half-time gave Dundee a well-merited lead but with Hearts on top after the break, a McPherson header and another by Colquhoun made it 2-2 with 17 minutes remaining.

However, the Dark Blues rolled up their sleeves and when Shaw pressurised Hearts keeper Henry Smith into miskicking across his penalty box, Paul Tosh crashed home a third goal for Dundee.

With the atmosphere near-electric, Hearts threw everything into attack and, two minutes from time, Willie Jamieson headed the ball down for another Dens "old-boy", Alan Lawrence, to level the scores. Four minutes into extra-time, Morten Wieghorst brilliantly shimmied past a couple of defenders before firing a dipping shot past Smith and into the net.

But with 107 minutes played, John Robertson equalised with a strongly disputed penalty and, after a nail-biting finale, it was on to penalties! McQueen and McCann netted before Tosh missed but Henry Smith also failed to score before Anderson and Jim Duffy took the shoot-out to sudden death. Jamieson beat Pageaud only to hit the post and then Wieghorst wrote himself into the Dens Park history books when he calmly beat Smith to give Dundee a 5-4 win on penalties.

It had been an incredible night and home fans in the crowd of 9,528 danced with delight as hundreds more ran on to the pitch to join the celebrations. The Dens Parkers had been ahead three times only for Hearts to equalise but, in the end, justice had been done and they were through to the last four.

Jim Duffy had come on as Dundee's third substitute and afterwards he could not hide his delight: "Morten was superb and his goal was nothing short of magnificent. It was an amazing tie, the sort all football fans want to see. It feels fantastic but I think it's only after all the emotion has settled down that we will realise what we've achieved."

Good fortune saw them paired with First Division rivals Airdrie while Aberdeen would face Rangers. Meanwhile, the in-form George Shaw netted twice in a 5-1 league win at Dumbarton before a Billy McKinlay hat-trick gave Dundee United a 3-2 win in the local derby at Dens. Dundee had played well but careless defending and a spectacular 25-yarder by McKinlay had sealed their fate.

By the semi-final on October 25th, the Dark Blues had slipped to fourth in the league and all at Dens recognized that Airdrie - Scottish Cup runners-up in 1992 and 1995, beaten League Cup semi-finalists (to Raith Rovers) and B&Q Cup winners (against Dundee) in 1994 - had a fearsome cup pedigree.

However, on a windy night, the Dark Blues enjoyed the support of almost three-quarters of the near 9,000 crowd and by kick-off, McDiarmid Park was a veritable cauldron of noise. Dundee stormed into attack only to miss a number of chances but although Airdrie hit back, it was the Dark Blues who broke the deadlock just before the interval.

Tommy McQueen raced up the left and although his cross went right across the box, Paul Tosh was on hand to smash the ball home. The large Dens contingent roared with joy but with Airdrie pushing forward and Jim Duffy's side content to hit on the break, they had little to cheer in a disappointing second half. With only seven minutes left, Dundee looked home and dry but when John Davies helped on a Paul Harvey corner, Peter Duffield stooped to head the equaliser.

That was a stunning blow for, by then, the Diamonds were looking ominously strong. However, with two minutes remaining, George Shaw sent the ball wide to Neil McCann. The winger sped into the box and with everyone expecting a cross, the Scotland Under-21 international flighted the ball over Martin's head. The ball dipped before going into the net off the inside of the far post and, after a moment's hesitation, the Dundee fans leapt from their seats to celebrate!

At last, the final whistle went and the Dark Blues were

through to their first major final for 15 years. "Hail, Hail the Dee are here" rang around the stands as the players were cheered to the rafters and it was fully 10 minutes before the jubilant fans poured from the ground into their coaches and cars for the happy trip home.

Now last year's B&Q Cup Final disappointment could be forgotten as the players returned to Dens for a party while thousands of fans crowded into bars and clubs where celebrations continued long into the night. It had been a battle rather than an exhibition of stylish football but Dundee had grafted away and, in the end, had outfought Scotland's most reknowned cup fighters.

With skipper Neil Duffy missing through injury, Ray Farningham - a diehard Dens fan - had performed tenaciously in midfield. Jim Duffy and Morten Wieghorst were also standouts but it was Neil NcCann who had netted the all-important winner and speaking to *The Daily Record*, he confirmed: "I've been taking stick in the dressing room because the boys said it was a fluke. But I meant it all right and was delighted to see the ball go in. When I turned towards the crowd and saw their faces it was absolutely brilliant. Reaching the final means so much to everyone connected with Dundee and I'm delighted to have scored the goal that got us there."

In the league, 10 points from their next four games, including a 3-2 win over Dundee United left Dundee just a point behind leaders Dunfermline. The Tannadice derby had been the ideal preparation for the League Cup Final and, with

Neil McCann celebrates his dramatic last-gasp winner against Airdrie. BELOW - Paul Tosh and Jim Hamilton rejoice as Dundee reach their first major final since 1973. Mirrorpix/DC Thomson

Wieghorst again pulling the strings and Tosh in great form down the right, two quickfire headed goals by Shaw put the Dens men in command. Three minutes after the break, a Wieghorst header made it 3-0 but United then took control and goals by Brewster and Malpas made it a nervy final 20 minutes for Dundee.

The Dark Blues had gained revenge for their earlier derby defeat at Dens but the left-footed Vrto had looked somewhat vulnerable at right-back - a problem position since the departure of John McQuillan. Just as alarmingly, United, who had switched things after the break, had been allowed the freedom of midfield without any tactical adjustment by the Dens Parkers.

Sky high - Morten Wieghorst heads home in the 3-2 triumph over Dundee United at Tannadice. BELOW - Celebrations after George Shaw's first goal. DC Thomson

Nevertheless, Dundee appeared to have found a winning formula with just two defeats in 21 games. Player-boss Jim Duffy had successfully employed a flexible 4-4-2 system by utilising three attacking midfielders. Out wide, the tireless Paul Tosh was playing with great consistency while Neil McCann, who had previously run United ragged at Dens, remained a hot handful for opposing defenders.

In central midfield, 20-year-old Andy Cargill, earlier nominated by Jim Duffy for a Scotland Under-21 cap, had impressed with a series of energetic displays before making way for the more experienced pairing of Morten Wieghorst and Neil Duffy in October. The big Dane was given the freedom to push forward while Duffy - appointed skipper after Dusan Vrto began the season on monthly contracts, was content to play a holding role in front of the defence.

Michel Pageaud remained a commanding figure in goal and despite the occasional deployment of Neil Duffy, Roddy Manley and Dusan Vrto were the favoured central defenders until the Slovak's foot injury allowed Jim Duffy to return. The cultured Tommy McQueen had brought a touch of class to the number three jersey but the right-back problem position was first filled by Kevin Bain then Ray Farningham before Dusan Vrto's recent switch.

Up front, Jim Hamilton had formed a promising partnership with the lively George Shaw after Gerry Britton, who now sported a Roberto Baggio-style pony-tail, had earlier been sidelined by injury. Hard to dispossess and strong in the air, the Scotland Under-21 striker was the club's top scorer with 11 goals and with Shaw also finding the net on a regular basis, Dundee had high hopes for Hampden.

The derby win, which was featured on BBC Sportscene, was the prelude to a week of Coca Cola Cup Final fever in Dundee as the Dark Blues came under intense media scrutiny. Most had identified the skill and surging runs of Morten Wieghorst plus the pace and penetration of Neil McCann as Dundee's top assets and with Aberdeen also bang in form, a footballing feast was widely anticipated.

With the match being televised live on both BBC and Sky, there were predictions that Dundee's support might number less than 10,000 but, in the event, around 16,000 fans made

the trip to Hampden on Sunday, November 26th. It was a day of great excitement and as kick-off approached, the dark blue, red and white of the Dundee fans, many with scarves and favours from a much earlier era, contrasted vividly with the red and white of the Aberdeen supporters who were seated from the halfway line round to the traditional Celtic end.

The Dark Blues were now just 90 minutes away from their first major trophy success since 1973 and for the third successive week they fielded an unchanged team. Skipper Neil Duffy replaced Ray Farningham in the only alteration from the semi-final. Dundee - Pageaud; Vrto, Manley, J. Duffy, McQueen; Tosh, Wieghorst, N. Duffy, McCann; Shaw and Hamilton. Subs. Britton, Farningham, Anderson.

Aberdeen - Watt; Grant, Inglis, Smith, McKimmie; Miller, Bernard, Jess, Glass; Shearer and Dodds. Subs. Robertson, Hetherston, Stillie. Referee - L. Mottram (Forth).

Under Roy Aitken's management, Aberdeen had narrowly escaped relegation six months earlier but although their semi-final win over Rangers made them firm favourites, Celtic's shock defeat by Raith Rovers in last year's final ensured there would be no complacency.

Having studied Dundee, the Dons had laid their plans accordingly and right from kick-off, they began at whirlwind pace. Wieghorst, McCann and Tosh were regarded as Dundee's key men but with Grant and McKimmie pushing right up on the deep-lying wingers and Wieghorst also denied space and time on the ball, Aberdeen took control.

After five minutes, the tricky Joe Miller was switched to the left alongside Stephen Glass to exploit Vrto's discomfort at right-back and soon Dundee's noisy support was silent as shots rained in on Pageaud's goal. Only stalwart defensive work kept the scores level, but 11 minutes from the interval Aberdeen finally made the breakthrough. Glass beat Vrto and his low driven cross was deflected up and across the goal by a last-gasp Neil Duffy tackle.

The bounce beat the inrushing Shearer but, momentarily distracted, Michel Pageaud could only get a hand to the ball and Billy Dodds ran in to score from five yards. Disappointingly, Dundee had created only one real chance, a Neil Duffy header which was tipped over by Michael Watt. Aberdeen had dominated to an embarrassing extent but Dundee, surprisingly, made no changes either in personnel or tactics, and within 30 seconds of the restart they found themselves 2-0 down.

Glass again eluded Vrto before crossing from near the corner flag. Duncan Shearer timed his run perfectly and with defenders slow to react, he stole between Jim Duffy and Tommy McQueen to head powerfully past Pageaud from six yards. In 55 minutes, Gerry Britton replaced Paul Tosh with 17-year-old Iain Anderson coming on for Neil McCann soon afterwards but although Dundee began to put some moves together they never looked like getting the goal which could have brought them back into the game and given their fans some measure of consolation.

It had been a great occasion for the Dark Blue army but the game itself had been a major disappointment. Pageaud, Jim Duffy, Manley, McQueen and the busy Shaw had played well but too many others had frozen on the day. Despite a fine performance by Aberdeen, particularly Stephen Glass, Dundee had played well below their capabilities and had rarely troubled their Premier League opponents.

Everyone knew that the Dens men - assembled for around £600,000 compared to the £3.5 million spent by the Dons - needed to be at their best to win but they had not shown their usual flair and again displayed a lack of tactical flexibility. The battle had been lost in midfield where Wieghorst and Neil Duffy were outmanuevered by the more mobile Bernard, Jess and Glass and many fans were surprised that

the experience and commitment of Ray Farningham had not been utilised in this area, the Dundonian coming on at right-back with only nine minutes remaining.

Unknown to the fans, Neil McCann and Aberdeen's Scott Booth had both suffered thigh strains three days before the final. Booth failed a fitness test and was replaced by Shearer but McCann declared himself fit and, despite later admitting that his thigh "went" after only five minutes, he struggled on to no effect until replaced by Iain Anderson in 65 minutes.

"For whatever reason, too many players did not perform," said Jim Duffy. "The experienced men were fine but the youngsters were tense and appeared to find the occasion too big to handle. They seemed confident and relaxed in the run up to the final but it was probably only when the bus drew up at Hampden that they realised their massive responsibility towards the thousands of Dundee fans who were there to cheer them on."

Nevertheless, the Dark Blues bounced back and a 2-1 win over St Mirren at Paisley gave them the chance of going two points clear at the top in their next game against Dumbarton. Just days earlier, the basement club had lost 8-0 to Dundee United but with less than 3,000 at Dens on a bitterly cold night, the Boghead outfit stunned Dundee with a late equaliser in a 1-1 draw. The Dark Blues had conceded several late goals that season and defensive carelessness had again cost them dear.

To a large extent, the run to the Coca Cola Cup Final had papered over the financial problems for the club's future remained uncertain. According to the Dundee-based directors, Ron Dixon had not been in touch since his departure almost a year previously and, in their opinion, he would not be back. However, Dixon had been contacted by Peter Marr and at a meeting in Seattle seven days before the final, the Dundee businessman was quoted a figure of some £3 million to buy the club.

The absentee owner had returned to Scotland for the final and following abortive discussions with the Marr brothers, he masked his failure to conclude a deal by offering his 72% shareholding to "a group" which included vice-chair-man Malcolm Reid and manager Jim Duffy. Dundee fans had been hoping for somewhat wealthier benefactors and the gloom deepened when Morten Wieghorst, still signing monthly contracts, went to Celtic for £600,000 with £100,000-rated Parkhead defender Barry Smith, a Scotland Under-21 international, arriving in part-exchange.

On December 9th, Smith made his debut at right-back in the top-of-the-table clash against Dunfermline at Dens. After leading 2-0, Dundee finally went

Dens machine - the legions of Dundee fans were in fine fettle prior to kick-off.   DC Thomson

Dismal Dees - the players reflect on their poor showing in the final (left to right) Dusan Vrto, Paul Tosh, George Shaw, Jim Hamilton, Michel Pageaud, Neil Duffy and Tommy McQueen.   DC Thomson

down 4-2 and had Paul Tosh dismissed for a mistimed tackle. On a day when the Pars might have scored many more, Wieghorst's midfield craft was conspicuously absent while a clearly unfit Manley had remained on the park until after Dunfermline's fourth in 76 minutes.

Meanwhile, Jim Duffy announced that the proposed management buy-out was on "the back-burner" while wealthy USA-based Nigerian Prince Obie Okehi withdrew his interest in the belief that Dixon's £3 million valuation was three times the club's value. Malcolm Reid had speculated that the Dens boss might get half the estimated £300,000 windfall from the final to strengthen the team, but it was no surprise that the cash plus the Wieghorst fee went to Ron Dixon, whose £1.5 million interest-free loan - including the £570,000 repaid to the bank in 1994 - had enabled the club to continue.

Later, Duffy claimed that the chairman had stated that "The key was in the door" had the Dark Blues not reached the final but it is hard to believe that this was anything other than a "hard-sell" for, if the chairman had closed the club, he would have forfeited hundreds of thousands of pounds in transfer fees since all Dundee's players - like those of Third Lanark in 1967 - would then have become the property of the Scottish Football League.

Unusually, the AGM was held on December 29th and after voting that the club be re-registered as a private company to facilitate any future takeover, around one hundred increasingly disillusioned shareholders heard that operating costs of £1,017,216 - including £800,000 spent on greyhound racing facilities in 1994, a venture that ended after just 12 weeks with losses of £172,000 - had contributed towards a loss of £56,717 that May compared to a £66,742 profit a year earlier.

A recurrence of his thigh injury at training meant Neil McCann would be sidelined until February and, with the team beginning to slip down the league, something had to be done to arrest the decline. Jim Duffy's use of two attacking wide men put a big responsibility on the two central midfielders and even with Wieghorst, the team had sometimes struggled for the right blend. Now 35, Ray Farningham no longer had the stamina of old while ex-United pair Andy

Cargill and Roy McBain - the latter signed on a free transfer in September - lacked the defensive qualities to balance their undoubted attacking ability.

The sale of Mike Teasdale to Caley Thistle for £15,000 freed up some funds and, early in the New Year, Duffy paid £25,000 for 32-year-old Dumbarton midfielder Chic Charnley. Home fans were quick to appreciate his ability as the newcomer marked his debut by lofting home a fantastic goal from all of 40 yards in a 2-1 home win over Hamilton Accies at Dens.

However, Charnley had accumulated 12 red cards in spells at Clydebank, Hamilton Accies, St Mirren, Partick Thistle and Dumbarton and he was to experience yet another early bath in the Dens derby against Dundee United three days later.

Two-goal Robbie Winters earned United a 2-0 win but, midway through the second half, the winger was involved in controversy. As Chic Charnley moved away with the ball, Winters went down clutching his face and with referee John Rowbotham ruling that the midfielder had deliberately struck Winters with his trailing hand, Charnley was sent off.

Gary McKeown meanwhile had returned to action after a long-term knee injury and there was further encouragement with the reappearance of Dariusz Adamczuk. Signed by Dundee from Eintracht for £250,000 in August 1993, the Pole joined Udinese for £500,000 two months later, but before the Italians had paid his fee in full, he was loaned to Portugese club Belenenses.

Udinese then refused to complete their payments and eventually FIFA deemed him still a Dundee player and insisted that the Dens club settle the remainder of their debt to Eintracht while waiving the balance due by the Italians. Although Adamczuk returned to Dens in mid-1995, he insisted that he didn't want to resume his Dundee career but after appearing for Polish side Pogon Szczin, he finally returned to sign a new one-and-a-half year contract for the Dark Blues.

Still Dundee's headlong slump continued and by mid-February, they had slipped to fifth in the league while a disastrous 3-1 third-round upset by a Charlie Nicholas-inspired Clyde at Broadwood brought their interest in the Scottish Cup to a premature end. Nevertheless, on March 6th, the Charnley-inspired Dark Blues earned a 1-1 draw against league leaders Dunfermline at East End Park and a win in their next game against second-placed Dundee United at Tannadice would bring them within a point of their local rivals.

Once again, Dundee gave a good account of themselves but, with United 1-0 up, in almost identical circumstances to the Dens derby Winters fell theatrically - and Charnley was dismissed by referee Hugh Dallas. This appeared rough justice for, earlier, the Dundee midfielder had been kicked by Dave Bowman while on the ground, only for the official to turn a blind eye. Brewster made it 2-0 and when Jim Duffy, recently sent off at Clydebank, also got his marching orders, the Dens men were fortunate not to lose by a bigger margin.

The return of Neil McCann, recently the subject of a failed £500,000 bid by Dundee United, brought added drive but a 2-1 defeat by St Mirren at Paisley on April 6th finally extinguished their promotion hopes. Seven days later, just 1,454 fans - their lowest home league crowd since April 1937 - turned out for the visit of Clydebank and with just two wins from their last seven games, Dundee finished fifth behind Dunfermline, Dundee United, Morton and St Johnstone, 10 points adrift of the play-off place - their worst league placing in fifty-eight years.

Post-Hampden, only eight of 22 league games had been won and with just three wins from 16 meetings with the top four clubs and just five successes in 18 league games at Dens, the fans' frustration was reflected in an average home gate of only 3,600. The creative abilities of Wieghorst and the injured McCann had been sorely missed and, in terms of goalscoring, Dundee had ended 20 goals adrift of champions Dunfermline and Dundee United, who had spent over £1 million on Steven Pressley, Gary McSwegan and Owen Coyle before achieving promotion with a last-gasp play-off success against Partick Thistle.

Jim Hamilton finished Dundee's top scorer with 19 league and cup goals but although George Shaw had had another good season, Gerry Britton failed to reproduce his earlier scoring form, while Paul Tosh had slipped back to his erratic ways of old. The powerful Roddy Manley looked the part at centre-half but since December he had spent much of his time on the treatment table, which meant Neil Duffy dropping back into defence to the detriment of midfield.

Jim Duffy continued to turn out to the exclusion of Kevin Bain but his lack of pace meant the defence having to lie deep and two red cards along with a series of uncharacteristic mistakes reinforced the argument that the popular veteran would henceforth be better advised to direct operations from the sidelines.

Few doubted that Dundee's future lay in youth development and great encouragement was taken from the performances of the youth side, who, under the tutelage of John McCormack, had reached the final of the BP Under-18 Youth Cup before going down 4-1 to Celtic. Stuart Rafferty returned to Dens as commercial manager and, along with newly appointed youth coach Ray Farningham, he would co-ordinate the youth scheme, which was augmented by a bequest from the late Ken Ouchterlonie, a member of Dundee's promotion-winning side back in season 1946-47.

However, the future looked bleak and with debts spiralling out of control, vice-chairman Malcolm Reid - who, previously had been unpaid like the other directors - was now working full-time on £30,000 per annum to get the club back on an even keel. Admitting that there was no chance of Jim Duffy and himself

taking control unless Ron Dixon dropped his price to take account of the Bosman ruling, he praised the understanding shown by creditors but warned that Dundee now had to live within its means with monthly expenditure requiring to be slashed by £15,000 for the club to remain full-time.

Roddy Manley, Mark Hutchison, Paul Mathers, Roy McBain, Darren Magee, Marcus Dailly, Andy Matheson and Graeme Cadger were all handed free transfers while the promising Gordon Tannock was forced to retire through injury. It was also decided to scrap the reserve team and to the fans' dismay, it soon became clear that most of Dundee's best players would have to go.

His contract up, Michel Pageaud rejoined Valenciennes with Dundee no longer entitled to a transfer fee under the new Bosman ruling. Another fans' favourite Dusan Vrto returned to Banik Ostrava of Slovakia for £50,000. Gerry Britton was transferred to Dunfermline for £60,000 and after rejecting Dundee's offer of a new deal, Scotland Under-21 international Neil McCann looked set to join Sturm Graz of Austria on freedom-of-contract.

This would again have left the Dark Blues without compensation but at the last moment Jim Duffy managed to broker a £250,000 deal with Hearts. Sadly, this was around one third of his true value and considerably less than the £500,000 plus which Dundee United had offered although the Dens fans would never have forgiven the board had the inspirational winger been allowed to go down the road.

Indeed, Duffy had been the major obstacle to that deal, insisting that he would rather resign than see McCann join their local rivals. On leaving, the young winger expressed his gratitude to the club: "I signed for Dundee when I was a 13-year-old and I'd like to thank Jim Duffy and everyone else at Dens for giving me a chance and for everything they did for me."

The exodus continued and, on the eve of the new season, Dens skipper Neil Duffy was transferred to Dundee United for £200,000. There was no great furore, for, by then, little could shock an already stunned Dens support and, of last November's 14-player Coca Cola Cup Final squad, only seven players now remained. Of those, Jim Duffy, Ray Farningham and Tommy McQueen were at the end of their careers, leaving just Jim Hamilton, Paul Tosh, Iain Anderson and the unsettled George Shaw as the core of the Dundee team for the forthcoming 1996-97 campaign.

Top man - Jim Hamilton outjumps a Dumbarton defender in the League Cup at Dens. Robbie Raeside and Iain Anderson are the other Dundee players. DC Thomson

CHAPTER THIRTY

Lowest Ebb

Now locked into an increasingly downward spiral, the Dens Park club appeared ill-equipped for a promotion challenge and Jim Duffy, who had unsuccessfully attempted to form a takeover consortium, was under no illusions: "In the absence of someone willing to pump money into the club, we just have to make the best of it. I've got a job to do and will continue to do it to the best of my ability. The longer we stay in the First Division, the more money we'll lose but if we can't afford quality players it will be even harder to return to the Premier League."

It was therefore no surprise when the cash-strapped Dark Blues turned to the free transfer market with 38-year-old former Scotland goalkeeper Billy Thomson arriving from Rangers along with ex-Raith Rovers' central-defender Robbie Raeside and Scarborough's former Partick Thistle winger Kevin Magee.

Encouragingly, a new shirt sponsorship agreement with *The Firkin Brewery* plus a kit deal with the sportswear company *Avec* would bring the club around £110,000, while it was announced that Dundee would turn out in Arsenal style V-necked jerseys, which, white sleeves apart, were remarkably similar to those worn in the happier days of the late 1950s and 1960s.

A pre-season trip to Northern Ireland brought a mixed bag of results but it had given Jim Duffy the chance to experiment and also allowed the newcomers to settle in. Understandably, supporters' morale was at rock-bottom but although the opening two home games attracted crowds of less than 2,000, there was a heartening display from the pacy Kevin Magee, who scored a fine solo goal and created two others in a 3-0 Dens win over Stenhousemuir in the first round of the Challenge Cup.

Five days later, injury-hit Dundee were forced to field two 16-year-olds - goalkeeper Jamie Langfield and substitute midfielder John Elliot, as they recovered from the loss of an early goal to beat Second Division Dumbarton in the League Cup at Dens. Just 15 minutes remained when Robbie Raeside headed the equaliser and with extra-time looming, Jim Hamilton popped up to strike the winner.

Dundee's league campaign too began reasonably well with a 0-0 draw against Partick Thistle at Firhill, a 2-1 home win over promotion favourites Morton, then a 1-1 draw with Stirling Albion at Forthbank. By then, the squad had been further strengthened by the acquisition of the ex-St Mirren and Aberdeen defender David Winnie (29), from Hearts for £30,000, while former Dundee striker Iain Ferguson (34), arrived on a free transfer from the Northern Irish club

Chic Charnley - bags of skill but a poor disciplinary record. DC Thomson

Portadown.

"Fergie", who had gone on to play for Rangers, Dundee United, Hearts, Motherwell and Airdrie, was delighted to return to his first club: "Back in 1986, I wanted to make my Dens loan spell from Rangers permanent. I twice knocked back United but although that wasn't to be, I'm pleased to be back now."

It had been a low-key start to the season but there was great excitement when the third-round draw of the Coca Cola-sponsored League Cup paired Dundee with Dundee United at Tannadice on September 3rd. Although the newly promoted Tangerines had made a poor start to the Premier League, they had won three of the four derby clashes last term and once again were favourites to win.

The teams lined up: Dundee - Thomson; Smith, Winnie, Raeside; Tosh, Adamczuk, Bain, Charnley, McQueen; Shaw, Hamilton. Subs. Ferguson, McKeown, Magee. Dundee United - Maxwell; Pressley, Benneker, Duffy; Perry, McLaren, Bowman, McQuilken; Winters, McSwegan, Coyle. Subs. McKinnon, Shannon, Key. Referee W. Young

On a warm, humid evening, around 12,000 fans saw Dundee make a positive start only for Coyle to put United ahead after 20 minutes. The Dens Parkers battled back to level through a Jim Hamilton penalty and second-half play swung from end to end before the game moved into extra-time. The thrills continued when Hamilton thundered a shot off the bar, then Gary McSwegan hit a post. But with 97 minutes gone, Chic Charnley deftly rolled the ball along the edge of the United penalty box and Kevin Bain's deflected shot put Dundee 2-1 ahead.

Kevin Magee then cracked an angled shot off the post but with 10 minutes left, McSwegan made it 2-2 and with Tannadice in a ferment, the drama continued into a penalty shoot-out. In turn, Charnley, Tosh and McKeown scored for Dundee with McKinnon and Duffy doing likewise for United. Thomson then saved from McSwegan and after an ice-cool Iain Ferguson made it 4-2, the Dens keeper clinched matters when he again guessed right to block Owen Coyle's effort.

It had been a terrific derby and as the players celebrated victory against their closest rivals, noisy Dundee fans roared their delight. All the Dens men had played their part but none more so than Chic Charnley and the heroic Billy Thomson. The mercurial Charnley had shrugged off his previous derby dismissals and, showing great appetite for the fray, he took control of midfield where he displayed his full range of passing skills.

Billy Thomson - made vital penalty stops.

Prior to his crucial penalty stops, ex-United keeper Thomson had made a string of incredible saves and afterwards, in true "Mystic Meg" fashion, he claimed to have predicted to his team-mates that the draw would throw up a Tannadice derby!

"That's exactly how it happened and what a good night it turned out to be," said Thomson. "Over the piece, I thought we deserved to go through and I just knew I was going to save a penalty or two. We were all square when it came to Gary McSwegan and I sensed it was the one I was going to save. I decided to go to my right and saved it, then did the same against Owen Coyle and Dundee were through."

Now the big keeper forecast that the quarter-final draw would throw up a re-run of last year's final and, remarkably, he was again correct as Dundee were paired with Aberdeen at Dens. However, their chances looked bleak following home defeats by Airdrie (1-0), in the league and St Johnstone (5-1), in the quarter-final of the Challenge Cup. Jim Duffy had started against Saints but with the Perth side four goals up by half-time, the veteran was withdrawn and his 238th appearance for the club would be his last.

The introduction of 18-year-old Gavin Rae for injured skipper Tommy McQueen was Dundee's only change from Tannadice. Aberdeen, however, had amassed 32 goals in 10 games and with Billy Dodds and Dean Windass bang in form, they looked formidable opponents. In a fiercely fought encounter, there were nine bookings and the more creative players got little chance to flourish. But with the interval approaching, Dundee went ahead when Tosh shrugged aside the attentions of three Dons defenders before volleying a fierce 16-yarder past Nicky Walker.

After the break, Kevin Bain relieved the pressure when his shot hit the bar but with 19 minutes remaining, Dodds made it 1-1 with a penalty after appearing to dive when challenged by Thomson. Vehement protests saw Raeside and Windass booked and minutes later, the volatile ex-Hull striker was red-carded for a wild foul on Charnley.

The midfielder then rattled the Dons bar with a 30-yard free-kick but with just two minutes remaining, Jim Hamilton finished off a good move with a half-hit shot that squirmed beneath Walker for a dramatic last-gasp winner!

At full-time, there were joyful scenes amongst the Dens faithful who nine months earlier had endured an afternoon of misery against Aberdeen at Hampden. That close season, many had feared the worst after losing so many top players and all were agreed that manager Jim Duffy and his assistant John McCormack had worked wonders on a shoe-string budget.

Now into the last eight, the Dark Blues were paired with Hearts and four straight wins over East Fife (h) 2-0, St Johnstone (a) 1-0, Clydebank (h) 2-1 and Falkirk (a) 1-0 kept them on track for promotion despite a 2-0 reverse to Partick Thistle at Dens prior to the semi-final. Significantly, Chic Charnley had been an absentee after receiving the 15th red card of his career in a clash with Falkirk's Brian Hamilton at Brockville. On a greasy surface, both players had slid in for the ball but Charnley had brought up his boot and was immediately ordered off by Willie Young.

Charnley was a key man for, although short on pace and mobility, he had great skill on the ball and his pinpoint long-range passing regularly set up chances for his strikers. The influential midfielder had received a five-match ban but to the fans' relief, he was available for the Hearts match. Craig Tully replaced the suspended David Winnie but otherwise Dundee were at full strength as they attempted to reach their second successive League Cup Final.

For Hearts, Neil McCann would miss out through injury, and his replacement was Stuart Callaghan who, ironically, had refused to move in part-exchange for the ex-Dark Blue.

In an interview with Jim Black of *The Sun*, Jim Duffy admitted to being pleasantly surprised at how well his new-look squad had adapted: "I'd be lying if I said I wasn't concerned because with the season approaching we simply didn't have enough players. However, after discussing things with "Cowboy", we began at the back and started to find replacements as cheaply as possible. Given our circumstances, I am satisfied at reaching a cup semi-final and being well placed in the league."

There were over 5,000 Dundee fans in the near-capacity 16,000 crowd at the floodlit Easter Road semi-final on Wednesday, October 23rd. Although many had pondered the possibility of a high-octane clash between the temperamental Charnley and Italian "hard-man" Pasquale Bruno of Hearts, their attention would soon be focussed on uncharac-

Payback time - Jim Hamilton slots home a last-gasp winner against Aberdeen in the League Cup at Dens.
DC Thomson

Action stations - Jim Hamilton, Robbie Raeside and Paul Tosh pressurise David Weir, Gilles Rousset and Neil Poynton of Hearts at Easter Road. DC Thomson

teristic defensive lapses which would cost the white-shirted Dens Parkers dear.

Both involved the normally reliable Dariusz Adamczuk. In 20 minutes, he toe-poked the ball back to Billy Thomson, who tried but failed to control the ball with his chest and Darren Beckford, an early substitute for the limping John Robertson, netted at the second attempt. Dundee hit back only for Colin Cameron to make it 2-0 when Adamczuk conceded a penalty with a clumsy tackle on Callaghan.

After the interval, Dundee stormed forward only to lose a third goal on the break and although Hamilton pulled one back in 75 minutes, there would be no Hampden return. "We gifted them a two-goal start but did much better after the break," said Jim Duffy. "Overall, we've no complaints and now we've got to pick ourselves up for the league."

The Dens men remained First Division leaders but although the semi-final defeat was only their third in 16 games, they had recently begun to toil. Defensively, there were few complaints. Billy Thomson was a steady keeper with Barry Smith a revelation in his new sweeper role alongside an equally impressive Robbie Raeside and David Winnie in a back-three formation.

Dariusz Adamczuk had been a standout in his new position at right-back and he and Tommy McQueen were now the wide men in a five-man midfield. However, there was insufficient inventiveness from midfield and with Dundee too content to lie deep and an over-emphasis on the use of the long ball to unsupported strikers, much of the side's rythm had disappeared. Kevin Bain had given his all in an unaccustomed midfield slot but the absence of the suspended Chic Charnley only served to further highlight his limitations.

Indeed, with the experienced George Shaw now unavail-

able after refusing to sign another monthly contract and Paul Tosh off the boil, Jim Hamilton had become an increasingly isolated figure up front. Sadly, Iain Ferguson now lacked the pace to make any impact while Kevin Magee had the speed but too often flattered to deceive. In contrast, 18-year-old Iain Anderson continued to show some brilliant touches although the young winger still had much to learn.

Duffy was under no illusions, "At the start of the season we brought in Thomson, Raeside, Winnie, Magee and Ferguson but clearly these players were different to the ones we'd lost like McCann, Britton and Wieghorst. I knew we'd have to change our style of play to an extent and I felt we had to adopt a less open style of play and make ourselves more difficult to beat in a 3-5-2 formation."

This dearth of attacking options saw Dundee draw a blank in their next five matches to equal their ignominious league record of six games without a goal, away back in 1902. In fact, from Raeside's first-minute goal at Falkirk on October 12th until Iain Anderson's 62nd-minute header against the Bairns at Dens on December 7th, Dundee supporters endured an astonishing eleven-and-a-half hours of football without celebrating a league goal!

Dundee's 15 league games had produced only 10 goals and, by late November, there was mounting disquiet over the tactics with only 2,500 regulars turning up at Dens, half the number that had attended the semi-final at Easter Road. During this barren spell, Dundee had fielded a succession of trialists, including former West Ham, Manchester City and Everton midfielder Mark Ward, French midfielder Laurent Croce and Norwegian striker Ole Petter Skonner but none had merited a longer stay.

Meanwhile, the Dark Blues had slipped to fifth behind Partick, Airdrie and Falkirk with pace-setters St Johnstone a massive 12 points ahead. And when back-up keeper Gary McGlynn and striker Jerry O'Driscoll - two of the stars of Dundee's BP Youth Cup run - returned from a loan spell at Portadown, they were given their opportunity against East Fife at Methil on Tuesday, December 3rd.

There, goals by Robbie Raeside and Jerry O'Driscoll gave Dundee a 2-1 half-time lead in the appalling gale-force conditions but to the dismay of their fans amongst the 367 spectators, a floodlight failure resulted in referee John Rowbotham abandoning the game two minutes after the restart. However, there was a new freshness about the side and, four days later, an angled header from Iain Anderson and a late strike by young Gavin Rae put Dundee back on the winning trail with a well-merited 2-0 win over Falkirk before a crowd of just 2,198 at Dens.

Having previously instigated the sale of so many players, any visit by Ron Dixon was viewed with great trepidation. After an 11 month absence, the chairman had planned a visit but although his trip was cancelled, fans' fears proved well founded when Scotland Under-21 striker Jim Hamilton was transferred to Hearts for £250,000 in mid-December.

Jim Duffy appeared philosphical: "Obviously I'm sorry to lose a young player for half his true value but only six months of his contract remained and he refused our offer of a new one. The Bosman ruling means clubs must act in advance of players reaching the end of their deals and that is what we have done."

Tynecastle striker John Colquhoun rejected the chance of moving to Dens and Peterborough United's ex-Norwich and Bradford City striker Lee Power (24), was fixed up until the end of the season. Two months earlier, the highly paid Power had been available for £150,000 but the cash-strapped "Posh" had finally given him a free transfer in order to slash their wage bill.

Power's debut coincided with a much-relished 7-1 win over East Fife in the replayed match at Bayview. Then, following a 2-2 Boxing Day draw with Partick Thistle at Firhill, the rampant Dark Blues netted six without reply against the luckless Fifers at Dens. That left Dundee second and although still 10 points behind leaders St Johnstone with a game more played, 15 goals from their last three games made prospects for 1997 seem a whole lot brighter.

The financial realities were all too clear at the AGM in the Stakis Earl Grey Hotel on Sunday, December 29th. The accounts at May 1996 showed that the Coca Cola Cup run had brought a considerably increased turnover and along with the money from the Wieghorst sale, there had been a profit of £110,507 - and that despite a tax penalty of £53,800 incurred by Ron Dixon for mistakenly reclaiming VAT on the sale of the former Bowbridge Jute Mill site.

Unfortunately, that profit made only a small impact to leave Dundee's net liabilities at around £1.17 million, most of which was due to Dixon. Effectively, players were being sold to repay the chairman's earlier £1.5 million loan and the balance sheet to May 1997 would show that debts had fallen to just over £1 million after an operating loss of £192,852, mainly due to the falling revenue at the gates.

However, there were only so many saleable assets and the lack of investment together with the ongoing player exodus left many worried that Dundee might be heading for extinction like Third Lanark in 1967. Ron Dixon had dropped his selling price to £1.7 million but this was still three times the board's valuation and, within 24 hours, matters were exacerbated by the departure of Jim Duffy. The popular Glaswegian had accepted the manager's post at Premier League strugglers Hibernian, where, ironically, he replaced former Dundee boss, Jocky Scott.

There he would receive £80,000 per annum - almost three times his Dens salary - but according to *Bob Angus* in that night's *Evening Telegraph,* the money was not the issue: "As recently as early summer he would not have dreamt of leaving. However, in recent months he admitted privately that he was fed up at having to sell all his quality players, and at the way the club was being run and would consider an offer to move." He went on to describe Duffy's departure as ominous, commenting that many would see it as the biggest nail yet in Dundee's coffin.

Malcolm Reid expressed his sorrow at losing Duffy: "We

Methil magic - Kevin Bain and Jerry O'Driscoll watch Dave Winnie head home in the 7-1 victory against East Fife at Methil.   DC Thomson

Troubled times - the 1996 AGM with Jim Duffy on right alongside directors Harry Leadingham, Bob Hynd, Nigel Squire, Malcolm Reid (at microphone) and John Black. BELOW - New boss John McCormack with his first signing Hugh Robertson. DC Thomson

tried to get him to stay but he felt he'd gone as far as he could. Everybody knows what a great job he did with such meagre resources. Dundee Football Club owes Jim Duffy a great deal because he was more than just a manager - on occasion he even put his own money into the club, just as the current directors did, to keep it going. Jim's the best there is but in the end, we couldn't stand in his way."

Duffy's assistant John McCormack was made interim-boss but he got off to a disastrous start as Dundee crashed 7-2 to St Johnstone in the Ne'erday game at Perth. From kick-off, the normally dependable Robbie Raeside was troubled by Roddy Grant and it was the bustling striker who put Saints ahead. Chic Charnley equalised with a stinging half-volley from 18 yards but soon after the break, Dundee conceded another two bad goals to trail 3-1.

With the Leigh Jenkinson-inspired Saints running riot, Dundee fell 6-1 behind before their misery was further compounded 11 minutes from the end. Already booked for a rash foul on Dasovic, Charnley got involved in a fracas with Raeside and, despite appearing to be struck by his teammate, he was again sent off by Willie Young. O'Driscoll netted a penalty consolation but, by then, rampant St Johnstone had made it seven on a dark, dark day for the Dark Blues.

Later a shattered McCormack revealed: "I was convinced that some of the players wanted me out. I had changed the system that day and my first reaction was that some of them just didn't want to play for me. That night, however, some players and others in the game whose opinions I respect, called me and insisted that I stick with it. I went along with that advice and, after that, the players responded magnificently."

The new manager then got some vital breathing space when the away game against St Mirren fell victim to the weather, thus allowing him to bring in two "new" faces for the home match against promotion challengers Airdrie on January 11th. Former Scotland Under-21 international midfielder Hugh Robertson (21), was secured on a free transfer from Aberdeen and there was another boost when George Shaw, who had earlier spent a month at Home Farm of Dublin, returned after prospective moves to Stuttgart, Real Mallorca, St Johnstone and Dunfermline fell through.

Goals by O'Driscoll and Power brought a 2-1 victory and a delighted McCormack fielded an unchanged side for the next game against Clydebank at Dens. This meant that Chic Charnley, who had missed the Airdrie match through suspension, would not start and the midfielder stormed off after

being named as substitute. A few days later Charnley was released and soon afterwards he joined Jim Duffy at Hibs.

Charnley's departure was a big setback for he was rightly regarded as a great entertainer and a key man for the Dark Blues. However, with 16 orderings-off, including four while at Dens, the fiery 33-year-old had a disgraceful disciplinary record and he was just one booking away from a further five-match ban.

John McCormack pulled no punches: "I was prepared to quit over Chic Charnley. It was him or me and if he'd stayed at the club, I would have gone. Chic is a good player, a good friend and he was a big favourite with the fans, so it was a big decision. There were one or two internal incidents with him that I wasn't prepared to tolerate and that's why he was allowed to go."

Indeed, the midfielder's indiscipline was not confined to the field of play for he had continued the altercation with Raeside in the McDiarmid dressing room and the interim Dundee boss also revealed: "Chic was a regular absentee from training and he appeared to have a particular aversion to Monday sessions. We could have put him up for sale but I felt it was best all round if he was released."

At the end of January, Dundee went down 3-2 to St Mirren at Paisley but although Lee Power was ordered off and Jerry O'Driscoll missed a penalty, the new striking partnership showed great promise. The stronger and more experienced Power brought out the best in the eager O'Driscoll, who had now netted seven goals in eight games, and it was a pairing that augered well for the future.

A £300,000 St Johnstone bid for O'Driscoll was turned down and after first persuading the striker and other bright prospects like Barry Smith, Iain Anderson, Gavin Rae, Hugh Robertson, Craig Tully and Gary McGlynn, as well as the more experienced Dariusz Adamczuk, to sign new two-year deals, John McCormack himself had his own contract confirmed with an extension until May 1999.

It had been expected that McCormack would accompany Duffy to Easter Road and he admitted: "I was gutted when I realised I was not going because I had looked on it as a chance for me to go to a Premier League club which had some money. However, things have worked out for me here and I'm now glad Jim went for Jackie MacNamara as his assistant. I knew there was a boardroom split over my appointment so I gambled by suggesting that they pay me what they thought I was worth and in the end, I got a backdated pay rise."

Shock news - Paul Tosh joined Hibs for £200,000 along with Lee Power.

It was hoped that a good Scottish Cup run might bring in some much-needed cash and a 3-1 Dens win over Second Division Queen of the South set up a fourth-round thriller against Morton at Cappielow. With just five minutes left, Dundee trailed 2-1 only for Iain Anderson, scorer of a spectacular effort in the previous round, to magnificently volley home the equaliser off the underside of the bar.

In the dying minutes of the replay, Anderson had a penalty saved by Wylie before Thomson made a splendid diving save from a Lilley spot-kick. However, Thomson had only delayed the outcome with Morton substitute Barry Mason ending the stalemate in the second period of extra-time.

An O'Driscoll 30-yarder brought a 1-0 revenge win league over Morton in the league at Dens a few days later, but, by mid-March, any chance of finishing top had disappeared as Dundee lay third, 12 points behind St Johnstone, two behind Airdrie and one ahead of St Mirren. Seven games remained and the target now was second place and a play-off against the ninth-placed Premier League side.

There had been widespread speculation that a takeover was imminent but with Dundee still looking good for the runners-up spot, came the shock news that Lee Power and Paul Tosh had been sold to Hibernian for a combined fee of £200,000. None of the local directors had been consulted and when it emerged that Hibs boss Jim Duffy had negotiated directly with Ron Dixon in Canada, Dens managing-director Nigel Squire resigned in protest.

However, John McCormack felt the moves were in the best interests of the club and in an interview with *The Scottish Daily Mail,* he stated: "Both were free to move on at the end of season with Tosh unwilling to sign for more than a year and Power demanding far more than Dundee could afford. I was told to get some money in and if I hadn't agreed to transfer them I would have had to sell either Iain Anderson or Jerry O'Driscoll, or both."

Dundee property developer Michael Johnston, who had just tabled a £1.2 million bid for the club, declared himself angry and disappointed at the transfers and immediately withdrew his offer. The takeover situation was now coming to a head and in late March, Ron Dixon arrived back in Dundee to dispose of all his Scottish interests, including Ballygrogan Farm on the Mull of Kintyre and his home at St Maddoes near Errol, as well as Dundee Football Club.

Jim Duffy's departure had seen a renewed buyout bid by Peter and Jimmy Marr and after making a verbal offer in February, a formal written offer of £1.3 million to buy his shares and repay his loans was lodged the following month. Ron Dixon claimed that he had never regarded Michael Johnston as a serious contender before confirming that a deal with the Marr brothers was on the cards: "My time is up. I've been here five years and I will leave the club in a far healthier state than it was when I arrived."

"The future plans for the club have to be right for me because I don't want to come back here in a year and discover houses where the stadium used to be. Peter Marr appears to have all the personal qualities I regard as important for anyone wanting to buy the club for he is someone with a love of football and Dundee F.C. in particular."

However, although Dixon had wanted to have matters tied up by April 4th, a delay while the Takeover Panel studied all the relevant details of the transaction following a minority shareholder's complaint, saw him jet off on a business trip to Russia after resigning his directorship, and Malcolm Reid was left as acting chairman.

Meanwhile, the loss of Power and Tosh had blunted Dundee's promotion thrust and although unsuccessful with bids for midfielders Grant Johnson (Dundee United) and Billy Davies (Motherwell), and Clydebank striker James Grady, John McCormack beat the March 31st signing deadline to pay £70,000 for Clyde's ex-Partick Thistle and Sligo Rovers hitman Eddie Annand (24), scorer of 50 goals for the Broadwood side over the past two seasons.

There was no glory start for the new striker and after a 2-0 home defeat by Scottish Cup finalists Falkirk, both Annand and Adamczuk were dismissed as Dundee lost by an identical scoreline in the crunch game against Airdrie at Broadwood. That left the Dark Blues eight points in arrears, a lead that proved insurmountable as they finished third, two points behind Airdrie, who went on to lose 5-2 on aggregate to Hibs in the play-off for a Premier place.

However, the Dens men had trailed runaway leaders St Johnstone by a massive 22 points, and, had they reached the play-off and subsequently achieved promotion, the team would have virtually had to be rebuilt. There were a number of promising youngsters but too many others had been found wanting when the chips were down.

As one of the more experienced players, Dave Winnie ought to have led by example, yet, like Chic Charnley, he had twice been suspended after accumulating 12 bookings. Similarly, George Shaw's return had not been a success with John McCormack admitting: "I brought him back and made him the club's best-paid player but it was a mistake for somehow he no longer had the hunger of old."

CHAPTER THIRTY-ONE

New Ownership

Demoralised supporters could only wait and wonder whether the club would change hands for there was little future under the ownership of Ron Dixon. The Marrs' takeover bid was to drag on into mid-summer with the London-based Takeover Panel, concerned at earlier alleged improper dealings involving the club, taking a close interest in proceedings.

A £1.3 million deal, which included the repayment of Dixon's outstanding loans as well as 6p per share for his 72% holding, had been agreed. However, this was deemed unsatisfactory since minority shareholders who had paid 60p per share at the 1992 share issue would be well out of pocket. A figure of 14p per share was decided and in mid-June, the Marrs, who seven months earlier had bought the land bordering Sandeman Street behind the T.C. Keay end of Dens, were given the official go-ahead to take control.

The deal finally went through on June 17th but not before a worrying night for the prospective new owners. Along with their Glasgow-based team of accountants and solicitors, the Marrs spent the night thrashing out the final details over an open phone link to Dixon and his advisors in Vancouver, with another of the Marrs' lawyers in the Canadian city to present a banker's draft to Dixon on completion of the agreement.

At one point, the negotiations looked like collapsing and it was a relieved Peter Marr who confirmed: "Everything was signed and sealed just before dawn. We're 10 weeks behind schedule and over £100,000 worse off through additional legal and accountant's fees, but it's all been worth it to own the club we've supported since Primary School. Dealing with Dixon and trying to get the guarantees we needed was very, very difficult although that's just the way he does business. Previously, almost £1 million was misdirected on the dog-racing facilities but the good thing is we have taken over a club with very little debt."

"I think it is safe to say this is the start of an important new period in the club's history. Our principal aim will be to get people supporting us, both at the gate and through sponsorship. I think there is a lot of goodwill that has not been tapped recently and I would like to put that right. We genuinely have the best interests of Dundee F.C. at heart and will be doing everything we can to bring the good times back to Dens, though we will need the help of the Dundee people."

The takeover marked a close to Ron Dixon's five-year reign during which the club had spent three seasons in the First Division. Yet, in his early days, the Canadian had certainly splashed the cash for players like Leighton, Vrto, Wieghorst, Czachowski and Adamczuk. However, the disillusioned chairman-in-exile had long since made it clear that he would make no further investment and that players would have to be sold to recoup his loans to the club.

The remaining directors Malcolm Reid, Bob Hynd, John Black and Harry Leadingham, the latter a close friend of Michael Johnson and appointed just seven months earlier, would all depart. Peter Marr would become chief executive with his brother Jimmy as chairman. Derek Souter would return as marketing director, while Jim Connor, who along with Souter had excelled on the commercial side at St Joseph's Juniors, would become commercial manager with Brian Gray as his assistant.

Earlier, the law courts had judged that Souter had been unfairly dismissed by Dundee in 1992 and a four-year legal wrangle ended with the former commercial consultant due almost £300,000 from the club. In the interim, Souter had been awarded Ron Dixon's house in Errol as security but now he came to a financial arrangement with the Marrs as part of their deal with Dixon.

Previously well-known in local football circles through their involvement with Timex Amateurs and Tayport

A new start - new owners Peter and Jimmy Marr with Derek Souter (centre) brought fresh hope to the Dens Park club.
DC Thomson

Juniors, the Marrs' five-year spell in charge of St Joseph's had that season culminated in five trophy successes. The brothers were optimistic Dundee could return to the upper echelons of Scottish football and although refusing to set a timescale, they were hopeful that the club might soon see home gates of 5,000 to 6,000.

"I won't be making any promises I can't keep," said Peter Marr in *The Courier*. "I know the feeling for this club because there are addresses from all over the world on the 900-plus list of shareholders. Fans have phoned, knocked on my door and stopped me in the street to wish me all the best. Supporters like these deserve success and we'll be aiming to give it to them. In turn, if they back us by buying season tickets, help with sponsorship and generally get behind the team, the increased revenue will hopefully allow us to get better players."

Marr continued: "We want the young fans in this area to support Dundee and I'd like to see more kids in the streets wearing Dundee strips than United ones." The new chief executive also made no secret of his intention to overhaul the club's youth policy. Out went Stuart Rafferty and, although Ray Farningham remained as a youth coach, former Dundee striker Kenny Cameron (54), who had masterminded the rise of St Joseph's since leaving Dundee United in 1995, would take charge of Youth Development as well as visiting local schools and communities to coach youngsters.

Well respected locally and a highly regarded SFA staff coach at Largs, Cameron's coaching experience, particularly at Tannadice where he had been a key figure in United's successful youth development programme, made him the ideal choice for Dundee. The club already had some promising young talent and, that summer, Iain Anderson had turned in some brilliant performances for the Scotland Under-21s in the Umbro tournament at Toulon.

Jerry O'Driscoll, who had finished Dundee's top scorer with 11 goals, was another exciting prospect. However, in May, the Scots-born striker had opted for the Republic of Ireland Under-19s, who were to play in the World Youth Cup in Malaysia. O'Driscoll impressed in a friendly for the Irish against Belgium but after sustaining a shin injury in a later trial against Cork City, he was forced to withdraw from the glamour trip.

There had been rumours that a more experienced man such as Jocky Scott, Jimmy Nicholl or Kenny Cameron might become manager but John McCormack was given a vote of confidence by the new owners. Earlier, the Dens boss had handed free transfers to Kevin Bain, Gary McKeown, Tommy McQueen, David Winnie, Iain Ferguson and, for a second time, goalkeeper Barry Thomson. Andy Cargill and Dave Fisher had previously moved on, to Forfar and Montrose respectively, and now Dundee were left with just 12 full-time players.

Battle-hardened - Jim McInally was a key man in midfield.

McCormack believed Dundee required a nucleus of seasoned professionals and his first move was to fix up former Scotland internationals Brian Irvine (32), and Jim McInally (33), on two-year deals. The towering Irvine, surprisingly released after 12 years at Aberdeen, joined the Dark Blues in preference to Premier League Motherwell while McInally, who had previously played 11 games for Dundee while on loan from Celtic in 1984, cost £20,000 from Dundee United.

The signings continued with the arrival of 26-year-old Clydebank striker James Grady for £25,000 - one third of the fee Dundee had offered prior to the March transfer deadline. Lee Maddison (24), a full-back, and midfielder John McGlashan (30), the latter a life-long Dark Blue, were fixed up on free transfers from Northampton and Rotherham, respectively, while Darren Magee, a 21-year-old midfielder who had battled back to prominence with Pollok Juniors after his release by Dundee in 1996, returned to Dens.

Encouragingly, over 3,000 parents and young fans turned up at Dens for an Open Day before a trip to North-West England brought wins over Third Division Macclesfield (3-0), and Vauxhall Conference sides Lancaster City (2-0), Barrow (3-0), and Morecambe (1-0). On their return, Dundee drew 1-1 with Portsmouth and former Chester and Tranmere central-defender Dave Rogers (21), was signed on freedom-of-contract after a successful trial against the English First Division side.

Although Billy Thomson's first-team career was over due to a recurring back injury, the one-time Scotland international would remain as goalkeeping coach. That left Garry McGlyn as the only goalkeeper at Dens and, when ex-Hearts goalie Gary O'Connor was released after a period on trial, Dundee paid £100,000 for Livingston's Robert Douglas with the £30,000-rated Kevin Magee going to Almondvale.

After so long in the doldrums, things were buzzing at Dens. The backroom staff of football coaches Kenny Cameron and Ray Farningham, sprint coach Harry Hay and physio Jim Crosby was further augmented by former St Joseph's kit manager Willie Dryden, while groundsman Willie Robertson was given a budget to purchase some much-needed new equipment!

John McCormack was upbeat about Dundee's chances: "I have managed to bring in eight new faces and there is now a hardness about this squad which pleases me. Guys like Irvine - for whom two bids have already been refused - and McInally have been through it all before and they know what it takes. My hope is that they can transfer that spirit to the rest of the team."

Now "Cowboy" took the welcome but recently unprecedented step of naming his team 24 hours before kick-off. For the Dens opener against Falkirk on Saturday, August 2nd, Dundee fielded: Douglas; Smith, Irvine, Rogers; Adamczuk, McInally, Magee, Maddison; O'Driscoll, Annand, Grady. Substitutes - Elliot, Anderson, McGlashan.

On a sunny day, over 4,500 fans turned up as Dundee ran out 3-0 winners against the 1997 Scottish Cup runners-up. Robert Douglas had all the physical attributes of Manchester United's Danish international Peter Schmeichal and the new keeper quickly paid his way with a superb one-handed save from a Kevin James header before Jerry O'Driscoll powered home the opener. On the hour, Annand added a second and

On the spot - Jerry O'Driscoll grabs the opener in the 3-0 win over much-fancied Falkirk at Dens to get Dundee's promotion challenge off to the best possible start. Sadly, the talented young striker would not fulfil his early promise.   DC Thomson

just on full-time, 17-year-old substitute John Elliot fired a penalty past Nelson to get Dundee off to a cracking start.

That scoreline was repeated against Partick Thistle at Firhill and the Dark Blues maintained their 100% league record with a 1-0 victory over St Mirren at Dens. In the League Cup, it took a last-gasp goal by O'Driscoll to break the stalemate at home against East Stirling but they would progress no further. In the next round, Aberdeen departed with a 3-0 win but although Dundee also made an early exit from the Challenge Cup, losing 1-0 to Airdrie at Broadwood, cup progress was secondary to the primary objective of promotion.

In late August, McCormack's men squandered a two-goal lead in a 2-2 draw against much-fancied Raith Rovers at Dens. The loss of Grady with concussion and Adamczuk with a rib knock disrupted their rythm but with Raith taking a more positive approach, Dundee lost control of midfield and, in the end, were fortunate to take a point.

The manager had set his team out to play in either a 3-4-3 or 3-5-2 formation but a lack of composure in the crucial "boiler-house" area of the team now threatened to derail their efforts. Wing-backs Adamczuk and Maddison were reliable defenders, the Pole providing attacking options down the right, with Iain Anderson wide on the left. Grafting incessantly, Jim McInally provided vital cover in front of the back three and, alongside him, in a more forward midfield role, lay Darren Magee, a player of great stamina and commitment but without the composure or flair to ensure that Dundee controlled the vital midfield area.

To remedy this, the Dens boss exchanged the unsettled George Shaw for Dunfermline's attacking left-back Derek Fleming before signing St Mirren midfielder Russell Kelly on freedom-of-contract. Eddie Annand had formed a useful partnership with James Grady, but although he netted his fifth goal in Dundee's 2-1 win at Ayr, their five-game unbeaten league run ended in a 2-0 defeat to Sandy Clark's strong-going Hamilton at Dens on September 20th.

However, the Dark Blues bounced back with another three straight wins before a John Elliot goal earned a 1-1 draw at Falkirk in late October. Dundee had been in pole position from the outset and after 10 games, they remained top, two points ahead of Hamilton with Raith Rovers and the Bairns just a few points further behind.

Dave Rogers had emerged as a determined defender with a sense of humour much appreciated by the Dundee fans. Soon after crashing home a late penalty in the 1-0 home win over Airdrie, the defender went off injured and later claimed that he had been kicked by Airdrie boss Alex MacDonald as he limped past the away dugout. The jovial Liverpudlian also claimed to have told MacDonald: "Thanks very much, we have three points and you don't. Have a nice trip home and I'll see you next time!"

Later MacDonald remarked: "Anyone who knew me as a player would know that if I'd kicked him, he would have been stretchered off." The SFA, though, were unimpressed by the widely publicised dialogue and although John McCormack later apologised, saying the player had stumbled over the leg of Airdrie coach John Binnie rather than MacDonald, both Rogers and McCormack were fined for bringing the game into disrepute.

However, five points - all at home - were dropped from the next four games although there was a battling 1-0 win against Raith Rovers at Stark's Park. Over 30 minutes remained when Derek Fleming was sent off for a a bad tackle on Craig Dargo, but, soon afterwards, Jim McInally ran fully 50 yards to head home a superb cross by Grady. As time ran

Turning point - James Grady celebrates his hat-trick at Ayr where Dundee recovered a two goal deficit to win 5-2.

Mirrorpix

out, Robert Douglas was forced into a series of breathtaking saves but Dundee held on and, later, McInally declared: "We're confident as opposed to arrogant but it's important that we now go on to win our home games and show a bit more creativity."

On November 29th, Dundee travelled to Cliftonhill for a vital clash against second-placed Hamilton, who, temporarily homeless, were renting the tumbledown Coatbridge ground from lowly Albion Rovers. The opening period was a battle for midfield supremacy but with half-time looming, James Grady broke the deadlock with a fierce 18-yarder that was deflected past Ferguson. That was his first of a hat-trick as Dundee went on to win 4-0, with Russell Kelly excelling in an attacking midfield role, just 24 hours after a deal for creative Raith Rovers midfielder Paul Harvey had collapsed due to his excessive wage demands!

Another five points from their next three games left Dundee seven points clear of Raith with Falkirk a point further adrift. Now with 1997 coming to an end, back-to-back home games against their closest challengers would provide the sternest test yet of the Dens men's promotion hopes. But, there was to be little festive cheer as they went down 1-0 to Falkirk then had to settle for a share of the spoils in a 1-1 draw against Raith on January 3rd.

Indeed, the slick-moving Bairns, who had scored through David Moss, had looked more like league leaders than Dundee and after the match, an upset John McCormack commented: "Once again we've flopped in our own backyard. I'm as demented as the fans and maybe I've been too loyal to some players. We have been working hard and grinding out results but maybe now is the time to get another couple of bullets in our gun."

Dundee's defence was second to none. Robert Douglas was regarded as one of Scotland's brightest goalkeeping prospects, while the aerial ability and the never-say-die attitude of Brian Irvine and Dave Rogers plus the all-round

defensive abilities of Barry Smith had been a major factor in Dundee's record of conceding just 10 goals in 20 league games.

However, there remained a lack of creativity from midfield and equally there had been a desperate lack of punch up front with Dundee failing to score in four out of their five home games prior to drawing with Raith.

James Grady was top scorer with eight goals, two more than Eddie Annand, who had managed just one goal in 14 games since September 13th. The ex-Clyde hitman was capable of some spectacular strikes but Grady had quickly become the fans' favourite with his non-stop, all-action style of play.

Initially, McCormack had fielded Annand, Grady and O'Driscoll before reverting to two strikers when Iain Anderson was restored to the team. O'Driscoll and Annand were each tried alongside Grady and when the Annand-Grady partnership flourished, O'Driscoll was restricted to short spells as a substitute. Great things had been expected of the Aberdonian but he struggled to make an impact due to a lack of fitness, initially due to missing much of pre-season training because of his shin injury.

Now John McCormack sought to remedy the recent goal drought and, in late December, he paid £25,000 for 28-year-old Stirling Albion striker Steve McCormick, who had been a prolific scorer for the Forthbank club. On January 3rd, the giant hitman made his debut against Raith and despite his lack of match practice, showed some clever touches.

It was an entertaining match despite the gale-force wind and rain but once again the visitors looked the more accomplished side and, worryingly, Falkirk's 6-0 victory over Stirling Albion had moved them within three points of Dundee. John McCormack was blunt: "We've now dropped 17 points from eleven home games compared to just four on our travels. That is unacceptable and has to be addressed soon if it is not to cost us the title."

A week later, things looked dire when Dundee trailed 2-0 to Ayr United after 14 minutes at Somerset Park but there was a spirited fightback. Brian Irvine headed home a Maddison free-kick and a quick one-two by Grady and McCormick put them ahead after 28 minutes. It was a remarkable turnaround and as the blitz continued, James Grady added another two to complete his hat-trick in a timely 5-2 win for the Dark Blues.

Later that month, Dundee overcame St Mirren 4-2 in the third round of the Scottish Cup at Dens. But, although four goals ahead and with Saints down to nine men - Alan Combe and Andy Roddie were sent off - soon after half-time, they again ended up struggling, a pattern that was repeated in the league game against Hamilton at Dens

A McCormick goal to the good, the jitters kicked in after the interval and after Adamczuk was red-carded for a wild tackle near the end, the Accies grabbed a last-gasp equaliser. Players and fans alike were stunned and, once again, the lack of a midfield playmaker - another bid to sign Motherwell midfielder Billy Davies had failed due to his personal demands - who could hold the ball and dictate the tempo of the game, had cost them dear.

Away from home, Dundee had often employed a five-man midfield and their ability to hit on the break had been highly successful. But although the team had a wonderful rapport with their large travelling support, the home crowd were becoming increasingly unhappy at the lack of entertainment at Dens.

Many felt it was only a matter of time before Dundee's lead at the top was whittled away and the directors, too, were deeply concerned, especially at the home record of just four wins from 12 league games. Now, they insisted that the players should, like St Johnstone, work a six-day week and undertake extra training in the afternoons, a directive that did not sit well with the manager, who later revealed that for the first time he felt under real pressure.

On February 7th, the Dark Blues bounced back with a 3-1 win over Stirling Albion at Forthbank to go five points above second-placed Raith Rovers, who had recently defeated Falkirk. In his post-match interview, John McCormack declared: "We're bang on course for promotion and have been all season." However, it was already too late for the Dens boss and the following day he was sacked after being summoned to the ground from his Glasgow home.

At a press conference on Monday, February 9th, Jocky Scott - one of the most prominent figures in the club's post-war history - was named as Dundee's new manager on a two-and-a-half year contract. Scott had spent 24 years at Dens as player, coach and manager and since leaving them in 1988, he had also managed Aberdeen (jointly with Alex. Smith), Dunfermline and Arbroath. He was then assistant-manager and latterly caretaker-boss at Hibs before accepting a coaching job with Dundee United.

Scott expressed sympathy for his predecessor and admitted that he was in a no-win situation for the fans would now judge anything less than promotion as failure. However, he

Shut-out king - Rab Douglas went from strength to strength in goal.

was confident of success: "I've met the players and told them the Premier League is the only place to be." Scott intimated that an assistant-manager would be appointed and that every member of the playing staff, including the transfer-listed Robbie Raeside and the out-of-favour Gavin Rae and Jerry O'Driscoll, would get their chance while moves would also be made to strengthen the squad.

In an interview with "Bob Angus" of *The*

Rock steady - Brian Irvine heads clear against Partick Thistle. His experience was crucial in the promotion battle. DC Thomson

Evening Telegraph, Peter Marr gave his reasons for John McCormack's sacking: "I would start by saying no-one can question the amount of hard work John put in at Dens. However, that could not change the fact things were not heading in what we felt was the right direction and we had to act. We feel John has taken us as far as he can. Replacing him was a hard decision and it would have been easy to use our league position to put off making it, but that would not have been the right thing to do."

Vice-chairman Derek Souter concurred, adding: "We inherited John McCormack but we feel Jocky Scott is the man to take us forward. Football is now a professional business with serious levels of investment. If our man fails, at least it will be our man. It's not only what you see on the park but what you see off it as well, it's the delegation, control, training, organisation and all aspects and if you've been in business you know. It was a hard decision and we knew we'd be damned if we did it and damned if we didn't."

Understandably, McCormack was bitter about his departure: "Firstly, I can hold my head high over what I achieved at the club. They are on course for promotion and every player I signed has done a shift. James Grady has been brilliant and Dave Rogers outstanding, as have Brian Irvine, Jim McInally and others. If Dundee go up, it will be because of the work I've done - if they don't, it'll be because the board have made a mess of it. After previously being told I had two years, I was informed in November that I had to get the team up this season, presumably because of the breakaway talk."

He then claimed the directors had ordered him to sign a player he didn't rate: "At a board meeting last week, I was told that I had 24 hours to sign a player they wanted. I even went as far as interviewing him but he didn't impress and I didn't rate him an asset to the club. The board still wanted me to sign him but if I did, who would be picking the team?"

"When I told them I wouldn't be signing this player, I gave them eight alternatives ranging from £15,000 to £175,000 but although they said they'd discuss them, they'd obviously made their minds up about me by then. I tried to bring in first Peter Weir, then Paul Hegarty as assistant-manager but financial arrangements were the stumbling block. Last week, I gave them two other names I would have liked but again they didn't get back to me."

The west coast media, many of whom were unfamiliar with Dundee's poor home performances, were incredulous. But although Jim McDonald and Jack Jolly, who were Dundee scouts in central Scotland, resigned in protest, fans mostly agreed with the decision although there was great sympathy for McCormack.

Robin Grimmond, editor of the Dundee F.C. fanzine *Eh Mind O' Gillie*, explained: "Anyone who watched the team regularly must have realised there was something wrong. They have not been playing well and are almost top of the league by default. It's sad to see a good clubman like Cowboy go but it had to be done. My hope is that he is properly looked after financially because while he may not have been the man for the job, you could not question his commitment to Dundee."

There was considerable feeling for McCormack in the

dressing room but veteran defender Brian Irvine, who had earlier spent three years under Scott at Aberdeen, rated the new manager highly: "He's one of the best in the business and it's now up to us to help him complete the task which John started."

Scott's first test came with the visit to Dingwall in the fourth round of the Scottish Cup against

On the run - Eddie Annand and Iain Anderson against Ross County. DC Thomson

Third Division Ross County. The former Highland League team, who included former Dens Parker, Roy McBain, had defeated Airdrie at the previous stage and around 1,000 Dundee fans had made the trip north to take their places amongst the 4,500 crowd at Victoria Park.

In 54 minutes, Douglas was beaten by a spectacular lob from Derek Adams but the introduction of Adamczuk lifted Dundee and within eight minutes, the galloping Pole crossed a great ball for John McGlashan to head past Nicky Walker. In the end, it could have gone either way and the new manager was glad to get the first game under his belt without mishap.

Adamczuk, Annand and Raeside replaced Tully, McCormick and Fleming for the Dens replay on February 17th, but County again made it tough, twice hitting woodwork in the first half. Soon after the break, Eddie Annand thumped a powerful left-foot shot past Walker and with the deadlock broken, Dundee went on to win 3-0.

With Smith, Irvine and Rogers forming an impressive defensive unit, Robbie Raeside had found himself out of the picture and, transfer-listed at £25,000, he had almost joined Ayr United. Now, he had marked his return with a fine headed goal and the former Raith man would play his part in the crucial months ahead.

Four days later, a late Steve McCormick goal gave Dundee a 1-0 win over Airdrie, their first at home in three months. That put them eight points clear at the top and to bolster his squad, Jocky Scott brought in out-of-favour Hearts striker John Robertson (33), on a month's loan. Over the past 15 years, the former Scotland international had been a prolific goalscorer for Hearts and although managing just one goal for Dundee, his experience proved invaluable, his loan spell coinciding with victories over Partick Thistle (a) 2-1, St Mirren (h) 1-0, Morton (h) 2-0 and Hamilton (a) 2-1 as the Dark Blues continued to set the pace at the top.

Within 60 seconds of kick-off, James Grady scored the vital goal against St Mirren, but long before the end, the

So near - Robbie Raeside outjumps the Rangers defence to head for goal in the Scottish Cup quarter-final replay at Dens. DC Thomson

Dundee fans were desperately whistling for full-time. John Robertson had his own theory about the problem: "Previously, I wondered why the home record was so poor compared to away form. I think it's because players are scared to be the one to make a mistake at Dens. If the fans here really want Premier League football they must try and help the players relax and the best way to do that is to get behind the team."

Now, Dundee could concentrate on their Scottish Cup quarter-final clash against Rangers at Ibrox on Monday, March 9th. Although the game was televised live on BSB-Sky, almost 3,000 Dundee fans made the trip, their first visit to the Govan ground since 1994. And, with John Robertson cup-tied, Jocky Scott sprang a surprise by recalling the more competitive Darren Magee in preferrence to Iain Anderson in a three-man central midfield.

In a fiery opening, Negri thundered a shot off the bar but although Rangers continued to hold the territorial advantage, a series of brilliant saves by Robert Douglas and sterling defensive work kept the Light Blues at bay in a no-scoring draw. Robertson's comments had been taken to heart and Jocky Scott was full of praise for the Dundee fans in the 40,309 crowd: "The only thing that topped the team's performance was that of the fans who were magnificent. I've been to Ibrox with a few clubs but I've never heard an away support make so much noise for so long."

The new boss had already shown a refreshing willingness to make tactical changes and McCormick and Anderson replaced Annand and Rogers for the midweek replay nine days later. Once more, there was live BSB-Sky coverage, and for the first time in years Dens housed a near-capacity 12,500 crowd with the 7,000 home fans in the South Enclosure and Provost Road end providing a colourful mass of dark blue, red and white.

Belying their billing as underdogs, Dundee took Rangers by storm and in 11 minutes, James Grady took advantage of a goalmouth melee to curl the ball into the net. However, Rangers were soon level, Gough nodding back a long throw by Vidmar for the ever-alert McCoist, now 35 years old and back in the side along with Ian Durrant, to glance home.

And although Dundee battled back, a well-worked 54th minute free-kick saw McCoist beat Douglas with a low shot. The Dark Blues were unable to retrieve the tie, but it had been a gallant effort and that weekend, they recovered from the loss of an early goal to win 2-1 against Hamilton at dilapidated Cliftonhill.

Although upset at losing Lee Maddison with a fractured ankle, Dens boss Scott was delighted at the result: "The Rangers match took its toll mentally as well as physically and to go from playing before a full-house to just 1,800 here was difficult." He appealed for the fans' backing in the next home game against Stirling Albion and pointed out that there were some tricky away games in prospect over the next few weeks.

Both players and fans responded well and two marvellous strikes from Eddie Annand - a stunning overhead kick, then a lofted shot from the edge of the box for the second - gave a more confident-looking Dundee the points and with a 12-point margin over their closest rivals, another seven points from the last six games against Airdrie (a), Raith Rovers (a), Ayr Utd. (h), Falkirk (a), Partick Thistle (h) and

Strike force - Steve McCormick and James Grady celebrate at Airdrie.

St Mirren (a) would then ensure that the title was bound for Dens.

On April 4th, Dundee faced a major hurdle against Airdrie at Broadwood and, once again, they opted for a three-man central-midfield of Brian Grant - the experienced 34-year-old ex-Aberdeen midfielder recently signed for a nominal fee from Hibs - Jim McInally and Darren Magee.

On a muddy surface, battle-hardened Airdrie did most of the early pressing but it was the Dark Blues who went ahead after 17 minutes, Eddie Annand shrugging off Sandison and Jack before slipping the ball past Martin.

A Kenny Black free-kick rattled the junction of post and bar before Steve Cooper equalised and with Dundee seemingly content to hit on the break, there were a number of near escapes. However, with 18 minutes remaining, Jocky Scott replaced Grant with the pacy Iain Anderson then brought on Steve McCormick for Annand. That provided added impetus and with four minutes left, a quickly taken Anderson free-kick was cut back by Grady and McCormick slid in at the far post in to net the winner!

It was fitting reward for the gangling striker who had given his all since arriving at Dens and, at the end, players, officials and fans celebrated noisily on receiving confirmation that second-placed Raith had lost at home to Morton in the dying minutes.

That was Dundee's seventh successive league win and with a 15-point lead with just five games left, a grinning Jocky Scott acknowledged: "We are nearly there. It was a tough game on a slippery surface and although we had two players booked, I was really pleased at our discipline."

Just one point was required to clinch the championship and, on Saturday, April 11th, there was great excitement amongst the near 7,000 crowd at Stark's Park. There was one change, Iain Anderson returning in place of Brian Grant as Dundee lined up: Douglas; Raeside, Irvine, Smith; Adamczuk, McInally, Magee, Rogers; Anderson, Annand, Grady. Subs. - Tully, Grant, McCormick.

Despite the heady atmosphere, Dundee looked nervy and hesitant and it was Jimmy Nicholl's side who won the 50-50 challenges and pushed forward at every opportunity. By half-time, the sunshine had given way to dark skies and heavy sleet and there was another setback for Dundee when Brian Irvine was forced to remain in the dressing room with an achilles injury.

Shortly after the restart, Raith went ahead when Paul Hartley beat Rogers to slip the ball past Douglas. At last, Dundee stepped up a gear and in 59 minutes, Adamczuk was downed after a powerful run down the right. From just over the halfway line, Iain Anderson flighted the free-kick

Magic moment - Eddie Annand heads the equaliser against Raith to clinch the First Division Championship.   Dave McRitchie

beyond goalkeeper Guido van de Kamp to the far post and up soared Eddie Annand to direct his header into the far corner of the net!

The travelling fans roared their relief but after a brief spell in control, Dundee fell back. Soon they had six men strung along the box and this would prove highly effective amidst the nerve-jangling tension near the end. The Dark Blues held on for a 1-1 draw, a result that secured their promotion as First Division Champions and sparked jubilant scenes amongst their 5,000 supporters ranged around three sides of the Kirkcaldy ground.

Later, Jocky Scott admitted: "It wasn't Dundee's best performance of the season, but with so many fans following us here, the result was the main thing. It's great to be going back up to the Premier League and the players deserve the credit for taking us there. We've been lucky to avoid injuries and suspensions but the determination shown by our core of 14 or 15 players has been first class. We can now afford to relax a bit until the end of the season which is maybe just as well as the last few minutes of that game seemed to go on for ever."

As a gesture to their fans, the board decided to make the home game against Ayr United a gala occasion with reduced admission prices and pre-match entertainment. Dens Park was suitably bathed in sunshine as an 8,104 crowd - their largest home league gate of the season - gave the new First Division Champions a rousing reception when they took to the field but, within five minutes, there was silence as Dundee fell a goal behind.

James Grady netted with a 34th minute penalty but later missed another and the score ended 1-1. The large crowd remained to see Scottish League secretary Peter Donald present the First Division Championship trophy to skipper Barry Smith. But although the home players who were now bedecked with scarves and coloured hats, went on a lap of honour before the cheering fans, many were disappointed at Dundee's failure to win.

Indeed, with the title and promotion assured, the season ended in anti-climax with three defeats but the main objective had been achieved and, as a bonus, the players were rewarded with a sunshine holiday to Majorca.

After four years in the First Division - Dundee's longest-ever peace-time spell out of top flight football - failure to go up would have been a bitter blow. The Dark Blues had done well to overcome the challenge posed by Falkirk and Raith Rovers - both good footballing sides - but, based on a strong, well organised defence, they had shown great consistency to string together an impressive 14-game unbeaten run during which the championship was clinched at Stark's Park.

Chief executive Peter Marr declared himself a happy man: "I've been a Dundee fan all my life and as a boy can remember crying when a game against St Johnstone was called off because of snow. Myself, Jimmy and Derek Souter are not in this to make a quick profit. We're in it for the long haul and that is because we care about the club. We expect our turnover to treble next season and that should help provide funds for the manager. We went for Ian Durrant back in November and nobody should doubt our ambition."

Fittingly, Jocky Scott was named Bell's First Division Manager of the Month for April. The Dens boss had kept the players on their toes by altering the team as occasion dictated and, in the end, had successfully negotiated a hazardous run-in to take the title. Clearly, there had been results of great significance - the 3-0 success over Falkirk got John McCormack's fledgling side off to a great start, while away wins over Raith and Hamilton in November restored morale after some shaky home form.

Then, with just two wins from their previous seven games, Dundee's comeback from two down to win 5-2 at Ayr in January was a defining moment before another major hurdle was negotiated with the 2-1 success over Airdrie on April 4th. Had Dundee and Raith's results been reversed that day and the Dens men then lost at Kirkcaldy, their lead would have been down to six points. And with a hazardous trip to Falkirk, it would have meant a frantic finale!

Scottish League First Division 1997-98							
	P	W	D	L	F	A	Pts
Dundee	36	20	10	6	52-24		70
Falkirk	36	19	8	9	56-41		65
Raith Rovs.	36	17	9	10	51-33		60
Airdrie	36	16	12	8	42-35		60
Morton	36	12	10	14	47-48		46
St Mirren	36	11	8	17	41-53		41
Ayr Utd.	36	10	10	16	40-56		40
Hamilton	36	9	11	16	43-56		38
Partick Th.	36	8	12	16	45-55		36
Stirling Alb.	36	8	10	18	40-56		34

Robert Douglas had made 17 shut-outs, conceding just 24 league goals, and, in March, he was rewarded with a Scotland 'B' international cap against Wales at Broadwood. Goalkeeping coach Billy Thomson was full of praise for the ex-bricklayer and part-time fireman: "John McCormack sent me to watch him in a summer tournament at Livingston and I was impressed. He had great presence and I loved the way he came for crosses. He's only 25 and learning all the time. If he continues to improve, he could well carve an international future for himself."

Dundee F.C.'s 1997-98 First Division Championship winning squad after clinching the title against Raith Rovers at Stark's Park. (BACK, left to right) Brian Irvine, Harry Hay (sprint coach), John Elliot, Dave Rogers, Russell Kelly, Rab Douglas, Darren Magee, Steve McCormick, Robbie Raeside, Craig Tully, Gavin Rae, Jerry O'Driscoll. FRONT - Lee Maddison, Jim McInally, Iain Anderson, Barry Smith, Eddie Annand, James Grady, Brian Grant, Dariusz Adamczuk. Inset - the managers, John McCormack (left) and Jocky Scott (right).

Alan Richardson Pix-AR

Jim McInally and Brian Irvine were both in the twilight of their careers yet their influence had been immense, the redoubtable Irvine forming an excellent partnership alongside Barry Smith at the heart of the iron-curtain Dens defence. Polish international Dariusz Adamczuk remained a firm favourite and, although frustratingly inconsistent, there was no doubting Iain Anderson's ability which had earned him ten Scotland Under-21 international caps. The young winger's trickery and imagination had often been the key which unlocked opposing defences and a significant number of goals had resulted from his surging runs and crosses.

Up front, 18-goal James Grady had been a real buzz-bomb while strike partner Eddie Annand had contributed 14 goals despite suffering a loss of form over the winter months. Indeed, Grady, who had finished Dundee's top scorer with 18 goals, was voted the SPFA's First Division Player of the Year ahead of team-mate Robert Douglas, David Moss (Falkirk) and Alex. Bone (Stirling).

Barry Smith, though, had been a key man and Jocky Scott paid a glowing tribute to his skipper: "Barry has been absolutely superb for us all season and I was surprised that he wasn't in the running for the SPFA prize. He is consistent, makes the big tackle when it is needed and leads the team very well."

No fewer than eleven of the title-winning squad had been signed by John McCormack and his contribution to Dundee's title win was widely acknowledged. Cowboy's gesture in sending a congratulatory fax to Dundee's management and players was much appreciated and several players would later enjoy a celebratory meal with their former boss in Glasgow.

Earlier, McCormack, frustrated at the board's failure to offer him compensation, had instructed an arrestment of Dundee's share of the proceeds from their Scottish Cup tie at Ibrox. This was to ensure there was money in place to

meet a possible court action for lost earnings from the remaining 16 months of his £40,000 a year contract as well as a £10,000 commission he claimed was due for selling Paul Tosh and Lee Power to Hibs.

Peter Marr said: "We think it ridiculous that the players were sold while Dundee still had a chance of achieving the play-off spot and there's no way we'll agree to pay a five-figure sum as a commission." It was to prove an increasingly acrimonious dispute but in the end an out-of-court settlement was agreed.

Now Dundee could now look forward to life in the newly formed Scottish Premier League which, in May, had finally received SFA approval after an earlier special meeting of the Scottish League voted 58-20 to allow the 10 clubs to depart. It would be one up, one down in the new set-up, although the league would expand to a minimum of 12 clubs in season 2000-2001. The SPL would negotiate their own TV deals, there would be an annual winter break in January while the formation of a new under-21 league would allow teams to field three over-age players.

To comply with the new SPL rules, Dundee now had to ensure that they had a 10,000 all-seated stadium by next July. In 1997, Peter Marr had asked town planners to identify any areas of Dundee large enough for a stadium, ideally with no buildings requiring demolition. Rumours that the club intended building a new stadium at the grounds of St John's High School proved unfounded and, that January, plans to redevelop Dens were displayed in the local press after their approval by Dundee City Council.

However, the board's preferred option remained a new purpose-built stadium and both Linlathen School - later sold to a supermarket - and Riverside Drive were mentioned as possible sites before *The Evening Telegraph* speculated that Dundee's first choice was a £5-million 14,000-capacity stadium at Caird Park with training pitches, extensive car parking and a soccer school of excellence.

On April 11th, Peter Marr had declared: "Our preferred option remains moving to a brand-new stadium somewhere in the city. Starting from scratch we could build a ground to our own specification and it would still cost less than redeveloping Dens. Caird Park isn't feasible because we need to start work soon and the fact that it was a gift to the city - by Sir James Caird in 1916 - means certain lengthy legal procedures would have to be followed. It's possible there could be other sites but we need 15 acres and that's a lot of land."

Soon afterwards, there were abortive talks with the council and, with time fast running out, it was decided to proceed with the redevelopment of Dens Park. In May, John Barr Construction were awarded the £2.7 million contract to build two 3,075-seater stands, one behind each goal, with new floodlighting to be installed in the existing floodlighting pylons to meet the higher levels set by UEFA.

Inspirational skipper - Barry Smith led Dundee to promotion glory. Darius Adamczuk and Lee Maddison guard the posts.

CHAPTER THIRTY-TWO

Dundee are Back

It was to prove a busy close season as Dundee steeled themselves for the rigours of the newly formed Scottish Premier League. The Dens men had deservedly won promotion but despite impressing against Rangers in the Cup, many fans questioned whether they could consistently produce that form at the top level.

Most regarded Rab Douglas, Dariusz Adamczuk, Brian Irvine, Barry Smith, Iain Anderson and perhaps James Grady and Eddie Annand as being of Premier League standard but all recognized that new blood was needed if Dundee were to survive, far less be a force in the land again.

Well aware that reinforcements were required, Jocky Scott's priority was to bring in players of Premier League experience. However, his first move was to appoint an assistant-manager in the form of Jimmy Bone, a player of many clubs who had been manager of St Mirren and East Fife before coaching at Dundee United and Dunfermline.

Anderson apart, Dundee had long lacked a creative spark in midfield but, moves for Manchester United's Grant Brebner - who had impressed while on loan at Hibs, ex-Dens Parker Andy Dow and Raith Rovers skipper Danny Lennon proved unsuccessful. Scotland Under-21 internationals Brebner and Dow opted for English Second Division Reading (£100,000), and Aberdeen (£75,000), respectively, while Lennon chose to remain and sign a new deal for his First Division club.

Jocky Scott had made a couple of cross-Channel trips to France and Belgium as well as visiting England but though nothing materialised on that front, there were soon five new faces at Dens. Midfielders Shaun McSkimming and the Frenchman Eric Garcin, as well as strike pair Willie

Falconer and Tommy Coyne were all obtained from Motherwell, the first three on free transfers with Coyne and former Hibs right-back Willie Miller, (28), moving to Dens on freedom-of-contract.

Now thirty-five years old, Coyne had rejected overtures by Motherwell and Kilmarnock before signing a two-year deal for Dundee where he had netted 60 goals prior to joining Celtic for a Dens record fee of £500,000 back in 1989. Although overlooked by Scotland, The Republic of Ireland were grateful to harness his talents and Coyne had starred at the 1994 World Cup Finals in America before finishing Motherwell's top scorer with 14 goals last term.

Of course, McSkimming (28), was another former Dark Blue who had gone to Kilmarnock for £40,000 in 1991 before later moving on to Motherwell for four times that amount. Willie Falconer, (32), was another experienced campaigner who had previously turned out for Aberdeen, Watford, Middlesbrough, Sheffield United and Celtic while Garcin, (28), had looked a class act at Motherwell.

There was plenty of other interest for the Dens faithful. Close season improvements to the main stand included additional toilets and catering facilities although plans to put bucket seats in the South Enclosure were put on hold. Lack of finance remained a problem and rather than install under-soil heating, the board chose to invest £60,000 on an inflatable hot-air dome with another £50,000 spent on equipment for the Bobby Cox fitness suite.

On the commercial side, business was booming. All five hospitality lounges were sold out for the season as was the trackside hoarding advertising, while season ticket sales had

Dens Park reinforcements - (left to right) Willie Falconer, Eric Garcin, Shaun McSkimming and Tommy Coyne. DC Thomson

more than doubled to 1,770. A £100,000, one-year, shirt sponsorship deal was agreed with Scottish Hydro Electric and there would also be income from replica home and away kits which the fans themselves had helped choose via a telephone poll conducted by *The Evening Telegraph*.

Jocky Scott had opted for a low-key pre-season build-up and results of note included a 1-0 win over Kevin Keegan's Fulham at Dens - where Eric Garcin and 30-year-old trialist central-defender Stephane Pounewatchy impressed - as well as victories over Northern Conference sides Kidderminster Harriers 2-1 and Southport 5-0 in North-West England.

Interviewed on the eve of the new campaign, Jocky Scott commented: "We're quietly confident for as well as the promotion-winning men, we've brought in others with Premier experience and my aim is to build a squad capable of playing different tactical systems as the occasion demands. However, we have to adjust to the faster pace of the higher level while ensuring we're as good defensively as we were last season and we've also been working hard at retaining possession."

"There's not a lot between the top of the First and the bottom of the Premier but the big test is playing consistently well at the top level. Most of the new signings are attacking players so we will go out to try and win games, but, in the end, success or failure will be judged on whether or not we stay up. That's the short-term plan. The long-term aim is to make Dundee the number one club in the city again."

However, the Dark Blues were to make a disastrous start to the new season. Wing ace Iain Anderson would miss the opening games due to tendonitis of the knee while Eddie Annand was another absentee from the August 1st opener against Aberdeen at Dens due to suspension. Prior to kick-off, chairman Jimmy Marr unfurled the First Division Championship flag, but the occasion fell flat for the home side with first-half goals by Jess and Hignett setting the Dons up for a comfortable 2-0 win.

Worryingly, Dundee's defence had shown an uncharacteristic loss of concentration while Tommy Coyne failed to score with a penalty and struggled to cope with the pace of the game. Starting with four at the back, the home midfield had been overrun in the first period and it was only after switching to a more familiar 3-5-2 system that Dundee had held their own.

Seven days later, yet another insipid Dens performance saw Dundee crash out of the League Cup, a shock 1-0 defeat to Second Division part-timers Alloa costing them a money-spinning third-round tie against Rangers at Ibrox. And when they then went down 2-0 at Dunfermline and lost 1-0 to St Johnstone at Dens,

Dens sparkler - Iain Anderson brought flair to midfield. DC Thomson

Safe hands - Rab Douglas was a key man as Dundee fought for survival.

Dundee fans were plunged into the depths of despair.

After four games, the Dark Blues were out of the League Cup but far more worryingly they were anchored to the foot of the league. And, having lost the last three games of last term, they had now gone seven competitive games without a win and had failed to score a single goal!

With the season just three weeks old, many predicted that Dundee were heading straight back to the First Division and, with the next three fixtures against Celtic (h), Hearts (a) and Dundee United (h), it was already rumoured that Jocky Scott faced the axe if an improvement was not forthcoming.

Nevertheless, with Robbie Raeside recalled, the team had looked considerably sharper and better organised against St Johnstone before a lowly 3,641 crowd. Various factors such as the Sunday 6.05pm kick-off, rainy conditions, Dundee's poor home form and live coverage by BSB-Sky TV had all contributed towards the poor turnout but, perhaps in retrospect, admission prices should have been slashed, a ploy later employed successfully at Motherwell.

From the start of the season, there had been problems in central defence and even regulars like Barry Smith and Brian Irvine were axed as the manager sought a winning blend. There was no doubting the footballing ability of Pounewatchy but the strapping Frenchman looked no better than others at Dens and when he reputedly demanded a salary of £110,000, news of his release came as little surprise.

On August 29th, Dundee faced a tough task against Celtic at Dens Park and things got even harder when Eric Garcin retired with a groin strain after 10 minutes with his replacement, Brian Grant, later limping off with a calf strain! On the hour, Craig Burley put Celtic ahead but the Dark Blues hung on and, in the dying minutes, Eddie Annand thundered the ball past Jonathan Gould from the penalty spot for the equaliser.

Jocky Scott's men were learning fast and their improvement continued with a 2-0 victory over Scottish Cup holders Hearts at Tynecastle. The arrival of Willie Miller had meant Dariusz Adamczuk switching to central midfield and with Gavin Rae and Shaun McSkimming alongside him in place of McInally and Garcin, the Pole made his mark with two well-taken goals while the wing-backs Willie Miller and Lee Maddison also did well to stifle the trickery of Neil McCann and the mercurial Jose Quitongo.

That all-important first win lifted Dundee two points clear of bottom-of-the-league Dundee United, who were now managed by Paul Sturrock after the recent dismissal of Tommy McLean. On September 19th, the sides met in a 12,081 all-ticket clash at Dens but although the Dark Blues held the edge in a hectic first half, McSwegan headed home an Olofsson cross on the counter-attack soon after half-time. Dundee's defence were struggling against the Tannadice long-ball ploy and when Olofsson added a second in 67 minutes, there looked to be no way back.

Almost immediately, Annand responded with a fine headed goal and with the roving Anderson - just back from injury - a constant menace after coming on as substitute, Dundee threw everything into attack. Just four minutes of extra-time remained when Anderson's left-wing cross was nodded back by Falconer and Dariusz Adamczuk charged in to head powerfully for goal.

Sieb Dykstra got an arm to the ball but was unable to prevent it spinning into the net as the noise from celebrating home fans threatened to raise the roof from the main stand and South Enclosure. The score had ended 2-2 but it was a victory in all but name for the Dark Blues!

Dundee had found their feet at Premier League level and the next six games brought a further 10 points. However, on November 7th, they were brought back to earth with a crushing 6-1 defeat by Celtic before 58,000 at Parkhead. A controversial early penalty award by referee Stuart Dougal set the pattern and when Barry Smith was ordered off for a "last-man" tackle on Henrik Larsson in 18 minutes, the Dark Blues were in real trouble.

Annand pulled one back with a raging drive but 10-man Dundee were no match for the rampant Celts. Inspired by the clever prompting of Moravcik, the pacy Larsson, Burchill and O'Donnell tore gaping holes in their defence and only the introduction of Raeside alongside Irvine and ex-Hibs defender Gordon Hunter - recently signed on a three month contract - soon after the sixth goal in 66 minutes, helped avoid a real catastrophe.

The Dark Blues bounced back with a 1-1 draw against third-placed Kilmarnock at Dens, where former Scotland international half-back Doug Cowie, who had made a record 446 league and cup appearances for Dundee, was presented with a framed montage to mark the official opening of the latest hospitality area, The Captains' Lounge.

The following Sunday, Dundee made the short trip to Tannadice but it took some inspired defending to keep United at bay as the game entered its final stages. James Grady, who was back after missing seven games through injury, substituted for Tommy Coyne and with just eight minutes remaining, the wee striker ran on to an Eddie Annand head-flick and volleyed a spectacular 18-yarder into the top of the net! Douglas then had to make several heroic saves but, to the delight of their fans, the Dark Blues held on for their first derby success since September 1992.

Meanwhile, plans for the £2.7 million Dens redevelopment appeared to be on course with the announcement of a £1 million grant from the Scottish Sports Council Lottery Sports Fund with a further £366,800 grant and a £200,000 loan to come from the Football Trust. Dundee chairman Jimmy Marr insisted that plans were in place to raise the balance of just over £1.1 million but, significantly, he warned, "If we had not received this funding, it would have been impossible for us to carry on in the Premier."

Certainly, this came as a timely boost for earlier the directors had been stunned to learn that they were not to share the £5 million Sky TV handout. After deducting the legal fees involved in setting up the SPL and the £250,000 awarded to relegated Hibs and Falkirk - the latter denied promotion due to the change in rules - the remaining £3.5 million was divided between the other nine SPL clubs with Dundee excluded since "they had taken none of the risks." It was a decision vehemently disputed by the Dens board and an appeal was lodged.

In an effort to reduce their wage bill, a number of fringe players had been allowed to move on for small fees. Russell Kelly signed for Ayr United, Steve McCormick went to Airdrie after loan spells at Leyton Orient and Morton, Derek Fleming moved to Livingston, John McGlashan joined Ross County after a loan spell at Arbroath while Craig Tully

Flying Pole - Dundee's Polish international midfielder Dariusz Adamczuk powers home a header to net a last-gasp equaliser and earn the Dark Blues a 2-2 draw in the Dens Park derby.

Mirrorpix

would shortly move on to Ross County.

In November, Gordon Hunter and Eric Garcin were released. The 30-year-old defender was no longer fit enough for the Premier League but although the official line was that the injury-plagued Garcin, who had started only three games, had "failed to settle", chairman Peter Marr later claimed - at the AGM - that, his injury problems apart, he had been a disruptive influence amongst the other players.

Due to postponements, it was December 12th before the Dark Blues returned to action but by the start of the three week winter break in early 1999, they had gathered only four from a possible eighteen points. However, there had been a number of talking points - a magnificent 80-yard run had taken Dariusz Adamczuk past five opponents before he beat Alan Main to earn a 1-1 draw away to St Johnstone, while Iain Anderson snatched the ball from allotted penalty taker James Grady only to hit the post with a spot-kick as Dundee went down 2-1 at Motherwell!

There were also a couple of new faces. After losing out on Celtic's Malky Mackay, who joined Norwich City, and Scott Wilson who chose to remain with Rangers despite the clubs agreeing a £250,000 fee, Dundee paid £75,000 for Stoke City centre-half Steven Tweed, who had previously played for Hibs and Greek club Ionikis with left-back Lee Sharp, (23), arriving from Dumbarton for £5,000.

The towering Tweed, a former Scotland-Under-21 international, looked the part alongside Smith and Irvine, while the pacy Sharp, impressive in an attacking full-back role, cracked home a penalty as Dundee recorded a 2-1 win over Hearts at Tynecastle in late December.

It was good to see Hugh Robertson make his comeback after a loan spell at Inverness Caley Thistle following the trauma of his brother's death in 1997, but a 3-1 Dens derby defeat then left Dundee one point ahead of United and five above bottom-of-the-league Dunfermline by the break.

Worryingly, two of Dundee's top players, Dariusz Adamczuk and Iain Anderson, who were out of contract at the end of the season, had made it clear that they wished to

Programme - but was the local derby soon to disappear?

move on, and both were made available for transfer - at the right price.

An Aberdeen bid of £250,000 for Adamczuk was rejected, while St Johnstone's interest ended abruptly when the Pole's wage demands became known. However, on a more positive note, the Dens men would - due to a clause inserted in his contract at the time of his transfer from Dundee - receive an additional £350,000 from Hearts following Neil McCann's £1.8 million move to Rangers!

Just over three weeks later, Dundee returned to action but any hopes of a money-spinning Scottish Cup run were dashed by a 2-1 reverse to First Division Morton at Cappielow, with a 4-0 drubbing from Rangers following at Dens a few days later. With on-loan Coventry midfielder Gavin Strachan - son of former Dens legend Gordon Strachan - in the side, Dundee drew 0-0 at second-placed Kilmarnock, but a flu epidemic was then to bring major selection problems.

Despite ten members of Dundee's first-team squad suffering from illness, the SPL refused to sanction a postponement of the game against Motherwell at Dens. Steven Tweed was one of several affected who decided to play and, with just two minutes gone, he headed the only goal of the game.

However, Tweed could only last until half-time before he was replaced by Barry Smith, who had also left his sick-bed to play. Brian Irvine was another hero in a gritty, backs-to-the-wall finish but, for the first time in his career, the big defender was sent off after receiving a second yellow card for accidentally kicking Derek Adams while attempting to clear his lines.

Steady as she goes - Dundee skipper Barry Smith prepares to tackle Celtic's Swedish international striker Henrik Larsson with Dens team-mate Willie Miller ready to lend a helping hand.

DC Thomson

CHAPTER THIRTY-THREE

Desperate Days

Meanwhile, the city had been awash with rumours that the Dens redevelopment was in doubt. The work had initially been scheduled for the end of that month but on February 18th came the stunning news that Dundee's directors were prepared to consider a merger with Dundee United.

In a telephone poll conducted by *The Evening Telegraph* 58% of those calling in had apparently favoured a merger between the two city clubs and this prompted the Dens board to discuss the possibility of approaching their neighbours for amalgamation talks. According to Peter Marr, Dundee's financial prospects were bleak: "We lost £500,000 last season and we would have lost money again this term had it not been for the Neil McCann windfall. It's very difficult for a club like ours to operate on the gates we have been getting although if everyone who said they were Dundee fans came to the games it wouldn't be so bad."

"We had hoped for a 6,000 gate at the recent Motherwell match but got 4,187, of whom just over 3,000 were Dundee fans. I honestly don't know if a merger is possible but I've an open mind on the subject and would ask fans to do likewise. Rangers and Celtic are streets ahead of the rest and maybe one Dundee club could give them a challenge. However, what I do know is that the directors can't afford to go on losing large amounts of money."

Eight years earlier, the fans had experienced a similar situation under Angus Cook and were once again opposed to a merger which would spell the end of Dundee Football Club. The Dundee F.C. Supporters' Association which now consisted of 21 branches representing some 1,500 fans, urged supporters to write to the club to make their feelings known and plans were drawn up for a demonstration at the next home game against St Johnstone.

In an interview for *The Courier*, Bobby Cox, skipper of Dundee's 1961-62 championship winning side and a hospitality lounge match-day host, was vehement that the club should retain its separate identity and he voiced his fears that Dundee's 106-year-old history might fade into obscurity. Soon, a tidal wave of opposition had built up and with local newspapers inundated by an anti-merger e-mail petition, *The Evening Telegraph* published numerous letters of protest from agitated fans of both city clubs.

That weekend, Dundee, who were without the suspended Irvine, crashed 6-1 to Rangers at Ibrox but the over-riding priority was the continued existence of the club. Throughout the match, the 600-strong travelling support waved banners and loudly expressed their opposition to a merger, with

Loud and clear - Dundee fans at Ibrox make their feelings known about the proposed merger.
Mirrorpix

about one hundred remaining after full-time for an impromptu demonstration, which was widely covered by the media.

Two days later, the board bowed to the weight of opposition by agreeing to take no further steps towards amalgamation. In an interview with *The Daily Record*, Peter Marr broke his week-long silence: "The supporters have made their feelings clear and I've been overwhelmed by it all. I'm very touched by the emotion shown for the club but although our hardcore support has increased from 2,500 to 3,500, we require at least another 2,000 to show up on a regular basis. We also need the fans to back the forthcoming share issue. If those things happen, then we will have a chance."

"It's fair to say that the club's future is now in the hands of the supporters. I'd love them to show Jim McLean that Dundee are capable of emerging as a force again. Jimmy and I don't have any more money to put into the club. I reckon we've put in around £2.5 million but we'd rather lose that than merge with Dundee United."

"I'm speaking the truth here. I couldn't live with myself if I killed off Dundee F.C. because the club means too much to me. Let's not forget we also live in the city so you can imagine what it would be like for us. For as long as we are in charge, we will never actively seek a merger with Dundee United. The two new stands are the key to the future of this club and with them in place, we will have family facilities and cover for visiting supporters. I'm certain more fans will come to Dens as a result, then gradually we can look at redeveloping the South Stand."

In meetings with members of the business community and DSA representatives, the Marrs admitted that for the first time in their business lives they had had problems in obtaining a bank loan. Nevertheless, they would continue their attempts to raise the £1.1 million balance required and a few days later, a high profile "Buy a Brick" campaign was launched. Four thousand bricks for the new Provost Road stand would be available at £25 each and purchasers would have their name inscribed on their brick as well as getting a commemorative certificate.

The Supporters' Association remained supportive of the board and a spokesman declared: "Five years of strong leadership could turn this club around. We feel Peter and Jimmy offer the kind of direction that's long been lacking but they can't do the job alone." Stay-away fans were exhorted to come along to the Dens game against St Johnstone on Saturday, February 27th with the DSA urging: "If you care, be there!"

On a cold, windy afternoon, over 6,000 Dundee fans were amongst the 7,245 crowd but they found little to stir the blood as the well-organised Saints departed with a 1-0 win. However, the home supporters had rallied round and greatly encouraged, Peter Marr thanked them for turning out and also those who had donated their gate money despite being unable to attend. He apologised for the poor fare on offer and pledged that things would get better if the fans stuck with the club.

Already 1,800 bricks had been sold with many of the current players and former favourites like Neil McCann and Morten Wieghorst amongst the buyers but, in early March, a 2-0 defeat at Dunfermline dragged Dundee back into the relegation fray. In the dying seconds, Dariusz Adamczuk was sent off after getting a second yellow card - his eleventh of the season - for kicking the ball away and the volatile Pole received another red card for foul and abusive language on leaving the field.

There was no doubting Adamczuk's commitment but his subsequent six-game suspension was a huge blow, particularly as Dunfermline, Hearts and Dundee United were all now within three points of Dundee. Off the field too, problems were mounting. Demolition warrants had been obtained and Barr Construction had set up office in the T.C. Keay end car park but the builders refused to start work

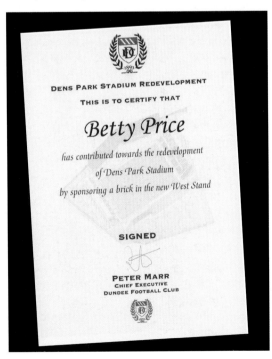

until all funding was in place and the SPL made it clear that Dundee would be expelled unless their ground was ready on time.

Nor would the various grants be released to Dundee until the club produced the balance of £1.1 million. As yet they had been unable to do this but, on March 4th, Peter Marr, Jim Connor and solicitor Jack Robertson flew to meet Italian-born lawyer and international businessman Giovanni di Stefano for talks in Brussels.

Prior to the Dunfermline game, *The Daily Record* had claimed that di Stefano had been a general in the Serbian military during the Yugoslavian Civil War of the early 1990s and was a close confidant of Zeljko Raznatovic, better known as Arkan, commander of the infamous Serbian Tigers and a suspected war criminal. The newspaper asserted that di Stefano was to take a 10% shareholding in Dundee and that some £800,000 had already been transferred, but although admitting to discussions, the board denied receiving any cash or issuing any shares.

Di Stefano was standing as an Italian Nationalist candidate in the forthcoming European elections and, in a letter to the Press Association, he acknowledged that his position as General Sales Agent to Yugoslavia for Iraqui Airways involved meetings with President Saddam Hussein and that his political life had also brought him into contact with Yassir Arafat and Gerry Adams although this did not mean he shared their beliefs.

These comments merely fanned the flames of controversy and although Peter Marr indicated that Dundee were interested only in football, the club came under enormous pressure to distance themselves from di Stefano. Club sponsors Hydro Electric maintained a diplomatic silence but there were suggestions that the Royal Bank of Scotland might terminate Dundee's banking facilities if the deal went ahead. The Bank of Scotland were also reported to be upset at the negative publicity generated in their first week as league sponsors while the SPL themselves were none too happy although apparently powerless to intervene.

By then, it was mid-March, and with three successive defeats and just nine games left, many fans worried that off-field events might affect the team, perhaps leading to relegation and even oblivion for the Dens Park club. On Saturday March 20th, Dundee faced a crucial test when they entertained a Hearts side without a win since early December. Robertson replaced the suspended Adamczuk, Raeside was brought in for Tweed and Steven Boyack, a recent £25,000 signing from Rangers, made his debut on the right side of midfield.

Initially, Hearts had the edge but Dundee were deadly on the break and twice before the interval they came close when Eddie Annand exploited the space behind the young wing-back Gary Naysmith. Soon after half-time, Barry Smith played in Annand and this time the striker cleverly lofted the ball over Rousset, adding a second 13 minutes later when Raeside nodded on a corner kick.

That was Dundee's fourth win over Hearts that term and now they had a six-point cushion over the beleaguered Tynecastle outfit. Steven Boyack, whose father was a life-long fan of the Dark Blues, had looked a class act and even

Netbound - Gavin Rae powers home a header against Aberdeen watched by team-mates Brian Irvine and Eddie Annand. DC Thomson

Hearts boss Jim Jefferies had been impressed by Dundee's organisation and all-round grit and determination.

Meanwhile, time was running out for the redevelopment and with a start date still to be confirmed, the SPL were running out of patience: "Although we are sympathetic, there's no prospect of the rules being bent for Dundee who have known for over a year what was required."

Previously, it had been thought that if the Dens men were close to completion by July 31st, the deadline might be extended. Alternately - like Celtic at Hampden - they might be allowed to groundshare or perhaps - like Hearts - play just away games early next season but with half the league under threat of relegation, it was unlikely Dundee would get the 50% backing required for such a waiver.

Initially, the Dens board had welcomed di Stefano's investment offer but there was considerable disquiet at his praise for Italy's wartime fascist leader Mussolini and his public condemnation of NATO air strikes against Slobodan Milosovic's forces after negotiations with Yugoslavia over the Kosovo situation had broken down and at the end of March, Peter Marr confirmed that the deal was off.

However, the uncertainty over di Stefano's involvement continued when it was reported that Companies House in Edinburgh had confirmed that £65,386 worth of Dundee F.C. shares had been allotted to his Italo-Yugoslav Airlines company. Dens vice-chairman Derek Souter, though, maintained that di Stefano had nothing to do with the club: "He is not a shareholder and never has been. His offer was made on March 24th but our Articles of Association allow us 14 days to accept or reject it, and, this period having elapsed, we will be notifying Companies House that it has been cancelled."

Recently, Robert Douglas had been in the Scotland squad

for the internationals against Bosnia and the Czech Republic but the big keeper was unable to prevent a 5-0 reverse to Celtic at Parkhead and it was now vital that Dundee took something from their trip to Motherwell. Falconer, Robertson and Boyack were recalled after their omission from the starting line-up against Celtic and there was a strong feeling that the manager had purposely held them back for the Fir Park clash.

At half-time, a nervous-looking Dundee trailed 1-0 to an early John Spencer strike but the sending off of defender Tony Thomas for a trip on Maddison was to prove crucial. Anderson was brought on for Miller and, in 64 minutes, Rae accepted a defence-splitting pass from Robertson before cutting the ball back for Falconer to equalise. Later, Robertson went off with a badly cut thigh but his replacement James Grady was to grab the winner with a splendid turn and shot from 20 yards out!

Defeats for Aberdeen and Motherwell meant they too were now involved in the relegation struggle and with just seven points separating the bottom six teams, the drama was set to continue. Meanwhile, it appeared that the board had finally made up the financial shortfall although last-minute negotiations meant it was lunchtime on Wednesday, April 14th before the first bulldozer moved into Dens.

This was a huge relief to all concerned with the well-being of the club but just 24 hours later came the astonishing news that Dundee United had failed in a second £2 million-plus attempt to take over the Dark Blues. That Monday morning, Jimmy Marr had pulled the plug just hours before a Tannadice press conference scheduled to announce the deal and a Dens Park spokesman commented: "Dundee F.C. will not entertain a takeover by Dundee United and have demonstrated their commitment to the club and fans by sanctioning this week's near £3-million redevelopment of Dens Park."

A confidentiality clause prevented those involved in talks from revealing details but it was understood that the new club would have played at Tannadice and that only an impasse over details like a new name - Sporting Club of Dundee had been mooted - prevented the deal going through. However, it had become increasingly clear that the SPL regarded a merger as the best solution to Dundee's redevelopment problem and that there had been considerable pressure on them to go through with the deal.

Supporters were stunned that there had been further talks and many worried that only demolition work was scheduled and that a takeover which would effectively kill off their club, might still be on the cards. Most now would not relax until the first steelwork had been erected and an ambiguously worded Dens Park statement the following day claiming that: "Dundee would not agree to a takeover by United which led to their name disappearing while United's remained intact", merely added to their concern.

Rumours abounded and, that Saturday, both *The Scottish Daily Express* and *The Star* insisted that the takeover would go through within two weeks, claims that Jimmy Marr denied, saying that the club had obtained a loan from the Bank of Scotland and that the over-riding priority was to have the two stands ready for the start of next season.

Jocky Scott was unhappy at the timing of the latest controversy just before that Sunday's match against Rangers at Tannadice, which Dundee had rented and, despite having recently lost 4-0 and 6-1 to the Premier League title favourites, he decided on a 4-3-3 formation with Iain Anderson in a wide-left attacking role.

In the early stages, Dundee came under siege but, gradually, they hit back and, in 22 minutes, Boyack crossed for Anderson to send a powerful header past Klos. Soon after half-time, Vidmar equalised but with Willie Miller again subduing the ever-dangerous Neil McCann, the Dens rearguard held firm in the face of intense Rangers pressure.

With Anderson at his tantalising best and Coyne holding the ball up well, Dundee continued to pose problems only for Grady to miss three great chances. However, the Dens men had done well to secure a point and Rangers coach Dick Advocaat was fulsome in his praise, saying: "On that form, Dundee would have taken points from any team on the planet."

Dundee were now level with Aberdeen and Motherwell and seven points clear of bottom markers Dunfermline and Jocky Scott believed that another two points from their last five games would ensure their survival: "This time we were determined to have a go and it paid off. I've tried ten men back against them and got gubbed so I thought if we're to get beaten again, we'd at least do it attacking!"

Giovanni di Stefano continued to insist that he would be involved at Dens and although the SPL accepted Dundee's faxed copy of a Companies House-registered Statutory Declaration nullifying their agreement to sell him shares, they found it strange that he continued to contradict Dundee's assertions. SPL chief executive Roger Mitchell warned that Dundee had until the end of May to satisfy them that the new stands were on track for completion by the deadline or face expulsion. And should that happen, he

United fail in second Dens takeover bid

£2m-plus deal collapsed after initial agreement

The end is nigh at Dens Park

EXCLUSIVE: Marr brothers re-open talks with United

FINAL SEASON FOR DUNDEE

Coming down - the famous Provost Road terracing and enclosure are demolished but would the new stands be going up?   Norrie Price

Nearly safe - Willie Falconer and the Dens fans celebrate Shaun McSkimming's headed winner against Kilmarnock. DC Thomson

questioned where they would stand as regards regaining admission to the Scottish League, suggesting that they might even have to restart in the Third Division.

It was then alleged that not only was a deal with di Stefano still possible at the end of the Kosovo conflict, but it was one which could involve him acquiring all of Peter Marr's 86.4% controlling interest instead of the 10% previously mentioned, a revelation that prompted Derek Souter to warn that he would review his position if the takeover went ahead.

The long-suffering fans were thoroughly fed up with all the conjecture and Saturday's home game with third placed Kilmarnock came as a great relief. There was a surreal atmosphere about Dens for, by now, the T.C. Keay end had been flattened, half the Provost Road end terracing had been ripped up and the West Enclosure demolished with around 5,000 fans confined to the main stand and South Enclosure.

Nevertheless, there was no doubting the almost fanatical enthusiasm of the home fans as Dundee ran out to the recently adopted theme tune of "The Great Escape". Just before half-time, a sustained spell of home pressure resulted in a rejuvenated Anderson speeding behind the Killie rearguard to volley home a Maddison cross and though the visitors levelled, there was no stopping the "New Dundee".

In 64 minutes, Boyack beat three defenders and his inch-perfect cross was headed home by McSkimming. That was the winner and the noisy home support, who throughout had sung and stamped their feet in the old wooden stand, gleefully chanted "Are you watching SPL!"

It had been another end-to-end thriller but the competitiveness of midfield anchor-man Rae and the attacking forays of Boyack and Anderson had given Dundee the decisive edge. Football-wise at any rate, the Dark Blues who had moved up to fifth, had virtually secured their place in the top flight and now, after months of bad press, media pundits such as

Steven Boyack - a touch of flair for Dundee. AR-Pix

Gordon Smith - in *The Sun* as well as on BBC Sportscene - began to talk up the Dark Blues.

Now, too, there was speculation that Dundee might lose the £1.4 million grant support from the government-funded Scottish Sports Council Lottery Sports Fund and the Football Trust should the di Stefano takeover proceed. But on Thursday, April 28th, two days after the deadline for the £2.5 million buyout, Jimmy Marr announced that Dundee had finally severed their links with the lawyer.

In an in-depth interview with Graeme Dey of *The Courier*, the Dens chairman spoke of the pressure that he and his brother had been under and of the relief he now felt: "I really see this being an end to all the doubts and controversy. Peter and I talk every day and we just decided it was time to end all the uncertainty surrounding the club's future and call a halt to this business."

Refuting di Stefano's claims that he effectively held a 10% stake in the club and had first option if the Marrs were to sell, the chairman continued: "I have no regrets about getting involved with Mr di Stefano in as much as you have to look at every option that becomes available but I would only want to do what is best for Dundee F.C. There is still a long, hard road ahead and we require to sell the remaining 1,500 bricks and need a successful share issue - put on hold due to the various distractions - in a few months' time."

"I'm not saying I would never sell my shareholding but there will be no further negotiations with Mr di Stefano nor a merger with Dundee United and we hope the support will throw their weight behind our efforts to match the fantastic job done on the park this season by Jocky Scott and his

High and mighty - Eddie Annand watches Brian Irvine head Dundee's opener in the 2-0 win over United at Tannadice. Mirrorpix

coaching and playing staff."

"The majority of the funding required to build the new stands is, as it has been for the past four to six weeks, in place. But obviously, the less money we need to borrow the better. Looking back, we possibly tried to do too much ourselves and like everyone does, we've made mistakes. Now though, we are talking to potential investors and we will look to bring other people to the boardroom, people who will share some of the workload and benefit the club."

Now everyone could look forward to that weekend's Tannadice derby which carried an extra edge after all the recent takeover talk involving Dundee United - themselves still in serious danger of relegation. Eddie Annand replaced James Grady but otherwise Dundee retained what had been a virtually unchanged team for the past three games - Douglas; Miller, Irvine, Smith, Maddison; Boyack, Rae, McSkimming; Anderson, Annand, Falconer. Dundee United fielded - Dykstra; Skoldmark, de Vos, Patterson, Malpas; Easton, Hannah, McCulloch; Miller, Dodds, Olofsson.

Over 11,000 turned out on a gloriously sunny day and to the delight of their fans, the Dark Blues almost totally dominated proceedings. Time and again, they tore United apart but, frustratingly, were unable to apply the finishing touch. Veteran left-back Maurice Malpas got a first-half roasting by Iain Anderson but although United showed some improvement after replacing him with Eustace, Dundee remained the masters.

In 67 minutes, they finally made the breakthrough as Hugh Robertson swung over a corner and Brian Irvine rose

to power a header down and into the net. Near the end, United's Northern Ireland international defender Darren Patterson was sent packing for yet another foul on the industrious Annand. The striker limped off to be replaced by Grady and with full-time looming, a defence-splitting pass by Boyack allowed the substitute to fire in a shot which hit Dykstra's heel, then slowly rolled into the net to make it 2-0 for Dundee.

Dens boss Jocky Scott was delighted: "Now we're mathematically safe. This was a great result and a great day for Dundee. A lot of people said we were not good enough for the Premier League and we were determined to prove them wrong. We've now done this and it's a tremendous feeling. I always said we'd stay up and I'm delighted we've achieved this with more than just spirit. Today, we showed how well we can pass the ball and control a game."

Now seven points ahead of their rivals, the Dark Blues, were again the city's top dogs, and while their supporters poured into the surrounding streets to celebrate, disgruntled United fans remained to demonstrate. A Dens signing target since the start of the season, Steven Boyack had proved an absolute bargain at £25,000, his direct running making him a constant threat at Tannadice where he showed great skill and awareness and was always willing to bring his teammates into play.

Dundee were on a high and it was little surprise when they returned from Aberdeen with a 2-1 win - their first over the Dons in the league since Hogmanay 1988 and their first league success at Pittodrie since March 1976 - then followed that up with a convincing 3-1 win over the already-doomed Dunfermline at Dens.

After the Pars game, there was an emotional farewell from the departing Dariusz Adamczuk and Iain Anderson, the Pole throwing his jersey to eager fans in the South Enclosure while Anderson ran to the lower part of the main stand to present his top to a young disabled fan.

Brian Irvine too was on his way and the popular defender also went to the crowd, kissing the badge on his jersey before waving an emotional goodbye. Unbeaten in their previous six games and with six wins from their last eight matches, it was Dundee's best-ever Premier run and, now certain of fifth place, it was also their highest league position since season 1974-75!

On Sunday, May 23rd, the campaign ended in anti-climax with a 1-0 to UEFA Cup qualifiers St Johnstone before a 10,575 capacity crowd at McDiarmid but Dundee had had a fine season, far exceeding their primary aim of remaining in the cut-throat SPL.

Those outwith Dens, too, recognized the club's contribution with Jocky Scott being named the Bank of Scotland's SPL Manager of the Month for May. It was a tribute well deserved since the Dens boss, along with assistant-manager Jimmy Bone, had done a marvellous job in keeping the players motivated during the long weeks of uncertainty in possibly the most unsettling period to date of Dundee Football Club's proud 106-year-old history.

Jocky Scott - guided Dundee to their best placing in 25 years.

CHAPTER THIRTY-FOUR

Taking Stock

By finishing fifth, Dundee had earned themselves a welcome £331,364 in prize money - £221,137 more than had they merely survived in ninth place, while another £513,610 had been taken from television appearances. However, Dundee's Premier League future remained dependent on the completion of the Dens Park redevelopment by the July 31st deadline.

By mid-May, the demolition and excavation work was finished and fans at the final home game against Dunfermline were encouraged to see that both ends had been completely flattened with concrete foundations clearly in evidence at the T.C. Keay end.

The following Saturday, *The Sporting Post* had shown workmen erecting steel girders and roof beams for the new stand at the T.C. Keay end of the ground. By then, hundreds of anxious fans were making a daily pilgrimage to Dens in order to chart progress and by early June, there was an identical steel skeleton at the Provost Road end with prefabricated concrete steps also beginning to appear behind both goals.

In recent years, Barr Construction had transformed the grounds of Celtic, Hibs, Kilmarnock, Dunfermline, Airdrie, Raith and Livingston and now they were working round the clock to beat the deadline. Bill Barr, though, was confident: "After all our experience we have everything down to a fine art. The steel is prefabricated then delivered to be bolted together like a giant Meccano set. That's why we can guarantee football clubs an accurate time scale."

On June 11th, Dens officials met their SPL counterparts for crucial talks in Glasgow. Chairman Jimmy Marr presented Barr Construction's written report which indicated that the redevelopment was well on schedule and the SPL, then in the process of formulating fixtures for the forthcoming season, accepted Dundee's assurances.

Aterwards an elated Jimmy Marr commented: "We are delighted the SPL has confirmed our place in the league next season, particularly after our highest top league finish for a quarter of a century. Now it's all systems go for the new campaign and hopefully we can provide our loyal fans with entertaining football in a modern stadium they can be proud of."

Football supporters around the country had wished Dundee well in their battle against adversity and John Brown of *The Evening Telegraph* accurately summed up the feelings of the beleaguered Dark Blues: "The two new stands are similar in many ways to those built at several other grounds but it's the symbolic nature of the new structures that is intriguing - one team's fight against adversity, expulsion, bankruptcy, takeover and, it seemed, the entire world!"

The meteoric rise of the new stands was to mark a watershed for the Dens Park club for another spell in the First Division might well have been disastrous. How then, one wondered, would the funds for redevelopment have been raised and, indeed, might the Marrs, faced with escalating losses, have decided to walk away?

The race is on - the construction work has begun with the first columns for the new Provost Road stand pointing skywards. Fotopress

Nearly there - the stands are taking shape and the finishing line is in sight. Fotopress

The Dark Blues could have faced a bleak and uncertain future - perhaps similar to that of Falkirk - but, in the end, the redevelopment was finished ten days ahead of schedule. The stands had been erected in just 78 days and great credit was due to Barr Construction whose workmen had often worked 16 hours a day to ensure completion.

In addition, a new floodlighting system, similar to that at the "new" Hampden and Parkhead and providing four times as much light as previously, had been installed by local firm DC Electrics. The cost was £170,000, but this time there was no problem in raising the funds.

The construction of the two new 3,075-seater stands, resplendent with dark blue plastic seats, now gave Dens a 10,078 all-seated capacity (main stand 3,528, its enclosure 400), which would rise to 11,856 after 1,778 individual seats were installed in the covered area of the South Enclosure. A certificate of fitness was duly issued by the Tayside Sports Ground Safety Team and, on July 27th, SPL chief executive Roger Mitchell came to view the redeveloped stadium.

The SPL supremo was all smiles as he declared that Dundee's efforts were an example other clubs with Premier aspirations should seek to follow: "When you see the stadium now, you have to take your hat off to Dundee. It is fantastic and to do it so quickly is phenomenal. Peter and Jimmy Marr have been under a lot of pressure and what they have achieved should not be underestimated."

"We are committed to minimum standards for stadia but the SPL's hardline stance has only ever been business not personal," he insisted. "It is a relief that we did not have to use the sanctions we have available. Dundee are one of Scotland's most historic clubs and it would have been a disaster if they hadn't made the deadline."

It was a proud day for Jimmy Marr: "On August 19th, it will be one hundred years since Dundee started playing at Dens Park and I think they will still be here in another hundred years. When my brother and I took charge one of our aims was to give the fans modern facilities to enjoy so this is a brilliant day for us as well as a great day for the club."

Following a newspaper poll of fans, the club revealed that the new stands were to be named after the legendary Bob Shankly and Bobby Cox, respectively manager and captain of Dundee's 1961-62 Championship winning side. A delighted Cox declared: "I regard this as a big, big honour and I'm particularly pleased that the Provost Road end will have my name as I was born just a few hundred yards away."

Plans had also been made for a second phase of construc-

tion comprising a £2.5m four-level south stand with offices, hospitality suites, viewing boxes, a function suite and a new boardroom - which would take the capacity to 14,000 - while the final stage would incorporate a modern 4,000-seater main stand. All that, though would depend on the club's future finances.

At the end of last season, vice-chairman Derek Souter had resigned from the board while Peter Marr had become a tax-exile in Majorca after selling *The Mardi Gras* nightclub for an estimated £3 million. On match days, the Dens chief executive regularly flew back to Scotland but although his influence would remain, new directors Jim Connor and local solicitor Ritchie Robertson - the new company secretary in place of Blackadder, Reid & Johnston - would assume the day-to-day running of the club along with Jimmy Marr.

Connor had been a key man in reviving Dundee's financial fortunes and he enthused: "Things are buzzing on the commercial front and although we only made a profit of £77,197 last term - the first since 1996 - that compares well with a £657,788 loss in 1997-98 and I'm sure there are exciting times ahead."

"When we came to Dens, only around 20 to 30 fans were in hospitality on match days but now there are as many as five hundred in the lounges, which is why we recently opened another one - The Captains' Lounge. Commercial income is up tenfold to £600,000 with turnover increasing from £700,000 prior to our arrival to nearly £3 million now."

"The buy-a brick scheme was a big success and only 800 bricks from the original 4,000 remain. We recently received £188,000 of the Neil McCann money from Hearts and the balance is to follow in December. The club are also to unveil a new strip, which for the next three years, will be supplied by Xara. There is to be a new shirt sponsor, Ceramic Tile Warehouse, as well as a new boot sponsorship deal with Umbro, and we expect the three deals to bring in around three-quarters of a million pounds."

There was an ever-increasing "feel-good" factor about the club. Allied to their fine end-of-season form, the construction of the new stands had been the catalyst for a great wave of enthusiasm amongst Dundee fans and, encouragingly, season ticket sales for the new campaign were again almost doubled from 1,770 to 2,800.

Meanwhile, on the football front, Jocky Scott's team planning had not been helped by all the earlier uncertainty. Two of Dundee's top stars, Iain Anderson and Dariusz Adamczuk had moved on under the Bosman ruling and though expected, this was a big setback for the club. The 29-year-old Polish international signed a four-year contract for Rangers while Anderson finally joined Toulouse in mid-July.

In both cases, Dundee had lost out on compensation. Celtic had agreed to pay a £40,000 fee for Adamczuk in April but although the Parkhead club backed out due to his £8,000 per week wage demands, the popular Pole later told *The Scottish Daily Mail*: "It was always my intention to achieve freedom of movement by seeing out my contract at Dens. And although I have no guarantee of a regular place, joining Rangers gives me the best opportunity of winning medals and playing in the Champions League."

A host of English clubs, including Chelsea - with whom he had spent a trial period - Sunderland, Bolton, Wolves and Fulham, had been keen on Anderson and although Dundee United made an abortive attempt to lure the Dens wing ace, the others lost interest when Peter Marr mentioned a figure of £500,000 as compensation for the 22-year-old.

England had always appeared to be Anderson's preferred destination and with the player still under 24 years of age, Dundee would have been entitled to compensation. But with only French clubs Toulouse and Strasbourg making firm offers, the ten-times capped Under-21 international opted for a two-year deal with French Second Division club Toulouse - a move which would deprive Dundee of a fee.

Jocky Scott believed that Anderson's career would have been best served by remaining at Dens for a further two seasons but he refuted the idea that Dundee might not have ended up empty-handed, had they asked for less: "No manager from down south called to verify the figure quoted and in my experience, they would have done had they been genuinely interested. In the end, no English clubs wanted to buy him, because, in my opinion, they hadn't seen him play regularly and didn't know him."

Meanwhile, club skipper Barry Smith, Gavin Rae, Lee Maddison, Hugh Robertson and Jamie Langfield had all been re-signed on three-year deals and there was a major boost when the popular Robert Douglas opted for a two-year contract extension which would keep him at Dens Park until 2002.

Liverpool, Chelsea, Rangers and Aberdeen had all shown interest but the attitude of the £1 million-rated Scotland squad keeper was refreshing: "Dundee took a chance on me when I was a part-timer with Livingston so it's nice to give them something back. I've just had a great season here and there's a lot to look forward to next term."

Many thought that Douglas might be sold in order to finance the new stands, but the board had resisted the temptation to sell with the Marrs adamant that top players would no longer be allowed to leave at bargain prices. Previously, Jim McInally, Brian Grant, Jerry O'Driscoll, Darren Magee, Gary McGlynn, Michael Dickie and Steven McDermott had

Brian Irvine - epitomised the fighting spirit at Dens. Mirrorpix

been given free transfers. January loan signing Gavin Strachan had been allowed to return to Coventry, while Brian Irvine signed for Ross County and Dave Rogers joined Ayr United after both rejected Dundee's offer of a one-year contract.

Many fans were upset that big Brian Irvine had been allowed to go after missing just three out of 72 league games in his two seasons with Dundee. The gritty defender had epitomised the fighting spirit at Dens and, in an in-depth interview with Graeme Dey of *The Courier*, the 34-year-old revealed that he had wanted to remain but was disappointed that his efforts had only merited a one-year deal rather than the two years for which he was looking.

Irvine would have relished the chance to assist in the development of 19-year-old centre-half Lee Wilkie. However, he had earlier been told that he was to be released and had no long-term prospects of a regular place. Hibs, Aberdeen and Dunfermline all showed interest but in the end Irvine opted for a three-year deal with ambitious Second Division outfit Ross County.

"That was so I wouldn't come up against Dundee," he explained. "I had a tear in my eye after the St Johnstone game and that night I couldn't sleep. I want to say a big thank-you to the Dundee fans who now have as special a place in my heart as those of Aberdeen. I am going with good memories and I sincerely hope the supporters enjoyed what we achieved as much as I did."

Jim McInally had been another key player in the recent Dens revival. Despite his lengthy Tannadice connection, he had been accepted by the Dundee fans and like Irvine had been a first-class ambassador for the club. However, he had lost his place to the up-and-coming Gavin Rae and, his job complete, the 35-year-old veteran left to become player-manager of Irish League club Sligo Rovers.

Earlier used as a right-back or an attacking midfielder, Rae appeared to be on his way out of Dens prior to John McCormack's departure. However, he had been given a fresh start by Jocky Scott who advised him and fellow

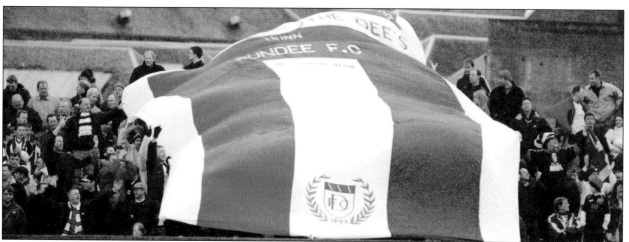

Flying the flag - the Dens Park faithful rally to the flag on the terracing outside the South Enclosure. DC Thomson

Aberdonian Jerry O'Driscoll to work hard on their fitness over the summer of 1998.

Rae had done just that and his dedication was to pay off as he made his breakthrough as a deep-lying midfielder. Soon he had established himself with some commanding performances and his season was to end with three appearances for the Scotland Under-21s.

In contrast, O'Driscoll, who had finished season '96/97 as Dundee's top scorer, had fallen from favour after a promising start to the promotion winning campaign. He failed to regain his earlier fitness and scoring form and after loan spells with Arbroath and Montrose, it was no surprise when he was released. His potential had been clear to all and his failure to make the grade was a tragedy for player, club and fans alike.

In last season's BP Youth Cup, Dundee had beaten Rangers and Hearts before progressing to the final against Celtic at Parkhead. And, despite losing 4-0, centre-half Lee Wilkie was one who particularly caught the eye. Indeed, there were signs of a promising youth set-up at Dens and youth development officer Kenny Cameron and coaches Ray Farningham and Billy Thomson were all handed new three-year contracts.

Meanwhile, the Dens redevelopment meant there was little cash available for signings and by the start of the 1999-2000 campaign, there were only two new faces. Michael Yates, a 19-year-old striker who had played for the Liverpool youth team alongside the prolific Michael Owen, was signed from Unibond League club Burscough Town, while right-back or midfielder Frank van Eijs, (27), arrived on a free transfer, having previously played for Mechelen of Belgium and Dutch Second Division clubs Fortuna Sitard and MVV Mastricht.

The Dark Blues warmed up for the new campaign with a number of friendlies against local lower league sides before completing their preparations with a 2-1 win over Inverness Caledonian Thistle in the Highlands. A clutch of continental trialists had been used, and as well as van Eijs, Portugese midfielder Nevees had looked impressive. His wage demands ended any possible deal, but Spanish striker Robert Matoute, formerly with Belenenses of Lisbon, was given an extended trial period and he later signed a three-month contract.

After finishing fifth and having upstaged their local rivals, some felt that Dundee should be pushing for a European place. However, Jocky Scott appealed for fans not to become unrealistic in their expectations: "After all they've suffered down the years they're keen for success to return to the club and I understand that because I want the same. But as manager I have to be realistic and recognise that this season will be very hard. I'm not being negative but I think we should be delighted if we can avoid finishing tenth. The aim is to avoid being relegated and, hopefully, build on the platform we've established in the coming years."

"Our target last year was simply to stay in the Premier League and a lot of people wrote us off early on. That only made the players more determined and you have to say they did tremendously well, especially coping with everything that was going on, on and off the park as they did."

"That's why, in the last quarter of the season, it was so satisfying to see them starting to get the credit they deserved from the media, particularly from pundits who'd knocked them earlier. Earlier in the season, six teams were involved in the relegation battle. But in the last quarter a gap developed between ourselves and Dunfermline and that cushion meant my players could relax and show they had the ability to play good football."

"Of course, I went to three up late on and formation-wise we looked a bit more positive. But I'd sought to have a positive approach throughout the campaign even when we had a 5-3-2 system."

Dundee F.C. Season 1999-2000 (BACK, left to right) Jack Cashley (masseur), Frank van Eijs, Robbie Raeside, Steven Tweed, Robert Douglas, Jamie Langfield, Lee Wilkie, Willie Falconer, Gavin Rae, John McCreadie (physio). MIDDLE - Kenny Cameron (youth development co-ordinator), Robert Matute, Shaun McSkimming, Lee Sharp, Mark Slater, Michael Yates, Graham Bayne, Ray Farningham (youth coach). FRONT - Harry Hay (sprint coach), Steven Boyack, James Grady, Willie Miller, Jimmy Bone (assistant-manager), Jocky Scott (manager), Barry Smith, Hugh Robertson, Lee Maddison, Billy Thomson (goalkeeper-coach). DC Thomson

CHAPTER THIRTY-FIVE

New Millennium

The manager had also talked of the importance of securing points early in the season but a disappointing start was to bring just one win from the opening four league games of the 1999-2000 campaign. Having convincingly beaten Dundee United in May, Dens fans eagerly anticipated a repeat in the opening-day fixture at Tannadice on July 31st. But despite recovering from a poor start to level through Falconer, the Dark Blues lost the winning goal in the dying moments of the game.

The following Sunday, Dundee entertained recently-promoted Hibernian and prior to kick-off, the newly constructed Bobby Cox and Bob Shankly stands were officially opened in a ceremony involving Dens Park chairman Jimmy Marr, Bobby Cox and the late Bob Shankly's son and daughter. The game itself provided great entertainment but although Dundee led 3-2 with only six minutes remaining, two late goals by Frank Sauzee and Kenny Miller gave the Easter Road side all three points.

A brilliantly headed double by Willie Falconer earned a welcome 2-0 win at Aberdeen but despite pushing Celtic all the way at Dens on August 21st, Dundee's inability to clear a long throw-in was punished when Henrik Larsson netted in a last-gasp victory for the visitors. The Dark Blues responded with a 2-0 success at Motherwell but when a 4-0 defeat by Hearts at Tynecastle was followed by a 2-1 home reverse to St Johnstone involving the loss of another two late goals, serious questions were again asked of the defence.

Robert Douglas remained a reliable keeper while the regular back four consisted of Willie Miller, Barry Smith, Steven Tweed and Lee Maddison and with the exception of Tweed for Irvine, this was the same rearguard that had performed so reliably at the end of last term. However, the loss of so many late goals - particularly at Dens - was now a major concern and individual lapses in concentration were costing the team dear.

The renewed optimism had all but disappeared and although a couple of fine goals by Steven Boyack and Gavin Rae ensured a 2-0 win at Kilmarnock, successive defeats to Rangers (h) 2-3, Dundee United (h) 0-2 and Hibernian (a) 2-5 meant Dundee had lost eight of their eleven Premier League games by October 23rd.

The Dark Blues lay second bottom, just four points clear of struggling Aberdeen, and although the bottom club would play off with the top team in the First Division rather than face automatic relegation, it remained a worrying period for the Dens Park club.

Emerging talent - a young Lee Wilkie jousts with the talented Celtic midfielder Lubomir Moravcik. DC Thomson

In an attempt to plug the gaps, manager Scott reverted to the 3-5-2 system which allowed him to blood Lee Wilkie. In his league debut against Celtic, the towering central defender did well against the formidable Mark Viduka and was unfortunate to get his marching orders for a couple of heavy challenges against Rangers. Wilkie then returned from his one-game suspension, only to again be sent off for another rash tackle as a depleted Dundee, who were without Miller, Smith and Maddison, were torn apart by a Russell Latapy-inspired Hibernian at Easter Road.

By then, both Wilkie and Rae were regulars for the Scotland Under-21s with reserve goalkeeper Jamie Langfield another Dark Blue to be included in the squad. But with two red cards from his first five games, the young defender would be used sparingly at club level over the next few months.

Up front, Eddie Annand and James Grady were struggling to find the net but Willie Falconer had hit a rich vein of scoring form. His goal at Easter Road was his ninth that term and after twice netting in a 4-0 triumph over Dumbarton at Dens, another two in a 3-1 win at Alloa ensured Dundee's place in the last eight of the League Cup.

However, league form was a concern and without the cash

to adequately replace their departed stars, a spate of injuries exposed the lack of depth in the Dens Park squad. Michael Yates - despite his spectacular angled goal against St Johnstone - and Frank van Eijs did not look up to Premier League standard while Lee Sharp lacked the defensive qualities to complement his undoubted attacking flair.

Earlier, a new share issue had been announced - the first since 1991 - and at the AGM in September, Peter Marr told shareholders that if a minimum of £201,500 was raised, there were companies prepared to plough serious money into the club: "If we can prove that the fan base is strong and supportive, two or three big investors will look upon us as a good investment."

In the event, around £350,000 was raised and as fans awaited developments, Yugoslav businessman Voya Novakovic, a London-based football agent understood to have extensive contacts, was appointed director of football. As he explained: "I will help Jocky Scott and his coaching staff to identify players to look at and it will also be my responsibility to expand Dundee's business contact base in Britain as well as further afield."

Novakovic declared himself unconnected to Giovanni di Stefano and, soon after his arrival, Italian midfielder Patrizio Billio and Argentinian right-back Walter del Rio - both available on freedom-of-contract from Crystal Palace - came to Dens on trial. Billio (25), formerly with AC Milan and Ancona, signed an 18-month deal but with sufficient cover in his position, del Rio was allowed to leave.

Out-of-favour Dunfermline central defender Craig Ireland (23), was secured on a one-month loan and later Dundee paid £50,000 to make the move permanent. On October 30th, both Ireland and Billio impressed in a 1-0 win over Hearts, an early goal by Steven Tweed providing Dundee with their first home league success of the season.

However, behind the scenes, an increasingly strained relationship between Jocky Scott and the new director of football saw Novakovic depart after just five weeks to concentrate on "other business affairs". The Yugoslav had set up a floodlit friendly with Aris Salonika of Greece to celebrate Dundee's £2.7 million ground redevelopment but although it was hoped that two of their Greek Under-21

internationals might stay at Dens on loan, nothing was to transpire.

Recently signed on a two-and-a-half year contract, ex-Southampton and Oxford forward Nicky Banger displayed a fine turn of pace in the 3-2 win over the Greeks. However, the 28-year-old Englishman was not fully fit and soon there were also doubts over his temperament when he was sent off for kicking an opponent as he made his league debut in the 1-0 defeat by Motherwell at Dens.

On Sunday, November 28th, the Dark Blues bounced back with their best result of the season at Ibrox. Ireland put them ahead with a powerful header from a McSkimming corner in 14 minutes and although Douglas saved an Albertz penalty, Rangers later equalised. However, Dundee were not to be denied and, deep in injury time, Boyack cleverly cushioned a Robertson crossfield pass and the oncoming Gavin Rae fired the ball past Rangers on-loan keeper Thomas Myhre.

That was Dundee's first win in Govan since September 1985 and it would also prove Rangers sole home league defeat that season. But, having previously been cup-tied with Dunfermline, Ireland was an absentee for the money-spinning League Cup quarter-final tie against Celtic at Parkhead. And although Wilkie came in and again kept a tight rein on Viduka, Dundee failed to play with the same belief they had shown at Ibrox.

Just before half-time, Mahe was dismissed for lashing out at Annand but Dundee failed to take the initiative and with extra-time looming, former Dens Park favourite Morten Wieghorst headed home the only goal of the tie.

The Dens men had lost a golden opportunity and despite enjoying the bulk of possession in their next match at Tannadice, a Tweed blunder allowed Dundee United's Portuguese striker Joachim Ferraz in for a late winner. It was the third time that Dundee had lost to their rivals that season and, defensive lapses apart, there was again an alarming lack of punch up front.

Two days after Christmas, Dundee could only manage a 1-1 Dens draw against St Johnstone in their last game prior to the winter shutdown. They lay eighth, six points above Kilmarnock with Aberdeen a further point in arrears. But

Knock-out punch - Gavin Rae slams home Steven Boyack's knockdown for a last-gasp winner against Rangers at Ibrox. Mirrorpix

Dawn of a new millennium - the new stands have transformed Dens Park and there is plenty of space for further development on the south side. Tannadice lies in the background.   SNS Group

despite recording excellent victories at Ibrox, Pittodrie, Motherwell, Kilmarnock and McDiarmid, the Dark Blues had achieved only one win and a draw in eight home games.

Now into the new Millennium, the four-and-a-half week break provided an opportunity to take stock but with Maddison, Miller, McSkimming, Banger and Raeside all injured, Dundee were hard pressed to field a team during a five-day break on the sunshine island of Cyprus. Nevertheless, local club Anorthosis Famagusta were beaten 2-1 and there was a 2-2 draw with Yugoslavian Premier League side FK Cukaricki although a couple of Italian trialists had been required to make up the numbers.

A lack of funds prevented any new signings and, on their return, Dundee failed to find the net in league games away to Hearts (0-2) and at home to Kilmarnock (0-0), a scoreline replicated in the Scottish Cup tie against Ayr United at Dens. The fans were fed up with the poor home form and at the end of a dire display against Ayr, the players were loudly booed from the field.

It had been hoped that Banger might provide much-needed penetration but another red card incurred against Killie made him an ever-increasing liability. The attacking flair of Iain Anderson was badly missed and though much was expected of Steven Boyack, other teams had taken measures to block his dangerous runs.

In an effort to freshen things, Boyack and Billio were dropped but without any quality replacements, it was to no avail. A hamstring injury then sidelined Billio for several

weeks but, on February 5th, a spectacular 35-yarder from Hugh Robertson set Dundee on the road to a morale-boosting 3-0 win at Motherwell.

The respite proved temporary and although Celtic had just sacked John Barnes after their Scottish Cup humiliation by Inverness Caley Thistle, the Bhoys coasted to a 3-0 win at snow-swept Dens. A twisted knee ruled Robert Douglas out of the cup replay at Ayr - previously postponed due to high winds - but after 180 minutes, neither side had managed to find the net.

As snow began to carpet the pitch, Rae swept home the opener early in extra-time only for Neil Duffy to head an equaliser. With no further score, the tie would be decided on penalties and when this failed to separate the sides, it was on to sudden death. Robbie Raeside and Barry Smith both netted but when Nicky Banger's effort was saved by Nelson, Ayr were through, 7-6 on penalties.

The Somerset Park side went on to reach the semi-finals and Dundee's failure to progress to the more lucrative stages came as a severe financial blow. Ireland had been absent due to cartilage trouble and without his steadying influence, the next four games turned out to be a defensive nightmare.

A 3-1 home defeat by Aberdeen dragged Dundee back into the relegation dogfight before things hit rock bottom in a 7-1 debacle against Rangers at Dens. In a Sunday night shocker broadcast live on Satellite TV, a clearly unfit Douglas returned to goal to spare young Jamie Langfield an ordeal - but the big keeper got scant cover from his defenders who were pulled all over the place by the rampant Rangers attack.

Jocky Scott's contract was due to expire in July and now he found himself under ever-increasing pressure. In a pre-match interview in *The Daily Record,* Peter Marr claimed that although not facing the sack if Dundee lost to Rangers, the manager would have to fight for his future just like the players. Recent home games had seen Scott subjected to abuse from a section of the support and during the Rangers game the Dens boss had angrily gestured towards them.

Afterwards he apologised, blaming his reaction on frustration at onfield events: "Rangers gave us a pummelling. They were simply lethal on the night but we gave them a hand with some poor defending and should at least have matched them in terms of workrate and attitude."

The nightmare continued with a 6-2 midweek thrashing from Celtic at Parkhead and, on March 4th, Dundee faced a vital match at Kilmarnock where defeat would leave them just a point ahead of the bottom-of-the-league side who had a game in hand.

Travelling fans feared the worst when the Dark Blues went two down but with 15 minutes left, Annand came off the substitute's bench to score before Grady headed a dramatic equaliser. At last, the fighting spirit was back and that result was to prove a turning point for the Dens Park club.

By mid-March the speculation over Jocky Scott's future intensified when it was announced that three Spaniards, striker Francisco Luna and centre-half Jose Mesas from Sporting Gijon and right-midfielder Javier Artero from San Lorenzo of Argentina, had been signed on loan until the end of the season. Peter Marr had instigated the moves through a players' agency operated by ex-Barcelona and Scotland star Steve Archibald, with whom he had become acquainted in Majorca - but the deals had not been done with Jocky Scott's approval.

According to Marr, there was no hidden agenda and the players had been signed to give the manager options: "We had the chance to get some players who have performed at the highest level in Spain. Whether they play or not is up to Jocky." However, the board's latest action coupled with their failure to offer Scott a new deal put a large question over whether they intended extending his two-year reign.

It was an uncomfortable situation and not one the manager wished to discuss as he concentrated on lifting the club to safety. Reinforced by Ireland's return, Dundee took a massive step with a 2-1 midweek victory over Hibs at Easter Road. Javier Artero justified his inclusion with several penetrating runs but, a goal down at half-time, Jocky Scott's tactical change from 4-4-2 to 4-3-3 had changed the game. Annand replaced Sharp but it was Falconer who proved the match-winner as he twice rose to head

home accurate crosses from Boyack, with the winning goal coming deep in stoppage time.

However, there was to be no respite for Scott and just 10 days later, his position was further undermined when the board announced the signing of West Ham defender Chris Coyne as well as Argentinian striker Martin Hugo Prest from Manchego in Spain and Celtic reserve forward Barry Elliot. Prest signed an 18-month deal while the others received three-year contracts but the trio had again been fixed up through Steve Archibald and it was also revealed that three Danish players - one a full international - had been lined up for next season.

On April 1st, Archibald's presence at Dens for the match against Hearts further fuelled rumours that he and former Barcelona team-mate Berndt Schuster would be Dundee's next management team. With the influential Patrizio Billio back in midfield, Dundee performed well in a no-scoring draw but it was a sad day for all associated with the club. That morning, former chairman and lifelong supporter Ian Gellatly had died at the age of sixty-one and, as a mark of respect, the players wore black armbands and there was a minute's silence before the game.

With eight games left, the possibility of a relegation play-off remained. And with Peter Marr adamant that no managerial decision would be taken until Dundee's league status was clear, the Dundee F.C. Supporters' Association called for board, management and players to pull together until safety was achieved.

With top scorer Willie Falconer suspended for the visit of fourth-placed Motherwell, "Paco" Luna, who had been so impressive as a substitute against St Johnstone, came in for him as Dundee lined up:- Douglas; Smith, Wilkie, Ireland, Maddison; Boyack (Artero), Rae, Billio, Robertson; Luna (Annand), Grady.

At half-time, the Dark Blues trailed 1-0 but, although James Grady had missed a bundle of chances, he equalised soon after the restart before being booked for "over-celebrating" at the Provost Road end! Grady then made it 2-1 but in 63 minutes, he was ordered off when referee Dougie McDonald gave him a second yellow card for allegedly div-

Buzz bomb - James Grady in all-out action against Motherwell at Dens with Francisco Luna and ex-Dark Blue Jamie McGowan ready to pounce.

Fotopress

ing after a Benito Kemble challenge. It was harsh justice and televised highlights on that evening's *Sportscene* clearly revealed that Grady had been fouled.

Earlier, Motherwell's McGowan had also been sent off and, with both sides down to ten men, the energetic Luna was a constant threat, a lung-bursting 60-yard run ending when he was brought down in the penalty box. Billio stepped up to crash home the spot-kick and soon afterwards Luna himself made it 4-1 with a header.

The recent re-opening of the South Enclosure had certainly delighted the home support who also appreciated the greatly improved attacking performance. In Luna they had found a new hero and Jocky Scott was full of praise for the newcomer: "Luna is lying knackered in the dressing room but our fans can take to a skilful guy who shows an appetite for hard work."

Luna was again on target with a flashing header in a 2-2 draw against Celtic at Parkhead. The continentals had brought a welcome touch of flair and, three days later, Luna's brilliance made him the target for tough tackling Aberdeen defenders at Pittodrie. After being booked, the Spaniard was substituted for fear he might retaliate but skill was to win through, his replacement Artero conjuring up a finely struck late goal in a 1-0 win.

Now eleven points clear of Aberdeen, safety was virtually assured and despite losing to Kilmarnock (h) 1-2 and Rangers (a) 0-3, Dundee - with three home games left - remained hopeful of a top half finish. Luna and Artero had become firm favourites and allied to the team's resurgence, the fans' enthusiasm had been rekindled. There was considerable disquiet at the treatment of Jocky Scott and Jimmy Bone but, equally, there was a growing acceptance that the board's ploy of signing quality continentals was the right direction in which to go.

In a *BBC Sportsound* interview prior to the Killie game, Peter Marr stated his intention to restore the Dark Blues as a major force in Scottish football. He acknowledged that Jocky Scott had done well but, while now admitting that a foreign coach was a possibility, said: "We have only used Steve Archibald in an agency capacity and that is the extent of the relationship. He has a lot of contacts but was never a contender for the manager's post."

On Saturday, May 6th, the managerial uncertainty was laid aside as Dundee prepared to meet Dundee United at Dens. Ex-Dundee and Scotland star Ian Ure was a guest as three changes were made from the side that had beaten Motherwell. Tweed replaced the injured Ireland, Artero came in for Robertson and Rae moved to the left, while Willie Falconer was preferred to Grady alongside Luna.

On a gloriously hot day, the players were grimly determined to avenge their last three derby defeats and by midway through the first half, Billio and Rae had established a stranglehold on midfield. It was one-way traffic and although Billio blasted a penalty over the bar, the game swung decisively in Dundee's favour when Ferraz was sent off for a crude backheader on Wilkie, who in November had lost two teeth and required plastic surgery to his mouth after a collision with United's David Hannah.

Four minutes after half-time, Dundee got the breakthrough

Dandy double - Willie Falconer netted twice in Dundee's 3-0 Dens derby win over United. DC Thomson

when Falconer headed home an Artero cross. Quarter of an hour later, a Rae-Boyack move culminated in Grady heading a second and, soon afterwards Falconer made it 3-0 when Grady unselfishly nodded a Boyack corner back across goal.

It had been a great team performance but the powerful running of Artero, the incisiveness of Boyack and the nonstop aggression of Grady - a half-time substitute for the injured Luna - had been key factors as Dundee ran United ragged in their biggest Dens derby success since 1973.

Seven days later, a Gavin Rae goal earned a 1-0 win over Hibs but Dundee were to pass up the opportunity of again finishing fifth when they lost 2-0 to Scottish Cup finalists Aberdeen. It was a disappointing finale and, by then, the managerial position had been clarified. Just 24 hours after their derby success, Jocky Scott and Jimmy Bone had been informed that their contracts were not to be renewed when they expired on July 9th.

Dundee's official statement had read: "The decision not to proceed with the current management team is no reflection on the abilities of either man. Nor should it be interpreted that the directors felt that the manager and his assistant had achieved all that they could for Dundee. The records of Jocky Scott and Jimmy Bone speak for themselves. But the unanimous decision of the board is that a change of direction at management level is the desired option."

Jocky Scott saw it somewhat differently: "I am angry, frustrated and very disappointed because we were given no reason for their decision. As far as I am concerned I have been sacked. That's football but there's a right way to go about it. This could have been done weeks ago but wasn't and it became the worst-kept secret in Dundee. I just wish the board had been honest with me."

Remarkably, Scott, who had comfortably achieved that season's target of consolidation, had spent only £210,000 in his 27 months in charge. Along with Bone, he had displayed commendable dignity throughout a traumatic period. Both were highly respected coaches and that summer Jocky Scott moved south to become manager of English Second Division club Notts County while Jimmy Bone later returned to South Africa to take charge of Premier club Umtata Bush Bucks.

Dundee F.C. Season 2000-01 (BACK, left to right) Juan Sara, Chris Coyne, Steven Tweed, Jamie Langfield, Rab Douglas, Derek Soutar, Craig Ireland, Lee Wilkie, Willie Falconer. MIDDLE - Jack Cashley (masseur), Dario Magri (club co-ordinator), Enzo Romano (fitness coach), Marco de Marchi, Mark Slater, Graham Bayne, Michael Yates, Hugh Robertson, Gavin Rae, Harry Hay (sprint coach), Billy Thomson (goalkeeping coach), Dario Bonetti (assistant-manager). FRONT - Walter del Rio, Steven Milne, Patrizio Billio, Fabian Caballero, Barry Smith, Ivano Bonetti (manager), Marcello Marrocco, Alessandro Romano, Giorgi Nemsadze, Javier Artero, Shaun McSkimming.

DC Thomson

CHAPTER THIRTY-SIX

Forza Dundee

Meanwhile, Dundee Football Club were indeed about to move in a completely new direction. Twenty-four hours after Scott and Bone had learned of their fate, a press conference was held at the Ballinard Hotel in Broughty Ferry. And there, Dens chairman Jimmy Marr informed the assembled media that Dundee's new management team would be Italian brothers Ivano and Dario Bonetti.

"Dundee have taken a major gamble in choosing the potential of the Bonettis over the proven track record of Jocky Scott," said Marr. "You have to live by the decisions you make in football and we are prepared to do that. We can't be right all the time but everything we do is because we believe it to be in the best interests of Dundee Football Club."

The Bonettis would be involved in a coaching capacity only, for it was rumoured that, along with fellow Serie 'A' stars Attilio Lombardo and Roberto Mancini, they had attempted to buy out the Marrs late last year. Three years earlier, the Italians had fronted an abortive bid to buy Grimsby and in 1999 they also failed in efforts to take over Hull City and the Italian club Genoa.

The Marrs knew of the brothers through their cousin Dario Magri, who had facilitated Patrizio Billio's transfer while at Crystal Palace. Originally keen on Ivano as a player, they had been impressed by his enthusiasm, ideas and contacts and felt a managerial role could be productive. Magri, a former London cab driver and a fluent linguist, would now be Dundee's footballing "co-ordinator". That would allow the brothers to concentrate on coaching with another Italian, Enzo Romano, coming in as fitness coach.

Dario Bonetti (38), an Italian international central defender, had starred for Brescia, Roma, AC Milan, Verona, Juventus and Sampdoria while Ivano Bonetti (35), had been a left-sided midfielder of distinction for Brescia, Juventus, Genoa, Atalanta, Bologna, Sampdoria and Torino. In 1995, Ivano joined English First Division Grimsby, where an infamous dressing-room bust-up with manager Brian Laws left him with a broken cheekbone. Bonetti received an out-of-court settlement, later moving on to Tranmere Rovers, then Crystal Palace before finally returning to Genoa.

Both had appeared in a European Cup Final - Dario for Roma who lost to Liverpool in 1984, and, along with Ivano, for Sampdoria in the defeat by Barcelona at Wembley in 1992. Ivano boasted a World Club Championship medal for Juventus after their triumph over Argentinos in 1985, while Dario had won a UEFA Cup winners' medal in 1990 when Juventus defeated Fiorentina, and both held a European Super Cup winners' medal as well as various others from domestic league and cup successes.

Italian job - Ivano and Dario Bonetti would form the new Dens Park management team.   DC Thomson

Clearly, the brothers had performed at the highest level and had learnt their trade from some of the biggest names in World football. Nils Liedholm, Arrigo Sacchi and Dino Zoff were amongst those who had managed Dario while Ivano had played for Dundee's old AC Milan adversary Giovanni Trappatoni as well as Sven-Goran Eriksson. Nevertheless, there were obvious concerns over their own lack of managerial experience which thus far had been confined to Italian Fifth Division club Sestrese.

Understandably, the media had sympathised with the outgoing Scott and Bone and when Dundee talked of a top-three placing by 2003, many were dubious. However, Motherwell chief executive Pat Nevin had first-hand knowledge of Ivano from his time at Tranmere and was convinced that the Dens Park board had made a wise move: "Bonetti was a very talented player whose standard of fitness and play was exceptional and he was also well liked by his team-mates."

It was late June before the Italians officially took over but by then, there had been a number of changes to the playing staff. Eddie Annand, Tommy Coyne, Robbie Raeside and Paul Clark had all been released while John Elliot joined Airdrie after refusing a one-year deal at Dens. Spanish defender Jose Mesas, who had not featured for the first team, had also been allowed to go.

Speed merchant - Spanish winger Javier Artero leaves Arthur Numan of Rangers for dead at Dens.
DC Thomson

After the Aberdeen game, fans' favourite James Grady had thrown his jersey and boots into the Bobby Cox Stand in a parting gesture. He had been keen to remain but, at the end of his contract and unable to agree terms with Dundee, he finally opted to join Eddie Annand at Ayr United.

Javier Artero and Francisco Luna had excelled in their short spell at Dens and this prompted Dundee to sign Artero on a three-year contract from San Lorenzo for a new Dens record fee of £300,000. A similar fee was agreed with Sporting Gijon for Luna but, to the fans' dismay, he pulled out of the deal due to his family's reservations over settling in Scotland.

The three Danish signings also fell through but in quick succession, Dundee secured Georgian international midfielder and captain Georgi Nemsadze (28), former Bologna, Juventus and Roma defender Marco de Marchi (33), and ex-Napoli and Genoa left-back Marcello Marrocco (31), with all fixed up on three-year deals.

De Marchi and Marrocco had been persuaded to utilise contr-actual "get-out clauses" to obtain their release from Vitesse Arnhem and Modena, respectively, while the 49-times capped Nemsadze - rated at £1.5 million while at Grasshoppers of Zurich, had arrived from Reggiana on freedom-of-contract. However, the former Dinamo Tblisi man's financial demands had earlier thwarted Hibs and signing him involved Dundee in an outlay of some £420,000.

De Marchi had starred alongside Roberto Baggio, Gianluca Vialli and Fabrizio Ravanelli in the Juventus UEFA Cup winning team of 1993 and, such was his popularity at Vitesse, that, on leaving, he had taken out a full page advert to thank his appreciative fans.

However, Bonetti was keen to blend the best of Scottish and continental football and he now persuaded Scotland Under-21 internationals Gavin Rae and Lee Wilkie, then

Patrizio Billio - whose fine end-of-season form had attracted interest from both Perugia and Stuttgart - to extend their contracts until 2003.

That summer, Dundee's pre-season preparations were based at a training camp at the ski-resort of Borno, high in the Italian Alps near Lake Garda close to the Bonettis' home town of Brescia. The snow-capped peaks provided a stunning backdrop for the 24-man squad's twice daily training sessions but when a glamour game against Udinese fell through, the Dark Blues played friendlies against Italian Fifth Division sides Polisportiva San Guiseppe and Borgorosso, who they defeated 5-0 and 7-0, respectively.

The departure of Grady and Annand and the failure to secure Luna had left Dundee short up front, and, in mid-July, Bonetti announced the capture of two highly rated Argentinian strikers, Juan Sara (24), for £80,000 and Fabian Caballero (22), for £133,000 from a Players' Agency on one-year contracts. Both had been playing in Paraguay where, after less than a third of the season, Caballero had netted 13 goals for Sol de America while Sara had scored six for Serro Portino. In season 1998-99, Caballero had been on the fringes of the Arsenal squad and though the target of late bids by Porto and Bari, he decided on Dens!

The Italian trip allowed the new management team to assess the players but there was a shock when Steven Boyack was made available for transfer along with Lee Maddison, Hugh Robertson, Willie Miller, Lee Sharp, Barry Elliot, Frank van Eijs and Nicky Banger. On their return, Sara and Caballero netted in a 2-1 win over Raith Rovers at Kirkcaldy but it was Boyack's energetic display as a substitute that had turned the game. However, the winger wanted to keep his options open when his contract expired in 2001 and mindful of losing Adamczuk and Anderson for no fee, Peter Marr supported Bonetti's decision.

Meanwhile, the Dark Blues received an unexpected bonus when Iain Anderson was transferred from Toulouse to Preston North End for £500,000. The winger had struggled to establish himself in France but a successful loan spell had helped Preston win the English Second Division and the deal became permanent. Dundee were entitled to compensation since "Ando", still under the age of 24, had joined another British club within 12 months of leaving Dens. A figure of £90,000 was agreed with the Dark Blues negotiating a 20% sell-on fee on any subsequent transfer.

Several hundred fans travelled to Blundell Park for Dundee's final warm-up game against Ivano Bonetti's former club Grimsby Town. The Dark Blues could only manage a 2-2 draw but there was certainly the promise of things to come when Nemsadze wriggled past a trail of defenders before netting a superb solo goal.

With the new season fast

Marco de Marchi - the former Juventus star was now at Dens.

approaching, enthusiasm amongst fans was sky-high as Peter Marr declared: "Dundee's primary aim is to finish in the top six of the Premier League. Thereafter, we want to achieve a level of success and consistency that will guarantee European football at Dens Park each season. We do not believe we are being unrealistic in striving to become the third force in Scottish football."

Clearly, his feelings of optimism were shared by the 2,000 Dundee fans who made the trip to Fir Park for the Premier League opener against Motherwell on Saturday, July 29th. Just three Scots made the starting line-up as Dundee fielded: Douglas; Smith (capt), Tweed, de Marchi, Marrocco; Artero, Nemsadze, Billio, Bonetti; Caballero, Sara. Subs. McSkimming, Falconer, Langfield, Milne, Bayne.

An eighth minute Billio goal set the scene for an exhilerating first-half display in which Dundee hit the woodwork three times. Bonetti himself was a stylish attacking midfielder but, soon after the restart, he was sent off when a rash challenge earned him a second yellow card. Dundee's ten men came under real pressure but with four minutes remaining, Artero completed a dazzling dribble past five home players to fire home the decisive second goal.

It had been a marvellous attacking performance and the following weekend over 7,000 fans were treated to an equally impressive 3-0 win over Dunfermline at a sun-drenched Dens. The Dark Blues were top of the Scottish Premier League and just as importantly, their skilful, flowing football had caught the imagination of the fans. Some likened the quality of play to that of the great Dundee side of the early 1960s although Ivano Bonetti was more realistic, "Our start has not surprised me because I was aware of the potential but we must keep our feet on the ground and remember our target for this season is to get into the top six."

In their third match, Dundee travelled to Easter Road and once again turned on the style, continually slicing through the Hibernian rearguard before Fabian Caballero shot high into the net from 16 yards. However, with Latapy and Agathe causing all sorts of problems, Hibs hit back to lead 2-1. It was a footballing classic but just on half-time, Caballero was scythed down by Mathias Jack and as the pair became entangled, the striker was sent off for an innocuous push while the German escaped with a yellow card despite a shocking two-footed tackle.

The game had been allowed to flow but this was harsh justice by the referee George Clyde, who had previously ignored several heavy home challenges including a blatant body-check by Jack on Billio in the lead up to Hibs second goal. In such a finely balanced match, Caballero's departure proved fatal and in a late collapse, three more goals were conceded with Billio sent off for a needless foul.

Without the suspended Caballero and Billio and with de Marchi and Bonetti injured, Dundee went down 2-1 to newly-promoted St Mirren at Love Street before the loss of yet another late goal meant they had to settle for a 1-1 draw against Hearts at Dens in late August. Nevertheless, there was the makings of a top quality side and there were high hopes of a good run in the CIS Insurance League Cup.

The powerfully built Caballero had emerged as a deadly striker with good technique and a powerful shot. Earlier, the

Strike force - Argentinians Fabian Caballero and Juan Sara were worth their weight in goals. Fotopress

Argentinian had bulleted home two stunning goals in a 3-0 win over Montrose at Dens. But although the third-round tie against St Mirren brought an opportunity of revenge, Dundee's midweek trip to Paisley was to end in disaster.

The Dark Blues were unable to handle Jose Quitongo and with 15 minutes played, four players had been booked by Tom Brown before Billio was sent off for a lunging tackle. Dundee had plenty of possession but in a crazy spell just after half-time they lost two goals and Lee Wilkie was dismissed for two successive bookings. Saints went on to win 3-0 but the nightmare continued with Caballero receiving a second caution - the equivalent of a red card - when a teapot struck the referee's dressing room door, although Dens officials later insisted that Tweed was the culprit!

Match officials appeared to have been influenced by comments from other SPL managers such as Dunfermline's Jimmy Calderwood and Alex. McLeish of Hibs who appealed for "strong refereeing" while referring to Dundee's "Latin" temperament. It was gamesmanship much reminiscent of McLeish's old mentor Alex. Ferguson and later the Dens Park club complained to the SPL. Jim Jefferies of Hearts then labelled the Dundee players "serial divers and shirt pullers" but it had been patently obvious that it was his side that had used such tactics after getting something of a runaround at Dens!

Nevertheless, Dundee's disciplinary record of six red cards and 21 bookings was fast overshadowing their new-found reputation for skilful play. Previously, the players had been briefed by former referee Bob Valentine and following an informal meeting with SFA refereeing officials, Ivano Bonetti declared that the club would not tolerate any further indiscipline.

Meanwhile, the foreign influx had continued with the arrival on "Bosmans" of Argentinian defender Walter del Rio (23), - previously rejected by Jocky Scott after appear-

Hit-man - Juan Sara turns away after netting the first of his hat-trick in the 3-0 demolition of Dundee United at Dens. DC Thomson

ing in Dundee's friendly against Aris Salonika - and former Lazio, Brescia and Verona midfielder Alessandro Romano (30). An economic passer of the ball, Romano was involved as Dundee - employing a more cautious 4-4-1-1 system with only Caballero up front - bounced back with a 1-1 draw against SPL Champions Rangers at Dens to dispel any notions that the Bonetti revolution was grinding to a halt.

On September 20th, fifth-placed Dundee entertained bottom-of-the-table Dundee United, who had failed to win any of their opening seven games. For long spells, the Dens men were on the defensive but, soon after the break, Sara netted from a tight angle after Combe could only parry a powerful 25-yarder by Caballero. Now it was all Dundee until a horrendous double challenge by McDonald and de Vos resulted in Caballero going off with a serious knee injury.

De Vos was red-carded although McDonald appeared to be the main culprit, while assistant-manager Dario Bonetti was sent to the stand after a touchline confrontation with the referee. Dundee continued to press and in 79 minutes, Sara headed home after Nemsadze had weaved his way past three men and, two minutes from time, the Argentinian notched his hat-trick with another header from an Artero cross.

That was Dundee's second successive 3-0 derby win at Dens but it had come at great cost. Caballero had sustained a ruptured ligament in one knee and with a partial tear in the other, the striker would undergo surgery at the Isokinetic Fitness Institute in Bologna where he would remain for a lengthy programme of recuperation.

Ivano Bonetti was bitterly upset: "We want to play entertaining football but some teams try to kick us off the park. United are the worst team for this I've seen and they tried to kick Caballero two or three times before he was injured. My brother was close to the incident and was very angry because he knows how important a player Fabian is for us."

There was a growing confidence at Dens with the fans relishing their football amidst an excitement that had not

been seen for many years. Meanwhile, Martin Hugo Prest had joined Airdrie, Lee Sharp went to St Mirren, while Steven Boyack remained after a £125,000 bid from Dundee United was rejected. Following an unsuccessful trial at Bolton, Boyack refused similar trips to Wolves, Notts Forest and Wigan but when he indicated his willingness to play for Dundee he was told that it would be best if he moved on.

In *The Courier*, a frustrated Boyack claimed that Bonetti had virtually ignored him during a discussion about his future: "The manager said I would remain here until another club met Dundee's valuation but he spoke to me while watching a football video and I only got 20 seconds of his time. No one has told me that I'm not good enough to play for Dundee and I've not become a bad player overnight but it's now best that I move on."

It was a no-win situation for both parties and, in October, the midfielder rejoined former team-mates James Grady and Eddie Annand at First Division Ayr United on loan. Lee Wilkie had missed Dundee's opening two games through suspension and with Steven Tweed, Marco de Marchi, Chris Coyne and Barry Smith all available for the central defensive positions, the then five-times capped Scotland Under-21 international had attracted strong interest from Tottenham, Notts Forest and Wolves before being allowed to spend seven days on trial with Leeds United at Elland Road.

Nothing came of this and the £1-million rated defender returned to play in five of Dundee's next eight games. However, the long-term absence of Caballero had come as a hammer blow to Dundee's plans and although it was rumoured that Francisco Luna was keen to rejoin Dundee after an unhappy loan spell in Mexico, nothing had transpired. Off the field came the sad news that former chairman Ron Dixon had been killed in a car crash in Mexico but soon there were better tidings for the Dens Park club. Repeatedly, it had been rumoured that a short-term replacement for Caballero was to be drafted in but few could have imagined the ensuing turn of events.

CHAPTER THIRTY-SEVEN

"The Bird"

That summer, Dundee had been linked with a number of top Italian stars such as Roberto Mancini, Attilio Lombardo and Claudio Caniggia. No-one had really believed that any would actually pull on the Dark Blue of Dundee but now it was believed that former Argentinian World Cup star Caniggia was due in the city for signing talks as was fellow Argentinian international, Beto Carranza!

Along with his close friend, the great Diego Maradonna, the 47-times capped Caniggia had formed one of the world's most famous striking partnerships, distinguishing himself at Italia '90 when Argentina lost 1-0 to West Germany in the final and again at the next World Cup Finals in America four years later. The 33-year-old striker had played for River Plate, Verona (alongside Dario Bonetti), Atalanta, Roma, Benfica and Boca Juniors before returning to Atalanta where he was now out of contract. However, there was also controversy, the long-haired Argentinian having served a 13-month ban after failing a drugs test while at Roma in 1993.

For days, Tayside had buzzed in anticipation and, finally on Tuesday, October 3rd, Ivano Bonetti informed a packed Dens press conference that Dundee had indeed signed Caniggia and Carranza: "I have dreamed of bringing Claudio to this club and today it has come true. When Caniggia plays, everyone wants to watch for he is one of the biggest names in world football. He has come here to help his friends and he hopes to play himself back into Argentina's team for the 2002 World Cup."

Dens director Jim Connor admitted he was still in a daze after the signing: "These are incredibly exciting times for Dundee Football Club. Claudio will be a huge influence on the team but there will also be great commercial benefits." And according to Javier Artero, his new team-mates were just as happy: "Much has been said about how excited the fans are about Claudio's arrival but I can assure you that the players are just as happy."

In addition, there was confirmation that former Argentinian international Beto Carranza, (27), a friend of Walter del Rio, had also signed. The speedy midfielder had earned nine full caps while at Racing Club, Boca Juniors, Independiente and San Lorenzo until suffering a career-threatening knee injury. However, he appeared to have recovered, going on to play for Vera Cruz of Mexico then Peruvian outfit Universitario de Deportes and had impressed in a short trial spell at Dens.

However, the signing of Caniggia - comparable to that of Dens Park legend Billy Steel in 1950 - had captured the imagination of the fans and soon the club shop was doing a roaring trade selling replica strips with Caniggia's name and squad number 33 on the back. The Argentinian star would make his debut at Aberdeen and Dundee's 2,500 ticket allocation was quickly snapped up.

Somewhat short of match practice, Caniggia would start on the bench. This was disappointing for the large Dundee contingent - hundreds of whom sported Caniggia wigs - but they were soon treated to some wonderful flowing football in the sun before player-manager Ivano Bonetti scored with a delightful 25 yard chip over Ryan Esson.

Just before half-time, there was near hysteria when Caniggia came on for Milne. And although Gavin Rae's sending-off for retaliation on Phil McGuire made things harder, the pacy Argentinian - nicknamed "El Pajaro" or "the Bird" - set the seal on a memorable afternoon when he raced on to a perfectly weighted Nemsadze pass and slid the ball inside the far post in the dying seconds. It had been a dream debut and there were great celebrations amongst the fans.

Superstar - former Argentinian World Cup star Claudio Caniggia made an electrifying start with two goals in his first two games for the Dark Blues. Jimmy Lorimer

Caniggia fever - Dundee supporters go wild as their newest hero nets on his debut to clinch a 2-0 win at Aberdeen.　　DC Thomson

However, it was farewell to another Dens star when Robert Douglas threw his jersey to the crowd at the end of the game. The popular goalkeeper was Celtic-bound with the Dark Blues to get £1.2 million plus another £200,000 dependent on appearances for Celtic and Scotland.

In an interview with Derek McGregor of *The Sun,* the Scotland squad keeper declared: "I'm sad to leave when things are starting to take off at Dens. Ivano has brought in several gifted players and I'm sure Dundee will go from strength to strength. I feel very emotional because the fans have been brilliant to me and I hope I've been as good for them. I could have left on a Bosman but I signed a new deal and I'm pleased Dundee will get a good transfer fee because they always looked after me."

The following week, Caniggia made his home debut against Motherwell. However, slack defending meant the loss of two early goals before Dundee's new hero expertly screwed the ball over the keeper and into the back of the net. That sent the 8,000 fans wild with delight and although Dundee were unable to level the scores, the fair-haired Argentinian had looked every inch the superstar with his blistering pace and lightning twists and turns.

Scotland Under-21 international Jamie Langfield had been in goal but now Dundee brought in the experienced Marco Roccati, (25), on loan from Bologna until the end of the season. Formerly at Torino and AC Milan, the 6'6" ex-Italian Under-21 international had signed from Ravenna for £1.3 million in 1998, though he had mostly been understudy to former Italian international keeper Gianluca Pagliuca.

However, Roccati was unable to prevent defeats at Dunfermline and at home to third-placed Hibernian and, on November 11th, Dundee went up the road to play a Dundee United side who had taken just two points from 15 games and, without a home win in almost a year, lay eight points adrift at the foot of the table. Willie Falconer was recalled to play alongside Caniggia and Dundee's stylish passing and movement was in stark contrast to United's long-ball game. With half-time approaching, the veteran striker cleverly

played in Caniggia and the Argentinian sped through to pick his spot in the net.

From then, Dundee were happy to hit on the break and, in 73 minutes, a rapier-like movement down the right brought a second. Controlling a pass from Smith, Caniggia back-heeled to Nemsadze, who ghosted past two defenders before brilliantly lofting the ball up and over the helpless Combe.

Later, Tannadice boss Alex Smith claimed that United had been "mugged" but in truth they had been outclassed with Smith grudgingly admitting that he didn't have the luxury of any World Cup stars in his team! However, one of Dundee's key men was Ivano Bonetti, who showed great courage in holding the ball amidst some fierce tackling, calmly dictating play with great skill and vision.

Seven days later, St Mirren were routed 5-0 at Dens and although two-goal Caniggia was again the star attraction, Gavin Rae received great praise from Bonetti. Virtually an ever-present last term, the 22-year-old midfielder had only recently regained his place from Patrizio Billio and now Bonetti - who claimed Rae could be worth £10 million - predicted he would go on to play for Scotland. In contrast, Billio, formerly a close friend of Bonetti, had become unsettled and he was put up for sale for £400,000.

The Dark Blues continued to play some breathtaking football but could only manage one point from their next three games against Hearts (a) 1-3, St Johnstone (h) 1-1, and Celtic (h) 1-2. Beto Carranza had burst to prominence with a marvellously struck goal from a free-kick against Hearts and, along with Nemsadze and Caniggia, he repeatedly took the eye with his brilliant dribbling skills and penetrating runs against St Johnstone.

For long spells, Dundee had dominated proceedings against Saints but, just as at Tynecastle, the loss of a late goal would prove their downfall, with the Perth equaliser arriving in the 95th minute despite the fourth official previously indicating two minutes of injury time. It was a similar story against league leaders Celtic in a Sunday Sky TV spectacular. The Dark Blues lost an early goal as well as the influential de Marchi through injury but soon their swift interchanging brought them almost total control and a 55th-minute equaliser when Tom Boyd headed a spectacular own-goal. Celtic, however, were the stronger in the latter stages and when an attempted clearance by Chris Coyne ricocheted across goal after a corner, the unmarked Agathe headed a last-gasp winner.

Nevertheless, Dundee were gaining a host of new admirers. Celtic boss Martin O'Neill and St Johnstone manager Sandy Clark were mightily impressed while former Dundee, Hearts and Celtic star Tosh McKinlay - at Dens on behalf of *The Scottish Daily Mail* - commented: "I was very impressed by Dundee and thought they were most unfortunate not to take something. After taking some time to adjust to the Scottish game, Bonetti has been a breath of fresh air with the way his team plays."

"Caniggia is different class. People thought he had been put out to grass but he does his bit to drop off and link with the midfield players and still looks capable of playing at the highest level. However, like Sara today and Bonetti and Carranza last week, he failed to take his chances to kill the game and Dundee need to turn the good play into points."

The following week they did just that, returning from Kilmarnock with a 3-2 win after overcoming a two-goal deficit. Twenty-year-old Stevie Milne, last season's Third Division Player of the Year after scoring 19 goals while on loan at Forfar, netted twice and proved an excellent deputy for Caniggia who had been to South America on business.

The Argentinian returned for the pre-Christmas visit of Aberdeen while a fit-again Marco de Marchi replaced Australian Under-21 international Chris Coyne, who had been a defensive stalwart against Celtic and Kilmarnock. A steel band provided plenty of background rythm and home fans in the 9,000 crowd were certainly treated to a pulsating performance in a 2-2 draw. Goals by the on-song Carranza, then Sara put them 2-1 ahead with an hour gone and Dundee looked sure to go on and win.

However, the game ended in controversy, Stavrum equalising when Aberdeen referee Alan Freeland, who had earlier denied Caniggia a clear penalty, awarded the Dons a soft spot-kick for a push by Barry Smith. After full-time,

Beto Carranza - on his day the former Argentinian international was a real handful for opposing defenders. DC Thomson

Masterclass - Ivano Bonetti and Steven Tweed celebrate the 2-0 win over Dundee United at Tannadice.

Caniggia received a second yellow card for dissent but although the Argentinian was suspended for the Boxing Day clash at Motherwell, Milne again did well as Dundee won 3-0 at a freezing, foggy, Fir Park.

On January 2nd, Dundee lost by an identical scoreline to Hibs in the last match prior to the demolition of the famous old Easter Road stand, a result that left them sixth after 23 games but, though there was again a three-and-a-half-week long winter break, there would be plenty of talking points for the Dens Park supporters.

Fans had queried how Dundee could afford the sky-high wages of the continentals now at Dens. But in an earlier interview with *The News of the World,* Majorca-based chief executive Peter Marr had revealed: "A lot of new guys have arrived but we have only actually paid one fee, for Artero. It's all done on a cash flow basis and obviously we are taking a bit of a gamble. Our wage bill has increased quite substantially but we are looking to offset that in other ways."

"We're hoping to get money back through increased gates, a better league position, more TV money and by looking to become more marketable. But essentially we are copying an approach that Primera Liga sides like Real Mallorca have used to great effect. A few years ago they were struggling in the Spanish First Division until they began to bring in a lot of talented but little known foreigners."

"Each summer, a couple are sold for big money and replacements are brought in from South America or elsewhere. We've been building up contacts all over the place and they're the key to the success of this strategy. That's why we went for the Bonettis because Ivano in particular knows an incredible number of footballing people throughout the world. Caniggia was Dario's team-mate at Verona, while it was Ivano's contacts who helped bring in the Argentinians from Paraguay as well as the others."

By January, several of the fringe players had moved on. Lee Maddison joined Carlisle, Barry Elliot signed for Berwick Rangers after a loan spell at Airdrie and the Steven Boyack saga ended when he was transferred to Hearts for £50,000. After a spell on loan at Ayr, Hugh Robertson joined Ross County and, of those originally for sale, only Willie Miller, Frank van Eijs and Nicky Banger remained with Craig Ireland and Patrizio Billio now added to the list.

Lee Wilkie's future was also unclear for, after that bizarre own-goal for St Johnstone when a cross skidded off him, struck Roccati then rebounded back off him and into the net, there was a training ground bust-up with Ivano Bonetti. Told that his Dens career was over, Wilkie was ordered to train with the Under-21s and although a "clear the air" chat saw him back on the bench at Easter Road, he was loaned to Plymouth Argyle to allow clubs like Everton, Sheffield Wednesday and Preston North End to monitor his form.

Meanwhile, Dundee announced that they had rejected "a serious money move" by FC America of Mexico before persuading Claudio Caniggia to sign a new two-and-a-half year deal. It was believed the striker would get around £10,000 per week with Peter Marr commenting: "It is a massive deal for us - easily the largest amount of money this club has ever invested in a single player. However, with extensive ESPN television coverage in South America, the higher profile Claudio has brought us has already generated a significant amount of revenue and we believe there are other exciting commercial opportunities to come."

One such opportunity involved a Dens glamour friendly against Serie 'A' giants Napoli with a guest appearance by the great Diego Maradona. For days, there was speculation that Dundee would pay the controversial, out-of-condition 40-year-old £250,000 appearance money in the hope of recouping the cash through the sale of TV rights, gate receipts and sponsorship deals. However, the deal collapsed when Maradona - recently served a £16-million tax bill from his time in Italy - turned down Napoli's offer of a coaching position upon which the friendly depended.

Earlier invitations to tour South America had been dismissed as impractical and when a trip to Dubai also fell through, Dundee returned to Italy, this time to Riccione on the Adriatic coast. There, they underwent a seven-day training programme used by Juventus and, in a closed-doors game, defeated the local Serie 'C' side by five goals to one.

In late January, the Dark Blues returned to domestic action, drawing 0-0 with Falkirk in the Scottish Cup before going down 3-2 to Dundee United in a 11,724 derby sell-out at Dens. On a heavy pitch, their lightweight midfield of Artero,

Happy days - Dundee players celebrate a goal against Celtic at Dens Park.
Fotopress

Cash flow - Rab Douglas joined Celtic for a record £1.2 million.

Nemsadze, Romano and Carranza was unable to match United's more determined approach.

Ivano Bonetti, who was recovering from a calf strain, came on in midfield for the injured Shaun McSkimming but it proved a costly gamble when he had to retire after tearing his calf muscle and he would not appear again that season. His influence was missed and over the next few weeks, Dundee's top-six hopes receded after defeats by St Mirren (a) 1-2, Dunfermline (h) 0-1 and Rangers (h) 0-1 made it five successive league losses.

There had, though, been mitigating circumstances. After putting Dundee ahead with a superbly executed overhead kick at Paisley, Juan Sara, earlier booked for lifting his jersey to display a T-shirt declaring "I can do everything through Christ", received a second yellow card for an innocuous midfield handling offence, and his controversial dismissal, at a time when Dundee had been well on top, had swung the game St Mirren's way for the third time that term.

An understrength Dundee had been abysmal against Dunfermline but they had given Rangers a torrid time at Dens. Repeatedly, the surging runs of Caniggia and Nemsadze's close control and clever dribbling carved gaping holes in the Ibrox defence only for Sara to twice miss penalties before Rangers went on to grab a late winner.

Meanwhile, the Dark Blues had made progress in the Scottish Cup. On Monday, February 12th, they matched First Division promotion challengers Falkirk for endeavour and their superior skill paid off when two late goals by Sara and Caniggia - the latter following a lung-bursting run by Artero - set up a fourth-round clash against Hearts at Tynecastle. There, Sara put them ahead but although Roccati made a splendid double save from a Colin Cameron penalty, Dundee finally succumbed to incessant home pressure when Juanjo equalised near the end.

Marco de Marchi continued to be troubled by injury. In the first two months of the season, he missed five games through a niggling hamstring complaint and also came off during the Dens derby against Dundee United. In December, the Italian lasted just six minutes against Celtic and, though he declared himself okay to face Aberdeen two weeks later, he looked far from fit and it was little surprise when he then broke down in the pre-match warm-up at Motherwell.

In late February, de Marchi finally returned and did well at left-back against Rangers and again in a 3-2 away win over St Johnstone. Dundee looked in fine fettle for the Scottish Cup replay against Hearts on Wednesday, March 7th, with many feeling that they were just the sort of flair team that could go all the way in the cup. After a slow start, Dundee looked to have the edge but with 34 minutes played, Dens Park was stunned when Marco de Marchi was sent off.

TV footage later revealed that, while John Underhill had been booking Lee Makel, the Hearts midfielder had stood on the foot of de Marchi, who had kicked him in retaliation, an action brought to the referee's attention by the South Enclosure linesman. Ten-man Dundee battled on only to go down to a late goal and their cup dream was over. The loss of the experienced de Marchi had been a crucial factor and the following day, the Italian defender was made available for transfer.

Meanwhile, Dundee's squad had been bolstered by the arrival of 19-year-old Georgian international defender Zurab Khizanishvili as well as two midfielders, the Argentinian Beto Garrido (26), formerly of Boca Juniors and Lerida of Spain, and an Australian, Mark Robertson (23), whose father Alex had been on Dundee's books in the 1970s.

The highly rated Georgian, who had signed an 18-month deal with Dundee rather than Premiership-bound Fulham, already had 10 full caps and it was hoped he would flourish under the tutelage of Georgian skipper Georgi Nemsadze at Dens. The former Locomotiv Tblisi player had become a free agent when his club went defunct and although Dundee's initial application for a work permit was rejected, it was granted after an appeal, which included a glowing testimony by Arsenal boss Arsene Wenger.

However, footballing matters were put firmly in perspective by the sudden death of Dens Park kitman Willie Dryden (54), who had worked alongside Peter Marr and Jim Connor at St Josephs. A shocked Connor said: "Willie was the type of person who was always there for everyone and nothing was ever too much trouble. He will be sorely missed by everyone at Dens Park."

On Wednesday, March 14th, Dundee paid a fitting tribute to their popular bootmaster with a 2-0 win over Rangers at Ibrox, a victory described by Roger Hannah of *The Scottish Daily Mail* as: "A Caniggia-inspired performance of verve and dynamism which stunned the fallen champions." In 14 minutes, the long-haired Argentinian despatched a powerful shot in off the near post but, despite Craig Moore's dismissal early in the second half, it took a flashing injury-time header by Stevie Milne to secure a 2-0 win after a constant home onslaught.

The Dark Blues had been deadly on the break but their home form was far less effective. Nevertheless, Dundee remained the great entertainers with BBC Scotland's Chic Young labelling them "The Haarlem Globetrotters of Scottish football" and although they faced away fixtures against Celtic and Aberdeen before the 33-game split, the possibility of a top-six place remained.

In the midweek game at Parkead, Jamie Langfield - the subject of an abortive move to Cardiff City - replaced Marco Roccati, who had injured his back in the pre-match warm-up. The youngster made several superb saves but although Dundee looked set for a 1-1 draw after controlling play for long spells with their slick passing movements, Barry Smith was sent off before Mjalby bundled home a last-gasp winner.

Nevertheless, it had been a heartening performance and with sixth-placed Dunfermline just three points ahead, Dundee, who held a superior goal-difference, had to beat Aberdeen and hope the Pars would lose at Kilmarnock. The Dark Blues, without the injured Caniggia, were surprisingly lethargic in the first half but a half-time pep-talk brought new urgency to their play. Within six minutes, Nemsadze put them ahead and soon afterwards, Caballero, who had just recently returned, fired in a second.

That was Dundee's fifth successive win at Pittodrie but the drama continued after full-time, for four minutes remained at Rugby Park. Soon it was all over and with Killie holding on to win 2-1, there were wild scenes of jubilation amongst the fans as well as the Dundee players and officials who had remained on the field.

Ivano Bonetti was delighted: "My players were tired but played with their heart. The top six was the target and to get there was like winning our own league. I believe we could have had 55 points rather than the 41 we got, but we know where the problem is and what we have to do to fix it!"

There had been another masterful performance by Georgi

On target - Willie Falconer heads for goal against Dunfermline but the influx of foreigners limited his appearances. DC Thomson

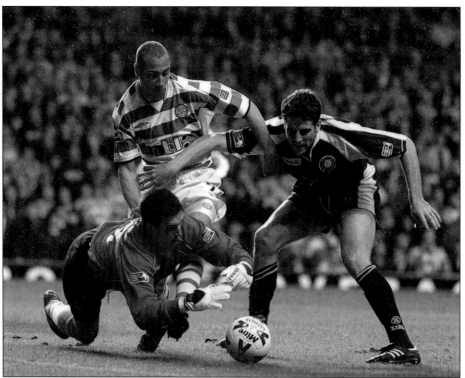

Heat of battle - Jamie Langfield dives to grab the ball from the feet of Celtic dangerman Henrik Larsson at Parkhead while Chris Coyne stands firm.

SNS Group

had merited.

On May 19th, the curtain came down on a season of fine football and despite losing 2-0 to Hearts in Edinburgh, the 3,000 travelling supporters showed their appreciation by singing "Ivano-Dario" non-stop for the last 20 minutes!

That night, the Dundee F.C. Supporters' Association held their Player of the Year Dinner at the city's Hilton Hotel, where Georgi Nemsadze and Gavin Rae each picked up a handful of awards - significant choices since, by then, it had become clear that Claudio Caniggia was on his way to Rangers.

The pacy Argentinian had captured the imagination of the footballing public and, along with Russell Latapy and Frank Sauzee of Hibs and the ultimate winner, Celtic's 53-goal striker, Henrik Larsson, he had been in the running for the prestigious Players' Player of the Year award. Earlier, it had been rumoured that he was heading for Celtic but, when the March 31st signing deadline passed, it was thought he might just remain.

Nemsadze whose midfield brilliance was perfectly complemented by the power and directness of Gavin Rae. And with reported interest from English Premiership clubs as well as Rangers, Dundee ensured that Rae signed a new three-and-a-half year contract.

Scotland international team boss Craig Brown was yet another admirer and later that month, the young Aberdonian was given his full international debut in Poland to become the first Dundee player to play for Scotland since Robert Connor in 1986.

Few could deny that Dundee merited their placing for, even prior to Caniggia's arrival, their play had provided great entertainment. But all too often they had failed to get the results at Dens, a statistic further highlighted by defeats from Rangers (0-3), and Hibernian (0-2), before goals by Sara and Carranza with a penalty finally brought a 2-1 win over Kilmarnock on May 5th - their first home victory in five-and-a-half months!

Fabian Caballero's return had come as a major boost and, eight days later, the powerful Argentinian had further cause to celebrate when he notched a first-half double in Dundee's 2-0 win over Celtic at Parkhead. The first was a glorious effort when, with his back to goal, he brilliantly turned Vega before curling the ball past Gould. However, soon afterwards, the cultured Khizanishvili was controversially sent off after a tussle with Henrik Larsson.

Certainly, there had been a spot of jostling while the pair chased a long through ball but although TV footage later indicated that it had been the Georgian who was tripped, Tom Brown allowed Larsson to run on and shoot wide before returning to dismiss the grounded Khizanishvili and award a free-kick to Celtic! However, the ten-man Dark Blues were not to be denied and a second strike by Caballero earned them the result their earlier displays against Celtic

That would prove a forlorn hope for Caniggia was desperate for a recall to the Argentina squad for the 2002 World Cup Finals in Japan and, perhaps feeling he had a better chance of a regular game at Ibrox, he opted for Rangers. It was May before the move went through after David Murray refused to deal with two seperate agents - apparently not an uncommon situation with South American players. By then, Dark Blue fans were fed up with the whole affair but they had the consolation that Dundee had banked some £850,000, a substantial fee for a 34-year-old. And, this early, their speculate to accumulate investment strategy looked sound.

Now the Caniggia cash could be used to secure the permanent transfers of Fabian Caballero - for a new Dens Park

record outlay of £600,000, Juan Sara (£500,000) and a third Argentinian player Beto Carranza (£200,000), with all three given new three-year deals. Meanwhile, Georgi Nemsadze signed a two-year extension which would keep him at Dens Park until 2005, with midfielders Alessandro Romano and Beto Garrido both handed one-year contracts.

CHAPTER THIRTY-EIGHT

Brief Foray

There would be little break for most of the Dundee squad that close season. The Dark Blues had opted to enter the Intertoto Cup and, just four weeks after their final SPL match at Tynecastle, they returned to action against FK Sartid of Yugoslavia with the incentive of a lucrative tie against Munich 1860 should they progress to the second stage.

It was Dundee's first European foray since their UEFA Cup clash with RWD Molenbeek in October 1974, yet four key men would be marked absent. Beto Carranza was permitted to return to Argentina for the birth of his daughter, Georgian internationalists Georgi Nemsadze and Zurab Khizanishvili were excused after playing two World Cup qualifying games, while Steven Tweed was unavailable after his recent hernia operation.

Unlike other European club competitions, the Intertoto Cup was played at weekends in midsummer and with just 6,500 in attendance on Saturday, June 16th, a somewhat surreal atmosphere surrounded the first-leg tie at Dens. The Dark Blues fielded - Langfield; Smith, Wilkie, Coyne, Marrocco; Artero, Robertson, Romano, Rae, Garrido; Sara. Subs. - Milne, Bonetti, Caballero.

Surprisingly, Dundee began with just Juan Sara up front and Sartid rarely came under any pressure. At half-time, Stevie Milne was introduced and the switch to 4-4-2 brought a marked improvement. However, with the Yugoslavs blatantly time-wasting it was not until the final minute that Dundee went close, a skidding drive by Fabian Caballero flying just wide of the right-hand post.

It had been dull fare and, sadly, the second-half introduction of Ivano Bonetti for Beto Garrido had proved a retrograde step. It was his first appearance since January's brief showing against Dundee United, but, now 36 years old, the Dens player-boss looked well off the pace and henceforth would concentrate solely on his managerial duties.

Mindful of the NATO air-strikes on Belgrade during the Kosovo conflict in 1999, the Foreign Office advised Dundee fans not to travel to Serbia for the return. Consequently, only eight Dens diehards made the trip to the Gradski Stadium in Smedevero although, in the event, both they and the official Dundee F.C. party were warmly welcomed by their Yugoslavian hosts.

Caballero for Robertson was the only change from the first leg and, just four minutes after kick-off, the Argentinian cleverly chested home a headflick by Rae. It was a dream start but despite earlier concerns about the heat and the fanatical home support, controversial refereeing by M. Marinov of Bulgaria was to prove a major factor in Dundee's demise.

In a three-minute spell, Sartid twice converted questionable penalty awards and just before half-time, the unmarked Aleksic made it 3-1 from a corner. In 60 minutes, Sara reduced the deficit when he headed home after a fine run and cross by Cabellero. However, with 15 minutes left, Caballero was red-carded for retaliation and the subsequent gamble of putting on Milne for Wilkie backfired as Sartid went on to win 5-2.

Sloppy defending had contributed to Dundee's downfall

Intertoto action - Stevie Milne looks on as Fabian Caballero takes on the FK Sartid defence in the first-leg tie at Dens.

DC Thomson

but there were strong suspicions over the referee's impartiality. At the first penalty a Sartid player had left studmarks on Jamie Langfield's arm before going down, a powerful shot had clearly played Chris Coyne's arm for the second and by the end, five Dens players had been booked.

Talking in *The Scottish Daily Mail*, Coyne protested: "The Sartid boy lashed the ball straight at me and when it hit my arm, I just knew the ref would give a penalty. We were getting so frustrated, working our socks off for absolutely nothing and most of the bookings were for talking to the referee."

Asked if he felt the Bulgarian official had been bribed, the Dens stopper replied: "Something went on. No way was he impartial. The only thing that did go our way was Alessandro Romano being booked twice and not getting sent off but that just shows what the referee was like!"

After the game, there was uproar in the Dundee camp with an outraged Ivano Bonetti talking of match-fixing and even suggesting that the club might make an official complaint to UEFA. However, in the knowledge that the governing body rarely upheld protests against match officials and, indeed, that Dundee themselves might face sanctions should their protest fail, no further action was taken.

Meanwhile, fans were unsure of the club's current finances although the June AGM had revealed that Dundee F.C. Holdings plc - created in 1999 to allow public share issues since the club had reverted to Limited Company status in 1995 - of which Dundee F.C. Ltd. was a wholly owned subsidiary and whose parent companies were Macrocom 399 and P&J Taverns, had made a £421,000 loss in 1999-2000. Wages were £1,720,553 or 68% of the £2.5m turnover.

As expected, Marco Roccati had returned to Bologna while Willie Falconer and Shaun McSkimming were released along with Frank van Eijs, Mark Slater, Marco Russo and Jonathan Kelly. However, Steven Tweed, a stalwart at

centre-half for the past two seasons, was a shock addition to the open-to-transfer list, which also included the out-of-favour Patrizio Billio and Marco de Marchi, as well as Willie Miller, Craig Ireland, Nicky Banger and Michael Yates.

Goalkeeping coach Billy Thomson, under whose keen instruction Robert Douglas had progressed to the full Scotland international squad, was another to depart.

Soft-shoe shuffle - Georgi Nemsadze was a class act for Dundee. DC Thomson

His position had been undermined by the arrival of Luciano Bodini - reportedly brought in at the insistence of Rocatti's club Bologna. Then when Bodini - like fitness coach Enzo Romano before him - returned to Italy, the appointment of another Italian goalkeeping coach Claudio Bozzini meant there was little future for Thomson at Dens although a short while later, he did well to land a plum post in the new youth set-up at Rangers.

Club captain Barry Smith was given a new three-year contract as were Jamie Langfield, Stevie Milne, Derek Soutar, Lee Mair, Gavin Beith, Barry Forbes and Colin Boylan. However, Dundee had been unable to get a work permit for 20-year-old Georgian international defender Edik Sajeaia, who had played insufficient internationals over the past two years, and they also failed in an ambitious move to persuade the prolific ex-Rangers striker Marco Negri to return to Scotland.

Nevertheless, it was believed that two Argentinians, 28-year-old FC Colon central defender Luis Medero, a former Boca Juniors team-mate of Carranza, Garrido and del Rio, and Under-21 international goalkeeper Julian Speroni, (22), would soon join the club on freedom-of-contract.

Looking ahead to the new campaign, Ivano Bonetti declared that fifth place was a realistic target for Dundee. He played down Claudio Caniggia's departure and insisted that a fully fit Caballero - with six goals from his 14 games compared to Caniggia's eight from 24 - could be just as influential and, indeed, was likely to score more goals.

That was a mouth-watering prospect and, following their brief flirtation with the Intertoto Cup, the Dens players were given another short break before once again flying to Italy for their pre-season preparations. There they routed Equipe Romagna - a team of out-of-contract Italian professionals before returning to defeat Luton Town 3-2, a game which was played behind closed doors due to ongoing electrical work at Dens Park.

Heads you win - Dundee striker Juan Sara sends a scoring header past Nick Colgan of Hibernian at Dens. DC Thomson

On Saturday, July 28th, Dundee's 2001-02 campaign began with a 2-2 draw against Dundee United at Tannadice before wins over Hibernian (2-1) and Livingston (1-0) took them to third place behind Celtic and Rangers. Juan Sara made a fine start, netting in each of the three opening games, while Fabian Caballero, missing at Tannadice through suspension, appeared to have overcome his injury problems.

The popular Caballero did particularly well against Hibs, first crossing for Sara's headed opener then cleverly creating space to fire home the winner. Hibernian had featured the exciting full-back Ulises de la Cruz as well as ex-Dens striker Paco Luna and the game provided top quality entertainment for the near 10,000 crowd.

Almost 8,000 returned for the visit of newly promoted Livingston but despite some spells of superb football, the Dark Blues had struggled in the latter stages of all their opening games. At Tannadice, where Ivano Bonetti had failed to use any of his substitutes, Dundee conceded a last-gasp equaliser. Only fine goalkeeping by Langfield and a large slice of good fortune prevented a repeat against an eager Almondvale side but the next four games against Hearts (a) 1-3, Rangers (a) 0-2, St Johnstone (h) 1-1 and Celtic (h) 0-4 were to bring just a solitary point.

At Ibrox, Dundee again proved they could compete with the Old Firm though the game would be best remembered for two late flare-ups and some controversial post-match comments. Former Dark Blue Neil McCann was dismissed for an uncharacteristic two-footed lunge at Barry Smith while Beto Carranza later got his marching orders for a retaliatory kick at Fernando Rickson - an action which would cost him a fine of two weeks wages.

There was no doubting Ivano Bonetti's frustration and afterwards he said: "Caniggia, Latapy and Amoruso apart, I wouldn't want any of their players in my team. For 70 minutes there was only one team out there and although we didn't win, we're getting to where we want to be."

On September 11th, the world was stunned after terrorists hijacked four American passenger aircraft. Two were flown into the twin towers of the World Trade Centre in New York causing their collapse, a third plane hit the Pentagon and with a total of over 3,000 victims, it was a sombre crowd that observed the minute's silence when Dundee met Celtic at Dens a few days later.

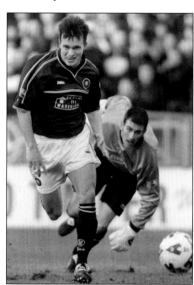

As at Ibrox, Dundee controlled play for long spells only to trail 1-0 at half-time. The loss of a second headed goal in 59 minutes from another set-piece meant there was no way back. But, in the post-match press conference, Bonetti suggested that Chris Sutton was more suited to a swimming pool than a football field and was fiercely critical of referee Alan Freeland for awarding the free-

Local talent - Stevie Milne made his mark alongside the big-name stars.

Enforcer - former Serie 'A' midfielder Alessandro Romano in a tussle with ex-Dark Blue Paco Luna of Hibs. DC Thomson

kicks which had led to the first two goals.

He also felt that Walter del Rio had been unfairly dismissed although his defender, who had already been shown a yellow card, had recklessly lunged into a challenge to earn his second booking. With just two wins from their first seven games, the Dens boss appeared unable or unwilling to recognize his own team's failings and his comments were guaranteed to upset the footballing authorities.

Indeed, both Bonettis had already felt the wrath of the SFA disciplinary committee, Ivano receiving a severe censure for angrily flinging away his jacket after Khizanishvili's dismissal at Parkhead with Dario given a three month dug-out ban for his aggressive behaviour after the home game against Kilmarnock in May.

On the field, Georgi Nemsadze continued to pull the strings but though the team remained similar to that of last term, there was too little end product to Dundee's skilful play. One absentee was Javier Artero, who, just prior to the start of the season, had taken ill before tests at Ninewells Hospital revealed he was suffering from multiple sclerosis, a disease which attacked the body's nervous system.

Subsequent tests showed that the player had a mild form of the disease and he was advised that he would be able to play again. Overwhelmed by hundreds of messages of support, Artero wrote a public letter of thanks to his well-wishers, including former Dark Blue Brian Irvine who had recovered from a similarly traumatic experience.

The strong-running Spaniard had been missed but just as significantly, Dundee looked vulnerable in central defence. Earlier, Ivano Bonetti had informed Peter Marr that he wanted a more mobile, creative style of central defender and, by mid-September, the out-of-favour Steven Tweed, Chris Coyne and Craig Ireland had all been allowed to move on. Ireland rejoined former boss Jocky Scott at Notts County for £50,000, German Second Division outfit Duisburg paid a similar amount for Tweed while Luton Town parted with £70,000 to snap up Coyne.

By then, Bonetti had agreed a three-year deal with the experienced Argentinian defender Luis Medero but delays in processing his and Julian Speroni's application for Italian

On the ball - Javier Artero returned to action against Hearts but illness was to curtail his footballing career. DC Thomson

passports - to which they were entitled through their ancestry - meant neither could turn out for Dundee. By mid-September, Speroni had received his documentation but, by then Medero had got fed-up and instead he signed for Argentinian champions San Lorenzo.

The ongoing feud with Ivano Bonetti meant Scotland Under-21 international Lee Wilkie was also surplus to requirements and this brought interest from Serie 'A' club Perugia, as well as Everton, Sheffield Wednesday and Portsmouth. Dundee were now looking for £350,000 but although First Division Portsmouth, under the management of former Dens duo Graham Rix and Jim Duffy, were particularly keen, "Pompey" could not afford the fee.

Instead, it was Walter del Rio, whose previous seven appearances had all been at full-back, who was the surprise choice to play alongside Khizanishvili in central defence. However, although the Argentinian did well enough in his new role, neither he nor his Georgian partner were sufficiently dominant in the air. At Tannadice, their failure to deal with high cross balls had cost Dundee two points, while the aerial power of Celtic's Sutton and Larsson had also caused major problems.

A bright start to the season saw Jamie Langfield rewarded with a second Scotland Under-21 cap against Croatia, and the young keeper was also included in the Scotland squad for the World Cup qualifier in Belgium. Gavin Rae made the Scotland squad against Latvia, while the selection of Mark Robertson for his first full Australian cap against 2002 World Cup Finals co-hosts Japan, only further served to emphasise the cosmopolitan set-up at Dens.

Former Reggiana midfielder Dario Morello, (32), an ex-Genoa team-mate of Ivano Bonetti, who had impressed in the pre-season game for Equipe Romagna, was paraded as a new signing at Dens but, strangely, the once injury-plagued Italian was said to have decided against remaining and returned home.

The arrival of midfielder Lucas Gatti (23), and ex-Dundee United forward Beto Naveda (28), swelled the Argentinian contingent to eight and, fittingly, Dundee now sported a version of the Argentinian national jersey as their away kit - a strip which certainly proved popular with the fans.

However, things were not quite so interesting on the park and although a Gavin Rae thunderbolt got the team back on the rails with a 1-0 win at Kilmarnock and there was a 2-0 CIS League Cup second-round success at Hamilton, Dundee remained unconvincing. Few who witnessed these performances were convinced they had turned the corner, and this view was confirmed by subsequent league defeats from Aberdeen (h) 1-4 and Dunfermline (a) 1-0.

Now into October, the Dark Blues lay ninth, two points above second-bottom Motherwell. They remained capable of turning on the style but although Carranza had given Thomas Solberg a torrid time prior to Caballero's brilliantly chipped equaliser, suicidal offside tactics against speedy Dons attackers like Darren Mackie and Hachim Zeruouali were doomed to failure.

Meanwhile, Dundee were now in dispute with Patrizio Billio and Marco de Marchi. In April, the players had publicly complained that they were being frozen out and the following month, they were subjected to a number of disciplinary measures by the club. The pair appealed to the SPL, who ruled that the club were justified in fining them two weeks wages for failing to return and prepare for the Intertoto Cup tie against Sartid, but wrong to impose a further two fines, and those findings were then endorsed by the Scottish Football Association.

Dundee's onfield problems were further highlighted by a shock exit at the hands of First Division Ross County at Dingwall. The team looked ill-prepared, especially when former Dens favourite Brian Irvine rose unchallenged to head an early opener and the 2-1 defeat was to deprive them of a lucrative quarter-final tie against Rangers at Dens. Dundee had rarely threatened and to the disgust of fans who had made the long midweek trip north, too many players had lacked the will to win.

In fairness, a number of key men had been missing, for, as well as Artero, the influential Nemsadze was out with a cruciate ligament injury while Marcello Marrocco had suffered a herniated spinal disc. Both would require surgery while Sara, the club's top scorer, again had tendonitis of the knee and Caballero was dogged by a persistant hamstring problem.

Dundee's lack of reserve strength was now exposed with Gatti and Naveda not up to the required standard and youngsters like Barry Forbes and Colin Boylan not yet ready for regular first-team football. Thus far, Dundee had netted a meagre nine goals in winning just three of their 10 league games. With only eight wins from 26 matches since the start of the year and a poor home record, the Bonetti revolution looked to be in trouble but a flurry of transfer activity was once again to bring renewed hope.

Global view - Ivano Bonetti with internationalists Zurab Khizanishvili (Georgia) and Mark Robertson (Australia). DC Thomson

CHAPTER THIRTY-NINE

More New Faces

Ivano Bonetti had more than one target in mind as he sought to recast his defence. For a number of months, the Dens boss had trailed Fan Zhiyi of Crystal Palace and, on October 15th, the Chinese international defender was persuaded to sign a two-and-a-half-year deal with Dundee despite interest by English Premiership clubs, Everton and Fulham.

The Dens Parkers had paid £300,000 for his transfer but with salary and bonuses it was anticipated the total outlay could be £1.8 million. However, the 32-year-old Chinese captain was regarded as a national hero, particularly by the 12 million inhabitants of his home city Shanghai, and though his international commitments had meant conflict with Palace boss Steve Bruce, Peter Marr was confident that Dundee would enjoy substantial commercial spin-offs.

Within 48 hours, the arrival of Georgian international midfielder Temuri Ketsbaia from Wolves came as another major signing coup. Just 15 months earlier, the 33-year-old who had also played for Dynamo Tiblisi, Anorthosis Famagusta and AEK Athens, had cost the English First Division side £900,000 from Newcastle United. But, now out of favour and with Dundee willing to pay the final six months of his contract, Wolves - who had recently baulked at Dundee's £7-million valuation of Fabian Caballero - waived the £400,000 fee which they had earlier demanded.

Having secured the 45-times capped Ketsbaia - Georgia's all-time top scorer and a huge favourite at Newcastle - Dundee confirmed their interest in Polish international captain Marek Kozminski, a left-sided midfielder with Italian Serie 'A' club Brescia. Nothing transpired but soon Massimo Beghetto, a 32-year-old left-back formerly of Bologna, Vicenza and Perugia was signed on freedom-of-contract until the end of the season.

On October 27th, Ketsbaia and Beghetto made their debuts in a 2-1 win over Hibernian at Easter Road but it was two young Scots who took centre stage. Gavin Rae - The Bank of Scotland Player of the Month for October - ran half the length of the field to score and although Hibs levelled, a late winner by Dens substitute Stevie Milne sent the travelling support into raptures.

Three days later, Ketsbaia made his mark as Motherwell were defeated 3-1 at Dens. First he netted after a typical surging run, later setting up Caballero who scored with a fine curling shot. Beghetto had impressed as a reliable defender and when Fan Zhiyi arrived from China later that week, the 8,500 home allocation for the Dens derby against Dundee United was quickly sold out.

A crowd of 11,571 witnessed the Chinaman's debut but there was to be no dream debut. In fact, it was United who looked the more committed until a spell of home pressure saw Carranza equalise with a penalty just on half-time. Fan had already been booked for a reckless first-half challenge and in 63 minutes a second yellow card for allegedly diving after a lunging McIntyre tackle meant an ignominious exit.

It was harsh justice by referee Stuart Dougal but bolstered by the substitution of skipper Barry Smith for Milne - himself a 16th-minute replacement for the injured Caballero, Dundee held out for a draw. Already due to fly out for the Chinese National Games, Fan was unaffected by his one-game suspension and would not return until the game against Rangers in late November.

The week before, a hard-fought 1-1 draw with Hearts had featured a fine headed equaliser by 20-year-old Dave Mackay, who, only recently recalled from a loan spell at Arbroath, had performed solidly at right-back. Fan Zhiyi was back and, ably supported by Khizanishvili, he kept a tight rein on Rangers £12 million striker Torre Andre Flo.

On December 15th, the Chinese star struck a magnificent goal against Celtic at Parkhead in 17 minutes but things turned sour after a stylish first-half performance. Soon after half-time two soft goals were conceded, Zurab Khizanishvili had to be stretchered off and when a floodlight failure entailed a 15 minute stoppage, there was no way back. Ivano Bonetti had finally been able to field his preferred formation

Star quality - the arrival of famous Georgian international Temuri Ketsbaia was another major coup for Dundee.   DC Thomson

but his first-choice back three of Khizanishvili, Fan and del Rio looked alarmingly vulnerable to the high cross ball. In the end they lost 3-1 and when a subsequent 2-1 home defeat by Kilmarnock left them with just one victory in eight games, some serious questions began to be asked.

Earlier proposals to extend the Bonettis' contracts until 2006 had been

Far East - Fan Zhiyi was also the Chinese international captain.

put on hold with Peter Marr later explaining his decision in *The News of the World*: "The honeymoon period with the fans is over for Ivano. Last year he was praised because of the exciting football we played but he is now being criticised and it will be interesting to see how he handles it. We have not moved forward as we should have although perhaps expectations were unrealistically high after last term."

"I honestly believe much of the criticism is unfair in light of the injuries to key players such as Nemsadze and Khizanishvili. It would be much fairer to wait and see how we do when everyone is back for the start of next season. Ivano is entitled to that chance and that's why we'll leave the contract extension situation on ice for now."

Khizanishvili's injury had been diagnosed as a torn cruciate ligament and he, like Nemsadze, would be out for the rest of the season. And with Romano - who last term had been out for two months with pancreatitis - again sidelined, this time with an intestinal problem, and Rae missing for three weeks with an ankle injury, there appeared no end to the catalogue of injuries and illness at Dens.

To strengthen the squad, Kiko Torres, a 25-year-old Spanish midfielder recommended by his former Real Madrid youth colleague Javier Artero, and Algerian-born striker Khaled Kemas, formerly of Paris St Germain, were signed until the end of the season. However, the biggest plus was the form of Temuri Ketsbaia. The balding Georgian had become a major influence and his drive and shooting power made him a big favourite with the fans.

As part of Scotland's bid with the Republic of Ireland to co-host the 2008 European Championships, it was proposed that the two Dundee clubs take advantage of generous Scottish Executive funding and build a new 30,000-seater shared stadium at Caird Park. Tentative agreement was reached on a basic 20,000 with temporary stands to achieve the required capacity, but although outline planning permission was obtained from Dundee City Council, all plans went "on hold" in December when UEFA instead accepted a joint-bid by Austria and Switzerland.

There would be no winter break due to that summer's World Cup Finals and on Sunday, January 6th, Dundee entertained Falkirk in the third round of the Scottish Cup. A year earlier, the pair had met at the same stage of the competition but although the Bairns deteriorating financial situation had meant the sale of many of their best players, Dundee again made heavy weather of things.

With eight minutes left, Milne put Dundee ahead only for

Falkirk to level in the dying seconds. In the midweek replay at Brockville, it took a well-struck 30-yarder by Fan to separate the sides although Caballero spurned a great chance to kill the tie. His weakly hit penalty was saved by Hogarth and only a brave second-half penalty double stop by Speroni saved the day for Dundee.

Dens defender Lee Mair had impressed for Falkirk where he was on loan along with Lee Wilkie. In October, Wilkie had made a premature return from a loan spell at Notts County with his former Dens boss Jocky Scott commenting: "Lee has returned to Scotland by mutual agreement because things have not worked out for him down here. He is not the player I worked with when manager at Dundee."

Wilkie was then told by Ivano Bonetti that he had no future at Dens but despite joining Falkirk on loan, he was not allowed to play against the Dark Blues in the cup! Meanwhile, Jamie Langfield lost his place to Julian Speroni after a poor showing in a 4-2 league defeat at Motherwell. And although an opportunist Fan Zhiyi goal earned a 1-0 home win over Hibs, only one point was taken from the next three games, all away, against Dundee United, Aberdeen and Rangers.

Dundee's problems were not confined to onfield matters. The under-fire Ivano Bonetti - abroad "on club business" had been posted absent for the Motherwell game but, more disturbingly, Patrizio Billio had been headbutted soon after leaving Dens with Marco de Marchi the following day. A local man and Paul Marr - Peter Marr's son, who was Dundee's director of football from 2001 to 2003 - were charged in connection with the incident but both were later cleared.

Without the injured Ketsbaia and Rae, the Dark Blues had survived a tricky fourth-round Scottish Cup tie at Firhill on January 26th. Just after half-time, they went behind and although Torres hit a stunning equaliser, the final whistle came as a welcome relief. Around 8,000 fans turned out for the Dens replay on Wednesday, February 6th. And with the quarter-final draw throwing up a home tie against Inverness Caley Thistle, the prospect of a place in the Scottish Cup semi-finals - something last achieved in 1987 - was a huge incentive for Dundee to overcome their First Division opponents.

Smith was switched to left-back for the injured Beghetto while Milne and Kemas were preferred to Sara and

Razzle-dazzle - Fabian Caballero on the run against Hibs at Easter Road watched by Kiko Torres. DC Thomson

Caballero up front. However, Ketsbaia and Rae were back and, fresh from an encouraging performance at Ibrox, Dundee were confident of success:- Speroni; Mackay, Fan, del Rio, Smith; Carranza, Torres, Rae, Ketsbaia; Kemas, Milne. Subs. Sara, Caballero, Robertson.

In 17 minutes, home appeals for a penalty were ignored when an Alan Archibald challenge resulted in Carranza's departure with a knee injury. Mark Robertson substituted but within six minutes, ex-Dark Blue Gerry Britton hooked home a spectacular opener. Dundee were struggling against their lower league opponents but in 37 minutes the ineffectual

Spot on - Juan Sara levels with a penalty but First Division Partick Thistle hit back to win.   DC Thomson

Kemas was replaced by Sara and, soon after the restart, the Argentinian levelled the scores via the penalty spot.

Sara's ability to hold the ball had changed the pattern of play and Dundee looked likely to go on to win. However, with eight minutes left, Fan was sent off when an on-going feud with Britton saw him receive two yellow cards in quick succession. That left the Dark Blues in disarray and soon afterwards Andy Gibson netted the winner for Thistle.

It was yet another humiliating cup exit at the hands of lower league opposition and with just two wins from thirteen SPL games since the start of November, things looked bleak. With Ketsbaia well policed, Dundee had struggled in the opening period but ultimately Fan's indiscipline had cost them dear. With two red cards in his short Dens career, there was a huge question mark over his temperament and also over his concentration in central defence.

However, unlike de Marchi a year earlier, Fan incurred no disciplinary action from the club. The powerfully built Chinaman was certainly a charismatic figure with bags of skill and many felt he might have been better utilised in midfield where he would have been better able to utilise a powerful shot which had already brought him three goals.

Fan's presence attracted hundreds of local Chinese students as a Torres goal earned a 1-0 league win over St Johnstone at Dens but, with Ivano Bonetti surprisingly allowed three weeks off for his wedding in Italy, a single point from the next four matches against Dunfermline (h) 2-2, Celtic (h) 0-3, Kilmarnock (a) 2-3 and Aberdeen (h) 2-3 left the Dark Blues second-bottom, nine points adrift of the top six after 30 games.

There were major problems in defence and with Dundee repeatedly struggling in the latter stages of games, the players' stamina was open to question. After netting twice in the opening minutes against Dunfermline, the Dark Blues had to be content with a draw despite the Pars having Crawford dismissed for a 74th minute foul on Speroni. The defensive woes continued against Celtic and on March 2nd, the loss of another two late goals cost them the points at Kilmarnock.

Now Dens boss Ivano Bonetti acknowledged what had long been obvious: "We must learn to defend crosses better.

Too often our players watch the ball and lose their man." However, his advice went unheeded and the slipshod defending continued against fourth-placed Aberdeen at Dens where Fan was an absentee after being loaned to Cosco Shanghai to enable his participation in China's World Cup Final preparations.

The goalscoring form of Temuri Ketsbaia was one of the few highlights for demoralised Dens fans and the Georgian, scorer of a fine goal at Rugby Park, earned a penalty against Aberdeen when he was downed in the box. Juan Sara converted before Ketsbaia made it 2-0 with a blistering low shot but, although the on-song Dark Blues looked set for victory, yet another second-half collapse saw them go down 3-2 with Romano dismissed for spitting at Leon Mike just seven minutes after coming on as substitute.

It was as well that St Johnstone had had such a poor season otherwise Dundee could well have been dragged into the relegation dogfight. This state of affairs could not be allowed to continue and, at the insistence of chief executive Peter Marr, the out-of-favour Lee Wilkie was recalled for the midweek clash with Livingston at Dens. The move was an instant success and the big defender gave Livy dangerman David Fernandez little chance to shine as Sara netted twice in a convincing 2-0 win.

On March 16th, Temuri Ketsbaia - whose shooting was reminiscent of the great Alan Gilzean - thundered home two glorious 25-yarders in a 2-0 home win over Motherwell. Sadly that would prove his last appearance at Dens for, soon afterwards, he sustained a bad knee injury while playing for Georgia against South Africa and later decided that his future lay elsewhere.

Wilkie, however, had brought much-needed solidity to defence and his return was a key factor as Dundee managed four wins and a draw from their last eight games. His form had not gone unnoticed by new Scotland boss Bertie Vogts and, along with Gavin Rae, he was selected for a Scotland XI against Dundee United.

The big centre-half did enough to merit inclusion in Scotland's squad for the summer tour of the Far East. He appeared as a half-time substitute against South Africa then played from the start in the 4-0 win over a Hong Kong XI.

Safe hands - Julian Speroni in action against Motherwell at Dens. Fotopress

there were now grave doubts over the prospects of the Bonettis and their Italian entourage. Dundee's season had ended with a 2-1 defeat at Motherwell, where a disgruntled Ivano Bonetti had stunned the media with his post-match comments about referee Willie Young.

Both sides were awarded penalties but, in *The Scottish Daily Mail,* Bonetti claimed: "When I saw this referee, it was like starting 2-0 behind. He puts Dundee in trouble all the time and it cannot be a coincidence with him. I hope this is his last game and he can get his pension and retire. You can make many mistakes but this is the only referee in my life who is dishonest. All the time in the game he watches our bench. Maybe he is in love with Dario or me - but he is a joke and I want to tell you how angry he makes me. He has a party through the night when Dundee lose."

Dundee quickly distanced themselves from his controversial remarks and later the whistler threatened legal action against the Dens boss if an apology was not forthcoming. However, when invited to explain his comments to the SFA, Bonetti claimed he would be unable to attend since he was going to the World Cup Finals in Japan. This, though, was news to the club who now suspected that the possibility of a touchline ban did not worry him because he had no intention of returning.

Just hours after the Motherwell game, Ivano Bonetti had assured fans at the DSA dinner at Dundee's Hilton Hotel that he would see out the final year of his contract. However, this appeared to be contradicted by the club's revelation that the Bonettis and their coaching staff had given up their Scottish homes and moved their belongings back to Italy, while the manager had also cleared personal effects from his office at Dens.

Peter Marr was unhappy at all the continuing uncertainty but, although denying that Dundee were to sack the Italians, he did

It was a remarkable turnaround for the once £1m-rated stopper whose disagreement with the manager had threatened his future in the game. Since then, his transfer value had fallen dramatically and it had taken a derisory bid of £25,000 from their local rivals Dundee United before the board had finally seen sense.

The future looked bright for Wilkie but

suggest that the Bonettis should consider their position. And perhaps significantly, it had already been decided to dispense with physio Giovanni Grassi and goalkeeping coach Claudio Bozzini, with the position of club co-ordinator Dario Magri also under review.

Ivano Bonetti, meanwhile, maintained that the management team would be back to take charge of pre-season training. In June, Jim Connor and club spokesman Niall Scott flew to Milan but their meeting with the Bonettis proved inconclusive and, with the start of the new campaign fast approaching, doubts over their position persisted.

However, on Monday, July 2nd, the Bonetti brothers and Dario Magri did indeed return to Dundee, arriving half-an-hour after the start of pre-season training under Kenny Cameron, Ray Farningham and Steve Campbell at Caird Park. There they shook hands with the coaches and players before driving off to prepare for a meeting with the Marrs at Dens that evening.

The Italians remained tight-lipped as they left the talks but, just minutes later, Peter Marr emerged to announce: "After discussions with the Bonettis, it has been decided to mutually terminate their contracts forthwith." And now, after two eventful years, the Italian-led revolution had come to the end of the road.

When Ivano Bonetti was appointed, the theory was that he would use his contacts to bring in big-name players and sell others to balance the books. But, as Peter Marr explained to Ron Scott in *The Sunday Post:* "Ivano was good at bringing players in but he couldn't get them out. That's where the plan fell down. Everything was compared to life in Italy, so he didn't bother with the reserve and youth sides because the head coach doesn't do so there."

"The final straw came when he criticised Willie Young and that's when I decided things would have to change. I know the idea of employing Ivano and his brother Dario was mine but it just didn't work out the way I hoped. You have to be big enough in this game to hold up your hand when things don't work out."

Where did it all go wrong? - that could be what Ivano Bonetti is asking his brother Dario with substitute Dave Mackay and co-ordinator Dario Magri looking equally bemused. DC Thomson

CHAPTER FORTY

Razzle, Dazzle Dundee

Two days later, former Dens boss Jim Duffy was named as Bonetti's successor but not before the Paraguayan football club owner and players' agent Francisco Ocampo rejected the job. A few weeks earlier Jimmy Marr and Jim Connor had flown to Paraguay to resolve a dispute over payments due to Tactuary - one of Ocampo's clubs - for Juan Sara's transfer, but denied that the South American was in the running for the manager's post.

Instead, the board turned to 43-year-old Duffy, who had recently been linked with a top post at Dundee United's proposed Football Academy. His appointment was somewhat controversial for some fans regretted the end of the Bonetti era, while others felt the former Dens manager had left them in the lurch when he joined Hibs, five-and-a-half years earlier. Some, too, questioned Duffy's managerial record, particularly his 13 months with the Easter Road club, who had been relegated despite his numerous forays into the transfer market.

Others, however, felt that managerial change was long overdue and that Duffy, so impressive as master of ceremonies at the 2001 DSA dinner, was just the man to steady things and regain media respect for the club after several months of negativity. They believed he had learned from his mistakes and had gained invaluable experience as youth coach under Gianlucca Vialli at Chelsea and as assistant-manager at First Division Portsmouth, while also observing training methods at Real Madrid, Barcelona, Arsenal and Liverpool.

His spell in England had provided Duffy with many useful contacts and at Stamford Bridge he had dealt with players of many differing nationalities. For his part, the straight-talking Glaswegian was delighted to return to Dens although he appreciated the fans' concerns: "The club has built up a tradition of playing attractive and exciting football, particularly over the past couple of years under Ivano, and I hope to continue playing the same way."

However, Scottish Football was experiencing its worst-ever financial crisis. That summer, Airdrieonians, £3m in debt, had gone to the wall and when their attempt to resurrect themselves as Airdrie United saw them passed over in favour of Gretna for entry to the Third Division, the Lanarkshire men bought out ailing Clydebank, who were homeless since having to sell Kilbowie six years earlier.

Now, just like Third Lanark in 1967, the Bankies were history but with Motherwell in administration it was clear that many top-league clubs were also in trouble. At May 2002, most other SPL clubs, notably Rangers (£50m), Hearts (£17m), Celtic (£16m), Hibs (£13m), Aberdeen (£8m) and

Duff's back - Jim Duffy was back at Dens for a fourth time.

Dundee United (£5.5m), were heavily in the red and with debts of some £7.7 million, Dundee F.C.'s finances also seemed to be getting out of control.

Worryingly, too, the Dens accounts which showed a loss of £2.5 million with wages of £4,346,519 exceeding their annual turnover by £1 million, were always a year behind making it hard to assess their current position.

The SPL's failure to successfully renogotiate another lucrative contract with B-Sky-B was of major significance and without any major transfer income, an end-of-season Dens clearout saw the departure of no fewer than 14 out-of-contract players - Walter del Rio, Alessandro Romano, Beto Garrido, Massimo Beghetto, Kiko Torres, Willie Miller, Khaled Kemas, Gerardo Traverso, Umberto Fattello, Michael Hankinson, Graeme Thomson, Graeme Bayne, Keith Gibson and Richard Montgomery.

Several months earlier, Goran Jugovic - who never came near to first-team action - had joined Stirling Albion, Lucas Gatti and Beto Naveda had been released in March, and Mauro Vargiu - earlier banned for four months by the Italian FA for showing "sporting disloyalty" to Cagliari by joining Dundee - signed for Serie 'B' club Pistoise for a small fee.

The in-dispute Patrizio Billio and Marco de Marchi had also gone after FIFA ruled that their contracts, which had another year to run, should be terminated, though it was not clear whether they were due any compensation. Marcello Marrocco, too, would depart after receiving a settlement on the remaining nine months of his contract, while Javier Artero decided to hang up his boots. The Spanish wing-ace was in good health but after struggling to regain full fitness he would now combine a journalistic career in Madrid with duties as an international scout for Dundee.

Fan Zhiyi was another who would not play for the club again. His registration with the SFA and SPL had been cancelled on the understanding that he would rejoin Dundee on the same terms he had previously enjoyed. However, on returning from Cosco Shanghai, he refused to re-register, claiming that the deal on offer was different from before. The impasse continued beyond the August 31st transfer deadline but, although this ruled him out of football until the next transfer window in January, the out-of-contract Chinese star secured his future by signing for Cardiff City.

Happiness - Steve Lovell and Nacho Novo celebrate the big Englishman's double in the 2-1 win over Hearts at Tynecastle. Mirrorpix

Fan's departure would further reduce the wage bill but although it had been claimed the highly-paid Temuri Ketsbaia might remain as a player and assistant-manager, the popular Georgian, whose wife was a Greek Cypriot, confirmed his earlier decision to join Anorthosis Famagusta on the sunshine island of Cyprus.

Ketsbaia's departure left Dundee with just thirteen senior players from a total of 33 who had appeared the previous season. That included Julian Speroni, who had signed a new three-year deal, plus 23-year-old Spanish striker Nacho Novo, who was secured from Raith Rovers for £100,000 and Venezuelan left-back Jonay Hernandez (23), on freedom-of-contract from Real Madrid, where he had been understudy to Brazilian international Roberto Carlos.

A trip to the Romanian capital of Bucharest gave Jim Duffy the chance to observe his new charges in Astoria Cup games against Sportul Studentesc (0-3), and Rapid Bucharest (1-1), and a challenge match against Electro (1-0), but defeats in friendlies against Preston North End (0-2), and Rapid Bucharest (1-3), at Dens left many wondering what lay in store for the Dark Blues.

In the event, the fans were pleasantly surprised when a spirited Dundee dominated much of their SPL opener, a 1-1 draw with Hearts before nearly 8,000 at Dens, and, playing an adventurous 4-3-3 system and attacking at every opportunity, they were rewarded with a cracking goal by Caballero. Then came defeats at Rangers (0-3), and Dunfermline (2-4), where Dundee had twice led through Nacho Novo, who was later sent off after a couple of impetuous fouls on Scott Wilson.

A win was desperately required and it finally came on August 23rd with a 2-1 success against Hibernian at Dens.

High-profile efforts to secure ex-Newcastle, Spurs, Lazio and Rangers midfielder Paul Gascoigne had foundered but Steve Lovell was signed on freedom-of-contract from Portsmouth and the 24-year-old striker came off the substitute's bench to score Dundee's last-gasp winner.

A few days later, the squad was further strengthened by the arrival of Fulham reserve central-defender Tom Hutchinson (20), for £50,000 and former Spurs and Newcastle midfielder Gary Brady (25), from Portsmouth on freedom-of-contract. Hutchinson played alongside Lee Wilkie in the 0-0 draw against Dundee United at Tannadice where both excelled in the tough aerial jousts against Steven Thomson. And, by October 26th, Dundee had lost just one of their previous nine league games.

There was now real competition for places and with only seven goals conceded in that spell, it was clear that Jim Duffy had added a touch of steel to the side's silky play. There was also a much-improved team-spirit for, unlike previously, the new boss had insisted that players, irrespective of nationality, mix properly in the dressing room.

A reliable and often inspirational goalkeeper, Speroni was similar in style to Scottish international Thomson Allan from the successful Dens side of the early 1970s. Dave Mackay, Tom Hutchinson, Lee Wilkie and Jonay Hernandez soon established themselves as the defensive regulars with Barry Smith now successfully utilised alongside Georgi Nemsadze and Gavin Rae in a three-man midfield.

However, Dundee's new-found solidity had in no way diminished their reputation for free-flowing football and players like Caballero and Nemsadze continued to provide the flair and imagination with Nacho Novo an exciting addition up front.

Initially, Sara had partnered Caballero with Novo - who had netted 28 goals for Spanish Third Division side Huesca in 2000-01 before scoring 22 goals from 38 games for Raith Rovers last term - wide on the right. However, there was not enough pace down the middle and soon Lovell replaced Sara, Novo was given a roving commission while Caballero dropped into the "hole" between midfield and attack. Now two stones lighter, the rejuvenated Argentinian was a revelation in his new role, which allowed him more space in which to operate and get forward for a shot.

The introduction of Steve Lovell had brought a dash of power up front and, in late October, the big Englishman's double gave Dundee a 2-1 win over Hearts at Tynecastle to put them joint fifth. This improvement in form had brought hopes of an extended League Cup run but despite a comfortable 3-1 home win over Queen of the South, a midweek trip to Firhill in the fourth round saw Dundee go down to a late goal by Martin Hardie.

In the league too, Dundee began to falter, losing three successive games before bouncing back with a 3-2 win over Dundee United at Dens on November 23rd. For the first hour, Dundee had been magnificent. A brilliant run and cross by Novo allowed Caballero to open the scoring with a classic downward header, the Argentinian added another with a deflected shot which flew in off Lovell's back and soon after half-time Hernandez made it 3-0.

A slaughter looked on the cards but United hit back to score twice and although the Dark Blues might well have extended their lead, there were some anxious moments before the fans could finally celebrate. The previously watertight defence had begun to leak goals and after allowing Dunfermline - 3-2 winners at Dens - to come back from two down, it had almost been a similar story against United.

Georgi Nemsadze was now fully recovered from his cruciate ligament injury and, along with the fabulous Caballero, he had been the star performer against United, where he had dribbled past opponents with ease, repeatedly carving the Tannadice defence apart with a series of well-weighted passes. Some felt that Dundee's tactics were overly cavalier and that a switch to 4-4-2 after going a couple of goals up might have stiffened midfield but the following Saturday was to bring worries of a different kind.

Nemsadze, rumoured to have been set to join Celtic had they progressed to the group stage of the Champions League, was carried off with a knee injury in the 1-1 draw at Livingston. And although the diagnosis was severely bruised knee ligaments, it would be five weeks before the midfield playmaker returned.

In his absence, Dundee demolished Partick Thistle 4-1 at Dens but without the Georgian's creative influence, just one point was taken from the next six games to leave the Dark Blues seventh, eight points behind sixth-placed Kilmarnock by the start of the three-week winter break on January 3rd.

The loss of Tom Hutchinson with knee ligament damage was another setback but there had been other self-inflicted problems. With 31 minutes on the clock at Parkhead, referee Dougie McDonald had pointed to the spot after Lovell was downed by Balde. Novo, who had scored from the spot against Livingston, looked set to take the kick until Caballero intervened and a heated argument then ensued.

Eventually, the Argentinian prevailed only for Douglas to save his weakly-hit effort.

Until then, Dundee had matched the home side, but almost immediately Hartson scored with a brilliantly executed overhead kick and Celtic were on their way to a 2-0 win. It was an embarrassing incident, identical to the one at Dens several months earlier when Sara had netted from the spot against Aberdeen despite Caballero and Carranza trying to muscle in. However, Jim Duffy would not accept such a lack of professionalism and, henceforth, would nominate a penalty-taker for each game.

It had been a roller-coaster campaign for Lee Wilkie. His fine early-season form had seen him rewarded with further international caps in Iceland, and against Canada at Easter Road, but despite excelling for Scotland, the big defender began to show signs of overconfidence and, increasingly, there were concerns over his self-discipline.

Already booked against Dunfermline, he was later sent off for dissent though home fans could sympathise with his frustration as referee Alan Freeland repeatedly ignored the backing-in of his direct opponent Craig Brewster. The lesson went unheeded and Wilkie again got his marching orders in the Boxing Day clash with Aberdeen at rain-sodden Dens. In both cases, the big defender had put himself under pressure with an initial booking and thereafter had been unable to maintain his discipline.

Now, however, manager and players could reflect on matters with a week-long trip to Trinidad and Tobago - courtesy of sponsors BP Amoco and the TGI Friday Restaurant Group - which allowed them to top up their fitness levels beneath the hot Caribbean sun. There would be double daily training sessions which would culminate in two friendlies with the Dens party also lined up to attend a string of official functions.

The results - a 3-0 reverse to League Champions San Juan Jabloteh in a closed doors match in Tobago's Port of Spain and a 2-1 defeat to a President's XI in Trinidad - were

Brilliant - Fabian Caballero completes a great move with a scoring header against Dundee United at Dens. Mirrorpix

disappointing but the Dark Blues had made the most of their excellent training facilities while also cultivating a useful relationship with FIFA vice-president Jack Warner's club Joe Public. In addition, the trip had allowed Georgi Nemsadze to get himself match-fit and this would prove a key factor as Dundee jetted back to a potentially hazardous Scottish Cup tie away to Partick Thistle on Saturday, January 25th.

With Caballero (suspended) and Lovell (injured) both unavailable and Sara on loan to Coventry City for the rest of the season, Novo and Milne were up front with Lee Mair at left-back in place of groin injury victim Jonay Hernandez. Right from kick-off, the Dens men took control with a rejuvenated Nemsadze pulling the strings in a four-man midfield. A goal had to come and with 31 minutes played, the Georgian brilliantly curled a free-kick beyond the wall and past Kenny Arthur for the opener.

Thistle pushed but although they could find no way past Lee Wilkie and Zurab Khizanishvili in central defence, it took Dundee until nine minutes from the end to grab the decisive second goal, when Gavin Rae played a one-two with Nacho Novo before rattling home the rebound after his first effort was blocked.

It was a great result, which, incredibly, would lead to a near three-month, 14-game unbeaten run which would propel Dundee into the top six of the Premier League and see them reach the Scottish Cup Final for the first time since 1964.

Three days later, a battling performance at Dunfermline saw Dundee return with a 1-0 victory in the league. The defence had shown great concentration against the ever-dangerous Brewster and Crawford but a heavy snowstorm was to cause the abandonment of their next match against Hibs at Dens after just 26 minutes with Dundee leading 1-0 through a cracking shot by Caballero.

Then came a 1-1 draw against Dundee United at Tannadice, where an exquisite outside-of-the-foot pass by Caballero allowed Nacho Novo to angle a low shot at the far post to equalise an earlier headed own-goal by Dave Mackay. From then on, Dundee dominated but despite United going down to ten men after Charlie Miller's dismissal, they were unable to grab the winner.

Dundee had been boosted by the arrival of Mark Burchill (22), on loan from Portsmouth until the end of the season. The bustling striker, signed for £900,000 from Celtic - where he had scored a bundle of goals - in August 2001, had worked well with Jim Duffy at Portsmouth and, now recovering from a knee injury, he was prepared to take a big wage cut to come to Dens.

Meanwhile, it appeared

Lee Wilkie - now first-choice at centre-half for Scotland . Fotopress

Happy days - Dundee enjoyed a 14-game unbeaten run in the early months of 2003 . Fotopress

that Dundee's two-year shirt sponsorship deal with J-Search had collapsed. According to *The Sunday Mail*, only £30,000 of the £120,000 due that year had been paid with the newspaper suggesting that Jini Global owner Bob McCallum - a long-time Dundee fan - might be in financial difficulty after selling his £1 million mansion and moving to a much smaller house. This made an extended cup run even more important and, on February 22nd, Dundee entertained Premier strugglers Aberdeen in the fourth round of the Scottish Cup.

Ominously, the Dark Blues had only twice beaten the Dons at Dens since 1975 but that apalling record was about to change. Caballerro, Novo and Lovell repeatedly tore gaping holes in the Dons defence and, in 22 minutes, an inch-perfect pass by Caballero allowed Lovell to outpace Deloumeaux and knock the ball past the outrushing Preece. Just before half-time Nemsadze threaded the ball through for Novo to make it 2-0 and there was no way back for the Pittodrie side.

Roddy Thomson of *The Scottish Daily Mail* had been highly impressed by Dundee: "They played committed, skilful and pacy football at such a high tempo that Aberdeen's initial 3-5-2 formation was swamped in midfield by Dundee's 4-3-3. On his day, you will struggle to find a better all-round footballer in Scotland than Georgi Nemsadze. And when Fabian Caballero, too, is hinting at a full return of his abundant talents, no wonder Aberdeen were ripped apart."

Aberdeen boss Steve Paterson had gambled with three against three at the back and in *The Courier,* Barry Smith admitted the Dons formation had played straight into Dundee's hands: "With the pace our strikers have, that gave us the chance to play it down the sides and get running at their defence which paid off."

"Working as a team we were able to prevent them from playing and we felt in control for virtually the full 90 minutes. I think the manager has got us playing more for each other than used to be the case and the work-rate from everyone including the foreign lads, is different class."

The draw was kind to the Dark Blues although it would be fully a month before they played their quarter-final tie against First Division leaders Falkirk. By then, favourable league results against Hibernian (h) 3-0, Partick Thistle (a) 3-1, Livingston (h) 0-0, Killie (h) 2-2, and Aberdeen (a) 3-3, had stretched Dundee's unbeaten run to nine games, and, with two games left before the split, they lay sixth.

For long spells of those games, the Dark Blues had looked a class above their opponents. However, on occasion they had lacked the killer touch and, sometimes, the luck to finish them off, while defensive lapses had also been costly with 2-0 half-time leads surrendered to both Kilmarnock and Aberdeen.

Nevertheless, this run of form was the perfect riposte to those who had bemoaned the end of the Bonetti era. For there was not only bags of skill and free-flowing football, but also a greater determination and, with a number of potential goalscorers, here was a team that had found the winning way.

There had certainly been some mouth-watering fare for supporters with Nemsadze at his tantalising best and Caballero in a particularly rich vein of form. There were signs too that the fans were coming back with the midweek games against Hibs and Livingston attracting crowds of 8,400 and 7,500, respectively, as fans took advantage of the board's "two for a tenner" offer.

Lee Mair had done well at left-back before a couple of below-par performances saw the left-footed Jonay Hernandez recalled for the Scottish Cup quarter-final tie against Falkirk - shock 4-0 conquerors of Hearts in an earlier round. By then, SPL clubs Kilmarnock, Hibs, Aberdeen, Dundee United, Partick Thistle and Livingston were also out, and although the Old Firm remained, there were now genuine hopes that Dundee could go all the way.

There was plenty of noise from the 7,403 all-ticket crowd at the soon-to-be-demolished Brockville but although Trinidadian speed-merchant Collin Samuel had netted a hat-trick against Hearts, he was well held by Hernandez and it was veteran striker Owen Coyle who put Falkirk ahead in 58 minutes. Nacho Novo sped through on to a wonderfully-weighted lob by Caballero to ram home the equaliser soon afterwards but in a tense finish the scoreline remained 1-1.

Dundee's form had brought them plenty of positive publicity but although Dave Mackay, Lee Mair and Steve Milne had all done well, they were consistently overlooked for the Scotland Under-21s. Since January, Lee Wilkie had been a tower of strength but perhaps mindful of the penalty he had conceded for handball

against Portugal as well as his withdrawal from the "Futures" game against Germany in December - he had been omitted from Scotland's squad to face the Republic of Ireland.

Now, however, Wilkie, who had recently scored against Killie and Aberdeen, was recalled for the vital European Championship game against Iceland at Hampden. It was story book stuff for, with 20 minutes remaining, the Dens defender headed the winner in a 2-1 triumph, making him the first Dundee player to score for Scotland since Alan Gilzean's goal against Northern Ireland in November 1964!

The big games were coming thick and fast and, on Sunday, April 6th, Mark Burchill netted his first goal for Dundee in a 1-1 draw with Celtic at Dens. The Dark Blues were disappointed not to have won although the match was ideal preparation for the replay against Falkirk in midweek. Now, too, there was the added incentive of a semi-final against First Division Inverness Caledonian Thistle, shock 1-0 conquerors of Celtic. And with almost 10,000 fans in the ground, it was something like the good old days at Dens.

Dundee missed a couple of early chances but, inspired by the youthful Mark Kerr and Lee Miller, it was the Bairns who dominated much of the first half. In 31 minutes, Taylor scored with a thumping shot but that only inspired Dundee to raise their game and, two minutes from the interval, Caballero equalised with a splendidly struck low shot into the far corner of the net.

Thereafter, the Dark Blues held the edge in a cup-tie thriller and although Falkirk brought on Samuel and Dundee replaced Milne and Novo with Lovell and Burchill, the scores remained level at full-time. However, the introduction of two fresh strikers had given Dundee fresh impetus and three minutes into extra-time, Burchill raced on to a harmless-looking long ball to lob the stranded Ferguson before Lovell netted a glory double to seal a 4-1 win.

That put Dundee high and dry into the last four and three

Clincher - Mark Burchill puts Dundee ahead in extra-time in the cup replay against Falkirk. SNS Group

277

days later a 2-1 win at Motherwell ensured a top-six finish and set them up nicely for the Hampden semi-final clash with Inverness Caledonian Thistle. Initially, the game had been scheduled for the Monday night before the combined protests of Dundee, Falkirk and ICT finally persuaded the SFA to bring the match forward to the afternoon of Sunday, April 20th.

There were around 10,000 Dundee fans in the 14,429 crowd but just over a quarter of Hampden's capacity was filled and, clearly, a smaller, but more geographically accessible stadium like Pittodrie would have attracted a bigger crowd and provided a better atmosphere as befitted a Scottish Cup semi-final.

Dundee were strong favourites and were along the usual lines although they were without influential skipper Barry Smith, who was suspended, while Mark Burchill - who had scored in each of the last three games - had withdrawn after his partner had given birth. Smith was replaced by Garry Brady with Stevie Milne getting the nod alongside Fabian Caballero and Steve Lovell up front. However, the Dens men made a shaky start and, with seven minutes played, only a spectacular Speroni save diverted a long-range Dennis Wyness effort on to the post.

Throughout the first half, Dundee struggled to find their rythm against opponents who regularly kept eight men behind the ball. It was a scrappy game and soon after the restart Lee Wilkie was booked for a body-check on Barry Robson. On the hour, Dundee came close when clever play by Brady released Caballero but although the Argentinian lobbed the grounded keeper, the ball sailed over the bar.

The introduction of Nacho Novo injected new life into Dundee and, with 12 minutes left, they finally made the breakthrough. Caballero dribbled his way in from the left and from his cut-back, Nemsadze's half-hit strike trundled past the unsighted Mark Brown at his right-hand post. The Dens fans roared with joy and although Dundee might have got another, the final whistle came as a relief and sparked wild scenes of celebration in Hampden's South Stand!

It had been a dour struggle but Dundee had earned their place in the Scottish Cup Final and they would also return to mainstream European competition for the first time since 1974. Dens boss Jim Duffy was delighted for his players and he was also full of praise for Peter and Jimmy Marr: "I am so pleased for them for they are true Dundee supporters. They've invested so much time and money in the club and deserve this. Dundee have had some phenomenal sides since 1964 but for one reason or another they never got to the Scottish Cup Final."

"Now we are there and that speaks volumes for my players. Today they had to show a really determined mentality and dig out the result. We have had plaudits for playing good football this season, and deservedly so - today we deserve plaudits for perseverance."

However, there were mixed emotions for Lee Wilkie whose booking meant he would miss the final. After the match, he had twice been assured by an SFA official that he only had one booking in the tournament but it was later confirmed that he had also been yellow-carded against Partick Thistle. The young defender was devastated and with good cause for, although Jim Duffy appealed to the SFA for clemency, it was to no avail.

In the final, the Dark Blues would play Rangers who had defeated Motherwell 4-3, but with almost six weeks until the big day on May 31st, five SPL games remained. Without Nemsadze and Khizanishvili, who were on international duty, Dundee's unbeaten run finally ended with a 1-0 home reverse to Kilmarnock but then came an incident-packed 2-2 draw with Rangers at Dens.

With less than a minute played, Lee Wilkie conceded a bizarre own-goal as he tried to block a cross. But although the Dark Blues went 2-1 ahead courtesy of two stunning long-range strikes by Cabellero, Wilkie twice conceded rash penalties. Barry Ferguson sent the first over the bar then, eight minutes from time, had his second effort saved by Speroni before referee Rowbotham astonishingly awarded title-chasing Rangers a third spot kick when Mackay - who

One on one - Fabian Caballero was unsuccessful with this lob against Inverness Caley Thistle's Mark Brown in the Scottish Cup semifinal but later the Dens playmaker created the opening for Dundee's winner. Caley's Bobby Mann looks on . DC Thomson

looked to have been pushed - handled, and this time Arteta made no mistake.

It was a disappointing result but although Dundee had excelled, with the fit-again Carranza making a welcome return in what was a marvellous advert for the Scottish Cup Final, they then failed to win any of their remaining league games, drawing 2-2 with Dunfermline at Dens, before losing 6-2 away to title-chasing Celtic and by 1-0 to Hearts at Tynecastle.

Worryingly, 10 goals had been conceded in three games with Wilkie having another shocker before being substituted at Parkhead. After missing two games with a groin strain, Caballero returned at Tynecastle and was fortunate that referee Willie Young gave him a yellow card rather than a red which would have ruled him out of the final when he appeared to catch Andy Webster with his elbow.

Now all efforts could be concentrated on the Scottish Cup Final and, with Tayside swept by cup fever, Dundee's initial 16,500 allocation was quickly sold out before the club took delivery of an additional 4,000 tickets. The club shop did a roaring trade with all sorts of merchandise being snapped up in addition to 3,000 replicas of the new home strip which Dundee had been given permission to wear in the final by the SFA.

There would also be a new sponsor's name on the Dark Blue jerseys for, after the collapse of the Jini Global/J-Search agreement, a new deal was agreed with Magners Irish Cider. Commercially, Dundee were excelling themselves and although the high-flying Ibrox side had won the League on goal-difference over Celtic after a 6-0 last day destruction of Dunfermline, Dundee's recent five-star performance against the Ibrox side had convinced players, fans and neutrals alike that they could win the Scottish Cup for the first time since

away back through the mists of time in 1910.

Certainly, Jim Duffy had every confidence in his players: "In their run to the final the team has shown different qualities at different times. Against Aberdeen and Partick Thistle they played very well while we dug in to get through against Falkirk and Inverness. To win the Cup I believe we will need a combination of both these qualities."

"We're not daft enough to think we can dominate the 90 minutes but we can create things and be positive. The players will need to show a mental toughness but I really believe they need have no fear. Dundee are capable of winning a one-off game against any team in Scotland."

Now all media attention was centred on the two finalists with Dens old boys like Doug Cowie, Bert Slater and Kenny Cameron - scorer of Dundee's goal in the 1964 Scottish Cup Final discussing their previous Cup Final experiences and talking up Dundee's chances of success this time around.

In *The Daily Record,* Jocky Scott, now a coach at Sunderland, and former Dens player and coach and Dundee United supremo Jim McLean, also wished Dundee well. McLean warned that the Dark Blues would have to be at their best and carry some luck to win, while Scott said: "It's good to see Dundee back in a final and I hope they show no fear and perform like they did against Rangers recently. I spent almost 25 years there as a player, coach and manager and you don't spend so much time at a club without having feelings for them."

The Dens boss had some difficult decisions to make for, in recent weeks, Rangers had steam-rollered their opponents into submission and scored goals galore. Should he take an overly cavalier approach and incur a heavy defeat, he might regret it but, equally, there would be condemnation if Dundee played it tight and lost in a poor spectacle. Either

Gritty and gallant - but there was no glory for Gavin Rae in the Scottish Cup Final against Rangers.
Mirrorpix

way, nine players appeared certain starters with the battle for the remaining two jerseys between Novo, Milne, Burchill, Brady, Carranza and Mair.

Although preferring an attacking 4-3-3 formation, Duffy had successfully employed 4-4-2 in the recent game with Rangers. Then, Carranza had played wide right restricting the forward runs of Arthur Numan although the industrious Garry Brady, who had just signed a new one-year deal, was another possibility in a midfield four. Duffy knew that his defenders would have to be at their sharpest to counteract the movement and craft of Rangers, and after declaring himself happy to field Zurab Khizanishvili - rumoured to be joining Rangers when his contract expired in June - he had to decide on a replacement for the suspended Lee Wilkie.

With Tom Hutchinson ruled out due to a shin knock sustained while making his comeback in an Under-21 game, he could play Lee Mair, who had done well at centre-half, left-back and in midfield, or move Barry Smith from midfield. As Dundee's top scorer with 15 goals, Steve Lovell would certainly start as would Fabian Caballero, who was widely rated as the potential matchwinner for Dundee.

Prior to pre-season training, the Argentinian had weighed almost four-teen-and-a-half stone. However, Duffy had persuaded him to cut out junk food and soon extra training sessions saw the striker shed two stones. Since then, his form had been sensational and in an interview with Ron Scott of *The Sunday Post*, Jim Duffy declared: "Fabian is good enough to play at the very highest level. He could easily play in the English Premiership where there are a lot of players who couldn't lace his boots."

On the night before the final, the Dens party stayed at the picturesque Gleddoch House Hotel which overlooked the Clyde

estuary at Langbank, a few miles from Glasgow and Cup Final Saturday would prove a scorcher as thousands of Dundee fans - many from the far corners of the globe - made their way to the west coast city. At 1.30pm the team bus arrived at sun-drenched Hampden and the dark-suited players and officials, accompanied by 1964 skipper Bobby Cox, filed into the stadium. And by 2.45pm most of the Dundee supporters had completed their pre-match refreshments and streamed from their various hostelries to take their seats at Hampden Park.

It was an incredible sight as almost 20,000 fans in the dark blue, red and white of Dundee, centred on the traditional "Celtic end" but filling almost half the stadium, provided a backdrop of colour and waving flags as well as creating a veritable cacophony of noise. Both teams lined up in 4-3-3 formation. Dundee: Speroni; Mackay, Khizanishvili, Mair, Hernandez; Smith (capt), Nemsadze, Rae; Caballero, Lovell, Burchill. Subs. Novo, Milne, Brady, Carranza, Langfield. Rangers: Klos; Ricksen, Moore, Amoruso (capt), Numan; Malcolm, Ferguson, McCann; Arveladze, de Boer, Mols. Subs. Ross, Thomson, Muscat, McGregor, McLean. Referee: Kenny Clark.

Dundee had brought an 18-man squad to Hampden and, as expected Steven Robb and Gavin Beith took their places in the stand. Lee Mair would partner Khizanishvili with Mark Burchill preferred to Nacho Novo or hamstring doubt Stevie Milne. For Rangers, former Dens ace Claudio Caniggia, Peter Lovenkrands and now Spanish midfielder Mikel Arteta were out through injury and Bob Malcom - normally a central defender - was drafted into midfield to counter the creativity of Caballero and Nemsadze.

Rangers made a whirlwind start but with just four minutes played, a penetrating run by Gavin Rae ended with Barry Smith firing in a fierce 25-yarder which beat Klos only to come crashing back off a post. There was certainly no sign of Dundee freezing and, soon afterwards, Lovell broke clear only for Klos to make a brave block as the striker prepared to shoot.

Rangers went close on a couple of occasions but

No luck - a thundering drive by Dens skipper Barry Smith rebounds from the post in the Scottish Cup Final at Hampden.
SNS Group

Dundee were competing well and Rae shot just over. Indeed, the Dens men - 10-1 underdogs - were looking the more composed side and by the interval their supporters were increasingly optimistic about the outcome. At half-time Mols went off with Maurice Ross coming on at right-back and Ricksen going to midfield but, with Dundee continuing as they had left off, Rangers made another substitution when Steven Thomson replaced Arveladze within 10 minutes of the restart.

A 40-yard run by Lovell gave Caballero a chance but a moment's hesitation saw him thwarted by Amoruso just inside the box. Moore then followed Arveladze into the book for a cynical foul on Burchill and the Australian might well have seen red for a similar offence on Nemsadze. Things were going well for Dundee but with Nacho Novo all set to replace an ineffectual Burchill, it was Rangers who went ahead in 65 minutes.

Khizanishvili needlessly fouled Thomson near the right touchline, and when McCann sent in an inswinging free-kick, Amoruso beat a hesitant Speroni - whose nose had been broken in a training-ground collision two days earlier - to head home from six yards. The introduction of Novo within six minutes gave Dundee fresh impetus with Rangers, who had also replaced Numan with Muscat, beginning to look leg-weary in the heat.

With 15 minutes left, Novo failed to connect properly with a Hernandez cross, later cutting the ball back into a crowded penalty box when he might have shot - albeit from a tight angle. First Milne, for Mackay in 78 minutes, then Brady, for Rae six minutes later, were brought on, but with Amoruso and Moore rock-solid down the middle, Dundee created few genuine scoring chances.

This pattern continued throughout the four minutes of added time and when a rushed shot by Milne bobbled past the post, Dundee's last chance had gone. The players looked devastated as they collected their losers' medals before going to salute their fans. However, the result had been in doubt until the last whistle and, unlike 1995, the team had done the fans proud. Dave Mackay, Gavin Rae, Barry Smith and Lee Mair had been immense with Lovell, Novo and Khizanishvili also performing well although the Georgian - never the best in the air - had lost Amoruso at the goal.

Although disappointed, Jim Duffy was proud of his team: "All you can ask of your players coming to a stage like this is to show mental toughness and belief, and they did that. They were outstanding from start to finish and gave every ounce of effort they had. When you look at the quality of the Rangers team and the money they've spent we have something to be proud of."

Gavin Rae admitted that Dundee hadn't shown the attacking ability of which they were capable: "Everyone was gutted with the way we lost. We didn't create too many chances, but neither did Rangers. We went there to play our normal game - it's just a shame the way it turned out."

Nevertheless, many felt that Dundee had lost a golden opportunity with Murdo McLeod of *The Daily Record* commenting: "If ever there was a day when Dundee were going to win the Scottish Cup, it was Saturday and Jim Duffy and his players will live with deep disappointment for the rest of

Nacho Novo - brought on too late to influence the result. Fotopress

their lives. Rangers looked done as the game wore on and the sun blazed down."

"They were there for the taking and the Dens men knew it. But they couldn't quite find the killer pass to create a goal which would have taken the game to extra-time. Even Alex. McLeish admitted that another 30 minutes would have been a step too far for his team but sadly it was not to be. Dundee are not a club who find themselves in Cup Finals that often and I feel for their fans, who were fantastic."

In *The Sun*, Bill Leckie observed that Dundee's flair players like Caballero, Nemsadze and Burchill had failed to conjure up their usual magic although mindful of the Dens clash three weeks earlier, a hard-tackling Rangers side had denied Caballero in particular the time and space in which to manoeuvre.

Jim Duffy had got his tactics just about right - Leckie had observed him urging his back-four forward to provide support for the midfield and front men - and had come close to causing a major upset. However, that little bit of luck so necessary in a Cup Final against either of the Old Firm, had not been forthcoming and had Smith's shot gone in, it might well have been a different story.

It could be argued that, in such hot conditions, Nacho Novo or Beto Carranza might have been a better bet to start rather than Mark Burchill. However, since January, the Dens boss had cleverly juggled his strikers, perming any two from Lovell, Novo, Milne and Burchill, with the other pair providing fresh impetus from the bench - a ploy that had paid rich dividends.

Duffy, the Bank of Scotland Manager of the Month in January and March - had, unlike Bonetti before him, successfully blended the foreigners' flair with the commitment of the British players and the final had been a grand day out after a season of marvellous football. And while disappointed but nonetheless proud fans filled the city's pubs and clubs, the official Dundee F.C. party held their own party at the city's Apex Hotel.

There, Peter Marr praised his manager and players for reaching the Scottish Cup Final and gaining a place in Europe: "We outplayed Rangers for large parts of the game and our wonderful fans out-sang theirs from start to finish. Rangers gave us the respect we deserved and Alex McLeish's decision to replace an attacker with a defender to try and snuff out the threat posed by Caballero showed we had them worried. I genuinely believe if we could have taken the game into extra-time, we would have won it for we were looking stronger and hungrier as the game went on."

Dundee F.C. at the start of Season 2003-04 (BACK, left to right) Jim Law (physio), Paul Mathers (goalkeeper coach), Ray Farningham (coach), Brent Sancho, Callum Macdonald, Julian Speroni, Derek Soutar, Jonay Hernandez, Tom Hutchinson, Brian Duncan (kit-man), Robbie Raeside (physio), Jack Cashley (masseur). MIDDLE - Dr. Phyllis Windsor, Fabian Caballero, Neil Jablonski, Gavin Rae, Lee Mair, Lee Wilkie, Juan Sara, Steve Lovell, Dave Mackay, Garry Brady, Ernie Ferguson (boot-man). FRONT - Steven Robb, Mark Robertson, Georgi Nemsadze, Nacho Novo, Jim Duffy (manager), Barry Smith, Tom Cowan, Steve Milne, Beto Carranza.

DC Thomson

282

CHAPTER FORTY-ONE

Eye of the Storm

The approach of the 2003-04 season was eagerly awaited by players and fans alike. For the first time in 29 years, Dundee would be involved in a major European competition and, having performed so impressively in the second half of last season, many felt that further progress could be made. However, behind the scenes, there were major concerns over the club's finances and these would become all too apparent over the next few months.

Pre-season preparations included a sponsored trip to the USA with Dundee based in Raleigh, North Carolina. Raleigh CASL Elite were defeated 5-0, there was a 1-1 draw against Honduran Cup holders CD Marathon and, on their return, the Dark Blues rattled in 12 goals in pre-season friendly wins at Raith Rovers (4-1), Northampton (4-2), and Kettering Town (4-0). Beto Carranza had been in dazzling form, Juan Sara looked impressive after his loan spell at Coventry and with Steve Lovell knocking in the goals, there was indeed plenty to look forward to.

The squad had been bolstered by the arrival of Trinidad and Tobago international defender Brent Sancho and the former Clyde and Rangers left-back Tom Cowan, (33). Jim Duffy had been impressed by Sancho during Dundee's Caribbean trip and, after obtaining a work permit on appeal, the 26-year-old was signed from San Juan Jabloteh, while the experienced Cowan, who had also played for Sheffield United, Huddersfield, Burnley and Cambridge, was secured on a free transfer from cash-strapped York City.

The departure of Zurab Khizanishvili to Rangers on freedom-of-contract, while not unexpected, was a setback and would prove fiercely controversial. A knee injury and subsequent complications would sideline Stevie Milne for many months, while Fabian Caballero had returned from Paraguay well short of match fitness after failing to join the training camp in North Carolina due to his pregnant wife being unwell.

On August 9th, the talented Argentinian was left on the bench for the opening Premier League game at Motherwell but Dundee made a great start to the new campaign with a well-deserved 3-0 victory in the sun.

The UEFA Cup preliminary round draw had paired the Dark Blues with the little-known KS Vllaznia from Shkoder in the north of Albania.

However, the former Communist state was a European backwater and, allied to British Embassy security concerns, the news that Vllaznia's president had recently been shot dead in nearby Montenegro meant that only around one hundred Dens diehards made the trip to Albania for the first leg five days later.

It was something of a nightmare three-hour journey from Tirana, the capital, to Shkoder on a bumpy sub-standard road in temperatures reaching 100 degrees. The end of Communism a decade earlier had precipitated the collapse of industry in the northern city whose crumbling infrastructure and poverty-stricken inhabitants came as a real culture shock to the visitors.

Dundee were unchanged from Fir Park and, once again, they lined up in 4-4-2 formation: Speroni; Mackay, Wilkie, Mair, Hernandez; Smith, Rae, Nemsadze, Brady; Lovell, Novo. One of the most fascinating aspects of European competition is in assessing the strength of the opposition - particularly the lesser-known Eastern European sides.

But although Vllaznia were useful enough in possession, the Dark Blues settled quickly before a crowd of 11,000 at the Loro Borici Stadium. A number of chances went abegging but in 41 minutes Steve Lovell put Dundee ahead and another strike from Nacho Novo ensured it was a suitably triumphant Euro return.

Meanwhile, bookmakers, alarmed

Sunny days - Dundee returned to mainstream European competition with a UEFA Cup trip to northern Albania where they met KS Vllaznia.

Bob Slessor/Kenny Ross

On the spot - Juan Sara turns away after putting Dundee 2-0 up against KS Vllaznia at Dens.   DC Thomson

by large amounts of money being placed on Dundee to win, had stopped taking bets, although suggestions that Vllaznia, whose players had threatened to strike after non-payment of their wages, had thrown the game, were angrily dismissed by manager Jim Duffy.

That Sunday, Dundee returned to the bread and butter of domestic football but, disappointingly, they went down 2-0 to Dunfermline at Dens. A Nacho Novo double - the first with a breathtaking volley - then brought a 2-1 home win over Livingston and on Thursday, August 28th, Dundee faced KS Vllaznia in the return game at Dens.

There was one change from the first leg. Beto Carranza replaced Gary Brady and, within two minutes, a brilliant defence-splitting pass by the little Argentinian allowed Novo to fire home. Sadly, Carranza's injury jinx continued when he had to retire with a thigh problem but, just before the break, his replacement, Juan Sara, added a second goal. Soon after half-time, Gavin Rae thundered a ferocious 22-yarder in off the bar and near the end, Nacho Novo completed a 6-0 aggregate rout.

It had been an enjoyable night for the big crowd - officially given as 8,254 but appearing to many to be more like 10,000 - with the well motivated and physically stronger Dark Blues totally eclipsing their Albanian opponents.

Jim Duffy was delighted: "We got a great reaction from the public tonight and the fact they got right behind us made for a terrific atmosphere." However, there was to be no easy passage, the draw for the first round proper - held in the glamourous setting of Monte Carlo - pairing Dundee with AC Perugia of Italy, with the first leg tie to be played at Dens Park on September 24th.

League form was somewhat indifferent, a 1-1 draw at Kilmarnock preceding a dismal 1-0 Dens defeat to a ten-man Celtic, who had lost Didier Agathe for a last-man challenge on Novo in 25 minutes. With an extra man it was expected that Jonay Hernandez - earlier awarded his first cap for Venezuala - would provide the width to penetrate the deep-lying Parkhead defence but, repeatedly, he failed to get over a telling cross.

Tom Cowan came in at left-back for the match against Aberdeen and it was to be a glorious home debut for the much-travelled veteran. With Caballero and Nemsadze at their tantalising best and Sara causing the Dons problems in the air, Dundee dominated. It fell to Cowan to open the scoring with a spectacular 35-yard shot high into the net and, near the end, Novo added another to earn fourth-placed Dundee their first home league win over Aberdeen since

away back in December 1988.

With just six weeks of the season gone, there had been plenty for Dens fans to discuss. Magners Irish Cider had provided Dundee with a jersey sponsorship deal for the Scottish Cup Final and that summer the pair struck a new one-year sponsorship agreement. Then, in early August, Giovanni di Stefano, who had been so close to making an investment in 1999, was appointed to the board.

As a lawyer, Di Stefano had made his reputation advising the defence in high-profile criminal cases in English and international courts. Peter Marr believed it was a good move for Dundee: "He's enthusiastic, very wealthy and maybe he can help us financially as well. Hopefully, he will buy shares but what he will certainly provide is his financial and commercial expertise as well as his worldwide connections."

Rumoured to have a personal fortune of £300 million, di Stefano declared himself willing to invest some £26 million, which he claimed to have made from the sale of his shares in FC Obilic of Belgrade, into Dundee. He pledged to redevelop the south side of Dens by erecting a six storey building that would incorporate commercial developments as well as a new stand, which would increase the ground capacity to over 18,000.

Di Stefano talked of new deals for players like Caballero, Rae, Smith, Sara, Mair, Mackay, Milne, Carranza, Brady, Langfield and Robertson, who were all out of contract in June 2004. He also hinted that Dundee's challenge to the Old Firm would shortly be enhanced by a couple of big-name signings. This caused great excitement amongst the fans but although many were cynical, others wondered if di Stefano might be Scotland's answer to Russian billionaire Roman Abramovich, who had begun to invest heavily in English Premiership side Chelsea.

Two of the players mentioned were strikers - Motherwell's Scotland international, James McFadden, and Chelsea's England Under-21 international, Carlton Cole. And when it was revealed that Dundee had offered £600,000 for the 'Well star, Dens fans sat up and took notice. The bid was rejected as was an increased offer of £750,000 and although McFadden eventually joined Everton for £1.4 million, supporters were somewhat reassured that Dundee appeared

Super saver - the cat-like Julian Speroni was a popular figure in goal during his time at Dens Park.   Fotopress

Flying high - Dundee centre-half Lee Wilkie soars high to head the equaliser against Perugia in the UEFA Cup tie at Dens. SNS Group

to have the wherewithal to bid, for, 10 days earlier, the club had announced a loss of £6.6 million - an incredible £4.1 million more than a year earlier - for the financial year ending on May 31st, 2002.

It was understood that debts then - 16 months earlier - totalled an astonishing £14.6 million though di Stefano, who was seeking to control the debts by transferring Dundee's account to a foreign bank, insisted that money was available for signings. By then Cole had joined Charlton on loan and with the August 31st transfer deadline imminent, there were also unsuccessful moves for other high profile players.

Amongst those were Georgian international winger Georgi Kincladze (most recently with Derby), Atletico Madrid midfielder Dani, Aston Villa's giant striker Peter Crouch, Deportivo de La Corunna's Brazilian midfielder Djalmina - rumoured to have been offered £8,000 per week - and former England international Paul Gascoigne.

Initially, the only signing was 19-year-old Dundee-born midfielder Mark Fotheringham - once the most sought-after youngster in Scotland - on a free transfer from Celtic in lieu of cash due after Robert Douglas had made five competitive appearances for Scotland. But soon, Dundee were back in the headlines with a couple of big-name captures.

In came Craig Burley, the former Chelsea, Celtic, Derby and Scotland midfielder, followed by the world-famous ex-Juventus, Middlesbrough, Lazio, Derby and Italian international striker Fabrizio Ravanelli. Both were free agents but neither would come cheap and despite Dundee's seemingly precarious financial position, their arrival seemed to

confirm that the money was there at Dens.

In recent seasons, Burley (31), had been plagued by knee problems while Ravanelli - nicknamed "The White Feather" due to the premature greying of his hair - was now almost 35-years of age. Both were awarded two-year deals but though confirming that he had identified Burley as a target, Jim Duffy denied that Ravanelli had been forced on him although he hinted that the ageing striker should only have been signed until the end of the season.

On Thursday, September 24th, it was back to UEFA Cup action against Perugia. The Italians had finished tenth in Serie 'A' but had qualified for the UEFA Cup via the Intertoto Cup after defeating AC Allianssi (Finland), Nantes (France) and VfL Wolfsburg (Germany). And with the tie going out live via the BBC and Italian Television, Jim Duffy described it as the biggest game at Dens in 30 years.

However, the pre-match build-up was somewhat overshadowed first by Burley and Ravanelli's arrival then by incredible claims from Giovanni di Stefano that Dutch international midfielder Edgar Davids - on £50,000 a week at Juventus - was a Dens Park transfer target! All this was news to Jim Duffy and, disturbingly, it appeared to contradict the manager's earlier assertion that it was his job to identify players and the board's to finance them!

Meanwhile, Perugia had been watched by Duffy's ex-Dundee, Chelsea and Portsmouth colleague Graham Rix with the former England international reporting back that they were an industrious, well-disciplined team who had played impressively in a 1-1 draw with European Champions AC Milan in Perugia.

Party time - over 2,000 Dundee fans of all ages followed Dundee to Perugia and a great time was had by all. N Price

Dundee again opted for 4-4-2 with Sara replacing Carranza at left-midfield from the home tie against KS Vllaznia, with the white-clad Perugia going for a 4-3-3 formation. The near-capacity (11,800) crowd - the official figure was 9,911 - were treated to a pulsating game but, without the power of Caballero - suspended for three games after his red card in the Intertoto tie at Sartid - and with Burley and Ravanelli ineligible, Dundee were hard pushed to contain their Italian opponents.

Five minutes after half-time, Perugia went ahead when di Loretto shot high past Speroni following a short corner. Dundee then lost Lovell with a twisted knee but in 63 minutes Lee Wilkie made it 1-1 when he connected with a corner and sent a powerful header inside the far post, with the predatory Novo trying to claim the final touch. That set Dens alight but although enjoying a ten-minute spell of domination, Dundee failed to capitalise and, eight minutes from time, slack defending allowed Fusani to hook home a second goal for Perugia.

It was a cruel lesson for although the physically powerful Italians had held the edge, Dundee's battling display had merited a draw. There were further fine performances at Ibrox and Tynecastle but the loss of late goals again cost them dear as they went down 3-1 to Rangers then lost a two-goal lead in a 2-2 draw with Hearts.

On October 15th, the official Dundee party flew direct to Perugia for the second leg with around 2,500 fans of the Dark Blues also making the journey to lend their support. In the day-and-a-half prior to the game, there was a real carnival atmosphere as the fans, many resplendent in kilts as well as their Dundee tops, gathered in the Umbrian university town, which lay around 50 miles north-east of Rome and whose population numbered some 200,000.

There were colourful scenes as the fans thronged Perugia's main square but Wednesday night's late-night merrymaking came to a halt after a hail of missiles from Italian thugs provoked a number of skirmishes. However, the behaviour of Dundee's good-humoured fans was praised by the local police chief and next day the Dark Blue army was back in force, enjoying the local hostelries and utilising the cathedral steps as a focal point to wave flags and sing their songs.

In the event, the pre-match build-up was to exceed the excitement of the game itself, which was played on a bitterly cold night at the Renato Curi Stadium. Caballero replaced the injured Lovell with Sara moving up front but despite great support from their fans in the 8,000 crowd, Dundee made little impact. It took a splendid Speroni save to push a fierce shot from the bustling English striker Jay Boothroyd on to a post but a Jim Duffy pep-talk resulted in a more positive approach to the second half.

Getting little change out of Perugia's central defenders, Sara dropped a bit deeper and soon there were several lightning moves up the right. Rae, twice, and Novo all came close with Wilkie coming up to fire just past, but with 19 minutes remaining, Dens hopes were shattered when home substitute Margiotta made it 3-1 on aggregate from close in after Speroni had saved his first effort.

Dundee had created more openings than in the first leg, but, just as lapses in concentration had cost them dear at Dens, their failure to take their chances in Italy meant a premature end to their UEFA Cup adventure. Nevertheless, it had been a trip to remember and now it was hoped the addition of Burley and Ravanelli might help Dundee gain a high enough placing to ensure a swift return to European football.

In his debut against Partick Thistle, Ravanelli put Novo through to score but the Italian's pace had gone and, disappointingly, just five points were taken from games against Thistle (h) 1-0, Dundee United (a) 1-1, Hibernian (h) 1-1, and Motherwell (h) 0-1. For much of the first half the Dark Blues gave United the runaround and at half-time, they led through a Novo penalty. However, allied to an Ian McCall tactical switch, the loss of Jonay Hernandez and Scottish international midfielder Gavin Rae - who had recently gained his sixth full cap against Germany - swung things United's way and Dundee were fortunate to survive.

Craig Burley made his starting league debut against Hibs only to get his marching orders for a reckless challenge on Tam McManus after just 23 minutes. The fans expected better from a player of his experience and although his teammates battled hard for a point, their subsequent reverse to Motherwell was to prove the prelude to desperate days of an altogether different kind at Dens.

Big deal - Fabrizio Ravanelli celebrates his League Cup hat-trick against Clyde with Nacho Novo. Ravanelli and Craig Burley (inset) got huge salaries but their stay was short-lived. SNS Group

CHAPTER FORTY-TWO

Oblivion Beckons

Off the field, a succession of events was about to plunge Dundee Football Club into the depths of despair. First, the Inland Revenue began court proceedings for recovery of £72,000 due for PAYE but no sooner had Giovanni di Stefano settled the matter with a personal cheque, than Dundee United went public over Dundee's failure to hand over £83,000 of ticket money from the recent derby.

The fierce war of words which broke out was clear evidence of the mounting financial pressure following the Bank of Scotland's ultimatum that it would not allow overdraft facilities of its 10 SPL clients to drift any further into the red. Dundee were reeling and, on November 14th, they were stunned when an SPL tribunal ruled that they were not entitled to any compensation for Zurab Khizanishvili, who had been 21-years old when he left Dens.

Earlier, the Ibrox club had offered £75,000 but, with the Georgian having already played 21 full internationals - eleven while at Dens - this had immediately been rejected. And, heartened by the £2-million compensation paid by Manchester United for Sunderland's David Bellion (20), Dundee were optimistic that they would get £200,000 to £300,000, particularly as they would be represented by top London QC Jim Sturman as well as Giovanni di Stefano himself.

Rangers, however, had raised four technical points to argue that Dundee were entitled to nothing. Three of these were rejected but the fourth - namely that Dundee's letter indicating a desire to discuss new terms was not an offer of employment - was accepted as valid, and effectively meant Khizanishvili was a free agent.

Peter Marr was devastated and, in an interview with Ron Scott of *The Sunday Post*, he maintained that it was a procedure which had been followed for many years: "We feel robbed and cheated about the decision. It appears to us that they are making up the rules as they go along. When we sent Zurab a written offer to remain with Dundee, both the SPL and SFA received a copy but neither stated there was anything wrong. Now we are being told that because an official contract was not included, it constitutes a technicality. Why did they not tell us at the time?"

That came as a crushing blow and although Lee Wilkie did well to

Last straw - no fee for Zurab Khizanishvili

Dens director Giovanni di Stefano. DC Thomson

subdue the deadly Ruud van Nistelrooy in Scotland's 1-0 defeat of Holland at Hampden, storm clouds were fast gathering over Dens. A few days later, Wilkie and Gavin Rae were both in the starting line-up as Scotland crashed 6-0 in the Amsterdam return and, on their return came the bombshell news that Dundee were about to go into administration.

For the first time, Peter Marr admitted that the club was in serious financial trouble, but although he and the other Dundee-based directors accepted that voluntary administration was inevitable, Giovanni di Stefano voiced his opposition. He hinted that he might take legal action against the board's plans but Peter Marr was quick to respond: "Gio is all bluff and bluster. He can talk all he wants but we see this measure as the only way forward. Wages are bleeding this club to death and there will have to be victims for Dundee to survive. The losses have to stop and going into administration is the only way forward."

That Saturday, the Dark Blues lost 2-0 on the new "plastic" pitch at Dunfermline but by then, the main concern was the survival of the club itself. In recent years, Hamilton, Raith Rovers, Falkirk, Partick Thistle, Morton, Airdrie, Clydebank and Motherwell had all had major financial worries but Dundee were the biggest club yet to be affected, with their debts believed to exceed those of all these clubs combined.

At lunchtime on Monday, November 24th, Dundee formally went into administration after an application was made to the Court of Session in Edinburgh. Tom Burton and Fiona Taylor of accountants Ernst and Young were appointed joint administrators but the staggering news was that their debts now topped the £20 million mark.

Burton, who was Ernst and Young's corporate restructuring chief, had led successful administrations at Gillingham and Portsmouth as well as the restructuring of Brighton but Portsmouth's debt had only been £8 million with average gates of 11,000 and he was cautious about Dundee's prospects: "This move stops the clock running on the club's debts and gives us the ability to restructure its operations and debts. However, the club is in a critical financial position and solutions to its problems will not be easy to find."

Di Stefano no longer planned to mount a legal challenge to the administration but, insisting that he would not be made the scapegoat for those that had accrued the liabilities, he

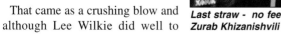

Hamilton), Gavin Beith (at Peterhead), Kris Brash (at Montrose), and Steven Vanderdeyl (at Cove Rangers).

They were joined by youth development chief Kenny Cameron, community coach Kevin Lee, goalkeeper-coach Paul Mathers, assistant-physio Robbie Raeside and European scout Javier Artero, as well as five office-based staff including commercial director Jim Connor, commercial manager Tommy Dickson and accountant Ian Coyle. Jim Duffy had undertaken the difficult task of telling the players the dire news and later he remarked: "I feel shattered and it will take a long time before the damage is repaired. This action has bought us time but I have been told that we will definitely need to sell a player in the January transfer window."

Tom Cowan, who had an offer to join Carlisle, had volunteered to go. He had been through a similar experience at York as had Lovell at Portsmouth and Bournmouth but for most of the players there was bewilderment mixed with anger as they left Dens to face the media. A clearly stunned Georgi Nemsadze struggled for words: "It was very emotional in there. In my time here we built up a very good team but now it's all gone. I don't know what I'm going to do."

suggested in *The Courier* that the Marrs might have struck a "covert agreement" with the Bank of Scotland so that their companies might be treated more leniently and that that was the motivating factor for going into administration. However, although accepting that the Marrs' businesses were closely intertwined with the club, his theory was refuted by Dundee spokesman Niall Scott.

Peter Marr had been on business in Egypt when informed that the Inland Revenue were threatening to wind up the club over another unpaid tax bill of £750,000. The Dens boss was unsure about di Stefano's claim to have put up a personal guarantee to pay this and explained: "If the club had been liquidated, that would have been the end for Dundee F.C., so, after speaking to the Bank of Scotland, we decided to follow new Government legislation and go into voluntary administration to try and save the business. The club will immediately be put up for sale but if no-one comes in and makes an offer, we fully expect to be here when the club comes back out of administration."

He acknowledged that the club's speculate to accumulate policy had been an expensive mistake: "We have been paying players too much and with the collapse of the transfer market we struggled to move players on. Ivano Bonetti got them in but only managed to sell Douglas and Caniggia. I think you'll find that clubs in other countries who did likewise, are in exactly the same situation."

The following day, the full reality of Dundee's predicament hit home as 25 employees, comprising players, backroom staff and office workers were axed. The players shown the door were Georgi Nemsadze, Fabian Caballero, Fabrizio Ravanelli, Juan Sara, Craig Burley, Beto Carranza, Jamie Langfield, Tom Cowan, Colin Boylan, Matt Engele, Mark Robertson (on loan at St Johnstone), Barry Forbes (at

Juan Sara, too, was astonished at the situation: "I am very angry and I don't believe the law here. I cannot believe that employees can be sacked like this. You come into work one day and they tell you you have been dismissed, you have no rights, you no longer have a contract, you are not getting your money and to go home."

Despite his promises of massive investment, Giovanni di Stefano did not appear to have been of any great financial benefit and, earlier, in *The Courier* a club source had revealed: "Gio paid a tax bill of £72,000 and Ravanelli's wages but there is a dispute over the extent to which Burley has been paid and we are at best only slightly financially ahead in our dealings with him. Since he became a director in August we have had three months of totally unfulfilled

Money man - administrator Tom Burton would decide whether Dundee F.C. had a future. DC Thomson

Alive and kicking - Mark Fotheringham fires in a shot against Hearts soon after Dundee went into administration.   DC Thomson

promises of investment. It reached the stage where the club had to take action to safeguard itself."

Peter Marr, though, refused to blame the Anglo-Italian for Dundee's predicament, saying: "I don't want to criticise Gio - he came in, tried to help but it has not come through and it's as simple as that. That should be put to bed and it is now about going forward. We need to get things sorted out then hopefully it will be a lot better."

After the sackings, di Stefano, whose position on the Dens Park board had still not been ratified by the SFA, had attempted to have Ravanelli reinstated at his own expense. However, it was pointed out that, legally, having made the former Italian international redundant, Dundee would have to re-hire him, then be responsible for the remaining 21 months of his £260,000 per annum contract.

Tom Burton said that it would only be considered if the entire cost of the contract was paid up front but, after consulting Jim Duffy, he decided that if the money was available, it would be better spent on more than one player. Conversely, Kenny Cameron and Kevin Lee were regarded as key elements of Dundee's youth development programme and both were re-instated on a consultancy basis after funding was produced by local businessmen.

The dismissals had cut the losses from a crippling £100,000 to £60,000 per week with Burton revealing that Dundee had been previously expending over 150% of their income on wages: "You don't need to be a specialist in corporate restructuring to know that that situation cannot continue. We're only part of the way towards getting to a position of breaking even and for a start, I'll be happy to get us back to a manageable level of losses."

The administrator was aware of the strong sense of goodwill from the local population and he appealed to sponsors and fans to dig deep. He noted that although some 18,000 Dundee fans had been at the Cup Final, only 6,000 regularly came to Dens and he exhorted the missing thousands to attend home games.

After a week of trauma, the trip to Livingston came as a

relief and travelling fans were rewarded by a last-gasp Mark Fotheringham equaliser in a 1-1 draw. However, when bottom-of-the-league Partick Thistle made Jim Duffy their target after sacking Gerry Collins, fans feared the Dens boss might be lured by the relative stability of Maryhill. Many felt that his departure could send the club into freefall but players and supporters got a tremendous boost when the highly-respected Duffy pledged to fight on at Dens.

In October, a quickfire Ravanelli hat-trick after coming on as a 70th-minute substitute, had helped Dundee to a 5-2 League Cup win over Clyde at Broadwood. That set up a quarter-final tie against Hearts and, on Wednesday, December 3rd, the visit of the third-placed Edinburgh side - Dundee's first home game since administration - appeared to have attracted considerably more than the 7,130 official attendance. It was an emotional night and lifted by a noisy home support, the Dark Blues hammered away at the visiting defence throughout the first period.

Hearts hit back after the interval only to find Lee Wilkie in inspirational form as he repeatedly thwarted their giant Dutch striker Mark De Vries. It was an enthralling encounter and as the excitement continued into extra-time, 18-year-old Dundee substitute Bobby Linn finally broke the deadlock when he pounced to hit a 107th-minute winner after Nacho Novo's shot rebounded from a post.

That meant the Dens men could expect some £250,000 from their share of the pooled gate money, the semi-final draw pairing them with the unfancied Livingston, while Hibs, shock conquerors of Celtic - would meet Rangers in the other tie. By now, the Dundee Supporters' Association had launched the Dee4Life fund-raising campaign with Blue Nose Day and a promising start was maintained when a bucket collection at the Hearts tie raised in excess of £12,000.

Only thirteen players with much first-team experience remained. And with Rae, Sancho, Milne, Hutchinson and Lovell struggling through injury and Robb (Raith Rovers), Soutar and Jablonski (both Brechin City), on loan and unable to be recalled until January, there were major selection problems. Nevertheless, the team continued to play entertaining football, netting four goals in a 3-2 defeat to Celtic at Parkhead and a 2-2 draw at Aberdeen.

Meanwhile, hopes of fresh investment by Vladimir Romanov, who owned the Russian-backed Ukio Bank in Lithuania, fell through - as had his approaches to Dundee United and Dunfermline - after a meeting in London. There was to be no quick fix and administrator Tom Burton warned that the club's fate still hung in the balance: "We have been at the club just short of a month and have halved the weekly operating losses to around £50,000 per week. However, no-one should hope for anything more than just staying alive to see another Christmas and, yes, the worst-case scenario is that the club could go into liquidation."

"If that was the case, there would be automatic expulsion from the SPL although they could re-apply to the Scottish League and work their way back up again. However, the ground would have to be sold because if the business could not be sold as a going concern, it would have to be sold piece by piece. The team's achievement in reaching the CIS Cup semi-final has helped greatly but the cash flow is crucial so the fans should keep coming up with ideas and I would say I have been amazed by the energy and commitment shown by so many people."

However, with insufficient funds to get to the end of the season, income was required via player sales in the January transfer window even though it would be detrimental to the team. The loss of 16-goal Nacho Novo would seriously undermine their prospects while Speroni's departure would cause a major goalkeeping crisis for the League Cup semi-final since Derek Soutar was already cup-tied at Brechin, leaving 17-year-old John McCafferty as the only option.

Lee Wilkie had attracted interest from Shaktar Donetsk but he found a move to the Ukraine unappealing. His Scotland colleague Gavin Rae, who was out of contract next summer, became the main focus of transfer speculation only for Rangers to display little festive spirit in giving Dundee just two hours to accept a lowly £50,000 bid.

This was rejected as was an increased bid of £100,000 and, when the Ibrox club returned with an offer of £125,000, it too was turned down on the understanding that the Marrs would underwrite that amount should Rangers walk away. These moves had occurred in the lead-up to the home match with Rangers on December 28th but, with both Rae and

Star quality - but soon Dens stars Gavin Rae and Nacho Novo would join Rangers as financial cuts bit deep.   DC Thomson

former Dark Blue Khizanishvili out through injury, the Light Blues departed with a 2-0 win.

Earlier, Jim Duffy had accused the Ibrox club of using "bully-boy tactics" in attempting to get an international player for a derisory sum but, with a number of English clubs showing interest, the two clubs finally struck a deal on December 30th. In the end, Dundee got the £250,000 they had held out for, less the £37,000 deposit which Rangers had initially put down for Khizanishvili.

Rae had been a grand servant in his 10 years at Dens and his driving midfield play would be missed. The Scotland international had stated his willingness to go anywhere so the club would get as big a fee as possible and Tom Burton echoed the fans' appreciation: "Gavin recognised that his move could ease our situation and his professionalism has been exemplary. We completed the transfer on our terms and, if we have to consider any further activity in January, this will only happen if a deal is acceptable to the club."

In recent weeks, little had been heard from Giovanni di Stefano but with New Year approaching, he responded to suggestions that he had not delivered: "Having arrived in August, I was effectively given two months to refinance £20 million. I managed to do £12.5 million of refinancing only to have the plug pulled from that by the club going into administration. What more could I have done?"

"I live in the real world and I am clear that with debts approaching £20m Dundee will be liquidated unless the Bank of Scotland, who are owed nearly £14 million, write off or write down the overdraft to £1 or 2 million. No-one is going to come in, pay off the debts and start again."

He revealed that he had registered the name Dundee City F.C. at Companies House - the Angus Cook version from 1990 had lapsed - to replace Dundee F.C. if they became defunct. He did, though, acknowledge that for that to happen, football and governmental authorities would have to adopt new legislation, similar to that in Italy, where financially crippled Fiorentina, who had been relegated from Serie 'A' to Serie 'C2' due to financial irregularities, had recently been permitted to leapfrog others into Serie 'B'.

Meanwhile, it was understood that di Stefano had offered £835,000 for Dens Park Stadium and the car park, proposing a 125-year lease at a nominal £2,000 per month and guaranteeing to charge no more than 10% of the purchase price for the first five years. He denied that he wanted to sell the ground on at a huge profit but his offer was turned down by the administrator who also rejected di Stefano's claim that he had been unable to purchase the ground since it was owned by parent company, Dundee F.C. Holdings.

"Contrary to speculation placed on various internet message boards over the past few days, I can confirm that the stadium is owned by Dundee Football Club Ltd and has been since 1920," he said. "We are concerned about the effect that inaccurate speculation of this kind can have at a time when supporters, directors and the club are working so hard to ensure the long-term survival of the club."

Since the onset of administration, many had dreaded a severe winter and the subsequent revenue loss from postponements. Their concerns were justified for although the Rangers game - attendance 10,948 - had beaten the weather, the home match against Hearts on Saturday, January 3rd, had to be postponed due to snow and frost.

The rescheduled game went ahead the following Tuesday and not only did Dundee lose 2-1 but just 6,387 fans - around 3,000 less than expected for the holiday weekend fixture, paid their way in - a financial loss the Dark Blues could ill afford. The hot-air dome had never provided satisfactory pitch protection and now club officials agreed that it would be prudent to invest in undersoil heating.

Tom Burton confirmed that the £150,000 installation costs had been included in his projections for next season and he appeared increasingly optimistic that the Dark Blues would manage to raise the £350,000 required to survive until the summer and might actually break even in 2005-06.

Derby delight - Steve Lovell crashes the ball past Paul Gallacher to ensure a morale-boosting 2-1 win over Dundee United at Dens .
DC Thomson

The financial situation was further improved by the Scottish Cup third-round draw which paired Dundee with Aberdeen at Pittodrie. Over 11,000 turned out but although the injury-hit Dark Blues dominated the first period, the ordering-off of Mark Fotheringham for a second yellow card meant a backs-to-the-wall battle to escape with a 0-0 draw.

The cash-strapped Dens men got a £125,000 windfall when B-Sky-B broadcast the January 21st replay live but little was to go right on the pitch. Behind after just four minutes, Dundee quickly levelled when Robb prodded home Jablonski's netbound header after a Novo shot was parried by Preece. The fast interchanging of Novo, Robb and Linn caused the Dons problems but after the break, the visitors took control. With 13 minutes left, Heikennen fired home after the ball took a bad bounce off Smith, Zdrilic making it 3-1 before Novo got a late consolation.

In Dundee's fragile financial situation, the early Scottish Cup exit was far from ideal although there was a League Cup semi-final to come. Just four days earlier, Dundee had recorded their first league win in 10 games when late goals by Novo and Smith gave them a crucial 2-1 win over Partick Thistle at Firhill, leaving them with a nine point cushion over the bottom-markers.

Earlier, Thistle chairman Tom Hughes had claimed that Dundee should be relegated due to the financial chaos at Dens and there was further controversy when the Dark Blues, who had failed to persuade Caballero and Nemsadze to return to Dens on vastly reduced salaries, signed Portsmouth midfielder Neil Barrett (22), and Chelsea's German Under-21 international striker Sebastian Kneissl, on loan until the end of the season with their wages to be paid by local businessmen.

Hughes, SPFA assistant-secretary Fraser Wishart and sacked Dark Blue Craig Burley were outraged that clubs in administration, who had previously sacked players, were allowed to make loan signings, a criticism echoed by Raith Rovers, who had recently rejected Dundee's bid to take the First Division's top scorer, John Sutton, on loan and instead sold him to Millwall for £80,000.

On Sunday, January 25th, Dundee United fans threw monopoly money as Dundee took the field for the Dens derby, but it was the Dark Blues who had the last laugh. Inspired by the energetic Brady, Dundee dominated only for Billy Dodds to put United ahead with a 44th-minute penalty after Brent Sancho - an earlier substitute for the injured Lee Wilkie - had needlessly downed Charlie Miller.

Early in the second half, Fotheringham directed a free-kick to the far post, and when Sancho hooked the ball back, Novo bundled home from a couple of yards. In 69 minutes, a superb diagonal pass by Milne saw Lovell beat Wilson with his left foot before brilliantly sweeping the ball high past Gallacher with his right to give Dundee a 2-1 win!

And when the Dark Blues managed a 1-1 draw against Hibs at Easter Road, they appeared in fine fettle for the CIS League Cup semi-final against Livingston at the same venue on Tuesday, February 3rd. Sensibly, the Scottish League had moved the tie from Hampden but despite Dundee's 5,000-plus travelling support, there was a disappointing Livy turnout in the 7,231 crowd. Dundee: Speroni; Mackay, Sancho, Mair, Hernandez; Smith, Fotheringham, Barrett, Brady; Novo, Lovell (Milne). Livingston: McKenzie; Rubio (Pasquanelli), Andrews, Dorado; McNamee, Lovell, Makel, O'Brien, McAllister; Lilley, Fernandez.

The darting Nacho Novo, who remained at Dens despite interest from Rangers and Valencia, was a constant menace as he sped on to a series of long diagonal balls but in 10 minutes he shot straight at McKenzie when it looked easier to score. Just prior to half-time, the Almondvale side had a "goal" chalked off for offside and with a striker, Pasquanelli, on for Rubio, they dominated much of the second period, going close on a couple of occasions.

By the closing stages, Dundee looked the likelier to score but with just 60 seconds left, Mair and Sancho allowed a speculative ball to bounce through and, as Speroni hesitated,

Dangerman - Stevie Milne troubles Livingston in the League Cup semi-final at Easter Road .   DC Thomson

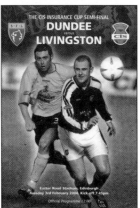

Pasquinelli went down in a tussle with Mair. Recently, Dundee had got the benefit of the doubt when Smith upended Grady in the box at Firhill but this time match referee Mike McCurry awarded a penalty and Derek Lilley stepped up to fire home the winner.

There was no disguising the disappointment as the fans trooped from the ground and the belief that the Cup had been there for the taking was only exacerbated by Hibernian's subsequent defeat of Rangers. Rae and Wilkie had been missed but, just 48 hours earlier, it had emerged that Livingston were also going into administration. And, according to Jim Duffy, that had piled the pressure on Dundee: "We were told the result could decide which club made it out of administration or not and perhaps that made the more creative players err on the side of safety.'

"We ran around, tackled and chased but didn't play with the head and, as far as purely football matters are concerned this is the worst I've felt in a long time. It was always going to be a tense match but we didn't play the way we can, made a mistake and got punished."

A top-six placing remained a realistic target, while the cash-strapped Dark Blues also had the incentive of an extra £60,000 per league position. But with skipper and defensive midfielder Barry Smith joining Scotland centre-half Lee Wilkie on the sidelines with a jarred knee, Dundee managed just one win from their next eight games with some heavy defeats. It had been hoped that rest and physiotherapy would lead to a full recovery by Wilkie but a recurrence of his knee injury at training resulted in surgery to his cruciate ligament and it would be December before he returned to action.

On February 15th, around 100 shareholders attended the 2002 AGM of parent company Dundee F.C. Holdings plc at Dens but, by then, Jim Connor, who had lost his paid commercial post, and Giovanni di Stefano had both resigned from the board. There was now a realistic acceptance of the club's difficulties rather than anger at the men in charge and, repeating their intention to continue if no-one bought the club, the Marrs pledged to bring several local businessmen as well as a fans' representative on to a new enlarged board.

Meanwhile, the Dee4Life fund-raising campaign had gone from strength to strength and by March, they had raised £153,000. Jim Duffy did his bit by donning diving gear and plunging into a shark-filled tank at the Deep Sea Aquarium at North Queensferry to raise £1,000, while Bobby Cox, Tommy Coyne and Brian Irvine were amongst a great many ex-Dundee stars who rallied round to help out.

In recent years, the DSA - comprising some 30 branches worldwide - had evolved into a highly-organised group and with the official club website Dundee F.C. Online as a focal point, numerous fund-raising ideas were accumulated and the best ones prioritised and actioned. It was time-consuming work but for those involved there was but a single aim, to ensure the survival of Dundee Football Club.

The struggle had become even harder with an SPL ruling that any club in administration after May 31st would start the 2004-05 season with a 10-point deduction and would be unable to sign new players. That left Dundee little time to sort out their affairs and an angry Tom Burton commented: "Football is not above the law and the penalties now faced by clubs entering administration after the end of this season may run contrary to the Enterprise Act 2003 which places the emphasis firmly on the survival of companies."

On March 5th, a meeting of creditors at Dens approved plans to renegotiate repayment of a large part of Dundee's debts in the hope it would enable the club to come out of administration via a Creditors' Voluntary Arrangement (CVA), by May 31st. The administrator listed total liabilities as £22.9 million, but this included contingent and other liabilities of £2.5 million - £1.3m for SportScotland and Football Trust grants, with another £1.2m for players' unexpired contracts.

Those contingencies would only become due in the event of liquidation or, in the case of the grants, disposal of the stadium. Once other assets were taken into account, that figure fell to £18.3m. The largest portion of debt (£14.7m), was due to holders of standard securities and floating charges, headed by the Bank of Scotland with debts of £13.8m and Lombard North Central (£740k), who, as secured creditors, would get preferential treatment in any financial settlement.

Amongst the ordinary unsecured creditors were the Inland Revenue, who were due £853,679 for PAYE and National Insurance, HM Customs and Excise, due £548,926 for VAT, current employees (£117,000), P&J Taverns and other Marr-related debts (£1.9m), with another £1.1 million due to 137 trade creditors who were mostly local businessmen. Others included Ivano Bonetti (£927,000), and Giovanni di Stefano (£35,000), with claims for outstanding loans, while Dinamo Tblisi were due £395,000 and Tacuary Futbal Club £228,000.

Burton was happy at the outcome but just days later came the shock news that the administrators - under pressure by Dundee's major creditor the Halifax Bank of Scotland - had been in talks with Dundee United to facilitate a tenancy arrangement at Tannadice from the start of season 2004-05.

It was understood that the bank had pressurised United, themselves £6.5 million in debt, and wanted to "buy" both grounds - Dens to be sold off, with Tannadice to be revamped in neutral colours and renamed the City of Discovery Stadium - where both clubs could play on an equal basis. The proposal was rejected by United but for those of a Dark Blue persuasion, the arrangement was even less palatable and there was immediately fierce opposition.

Dee4Life chairman George Knight echoed the feelings of most Dundee fans: "This club is on its knees and could die - but if it is to die then it is as well dying here than down the road. I am dismayed and dejected that we might be made to share with United because if it happens, regardless of the terms, it will be the death knell for the club as the fans will not support it."

Peter Marr, too, was far from happy: "My brother Jimmy and I don't want Dundee to go down the road and neither do the fans. I believe that, financially, it would make little difference whether we went there or not. In 1999, SportScotland and the Football Trust provided £1.3m in grant aid for the new stands and for a 20-year period, they can reclaim a diminishing proportion of the money should Dens cease to be used for football. As of today, they would, as secured creditors, be due around £600,000."

"There is also the money we borrowed to build the stands, so, in all, the club would be paying something like £2.1 million just to go to Tannadice. If we remain calm and keep pulling together, we can see Dundee playing on at Dens until, hopefully, we can come up with a plan that sees a new joint stadium built."

On Saturday 13th March, the Dee4Life fund-raising campaign was launched as a registered Supporters' Trust and soon membership had exceeded 3,000 - by far the largest in Scotland. Earlier, they had agreed to give £10,000 per month to Dundee F.C. but now the Trust resolved to retain the balance of £130,000, fearful it might disappear into a financial black hole unless certain conditions were met.

There was huge opposition to the Tannadice move with some fans arguing that it might be preferrable to go into liquidation and restart as a new club in the Third Division of the Scottish Football League. However, SFL rules stated that a club would have to honour all "football debt" accrued by its former self before gaining entry, meaning the "new" Dundee could start off heavily in debt due to liabilities to ex-Dundee F.C. employees such as Ivano Bonetti and the sacked players. In addition, the SFL reserved the right to treat each case on its merits and would not be bound to admit a new Dundee club ahead of other applicants.

Rumours that the Lithuanian consortium were prepared to construct a new stadium for both city clubs came to nothing as did Giovanni di Stefano's latest suggestion that Dee4Life link up with him to make a £1-million offer for Dens Park. On March 29th, the SPL approved various ground-sharing proposals, including one for Dundee to play at Tannadice although Tom Burton stressed that it was only one of three options, the others being the status-quo at Dens, or remaining at Dens with ownership transferred to a third party, such as the bank and the debt restructured.

Carnoustie property developer Bruce Linton of James Keiller Estates then proposed building a 12,000-seater stadium for both city clubs, south of the Kingsway and to the west of Kings Cross Road. There would also be sufficient land for a youth academy and, in exchange,

Linton would get Dens and Tannadice plus the area in between - worth some £3m in total - for development.

One drawback of the Linton scheme was the three-year timescale and although Dundee continued to show interest, Dundee United quickly distanced themselves from the proposal, claiming that the building costs were prohibitive - a stance which brought accusations from Dundee that sharing Tannadice was primarily designed to alleviate United's large debt rather than save the Dark Blues.

Later, former club sponsor Bob Jamieson proposed a new share issue to double the number of shares, with himself and Dee4Life paying £650,000 for a 51% controlling interest. He hoped the Marrs would remain on board but appeared to suggest cancelling existing player contracts and capping salaries. However, this was never likely to appeal to Dundee F.C.'s parent company Dundee F.C. Holdings plc, in which the Marrs then held an 86% stake. Neither did it appeal to the administrator, while Dee4Life also distanced themselves from his bid, which was subsequently withdrawn.

The innovative fund-raising schemes run by Dee4Life, the DSA and the Business Development Club continued apace and fuelled by publicity from the likes of Dundee East MP Iain Luke and Courier columnist Jim Crumley, they got tremendous support from the local community. Dee4Life merchandise was sold at Dens, while events included a fashion show at the Bonar Hall, a Sportsmans' Dinner at the Invercarse Hotel, an Easter Ceilidh at Forfar, various Burns Suppers, Football Quiz nights, various dominoes, cards and darts nights, a Ladies Night at the Marquee, a Gourmet Dinner in Broughty Ferry, while Dee Aid at Chambers Bar featured several local bands.

There was a Grand Raffle, a Smart Car raffle, a Best Dundee Tatoo competition, a sponsored Headshave, various bands including Jump The Q played before 1,200 clubbers at "Doo at The Vue". CJ Laing's Spar shops launched Dundee F.C. spring water, there was a sponsored Scroll of Honour in the Bobby Cox stand, ASDA in Dundee introduced a new range of DFC leisurewear, while a giant sponsored flag was later paraded before home games at Dens.

Fans from other clubs, too, rallied round, particularly at the Dens Park bucket collections. A "Night with Tam Cowan" was compered free of charge by the Motherwell-supporting football comedian. His BBC Radio Scotland colleague and St Johnstone fan Stuart Cosgrove made a generous donation, BBC sports pundit Jim Spence also did his bit,

To the rescue - Dens skipper Barry Smith clears from Nuno Capucho of Rangers with Lee Mair on hand to assist.   DC Thomson

while Dundee United fan Ricky Ross, former lead singer of Deacon Blue, donated a framed "Gold Disc" for auction. Soap stars from Coronation Street and Emmerdale turned out against a Dundee All Stars XI, while other celebrities like master chef Gordon Ramsay provided signed items for auction in a quite overwhelming display of goodwill.

Recently, Tom Burton had discussed Dundee's position in an interview with Roddy Isles of *The Courier*: "We are now trading on a level basis and there is a fairly clear path to the end of April, when we have to come up with a realistic package for the future. However, if the club survives, there will be no more big-wage players because you cannot do that on gates of 7,000 to 8,000. Dundee had outgoings comparable to Southampton, who have a well-utilised 30,000 capacity stadium as well as receiving English Premiership-level TV money."

"There will have to be some compromise between the existing directors, creditors, fans and fans' groups like Dee4Life. I know there is a lot of anger at Peter and Jimmy Marr. But if they hadn't put their hands in their pockets to provide more money on day one of administration, then we wouldn't be here because someone had to pay for that process. They have stood up and said they were wrong and we now have to move on from there."

"Our primary responsibility is to ensure the survival of the company and get as much back for the creditors as we can. We have no objective other than to get things sorted in the short term and in doing that give a reasonable chance of a long-term future for the club. It is a mixture of people writing off some level of debt and people having to take a long-term view on matters."

On Thursday, April 9th, there was welcome news when the administrator announced that Dundee would remain at Dens Park next season. He acknowledged the massive opposition to renting Tannadice but stressed that Dens was not a permanent solution: "We now have the breathing space to look in detail at a range of options, including redevelopment, ground-sharing at a neutral stadium or the building of a new stadium in Dundee."

The Halifax Bank of Scotland had finally accepted Burton's assertion that moving down the road was not a particularly attractive financial proposition although it still wanted to see radical cost-reducing changes to the way in which football was structured in the city and was likely to actively "encourage" both clubs to come together in some form the following summer.

That Sunday, Dundee faced Dundee United at Tannadice and although there was no official boycott, many fans did just that and just over 2,000 - less than half the number that usually followed Dundee across the road - went along. United were strong favourites but, despite the absence of the suspended Nacho Novo, Dundee again did themselves proud. And although on the defensive for much of the first period, the Dark Blues led 2-0 at half-time.

Stevie Milne was the key man. In 17 minutes, his near-post cross allowed Steve Lovell to head home before Milne, himself, finished off a lightning break by thumping a powerful 25-yard shot low past Gallacher. In the end, Dundee had to be content with a 2-2 draw, and McCall's Tangerines went on to finish fifth with the Dark Blues two places behind.

For a number of months the Marrs and Dee4Life had not seen eye to eye. There was resentment from the fans at the mess the directors had got the club into, while the Marrs felt that, since they had paid some £700,000 for the administration and were soon to lose millions in guarantees, Dee4Life should hand over their funds to help save the club.

On Monday 19th April, a three-hour meeting between the Marrs, Tom Burton and Dee4Life's three-man delegation comprising George Knight, Scott Glenday and John Langlands, took place at Dens - surprisingly, the first time all three parties had sat at the same table.

The club provided Dee4Life with their two-year business plan, which had the backing of HBOS. By then the Trust had donated £50,000 to aid cash flow and having accepted the plan, they agreed to raise their contribution to £150,000 in exchange for a 5% holding of special Class 'A' shares with full voting rights and a guaranteed place on the board for a Dee4Life Trust representative.

Soon afterwards, HBOS called in their guarantees from the Marrs, whose £5.3m payment for an additional 6% shareholding would drastically cut the club's £13.8m debt to their major creditors. There was now a feeling of increasing optimism and, on May 26th, creditors approved proposals for a CVA, a technical device for the restructuring of debt.

The alternative had been liquidation but now the club would avoid the penalty of a 10-point deduction for next season. The agreement would allow for preferential and secured creditors to get a 25% share of net funds from player sales during transfer windows that summer and in January 2005 but there were only minimal prospects of a return for ordinary creditors.

Tom Burton emphasised that the company's future finances were highly volatile and that its future viability depended on the sale of at least 3,600 season tickets, TV appearance money and a strict adherence to budgets. On a more positive note, cash flow projections indicated that the club could break even in the coming season or the year after, assuming the number of fans buying season tickets and attending games remained at 2003-04 levels.

Fund raiser - Jim Duffy and a young helper are ably assisted by Dee4Life Trust committee members (from left) Alan Laing, George Knight, Shaun Fitzimmons, Scott Glenday, John Langlands and Fraser MacDonald. DC Thomson

CHAPTER FORTY-THREE

On Thin Ice

On the eve of the 2004-05 season, much of the uncertainty over the immediate future was removed with the news that Dundee were officially out of administration. There had been a net write-off of £3.23m as well as a £1.5m write-off in loans from the Marrs. And with ongoing cuts to operating costs, the calling in of the bank's guarantees as well as a new agreement with HBOS to convert overdraft borrowings into a long-term loan, it was understood that the club's debt would be reduced to £7 million.

Dundee would have to operate within tight financial restraints but having recently been so close to extinction, it was a significant milestone for the Dens Park club. Peter Marr admitted: "My brother and I have held our hands up to the mistakes we made in chasing a dream to make Dundee a major force in Scottish football."

"That's in the past now and part of the deal to bring us out of administration was dependent on us pledging a further £6 million to the club to guarantee its future. We believe Dundee F.C. can rise again. But we can't do this on our own although the fans have already shown overwhelming loyalty to the club."

For his part Jimmy Marr remarked: "I don't believe coming out of administration should be a cause for celebration but rather a quiet relief that the hard work, loyalty and energy of our staff, our fans and the administrator has turned the club around when many predicted it couldn't be done. The supporters' response to our plight in the form of Dee4Life will always be part of the club's folklore and the changes proposed at board level will give them an even stronger voice in the way the club runs its affairs."

Marr, of course, was referring to Dee4Life chairman George Knight, who, along with local businessmen Willie Barnett, Frank Esposito, Ross Dow and Bob Brannan had been appointed to the board. Brannan, a lifelong Dundee fan and group managing-director of whisky giant William Grant & Son, had briefly been chief executive with Rangers. Now, at the behest of HBOS, he became chairman at Dens, where his financial background would be of great benefit in guiding the club through the hazardous post-administration era.

Last season, Dundee had lost just one of their final eight games but that feel-good factor had disappeared with the departure of five first-team players. The scoring exploits of top scorer Nacho Novo, who had netted 34 goals in his two seasons at Dens - and the brilliance of Argentinian goalkeeper Julian Speroni had not gone unnoticed and it was little surprise that both moved on - Novo to Rangers for £500,000 with Speroni joining English Premiership newcomers Crystal Palace for £750,000.

Class act - Dundee's Trinidad & Tobago international defender Brent Sancho battles with Celtic's Stilian Petrov. DC Thomson

The Dark Blues had got the fee they wanted for Novo but only after the Spaniard - who, like Adamczuk before him, had rejected overtures by Celtic - waived his £50,000 share of the deal to ensure that he joined former Dens team-mates Gavin Rae and Zurab Khizanishvili at Ibrox.

As part of his contract, Speroni got around £250,000, while Novo's old club Raith Rovers were due 15% of his fee. But, with Dundee still in administration and Raith regarded as an unsecured creditor under the terms of the Enterprise Act, the Kirkcaldy club had little option but to accept a compromise figure of much less.

Henceforth, Dundee's wage levels would be drastically cut and, attracted by much more lucrative offers, Stevie Milne (Plymouth Argyle), Lee Mair (Stockport County), and Dave Mackay (Oxford United), all moved south on freedom-of-contract. The cash-strapped Dark Blues had received substantial transfer fees for Novo and Speroni but there would be no such compensation for their other trio of top-team stalwarts, of whom Mair and Mackay had come close to agreeing new improved deals shortly before the club went into administration.

The harsh realities of financial life were all too clear with this latest exodus leaving just Barry Smith, Steve Lovell, Jonay Hernandez, Garry Brady and Steven Robb from the 18-man Scottish Cup Final squad of just 14 months earlier, as well as long-term injury victim Lee Wilkie. However, there was better news when club captain Barry Smith - after accepting a substantial wage cut - and Garry Brady signed new two-year deals, while the fast-growing Magners Irish Cider extended their sponsorship for another season.

Jim Duffy's loyalty was rewarded by a contract extension until 2006 and, to plug the gaps, the Dens boss made six new signings. In came centre-half Bobby Mann (29), a Dundonian who had just skippered Inverness Caley Thistle to the First Division Championship ahead of Clyde, and two strikers - former Raith target John Sutton (21), from Millwall on a one-year loan, and Glenn Larsen (20), formerly with the Norwegian club Vaalerenga.

There were also two midfielders - ex-Dens favourite Iain Anderson who had since had spells at Toulouse, Preston North End, Tranmere Rovers and Grimsby Town, and Dundee's former loan signing Neil Barrett who had reached a settlement with Portsmouth, as well as 28-year-old Trinidad and Tobago international and former Reading goalkeeper Kelvin Jack.

All with the exception of Sutton, brother of Celtic star Chris Sutton, had been signed on freedom-of-contract and, with so many changes, pre-season games, which included a short tour of Northern Ireland, brought a mixed bag of results. With a much-reduced but still worrying level of debt, it was crucial that Dundee remained in the Premier League though most believed that newly-promoted Inverness Caley Thistle, who would expend considerable resources to groundshare with Aberdeen, remained the prime candidates for relegation.

In the event, the new-look Dark Blues managed just four points from their opening four games although there was more than a measure of solace from a 2-1 derby triumph against Dundee United at Tannadice! Steve Lovell slotted home a penalty then, soon after half-time, he laid on a second for fellow Englishman John Sutton to set Dundee on the road to victory.

On August 28th, an astonishing comeback saw Dundee share eight goals with Hibernian at Easter Road. After 50 minutes, the Dark Blues trailed 4-1 but the introduction of Brady and Larsen as substitutes helped turn the tide and a last-gasp leveller by Venezuelan international Jonay Hernandez made it a memorable day for the travelling fans.

A Lovell hat-trick propelled Dundee to a 4-0 League Cup victory over Forfar Athletic at Dens but they went out at the next stage, a double from ex-Dark Blue Jim Hamilton giving the cup holders Livingston a 2-1 win after extra-time. Their small and relatively inexperienced squad looked short of the quality required for the SPL and soon adverse results in the league left Jim Duffy's men near the foot of the table.

Their cause was most certainly not helped by the regular absence of

Derby joy - Jonay Hernandez and John Sutton celebrate at Tannadice.

Derek Soutar - Dundee and Scotland Under-21 international keeper. Fotopress

Brent Sancho and Jonay Hernandez, whose international duties involved them in long, tiring flights to Central and South America.

Often they returned late on a Friday night, a delay in flights causing Brent Sancho to miss the home game against Motherwell, while Jonay Hernandez was deemed unready for the Kilmarnock match at Dens. And with the new-look defence, which now included youngsters like Stephen McNally at right-back and central-defender Callum MacDonald, requiring extensive coaching, this situation was far from ideal.

Steven Robb was increasingly being utilised at left-back and, having earlier raced 70 yards to net a magnificent goal against Livingston in the League Cup, he repeated the feat in a 3-1 win over Kilmarnock at Dens on October 16th. However, that month, two successive 2-1 defeats, at home to Dunfermline then to Inverness Caley Thistle at Pittodrie - the latter a real shocker - saw the Dark Blues embroiled in what would become a season-long relegation battle along with Dundee United, Dunfermline, Inverness Caley Thistle and Livingston.

Italian defenders Fabio Macellari and Lorenzo Cresta arrived on trial only to prove beyond Dundee's budget. And although spirits were raised by Fabian Caballero's return - aided by a £10,000 contribution from Dee4Life - and the arrival of Brazilian striker Alex Cordeira (24), formerly of Greek club Apollon Kalmarias, FC America and Vasco da Gama of Brazil, the next 10 games brought just seven points, with heavy defeats at the hands of Hearts (a) 0-3, Motherwell (a) 0-3, Hibs (h) 1-4, Rangers (a) 0-3, Killie (a) 1-3, and Dunfermline (a) 1-3.

There had, though, been some memorable moments, particularly at Dens, where a Lovell double had ensured a 2-2 draw with Celtic, and 1-0 wins over Dundee United and Aberdeen had maintained Dundee's recent supremacy over their North-East rivals in the league. On November 6th, Dundee had taken a first-half pounding from United with the left-footed Barry Robson causing mayhem down their right until injury necessitated the substitution of Steven Robb. On came Garry Brady to midfield and with Callum MacDonald - struggling at right midfield - going to left-back, Dundee were transformed.

After half-time, the Dark Blues took a more direct approach and with Lovell a constant threat down the middle, first Innes then Wilson (for a hotly-disputed last-man handball) were sent off. However, an increasingly nervy Dundee looked incapable of exploiting their two-man advantage and only six minutes remained when substitute John Sutton popped up at the far post to head the only goal of the game.

Derek Soutar was now first-choice goalkeeper but although sickness meant Kelvin Jack began the derby, the

Trinidad and Tobago man had to retire with a torn thigh muscle after 26 minutes. Soutar then came off the bench to play a blinder and a continuation of that form saw the Dundee-born custodian rewarded with an appearance for the Scotland Futures team against Germany in Mannheim to add to his earlier collection of eleven Scotland Under-21 international caps.

However, there was no disguising that Dundee were in serious trouble and by early 2005 they again found themselves anchored to the foot of the table. Too often they had looked a soft touch, particularly away from home, where to the dismay of traditionalists they regularly wore their dark blue and light blue striped "away" outfit, and recent 3-1 reverses to fellow strugglers Killie and Dunfermline made it clear that changes were required.

Jim Duffy concurred: "If we can change things about then there can be no complaints from those who hold the jerseys. The trouble is that we have been making basic errors and we need to show greater resilience and determination to get decent results. Concentration levels have to be better as we have been losing too many simple goals."

At an Open Forum in November, Bob Brannan revealed that the club's wage bill was down to £25,000 per week but stressed that Dundee would still have to finish in the top six to break even. He did, however, refuse to be drawn on whether there was a contingency plan in the event of relegation.

In an earlier interview with *The Daily Record*, Peter Marr admitted that the bank would continue to run Dundee's affairs, saying: "We are safe at Dens in as much as the bank and a property company have an option on the stadium but to get it would cost them the £7m debt which is left. That threat will be there until we completely clear the debt - in the form of a mortgage - which is going to take about 15 years."

"Administration cost us some £700,000 but it highlighted the financial situation and where the money was going. Now we have strict controls, we don't take any of the gambles we did in the past and we are working on a tight budget. The next twelve months will be all about stabilising the club and surviving in the league."

Survival would soon become Dundee's only concern, for by early January, they were out of the Scottish Cup after losing 2-0 to high-flying Hibernian at Easter Road. Spearheaded by Gary O'Connor and Derek O'Riordan, the youthful but highly talented Hibs side were producing sparkling, inventive football and the Dark Blues did well to keep things in doubt until near the end.

There had been a number of changes at Dens. Gordon Wallace returned to coach part-time, but, in September, Head of Youth Development, Kenny Cameron and boot-man Ernie Ferguson were victims of a cost-cutting exercise. Another to go was the promising Bobby Linn, his contract terminated "by mutual consent" after serious breaches of club discipline, which included his failure to attend training for the League Cup tie against Livingston.

In the summer of 2005, no fewer than sixteen players would be out of contract. And with a much-reduced budget, few would be retained. Accordingly, soon after the opening of the January transfer window, the latest exodus began. Jonay Hernandez, who had recently looked less than committed, joined Spanish club Cordoba, while fringe men Dougie Cameron, Neil Jablonski, Chris Hegarty and youth player Michael McGowan were also allowed to go.

Lee Wilkie had finally returned to action but, despite interest from Monaco and English First Division Leicester City, the big defender accepted a new two-year deal at Dens due to his strong family ties in Dundee. Soon, Steven Robb, Derek Soutar, Callum MacDonald and Stephen McNally followed his example before Tam McManus arrived on a free transfer from Hibernian. But although the Easter Road attacker opted for Dens rather than Motherwell, other signing attempts were to prove less successful.

The departure of Hernandez had left Dundee short of a natural left-back but efforts to lure Dean Gordon, formerly of Middlesborough and Crystal Palace, Adam El Abd (Brighton) and Scott Morrison (Aberdeen), on loan came to nothing. In another move, Jim Duffy came close to re-signing Lee Mair but that deal too was doomed to failure.

Dandy double - there was little to cheer in season 2004-05 but Steve Lovell brought some joy by netting twice in the 2-2 draw with Celtic at Dens.
Mirrorpix

Unhappy at Stockport, Mair looked to be on his way to Dundee United on a one-and-a-half year deal until the Tannadice club indicated they would first have to offload players. The Dens boss, who had maintained contact, offered Mair a two-and-a-half year contract only for the player and his agent Paul Cherry (who Dundee could not afford to pay) to use the Dens offer as a lever to negotiate a similar length of contract on better terms at United.

Jim Duffy was outraged: "The unscrupulous world of football has reared its head again and frankly I feel betrayed." Dundee instead had to settle for Ugandan-born ex-Chelsea, Brentford and Mansfield defender Joel Kitamarike, while another 20-year-old, striker Aaron Conway, was later signed on a short-term deal after being released by Dundee United.

On January 15th, a battling performance brought a timely success against Inverness Caley Thistle at Dens. Several brilliant saves by Soutar kept the visitors at bay before Robb - a recent Caley Thistle signing target - fired home a fierce low shot. Tam McManus had brought a welcome injection of pace and, soon after half-time, he headed a second goal, before John Sutton secured the points with a penalty.

At last, Dundee appeared to have turned the corner, and draws against Hearts (h) 1-1 and Dundee United (a) 2-2, then a 2-1 home win over Motherwell courtesy of a Lovell brace lifted them to tenth, eight points clear of bottom-placed Livingston. Fortune had smiled on the Dark Blues for, with their three-man midfield outmanoeuvred by United's four, they had twice trailed their hosts, while Soutar had performed heroics against Motherwell who managed eighteen shots to Dundee's eight.

It proved a false dawn as four successive defeats, including a 1-0 reverse to Livingston at Dens, plunged Dundee back into the relegation mire. In early December, the Dark Blues had suffered an identical result immediately after Livvy's new management team of Richard Gough and former Dundee boss Archie Knox replaced Alan Preston and Alan Kernaghan, and this had been a similarly dismal display.

Jim Duffy was devastated: "The way we began was a disgrace, we lacked passion and there was no enthusiasm. At half-time, we tried to lift the players and stressed how

Midfield battler - Garry Brady gave his all for Dundee. DC Thomson

important this game was but even then we were mediocre at best. Livvy came here battling for their lives and showed the fighting qualities I expected from my players."

To relieve the pressure on Duffy - who it was understood saw no requirement for an assistant-manager - Gordon Wallace was made full-time general manager to deal with contracts, scouting and development as well as continuing his coaching duties. Onfield, the players bounced back with a draw at Aberdeen (1-1) and home wins over Kilmarnock (1-0) and Dunfermline (2-1) put them nine points ahead of new "basement-boys" Dundee United and seven ahead of 11th-placed Livingston although both had a game in hand.

With just six games left, Dundee were close to securing their place in the SPL. On April 9th, an early knock to Barrett allowed the more creative Fotheringham to come on and play an influential role in the victory over Dunfermline. A goal down, Dundee fought back for Lovell to level with a penalty before Brent Sancho headed the winner. However, in the flush of victory few could realise the impact that the loss of Lee Wilkie - stretchered off earlier in the game with a recurrence of his knee injury - would have on their fortunes over the next few weeks.

The big defender had been a key man as Dundee edged their way to safety and now his absence would be keenly felt. Ten days later, the talented Mark Fotheringham featured in the Scotland Futures team which lost 2-1 to Austria in Vienna and such was Wilkie's form that it had been widely predicted that he too was to have been included by new Scotland boss Walter Smith, the successor to Bertie Vogts.

In the last game before the "split", the Dark Blues travelled to face Inverness Caley Thistle, who having met the new 6,500 seater criteria were back at Inverness and battling hard for a place in the "top six". Dundee should have been no less motivated but a sluggish start saw them go three goals down before pulling things back to 3-2. The following week brought a much-improved performance at Kilmarnock but the loss of a late goal, and with it all three points, meant the Dens derby on April 30th took on a huge significance.

Remarkably, Dundee were unbeaten in the last nine local derbies and once again they went for a 4-3-3 formation against the 4-4-2 of United. Both teams made a nervy start but, in 18 minutes, Fabian Caballero - so often an inspiration in the hectic derby

Spot on - John Sutton nets a penalty against Inverness Caley Thistle to secure a 3-1 win at Dens. Mark Fotheringham and Neil Barrett are the other Dundee men. DC Thomson

atmosphere - had to go off with a hip knock after some tough treatment from the United defenders. John Sutton came on to join Steve Lovell and Tam McManus but as the visitors took a grip on proceedings and continued to pour men down the left, it became a one-way traffic towards the Dundee goal.

In the second half, Dundee's tactics remained unchanged and soon after the restart Mark Wilson's free-kick trundled past their defensive wall and into the net beyond an unsighted Soutar. That brought the Dark Blues to life but although Lovell thundered home a 64th minute penalty, McIntyre restored United's lead soon afterwards. Dundee's derby luck had deserted them and, three minutes from time, the dismissal of McManus for a kick at Barry Robson ended any hope of salvaging a point, and also ensured his suspension for what was now an absolutely crucial match at Dunfermline.

Action man - Tam McManus heads past United keeper Nick Colgan to extend Dundee's unbeaten derby record to nine games.   DC Thomson

Just three games remained and with only four points separating the bottom four clubs, there were over 2,500 Dundee fans in the 8,300 crowd at East End Park. A dismal 2-0 defeat at Livingston had sent the Fifers to the bottom and in a last-ditch gamble Davie Hay was sacked and general manager Jim Leishman - the inspirational, self-styled "bard of Fife" - was once again put in charge of the team.

Both Livingston and Dundee United, who had sacked Ian McCall some weeks earlier and given interim control to ex-Dens skipper Gordon Chisholm, had benefited from a managerial change and for the third time that season Dundee would be up against similarly motivated opponents.

Recently, Dunfermline had installed a new artificial pitch but although better than the previous version, it was to play its part in Dundee's downfall. Last term, Derek Soutar had been stretchered unconscious from the rain-soaked "plastic" and now, with just 90 seconds played, he fumbled the ball and Derek Young was there to knock in the opener.

For the next 27 minutes, it was mostly Dundee but, thwarted by the inspirational Stillie, they were hit by a stunning double-whammy - a collision between Soutar and MacDonald causing the second goal before MacDonald put the ball in his own net. It was a comedy of errors that would end in a 5-0 rout but the nightmare was all too real with the Dark Blues now bottom behind the Pars on goal-difference, though still within three points of ninth-placed Livingston.

It was a devastating result for Dundee, whose outfield play had been good - they had won more corners and had more shots. But Derek Soutar - at fault for three goals - and Callum MacDonald had looked distinctly uncomfortable on the surface and it was noticeable that, when under pressure, Stillie, with more experience of the pitch, tended to punch clear whereas Soutar had tried to hold the ball, which when it hit the surface, tended to go somewhat "dead".

Nevertheless, with Jack injured, Soutar was retained in preference to Francois Dubourdeau for the penultimate game against Inverness Caley Thistle at Dens. McNally, Fotheringham and Caballero were replaced by Sancho, Robertson and McManus with MacDonald switched to right-back. A determined Dundee made most of the first-half running and McManus was unlucky when he hit the post with a direct free-kick.

In 47 minutes, the near-7,000 crowd went wild as Brent Sancho met a corner to power a header high into the net and, soon afterwards, Lovell was unfortunate when his powerful angled shot came back off the bar. With any luck, Dundee ought to have had a comfortable lead but, with Caballero virtually anonymous after replacing the industrious Garry Brady - off injured at half-time - Caley Thistle, who had earlier looked disinterested, gained the initiative and poured forward.

With just two minutes left, Dundee looked like holding on until a long throw broke to Golabek and despite Sancho's heroic goal-line block, Fox hit home the equaliser. The Dark Blues were devastated and 24 hours later their position became even worse when Dunfermline managed a 1-0 win at Tannadice. Barring a mathematical miracle, the Pars were safe and now it was a three-way battle between Dundee, Dundee United and Livingston to avoid the drop.

SPL (bottom placings) May 21st, 2005				
	P	F A	GD	Pts
Dunfermline	37	43-56	-13	34
Livingston	37	33-60	-27	34
Dundee United	37	40-59	-19	33
Dundee	37	36-70	-34	32

Saturday, May 21st would be the decisive day for the Dark Blues, who, having managed just one away win all season and with by far the worst defensive record in the SPL, faced a win or bust situation against Livingston at Almondvale. A draw, however, would suit Livingston while a similar result against Inverness Caley Thistle in the Highland capital would also ensure Dundee United's survival.

There could be no doubting the importance of the Almondvale clash and, in an interview with *The Scottish Daily Mail,* Barry Smith said: " I've played in Europe, a Cup Final and in hundreds of league games but this one is the biggest of the lot. There have been many highs and lows over the past 10 years and we're now in the situation where a win this weekend would be a massive high because of what survival means to the club."

Jim Duffy felt that the middle of the park was the key area: "Our midfield has probably been the most disappointing part of the team. You can have the best front players in the world but if they aren't getting the service, then they will struggle for goals. Individuals have done well in patches but no-one has shown consistency and as a unit, they've not created enough. If they can play better on Saturday, then the front players will have the opportunity to deliver."

Steven Robb - given new role at left-back.

Recently, the hard-working Garry Brady had been in good form but the experienced midfielder would miss out after failing to recover from injury and Dundee fielded: Soutar; McNally, Sancho, Mann, MacDonald; Anderson, Smith, Barrett, Robb; Lovell, McManus. Livingston - McKenzie; Dair, Deloumeaux, Dorado, Bahoken; Easton, Vincze, O'Brien, McMenamin; Lilley, Kachloul.

Over 4,000 Dens fans made the trip to West Lothian but at 2.45pm, the gates were closed after the 3,700-seater away end was filled, even although the 8,968 crowd was well short of the ground's 10,000 capacity. Those in charge refused to utilise the available space by compressing the Livvy fans and mayhem ensued as around six hundred Dundee supporters remonstrated with police and stewards on finding themselves locked out. It was a powder-keg situation but, undaunted, the unwanted fans scrambled up an adjoining hill to lend their vocal support and spectate as best as they could amidst the intermittent rain.

Dundee began well and, in 17 minutes, Bobby Mann nodded the ball back across goal from a corner and Callum MacDonald sidefooted home. Livvy were soon level as Hassan Kachloul - soon to be the centre of controversy - beat Barry Smith before crossing for Craig Easton to head home unchallenged at the far post.

Thereafter, it was dull fare with both teams anxious to avoid any careless mistakes. In 66 minutes, Sutton replaced Robb as Dundee went to 4-3-3 and in a last throw of the dice, Caballero (82 minutes), and Scott Robertson (88), were brought on as substitutes for Barrett and Anderson.

As the game wore on, Livvy retreated into a defensive shell but in a nervy, tension-ridden atmosphere, Dundee's passing was erratic and they were unable to apply consistent pressure.

The referee allowed six minutes of added time but when Tam McManus cut in from the right only to see his well-struck shot rebound from a post, fans of the Dark Blues sensed it was not to be their day. The battle contin-

ued right to the end but despite forcing a number of late corners, Dundee never really looked like scoring.

At full-time, Livvy celebrated their survival but for Dundee there was only despair and their players sunk to the ground as the reality of relegation finally struck home. Young fans of both clubs staged a mini-pitch invasion and although there was no confrontation, it again illustrated the inability of Livingston and the local police to anticipate a potentially explosive situation.

It was a sombre Dundee support that slipped away from Almondvale and in Monday's *Courier*, Graeme Dey summed up: "Barry Smith and Bobby Mann were excellent with Soutar dependable but too many others were stricken with nerves. There was too much careless passing and careless is a word which perfectly sums up Dundee's exit from the top flight. There can be no denying that the legacy of administration and its ravages was a significant factor and Jim Duffy faced a difficult job in keeping Dundee up."

"But having been nine points clear with just six games remaining - even with Livvy and United having a game in hand, they should have avoided the drop." The local scribe rightly emphasised that Dundee owed a debt of loyalty to Duffy, without whom they may well not have survived administration, but, he concluded: "There's no hiding from the fact that taking two points out of a possible eighteen on a run-in which pitted you only against sides in the lower half of the league was desperate form."

The lengthy absence of key men like Wilkie and Anderson was highly significant but, equally, others had been posted missing when the going got tough. Caballero was one and the manager's belief that he might pull something out of the bag proved sadly misplaced and the creative Mark Fotheringham, who had performed well at Dunfermline with little reward, might well have been a better bet.

The worst-case scenario - in a football sense - had come to pass and when asked for his comments, a shattered Dee4Life Trust secretary Scott Glenday spelt it out in a few short words: "This is seriously bad news for all concerned with Dundee Football Club."

Down and out - a downcast Stephen McNally and Scott Robertson after the 1-1 draw at Livingston condemned the Dark Blues to the First Division. DC Thomson

CHAPTER FORTY-FOUR

Young Guns

Dundee now had to face up to the stark financial reality of relegation, for, despite a £250,000 "parachute" payment it was estimated that lost revenue from TV, gate income and other sources could total £1.5 million. However, the Halifax Bank of Scotland remained supportive and, contrary to widely expressed fears, the club would remain full-time after another round of cost-cutting.

Jim Duffy's future had been in doubt but, after discussions with the board, he accepted a 30% pay cut and would continue as manager. Other club employees also faced wage reductions of 20% to 30% but the biggest shock was the departure of reserve-team coach Ray Farningham and Under-19 coach Steve Campbell. Dundee were to scrap their reserves and with the youth set-up (Under-13s to Under-19s) now to be run by general manager Gordon Wallace, the pair were axed along with kit-man Brian Duncan and commercial sales executive Dave Forbes.

As ex-players and lifelong Dundee fans with a total of 21 years service on the coaching staff, Farningham and Campbell were understandably upset. No-one could dispute their success for half of last season's first-team squad had come through the ranks and it was thought that some three dozen players who had come through the Dens Park youth system were still playing in British professional football.

At the end of May, Dundee's hopes of remaining in the top flight had been revived when Dunfermline asked the SPL to investigate whether Livingston had broken the rules by signing midfielder Hassan Kachloul. The Pars were suspicious of newspaper comments by Livvy boss Richard Gough, which indicated that the Morrocan international, signed as an amateur outwith the transfer window on March 31st, may have been paid. If so and Livvy were given a three-point penalty they would be relegated and consequently Dundee also pressed for an inquiry.

On June 15th, the SPL board comprising chairman Lex Gold, Rod Petrie (Hibs), John McLelland (Rangers) and Eddie Thomson (Dundee United), found Livingston guilty of breaching transfer regulations by signing Kachloul as an amateur and paying him as a "commercial executive" at a remuneration comparable to professional footballers at Almondvale. The punishment was a £15,000 fine since they believed that Kachloul was a free agent at that time and could have been registered as a professional, and therefore Livvy had gained no competitive advantage.

In *The Scottish Daily Mail,* Dundee chief executive Peter Marr admitted to being "staggered" by the verdict: "We proved that Livingston doubled their points average in the games he played so how the SPL can say they didn't gain an

Dundee F.C. Legends - Barry Smith receives a gift from Bobby Cox at the start of his Testimonial season. DC Thomson

advantage is beyond me. This is a total farce and we will undoubtedly be appealing. I can't understand how a club can be found guilty and get off with a fine. In any other country they would have points deducted and they'd be down."

Within two days a Dens spokesman announced: "We have resubmitted our complaint to the SPL in light of new evidence suggesting that Mr Kachloul may not have been entitled to sign for Livingston as a professional player as it appears that he was registered as an amateur player at Reading and played two reserve games for them."

"FIFA rules are explicit that he would not have been entitled to sign professional forms for any club until a new transfer window. That is completely at odds with the SPL's findings and, if true, means the decision that Livingston were guilty of a technical rather than an actual breach is groundless. If this is no longer a technical breach and Livvy have gained a competitive advantage then the punishment must be a points deduction."

In the event, the Dark Blues had no right of appeal since they were not directly involved and instead they took their case to the Scottish Football Association. On July 12th, the SFA board sub-committee, which comprised of Lord Ranald McLean, John McBeth (ex-Clyde), and Dick Shaw (QOS), met and ruled that Dundee did have the right of appeal, although it appeared that there had been strong attempts by Livingston and the SPL to persuade the SFA otherwise.

Emerging from the meeting along with QC Paul Cullen, chairman Bob Brannan explained that Dundee's appeal could not proceed until Livvy's own late appeal against their fine was clarified, saying: "We believe that when our appeal is heard in full, Livingston will be awarded a much more severe penalty, which we trust will be a deduction of points and that, we hope, will result in our reinstatement."

However, on the eve of Livingston's SFA hearing due on July 20th, the Almondvale club withdrew their appeal after being granted a judicial review at the Court of Session in Edinburgh. Livvy wanted the civil courts to "examine certain actions taken recently by the SFA in connection with the registration", believing they would not have got a fair and independent inquiry from the SFA, who would have been sitting in judgement over actions by its own officials.

It was unclear when the judicial review might take place but the SFA assured Dundee that a decision on their appeal would be made on Monday, July 25th. Livvy could have tried to prevent this - with the risk that the courts might feel obliged to deal promptly with the whole matter themselves - but did not. And after 10 hours of legal deliberations, the SFA panel finally decided to uphold the original SPL ruling.

Bob Brannan told *The Courier* of his dismay at the verdict: "It wasn't until 6 o'clock this evening that the SPL finally revealed their position in a very technical, legal argument that won over the committee. We respect the SFA's decision but we feel that a £15,000 fine is not a fair penalty for the SPL to impose given the seriousness of the breach of the rules that took place.What is particularly disappointing is that the SPL have spent the last six weeks trying to block our right to appeal rather than argue the merits of the case."

Peter Marr too was bitterly upset: "I don't know why it came to this when, seemingly, what we are being told is that we could not supply the necessary paperwork to prove Hassan Kachloul was registered as an amateur while at Reading. Why didn't the SPL lawyer Roddy McKenzie tell us that from the start. We have had to hire legal counsel to fight our case and the bill for that is liable to run to thousands of pounds which, clearly, we can ill afford."

"It should not have taken until five days before the start of the season. They've dragged it out and, frankly, that's not good enough. Our hopes were raised when Livingston spoke about a judicial review. Honestly, it just saps your strength and faith in this game and in the people involved."

Dundee's only remaining recourse involved legal action to prevent Livingston commencing their SPL fixtures until the matter was resolved by the courts. However, the possibility of further crippling costs should that fail dissuaded the board from going ahead and now, with considerable reluctance, it was decided to drop the matter and focus on engineering a swift return to the SPL.

The Dark Blues were 6-4 promotion favourites but it would be no easy task since previously relegated clubs such as St Mirren (2001), St Johnstone (2002), still remained in the highly competitive First Division, while Partick Thistle (2004), had since been relegated to the Second Division. In addition, Dundee had lost some of their most influential players, top scorer Steve Lovell rejecting an offer from Leicester City before joining Aberdeen for £200,000.

Mark Fotheringham was transferred to SC Freiburg of Germany for £30,000. John Sutton returned to Millwall at the end of his loan spell, while the out-of-contract Brent Sancho, Fabian Caballero, Neil Barrett, Glenn Larsen, Neil Clark, Aaron Conway, Francois Dubourdeau and youth players Andy Reilly, John Voigt, Kevin Cummings and Garry McLaughlin were all allowed to go.

Those remaining were asked to take a pay cut, a proposal that, understandably, did not go down well. Derek Soutar went public with his grievances only for Peter Marr to say that the request was reasonable since the players themselves had played a major part in getting the club relegated. Marr also claimed that the keeper had unsuccessfully requested a release clause in his contract if Dundee went down.

It was a delicate situation since anyone officially offered but declining what was effectively a new contract would be entitled to a free transfer. All, including top earners Derek Soutar, Bobby Mann, Iain Anderson and Garry Brady would remain and although not all accepted the cuts, others had their contracts extended by a year, on the understanding that they would get their money in full if promoted.

Local hero - Bobby Mann celebrates his goal against Queen of the South with Simon Lynch, Tam McManus and Scott Robertson all keen to congratulate the big centre-half.

Mirrorpix

Quick start - Simon Lynch nets against East Stirling and would score in each of Dundee's first six games before finishing their top marksman with 18 goals. SNS Group

Meanwhile, Jim Duffy had brought in three strikers - former Celtic and Preston hitman Simon Lynch (24), 20-year-old Andy Ferguson (Ayr United) and 17-year-old Craig O'Reilly (Raith Rovers). Likewise, 24-year-old Australian defender Adrian Madaschi (Partick Thistle) and Arbroath attacking midfielder Gavin Swankie (21), were secured on "Bosmans", the Red Lichties receiving £20,000 - £10,000 from Dee4Life - compensation as Swankie, also a St Johnstone target, was under 24 years of age.

Another to arrive - as player and assistant-manager - was ex-Dens striker Gerry Britton (34), who had recently been a fringe player at Motherwell after an unsuccessful spell as co-manager with Partick Thistle. Kelvin Jack would remain after an abortive trial at Brighton while the injury-plagued Tom Hutchinson, who was now out-of-contract, was given a new three-month deal to prove his fitness.

The Dark Blues kicked off the new campaign with a 2-0 win over lowly East Stirling in the Bell's Challenge Cup at Dens. On August 6th, they followed that up with a 3-2 home triumph over last season's runners-up St Mirren, who, along with St Johnstone and Hamilton, were fancied to make a strong promotion challenge. In a pulsating encounter, Bobby Mann, Simon Lynch and Tam McManus got the goals as Dundee fielded: Jack; Smith, Mann, Madaschi, Dixon; Anderson, Robertson, Brady, Robb; Lynch, McManus.

At half-time, the score was 1-1 but with Dundee's midfield in danger of being swamped, Tom Hutchinson replaced young Paul Dixon as they went from 4-4-2 to 3-5-2. That switch turned the game and, continuing with three at the back, another four points were taken from Clyde (a) 1-1, and QOS (h) 3-1, to leave them top of the league, though, worryingly, form remained unconvincing against what had largely been modest opposition.

On Tuesday, August 23rd, those fears were realised in a humiliating 3-1 League Cup defeat by newly promoted Stranraer at Stair Park. The part-timers had looked fitter and better organised and, within 24 hours, the Dark Blues parted company with Jim Duffy, who received a settlement for the remaining 10 months of his contract. It was a unanimous boardroom decision for previously that year Duffy had twice been close to dismissal and, even this early in the campaign, there were signs of discontent amongst the fans.

Gerry Britton took charge but when it became clear that Dundee were looking elsewhere, he joined Brechin City as a player. The board were now keen on a team boss with a proven track record in the lower divisions. But although Stranraer boss Neil Watt - mastermind of two successive promotions on a shoestring budget - was interviewed, his Glasgow business interests prevented him accepting what was a full-time managerial post at Dens.

Instead, Dundee turned to former Middlesbrough, Manchester City and St Johnstone central-defender Alan Kernaghan (38), who had been capped 26 times for the Republic of Ireland, with former Dens youth coach Billy Kirkwood as his assistant. In season 2003-04, Kernaghan had been player-manager of the Clyde team that narrowly lost out on promotion to Inverness Caley Thistle and he was later assistant-manager to Alan Preston at Livingston before joining Falkirk as a youth coach after the pair were dismissed from Almondvale.

The new regime got off to a bad start, losing 2-0 to Airdrie United in the league at Dens before exiting the Challenge Cup by a similar scoreline at Hamilton. Fresh blood was urgently required and ex-Aberdeen and Motherwell striker Steven Craig (24) and former St Johnstone and Morton right-back Stuart McCluskey (27), both unattached, were fixed up on short-term deals.

However, it was soon clear that Dundee were ill-equipped for the promotion battle. By mid-November, they lay sixth after 15 games, twelve points adrift of league leaders St Mirren, who, having won the Challenge Cup, also had a game in hand. On October 22nd, Dundee battled to a 0-0 draw at Paisley, but the loss of two late goals meant they had to settle for a 3-3 draw at home to Clyde and morale hit rock-bottom with a 4-0 defeat at Airdrie, three days later.

A Tam McManus header earned a 2-1 win in a Dens thriller against St Johnstone but, on November 19th, the writing was on the wall after a 3-0 drubbing by strong-going Ross County at Dingwall. Dundee had been a huge disappointment and with just two wins from a dozen league and cup games since their arrival, there was little sign of any improvement under the new management team.

In fairness, Kernaghan had inherited the current players and it was little surprise that several were deemed surplus to requirements. Severance packages were agreed with Joel Kitamarike and Jacinto Ela Eyene, (23), a winger from Spanish Second Division outfit Alaves, who had been signed on a two-year deal by Jim Duffy two months earlier. Tom Hutchinson and midfielder Keiran Keane were allowed to go at the end of their three-month contracts while John Madaschi was another to leave after losing his central defensive slot to Callum MacDonald.

Matters had not been helped by the lengthy absence through injury of Iain Anderson (knee ligaments), Callum MacDonald and Steven Robb (cartilage operations) and although Stephen McNally made a short-lived comeback after a recurrence of the stress fracture to his lower spine, he would have to undergo surgery to save his career.

From late November, things began to improve. Injuries to McCluskey, (achilles tendon), then McNally saw Barry Smith redeployed to right-back

In charge - Alan Kernaghan and Billy Kirkwood Fotopress

and with Kevin McDonald, who had made his debut at Brechin aged sixteen, brought into central midfield alongside Scott Robertson, just two of the next 16 games were lost.

For 10 years, Smith had been a key player at Dens and his unswerving loyalty - he accepted a massive wage cut after administration and again after relegation - had deservedly been rewarded with a Testimonial season. The Dens stalwart had turned out in every outfield defensive position and for the past three seasons, he had played as Dundee's defensive "anchor" in midfield.

Jim Duffy had no doubts of his value, at one point rating him second only to Neil Lennon of Celtic as the SPL's best holding midfielder: "Every manager he has worked under has held him in high regard and Barry can consider himself very unlucky not to have been capped."

There was no doubt that the experience of Barry Smith and Bobby Mann had been a major factor in the recent revival. Mann, though, had been Dundee's outstanding performer - almost unbeatable in the air, he stood firm in the face of adversity and invariably displayed bags of composure on the ball. Inevitably, however, youth had been given a chance at Dens due to the financial situation.

Last season, the highly competitive Scott Robertson (20), had impressed as a substitute - a £50,000 bid by Leicester City was rejected - and now he and 18-year-old left-back Paul Dixon were first-team regulars. Both were fast and tackled well, with Dixon possessing a powerful shot and the ability to hurl throw-ins deep into the opposition penalty box. Morten Wieghorst "look-alike" Kevin McDonald too had impressed as a fine passer of the ball, looking particularly dangerous when he embarked on long penetrating runs.

On December 10th, the Dark Blues produced their best performance of the season to dump runaway league leaders St Mirren 4-0 at Dens. Kevin McDonald fired them into an early lead but as the Buddies hit back, Dundee survived a number of close calls before a devastating three-goal blitz by second-half substitutes Craig O'Reilly, with two, and Andy Ferguson settled matters in their favour.

Dundee had risen to the occasion but on Boxing Day their inconsistency was all too clear as a 2-0 half-time lead over Airdrie ended in a painful 3-2 Dens defeat after the loss of two late goals. Inexperience had seen panic set in and in February, home fans had to endure more of the same as struggling Queen of the South replicated that scoreline to extinguish any lingering hopes of Dundee being promoted.

The Dark Blues had certainly become harder to beat away from home but there were too many draws and a miserable scoring record meant scant entertainment for the long suffering fans. In contrast, St Mirren - under ex-Kilmarnock

defender Gus McPherson - were getting results with an exciting brand of attacking football as were St Johnstone, who had strikers of the calibre of former Dark Blue Steve Milne and ex-United man Jason Scotland.

The January transfer window saw Gavin Swankie go to Arbroath on loan but although Garry Brady, Simon Lynch, Tam McManus and Iain Anderson - some of the highest earners - were made available, only "Ando" (to St Mirren), moved on. Dundee had been keen on Stranraer skipper Allan Jenkins but they were unable to compete with ambitious Gretna, who signed him for £60,000 then spent another £70,000 on Ross County defender Martin Canning.

Dens fans had to content themselves with Colin Marshall (21), a right-sided midfielder who had played under Kernaghan at Clyde, on a free transfer from Stranraer, ex-York City right-back Graeme Law and unattached goalkeeper Andy Britton. Encouragingly, though, talented youngsters like Scott Robertson, Paul Dixon, Kevin McDonald, Bryan Deasley, Scott Murray, Craig O'Reilly and Scott Gates all signed extended contracts until 2008.

With Derek Soutar recovering from a cartilage operation, giant shot-stopper Kelvin Jack began the season in goals. However, injuries to Dundee's top two keepers allowed 18-year-old Scott Murray to get an extended run. The youngster performed well, at one stage recording five successive shut-outs - just one less than Bobby Geddes in 1980-81 and two short of the club record held by Bob Crumley back in 1907-08.

There had seemed little prospect of Dundee doing much in the Scottish Cup but they made a good start against struggling Stranraer at Dens. Once again the Stair Park side proved dogged opponents but, soon after half-time, a lung-bursting 60-yard run and cross by Dixon was swept home by O'Reilly, with Simon Lynch later clinching matters with a superbly executed second goal.

On February 4th, Dundee took nearly 2,000 fans for the fourth-round clash with Airdrie United in Lanarkshire. Craig O'Reilly dropped out and 17-year-old Bryan Deasley - like McNally and Robertson a local lad and lifelong Dark Blue - became the latest youngster to get his chance. The pacy striker was to the fore as the fired-up Dens men began with all guns blazing and although McDonald hit the bar, it was no surprise when Deasley put them ahead in 22 minutes.

At half-time, Dundee might have been four goals up but it was a different story after the restart. As Airdrie piled on the

Star quality - left-back Paul Dixon, seen tackling Airdrie's Brian McPhee, quickly made a big impression. DC Thomson

304

Up for the cup - Bryan Deasley bursts through a posse of Airdrie United defenders to crack the ball past keeper Robertson. Pix-AR

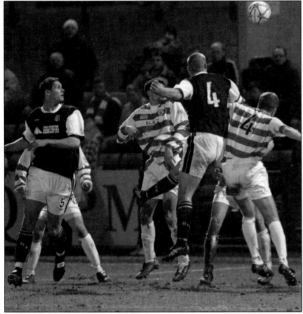

Netbound - Bobby Mann heads home in the quarter-final replay against Hamilton with Lee Wilkie looking on. Fotopress

pressure, McLaren levelled and by the end, it was desperate stuff as Mann and Robb headed netbound efforts off the line.

It had been a great cup-tie and with the fit-again Jack and McCluskey adding strength and experience, Dundee made another high tempo start in the replay. Deasley was a constant menace with his blistering runs and with only 10 minutes played he hammered home the opener. It was one-way traffic towards the Airdrie goal but the result remained in doubt until 18 minutes from time when Lynch made it 2-0 after good work by Brady and Dixon.

In the quarter-final, Kernaghan's men would meet Hamilton on the artificial surface at New Douglas Park. The previously out-of-favour Tam McManus retained his place after twice netting in the 3-3 draw at Clyde but he was to make little impact in a goal-less stalemate on a bitterly cold afternoon. Both sides hit woodwork and although Hamilton finished strongly, Dundee might have snatched it when Dixon's fiercely struck 30-yard free-kick was desperately pushed away by McEwan in the dying seconds.

The replay, which would be live on Sky TV, went ahead on Thursday, March 9th. Dundee had a great incentive for the cup draw had paired Hearts and Hibs with the winners of the

Dens tie to meet Second Division Gretna. Long-term injury victim Lee Wilkie appeared as a half-time substitute in the league match against Hamilton at Dens. But although the Scotland defender celebrated his return with a fine headed goal, Dundee's 4-2 defeat to virtually a reserve side looked ominous with Accies retaining their best players for the cup replay five days later.

A massive improvement was required if Dundee were to realise their Scottish Cup dream but with entrance prices slashed to £8 and £2, there were long queues as the 7,460 spectators waited to get in to Dens. Wilkie was preferred to MacDonald and with Barry Smith suspended, McManus was utilised on the right side of a four-man midfield.

Dundee did most of the early pressing but Hamilton looked the more dangerous until Bobby Mann headed the opener 11 minutes after half-time. Lynch made it 2-0 with a flashing header from a McManus cross but, for the third time that term, Dundee let slip a two-goal advantage, twice conceding goals from free-kicks outside the box with Jack looking far from blameless.

The Dark Blues looked down and out but they survived and, just two minutes into extra-time, Steven Craig, who had come on for Deasley, broke through to rifle the ball past McEwan. There were near things at either end but, inspired by Mann, Wilkie and Robertson, Dundee went on to win and, at full-time, there were wild celebrations at reaching the last four.

Tom Duthie of *The Evening Telegraph* waxed lyrical about the battling Dundee performance, singling out Bobby Mann and Lee Wilkie for special praise: "On a night not short on heroes, Mann was not so much a stand-in captain as the onfield general as he put in a they-shall-not-pass defensive performance. And for Wilkie to complete 90 minutes was amazing - that he was still able to give his all at the end of 120 is the stuff legends are made of. And as far as Dundee Football Club goes, this is a man who deserves that kind of status."

And with Barry Smith to return, Dundee, he felt, had every chance of reaching the Scottish Cup Final. Having just received £82,500 from Sky, Dundee could expect another £300,000 from their share of the pooled semi-final gate receipts and TV money, but the euphoria was short-lived. Less than 48 hours later came a humiliating 7-0 defeat at Airdrie and the following weekend a dreadful performance in a 1-0 home defeat to St Johnstone was exacerbated by a suspected recurrence of Lee Wilkie's knee injury.

At New Broomfield, Dundee's team had included only Barry Smith, Steven Craig, Callum MacDonald and Colin Marshall of any great experience. The Dens men had requested that the game be put back until the Sunday but when Airdrie refused, the Scottish League insisted it go ahead as scheduled.

Alan Kernaghan defended his decision not to play any of his cup-tie starting XI: "Having gone to extra-time two days earlier, there was no way I could have fielded those players because we would have ended up with lots of injuries. However, I should have changed the system earlier."

Few disagreed, though Dundee were later handed a £5,000 fine by the Scottish League, albeit suspended for three years. However, the biggest blow was the loss of Lee Wilkie - stretchered off when his suspect right knee buckled - and there were serious concerns that his career might be over.

Meanwhile, Dundee continued their preparations for the Scottish Cup semi-final with Gretna on Saturday, April 1st. Training was rescheduled to coincide with the 12.15pm kick-off - brought forward to accommodate live TV coverage by the BBC - there was a visit to Hampden to familiarise the players with the stadium, and it was also decided that the Dens party would stay in Glasgow on the Friday night.

Backed by wealthy benefactor Miles Brookson and shrewdly managed by Rowan Alexander, ambitious Gretna, had made great progress since joining the Scottish League four years earlier. The population of the Borders village numbered just 4,000 but their policy of bringing in seasoned professionals had paid off with two successive promotions and now they were set to play in the First Division.

There was a crowd of 14,179 at Hampden and although high-scoring Gretna were strong favourites, Dundee had the backing of over 8,000 noisy fans. Callum MacDonald replaced Wilkie but with Kernaghan opting for the experience of McCluskey rather than the attacking flair of McDonald, they lined up: Jack; McCluskey, MacDonald, Mann, Dixon; McManus, Robertson, Smith, Brady; Lynch, Deasley. Gretna: Main; Birch, Innes, Townsley; McGuffie, Tosh, Nicholls, O'Neil, Skelton; Deuchar, Grady.

Dee for life - Scott Robertson shows his grit in the Scottish Cup semi-final against Gretna.   DC Thomson

This time, there was no whirlwind start by the Dark Blues and although there were a couple of near things at either end, it was a largely uninspired contest. Gretna, though, began to find their rythm and, just on half-time, they went ahead when a sclaffed challenge by McManus sailed backward and spun off McCluskey's head to set Deuchar free down the left. The Gretna sharpshooter took the ball wide past Jack and, from a tight angle, his well-struck shot crossed the line.

After the break, Dundee resumed with McDonald on for McCluskey and Smith at right-back. This gave them added impetus but in 58 minutes they found themselves two goals behind. McGuffie beat Dixon then threw himself to the ground after colliding with Mann. The Dens centre-half had made no attempt to tackle but, astonishingly, referee Murray awarded a penalty and McGuffie scored from the spot.

Craig and Robb were brought on but Dundee were unable to break Gretna down and near the end a McQuilken cross deflected off Smith to make it 3-0. Little had gone right for the Dark Blues but it was fairy-tale stuff for Gretna, who went on to lose to Hearts in the final on penalties but would qualify for the UEFA Cup as runners-up.

Noticeably, Dundee had lacked the edge shown in earlier ties - Jack, MacDonald, McDonald, Robertson, McManus and Lynch had all previously had yellow cards and were perhaps wary of missing the final like Lee Wilkie in 2003 - and only Deasley had done much in a creative sense.

Many in the large Dens support blamed the manager for giving Gretna too much respect and for not having more of a go. Dundee had persisted with a deep-lying back four against old Dens hero James Grady and Kenny Deuchar - never the fastest of strikers - and the fans felt badly let down.

Rather than utilise the space wide of Gretna's back three, long high balls were repeatedly directed up the middle to Lynch and Deasley, who struggled to maintain possession. Indeed, Lynch made little impression and it was surprising that neither McManus or Craig were switched to the centre.

The cup run had diverted attention from what had been a miserable season and, when uninspiring draws at Ross County and Stranraer were followed by a dire display in a 1-0 home defeat to already-relegated Brechin, confidence in the management team hit rock-bottom. The headlines in *The Courier* read: "Dundee run ragged by slick Brechin", an uncomfortable fact and one not appreciated by the meagre 1,841 fans in attendance, who loudly vented their wrath at the home dugout.

It appeared that Kernaghan, who had utilised a rigid 4-4-2 system, had lost the dressing room and, with disgruntled fans threatening a season ticket boycott, both he and Billy Kirkwood were asked to "consider their position". Under their direction, Dundee had won just nine from 38 games (all competitions) and but for the points gathered by Jim Duffy and the two sets of caretaker-managers, they might well have been scrambling to avoid the relegation play-offs.

It was understood that the managerial duo were offered the equivalent of two months salary (an estimated £8,500 for Kernagahan) to resign but, with over a year of their contracts left, neither was prepared to do so. The stand-off lasted for another three days but on April 20th, the pair were sacked after just eight months in charge.

CHAPTER FORTY-FIVE

New Dundee

Barry Smith and Bobby Mann took charge for the last two games and Dundee ended what had been a dire season with a 3-1 win against Queen of the South at Palmerston. That was their first success outwith Tayside since beating Aberdeen in May 2004 and such was the style of their performance that Queen's boss Ian McCall likened their play to that of the "Galacticos" of Real Madrid!

It was, however, the last time that Barry Smith would pull on a Dundee jersey. The popular 32-year-old, who had made 424 starting appearances for the Dark Blues - a total exceeded only by Bobby Cox (433), and Doug Cowie (446), - rejected the offer of another year at Dens to join Icelandic club Valur on a two-year deal, saying: "I'm sad to go but it's a chance to go abroad which I simply could not pass up at this stage of my career."

The Dens veteran was leaving a club in disarray for, with the 2005 accounts still not published, still no sign of a new manager and no mention of season ticket prices or new shirt sponsors, there were even rumours that a return to administration might be on the cards.

In mid-May, the situation was somewhat clarified by appointments to two key positions. Jimmy Marr had indicated his intention to resign from the board and after nine years at the helm, Peter Marr stepped down as chief executive. Former Dark Blue Dave McKinnon, who had impressed in a similar role at Kilmarnock, took over and, soon afterwards ex-Falkirk, Millwall, Sunderland, Wolves and Rangers midfielder Alex Rae (36), was appointed player-manager.

Jocky Scott, just recently back at Dens as a youth coach, had looked a good bet for the manager's post, particularly after Peter Marr's admission in *The Sun* that he had erred in replacing him with Ivano Bonetti. McKinnon, though, perhaps also looking for an onfield leader, had gone for Rae, whose friend the ex-Hibs and Partick Thistle defender Davie Farell (36), a youth coach at Gretna, got the nod as his assistant - and soon the unfortunate Scott was on his way.

McKinnon had played for the Dark Blues in 1977-78 before continuing his career at Partick Thistle, Kilmarnock and Rangers. But, though confirming Bukta as Dundee's new kit supplier as well as a £50,000 jersey sponsorship deal with internet memorabilia company *signatures4U.com*, McKinnon now had to implement some harsh measures to appease the Halifax Bank of Scotland.

Dundee had failed miserably to adapt to the rigours of lower league football, finishing seventh in the 10-team First Division. Clubs like Ross County, Airdrie and Clyde - all on a lower budget than Dundee - had finished above the Dens under-achievers and now another clearout would ensure expenditure was cut to the bone.

New boss - Alex Rae would be player-manager at Dens. Fotopress

As well as Smith, Stuart McCluskey had gone - to Australia - while Kelvin Jack, Steven Craig, Colin Marshall, Graeme Law, Andy Britton and Robert Hendry were all allowed to leave at the end of their contracts. Once it became clear that Lynch was also going "Down Under", Craig was offered a two-year contract but he instead opted to join his local club Livingston, who gave him a three-year deal.

Kelvin Jack had been in the Trinidad and Tobago squad at that summer's World Cup Finals in Germany but his Dens form was erratic and he appeared somewhat injury-prone. And, as with Brent Sancho, it was never clear when he might return from international duty, for the big keeper had missed Dundee's trip to Dingwall after heading to the Caribbean for a celebration party following his country's decisive World Cup qualifier in Bahrein!

Indeed, most of Dundee's other top earners would also depart after being "offered" drastic pay-cuts. Garry Brady (to St Mirren), Derek Soutar (Aberdeen), Lee Wilkie and Steven Robb (Dundee United), Simon Lynch (Queensland Roar), and, eventually Tam McManus (Falkirk), all decided to move on, while even long-serving club doctor, Dr Phyllis Windsor joined the exodus, crossing the road to Dundee United soon after the start of the season.

There was considerable sympathy for the players who had signed contracts in good faith only to find that Dundee wished to tear them up and this particularly applied to fans' favourite Lee Wilkie. In June 2005, Dundee had paid £20,000 for the former Scotland defender - he earned 11 full caps while at Dens - to undergo his second knee operation which involved the attachment of a donor ligament by the world-renowned surgeon Dr Richard Steadman in Colorado.

Following his injury against St Johnstone, a scan revealed that the graft had failed and Dr Steadman advised that further surgery was not an option. That left the 26-year-old with the choice of retiring or building up the muscles around the joint and attempting to play on - as Willie Falconer had done for 15 years - without a cruciate. Any further re-occurrence could cause damage that might affect his daily life but, in the end, the big defender decided to take the gamble.

A severance payment was agreed but there then ensued a row over possession of a club jeep. In the end, a compromise was struck whereby the Land Rover Discovery was returned with Wilkie receiving a financial adjustment before signing a "pay-as-you-play" deal with Dundee United. Supporters wished him well but their concerns would now centre solely on the well-being of Dundee Football Club.

The accounts to July 31st, 2006 - actually published a year later - revealed that the Dark Blues remained in a precarious position. For although the wage bill had more than halved to £1.54m (79% of turnover) since exiting administration, and despite a second agreed write-off of £3.63m in 2005, and the various other measures, some £8m in liabilities - £6.8m due to HBOS for loans and bank overdrafts - still remained.

In 2005, Bob Brannan - by then group managing director of whisky firm Whyte & Mackay - had commented that: "Despite the improved financial position the club are saddled with an enormous and unsustainable burden of debt that would be difficult to service with SPL income, never mind the reduced revenues that result from relegation."

To achieve promotion, Dundee required substantial investment in players - impossible in their current financial situation. Should they fail to do so and earn a much-improved income, the debt was likely to rise, leaving the prospect of part-time football and even liquidation.

There had, though, been ongoing discussions with HBOS about a major restructuring. It was hoped the £7 million debt would be removed from the balance sheet to leave Dundee "debt-free" although in return, Dens Park could come under the ownership of a property company.

The stadium would then be leased back at an affordable rent with Dundee having security of tenure and a right of purchase over the ground in the future. The Marrs, who now held 92% of the club's shares, would relinquish control, reducing their holding to 25%, after the balance was sold, they hoped, to fans groups and members of the local business community. That could raise as much as £500,000 which would be utilised as working capital - something the club would require since they would no longer have the stadium as an asset to borrow against.

The Dee4Life Supporters' Trust, who already held 5%, determined to raise the £152,000 necessary to increase their holding to 26% - enough to give them the power of veto on any decisions concerning the future direction of the club.

The campaign to raise funds, aptly named *'Ure' Dundee*, was launched at Dens Park on Saturday June 3rd, with wealthy Gretna owner Brooks Mileson - a firm believer that fans should have a strong say in running their own club - as a guest speaker.

In order to concentrate minds an eight-week deadline was set and with the Trust contributing £50,000, the DSA £10,000 and

the Junior Dark Blues another £500, that left just over £90,000 to raise. In an act of great generosity, Mr Mileson pledged to donate £30,000 if the fans could raise the remainder and, remarkably, the target was met within the designated time-frame.

Already, eleven of last term's first-team squad had left and just prior to the new season, another two - the fit-again Stephen McNally (to Peterhead), and Andy Ferguson (Clyde), departed while Craig O'Reilly (East Fife) and Mark Allison (Forfar), went on loan. Alex Rae, meanwhile, had begun to rebuilt the team around himself, new club captain Bobby Mann, Scott Robertson, Paul Dixon and Gavin Swankie who was back after six months on loan at Arbroath.

In came former St Johnstone, Dundee United, Stockport, Aberdeen and 29-times capped Northern Ireland international defender Danny Griffin (28), former St Mirren and Livingston goalkeeper Ludovic Roy (29), ex-Dundee United, Reading, Kilmarnock and Morton winger Andy McLaren (33), who appeared once for Scotland - along with Gavin Rae - against Poland in 2001, Rangers reserve centre-half Gary McKenzie (21), and ex-Celtic midfielder Ross Harris (20).

A cracking goal by Bryan Deasley earned a 1-0 win over Craig Brewster's Dundee United in the Evening Telegraph Challenge Cup, as Dundee produced some encouraging pre-season performances. Last season, the young striker had been named as Bell's Young Player of the Year, and both he and teenage team-mate Kevin McDonald - Dundee had already rejected bids from Celtic (£75,000), and Everton (£100,000) for him - looked to have a bright future.

Realistically, little was expected of the drastically depleted Dark Blues, who would face strong competition, particularly from Gretna. Backed by the financial muscle of Brooks Mileson, the Second Division champions were again title favourites with Owen Coyle's St Johnstone and newly relegated Livingston also likely to be to the fore.

On August 5th, over 5,000 fans turned out for the visit of Partick Thistle but their enthusiasm was soon dampened by a 1-0 reverse with the newly-promoted Jags returning to inflict a second defeat - 3-1 in the League Cup - a few days later. Things were not going to plan and when a 1-0 reverse at Hamilton was followed by a humiliating 2-1 Challenge Cup defeat to Second Division Forfar Athletic at Station Park, Dundee could hardly have made a worse start.

The Dark Blues were desperately short of players and the situation was further exacerbated by injuries to Andy McLaren, Danny Griffin, Ludovic Roy, Bobby Mann with the strapping Gary McKenzie also out for a lengthy spell after an operation to remove calcification from his ankle.

To bolster the squad, Alex Rae brought in the experienced ex-Bolton, Motherwell and Livingston central-defender Gregg Strong, Queen of the South striker Derek Lyle, Kilmarnock forward Robert Campbell, and Rangers goalkeeper Calum Reidford.

A year earlier, 25-year-old Lyle had been sent off after a clash with Dundee's Tom Hutchinson but although deemed surplus to requirements at Palmerston, the energetic striker brought a much-needed directness in his debut against Clyde at Dens. Harris cracked in the opener and Lyle showed no sign of nerves as he thundered home a penalty before Gavin Swankie secured the points with a third.

On September 9th, Dundee were near full-strength for the top-of-the-table clash with Gretna at Raydale Park: Roy;

Dundee F.C. Season 2006-07 - the squad which defeated Dundee United to win the Evening Telegraph Challenge Cup - (BACK, left to right) Andy McLaren, Keith Shevlin (trialist), Alex Rae (player-manager), Callum MacDonald, Danny Griffin, Scott Murray, Ross Harris, Stephen McNally, Kevin McDonald, Gary McKenzie, Bobby Mann. FRONT - Bryan Deasley, Scott Gates, Scott Robertson, Ludovic Roy, Gavin Swankie and Paul Dixon. Inset - Andy Ferguson.
Fotopress

Griffin, Strong, Mann, Dixon; McLaren, K. McDonald, Robertson, Rae, Swankie; Lyle. In nine minutes, Derek Lyle fired home after an Alan Main blunder and the first-half blitz continued as Alex Rae, Andy McLaren and young Kevin McDonald found the net in a convincing 4-0 win.

Buoyed up by that success, they followed up with wins over Queen of the South (h) 2-1, and Airdrie United (a) 1-0, before a 1-1 draw against strong-going St Johnstone left them fourth, within four points of league leaders Gretna. However, Dundee were unable to maintain this form and by the end of the year, they had slipped back to seventh, a massive 16 points behind the high-flying Borders outfit.

With Deasley struggling through injury, Lyle and McLaren were left to carry the burden in attack for neither Campbell or Brian McGinty - the latter a short-term loan signing from St Mirren - looked the part. Even then, there was a distinct lack of firepower although matters were not helped by player indiscipline. By then, Derek Lyle, Alex Rae and Andy McLaren had all been dismissed with the ex-Tannadice man, previously sent off against Gretna at Dens, getting himself red-carded three times in the 2-1 reverse to Clyde at Broadwood in December.

McLaren had won over the Dundee fans with a combination of industry and pure skill, and his goal when he let the ball drop over his shoulder before smashing in an unstoppable shot in the 3-1 home victory over Ross County would long be savoured. However, the fiery front-man, who, years earlier had become acquainted with Alex Rae at Glasgow's Priory rehabilitation clinic when both were battling a serious drink problem, was a player who lived right on the edge.

With seven yellow cards, including two against Gretna,

already to his name that term, McLaren's first red at Broadwood came after his second booking when he tried to wrestle the ball from a Clyde defender in an attempt to speed up the restart after Swankie's late penalty had put Dundee back in the game.

In the subsequent mayhem, he received another two straight reds for "offensive, abusive and insulting language" towards referee Dougie McDonald and for striking Clyde's former Dark Blue, Michael McGowan. McLaren had let himself and the club down badly and, soon after receiving an eight-game ban from the SFA, he left Dundee "by mutual consent" following a meeting with Dens Park officials.

With the onset of the January transfer window, there were further departures from Dens. Gary McKenzie's return to fitness and the recent arrival of ex-Aberdeen and Hibs defender Gary Smith (35), on loan from Cowdenbeath, meant there was intense competition for the central defenders' jerseys. No longer in the plans, Callum McDonald signed for Peterhead after a spell on loan at Balmoor, Mark Allison joined Forfar, while John Boggan and Graham Hay were also released.

It was soon clear that the McKenzie-Smith pairing was the management's preferred choice and after submitting a transfer request, Bobby Mann joined Peterhead in late January. The 32-year-old Dundonian had swept the board at the Player of the Year awards in May 2006 but his contract was up that summer and with signs that he, like Gregg Strong (31), might be going "over the hill", both were allowed to go.

Last summer's cuts had brought savings of around £400,000 - a settlement had since been agreed with Alan Kernaghan - and now Alex Rae set about strengthening his squad. Gary Smith had looked fit and assured as had Jay Shields (21), a combatative full-back or midfielder, who had also arrived on loan some weeks earlier, and both had their contracts extended until the end of the season.

Clyde skipper Paul McHale signed a pre-contract agreement but the 25-year-old midfielder was soon on his way to Dens after the Bully Wee accepted a fee of around £5,000. Rangers reserve striker Bob Davidson (20), was also signed for 18 months, while Sunderland attacker Kevin Smith, (on loan), Dutch midfielder Khalid Hamdaoui (24), and ex-Aberdeen, Stranraer and Montrose centre-half Craig Higgins (21), were all fixed up on short-term deals.

Unlike last year, Dundee's Scottish Cup campaign was all too brief. Playing their fifth game in 14 days and affected by a flu virus, the Dark Blues looked a weary lot as they laboured to a 1-1 draw against Queen of the South at Dens. It was dull fare for the fans but the replay at Dumfries on Tuesday, January 15th would prove a ding-dong affair.

Just before half-time, Dobbie put Queens ahead but, three minutes into the second half, Lyle crashed home the equaliser. Dobbie made it 2-1 only for Deasley to nod home in 83 minutes and just when a close-in O'Connor goal seemed to have put Ian McCall's men through, Lyle made it 3-3 with a last-gasp leveller! Extra-time finished goal-less but there was no joy for Dundee in the penalty shoot-out, Barry John Corr saving from Lyle and Smith as Queen of the South went through to the fourth round, 4-2 on penalties.

Dundee, though, were undefeated in open play and by mid-February they had strung together a seven-game unbeaten run, which included taking an impressive 13 points from five league games. Undoubtedly, the highlight had been the 2-1 win over St Johnstone at Dens - an absolute thriller played out amidst driving rain with Gavin Swankie curling in the winner off the underside of the crossbar, just nine minutes from time.

Given little opportunity to shine under Alan Kernaghan before being shipped back to Gayfield, 23-year-old Swankie had again shown his trickery down the left. That season, the former "Red Lichtie" had consistently put over telling crosses and he had also weighed in with his share of the goals.

Quick-fire - Derek Lyle fires the ball home from the penalty spot on his debut against Clyde at Dens.
DC Thomson

Dens dazzler - Gavin Swankie weaved his magic on the wing.

The win over Owen Coyle's side, semi-finalists in the League Cup and Scottish Cup that term and, arguably, the best footballing side in the league, came as a big boost.

However, it would prove a false dawn for just a week later the Dens resurgence was well and truly over after a first-half blitzkrieg by a slick and street-wise Clyde saw the Broadwood men depart with a 4-1 victory.

Any lingering hopes of promotion had gone and subsequent defeats to Gretna (h), 0-1, and St Johnstone (a) 0-2, showed that the Dark Blues had much to do before they could class themselves as genuine promotion contenders.

Dundee could only look on as Gretna and the Perth side battled it out for promotion although supporters had long accepted that it would be a season of transition due to the financial problems at Dens. Nevertheless, much encouragement could be taken from their third-place finish. Home form was much-improved and the Dens men now at least had the nucleus of a promotion-challenging squad.

By March, much of the financial uncertainty had been resolved. Six of the Marrs' companies, including P&J Taverns, the ultimate parent company which held the controlling interest in Dundee F.C., went into receivership. That prompted the resignation of Peter and Jimmy Marr from the Dens Park board as Kroll, the receivers, put their 92% shareholding up for sale.

A number of offers were received but potential bidders had to show that they could manage the club's £8 million debt. It was another worrying period as fans awaited news of the club's new owners. But, in the end, a bid from a consortium comprising Dundee chairman Bob Brannan, chief executive Dave McKinnon, Dee4Life representative George Knight and local chartered accountant Ian Bodie was accepted as representing "the best deal for the company and the club".

A delighted Bob Brannan commented: "We're excited about it. We all know each other very well and see the future in much the same way. As a board, we have two primary goals - to create a stable platform for the club for many years to come and, of course, to get the club back to the Premier League as soon as possible without doing silly things with the finances."

He confirmed that they would sell 21% of their newly acquired holding to Dee4Life for £152,000 and would welcome new investment from other parties on the same basis - £7,500 per 1% of the shares. Their goal was to sell all the shares although any decision on share allocation would have to be unanimous. The most important thing they felt was not how much money someone wanted to put in but who they were and what their intentions might be.

It was also confirmed that HBOS had formally accepted their financial restructuring proposals, which would remove Dundee F.C. Holdings plc from the equation and leave Dundee Football Club 2007 Limited debt-free.

CHAPTER FORTY-SIX

On the Up

This agreement was signed on June 12th, allowing the chairman to relay the good news to some 1,500 members of the Dundee F.C. community at the Supporters' Rally in the Caird Hall that evening. As expected, the club would be intertwined with two other companies - Sandeman Properties Ltd and Deelite Ltd - Messrs Brannan, McKinnon, Knight and Bodie were the directors in control of all three, with the bank remaining in the background.

At the 2006 AGM, held at Dens Park on August 23rd, shareholders were told that Dundee F.C. Ltd was indeed debt-free. This would be reflected in the 2007 accounts due in October, with the AGM to follow a few months later. Dens Park Stadium, now under the ownership of Sandeman Properties, would be leased by Dundee F.C. with the club paying an estimated £3,500 per week - effectively the interest payments on what was a £3m mortgage.

This mortgage is repayable at any time and can also be reduced should the club progress to the latter stages of cup competitions - with a proportional reduction in Dundee's rental. The other £4m of debt, which HBOS are unwilling to formally write off, is now held by Deelite. However, it does not have to be repaid - and will not accrue interest - unless the club sell a player for over £750,000, in which case 50% of the fee would go towards reducing that debt.

It was also confirmed that proposals to redevelop the south side of the stadium were being considered. This would involve a new housing development facing on to Dens Road with Dundee Football Club benefiting from a cash injection as well as the construction of a new South Stand. According to Bob Brannan, the new stand, which would run the length of the south side, would require a capacity of 2,500 to 3,000 and would also have to be aesthetically pleasing.

Dundee had previously rejected the idea of a joint venture in case a collapse in the housing market meant the end for the club. However, ten building companies showed interest and J&E Shepherd (Chartered Surveyors) are scheduled to report back with their findings at the end of October once all interested parties have submitted their plans.

A "massive" retaining wall would be required, for, as well as sloping steeply down to Dens Road, there are contamination and drainage problems with the land on the south side of the ground. Talking about the proposals, newly appointed finance director Ian Bodie said: "It's like selling the family silver and we're not going to sell it on the cheap. But we want somebody credible to do this and you need people with a track record. There's a lot of engineering involved in it and it's not just the best price we'll be looking for."

Shareholders were impressed by the enthusiasm and profes-

New direction - Dave McKinnon, Ian Bodie, Bob Brannan and George Knight after taking control in March 2007. DC Thomson

sionalism shown by the board. For, not only had the club survived administration and its aftermath, but there were now plans to take the club forward. And in turn, chief executive Dave McKinnon was full of praise for Alex Rae and Davie Farrell.

He described their appetite for success, saying that the board were right behind them in the push for promotion and they hoped this would spread to the support: "We have taken a bit of a punt on the money available to the manager - a £300,000 loss was projected - although the wage structure remains intact. A lot of people have come to the club eager to perform. There is a huge hunger for success and there's a great team spirit amongst management and players."

However, having achieved a degree of financial stability, Dundee still have to fund the lease, maintain the ground and meets the salaries of players and staff. A meeting was held with members of the Business Development Club and, no longer faced by a mountain of debt, it is hoped that larger investors take up some of the remaining 71% of the shares.

Last season, Dundee were by far the best-supported club in the First Division and the willingness of fans to back the club, either by the purchase of season tickets - 2,500 were sold last term - or at the gate will continue to be crucial.

There is a big responsibility on the shoulders of manager Alex Rae and his assistant Davie Farrell, although the experienced Gordon Wallace is always there to give advice. Rae did well to take Dundee to third with limited resources and the use of 36 players for a second successive season certainly reflected the continuing turnover of staff.

Reflecting on his first season in charge, Rae told *The Evening Telegraph*: "I would say we have a nucleus of eight or nine players who I know are of the required standard. Now I need maybe half a dozen more who are experienced at this level and know what it is all about and if we get them we would be in with a shout in the promotion race."

Dundee could certainly count on Ludovic Roy, the versatile Danny Griffin, Scott Robertson, Gary McKenzie, Paul Dixon, Paul McHale, Gavin Swankie and Derek Lyle, while youngsters like Kevin McDonald and Bryan Deasley - the latter troubled by injury before penning a new deal until 2009 - will be all the better for having another season under their belts. Expectations are high but, like earlier starlets such as Andy Penman, Jocky Scott and Gordon Strachan, they require to be carefully nurtured.

Alex Rae displayed a good mix of skill and drive in midfield and he had clearly been a top class player. Sadly, though, he followed the "tradition" of earlier Dundee player-managers, Simon Stainrod, Jim Duffy (twice), and Ivano Bonetti in getting himself sent off twice as well as incurring several cautions. In fairness, Rae was the target of some wild challenges - he got little protection from match officials - but, sensibly, he has decided to step back from the action and henceforth will direct operations from the sidelines.

At the end of last season, Ross Harris, Craig Higgins and Khalid Hamdaoui, who were all out-of-contract, and loan signings Jay Shields, Robert Campbell and Kevin Smith were allowed to go. Craig O'Reilly was sold to East Fife for a nominal fee, Gary Smith joined Clyde as player-coach and Scott Murray moved on to Queen's Park near the end of the August transfer window.

An offer was made to Dyron Daal, who scored five goals in seven games while on loan from Aberdeen, but the big Dutchman, who had expressed an interest in playing football in the USA, instead signed for St Johnstone. There was further disappointment when Queen of the South right-back Eric Paton decided to stay at Palmerston while former St Johnstone and Port Vale striker Nathan Lowndes chose to join English League Two side Chester City.

However, by the eve of the new season, Dundee, who were offering a £20,000 promotion bonus, had made eight new signings. In came ex-Dundee United, Plymouth and Rotherham right-back David Worrell (29), Stirling Albion winger David O'Brien (23), ex-Paris St Germain, Hibs and Dunfermline winger Freddie Daquin (28), Czech Republic pair Jan Zemlik, a striker, and Milan Palenik, a centre-half, (both 29), former Dundee United, Kilmarnock and Ross County keeper Craig Samson (23), and the Slovenian striker Jani Sturm (25).

Rock steady - Milan Palenic helped to steady the defence. David Young

All arrived on freedom-of-contract apart from Daquin - like Roy a French national - who had been released by Dunfermline, while 21-year-old Craig Sives was signed on a year-long loan from Hearts.

The Dark Blues' summer signing spree came as a big boost to morale

Sky high - Gary McKenzie jousts with Alan Main of St Johnstone.

for what would clearly be a highly competitive First Division. Recently-relegated Dunfermline were a clear threat after beating Rangers, Hearts, Partick Thistle and Hibs to reach the Scottish Cup Final, where they narrowly lost to Celtic.

The Pars have a large, experienced squad, and were the hot favourites to make a swift return to the SPL, while St Johnstone - thwarted by Gretna's last-gasp goal from James Grady - are again likely to be a major threat. Now, though, boosted by the new arrivals, there was the feeling that the Dark Blues might just be able to cause an upset.

Alex Rae himself was under no illusions how tough it would be and in an interview with Joanna Moffat in the official club website *Dundee Football Club Online* as well as the club programme, he commented: "We've added some players and are hoping to improve on our third place finish last term. I know that from the off there will be a constant scrap to stay at the top."

"The supporters gave us their full backing last season and I would hope that can continue again this season. They've followed the club through thick and thin and I hope we can make a good start, get a bit of momentum going and get the fans coming out in good numbers."

"Initially when I came to the club, fitness levels were not great, that's why this close season has been so good with every player completing a personal fitness programme and returning above the level they were at last year. Last season, we struggled to get players in and by the time I came into the job many of the good players had been snapped up. But we've established good contacts with agents which allowed us to bring in more players on contracts rather than on loan, which was often the case last year."

"Davie Farrell knows about the lower leagues both through playing as well as his time at Gretna. I started out at this level but coming here reminded me how tough it was. We know that there must be a strong team spirit if you are to have any chance of success. However, I'm trying to instil a winning mentality and slowly but surely I'm moulding the team into the way I want them to be, which is strong and aggressive."

Certainly Rae appeared to have his own ideas. Last season, he had insisted that the Dens Park pitch be narrowed to give his defenders less width to defend. That resulted in a 16% drop in league goals conceded - from 50 to 42 - and it is a tactic he will continue with this time around.

And in the knowledge that his youngsters on the fringes of the first-team were unlikely to get much action at the start of the new campaign, Bryan Deasley (to Cowdenbeath), Brian Clark (Arbroath), Scott Gates (Forfar), were put out on loan to build up their fitness levels and gain vital experience -

Dundee F.C. 2007–08 (BACK, left to right), Gavin Swankie, Scott Robertson, Milan Palenik, Jan Zemlik, Gary McKenzie, David Worrell. MIDDLE - Gordon Wallace (general manager), Karen Gibson (physiotherapist), Paul McHale, David O'Brien, Paul Dixon, Craig Samson, Scott Murray, Ludovic Roy, Freddie Daquin, Kevin McDonald, John Sives, Davie O'Farrell (assistant-manager), FRONT - Scott Gates, Bryan Deasley, Derek Lyle, Alex Rae (manager), Brian Clark, Bob Davidson, Danny Griffin. Inset - Jani Sturm

DC Thomson

hopefully to later return and play their part in a Dundee promotion challenge.

Completing his interview, Rae admitted that player discipline - last year Dundee had the second-worst record in the First Division - had to improve and he also observed: "We must try to improve our away form this season. If we are to be challenging at the top of the league next April, we must look to pick up more points on our travels."

The Dark Blues took his remarks to heart and, buoyed up by an impressive 2-1 friendly win over Coca Cola Championship side Millwall, they kicked off the 2007-08 season with a 2-0 win at Livingston. The towering Jan Zemlik - 6'7" tall with a powerful physique - proved a real handful for the home defence and amidst the ensuing havoc, the industrious Bob Davidson twice cut the ball back for Scott Robertson to hammer home the vital goals.

Prior to the match, the omens had not been good. Livvy's first-choice strip was now an all-black outfit, meaning that Dundee as the away side were expected to change. Mistakenly, though, in the belief that the West Lothian side still played in yellow, the Dens Parkers had only brought their dark blue strip.

Dundee, who some years earlier had encountered a similar situation at Perth where they turned out in St Johnstone's change strip, were now offered Livvy's yellow tops. This suggestion was turned down by Dave McKinnon and, in the end, Livvy chairman Pearse Flynn sportingly agreed that the home side would turn out in last season's yellow strip.

It had been essential to get a good start in what promised to be a fiercely fought league campaign. And when Dundee followed their Almondvale triumph with a 2-1 home win over Queen of the South, then managed a 1-1 draw at St Johnstone before ending August with a decisive 3-0 win over Partick Thistle at Dens, there was an air of quiet satisfaction down Sandeman Street way.

Encouragingly, there was a new battling spirit about the Dark Blues and that is a basic ingredient for any side with promotion aspirations. One man who epitomised this new attitude was 6'4" tall defender Milan Palenik. The Czech had missed out at Livingston because his international clearance had failed to come through but thereafter he soon became established as a first-team regular.

As a trialist, Palenik had quickly endeared himself to the home fans, his never-say-die performance against Millwall earning him a standing ovation as he left the field. Alongside Palenik, Gary McKenzie is the preferred option although last term the big defender made a number of costly errors when caught lingering on the ball.

And when substituted after a dire display against Airdrie he angrily flung down the captain's armband before lashing out at water bottles in the dug-out. Diplomatically, Alex Rae maintained that the defender was "just demonstrating his passion" but, perhaps unsurprisingly, this season's captaincy has passed to goalkeeper Ludovic Roy.

Mackenzie has all the physical attributes to be a defensive colossus but, like Lee Wilkie before him, he needs to eliminate the fancy stuff and concentrate on his defensive play. Although just 21 years of age, he was made skipper after Bobby Mann's departure. But now, relieved of that burden and playing alongside the experienced Palenik, the big ex-Ranger appears to have adopted a more disciplined approach and will be a key player in the long months ahead.

On September 1st, the Dark Blues came from behind to record a 2-1 win over Clyde at Broadwood, a ground where good results had recently been thin on the ground. The Bully Wee, now managed by the ex-Dundee and Scotland international Colin Hendry, were disadvantaged by the sending-off of Joe Cardle after 25 minutes. But Dundee still had to battle hard before Paul McHale levelled with a 25-yarder and David O'Brien fired home the winner in 64 minutes.

Tale of two penalties - Derek Lyle fires home from the spot to make it 2-2 and take the CIS Insurance Cup tie against Livingston to extra-time at Dens. BELOW - Dundee keeper Craig Samson is the hero as he dives full length to save from Jason Kennedy.   David Young

Dundee had taken thirteen from a possible 15 points in their first five games and were second behind surprise league leaders Hamilton. Thus far, Dunfermline and St Johnstone had struggled to get results but in mid-Sepember, Alex Rae's men found themselves in a ding-dong battle with the Pars at Dens Park.

Dunfermline dominated the early stages and went ahead through Jim Hamilton but almost immediately Kevin McDonald equalised with a deflected shot. McDonald - the Irn Bru Young Player of the Month for August - and Scott Robertson - then took control of the midfield but soon play simply raged from end to end. Yet with 13 minutes left it looked like Dundee might grab all three points when they were awarded a penalty after the marauding Dixon was downed in the box.

Up stepped Derek Lyle but the on-loan former Scotland keeper Paul Gallacher anticipated his shot to save the day for the Fifers. A 1-1 draw was a fair result but concerns about Dundee's lack of penetration were soon borne out when they had to settle for a 2-2 draw with struggling Stirling Albion at Forthbank. They twice had to come from behind and this did not auger well for their CIS Insurance League Cup third-round clash against Celtic on Wednesday, September 26th.

In the first round of the Challenge Cup, an understrength Dundee had gone down 2-1 at home to Second Division Ross County. This was not appreciated by a number of fans - long-time shareholder David Ash vociferously made the point at the AGM - but it had been a strategic move to ensure the strongest possible team was ready for the important league clash with St Johnstone a few days later.

However, they had made good progress in the League Cup, where the luck of the draw had brought three successive home ties. Newly-promoted Morton were beaten 2-0 while Livingston were despatched on penalties after a 2-2 draw and extra-time. Early on, the Dens Parkers had struggled to impose themselves on a Greenock side whose fortunes had been transformed by Jim McInally, who, along with Ian McCall (Partick Thistle), Colin Hendry (Clyde), and Gordon Chisholm (QOS), was of course a former Dark Blue and now manager of a First Division club.

Livvy, too, made it hard and only an 86th-minute penalty by Dens substitute Derek Lyle kept Dundee in the cup as they came from behind for a second time. It was then on to extra-time but with no further score, the cup-tie would be decided on penalties.

With the score standing at 4-4, it was on to sudden death and Livvy's Des McCaffrey and Dundee's David O'Brien made it five apiece. However, Craig Samson then made a brilliant diving save to stop young Jason Kennedy and up stepped Jani Sturm to make it 6-5 and spark joyous celebrations amongst home players and fans.

Kevin McDonald - made a big impression in midfield. David Young

Mayhem - Jan Zemlik gives the Celtic defence all sorts of bother in the League Cup tie at Dens. David Young

Their reward was another home tie and this time it was a money-spinner against SPL champions Celtic. And with the game going out live on BBC TV, there would be a £70,000 cash windfall for Dundee, who lined up: Samson; Worrell, (Griffin), McKenzie, Palenik, Dixon; Daquin, McDonald, McHale (Davidson), Robertson, Swankie; Zemlik.

Celtic, who were through to the sectional stages of the Champions League, had been expected to rest some of their top stars but having lost their last two games and with Nakamura and McGeady injured, they selected a strong team: Boruc; Caldwell, McManus, Kennedy, Naylor; Donatti, Brown, Sno, Riordan; McDonald, Vennegoor of Hessilink.

Paul McHale returned as the sitting player in a five-man midfield but despite utilising Jan Zemlik as a lone striker, Dundee went close when Gavin Swankie hit the post with a swerving free-kick. From the corner, Zemlik headed against the bar but it was Celtic who took the lead, Scott McDonald stealing in to nod home a free-kick from the right touchline.

Dundee hit back and with Scotland defenders Stephen McManus and John Kennedy struggling against Zemlik, Boruc was forced into desperate saves from McKenzie and Swankie. Samson saved a Riordan penalty but when Boruc pushed away another Swankie free-kick and Venegoor of Hessilink made it 2-0 on the hour, the game looked over.

In 71 minutes, Kevin McDonald pulled one back following a long throw-in by Paul Dixon. But although the Dens men kept up the pressure - they won 12 corners to Celtic's eight - they were unable to conjure up an equaliser. Dundee had lost two bad goals but they had given the Parkhead side a real fright and the gate money from the 8,200 crowd along with the TV money and other income would cover almost half of their projected deficit for the season.

Celtic boss and former Dark Blue Gordon Strachan was full of praise for the home side: "It was a terrific game. It should help Dundee for although they did not go through, their fans showed that they are right behind them and they did themselves a lot of good tonight."

Happy days - Scotland Under-21 international Paul Dixon shows his joy after Milan Palenik has scored against Morton. David Young

Kevin McDonald, Scott Robertson, Paul Dixon and Gavin Swankie had all looked the equal of their Celtic counterparts. But although Swankie acknowledged the brilliance of Boruc in goal, he was quick to identify the top priority: "I thought my first free-kick was in, likewise the second and then the third! The main thing, though, is that if we play like that every week in the league, then not many teams will prevent Dundee getting back to the SPL."

A few days later, Dundee roared into an early lead against Morton, but the midweek endeavours had taken their toll. The Cappielow side levelled and only a late, close-in goal by Sturm when Robertson's header came down off the bar after great wing-play by Swankie, brought them all three points. Hamilton's 4-1 defeat by St Johnstone had brought Dundee within a point and the stage was set for a top-of-the-table clash at New Douglas Park in early October.

However, there was no joy for the Dark Blues or their 1,200 fans as they crashed to their first league defeat of the season. Chances were few and far between on the much-criticised synthetic surface but Alex Rae's 4-5-1 formation looked like getting a draw until an 83rd-minute lapse in concentration - Palenik was off injured - allowed McLaughlin to head home a free-kick, with a second following near the end.

Dundee bounced back with a 4-1 home win against Livingston, Bob Davidson levelling an early Livvy strike with a stunning 30-yarder into the top right-hand corner of the net before a three-goal blitz by Zemlik, Davidson and Lyle secured the points. Disappointingly, they could only manage a 1-1 draw at Partick Thistle but on Saturday, November 3rd, much-fancied St Johnstone - just four points dropped from their last seven league games - were defeated 2-1 at Dens.

Down 1-0 and struggling - it was the eleventh time in 16 games that they had lost the first goal - Dundee brought on McHale for Daquin. The ex-Ranger became the sitting midfielder and, augmented by the trickery of half-time substitute Gavin Swankie, Robertson and McDonald surged forward in support of their strikers as Dundee pounded the Perth goal. In 59 minutes, McDonald laid the ball off for Davidson to make it 1-1 and, right on full-time, the big midfielder buried a left-foot shot behind Main to send the home fans in the 5,518 crowd wild with delight!

Hamilton, meanwhile, had lost at Dumfries to leave Alex Rae's men just three points behind, with Saints now a further seven points in arrears after the first third of the campaign This term, Dundee are much improved and as well as their new-found resilience, they also showed great skill and awareness in defeating a talented St Johnstone team.

There is a growing belief surrounding the Dark Blues but how well equipped are they for the challenge ahead? In goal, Craig Samson looks the part after stepping in for calf-injury victim Ludo Roy, the full-back positions have mostly been filled by David Worrell and Paul Dixon, Milan Palenik and Gary McKenzie are solid down the middle, and the ever-reliable Danny Griffin provides excellent cover.

Martyn Corrigan - on a month's loan from Motherwell - brought a touch of class at right-back, while the successful introduction of Paul McHale has given the manager plenty to ponder as the ex-Ranger showed excellent leadership qualities while dictating the pace of Dundee's play.

McHale found himself sidelined due to the fine form shown by Kevin McDonald and Scott Robertson. The popular "Robbo" has again been a tireless worker and, along with Paul Dixon, he scooped most of Dundee's Player of the Year awards last season. Dixon and McDonald deservedly made a number of appearances for the Scotland Under-21's. Both are tremendous prospects and it would be no surprise if they eventually progressed to full international level.

The athletic Freddie Daquin remains something of an enigma on the right side of midfield but Gavin Swankie is a quality performer, and the return of the pacy David O'Brien from injury and the promising Brian Clark from his loan spell, will further strengthen Alex Rae's hand.

One concern was the lack of a cutting edge up front. Jan Zemlik and Jani Sturm have had their moments but more recently Derek Lyle - suspended for the first four league games and somewhat out of favour - returned to partner Bob Davidson. Lyle, who netted 15 goals last term, is a real buzz-bomb of a player, while Davidson - currently Dundee's top scorer with seven goals to his credit, has come on leaps and bounds this season. Bryan Deasley is now back at Dens and if fit, his pace and movement should bring added firepower to the Dens Park strike-force.

Left-sided defender or midfielder Eddie Malone has been brought in on loan from St Mirren but Dundee's title hopes may well hinge on whether their top players remain until the end of the season. Robertson, McDonald, Dixon, Swankie and Lyle are all in the final year of their contracts and it must be hoped that Dundee can offer attractive enough deals for them to remain at Dens, or that the club obtain decent transfer fees should they move on.

Bob Davidson - stunning strike against Livvy. David Young

Over the past few seasons, Dundee fans have shown a remarkable loyalty, passion and love for their club and it would be a major success story if the previously beleaguered Dark Blues could build on their early-season results and go on to achieve promotion.